Zapotec Monuments and Political History

Prehistory and Human Ecology of the Valley of Oaxaca

Kent V. Flannery and Joyce Marcus
General Editors

Volume 1 *The Use of Land and Water Resources in the Past and Present Valley of Oaxaca, Mexico*, by Anne V.T. Kirkby. Memoirs of the Museum of Anthropology, University of Michigan, No. 5. 1973.

Volume 2 *Sociopolitical Aspects of Canal Irrigation in the Valley of Oaxaca*, by Susan H. Lees. Memoirs of the Museum of Anthropology, University of Michigan, No. 6. 1973.

Volume 3 *Formative Mesoamerican Exchange Networks with Special Reference to the Valley of Oaxaca*, by Jane W. Pires-Ferreira. Memoirs of the Museum of Anthropology, University of Michigan, No. 7. 1975.

Volume 4 *Fábrica San José and Middle Formative Society in the Valley of Oaxaca*, by Robert D. Drennan. Memoirs of the Museum of Anthropology, University of Michigan, No. 8. 1976.

Volume 5 Part 1. *The Vegetational History of the Oaxaca Valley*, by C. Earle Smith, Jr. Part 2. *Zapotec Plant Knowledge: Classification, Uses and Communication*, by Ellen Messer. Memoirs of the Museum of Anthropology, University of Michigan, No. 10. 1978.

Volume 6 *Excavations at Santo Domingo Tomaltepec: Evolution of a Formative Community in the Valley of Oaxaca, Mexico*, by Michael E. Whalen. Memoirs of the Museum of Anthropology, University of Michigan, No. 12. 1981.

Volume 7 *Monte Albán's Hinterland, Part 1: The Prehispanic Settlement Patterns of the Central and Southern Parts of the Valley of Oaxaca, Mexico*, by Richard E. Blanton, Stephen Kowalewski, Gary Feinman, and Jill Appel. Memoirs of the Museum of Anthropology, University of Michigan, No. 15. 1982.

Volume 8 *Chipped Stone Tools in Formative Oaxaca, Mexico: Their Procurement, Production and Use*, by William J. Parry. Memoirs of the Museum of Anthropology, University of Michigan, No. 20. 1987.

Volume 9 *Agricultural Intensification and Prehistoric Health in the Valley of Oaxaca, Mexico*, by Denise C. Hodges. Memoirs of the Museum of Anthropology, University of Michigan, No. 22. 1989.

Volume 10 *Early Formative Pottery of the Valley of Oaxaca*, by Kent V. Flannery and Joyce Marcus, with ceramic analysis by William O. Payne. Memoirs of the Museum of Anthropology, University of Michigan, No. 27. 1994.

Volume 11 *Women's Ritual in Formative Oaxaca: Figurine-Making, Divination, Death and the Ancestors*, by Joyce Marcus. Memoirs of the Museum of Anthropology, University of Michigan, No. 33. 1998.

Volume 12 *The Sola Valley and the Monte Albán State: A Study of Zapotec Imperial Expansion*, by Andrew K. Balkansky. Memoirs of the Museum of Anthropology, University of Michigan, No. 36. 2002.

Volume 13 *Excavations at San José Mogote 1: The Household Archaeology*, by Kent V. Flannery and Joyce Marcus. Memoirs of the Museum of Anthropology, University of Michigan, No. 40. 2005.

Volume 14 *Excavations at Cerro Tilcajete: A Monte Albán II Administrative Center in the Valley of Oaxaca*, by Christina Elson. Memoirs of the Museum of Anthropology, University of Michigan, No. 42. 2007.

Volume 15 *Cerro Danush: Excavations at a Hilltop Community in the Eastern Valley of Oaxaca, Mexico*, by Ronald K. Faulseit. Memoirs of the Museum of Anthropology, University of Michigan, No. 54. 2013.

Volume 16 *Excavations at San José Mogote 2: The Cognitive Archaeology*, by Kent V. Flannery and Joyce Marcus. Memoirs of the Museum of Anthropology, University of Michigan, No. 58. 2015.

Volume 17 *Cueva Blanca: Social Change in the Archaic of the Valley of Oaxaca*, by Kent V. Flannery and Frank Hole. Memoirs of the Museum of Anthropology, University of Michigan, No. 60. 2019.

Volume 18 *Zapotec Monuments and Political History*, by Joyce Marcus. Memoirs of the Museum of Anthropology, University of Michigan, No. 61. 2020.

Related Volumes

Flannery, Kent V.
 2009 *Guilá Naquitz: Archaic Foraging and Early Agriculture in Oaxaca, Mexico.* Walnut Creek, CA: Left Coast Press.

Flannery, Kent V., and Joyce Marcus
 2003 *The Cloud People: Divergent Evolution of the Zapotec and Mixtec Civilizations.* Clinton Corners, New York: Percheron Press.

Marcus, Joyce, and Kent V. Flannery
 1996 *Zapotec Civilization: How Urban Society Evolved in Mexico's Oaxaca Valley.* London: Thames and Hudson.

Memoirs of the Museum of Anthropology
University of Michigan
Number 61

PREHISTORY AND HUMAN ECOLOGY OF THE VALLEY OF OAXACA
Kent V. Flannery and Joyce Marcus, General Editors
Volume 18

Zapotec Monuments and Political History

Joyce Marcus

Ann Arbor, Michigan
2020

Printed in the United States of America
ISBN 978-0-915703-93-7 (print)
ISBN 978-0-915703-96-8 (ebook)

Cover design by John Klausmeyer

Browse all of our books at sites.lsa.umich.edu/archaeology-books.
Buy our books at www.press.umich.edu.
Visit the Museum website at lsa.umich.edu/ummaa.
For permissions, questions, or manuscript queries, contact Museum publications in Ann Arbor, Michigan, by email at umma-pubs@umich.edu.

Library of Congress Cataloging-in-Publication Data

Names: Marcus, Joyce, author.
Title: Zapotec monuments and political history / Joyce Marcus.
Description: Ann Arbor : University of Michigan Museum of Anthropology, 2020. | Series: Memoirs ; number 61 | Includes bibliographical references and index. | Summary: "Zapotec is one of the major hieroglyphic writing systems of ancient Mesoamerica. This volume explains the origins and spread of Zapotec writing, the role of Zapotec writing in the changing political agendas of the region, and the decline of hieroglyphic writing in the Valley of Oaxaca."-- Provided by publisher.
Identifiers: LCCN 2019057056 (print) | LCCN 2019057057 (ebook) | ISBN 9780915703937 (paperback) | ISBN 9780915703968 (ebook)
Subjects: LCSH: Zapotec language--Writing. | Zapotec language--History. | Zapotec Indians--Civilization.
Classification: LCC PM4546 .M37 2020 (print) | LCC PM4546 (ebook) | DDC 497/.6811--dc23
LC record available at https://lccn.loc.gov/2019057056
LC ebook record available at https://lccn.loc.gov/2019057057

The paper used in this publication meets the requirements of the ANSI Standard Z39.48-1984 (Permanence of Paper).

Dedicated to the memory of Alfonso Caso (1896–1970),
a pioneer in the study of Zapotec writing

Table of Contents

Part IV. Funerary Rituals and Family Shrines

Part V. Declining Use of Hieroglyphic Writing

Part VI. Shifting Strategies in the Use of Zapotec Writing

List of Illustrations

Color plates following page 359

List of Tables

Acknowledgments

I began this study in 1972, when I received a grant from the Ford Foundation to study the ancient monuments of Oaxaca. With those funds I traveled to Mexico to photograph nearly one hundred carved stones. It soon became clear that many of those monuments also deserved to be drawn. So with additional funding (this time with grant RO-21433-75-460 from the National Endowment for the Humanities), I returned with an artist to record hundreds of additional stones within the Valley of Oaxaca and beyond (Marcus 1972, 1975, 1976a, 1976b, 1983d, 1983f, 1992a, 2002, 2008b).

I am grateful for the generous financial support from both the Ford Foundation and the National Endowment for the Humanities. The NEH supported my first two artists, Lois Martin and Mark Orsen, whose efforts were remarkable. Both of them studied the most eroded stones under different lighting conditions before drawing the carved surfaces. As the number of stones increased I added other artists to my team, all of whom succeeded in bringing to life eroded hieroglyphs and faint images that photography could not capture. Their artwork, which enhances the extant corpus of Zapotec art and writing, will facilitate future studies.

In the 1970s I found Zapotec monuments in cornfields, museums, churches, municipal buildings, restaurants, and houses (see, for example, Figures A.1, A.2, and A.3). Occasionally we were lucky to discover carved stones still *in situ* at archaeological sites (e.g., Flannery and Marcus 2003; Flannery and Marcus 2015:180–193; Marcus 1976a).

Many scholars encouraged me during the course of this study, and I want to thank as many as I can. Among the most enthusiastic was the late Ignacio Bernal. I am particularly sad that I cannot show my deep appreciation by presenting him with this volume. His encouragement never flagged. Every time we met, his initial question was, "How much progress have you made on the stone monument volume?" During one of those meetings he handed me a box of Agustín Villagra's sketches and said, "Hope these advance your work." They did.

I met Bernal for the first time in 1969, when he and Margaret Mead were awarded honorary degrees by the University of California at Berkeley. When I saw him again in 1972 he said, "Do whatever you can to further the study of the Zapotec by looking at their writing and art." Bernal himself had done much to advance such studies. He had published significant volumes on Zapotec sculpture and he had other volumes in press (e.g., Bernal 1967, 1968, 1973; Bernal and Méndez 1974; Bernal and Seuffert 1973, 1979).

During my initial meetings with Bernal, we often discussed the need to put carved stones into a sociopolitical framework. We both hoped that such an approach would lead to a deeper understanding of Zapotec social and political evolution. My goal was not to create a catalogue of monuments, but to shed light on their subject matter, their intended audience, their creators' sociopolitical agendas, and their relationship to the dirt archaeology of the Zapotec.

As Bernal noted, we have a long way to go before Zapotec texts are fully deciphered. Kaufman and Justeson (2004a:1109) have noted that, "most of what is widely understood about Zapotec (Sapoteko) writing is not linguistic." Most research on the Oaxaca monuments, in fact, has been conducted much the same way that Proskouriakoff (1960, 1963, 1964, 1968, 1973, 1993) proceeded in her study of Maya monuments. She discovered meaning without deciphering every prefix, suffix, and main sign. By analyzing the distribution of certain hieroglyphs and their association with specific dates and scenes, she was able to deduce which glyphs referred to birth, the capture of prisoners, inauguration, bloodletting, and death, without rendering them phonetically. The broad strokes of her work have stood the test of time.

One must aim high to add to the solid foundation laid down by pioneers like fray Juan de Córdova, Alfonso Caso, Lorenzo Gamio, Ignacio Bernal, Jorge Acosta, Howard Leigh, Heinrich Berlin, Guillermo Dupaix, Leopoldo Batres, Francisco Belmar, Fernando Sologuren, Marshall H. Saville, Eduard Seler, Constantine George Rickards, Robert J. Weitlaner, and Wilfrido Cruz.

Subsequent generations of scholars have made important contributions to the study of Zapotec writing, including José Alcina Franch, Kenneth Pike, John Paddock, Joseph Whitecotton, Michael Lind, Gordon Whittaker, José María Bradomín, Heather Orr, Marilyn Masson, Adam Sellen, Wiltraud Zehnder, Arthur Miller, Elizabeth Boone, Emily Rabin, Ron Spores, Víctor de la Cruz, Arturo Oliveros, María Teresa Fernández de Miranda, Gary Feinman, Nelly Robles García, Manuel Esparza, María de los Ángeles Romero Frizzi, Karl Taube, Javier Urcid, Roberto García Moll, Cira Martínez López, Ferdinand Anders, Andrew Balkansky, Steve Kowalewski, Marcus Winter, Richard Blanton, John F. Scott, Bernd Fahmel Beyer, Mary Elizabeth Smith, Maarten Jansen, Michel Oudijk, Thomas Smith Stark, Iván Rivera, Christopher Moser, Roger Reeck, Bas van Doesburg, Ron van Meer, Claude Baudez, and Ernesto González Licón.

In the course of my studies I have been encouraged by Heinrich Berlin, Tatiana Proskouriakoff, J. Eric S. Thompson, Howard Leigh, Lorenzo Gamio, John Paddock, Linton Satterthwaite, and Cecil Welte. I appreciate the encouragement and support of many scholars—Guillermo Algaze, E. Wyllys Andrews, Wendy Ashmore, Andrew Balkansky, Kathryn Bard, Claude Baudez, Brian Bauer, Cynthia Beall, Robin Beck, Véronique Bélisle, Marc Bermann, Richard Blanton, Elizabeth Boone, Duccio Bonavia, Geoff Braswell, Kathryn Brown, Jane Buikstra, Marcello Canuto, Bob Carneiro, Lacey Carpenter, Luca Casparis, Luis Jaime Castillo Butters, Guillermo Cock, R. Alan Covey, Jordan Dalton, Allison R. Davis, Beatriz de la Fuente, Christopher Donnan, Christina Elson, Barb Fash, Bill Fash,

Sonny Faulseit, Gary Feinman, Laura Finsten, Chelsea Fisher, Marta Foncerrada de Molina, Marcella Frangipane, Beatriz de la Fuente, Susan Gillespie, Ernesto González Licón, David Grove, Dan Healan, Doris Heyden, Judith Irvine, Laura Junker, John Justeson, Patrick Kirch, Conrad Kottak, Steve Kowalewski, Tom Levy, Olga Linares, Alfredo López Austin, Leonardo López Luján, Bruce Mannheim, Linda Manzanilla, Lourdes Márquez Morfín, Ramiro Matos, David Meltzer, Arthur Miller, John Monaghan, Craig Morris, Mike Moseley, Chris Moser, Linda Nicholas, Deborah Nichols, Henry Nicholson, Arturo Oliveros, Jo Osborn, John O'Shea, Patricia Plunket, John Pohl, Tatiana Proskouriakoff, Elsa Redmond, Don Rice, Prudence Rice, Nelly Robles García, María Rostworowski de Diez Canseco, Alberto Ruz Lhuillier, Jerry Sabloff, Paula Sabloff, Ed Schortman, Jack Scott, Sue Scott, Bob Sharer, R. Jason Sherman, Jorge Silva, Kenny Sims, Bruce Smith, Mary Elizabeth Smith, Michael E. Smith, Charles Spencer, Ron Spores, Charles Stanish, Karen Strier, Thelma Sullivan, Loa Traxler, Howard Tsai, Patricia Urban, Gabriela Uruñuela, Dudley Varner, Laura Villamil, Nan and Evon Vogt, Joe Whitecotton, Gordon R. Willey, Ryan Williams, Amy Winchester, Henry Wright, and Jason Yaeger. I also thank Charles Spencer (Curator of Mexican and Central American Archaeology, Division of Anthropology) and the American Museum of Natural History for granting me permission to publish their photographs.

I am particularly grateful to the talented artists—Katherine Clahassey, John Klausmeyer, Jane Mariouw, Lois Martin, Rubén Méndez, Mark Orsen, David West Reynolds, and Margaret Van Bolt—who contributed their considerable skills and expertise to this volume. John Klausmeyer designed the cover and pulled together all the illustrations for this book. I also thank the director of the Museum, Michael Galaty, for his considerable help and never-ending enthusiasm.

Two special people—Manuel Esparza, then director of the Centro Regional de Oaxaca, and ethnohistorian María de los Ángeles Romero Frizzi—opened doors for me to make this study possible. I am also very grateful for the considerable patience and editorial expertise displayed by Elizabeth Noll throughout production of the book.

Note about the variability in the spelling of Colonial Valley Zapotec (CVZ) words

Spaniards such as Feria (1567), Agüero (1666), Córdova (1578a, 1578b), and Levanto (1732) recorded the Zapotec language in dictionaries, grammars, catechisms, and ecclesiastical texts. To record the unfamiliar sounds they heard, they had to create their own conventions. Even within a single manuscript, the Spaniards spelled the same word in different ways. For example, in Córdova's 1578 dictionary of 30,000 words there are many instances in which the same word is spelled in three ways, often distinguished by the use of different accent marks. Some twentieth-century linguists thought that Córdova was recording differences in pronunciation among Zapotec speakers both in Tlacochahuaya and other towns nearby. Other linguists (e.g., Anderson and Lillehaugen 2016; Radin 1930; Smith Stark 2003) concluded that Córdova used acute, grave, and other accent marks to indicate stress, tone, and glottal stops in Zapotec. Furthermore, the presence and absence of some accent marks were said to be a result of printing decisions, since some sections of Córdova's dictionary feature many accent marks while other sections of the same dictionary have few (even on some of the same words). The sixteenth and seventeenth centuries can be characterized as an era of unstandardized spelling, and scholars of the twenty-first century are still unsure what all their accent marks meant. In this book I have tried faithfully to reproduce Córdova's spelling, but warn the reader that spelling is unstandardized.

TEXAS
ACV·904

Figure A.1 (opposite page, top). For more than 400 years, Zapotec monuments have been removed from archaeological sites and used in the construction of municipal and residential buildings. One such example is shown here and in Figures A.2 and A.3. Project artist Mark Orsen is perched on Dudley Varner's vehicle in order to get a better look at a carved stone set into the wall of a residence in the town of Santiago Matatlán, located near the southern end of the Tlacolula subvalley (see Figures A.2 and A.3).

Figure A.2 (opposite page, below). This monument, also illustrated in Figures A.1 and A.3, has been displayed for many years in the exterior wall of No. 12 Calle Independencia in Santiago Matatlán. I thank Rosa Silvia G. de Méndez and her family for granting us permission to photograph and draw the stone. I discuss this monument (which Caso [1928: Fig. 94] called Lápida 14) in greater detail in Chapter 16.

Figure A.3 (above). The stone now known as Monument 2 from Santiago Matatlán was probably removed from El Palmillo, a nearby archaeological site that has been most recently excavated by Gary Feinman and Linda Nicholas (Feinman and Nicholas 2001, 2002, 2005, 2011). Drawing by Mark Orsen.

Part I

Background

1

Before Writing

When the Spaniards arrived in Mexico in AD 1519, they encountered hundreds of ethnic groups speaking different languages. These indigenous societies displayed the full spectrum of social and political complexity. Some societies were highly mobile or semisedentary. Some lived in small villages. Others occupied large villages surrounded by smaller subordinate settlements. Most stratified of all were the states and empires with their hierarchies of cities, towns, villages, and hamlets.

Scholars wanted to explain how such impressive social and political complexity arose; they also wanted to decipher the hieroglyphic texts left behind by these societies (Anders et al. 1992a, 1992b; Balkansky 1998a, 1998b, 2002; Berlin 1958, 1959, 1977; Caso 1928, 1947, 1965a, 1965b, 1965c, 1966; Caso and Gamio 1961; Grube 2012; Holmes 1907; Justeson 1986, 2012; Justeson and Campbell 1984; Kelley 1968, 1976; Kerr 1989; Lacadena García-Gallo 2008; Langley 1986; Marcus 1976c, 1992a, 1995, 1996, 2001b, 2003c, 2006a, 2012; Méluzin 1992, 1995; Mora-Marín 1997, 2005, 2009, 2018; Nicholson 1973; Prem 1971, 1973; Proskouriakoff 1963, 1964, 1968; Saturno et al. 2006; Seler 1904a, 1904b; M. E. Smith 1973a, 1983; Thomas 1893; Trigger 1998; Urcid 2001; Wang 2014; Whittaker 1980, 1982, 1992, 2009, 2018; Wichmann 2004).

Among the Mesoamerican groups that utilized writing were the Aztec, Mixtec, Zoque/Isthmian, Maya, and Zapotec. The remote ancestors of the Zapotec (known as the *bini gu'la'sa*, according to Cruz [1936] and Royce [2011], among others) began their trek to the southern highlands during the last Ice Age. They hunted game and collected wild plants. They covered a lot of terrain as they moved from place to place, leaving behind their temporary campsites.

By 8000 BC, these people were occupying rockshelters and caves in the riverine depression we now call the Valley of Oaxaca (Table 1.1; Figures 1.1–1.3). The valley, which lies at an elevation of 1550 m, exceeds 2100 km^2 in extent. This valley provides the greatest expanse of level land for agriculture in the Oaxaca highlands. Between 8000 and 6000 BC, the initial foray into agriculture began.

Sometime between 1800 and 1600 BC, the ancestors of the Zapotec abandoned their nomadic existence and made a greater commitment to agriculture and sedentary life. Survey of the Valley of Oaxaca has revealed 2700 archaeological sites, some of which continue to be occupied (Blanton et al. 1982, 1993; Feinman and Nicholas 2017; Kowalewski et al. 1989).

Three subvalleys (or arms) comprise the Valley of Oaxaca: to the northwest lies the Etla arm; to the east, the Tlacolula arm; to the south, the Valle Grande (also known as the Zaachila-Zimatlán arm). Two key rivers, the Atoyac and the Salado, created the valley in the shape of an upside-down Y; it is surrounded by forested

Table 1.1. Archaeological periods (based on Feinman and Nicholas 2017: Table 1.1).

Mesoamerica	Oaxaca	Approximate date
Colonial era begins	Spaniards arrive in Oaxaca	AD 1521–1550
Late Postclassic	Late V (Late Monte Albán V)	AD 1300–1521
Early Postclassic	Early V (Early Monte Albán V)	AD 900–1300
Late Classic	Period IIIb–IV (Monte Albán IIIb–IV)	AD 600–900
Early Classic	Period IIIa (Monte Albán IIIa)	AD 250–600
Terminal Formative	Period II (Monte Albán II)	1 BC–AD 250
Late Formative	Late I (Monte Albán Ic)	300–1 BC
Middle Formative	Early I (Monte Albán Ia)	500–300 BC
Middle Formative	Rosario phase	700–500 BC
Middle Formative	Guadalupe phase	850–700 BC
Early Formative	San José phase	1150–850 BC
Early Formative	Tierras Largas phase	1400–1150 BC
Early Formative	Espiridión complex	1900–1400 BC
Preceramic	Archaic hunting and gathering	11,000–1900 BC
Late Ice Age	Paleoindian hunting and gathering	15,000–11,000 BC

mountains that rise to 3000 m. The valley's temperate climate averages 21° C, with 550 mm of annual rainfall concentrated in the May-to-September rainy season.

Early farmers in Oaxaca cultivated gourds, squashes, beans, maize, chile peppers, and avocados. They grew those domesticates, but they also continued to collect wild plants such as acorns, prickly pear, hackberry, and maguey. Oaxaca highlanders hunted deer, peccary, gophers, rabbits, mud turtles, and other animals. On the Oaxaca coast, early villagers fished and collected molluscs. These wild foods not only added protein to the diet but also provided highly desired variety to their meals even after agriculture had emerged.

By 1500–1200 BC, hamlets and villages were scattered over the Mexican landscape from the Basin of Mexico to the coast of Chiapas. Although these early villagers were linked to each other via the exchange of marine shell, obsidian, pottery, and jade, most settlements were politically independent, inhabited by societies that were largely egalitarian. The term "egalitarian" here does not mean that every adult was equal in status, only that he or she began life with no special inherited rights.

By the time an individual reached adulthood, he or she might have achieved significant prestige as the result of having long-distance trade partners, oratorical ability, prowess in battle, leadership skills, or mastery of ritual lore. Men's and women's economic roles were often different, and these differences were reflected in their use of separate spaces inside the house. Some Formative houses were divided into a woman's work area and a man's work area (Flannery and Marcus 2005; Marcus 1998a, 1999b). As a reflection of the different roles they played in life and society, men and women often received different grave goods at death.

Before 1100 BC, men's and women's rituals were often conducted in different locations. Some men conducted their rituals in one-room men's houses, often wearing costumes and ingesting powdered lime in conjunction with ritual plants such as tobacco, jimson weed, or morning glory (Flannery and Marcus 2005:13; López Chiñas 1937; Marcus and Flannery 1978). Women's ritual was conducted in and around the house; it included divination and the use of solid handmade figurines that stood in for recently deceased ancestors (Marcus 1998a).

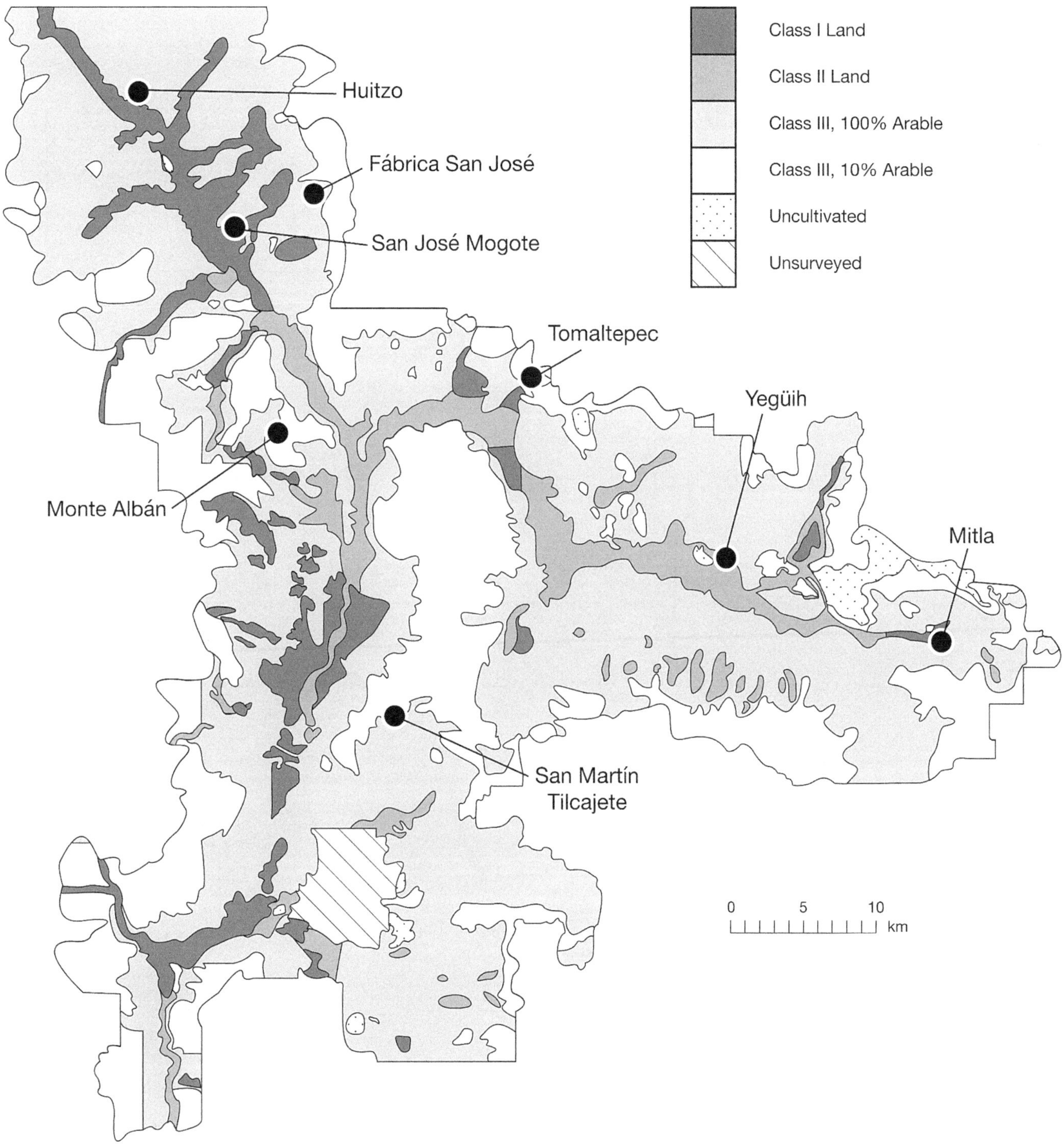

Figure 1.1. The Valley of Oaxaca, showing land classes and a sample of excavated archaeological sites.

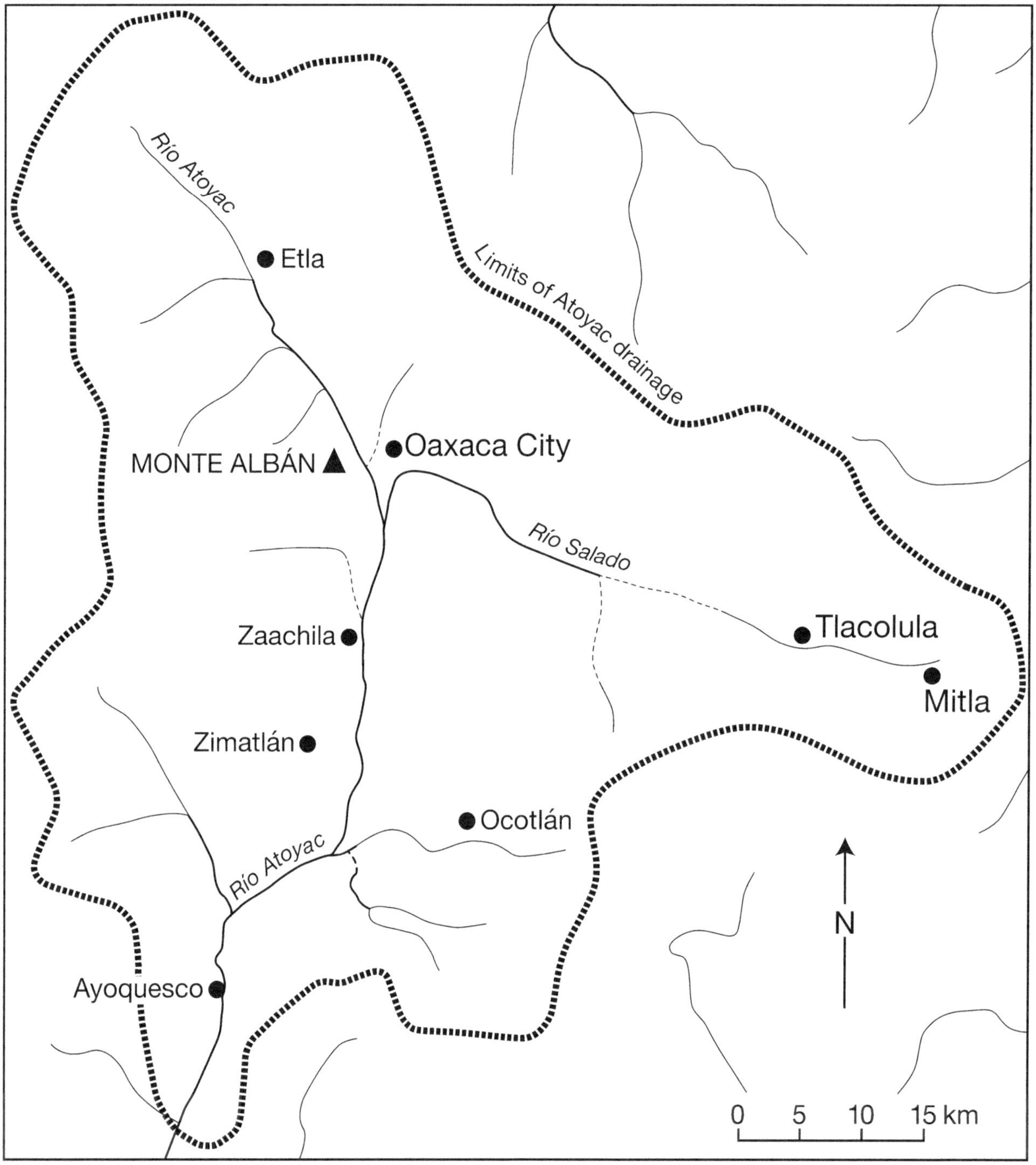

Figure 1.2. The limits of the upper Atoyac River drainage, showing a sample of modern towns and the site of Monte Albán.

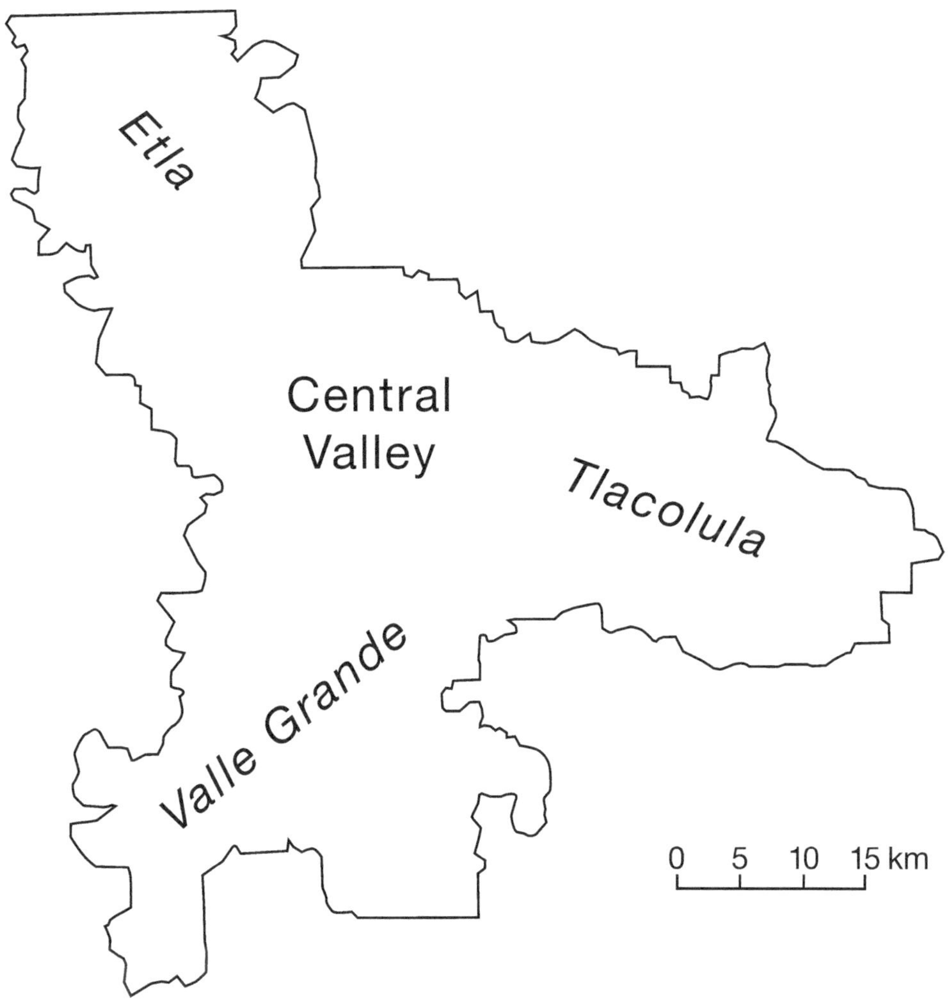

Figure 1.3. The subvalleys referred to in this volume: Etla (north), central, Tlacolula (east), and Valle Grande (south). Drawing by Kay Clahassey.

By 1000 BC a fundamental change in Zapotec society had occurred, creating a society in which some status differences were *inherited*, not achieved. One aspect of such a shift was ideological. The premise that "everyone is born equal" had changed to "some children are born with privileges based solely on who their parents are."

One line of evidence that suggests status was inherited was the appearance of burials with sumptuary goods such as magnetite mirrors, pearl oyster and spiny oyster ornaments, and jade earspools. Even children might be buried with vessels carved with symbols of sky (lightning) or earth (earthquake). Since such children were too young to have achieved high status through their own personal deeds and accomplishments, archaeologists infer that these infants and children had been born into high-status families and inherited their access to high-status goods.

A second line of evidence is the presence of deliberate cranial deformation. Since deformation to the bones of the skull had to be completed early in a child's life, such modifications long preceded any accomplishments the youngster could have achieved; it was a sign of elite ancestry.

Not only does the archaeological record from 1100 to 900 BC show fundamental changes in ideology, social organization, and inherited rights for the elite, it also reveals that political organization was changing. The era of separate, independent villages gave way to a time when small villages came under the control of larger ones. The emergence of such administrative hierarchies is one way that archaeologists infer the loss of political autonomy and the rise of chiefly territories. Leaders could now control labor and tribute from smaller subordinate villages. Such hegemonies or control hierarchies are of great interest to anthropologists.

The earliest hierarchies in Oaxaca appear to have had two levels—one large village with pyramidal temple mounds and smaller satellite villages that lacked temples. The development of three-level hierarchies was to come later. The trend to increasing complexity and hierarchy was not relentlessly upward, but oscillating and fluctuating. Three-level hierarchies sometimes broke down to two levels, then rose again to three. Archaeologists refer to this oscillating behavior as *cycling*, and they see it as a widespread dynamic in the evolution of complexity. In addition to fluctuations and oscillations in the political hierarchy, there was significant competition for administrative positions among villagers.

To be sure, one of the most difficult tasks facing archaeologists is to differentiate between an actual *administrative hierarchy* (in which some communities had political control over others) and a *site-size hierarchy* (in which sites of different size can be distinguished, but political control of smaller sites by larger sites cannot be demonstrated). Among the ways that archaeologists document political complexity is to show that some individuals had increasing control over labor and resources, that some had differential access to rare items, and that specialized personnel had emerged to direct labor and to sponsor feasts and conduct rituals.

Archaeologists also look for ways to document the evolution of rank into *social stratification*, the emergence of class-endogamous strata in which each stratum maintains itself by having its members take a spouse from within his/her own stratum. The individuals in each stratum occupied many different ranks, fulfilled different roles, and held diverse titles.

There is evidence that, by AD 1, an upper stratum had emerged in the Valley of Oaxaca that included a hereditary lord (*coquì*) and lady (*xonàxi*) and members of the royal court, as well as many ranks and categories of nobles (*joàna*), some of whom were becoming increasingly well defined. Within the lower stratum were commoners, farmers, landless serfs, and war captives converted into slaves.

The archaeological record reveals evidence of increasing competition, intervillage raiding, the burning of public buildings, and the taking of captives (e.g., Caso 1947; Redmond 1983, 1994; Redmond and Spencer 1983, 1994, 2006; Sherman et al. 2010; Spencer 1982, 2003, 2007; Spencer and Redmond 1997, 2001a, 2001b, 2003, 2006; Spencer et al. 2008). *All of these bellicose behaviors set the stage for the emergence of writing in the Valley of Oaxaca*, where hieroglyphic texts became one more tool to advance the sociopolitical strategies of ambitious individuals and families. Early texts provided the captions, labeling individuals, events, and scenes. Writing, as we shall see, first appeared in the context of competing hereditary leaders in pre-state Oaxacan society.

2

The Origins of Writing

Some of the earliest Zapotec monuments include hieroglyphs. This means that Oaxaca contributes one more case to a topic of general interest—the origins of writing worldwide—for which the literature is vast (e.g., Baines 1983, 1994, 1999; Coe 1976; Damerow 2006; Daniels 2018; Daniels and Bright 1996; DeFrancis 1989; Dibble 1940, 1971; Diringer 1962; Gelb 1952; Houston 2004; Justeson and Kaufman 1993; Kahl 2001; Keightley 1989; Marcus 1996, 2006a; Mattessich 2002; Michalowski 1993, 1994, 1996; Mary Pohl et al. 2002; Pope 1999; Postgate et al. 1995; Powell 2009; Prem 1971, 1973; Ray 1986; Regulski 2008, 2016; Restall et al. 2005; Rodríguez Martínez et al. 2006; Sampson 1985; Senner 1989; Trigger 1998).

We often hear both laymen and professionals voice the same question: "Why was writing invented?" Scholars have generally taken one of three positions: either (1) all writing systems were invented for the same purpose; or (2) each case is unique and its emergence requires a different explanation; or (3) a small number of explanations account for the appearance of most writing systems. As we will see, Position 3 is the one supported by our currently available data.

Scholars disagree on whether the appearance of writing was a sudden event or a slow process. Writing may emerge quite suddenly in some parts of the world, more gradually in others. At present we have no agreed-upon framework to explain the different rates of development and the spread of each writing system. In many parts of the world, writing systems are even thought to have been borrowed, adapted, refined, or emulated by neighboring regions.

Zapotec writing first appeared at just two sites within the Valley of Oaxaca—San José Mogote (ca. 600 BC) and Monte Albán (ca. 500 BC). Seemingly hundreds of years passed before Zapotec writing appeared on stone at other sites. The apparent monopoly held by Monte Albán is worthy of more study, as we try to determine whether it was real or merely a byproduct of decades of extensive excavation at Monte Albán. With extensive excavations at other key sites that date to the Rosario phase (700–500 BC) and Period Ia of Monte Albán (500–300 BC), we might be able to add other communities to the list of sites using the earliest Zapotec writing.

Even though we still lack fully satisfying scenarios that explain the emergence of each of the world's writing systems, I will try to show why Zapotec writing appeared before the state formed at Monte Albán. A special quality of Mesoamerican writing systems was the close relationship between image and text, between scenes and hieroglyphic captions, and between dates and events (as noted by Proskouriakoff 1960, 1963, 1964 and others since then). One function of early Zapotec writing was to label people and date events—to specify, name, and memorialize.

Figure 2.1. About 3300 BC, some of the oldest examples of Egyptian writing appeared on tomb "inventory tags." Cords could be inserted through the holes shown in the upper corners in order to attach these tags to sacks or jars. These specimens were found in Tomb U-j, Abydos (Umm el-Qaab). There is no consensus as to the meaning of the glyphs on the tags, but scholars have suggested that they convey either the place of origin or the contents of the offering (redrawn from Janák 2011: Fig. 7; Mattessich 2002: Fig. 1). Drawing by John Klausmeyer.

Old World Writing Systems

How many times in history has writing been invented? Almost everyone seems to agree that the correct answer is "at least twice." To begin with, writing was invented independently in the Old World and the New. Scholars, however, are not in agreement about the number of fully independent developments that appeared within each world area (see, for example, Damerow 2006; Daniels 2018; Daniels and Bright 1996; Gelb 1952; Justeson 1986; Pope 1999; Postgate et al. 1995; Powell 2009; Regulski 2016; Whittaker 2009, 2018).

Some scholars suggest that there were at least three fully independent inventions in the Old World (Sumerian cuneiform, Egyptian hieroglyphs, and Chinese characters), while others suggest six. They note that Mesopotamian writing on clay tablets and Egyptian hieroglyphs on sherds or ivory tags emerged at about the same time (ca. 3300 BC). Some consider their roughly contemporaneous emergence as evidence of coevolution, while other scholars think that they exemplify parallel evolution. The differences in style, format, content, and conventions would seem to support parallel evolution.

One of the most exciting discoveries that shed light on the emergence of Egyptian writing occurred in the 1980s, when Günter Dreyer reported on 190 bone and ivory tags from Tomb U-j at Abydos (Dreyer 1992; Dreyer et al. 1993, 1998). These tags, displaying one or more hieroglyphs (Figure 2.1), were found in what may have been the final resting place of King Scorpion of Dynasty 0, a tomb that may date to 3300 BC (Bard 2015; Hendrickx 2006; Kahl 2001:103–110; Mattessich 2002:196). The tags, which were apparently attached to bags and jars, display hieroglyphs that are thought to be the names of places where the objects were made and/or specify the quantity and kind of commodity. Of the 190 known tags, 43 display only numbers.

With approximately 525 texts now known for the era before Dynasty 1, Egypt's earliest writing would seem to be as ancient as that of the Near East. Sumerian writing initially focused on record-keeping—keeping track of rations and organizing receipts that listed, quantified, and categorized commodities, transactions, and supervisors. Early Egyptian texts often recorded proper nouns, labeling people, places, and objects associated with rituals and royalty (Baines 1989, 1994). Although Postgate et al. (1995:479) contrasted these functions as "utilitarian" versus "ceremonial," they conclude that "it seems probable that early writing systems were both developed for utilitarian purposes." By using the term "utilitarian" they meant that early writing emerged to serve administrative needs. This view downplays the fact that early Sumerian writing recorded economic transactions, while early Egyptian writing covered rulers' deeds.

The trajectory and pace of development of each writing system varied. Epigrapher Piotr Michalowski (1996:35) has argued that the earliest writing in the Near East "was invented as a whole and did not develop gradually" and that "the number signs may have been adapted from small clay counters that were used independently, or impressed on tablets." Most scholars agree that these clay objects functioned in a counting system, and that such counters existed long before writing appeared. Clay tokens could be sealed inside a *bulla,* a hollow clay envelope, to indicate the number of items being sent, somewhat similar to a bill of lading. In the 1950s, A. Leo Oppenheim (1959) noted that an inscription on the outside of a hollow clay *bulla* from the site of Nuzi in Iraq listed a number of animals, and the number of clay tokens inside that sphere matched the number written on the outside. Pierre Amiet (1966, 1972) reported similar findings at Susa in Iran, where the writing would have been an early form of Elamite.

These clay objects—from pebbles to geometric shapes—occurred all over the Near East for thousands of years before writing appeared (Zimansky 1993). Given that long time span, their extensive geographic distribution, and their variable shapes, some scholars see problems in viewing all of the clay tokens as direct precursors of writing (e.g., Lieberman 1980; Michalowski 1993; Zimansky 1993). Some scholars (Friberg 1999; Schmandt-Besserat 1977, 1978, 1979, 1992) do regard tokens as the impetus for writing and accounting. Friberg (1999:107) succinctly says "the early history of writing is also *the early history of counting and accounting"* [emphasis in original]. He underlines the important role of tokens in counting, noting that the largely undeciphered proto-Elamite script includes numbers that are nearly identical to numbers in Mesopotamian proto-cuneiform script.

Near Eastern scholars agree that cuneiform texts met the need to record economic calculations and transactions (Englund 1988, 1994a, 1994b; Green and Nissen 1987). Of the 5000 clay tablets found at Uruk in Iraq that date to around 3100 BC, 85% are economic texts, while the remaining 15% are lexical, including lists of people and professions (Nissen 1986:323). This system came to have about 800 signs, of which more than 60 were number signs (Figure 2.2). The presence of 60 different signs for numbers in proto-cuneiform reinforces our impression that quantification was very important and that certain number signs were used for different commodities. Several systems of numerical signs were used in cuneiform to quantify measures of grain, liquids, and units of time (Englund 1988, 1994a, 1994b; Friberg 1999; Nissen et al. 1993). Many of the 800 signs were pictographic, but a sufficient number of phonetic elements have been identified to confirm that Sumerian was the underlying language (Krebernik 1994; Michalowski 1990, 1996).

Sumerian cuneiform was predominantly monosyllabic. The majority of the 800 signs represent whole words, although some signs functioned as syllables in other contexts. Syllabic spellings were often needed to express personal names and homophones (soundalike words).

Even proto-cuneiform tablets included accounts, receipts, quantities, and lists. Proto-cuneiform was the subject of an important study by Damerow (2006), who isolated the following characteristics: (1) its structures were far from matching the syntax of a language; (2) phonetic coding played a minor role, if any; (3) its conventions were not yet uniform; (4) it was used in a restricted context, that of documenting administrative activities; (5) it had precursors in symbolic systems that were used for the same purpose; and (6) there was a coevolution of arithmetic and proto-cuneiform signs. In the preserved corpus of 6000 proto-cuneiform texts, there are more than 1500 nonnumerical signs. One hundred signs occur more than 100 times. In contrast, 500+ signs occur only once (Damerow 2006:6).

Precursors of writing included cylinder seals, sealed *bullae* with tokens inside, and sealed numerical tablets. Damerow concludes that writing developed in two stages—in its first stage, writing was fairly independent of phonetic coding; in the second stage, phonetic coding made new applications possible.

The oldest texts record early types of information processing that led to the projection of quantities needed. On the reverse side of the clay tablet shown in Figure 2.2 we see the projected total of grain that would be needed to produce the number of products registered on the obverse. As Nissen et al. (1993: Figure 32) note, this tablet attests to the calculation of "theoretical" values of grain use in the production of cereal products.

The earliest Egyptian writing appeared on tags and stone slabs that had been placed in royal tombs or discarded in ceremonial deposits. Among the earliest hieroglyphs were the royal throne and palace façade, both symbols of Egyptian kingship. The ancient Egyptians used their early hieroglyphs to label people and places. Well-known examples occur on carved stones—the Narmer Palette, Narmer Macehead, and Scorpion Macehead—associated with the reigns of two Dynasty 0 rulers named Scorpion and Narmer.

The obverse side of the Narmer Palette (Figure 2.3) depicts Narmer grasping a weapon in his right hand; in his left, he grasps the hair of a captive. Behind the captive's head are two signs (a harpoon and water sign), which might refer to his name or place of origin (possibly the Nile delta). Narmer's hieroglyphic name (Nar=catfish + Mer=chisel) is given in the square *serekh* immediately above his White Crown, the headdress worn by the kings of Upper Egypt. Behind Narmer's back is his servant, who carries a small (water?) jar (in his right hand) and the ruler's sandals (see left arm); the servant's hieroglyphic name combines a flower and another jar-like element. The very large hieroglyphs (on the right, above the captive) include a hawk grasping a cord tied to the nose of a bearded man in the land of papyrus (which may indicate the delta of Lower Egypt). In the lowest register are two more captives, whose names or hometowns are indicated by hieroglyphs near their faces. This side of the palette may record the conquest of Lower Egypt by Upper Egypt. The hieroglyphs clarify the contents of the palette—they supply proper nouns, labeling the individuals and places. Even though the depiction of Narmer shows him to be an important person—he wears crowns and is much taller than anyone else—we could not know his identity without the hieroglyphic captions that specify his name.

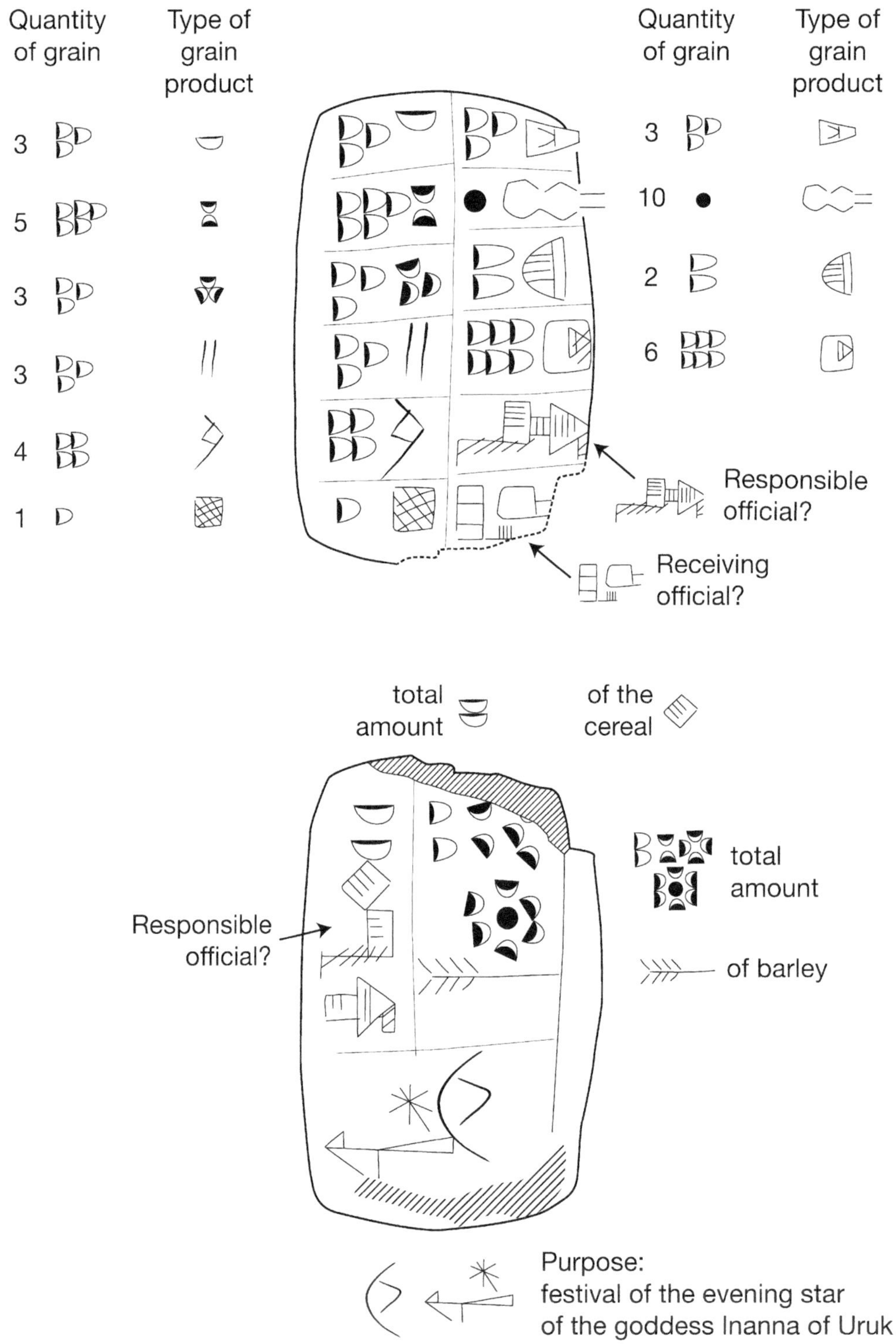

Figure 2.2. About 3200 BC, Mesopotamia developed its own form of proto-writing, called proto-cuneiform. As in the case of Egypt, word order was not standardized, nor was there a close rendition of the syntax of the spoken language. In contrast to Egypt, however, proto-cuneiform was used to maintain economic records. On one side of this clay tablet (*upper half of page*) we see 12 compartments, 10 of which include a number followed by a grain product. The last two compartments in the right-hand column mention the responsible official and the receiving official. The other side of the tablet (*lower half of page*) gives the projected total of grain to be used in a festival honoring the evening star of the goddess Inanna, patron deity of Uruk (adapted from Powell 2009: Fig. 5.1; Nissen et al. 1993: Fig. 32). Drawing by John Klausmeyer.

Figure 2.3. The obverse of the Narmer Palette shows a king named Narmer, who wears the White Crown of Upper Egypt. He grasps the hair of a captive in one hand and a club in the other. Hieroglyphs label the other four individuals depicted in the middle and lowest registers of the palette, including the two nude prisoners at the bottom. The name given hieroglyphically as Nar (fish) + Mer (chisel), which can be seen just above his White Crown, is located in a centrally placed rectangle or *serekh* between the heads of two bulls (redrawn from Emery 1961: Fig. 4).

Figure 2.4. The reverse of the Narmer Palette is divided into four registers. In the uppermost register we see two bulls flanking the hieroglyphic name Nar-mer, set inside a rectangular *serekh*. In the second register we can distinguish the standing figure of Narmer from all other standing individuals since (1) he is shown as exceptionally tall; (2) he wears the Red Crown of Lower Egypt; and (3) he is associated with his hieroglyphic name, which appears for a second time in front of his face. In the second register (from left to right) we see a servant, whose name is likely indicated by the hieroglyph inside the rectangle above his head; then we see Narmer walking behind another servant associated with a hieroglyphic caption, and four standard bearers. They all are traveling to see the beheaded corpses of Narmer's enemies. These ten decapitated men have their arms bound with rope and their heads between their ankles. The third register shows two animal wranglers, holding ropes around the elongated necks of two possible lions. Their intertwined necks are thought to signify the unification of Upper and Lower Egypt, which Narmer achieved. The circular depression surrounded by their elongated necks is the place where pigment could be ground on this elegant cosmetic palette. In the lowest register we see a bull attacking a walled town, a possible metaphor for Narmer successfully attacking a town (redrawn from Emery 1961: Fig. 4).

The name "Nar-mer" is given three times on the Narmer Palette—in the top register between the bulls' heads (on both sides of the palette) and, as we will see, in the second register in front of the ruler's head on the reverse side of the palette. The reverse side (Figure 2.4) has four registers. At the top we see the bulls' heads and hieroglyphic square (*serekh*) containing the signs for Nar+Mer. In the second register is the sandal-bearer, whose identity is indicated by a rectangle with a hieroglyph inside. The second, much taller figure, wears the Red Crown of Lower Egypt; in front of his face are the hieroglyphs Nar + Mer, inserted here to identify the ruler Narmer. There is a named assistant who carries water; other assistants carry wooden standards that may specify the names of districts and provinces.

All of these individuals are setting out to view a battlefield where ten nude captives have their arms bound with rope; these ten decapitated prisoners lie with their severed heads between their legs. These ten corpses probably symbolize the many who died; the hieroglyphic signs above them have been interpreted as a place in Lower Egypt. In the third register we see a circle, indicating the depression on the palette where cosmetic pigment would have been ground. This circular depression is surrounded by the long, intertwined necks of two animals. This intertwining may well symbolize the unification of Upper and Lower Egypt. In the lowest register is a bull that may also represent Narmer, battering his way into a walled town and taking a nude prisoner (see Emery 1961; Quibell 1898–1900).

Although it is difficult to settle on the exact number of times that writing was invented, it may have been anywhere from three to six in the Old World. Over the next few decades, scholars will try to determine with much greater precision whether there are five to ten cases of invention in the history of the world, or whether some apparent inventions were actually the result of borrowing and emulation.

Writing systems that appear after Egyptian and Sumerian are Proto-Indic and Indus script in Pakistan; Cretan Hieroglyphic (1800–1500 BC) found on the island of Crete; Linear A writing (1550–1450 BC) found on Aegean islands such as Melos, Thera, Kea, and Kythera; Linear B writing (1400–1200 BC) found in the Mycenaean palaces of Knossos on Crete and on the mainland at Mycenae, Thebes, and Tiryns; and Hittite writing in Asia Minor. Most of these writing systems are regarded as derivative rather than fully independent inventions, but the jury is still out.

Chinese writing, in contrast, is seen as a fully independent invention, even though it appeared long after Mesopotamian and Egyptian writing. Chinese writing emerged at ca. 1250 BC during the Shang dynasty, when oracle bone texts were incised on ox scapulae and turtle plastrons (Daniels 2018; Keightley 1989). Early Chinese texts consist of one to seven characters, some of which are thought to be the name of a clan or ancestor. Chinese texts on bronze can also specify the name of the person who made the bronze, and the name or title of the person for whom the bronze was cast (Boltz 1986:421). Shang writing is logographic, with each sign standing for a single word.

Like Egyptian writing, Chinese writing made use of the rebus principle (Boltz 1996). In Chinese, for example, the word *wang*, which means "king" and "to go toward," were both expressed by the same sign. In addition to homonyms and near-homonyms rendered by the same sign, there are characters expressing words linked semantically. Both the rebus use of characters and the multivalent use of characters increased the effectiveness of the Chinese writing system (Boltz 1996:193). To reduce semantic and phonetic ambiguity, Chinese writing developed semantic determinatives and phonetic determinatives. Japanese, Korean, and Thai writing systems emerged later, and are considered derivative in one way or another from Chinese writing.

As noted by Justeson and Mathews (1990:110), "in Sumerian, Egyptian, Chinese and Mayan hieroglyphic writing, rebus is repeatedly the prime basis for the development of nonlogographic phonetic values for signs that were originally logographs. … and tonal variation was legitimate in Mixtec rebuses." More than a century ago, Spinden (1913:31) noted that:

> Aztec writing can best be compared to the so-called 'rebus puzzles' which consist largely of pictured puns upon whole or partial words. The hieroglyphs are practically limited to place names, personal names, month and day names, numbers and principal objects of commerce. There are no word pictures for adverbs, adjectives or conjunctions, and no representations of abstract ideas. … the most important and interesting word signs are, as before remarked, rebuses in which separate syllables or groups of syllables are represented by more or less conventionalized pictures. The whole word picture is then made up of syllable pictures which indicate phonetically the word as a whole but which may have no definite relationship to the meaning of the word.

Daniels (2018:137) asserts that monosyllables seem to be a necessary precondition for a writing system to develop out of pictography, concluding that "writing began only for languages where almost everything you draw a picture of also has a pronunciation that is a single syllable." One example of rebus writing in English is "I saw Aunt Rose," a sentence that consists of four monosyllables (Figure 2.5). There are cases where words with more than one syllable also lent themselves to rebus writing. In future studies of Zapotec writing, it seems likely that scholars will find examples of rebus writing.

New World Writing Systems

Of the two earliest Old World systems (Sumerian and Egyptian), Mesoamerica's hieroglyphic writing was more like Egypt's in content and purpose. Egypt used logograms and syllabograms to label objects, to establish royal names and genealogies, and to record political and religious actions of the rich and powerful. The texts were usually intended for noble audiences.

The social setting in which writing emerged was dominated by the ideology of sacred power and the performance of royal

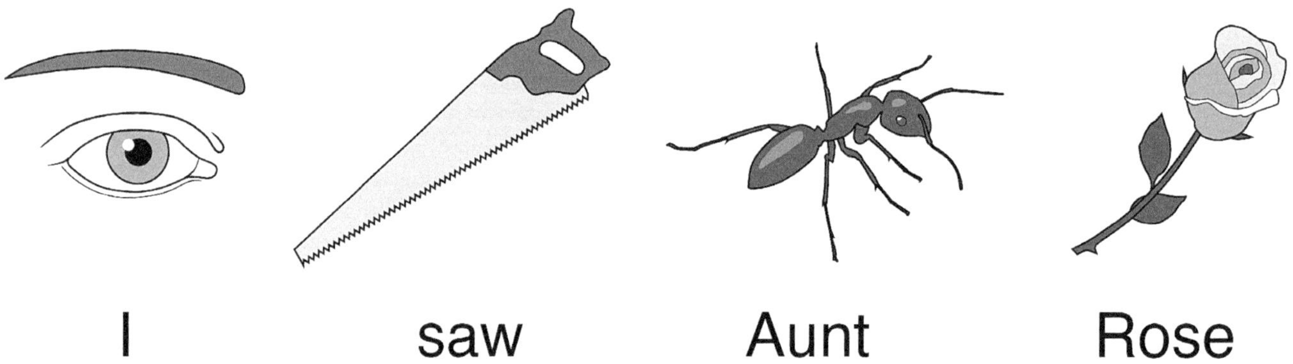

Figure 2.5. When two words (e.g., bear and bare) sounded alike in a particular language, and one of them was easy to depict, ancient scribes often used rebus writing to convey words that might be difficult to write. Such puns would work only for native speakers. For example, only a speaker of English can look at the depiction of an eye, a carpenter's saw, an ant, and a flower and read it as "I saw Aunt Rose" (redrawn from Marcus 1992a: Fig. 2.1). Drawing by John Klausmeyer.

ritual (Regulski 2016). "Available evidence suggests that the [Egyptian] hieroglyphic writing system was improved for purposes of high culture and display rather than for administration; but the latter no doubt also exploited such developments" (Baines 1999:885). Most of these statements about Egyptian hieroglyphic writing could be applied to Mesoamerica.

One fundamental contrast between Near Eastern writing and that of the earliest Zapotec or Maya was function—e.g., proto-cuneiform and cuneiform writing focused on lists and economic transactions, whereas Mesoamerican writing emerged to label people, places, objects, and events. Among the early hieroglyphs in the New World and in Egypt were proper nouns—names of leaders, victors, prisoners, and places, as we have seen in the Narmer Palette (see Figures 2.3, 2.4).

Mesoamerican texts included the exact dates on which events had taken place. The Maya, in particular, were able to anchor events in time more precisely than the Egyptians. We have seen Narmer taking prisoners and surveying the bodies of decapitated captives, but we do not know the precise day on which he performed these actions. In contrast, we often know the precise date that a Maya ruler took a captive; the Yaxchilan ruler in Figure 2.6 is shown taking a prisoner on May 9, AD 755. The monuments of the Maya and the Zoque/Isthmian people used a base date, a zero point, from which they calculated the number of days that had elapsed. They used the base date 3114 BC, which made it possible to anchor historic events in time.

The earliest Mesoamerican texts have ritual, social, and political content, often supplying names of individuals. What we do not see in the earliest texts are lists of commodities and the amount of each, as an accountant would record or a school boy would use to learn to calculate. Not until the sixteenth century AD do we see long lists of goods. At that time Aztec scribes were painting books that listed tribute (e.g., the Matrícula de Tributos 1980; Codex Mendoza)—the amount of each item and the name of each subject province. For example, the Codex Mendoza provided the names of 371 towns, grouped into 38 provinces, that paid tribute to Motecuhzoma, ruler of the Aztecs (e.g., Berdan and Anawalt 1997; Clark 1938).

Maya pottery, Zapotec stone monuments, and Mixtec codices sometimes depicted nobles sitting in their court while receiving gifts, food, or tribute, but the earliest Mesoamerican texts lack the lists of goods and the compartments that enumerate grains and animals, as we have seen in proto-cuneiform economic tablets (see Figure 2.2). Maya lords are depicted on some Classic vessels (AD 300–900) receiving cloth, cloth bundles (Figure 2.7), and bowls filled with gifts, food, or tribute (Kerr 1989; Marcus 2000:234; Reents-Budet 2006; Reents-Budet et al. 1994). Freidel et al. (2017) have identified possible counting sticks and tokens in Maya tombs, and they suggest that standardized shell objects may have been used as "all-purpose monies." One of the many purposes of these scenes on pottery, however, was to show the political and social power of a Maya ruler in his palace or temple,

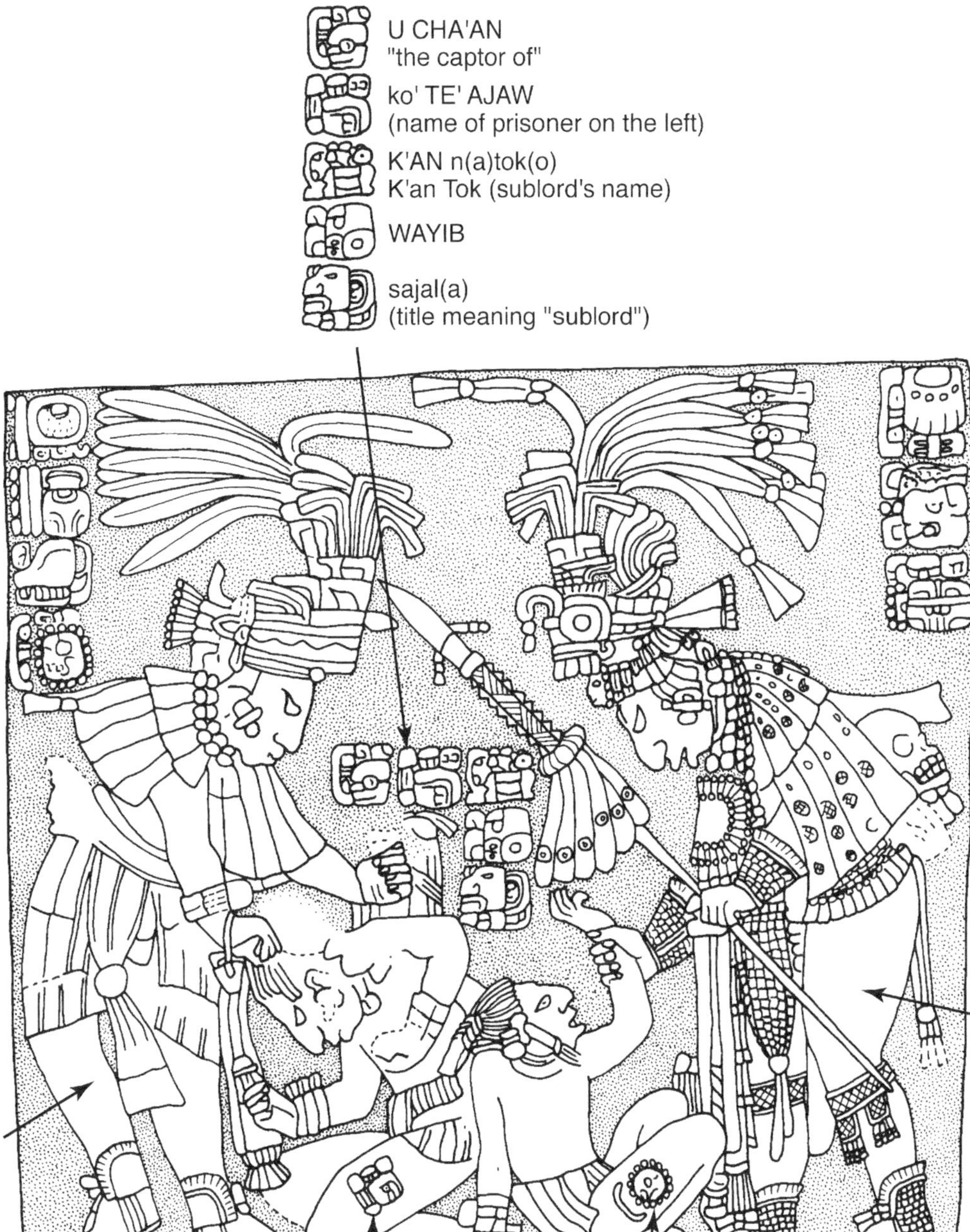

Figure 2.6. Both the Zapotec and Maya named important prisoners captured in battle. In this monument from Yaxchilan we see the Maya ruler Bird Jaguar (standing at far right) taking a prisoner by the wrist. That prisoner's name, Jeweled Skull, is incised on his right thigh. It is also given in the main text starting in the upper left corner, where we read: "in AD 755 was captured Jeweled Skull, his prisoner, Bird Jaguar, Lord of Yaxchilan." (From that time on, this Yaxchilan ruler would use "the Captor of Jeweled Skull" as one of his titles.) Standing at far left is the provincial governor K'an Tok Wayib, who has also captured a prisoner—in this case, by grasping his hair, much as the Egyptian ruler Narmer does in Figure 2.3. In the text associated with K'an Tok Wayib he is referred to as "the Captor of Ko'te' Ajaw." His prisoner's name is given twice—in the hieroglyphic text at the center of the monument and again on the prisoner's thigh (redrawn from Marcus 1992a: Fig. 11.52; Proskouriakoff 1964: Fig. 1). Drawing by John Klausmeyer.

Figure 2.7. In Mesoamerica, cloth was a highly valued item used for tribute, exchange, and gift-giving. Here we see scenes from three Maya vessels that show stacks of cloth used as gifts (*u yubte'il, hun pak yubte'*) or tribute (*patan*) (redrawn from Robicsek 1975: Figs. 72, 162, 166; Marcus 2000:234). The earliest Maya texts were not devoted to quantifying such commodities, but Late Classic texts on pottery do occasionally specify quantities of items. Drawing by John Klausmeyer.

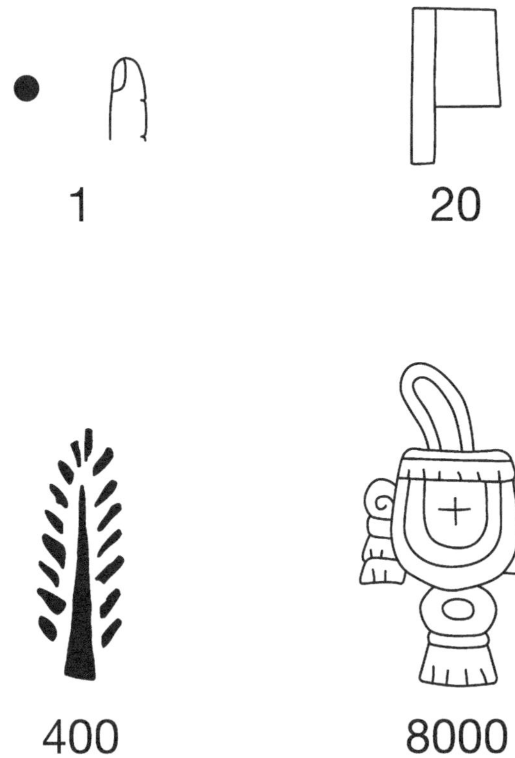

Figure 2.8. Like other Mesoamerican groups, the Aztec used a vigesimal system, which is based on multiples of 20. The Aztec used a dot or human digit to signify the number 1; the flag to signify 20; the feather/tree to signify 400; and a bag to signify 8000 (see Davletshin and Lacadena 2019). Drawing by John Klausmeyer.

rather than to list the quantities of each item he received. Although goods are occasionally quantified, detailed receipts for each and every commodity are not given. And some of these depictions of Maya lords receiving tribute were painted at least a millennium after writing first appeared in Mexico.

Only one group so far—the Aztec—used picture-writing to list the places and the amount of tribute exacted (Figures 2.8, 2.9). In Figure 2.9 we see part of one page in the Codex Mendoza that shows tributary towns in Tepeacac, a subject region that corresponded to most of the Mexican state of Puebla (Berdan and Anawalt 1997:98–101). The unique tribute demands imposed on Tepeacac included prisoners from Tlaxcala, Cholula, and Huexotzinco. Prisoners taken in war were listed as part of their tribute and their status as prisoners is indicated two ways—(1) by the central placement (at the top) of a symbol for warfare (a shield and obsidian-slotted weapon), and (2) by the disembodied heads of war captives from three different ethnic groups. Each head is linked to a hieroglyph that specifies the name of the ethnic group. Tepeacac was apparently the only province required to deliver war captives, and the only province required to pay tribute in lime, deer skins, and certain wood products.

The frequency with which war captives were to be delivered is unspecified, but other items were to be delivered every 80 days (e.g., 4000 loads of *tenextli* or lime, 800 deer skins, 4000 loads of canes, 8000 loads of canes for arrows, and 8000 loads of *acayetl* or canes filled with tobacco to be burned as offerings to the gods). The amount of lime demanded was substantial—4000 loads. While the Mixtec, Zapotec, and Maya may also have received regular tribute installments, we have yet to recover hieroglyphic texts that list the amount of each commodity and specify the delivery schedule for each.

In sum, there were at least two different stimuli for the origins of writing. One stimulus was to memorialize historic and ritual events, specifying the names of places and leaders. Another stimulus was the desire to keep detailed economic records that quantified the number of sheep, the amount of barley, and so on; such detailed accounting records could be consulted later.

The subject matter of early writing in Mexico was therefore more like that of Egypt; both those places created labels and proper nouns for events (Baines 1989; Berlo 1989; Houston 2004; Marcus 1992b, 2006a), rather than itemizing economic transactions.

Justeson and Mathews (1990) recognize two separate regional script traditions in Mexico: the Oaxacan and the Southeastern (e.g., Figure 2.10). They suggest that the Southeastern scripts (e.g., Isthmian and Maya) arose from the iconography displayed on ceremonial celts and that writing took shape before state-level political organization had emerged. Justeson and Mathews argue that the format of the iconography on ceremonial celts is columnar and that the clusters of motifs are broadly homologous with clause

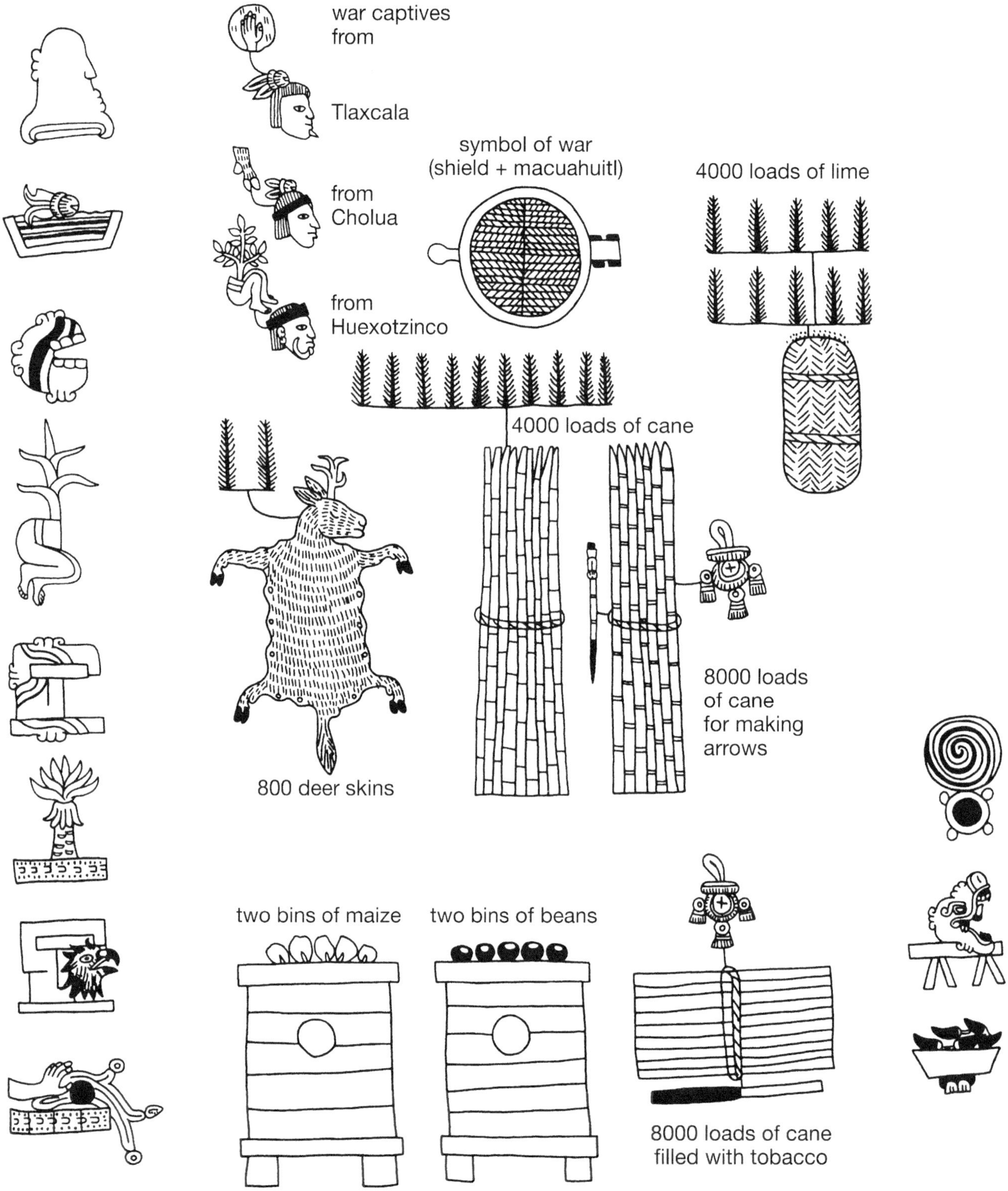

Figure 2.9. This page from the Aztec Codex Mendoza shows towns in the province of Tepeacac (in the column at left) as well as the items that those towns were required to deliver to the Aztec capital. Towns in this province had to deliver slaves, loads of lime, deer skins, and canes filled with tobacco, as well as bins of maize and beans (redrawn from Berdan and Anawalt 1997: fol. 42r). Note that the slaves (war captives) shown here are differentiated by hairdo, headdress, or facial markings; centuries earlier, the Zapotec of Monte Albán used similar methods to identify defeated places. Drawing by John Klausmeyer.

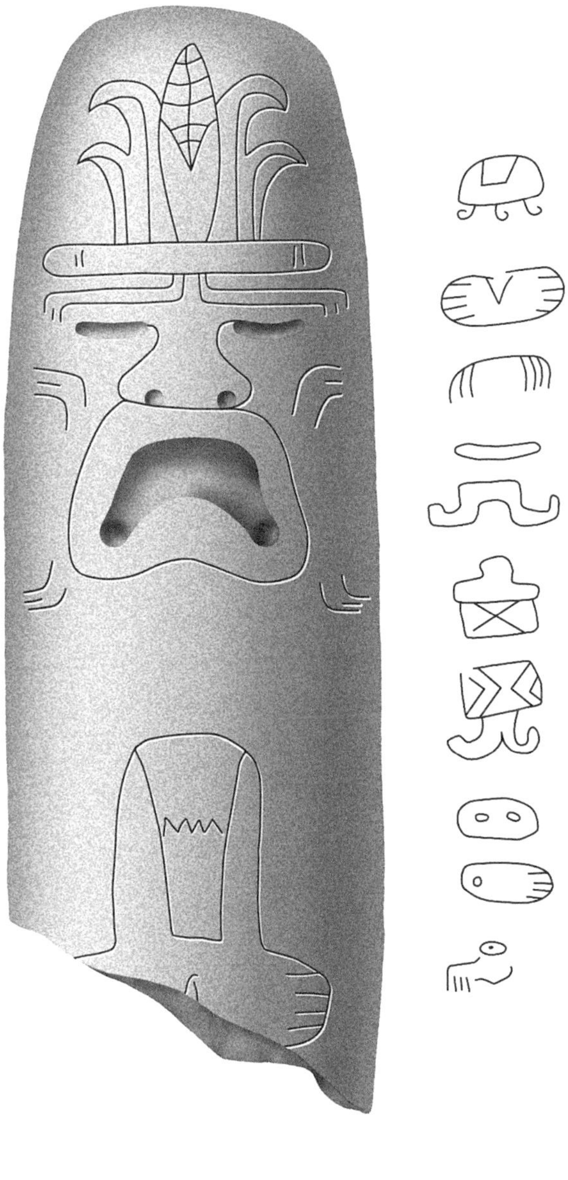

Figure 2.10. Organizing hieroglyphs in a column was typical of early Zapotec, Isthmian, and Maya writing. Some scholars (e.g., Justeson and Mathews 1990) suggest that this is because early texts were carved on celts, whose narrowness precluded placing hieroglyphs in long rows. Even later, when larger stone monuments were available, scribes continued to make the column their preferred way to arrange hieroglyphic texts. This celt from El Sitio, Guatemala, is carved on two sides. The front of the celt shows a figure with maize in his headdress. On the back of the celt we see an early column of hieroglyphs that have yet to be fully deciphered (redrawn from Navarrete 1974: Fig. 25). Height 21 cm. Drawing by John Klausmeyer.

Figure 2.11. This roller stamp from Tlatilco (Basin of Mexico) includes three logograms in a row, and could be considered a precursor to writing. After ink or paint was applied to the roller stamp, these three signs could be repeated over and over on cloth, paper, or the human body (redrawn from Franco C. 1959). Drawing by John Klausmeyer.

sequences in language. The long narrow shape of ceremonial celts inspired a format that led to hieroglyphs arranged in a column. Such celts are sometimes worn by early Isthmian and Maya lords, suspended from their belts (e.g., on Stela 31 at Tikal, Stela 114 at Calakmul, and on the Leyden Plaque; see Folan et al. 1995; Justeson and Mathews 1990; Schele and Freidel 1990; Taube 1996). Both the Oaxacan and Southeastern scripts used bar-and-dot notation for numbers; they used the column as an organizing principle to arrange signs vertically (Graham 1971; Marcus 1976c, 2006a; Prem 1973).

Even though the column was the principal Mesoamerican format, we occasionally see hieroglyphs set in a row. For example, an early roller stamp from the Basin of Mexico has three signs that seem to function as logograms (Figure 2.11). The profile head at left seems to depict maize emerging from a fissure in the Earth. The middle sign shows the four world directions (a motif which also appears on Early Formative pottery in Oaxaca; see Flannery and Marcus 1994; Flannery and Marcus 2005:332; Marcus 1989a). The sign at right later became the hieroglyph *k'in*, used by the Maya to refer to sun, day, and time (Marcus 2006a: Figure 1). Signs on such roller stamps, such as this one from the Formative village of Tlatilco, may be forerunners of Mesoamerican writing (Franco C. 1959; Kelley 1966). These roller stamps could have been coated with paint and then rolled over cloth, human skin, or other material to create continuous patterns. More than 300 such stamps have been recovered at the site of Tlatilco alone (Field 1967).

Mesoamerica eventually witnessed the emergence of several distinctive writing systems— Zapotec, Cascajal, Isthmian/Zoque, Maya, Teotihuacano, Xochicalcan, Mixtec, and Aztec—but not all are considered truly independent inventions (e.g., Berlo 1989; Houston and Coe 2003; Justeson 1986, 2012; Justeson and

Figure 2.12. Three hieroglyphs were arranged in a column on Monument 13, La Venta, Tabasco. These three hieroglyphs (especially the bird head) may provide the name of the individual depicted. They thus serve the same function as the hieroglyph on Monument 3, San José Mogote, Oaxaca, discussed in Chapter 6 (redrawn from Drucker 1952: Fig. 61). Drawing by John Klausmeyer.

Kaufman 1993, 1997; Kaufman and Justeson 2004b; Langley 1986; Macri and Stark 1993; Mora-Marín 2009; Mary Pohl et al. 2002; Rodríguez Martínez et al. 2006; Sáenz 1961, 1964; Saturno et al. 2006; Urcid et al. 1994; Winter et al. 1994). Zapotec writing was apparently one of the first to emerge, at approximately 650–600 BC. The next writing system—Isthmian/Zoque (also called Tuxtlan, Gulf Coast, La Mojarran, and Epi-Olmec)—seems sufficiently different from Zapotec to suggest that the idea of writing, rather than most of the hieroglyphs, may have been borrowed. The Zoque system was used at various sites along Mexico's Gulf Coast, perhaps as early as 500–300 BC (Figure 2.12). The oldest column of Maya text occurs at San Bartolo, Guatemala at ca. 300 BC (see Saturno et al. 2006).

From those initial examples of writing (Zapotec, Isthmian/Zoque, and Maya), multiple branches developed. Out of the greater Oaxacan tradition arose Ñuiñe, Cacaxtlan, Xochicalcan, and Mixtec. Out of the Isthmian/Zoque system—with its Long Count dates—arose the Pacific piedmont and later lowland Maya writing. The lowland Maya took the writing system to its greatest heights, capable of replicating the Mayan languages. Still later (AD 200–900), lesser-known writing systems appeared at several sites, including Teotihuacán, El Tajín, and Teotenango (Berrin 1988; Langley 1986). Finally, during the Postclassic period (AD 1200–1500), the Aztec or Nahua groups developed their system of writing (e.g., Lacadena García-Gallo 2008; Nicholson 1973; Whittaker 2018), which clearly owed a debt to earlier systems.

3

The Calendars of Mesoamerica

Like other Mesoamerican cultures, the Zapotec had two calendars. One was a secular calendar of 365 days (18 units of 20 days = 360 + 5 extra days). The other was a ritual calendar of 260 days (13 numbers x 20 day names).

When the 260-day calendar and the 365-day calendar were combined, the result was a 52-year Calendar Round with 18,980 differently designated days. Each year in the 52-year Calendar Round began with a different combination of number + day name. After 52 years had passed, the 53rd year returned to the same designation as the first.

Only four of the 20 day signs could begin a year (Boone 2000; Broda de Casas 1969, 1971; Caso 1928, 1965a, 1967; Morley 1915; Thompson 1950). Aztec years, for example, could begin only with one of the following days: Flint, House, Rabbit, or Reed (Figure 3.1). The year 1 Flint, for example, corresponded to AD 1428; 2 House began the next year, AD 1429; 3 Rabbit began AD 1430; 4 Reed began AD 1431; and AD 1432 corresponded to the year 5 Flint (Caso 1928:49). These number + day-name designations were sufficient to situate any year within a 52-year period, but not beyond that unit of 52 years.

Scholars have speculated as to when these calendars first appeared (e.g., Alcina Franch 1966, 1979, 1993; Caso 1967; Cruz 1935, 1946; Edmonson 1988; Malmström 1992; Miles 1952; Seler 1904a; Thompson 1950; Whittaker 1983). Current evidence suggests that the 260-day calendar came first, possibly appearing hundreds of years before dates were first carved on stone. Such time depth seems plausible simply because every Mesoamerican linguistic and cultural group used a 260-day calendar, and all its regional variants were similar in structure. That fact suggests that the calendar was in use before many of the ethnic and linguistic divisions took place.

Because the Aztec calendar is the best known, scholars over the years have found it tempting to use Nahuatl terms to explain lesser-known calendars such as those used by the Matlatzinca, Tarascan, Otomí, and Zapotec. To be sure, we have ample evidence to show that these calendars were not identical to that of the Aztec. Even the Aztec calendar itself was not uniform; different day names were used by residents of different Aztec towns, including Tenochtitlán, Texcoco, Tepepulco, Tlatelolco, Metztitlán, and Cuauhtitlán. A different day was chosen to begin each ethnic group's year as well (Kirchhoff 1954–1955). Caso (1967:39–40), Jiménez Moreno (1961), and Kirchhoff (1950), were among the first investigators to point out that different towns in Central Mexico began their years on different days.

Figure 3.1. Only four of the 20 day signs in the 260-day calendar could be used as year bearers. For the Aztec, those four day signs were Flint, House, Rabbit, and Reed. Here we see the year 1 Flint, which began the year AD 1428; 2 House or AD 1429; 3 Rabbit or AD 1430; and 4 Reed or AD 1431 (see Vaillant 1941: Pl. 63; Quiñones Keber 1995: fol. 31r). Drawing by John Klausmeyer.

The day names, their meanings, and the order of the 20 days are similar in the Zapotec, Mixtec, and Aztec calendars, but certainly not identical. Hieroglyphic variants for a subset of Zapotec day names also emerged over the course of time.

Zapotec Calendars

There is growing interest in the Zapotec calendar and writing system for two principal reasons: (1) the Zapotec use of the 260-day calendar, year signs, and year bearers on stone monuments is considered to be among the earliest in Mesoamerica, and (2) the Zapotec writing system has so far defied decipherment, although progress has been made—particularly on the nature and use of calendric signs.

The 260-day calendar has received attention for more than a century. One early scholar, Hans Gadow (1908:303), was impressed by how many day names in highland calendars referred to lowland tropical fauna. He surmised that the 260-day calendar used by the Aztec could not have been invented in the Basin of Mexico since at least five day names (crocodile, jaguar, monkey, king vulture, and iguana) were animals native to the tropical lowlands. In Gadow's own words (1908:303):

> In any case at least five, if not six, out of ten creatures being foreign to the plateau are, to my mind, strong evidence that these day-signs were not invented on the plateau, but were borrowed, and taken over by the Aztecs together with the ready made book.

One Mexican state that *was* home to all of these animals was the State of Oaxaca; thus all of these animals were known to the Zapotec. Hence the presence of tropical fauna in the Aztec calendar might simply reflect the adoption of aspects of earlier calendars. From the beginning, Zapotec day names included animals such as crocodile, monkey, and jaguar, all species known from the Isthmus of Tehuantepec.

Early scholars who studied Zapotec hieroglyphs (e.g., Caso 1928, 1947, 1967; Seler 1904a) usually began by studying dates, since dates—with their highly visible bars and dots—were well preserved on the carved stones (Figure 3.2). In addition to looking at the bars and dots, Caso compared the associated Zapotec day names to those in the Mixtec and Aztec calendars and relied on

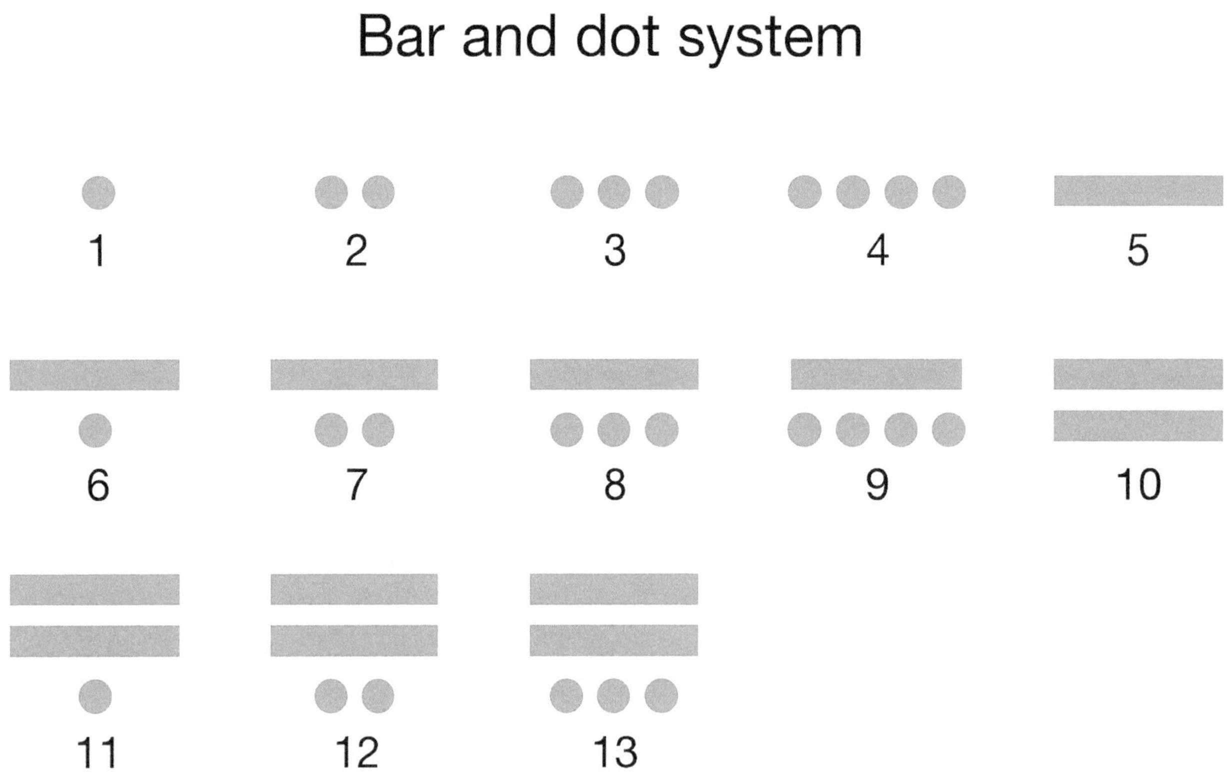

Figure 3.2. The Maya, Zapotec, and Isthmian ethnic groups wrote the numbers from 1 to 13 by using dots (that stood for 1) and bars (that stood for 5). The number 13, for example, would combine two bars and three dots. Drawing by John Klausmeyer.

sixteenth-century sources, particularly those written by fray Juan de Córdova ([1578a]1942, [1578b]1886). From Córdova's *Arte* and *Vocabulario*, Caso learned that the Zapotec had a 260-day calendar called *piye*, a 365-day year called *yza*, a month called *peo,* and a day called *copiycha*. He also learned that the Zapotec began each day at midday and ended it at the following midday (Marcus and Flannery 1978).

The Zapotec 260-day Calendar and Its Subdivisions

The Zapotec *piye* of 260 days was divisible by the following numbers: 2, 4, 5, 13, and 20. Dividing the *piye* by 20 results in 13-day units called *cocii* in Zapotec, and *trecenas* in Spanish. Division of the *piye* by 13 resulted in 20-day units, called *veintenas* in Spanish.

The Zapotec also subdivided their *piye* by four, which resulted in units called *cociyo*, each consisting of 65 days (Figure 3.3). Each *cociyo* was named after the day on which it began: to wit, *Cociyo quia chilla, Cociyo quia lana, Cociyo quia goloo,* and *Cociyo quia guilloo* (Córdova [1578b]1886:203–204). Each of the four day names—*chilla, lana, goloo,* and *guilloo*—was separated from the others by five intervening days, with *chilla* occupying the first position, *lana* the sixth, *goloo* the eleventh, and *guilloo* the sixteenth.

One of Caso's challenges was to match the sixteenth-century day names mentioned by fray Juan de Córdova to the hieroglyphs carved on the stone monuments of Monte Albán. The first of the day names, *chilla,* seems to correspond to the hieroglyph "CC." (The double letter "CC" had to be created because Caso originally included this two-headed crocodile sign with several other day names, all under his Glyph M [see Caso 1928: Figure 18, VII].)

Lana, goloo, and *guilloo* seem to correspond to Caso's Glyphs H, O, and L (Caso 1928). Although Glyph O (monkey) seemingly occupied the eleventh position, there has been some uncertainty about whether Glyph H occupied the sixth position and Glyph L occupied the sixteenth position (Figure 3.4).

Since some Zapotec day names (e.g., soot and cold) do not readily lend themselves to graphic depiction, it has been tempting to make Zapotec day names exactly match the much later Aztec and Mixtec day names. There are, however, some important differences. For example, the third day in the Zapotec calendar was the owl/night (Caso's Glyph F), while House occupied the

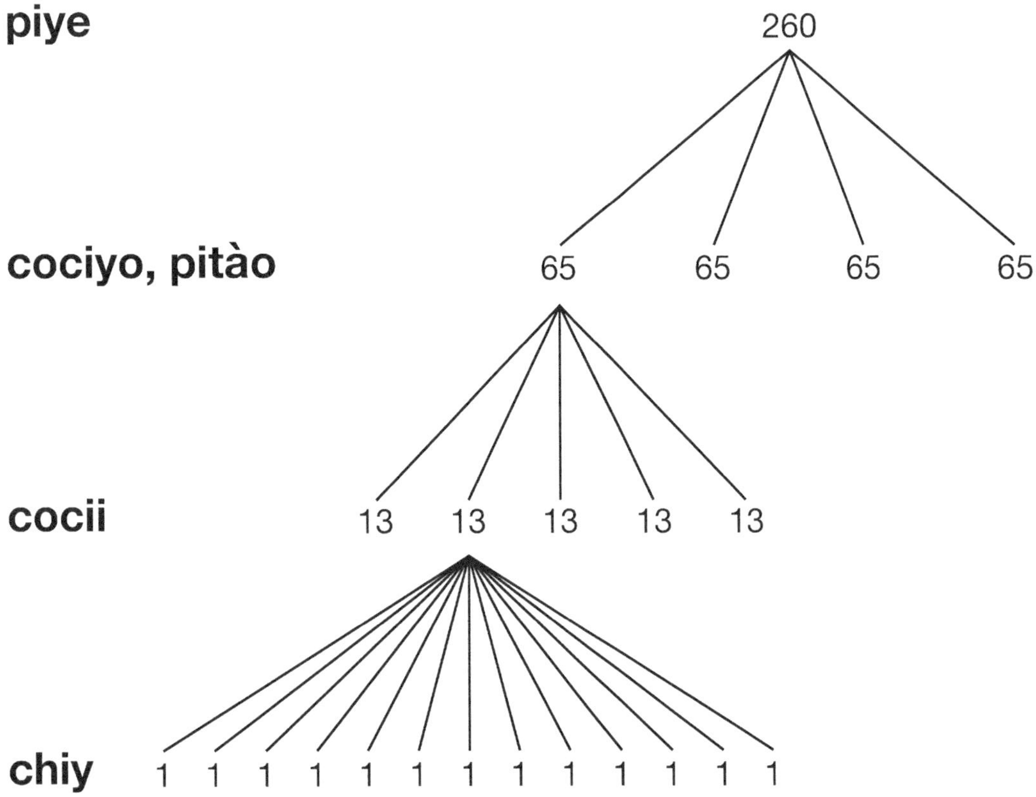

Figure 3.3. The Zapotec called their 260-day calendar *piye*. Here we see how the Zapotec subdivided the calendar's 260 days into units of 65 days (*cociyo* or *pitào*), units of 13 days (*cocii*), and individual days (*chiy*) (redrawn from Marcus and Flannery 1978: Fig. 3). Drawing by John Klausmeyer.

third position in the Mixtec and Aztec calendars. The Mixtec and Aztec calendars use eagle and vulture for day names 15 and 16; for those days, the Zapotec used Glyph J (maize) and Glyph L (motion or eye).

In addition to noting that the *piye* was divided into four *cociyo*, Córdova ([1578b]1886:202–203) revealed that units of time had animal patrons:

> Estos 260 dias que diximos, díuidianlos los yndios en veynte partes o tiempos, o meses, que salen a treze cada mes. Y para cada treze dias destos tenian aplicada vna figura de animal. s. Aguila, Mono, Culebra, Lagarto, Venado, Liebre &c. Los quales pintauan todos metidos en todas las partes o miembros de vn Venado, a donde pintaban las cabeças de cada vno de aquellos animales, de manera que aquella figura del Venado contenia en si estos veinte signos. Y cada vno de aquellos animales que eran veynte tenia treze nombres, y aunque todos estos treze nombres eran en si como vna cosa diferenciauandolos con les anadir o quitar letras, y con mudarles los numeros, como parece adelante. Como si dixessemos, Pedro quatro, y Perico cinco, y Periquillo seis, y Perote siete, y Pedroche ocho, que todos significan este nombre Pedro, aunque en diferentes maneras, y esto por les mudar letras y numeros como aquí parece.

Figure 3.3 shows the relationship among the *piye* of 260 days, the *cociyo* of 65 days, and the *cocii* of 13 days (Marcus and Flannery 1978: Figure 3). The importance of the *cocii*, even in the Colonial era, is revealed by a manuscript found in San Antonio Huitepec, District of Peñoles, Oaxaca. Although Huitepec is today a Mixtec-speaking community, it lies only 10 km from the Zapotec-speaking town of San Pedro Totomachapan, so van Meer (2000) thinks it likely that the latter town produced the manuscript.

The Huitepec manuscript shows how each 13-day unit (here called a *yoho*, or "house") required a different rite to appease a different entity. The first 13-day ritual was designated "For the Mountain"; the next was "Para atajar los animales." Others were designated "Para hacer suerte," "Oración para agua," "Para pedir los bacunos," "Para la siembra," "Para mal informar," "Para el rayo," "Para la casa," "Para quitar enfermo," "Para pedir todos los animales," "Para temazcal," "Para sacar el hechizo el cuerpo," "Oración para mujer," and "Para cueva." These rites were conducted at different locations near Huitepec, linking certain units of time to sacred places and specific prayers. The foci of these prayers (*oraciones*) could be *places* (mountains, sweatbaths, houses, caves), *goals* (to obtain more animals, a better harvest, more luck, good health, or avoidance of sickness), or *appeals to natural forces*

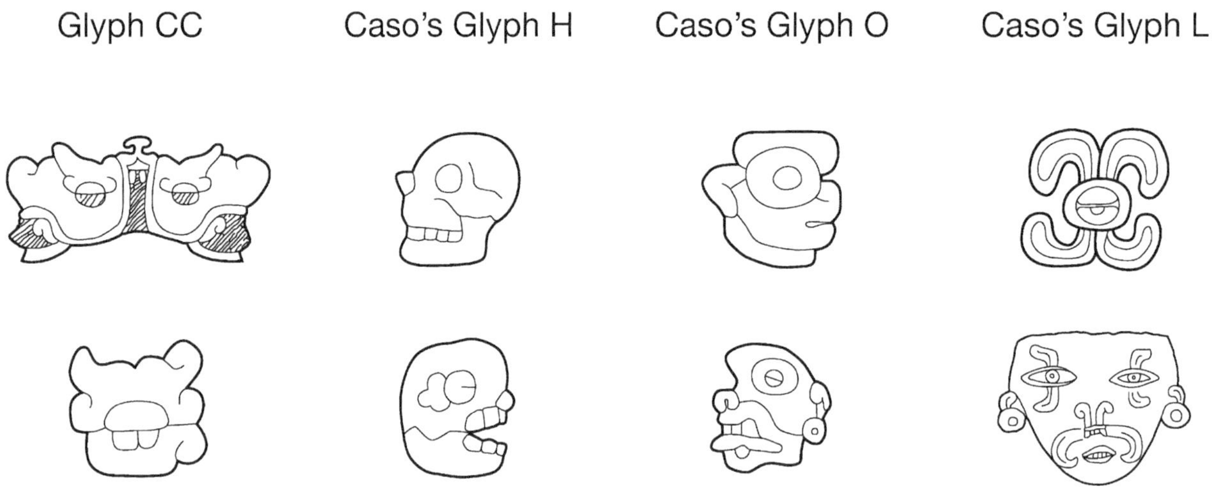

Figure 3.4. Only four of the 20 Zapotec day signs could begin a unit of 65 days (*cociyo*). These days—*chilla, lana, goloo,* and *guilloo*—corresponded to the first day (Glyph CC), the sixth day (Glyph H), the eleventh day (Glyph O), and the sixteenth day (Glyph L) (see also Figure 3.5). Drawing by John Klausmeyer.

(water, lightning). The Huitepec manuscript helps us understand the interrelationships among sacred time, space, and ritual.

Writing of the first 13-day period, van Meer (2000:51) emphasizes that we do not know whether we are learning about a ritual *for* the mountain itself, an offering left *on* the mountain, or a ritual aimed at a supernatural being who resided *in* or *on* the mountain. The clearest argument for the last (a ritual aimed at a supernatural being) can be found in the ninth 13-day ritual, which is explicitly dedicated to *Rayo* or Lightning, a supernatural[1] (Masson 2001; van Meer 2000:51–52).

While the Huitepec rituals had lasted into the Colonial era, comparable calendric rituals lasted into the twentieth century elsewhere in Oaxaca (Carrasco Pizana 1951; Weitlaner et al. 1958; Weitlaner and De Cicco 1962).

Zapotec Day Names in the 260-Day Calendar

Many translations of highland day names exist (e.g., Brinton 1893; Caso 1928:19; Caso 1967: Cuadro IX; Cline 1975; Córdova [1578b]1886; de la Cruz 1995; Edmonson 1988; Seler 1904a; Urcid 2001). Although there continue to be disagreements among scholars, Table 3.1 is an attempt to synthesize what we know about Zapotec, Mixtec, and Aztec day names (Caso 1928, 1967; Johnson 1936; M. E. Smith 1973a; Vaillant 1941).

Some of the Zapotec day names given in Córdova ([1578b]1886) have proven difficult to identify in the hieroglyphic record. There are three principal reasons: (1) some hieroglyphic day names occur infrequently; (2) the appearance of some day names is not easy to interpret; and (3) the meaning of some day names (e.g., black, soot, cloudy, cold) is difficult to depict. Some of Córdova's day names, however, can easily be depicted and identified; for example, the Zapotec seventh day was *china*, which means deer. Thus Caso (1928:54) found it easy to assign his Glyph

1. An occasional mistake made by some scholars of Zapotec religion is to consider every supernatural a "god." Many Mesoamerican religions had deities and deified ancestors, but they also had supernatural beings and spirits that were part of their natural world. Christianity, for example, has a celestial hierarchy with archangels, cherubim, and seraphim, all of which are supernatural beings but not deities. The Zapotec had many sacred beings, including certain royal ancestors and deified apical lineage founders. Key abilities included impersonation and metamorphosis, whereby important nobles could transform themselves into creatures with an array of special powers such as flying, communicating with animals and ancestors, impersonating animals, and sacrificing to the living and the deceased.

Table 3.1. Zapotec and Mixtec day names.

Zapotec day names			Mixtec day names
1. Chilla, chijlla	crocodile (Caso 1928:41; Marcus 1983b:145; Glyph CC; Urcid's V)		Crocodile, Peje-lagarto
2. Quij, laa	*cociyo*, rain, lightning (Caso 1928:41; Glyph M)	YEAR BEARER	Wind
3. Guela, ela	night, owl? (Caso 1928:33; Glyph F)		House
4. Gueche, quiche	iguana or lizard (de la Cruz 1995:159; Urcid's Ñ)		Lizard
5. Zee, zij	snake (Caso 1928:43; Glyph Y)		Serpent
6. Lana	black, soot (Caso 1928:35; cranium: Glyph H)		Death
7. China	deer (Caso 1928:34; Glyph G)	YEAR BEARER	Deer
8. Lapa	cut up, rabbit (de la Cruz 1995:161; Urcid's T)		Rabbit
9. Niza, queza	water (Caso 1928:43; Glyph Z)		Water
10. Tella	knot (Caso 1928:27; Glyph A)		Dog
11. Loo, goloo	monkey (Caso 1928:43; Glyph O)		Monkey
12. Pija	plant (Caso's bat; de la Cruz's grana) (Glyph N)	YEAR BEARER	Grass
13. Quij	flower (Caso 1928:31; de la Cruz's cane; Glyph D)		Reed
14. Gueche, eche	jaguar, *peche* (Caso 1928:28; Glyph B)		Puma/Jaguar
15. Naa	maize, mother (Caso 1928:36; Glyph J)		Eagle
16. Loo, guilloo	eye (Caso 1928:39; Glyph L)		Vulture
17. Xoo	force, temblor (Caso 1928:32, 1967; Glyph E)	YEAR BEARER	Motion
18. Opa, gopa	cold, stone (Caso 1928:43; Glyph Q)		Flint
19. Ape, gappe	cloudy? (Caso 1928:29; Glyph C)		Rain
20. Lao, loo	face of the lord (de la Cruz 1995:171; Urcid's X)		Flower

G—a deer's head—to the seventh position. Furthermore, Caso already knew that the Mixtec and Aztec used the head of a deer for the seventh position in their calendars (Figure 3.5).

Thus, the days that occupy positions 1, 6, 11, and 16 (*chilla, lana, goloo,* and *guilloo*) began each of the 65-day *cociyos*. The hieroglyphs in positions 2, 7, 12, and 17 were the year bearers (Caso's M, G, N, and E) (Table 3.1). The year bearers began the 365-day year (see also Boone 2000; Caso 1967; Morley 1915; Thompson 1950; Vaillant 1941) (Figure 3.6).

Zapotec Numbers

Córdova ([1578b]1886:197–198) devotes almost two full pages to numeral classification. He mentions *beni* or "person" as the term used to count humans, *mani* or "animal" to count animals, *kie* "stone" to count cocoa, grain, eggs, tamales, and round fruit, and *lati* "cloth" to count blankets, hides, and other such things. Numeral-classifier-noun phrases include *tobi kike beni* (one head person, one person) and *tobi lao liba'ana* (one sermon).

Various sixteenth-century sources supply lists of Zapotec numbers (Table 3.2). When used in a sentence to enumerate items, such cardinal numbers preceded the noun, just as in English. The terms for 10, 15, 20, and 400 (1 *ela*) are the stems or roots of higher numbers.

Comparing Valley of Oaxaca Numerical Terms

In Column 1 of Table 3.3 we see the numbers from 1 through 10 in nineteenth-century Zapotec. In Columns 2–4 we see the same numbers in twentieth-century Zapotec. By comparing these terms, we can see how conservative some numbers from 1–10 were; in contrast, the terms for numbers greater than 10—and especially above 20—have been subject to more linguistic change or drift.

Now we will look at numbers used in everyday counting, versus the special numbers used in the 260-day sacred calendar (Table 3.4). In the 260-day calendar, the number was fused to the day name (see Table 3.5) (Caso 1928, 1965a; Córdova [1578b]1886; Seler 1904a).

The fusion seen in Table 3.5 has been regarded as a byproduct of the 260-day calendar's antiquity (e.g., Caso 1928; Radin 1930). Some scholars (e.g., Urcid 2001; Whittaker 1983:127–129) have suggested that the prefixes are not numbers at all, but instead are

Figure 3.5. Here we compare the hieroglyphs for the 20 day signs in the Zapotec, Mixtec, and Aztec 260-day calendars. Note that many of the day signs in the Mixtec and Aztec calendars are more similar to each other than either is to the much earlier Zapotec day signs (see Boone and Smith 2003: Fig. 24.6; Caso 1967: Figs. 1-A, 1-B, Cuadro IX; de la Cruz 1995; Marcus 1992a: Fig. 4.15; Quiñones Keber 1995:279-282; M. E. Smith 1973a: Charts 1-2; Pohl and Urcid 2006; Vaillant 1941: Pl. 63). Drawing by John Klausmeyer.

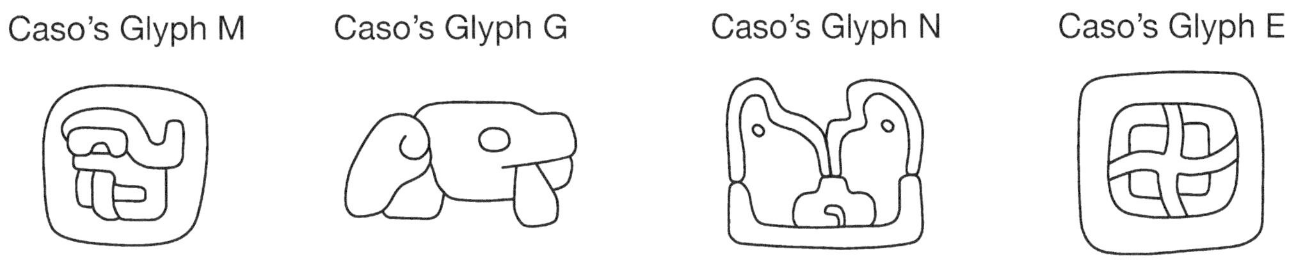

Figure 3.6. The Zapotec year bearers occupied the second, seventh, twelfth, and seventeenth positions; those positions corresponded to Glyphs M, G, N, and E (Caso 1928: Figs. 8, 10, 18, 19). Drawing by John Klausmeyer.

associated with the Lords of the Night, analogous to the birds or flying creatures (*volatiles*) associated with the Nahua calendar.

It should not surprise us that the Zapotec had special numbers for their 260-day calendar; similar numbers characterize other Otomanguean groups, such as the Mixtec (Caso 1956; Dahlgren de Jordan 1954:367; León 1933). For example, the Mixtec had a special vocabulary for numbers in the 260-day calendar and special terms associated with day names. Instead of saying *ee ndoo* (*ee* = one; *ndoo* = reed) for the day 1 Reed, the Mixtec calendar used *ca huiyo.* Instead of *ee idzo* for the day 1 Rabbit, the Mixtec calendar used *ca sayu* (M. E. Smith 1973a:23–24). The same Mixtec term, *ca*, was used for the numbers 1, 2, and 12; *co* was used for 1, 2, and 3; and *si* was used for 10 and 13 (Marcus 1992a:119; M. E. Smith 1973a:26). For the complete special Mixtec vocabulary used for numerical prefixes of calendar signs, see Smith's Chart 2 (M. E. Smith 1973a).

Both Mixtec and Zapotec are tonal languages (Leal 1950; Leal and Leal 1954; Pickett 1959, 1967; K. L. Pike 1945, 1948; Sicoli 2007; Stubblefield and Stubblefield 1991; Swadesh 1949, 1967). It is therefore worth considering that numerical prefixes in Mixtec and Zapotec could have had different tones, even when Colonial Spanish documents show them spelled the same way (Marcus 1992a:119; M. E. Smith 1973a:27). For example, when we see the word *pe* written in a Colonial document, we cannot be certain which number was intended, since *pe* could refer to 2, 5, 9, or 10 in Zapotec. In his dictionary Córdova ([1578a]1942) tried to indicate Zapotec tones by using accents and other diacritical marks; scholars, however, disagree as to the meaning of each mark (Caso 1965a:944, Caso 1967:84–85; Córdova [1578b]1886:204–212; Marcus 1983f: Table 4.2; Marcus 1992a:124–125; Smith Stark 2001, 2003, 2007).

Using the Arrangements of Bars and Dots to Date Monuments

Zapotec monuments can sometimes be "style dated" by studying the numbers. Whether a bar is bent or straight, decorated or undecorated can help to date a monument; whether dots were placed above the bar or below the bar is another clue. These general tendencies help us place some monuments in time, but there are exceptions. Justeson (1986:449) noted that "sign order is fixed in day names and month counts, with numerals always suffixed in the Preclassic below the sign to which they pertain; this is in keeping with Zapotec word order in the case of day names—the most ancient and the most frequent context of numerals—but not in enumerations. Sign order sometimes appears to be depictively rather than linguistically motivated."

The position of the dots relative to the bars does vary over time. After AD 300, most dots are shown *below* the bars (both as subfix and postfix), but sometimes the bars and dots appear as prefixes (e.g., on Stela 1 at Monte Albán). From AD 500 onward, bars usually have a diagonal band or ribbon that makes the bar look like a wrapped gift (Figure 3.7). Other Period IIIb monuments show decorated bars that are bent, curved, or floating; sometimes the bars are separated from the day name or the dots.

On some monuments (ca. AD 600–900), the scene may have been carved first, i.e. before the sculptor inserted hieroglyphs, whether day names or captions. This carving strategy may partially explain why the sculptor was left with insufficient space to insert the names and hieroglyphs, and why he decided to bend the bars to make them fit; this sequence of events may

Table 3.2. Zapotec numbers from Córdova ([1578b] 1886).

1 =	tobi, toobi
2 =	topa, tioopa, choopa, corropa
3 =	chona, choona
4 =	tapa, taapa
5 =	caayo, gaayo
6 =	xopa, xoopa
7 =	caache
8 =	xoono
9 =	caa, gaa
10 =	chi, chij
11 =	chi bitoobi (10 + 1)
12 =	chi tioopa (10 + 2)
13 =	chiñoo, chijño
14 =	chitaa (10 + 4)
15 =	chino
16 =	chinoo bitobi (15 + 1)
17 =	chinoo bitioopa (15 + 2)
18 =	chinoo bichoona (15 + 3)
19 =	chinoobi taapa (15 + 4)
20 =	calle
21 =	calle bitoobi (20 + 1)
25 =	calle bigaayo (20 + 5)
40 =	tua
60 =	ca yoono
80 =	taa
100 =	cayooa
200 =	chiá
300 =	chinóa
400 =	toobi ela
500 =	toobi ela cayooa
600 =	toobi ela chiá

Table 3.3. Comparing Zapotec terms for numbers.

	Valley Zapotec (1800s)	Isthmus Zapotec	Sierra Juárez	Yatzachi Zapotec
1	toobi	tobi	ttubi	to
2	tioopa/choopa	chupa	chuppa	chope
3	choona	chona	cunna	shone
4	taapa	tapa	tappa	tap
5	gaayo	gaayu'	gayu	gweya'
6	xoopa	shoopa	shuppa	shop
7	caache	gache	gaci	gashe
8	xoono	shono	shunu	shon, sh'on
9	gaa	ga'	ga	ga
10	chy	chii	ci'i	shi

Table 3.4. Everyday numbers versus numbers used in the 260-day calendar.

	Numbers used for everyday counting	**Numbers used in the 260-day calendar**
1	tobi, toobi	quia, que, qui, quie
2	topa, toopa, choopa, corropa	pi, pa, pe
3	chona, choona	ca, peo
4	tapa, taapa	cale, cala, pel
5	caayo, gaayo	pe, qua, peo
6	xopa, xoopa	que, qua, quala
7	caache	pi, pilla
8	xoono	ne, ni
9	caa, gaa	pe, pi
10	chi, chij	pilla, qua, pe
11	chi bitoobi (10 + 1)	ne, cala, pilla, ni
12	chi tioopa (10 + 2)	piña, peñe, piño
13	chiñoo, chijño	pini, pize, pici, piza, pice, pece

Table 3.5. Fusion of number and day name in the Zapotec calendar.

Number	**+**	**day sign**	**Fusion of number and day sign**
quia		chilla	(#1 + day sign) = quiachilla
quia		lana	(#1 + day sign) = quialana
quia		goloo	(#1 + day sign) = quiagoloo
quia		guilloo	(#1 + day sign) = quiaguilloo

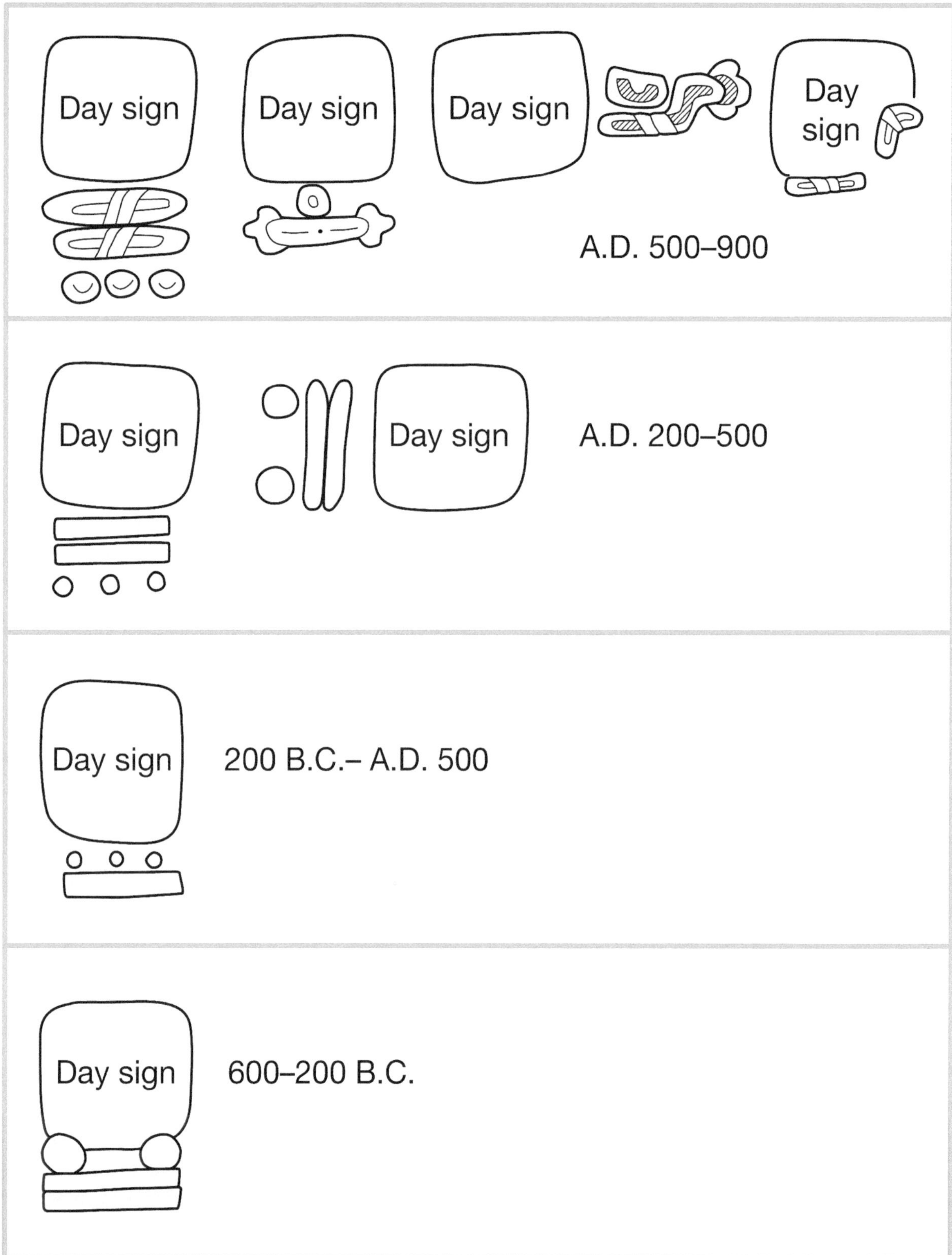

Figure 3.7. The style, position, and arrangement of bars and dots on Zapotec monuments varied over time. Thus it is tempting to "style-date" unprovenienced Zapotec monuments. Nevertheless, we must be cautious about style-dating since our sample of securely dated monuments remains limited, and we still do not know the full range of variation in any phase or period. Drawing by John Klausmeyer.

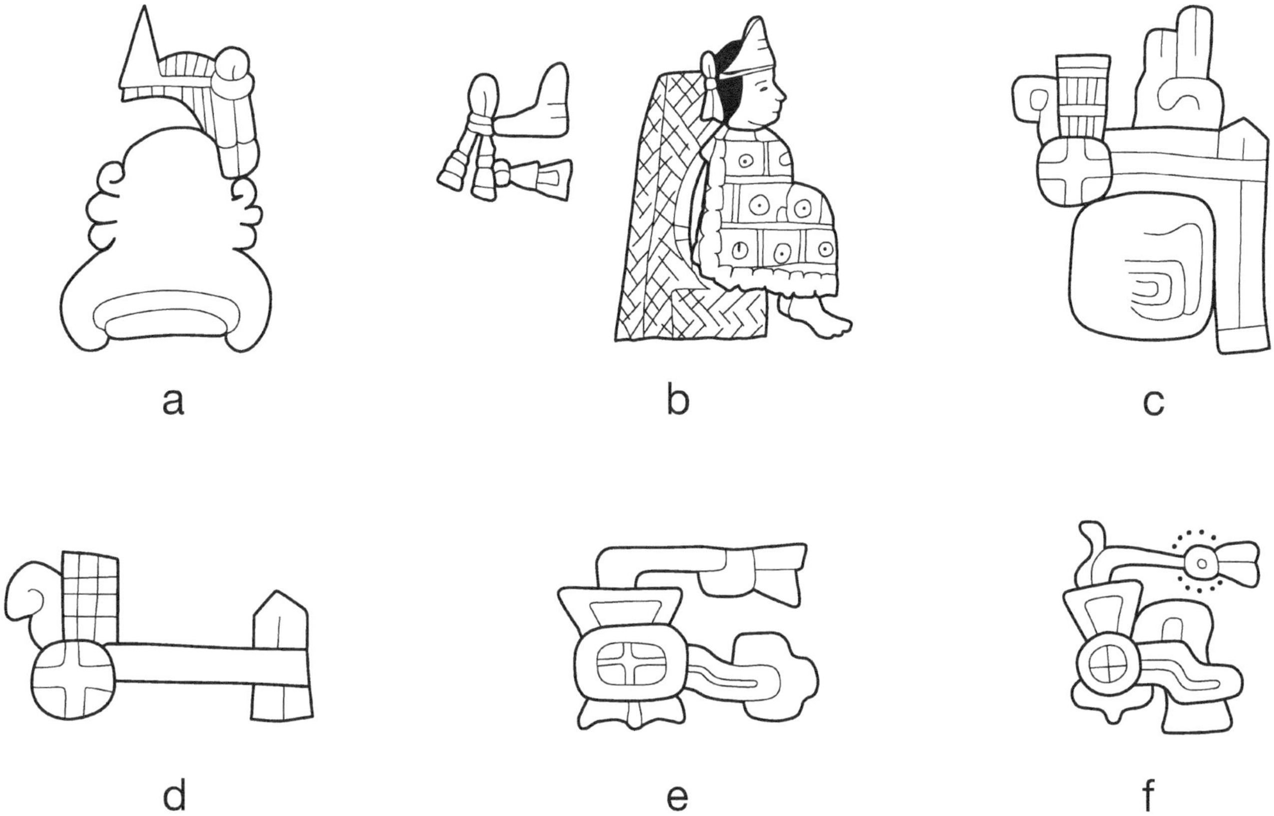

Figure 3.8. A headband or diadem was a symbol of rulership for the Aztec, Maya, and Zapotec. (*a*) The name of the Aztec town of Tecuhtepec combined the glyphs for headband + hill; (*b*) a headband was the name glyph of the Aztec ruler Motecuhzoma (*tecuh*[*tli*] = lord + *zoma* = frown in anger); (*c-f*) four examples of the way the Zapotec used the headband as a year sign (Caso 1928, 1947, 1965a; Marcus 1992a: Fig. 6.3; Peñafiel 1885; Codex Telleriano-Remensis fol. 31v; see also Saville 1922: Fig. 12). Drawing by John Klausmeyer.

explain why he separated bars from dots and numbers from day signs. Sometimes the stone carver placed the bars above the day sign and the dots below the day sign, or vice versa. When such placements are not near any of the people depicted, it can be difficult to determine which name goes with which individual.

The 52-year Calendar

Giving each year a name served two important functions: it was a shorthand designation for the year, and it influenced the luck for that year. Highland Mesoamericans looked upon their years in ways that were similar to the Chinese, who believe that each year has a good, bad, or neutral fate.

As mentioned earlier, only four day names could serve as year bearers and supervisors of the year, acting in ways that were similar to lords serving as protectors; these Zapotec day names occupied the second, seventh, twelfth, and seventeenth positions. Other Mesoamerican groups that used the same positions for their year bearers include the Tlapanec of Guerrero, the Cuicatec of Oaxaca, and the Ixil and Quiché Maya of highland Guatemala. In contrast, the Aztec, the Mixtec, and the Tzeltal, Chuh, and Jacaltec Maya used the third, eighth, thirteenth, and eighteenth days as their year bearers.

The Zapotec year bearer accompanies a year sign first identified by Alfonso Caso (1928:45–64). Caso (1928: Figure 21; Caso 1965a: Figure 11) interpreted the year sign as a headband with various ribbons and an ornament of turquoise attached to the front (Figure 3.8). Caso's identification of the year sign was a crucial step in our understanding of the Zapotec calendar. He did more than show that the Zapotec had four year bearers or overlords that protected and ruled each year; he showed that each compound—year sign + year bearer—designated the year's position in the 52-year Calendar Round. The presence of a year bearer and year sign shows the reader where to start reading. The year sign preceded the verb, the subject, and the object, following the typical word order of a Zapotec sentence, which was V + S + O (verb + subject + object).

The Zapotec Year Bearers

Zapotec year bearers always numbered four, but depictions of the year bearers changed over time. From 500 to 200 BC, depictions of only two of the four have been preserved: these were Caso's Glyphs E and M (see Caso 1928: Figure 21; Caso 1947:29; Caso 1965a:941; de la Cruz 1995; Urcid 2001). From 200 BC to AD 600, our sample of hieroglyphic texts with year bearers is larger, affording us the chance to find an example of each of the four year bearers—Glyphs E, M, G, and N (Caso 1928:45). From AD 600 to 900, new variants of Glyphs N and E appear (for example, an animal head may have been an alternative to Glyph N; a human head may have been an alternative to Glyph E).

Caso identified Glyph M as the face of Lightning (*Cociyo*) and Glyph G as the head of a deer (*china*). Caso assigned *Cociyo*/Lightning to the second position and Deer to the seventh position in the list of 20 days. He knew that "Deer" occupied the seventh position in other Mesoamerican calendars, and he knew that Córdova's term ([1578b]1886:204) for the seventh day was *china*, the Zapotec word for "Deer."

Caso (1928:31) identified Glyph E as turquoise, the precious stone that adorns the diadem in the year sign. He identified Glyph N as a stylized bat (Caso 1928:41). Over the last century many scholars have offered their opinions on the year bearers and the Zapotec calendar (e.g., Alcina Franch 1979, 1993; Brinton 1893; Cruz 1935; de la Cruz 1995; Edmonson 1988; Seler 1904a; Urcid 2001; Whittaker 1980, 1983).

It is noteworthy that as long ago as 1928, Caso was able to establish the key features of the Zapotec calendar, and he did so with a much smaller sample of texts and hieroglyphs than we have today. Brinton (1893) and Caso (1928, 1947) employed similar strategies: (1) they used Córdova (1578a, 1578b) to translate the Zapotec words for the 20 days, and (2) they compared the Zapotec day names to the day names of other Mesoamerican calendars, finding both differences and similarities. Many days in the Zapotec calendar were similar to day names in other highland Mesoamerican calendars (such as the Mixtec and Aztec), but not all.

We now know from Caso that Glyphs E, M, G, and N were the four Zapotec year bearers. And of the possible positions (given below), the first line (in bold type) is most likely the correct sequence (i.e., E in the seventeenth position, M in the second position, G in the seventh, and N in the twelfth).

M (2nd), G (7th), N (12th), E (17th)
M (2nd), G (7th), E (12th), N (17th)
E (2nd), G (7th), N (12th), M (17th)
E (2nd), G (7th), M (12th), N (17th)
N (2nd), G (7th), M (12th), E (17th)
N (2nd), G (7th), E (12th), M (17th)

4

Selecting Auspicious Names for Children

Zapotec children were named for the day on which they were born (e.g., Córdova [1578b]1886; Marcus 1976c:39; Marcus 1980; Marcus 1992a:206–210). When the day of birth was associated with bad luck, however, the diviner could wait a few days to select a more favorable day in the 260-day calendar. The Mixtec also sought favorable combinations (number + day) for their children. Whallon's (1992) statistical analysis of 1661 Mixtec noblemen's calendric names and those of 951 Mixtec noblewomen makes it clear that certain combinations were preferred.

The sixteenth-century Zapotec term for "day name" was *xiaa xiaa*, a term that had multiple meanings—birth name, celebration, planet, the sign under which one was born, and one's fortune (Córdova [1578a]1942:283v). These definitions emphasize the close relationship between one's calendric name, birth date, and destiny. The 260-day calendar was a kind of horoscope that allowed Zapotec diviners (*colaniy*) to foretell a child's future (Alcina Franch 1966, 1979; Córdova [1578b]1886:202, 204).

By avoiding inauspicious combinations of number + day name, Zapotec diviners probably increased the number of individuals with the same name. To distinguish among all those with the same name, the Zapotec and Mixtec often attached nicknames. For example, two Mixtec individuals born on the same day (e.g., 8 Deer) could be differentiated by calling one of them 8 Deer "Feathered Serpent" (Figure 4.1 a, b) and the other 8 Deer "Tiger Claw" (Figure 4.1 c, d). The Zapotec also added nicknames they called *lacha* or *laja'*, two terms related to the word for "name" (*laa*). Hieroglyphic examples of possible Zapotec nicknames can be seen in tomb murals (e.g., Tomb 105 at Monte Albán; see Caso 1938: Lámina IV; Miller 1995).

The 260-day calendar could even affect the selection of marriage partners. Among the sixteenth-century Mixtec, a man and woman were not supposed to marry each other if their names contained the same number. Thus 1 Deer (1 Cuaa) was not to marry 1 Water (1 Duta) (Caso 1967; Herrera y Tordesillas [1601]1947; M. E. Smith 1973a). Ideally, the number in the man's name should be higher than that in the woman's.

The 260-day calendar exerted tremendous influence over the lives of both Zapotec nobles and commoners (Marcus 1976c:39). A diviner could determine the benevolence or malevolence of each number + day to determine when maize should be planted or harvested, when war should be started, when nobles should marry, and so forth. In some areas of Oaxaca, such as Loxicha, the Zapotec continued to use the 260-day calendar well into the twentieth century (Weitlaner et al. 1958; Weitlaner and De Cicco 1962).

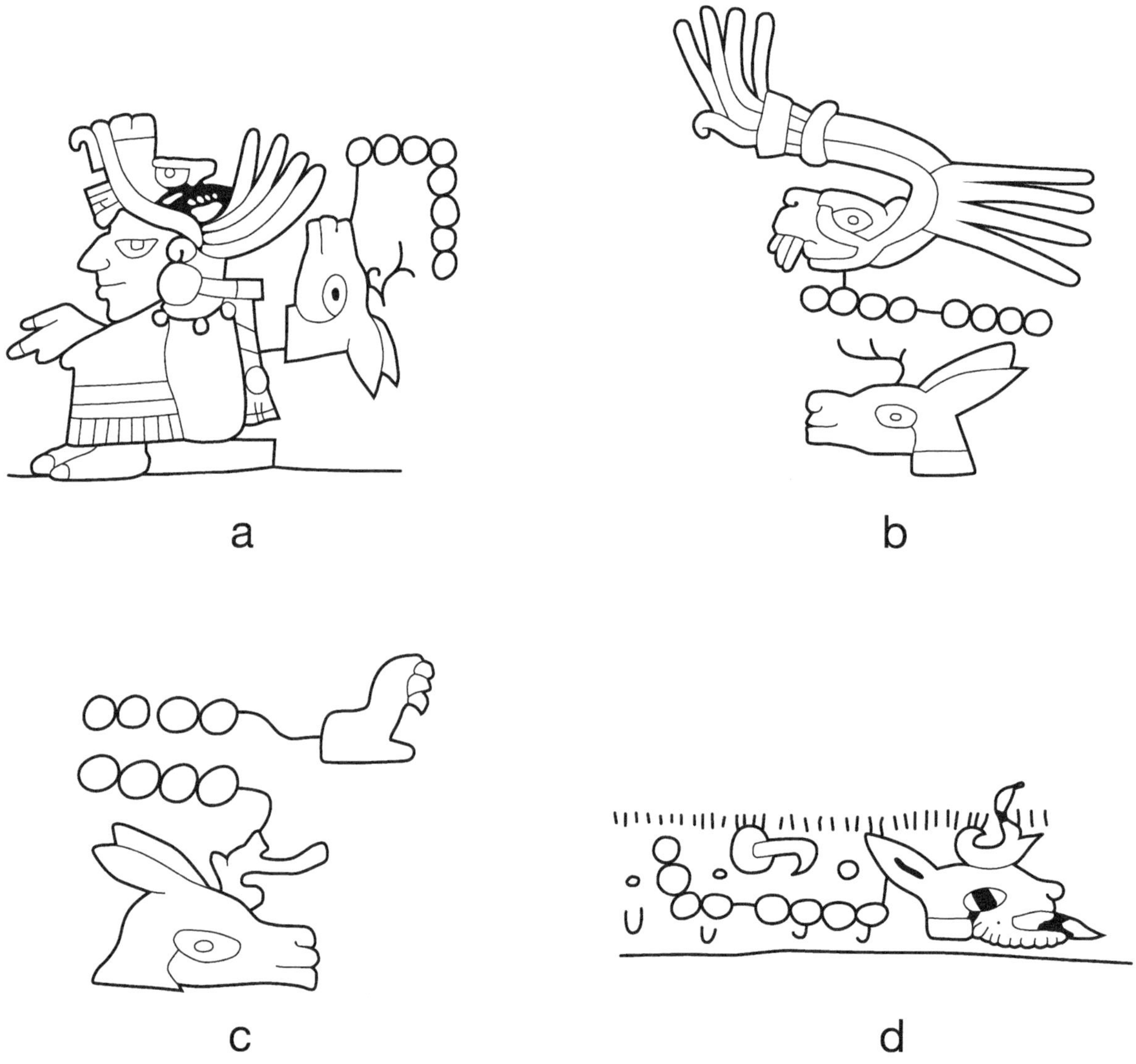

Figure 4.1. When two Mixtec lords were born on the same day, they needed a way to differentiate themselves. For example, two lords born on the day 8 Deer could do so by adding a nickname, as follows. One lord (*a*, *b*) added the nickname "Feathered Serpent." The other lord (*c*, *d*) used the nickname "Tiger Claw." (Illustrations *a*-*c* are from the Codex Bodley; *d* is from the Codex Nuttall.) Drawing by John Klausmeyer.

To write a name such as 6 Deer, the Zapotec used a bar for "5" and a dot for "1." The number might even be attached to the deer's head. Fray Juan de Córdova says that Zapotec nobles had names like Señora Cuatro Rosas (Lady 4 Flower), Señor Cinco Micos (Lord 5 Monkey), and Señor Veinte Leones (Lord 20 Jaguars, or Ocoñaña; see Caso 1949; M. E. Smith 1973a). (The name 20 Jaguars would be a personal nickname rather than a day in the 260-day calendar, since no number higher than 13 could occur in that calendar.)

Other day signs mentioned by Córdova include Crocodile, Snake, Deer, and Rabbit. Caso's hieroglyphs CC, Y, G, and T correspond to those four animals. The Zapotec calendar did not have a day that corresponded to "Eagle," although both the Aztec and the Mixtec used Eagle as their fifteenth day.

Position of the Number

In translating Zapotec texts from the Colonial era, Oudijk (2000) and Whitecotton (1990, 2003) always place the number *before* the day name, as in "2 Deer" or "1 Water." Examples include:

Pe + china, 2 Deer
Pece + chilla, 13 Crocodile
Quia + nica, 1 Water
Pela + quece, 5 Water
Ne + lapa, 8 Rabbit
Pila + xoo, 9 Motion or 9 Earthquake

In this regard, it is noteworthy that on the earliest Zapotec monuments, the numbers often appear *below* the day sign, as a postfix or suffix. It would appear that the shift to placing the numbers *before* the nouns occurred after the Zapotec had ceased to carve monuments, although there were some exceptions (e.g., Stela 1 at Monte Albán). This apparent shift has been discussed by linguist Yoshiho Yasugi (1995:156), who reached two conclusions: (1) Zapotec and Chatino are head-modifying or head-marking languages, whereby nouns precede qualifiers; and (2) it appears that numbers followed nouns until roughly AD 900, after which numbers came to precede nouns.

Evidently the pre-AD 900 Zapotec monuments followed the practice of placing numerical coefficients after day names; in fact, the Zapotec culture is unique in Mesoamerica in adhering to this convention both hieroglyphically and linguistically (Justeson 1986; Whittaker 1983:127). There is considerable evidence that ancient Zapotec was a head-modifying language, with numbers commonly postfixed to main signs. The last word on word order has yet to be written, since we still do not know how pre-AD 900 Zapotec texts were spoken.

Today's scholars also disagree on the reading order of elements within Zapotec compound glyphs. Just as with proto-cuneiform (Damerow 2006) and other early writing systems, it may be that the reading order of some early Zapotec hieroglyphic elements within compounds was not fully standardized. Justeson and Mathews (1990) also note that early texts may not fully match speaking order. They assert that "the best hieroglyphic evidence" that Zapotec was the underlying language of the Monte Albán script "is the suffixing of numerals to names of ritual calendar days, an exotic feature in Mesoamerican languages" and the fact that Zapotec is still spoken throughout the Valley of Oaxaca (Justeson and Mathews 1990:107). As we will see later in this chapter, there is another line of evidence, namely that early Monte Albán texts relied on puns (tone pairs) that work only if Zapotec is the language being used.

Digits that Signify Numbers and Birth-Order Positions

Caso (1947) was the first to notice that the Zapotec used human fingers as hieroglyphs in their early texts (e.g., on Stelae 15 and 17 at Monte Albán). He suggested that a finger might have had the value of 1, two fingers the value of 2, and so on. The fingers in those instances were serving as affixes, not main signs. It is not clear why two dots were preferred in some instances, and two fingers in others.

Caso was confident that the Zapotec were using digits as numbers because he had seen (1) Maya texts that used thumbs as numbers (e.g., Temple of the Cross at Palenque; Stela F at Quiriguá; see Thompson 1950:134–137) and (2) Aztec codices that used fingers as numbers (e.g., Codex Mendoza, Matrícula de Tributos) (Figure 4.2).

The Maya used thumbs with units of time (e.g., with a 20-year period called a *k'atun*; with a ca. 400-year period, a *b'ak'tun*; and with a day sign, Ahau). The Aztec also used a finger to indicate "1." Aztec tribute items such as cloth *mantas* were usually depicted without associated fingers; standard *mantas* may have measured 1 *braza* (ca. 1.67 m). When fingers were shown projecting from the top of a *manta*, however, those fingers apparently indicated that the cloth was to be longer than the standard length. Two fingers indicated a cloth 2 *brazas* in length; eight fingers indicated that the cloth was to be 8 *brazas* long (Figure 4.2c, d) (Berdan 1987:243). Caso also noted that the Zapotec sometimes used human fists as main signs. Because those fists were not day signs or affixes, Caso and others suggested that they might represent verbs.

After reading both Caso's (1928, 1947) description of the digits on early Monte Albán monuments and Córdova's ([1578b]1886:213–214) discussion of "the count of the fingers and toes which [the Zapotec] also use for the birth order of their children," I suggested years ago that the Zapotec might have elected to use some signs—fingers, or hands with fingers raised—to specify birth order (e.g., first-born, second-born, and so on) (Marcus 1972, 1983f:93; see Miller 1995; Oudijk 2000:142). According to Córdova ([1578b]1886:212–214), the Zapotec had two sets of terms to specify birth order—one set for sons and another for daughters. To distinguish daughters, they used the terms shown in Table 4.1.

Figure 4.2. In addition to bars and dots, Mesoamericans sometimes used human thumbs or fingers to represent numbers. Here we see Maya examples in which a thumb was used to signify "1." This thumb could then be combined with the day sign Ahau (*a, b*); with a *k'atun* or unit of 7200 days (*c*); or with a *b'ak'tun* of 144,000 days (*d*). For their part, the Aztec often demaded tribute in cloth (*mantas*) in various sizes and styles. In their tribute records, the Aztec usually depicted the cloth without fingers. However, to specify that a *manta* should be longer than the standard size, the Aztec did use fingers (*e, f*). Four fingers (*e*) indicated that the *manta* should be 6.7 m longer. Eight fingers (*f*) indicated that the cloth should be 13.4 m longer than a *manta* of standard length. (Illustrations *a, b* are from Stela F, Quiriguá; *c, d* are from the Tablet of the Cross, Palenque; *e* from the Matrícula de Tributos; *f* from the Codex Mendoza; see Berdan and Anawalt 1997.) Drawing by John Klausmeyer.

Table 4.1. Birth-order terms for daughters in Zapotec (Córdova [1578b]1886:213).

Zapotec term	Translation
zaa	first-born daughter
xoñi/xoni	second-born daughter
nijo	third-born daughter
laxi	fourth-born daughter
zee	fifth-born daughter
zayee	sixth-born daughter

In contrast, the Zapotec terms for the birth order of male children were the same as those used for fingers and toes. The thumb of the right hand was *yobi*; the second (or index) finger on the right hand was *tini*; the third finger was *tixi*; the fourth, *payo;* and the fifth, *yee*. Then the fingers on the left hand were counted, beginning with the thumb, *yobijye*; then the second finger, *teije*; the third, *texije*; the fourth, *xayoyye*; and the fifth, *pijye*. The toes were called by the same names as their counterparts on the hand. It follows, then, that the raised right thumb might designate first-born son, the second finger on the right hand second-born son, and so on. Given the similarity in pronunciation, this use of "thumb" for "first-born son" could be considered a pun (or a tone pair) in Zapotec.

Sixteenth-century documents show us that even after the Conquest, birth order remained a point of emphasis for the Zapotec, as Table 4.2 shows.

After a noble's first four sons had been designated, the family returned to the term for first-born (*yobi)* for the fifth son, but attached the ending *ye* to produce *yopiye*. If additional sons were born, the Zapotec continued adding the postfix *ye* to create the terms *tiniye/teyye, tixiye/texiye*, and so on. If an eleventh son was born, he would receive the name of the right big toe; later sons would receive the terms applied to the remaining toes on the right foot.

Let us now look at some sixteenth-century documents containing the terms for birth order. We will begin with a genealogy from San Lucas Quiaviní in the eastern Valley of Oaxaca (Oudijk 1998). The *Quiaviní Genealogy* mentions a noblewoman referred to as *Xonàxi Quie queche* (Lady 1 Jaguar or Lizard?), who presented her husband *Pichana Coquì Quiechilla* (Great Lord 1 Crocodile) with six noble offspring. They were:

> *cale* (was born) *yobi* (first-born son) *Coquì* (lord) *bilala* (2, 3, 5 ? House)
> *cale* (was born) *Coquì* (lord) *tini* (second-born) *palapia* (2 Grass?)
> *cale* (was born) *Coquì* (lord) *tixi* (third-born) *palachi* (2, 5 Jaguar or Lizard?)
> *cale* (was born) *Coquì* (lord) *payo* (fourth-born) *billa laba* (7, 10 Rabbit)
> *cale* (was born) *Coquì* (lord) *piye* (fifth-born) *quice* (1, 13 Serpent?)
> *cale* (was born) *Coquì* (lord) *piye* (sixth-born) *cacalana* (4, 8 Death)

Note that the fifth and sixth sons were both given the term *piye*. Oudijk (2000:142) suggests that they may have been twins; if that were the case, however, one would expect them to have the same calendric name, and they do not. Thus we may be dealing with a scribal error.

In another passage of the genealogy we read *alahatini cacabahalana cale yobi coquì balaa, tini pinielao, cale coquì tixi pilaha nelala*: "Here is {the woman who bore the following children} the first-born Lord 2 Monkey, the second-born 12?, the third-born, 8 Owl" (Oudijk 1998:22). This passage gives us

Table 4.2. Birth-order terms for sons.

Zapotec	Meaning	Sample clauses	Translations
yobi	first-born son	coquì+ yobi + ne lapa	(lord, 1st born, 8 Rabbit)
tini	second-born son	coquì + tini + cala lao	(lord, 2nd born, 4 Vulture)
tixi	third-born son	coquì + tixi + quie chilla	(lord, 3rd born, 1 Crocodile)
payo	fourth-born son	coquì + payo + pece naa	(lord, 4th born, 13 Maize?)
yopiye	fifth-born son	coquì + yopiye + peo china	(lord, 5th born, 3 Deer)
teyye	sixth-born son	coquì + teyye + pilla loo	(lord, 6th born, 7/10? Monkey)
texiye	seventh-born son	coquì + texiye + ne cee	(lord, 7th born, 8 Serpent)

a sentence construction with which we are now familiar (see the sixteenth-century texts studied by Whitecotton [1982, 1990] and Oudijk [1998, 2000]).

That construction is as follows:

(1) (verb = was born) + birth-order position + status (lord, lady) + (number + day name)
(2) (verb = was born) + status (lord, lady) + birth-order position + (number + day name)
(3) (verb = was born) + birth-order position + nickname + (number + day name)
(4) (verb = was born) + birth-order position + (number + day name) + from Town X
(5) (verb = was born) + nickname + birth-order position + 260-day name
(6) (verb = was born) + status (lord, lady) + nickname + birth-order position + 260-day name + place name

It seems to have been standard to give a status term or birth position immediately following the verb "was born." A woman's hometown might be mentioned at the end of a name clause. One noblewoman mentioned in the *Genealogy of Macuilxochitl* was named *xonàxi xilla tinelo* ça *toavayee xaquiya*, "Lady Cotton 8 Monkey [who comes from] Teotitlán del Valle," which includes her title, nickname, 260-day calendar name, and her hometown (Oudijk 2000:282).

Some of the most complete name clauses in sixteenth-century Zapotec manuscripts include as many as five elements, to wit:

(1) status term (such as lord or *coquì*, lady or *xonàxi*, noble or *joàna*);
(2) nickname (e.g., "Lightning-Creator," *Cociyoeza* or "Great Jaguar," *Pechetào*);
(3) birth-order position (such as first-born, second-born);
(4) 260-day calendar name (such as 8 Deer or 11 Water); and
(5) place of origin or hometown (often associated with women, because they presumably were marrying into the local dynasty and moving to that locale).

To be sure, it is rare to find all five components of a name clause. It does, however, seem to have been common to give a status term or birth position immediately following the verb "was born." The calendric name and hometown were usually found at the end of the name clause.

Most difficult to translate in these sixteenth-century texts are the names taken from the 260-day calendar. One reason is that Spanish scribes had no agreed-upon way to record Zapotec tones; without taking into account those tones, many numbers (for example, 2, 3, or 5) would be written the same way in published dictionaries. Another reason is that the numerical terms used by Zapotec diviners could differ from those used for everyday counting.

Applying the Lessons from Sixteenth-Century Sources

Based on what we have learned from sixteenth-century documents, what expectations do we have for ancient Zapotec writing?

First, we would expect many sentences to begin with a verb.

Second, we would expect the verb to precede the subject (many Zapotec sentences are Verb + Subject + Object).

Third, we would expect the names of Zapotec nobles to include as many as four elements:

status/title + birth order + nickname + calendar name

As discussed, individuals might also be given nicknames to distinguish them from people with the identical calendric name; well-known Mixtec examples of nicknames were given in Figure 4.1.

Now let us look at the Zapotec use of fingers and thumbs (Figures 4.3, 4.4). As mentioned earlier, Caso (1928) originally assumed that the use of human fingers was a complementary or alternative numerical system to the more frequently seen bars and dots. When I first suggested that fingers might in some cases refer to Zapotec birth order, I lacked sufficient evidence to confirm the suggestion (Marcus 1972, 1983f, 1992a). Thanks to the 1985 discovery of Tomb 5 at Cerro de la Campana, Suchilquitongo (Franco Brizuela 1993; Méndez Martínez 1988; Miller 1991, 1995; Trujillo de los Santos 1986), we now have additional evidence that fingers could be used as birth-order terms for male offspring.

The Cerro de la Campana tomb contained a genealogical register called Stela 5. This register, which dated to Period IIIb–IV, contained a text that is reproduced in Figure 4.4. It reads as follows:

Date + verb + title + subject + birth-order position + death + death date
Year 2N + was born + jaguar title + calendar name (12N) + 3rd-born? + bag glyph (*coti*) + 5N

Date + verb + title + subject + birth-order position + death + death date
Year 3N + was born + jaguar title + calendar name (12O) + 4th-born? + bag glyph (*coti*) + 7M

An approximate translation of these clauses could be:

Princess 12N was born in the Year 2N; this third-born offspring died on 5N.
Prince 12 Monkey was born in the Year 3N; this fourth-born offspring died on 7M.

Associated with the birth-order glyph are small symbols that may be *suertes para sortear*, items that could have been

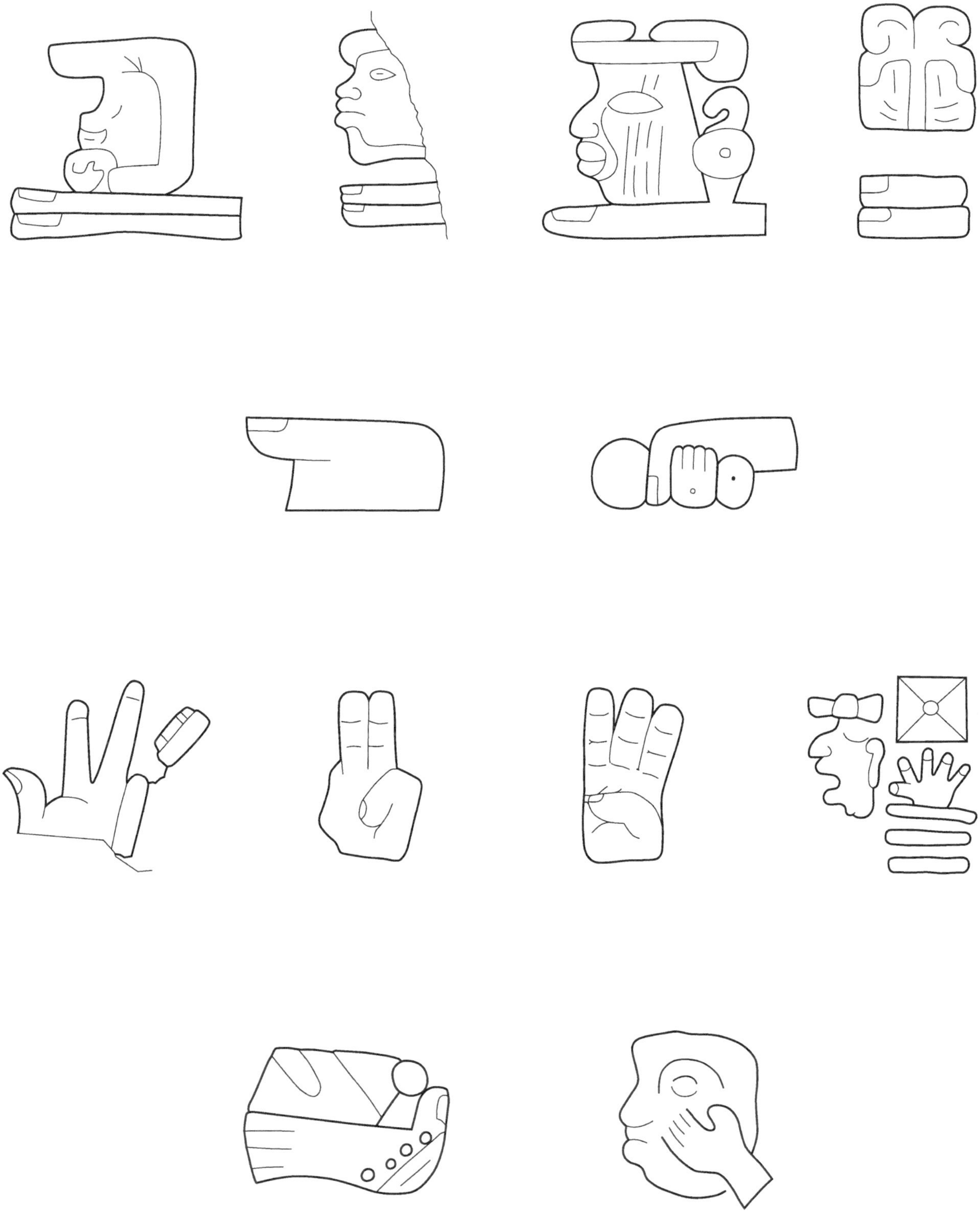

Figure 4.3. The Zapotec used fingers, thumbs, and hands to represent numbers, birth order, and verbs; here are some examples (see Caso 1928, 1947; Marcus 1992a:97). Drawing by John Klausmeyer.

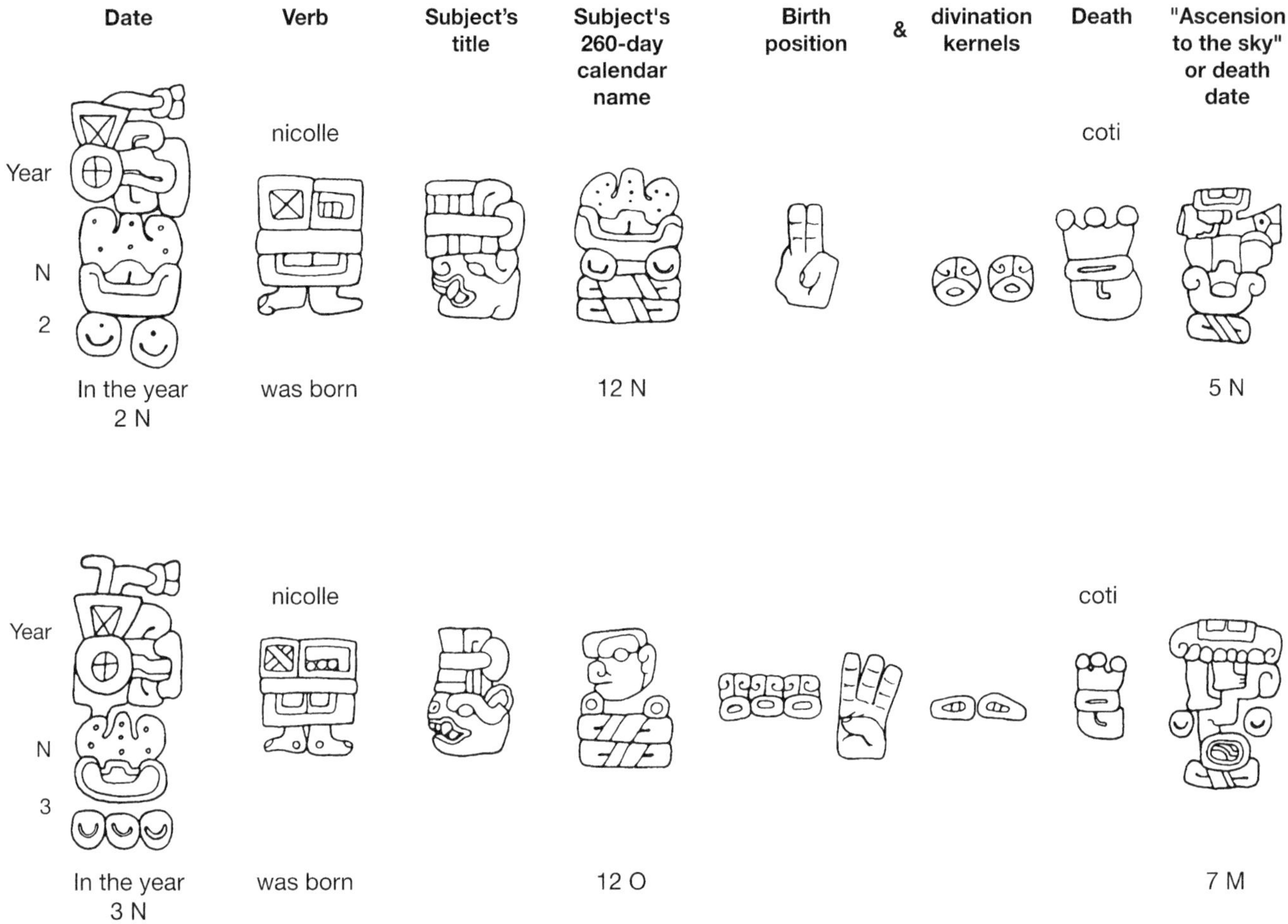

Figure 4.4. Birth order may be indicated in the hieroglyphic text on Stela 5, Cerro de la Campana, Oaxaca (see Chapter 12), which is shown here. We know that the sixteenth-century Zapotec used the prefix *ni* to create past participles such as *nicolle*, "was born." On Stela 5 we see hieroglyphic compounds that may well correspond to *ni* + *colle* and (*ni*) + *coti* (or *niguti*). We also see examples of human digits (thumb, index finger, and so on), which had the same sounds as the words used for birth order (Córdova [1578b]1886; Miller 1991, 1995). Drawing by John Klausmeyer.

used in divining rites. Three of those associated with 12 Monkey seem to be corn kernels, but the other two could be beans, seeds, jade beads, or something else. Although five possible divining symbols are associated with 12 Monkey, only two are associated with his sister.

The front of the stela shows Lord 13 Monkey propped up in a funerary box or wooden frame of the kind that was used to transport venerated ancestors from one place to another (Kidder et al. 1946; Marcus 2006b:226–229; Miller 1991, 1995) (see Chapter 12). On the sides of Stela 5 are name clauses that discuss the lives of Lord 13 Monkey's offspring (his daughter 12N and his son 12 Monkey). Since the death dates of these offspring are apparently given, it is possible that one of 13 Monkey's grandchildren or other relative commissioned the carving of the stone, and then oversaw its insertion into the tomb. As we shall see later in this book, the tombs of important people were regarded as family mausolea; reopening such tombs occurred for several reasons, including the placement of more family members and the placement of new offerings on the anniversary of interment.

A sixteenth-century document called the *Etla Genealogy* suggests that the word order of the text on Stela 5 may be particularly characteristic of the Etla region. While documents written outside the Etla arm of the valley usually present birth-order before calendar name, both the *Etla Genealogy* and the text on Stela 5 give the calendar name before birth order (Figure 4.4). The distinct Etla monument style is discussed in Chapter 12.

In this chapter we have seen how sixteenth-century documents can help us to interpret the inscriptions of the pre-contact Zapotec. We are, however, still a long way from understanding the grammar and degree of phoneticism of Zapotec texts. In Chapter 5 we examine some principles of Zapotec language to see what light they can shed on the inscriptions.

5

Looking at Zapotec Languages

We do not know how many Zapotec speakers there were in AD 1519. Kowalewski et al. (1989) have estimated that there may have been 160,000 Zapotec speakers in the Valley of Oaxaca alone. In the decades that followed, Zapotec speakers decreased in number owing to many factors—the introduction of Old World diseases, displacement and relocation of communities, infighting among local populations, and the Spaniards' never-ending demand for indigenous labor. The last seven decades of the twentieth century, however, witnessed a reversal, an actual surge in the number of indigenous speakers. The 1940 census recorded 94,000 Zapotec speakers; the 1950 census, 215,000; and the 1990 census, 400,000.

Today, if one includes areas outside the valley, there are an estimated 450,000 speakers of Zapotec. Not only have the numbers been on the rise, but so have speakers of other Indian languages in the State of Oaxaca (Figures 5.1, 5.2). Cultural and linguistic survival are the result of both modern medicine and indigenous policies that maintain corporate identity, community boundaries, village endogamy, and communal land ownership.

Although Zapotec speakers occupied a variety of environmental regions, occupants of both the lowlands and highlands featured mountains in their cognized world. Mountains served as territorial boundaries, defensible refuges, ritual altars, sacred summits, visible destinations, and named landmarks. Over the centuries, the Zapotec used various terms for mountains, such as *tani* and *daan* as well as *giya* or **guiya* (the asterisk indicates that **guiya* is a proto-Zapotec term, reconstructed from known variants).

Two thousand years ago, hieroglyphs that referred to mountains had begun to appear on Zapotec stone monuments. Although a few "mountain" or "hill" signs occurred during the period from 300 to 100 BC, it was not until AD 100 that the hill sign became common (see Chapter 6). This date was no accident; it coincided with the expansion of the early Zapotec state, a process making it advantageous to have a glyph referring to "hills" or "places" that Monte Albán claimed to have incorporated into its political sphere.

Linguistic Variants

Several variants of the Zapotec language are spoken today in the State of Oaxaca. A brief sketch of these variants may help to generate a list of expectations, some of which can advance the decipherment of Zapotec hieroglyphs.

Zapotec is a member of the Otomanguean language family (Fernández de Miranda 1995; Fernández de Miranda et al. 1960; Justeson 1986; Justeson and Kaufman 2010; Kaufman

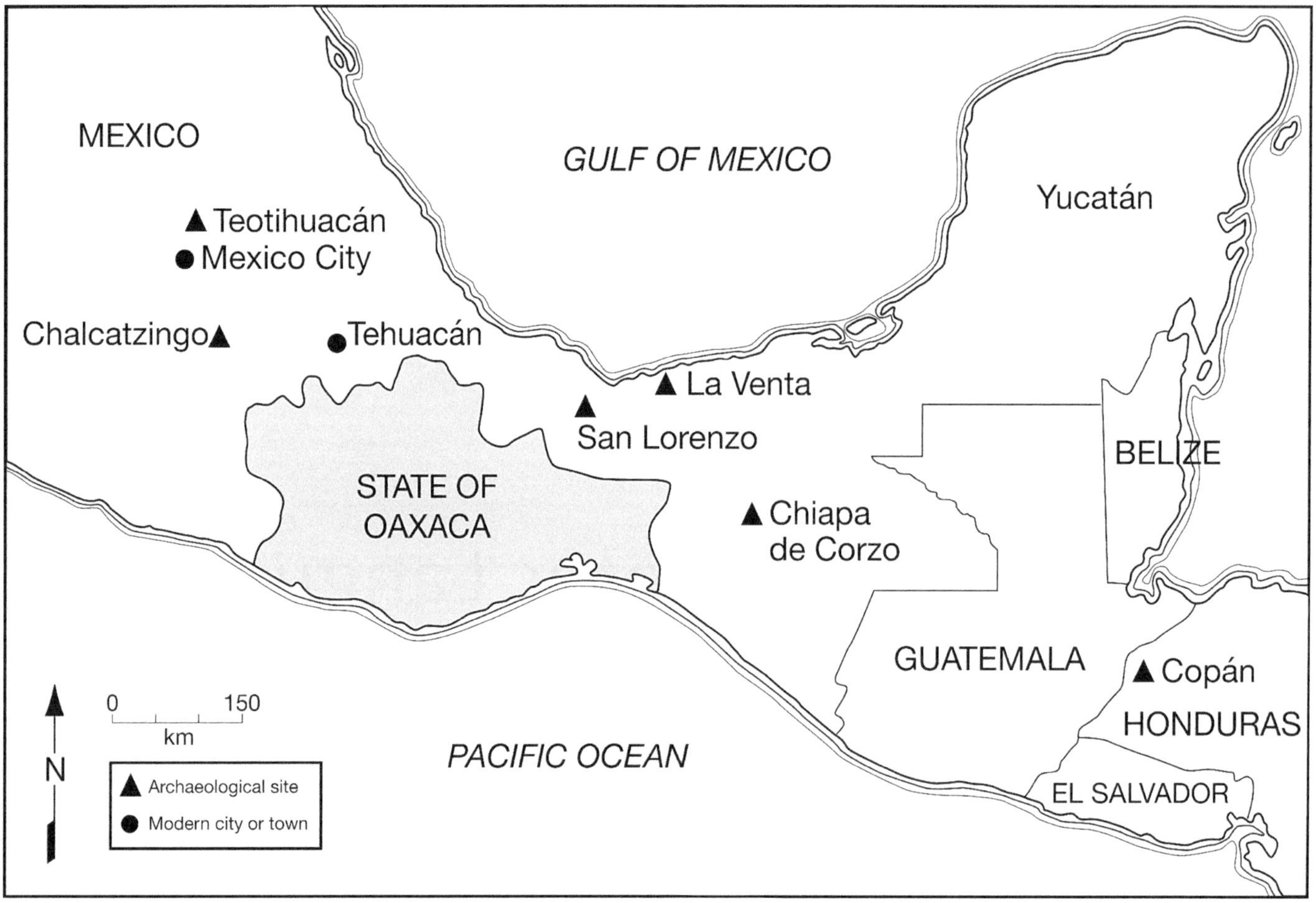

Figure 5.1. Map showing the State of Oaxaca, which lies southeast of the Basin of Mexico, south of the Gulf Coast, and west of Chiapas and Guatemala. Drawing by John Klausmeyer.

and Justeson 2004a; Marcus 1983a:4–5; Swadesh 1947; Yasugi 1995). The term Otomanguean combines "Otomí" + "Mangue," because Otomí marks the northern limit of the language family and Mangue the southern limit. Other members of the Otomanguean family include Mazahua, Chichimeca-Jonaz, Pame, Matlatzinca, Ocuilteca, Popoloca or Chocho, Mazatec, Ixcatec, Chiapanec, Mixtec, Cuicatec, Amuzgo, and Chatino. All these languages arose from an ancestral tongue called Proto-Manguean.

To create a subset of language groups within Otomanguean, Swadesh (1967:93) proposed the name "Oaxacan" for those Otomanguean languages located almost entirely within the State of Oaxaca. His Oaxacan branch included Mazatec, Chocho-Ixcatec-Popoloca, Amuzgo, Mixtec, Cuicatec, Trique, Chatino, and Zapotec. Of those, Swadesh concluded that Zapotec and Chatino were more closely related to each other than to any other member of the Oaxacan subset (Swadesh 1967:95). More recent linguistic research has confirmed Swadesh's statements about Zapotec and Chatino (Figure 5.3).

Among the early linguists interested in Otomanguean were glottochronologists, who established tentative dates for the divergences that took place within the Oaxacan subset. Armed with those dates, ethnologist Ralph Beals (1969) attempted to link language divergences to the archaeological sequence. One of those divergences began to take place around AD 100, when Zapotec/Chatino was still a single language. Such a divergence would accord well with archaeological data that suggest the following sequence of events:

(1) between 100 BC and AD 100, the early Zapotec state was expanding into regions outside the Valley of Oaxaca (Brockington et al. 1974; Gaxiola 1976; Marcus 1976a, 1980, 2008b; Marcus and Flannery 1996; Sherman et al. 2010; Spencer 1982, 1990, 1998, 2003, 2007, 2009, 2010, 2019; Spencer and Redmond 1997, 2003, 2006; Spencer et al. 2008);

(2) by AD 300 the Zapotec state had begun to shrink and many Zapotec speakers were returning to the Valley of Oaxaca, leaving remnant populations in their former colonies; and

(3) the retreat of the Zapotec from southwestern Oaxaca eventually stranded those speakers who came to be known as the Chatino (Marcus and Flannery 1996:201–202).

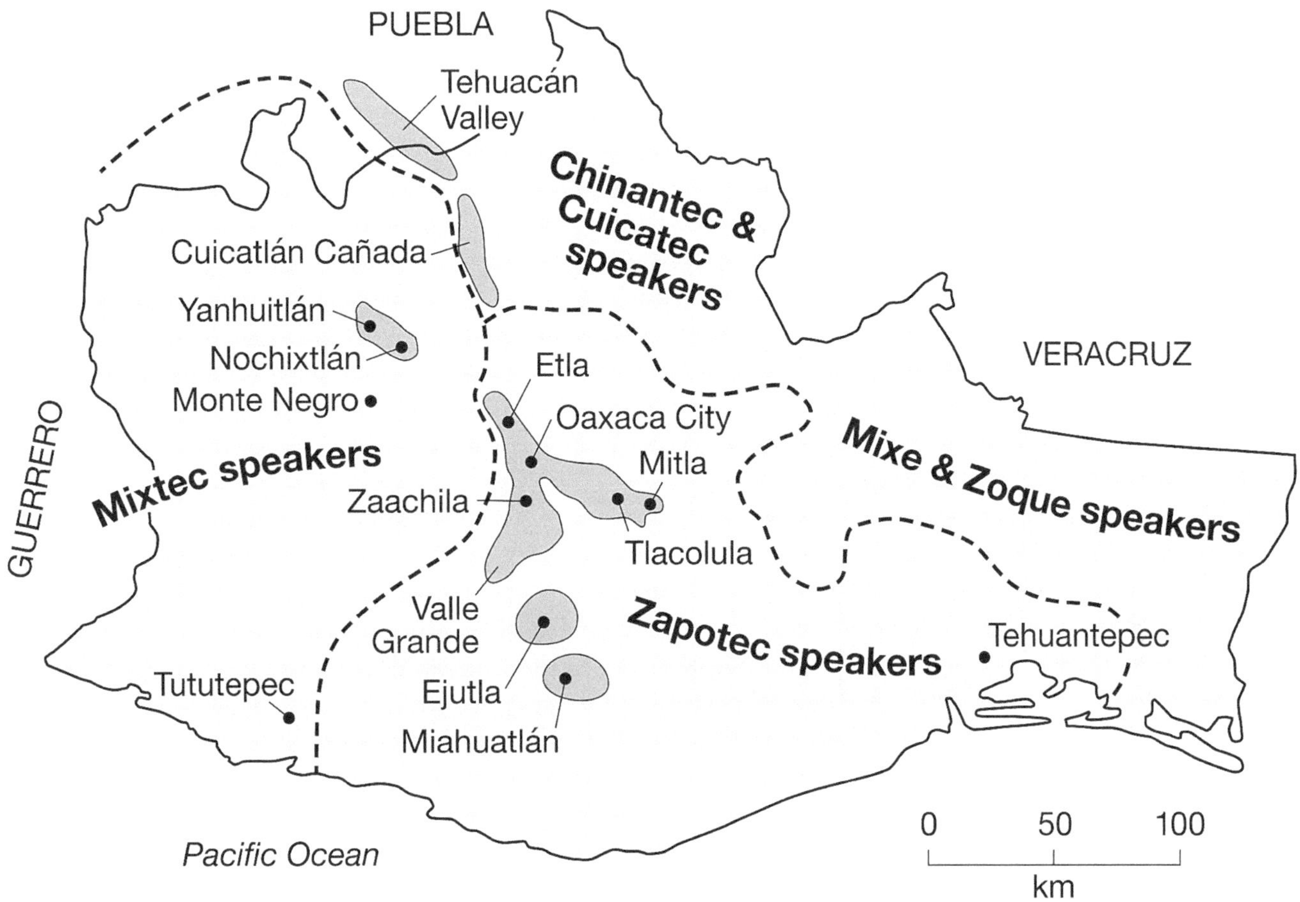

Figure 5.2. Unlike many states of Mexico, the State of Oaxaca includes speakers of many different indigenous languages. Drawing by John Klausmeyer.

Varieties of Zapotec

Prior to the twentieth century, most linguists regarded Zapotec as a single language with many dialects. These linguists used the term "dialect" to refer to mutually intelligible variants, reserving the term "language" for mutually unintelligible variants. More extensive work on the Zapotec language has led linguists to reassess whether or not some Zapotec variants were dialects or mutually unintelligible languages.

As early as the 1940s, a few linguists had begun to argue that some variants of Zapotec were mutually unintelligible, and suggested that the latter should be considered separate languages (Pickett 1967:292, Pickett et al. 1988:135; Swadesh 1947:220; Swadesh 1949, 1967). Swadesh (1949:419), in fact, compared the differentiation of Zapotec to the kinds of divergence that had taken place within Latin—the splits that led to the emergence of Catalan, French, Italian, Portuguese, Spanish, and Romanian.

Although some twentieth-century linguists divided Zapotec into six subdivisions (Valley Zapotec, Sierra Zapotec, Nexitzo, Villa Alta, Tehuantepec, and Miahuatlán Zapotec), recent studies point to the existence of more than 40 mutually unintelligible variants (Stubblefield and Stubblefield 1991:vii). During the 1990s, linguists began to find evidence to support what fray Juan de Córdova ([1578a]1942) had already noted in his sixteenth-century dictionary—that each Zapotec-speaking town revealed linguistic differences from its neighbors, and that such differences could be sufficient to make the languages unintelligible.

Diversification among Zapotec dialects seems to have accelerated after AD 1000. The good news is that the hieroglyphic texts I discuss in this book predate most of this diversification.

One example of the changes taking place after AD 1000 can be found in a word's final syllable. Some Zapotec languages retain the terminal syllable; in others, it has been lost. For example, the sixteenth-century word "animal" was *máni* or *mane* (Córdova [1578a]1942:29r). Some Zapotec-speaking regions still use *mani*; other regions shorten it to *man*; others, to *ma;* and some retain only the letter *m* as the initial consonant.

A second example is the word for water. In Córdova's parish, sixteenth-century Tlacochahuaya, the word was *niça*. The word *nisa* was still retained by twentieth-century Tlacochahuaya,

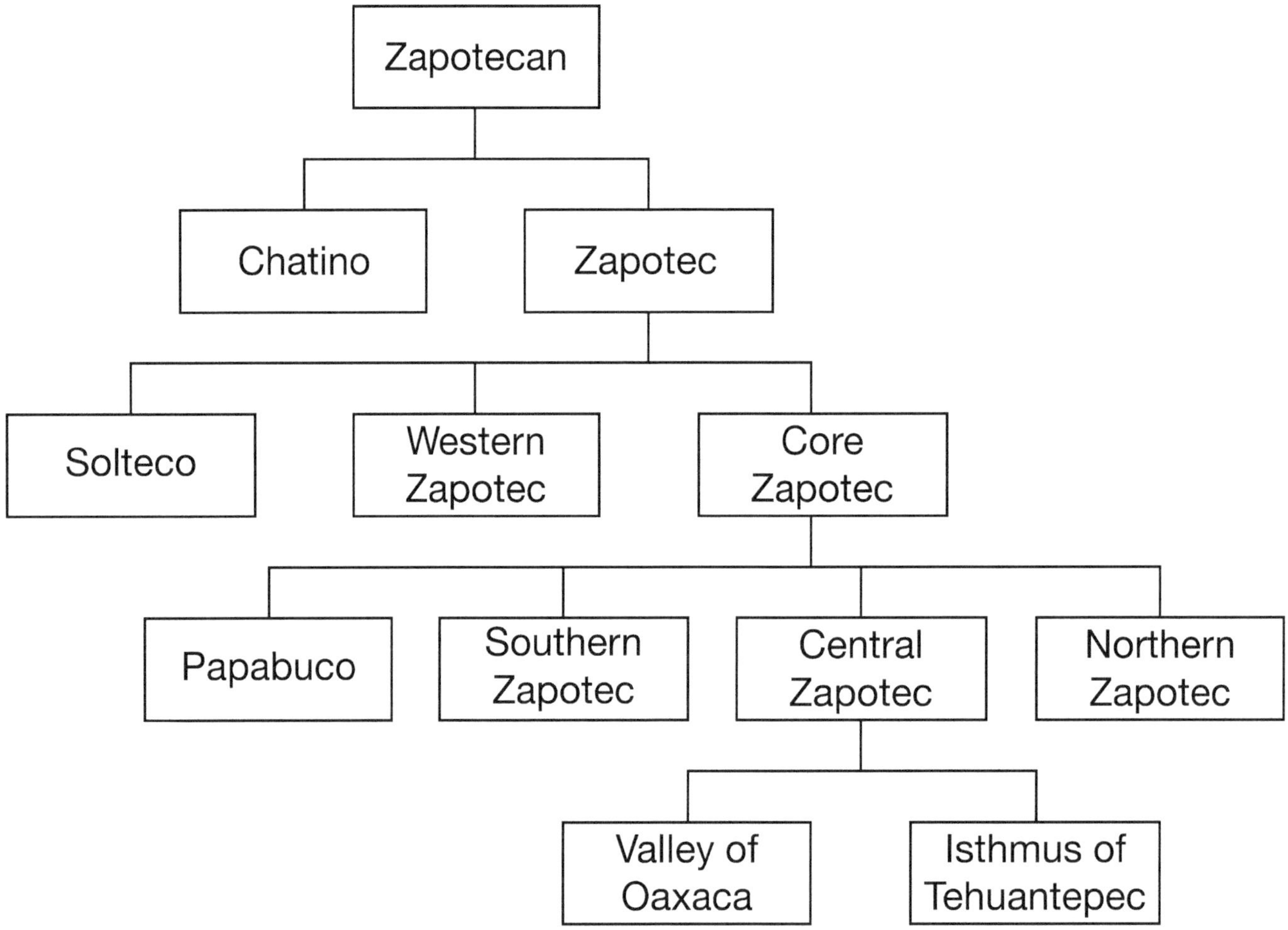

Figure 5.3. The Zapotecan language family (compiled from Broadwell 2015; Foreman and Lillehaugen 2017; Munro 2011; Smith Stark 2003, 2007). Drawing by John Klausmeyer.

Tlacolula, Zaachila, and Juchitán. In Mitla, San Antonino, Talea, and the Villa Alta towns, the term for water has been shortened to *nis*.

A third example of change involves word order. As mentioned earlier, Yasugi (1995) has argued that prior to AD 900, Zapotec numbers followed the nouns they modified. He expected to find that word order, because Zapotec (and its closest relative, Chatino) are head-modifying languages in which qualifiers follow nouns. We are not sure why nouns began to follow numbers after AD 900, but they did.

There is reason to believe that diversification and differentiation have accelerated over the last few centuries, converting what had once been different dialects into different languages. Today, estimates of the number of mutually unintelligible Zapotec languages range from as few as 4 (Hunn 1998:35) to as many as 62 (Pérez Báez 2011:945).

The Language Used by the Carvers of Valley of Oaxaca Hieroglyphs

Most Zapotec hieroglyphic inscriptions date between 600 BC and AD 900, meaning that they antedate much of Zapotec's later drift, divergence, and mutual unintelligibility. This is fortunate, because it likely means that ancient scribes in Etla, Tlacochahuaya, and Tlacolula were speaking mutually intelligible dialects.

In this chapter I present a few of the general principles of the Zapotec language to facilitate future decipherment. Useful material comes from many sources, including Alleman (1952); Anderson and Lillehaugen (2016); Angulo (1925, 1926a, 1926b); Angulo and Freeland (1935); Bartholomew (1983); Beals (1969); Beam de Azcona (2004); Belmar (1901, 1902, 1905, 1921); Black (2000); Boas (1913), Briggs (1961); Broadwell (2003, 2015); Butler (1980); Campbell (2011); Carnie and Guilfoyle

(2000); Córdova (1578a, 1578b, 1942); Earl (1968); Feria (1567); Fernández de Miranda et al. (1960); Foreman and Lillehaugen (2017); Galant (2011); Hunn (1998); Hunn and Acuca Vásquez (2001); Jaeger and Van Valin, Jr. (1982); Jones and Knudson (1977); Leal (1950), Leal and Leal (1954); Lee (2000); Levanto (1776); Lillehaugen (2006); Lillehaugen and Sonnenschein (2012); Lyman (1964); Lyman and Lyman (1977); MacLaury (1989); Marlett and Pickett (1987); Munro (2002, 2011); Munro and López (1999); Nellis and Hollenbach (1980); Nellis and Nellis (1983); Operstein (2003, 2012, 2017); Orozco y Berra (1864); Pérez Báez (2011); Pérez Báez and Kaufman (2016); Pickett (1953, 1955, 1959, 1960, 1967, 1990); Pickett et al. (1988); E. Pike (1948); Plumb (2019); Radin (1925); Reeck (1982); Rendón (1967, 1969, 1995); Robinson (1963); Rojas Torres (2009); Rosenbaum (1974); Sicoli (2007); Sonnenschein (2005); Stubblefield and Stubblefield (1991); Suárez (1990); Swadesh (1947, 1949, 1967); and Valdespino (1887).

Proto-Zapotec

To outline a few of the general principles we will look first at proto-Zapotec, then sixteenth-century Zapotec, and finally modern Zapotec. We will see that some features have great time depth and likely characterized the language spoken by those who carved the hieroglyphs in stone.

A number of linguists, including Fernández de Miranda et al. (1960), Pickett (1967, 1990), Suárez (1990), and Swadesh (1967), have contributed significantly to the reconstruction of proto-Zapotec. Swadesh's (1947, 1949, 1967) early work focused on glottochronology and on the phonemic structure. His collaboration with Fernández de Miranda and Weitlaner led to several important publications (Fernández de Miranda 1995; Fernández de Miranda et al. 1960; Swadesh 1967; see also Munro 2011; Operstein 2012; and Smith Stark 2001, 2003, 2007).

To reconstruct proto-Zapotec, Swadesh (1947) worked with four Zapotec languages and compared 94 cognate terms. Among those terms were nouns, adjectives, and numbers. Fernández de Miranda expanded Swadesh's sample to include seven Zapotec languages and 430 words; she included verbs, pronouns, prepositions, and adverbs, complementing the nouns and adjectives selected by Swadesh. Both Swadesh and Fernández de Miranda reconstructed the sounds (phonemes) that characterized proto-Zapotec; to indicate that a phoneme had been reconstructed for proto-Zapotec they preceded it with an asterisk.

According to Swadesh's orthography, the phonemes of proto-Zapotec were

*p, *t, *c, *k, *s, *š, *n, *l, *pp, *tt, *tc, *kk, *ss, *šš, *nn, *ll

According to Fernández de Miranda's orthography, on the other hand, the phonemes of proto-Zapotec were

*p, t, ¢, c, k, kʷ, ?, b, d, 3, g, s, š, z, z, N, n, L, l, r, R, y, and w (plus short and long vowels *i, e, a, o, u*)

The Sixteenth-Century Zapotec Languages

Our best sources on sixteenth-century Zapotec are a massive dictionary and an excellent grammar, both written by fray Juan de Córdova in 1578 (1578a, 1578b; see also Whitecotton and Whitecotton 1993). The author was born in 1503 in Córdoba, the city that provided his surname. He studied Latin and pursued a military career in Europe under Emperor Carlos V. At the age of 37, Córdova came to Mexico to join Francisco Vázquez de Coronado's expedition to Cíbola. After completing that expedition, Córdova decided to enter the order of the Dominicans.

Although he embarked on an entirely new career in 1543 at the age of 40, Córdova enjoyed such a long life that he ultimately spent 52 years in his second career, that of a priest. By 1549 Córdova was serving in the Convento de Santo Domingo in Oaxaca, which has since been converted to an archaeology museum (Museo de las Culturas de Oaxaca). Later he lived in poverty in the town of Tlacochahuaya, where he died in 1595 after having dedicated himself to writing his dictionary and grammar.

The variants of Zapotec spoken today in Tlacochahuaya and Tehuantepec are more similar to that recorded in Córdova's sixteenth-century dictionary than to other variants spoken throughout the State of Oaxaca (Marcus and Flannery 1978). Tlacochahuaya and Tehuantepec are localities that have remained relatively conservative, while many Zapotec dialects have diverged so much that they are mutually unintelligible today. Much of Tehuantepec's Zapotec-speaking population probably came originally from the Tlacolula arm of the Valley of Oaxaca and continued to maintain contact for some time.

Tones

All Otomanguean languages have tones that serve to distinguish otherwise similar words (Pickett et al. 1988; E. V. Pike 1948; K. L. Pike 1945, 1948; Swadesh 1949). Tone, usually defined as contrastive pitch, can occur on both vowels and syllables. Two words may be identical in every way except for pitch. This situation is unfamiliar for most speakers of English, to whom it makes no difference whether they say "doggie" with a low pitch or "doggie" with a high pitch.

Languages using pitch to create different meanings for words are called *tone languages*, and they are widespread; indeed, the *majority* of the world's languages are tone languages. For example, in the continents of Africa and Asia, most languages are tonal; in Africa alone there are more than 1000 tone languages. To be sure, the number of tones varies from one language to another. Spoken Thai, for example, has five tones, while Chinese has four tones.

Among the Zapotec languages, Sierra Zapotec has four tones (high, low, rising, and falling), while Tehuantepec Zapotec has only three (low, high, and rising). Unfortunately, we do not know how many tones Zapotec had between 600 BC and AD 900.

Córdova ([1578a]1942) clearly heard differences in tone during the sixteenth century, and he tried to record these differences. Many linguists note that Córdova used different kinds of diacritical marks, sometimes applying them to what seem superficially to be the same words. It is generally believed that some of his marks indicate differences in tone, while others indicate glottal stops and other sounds unfamiliar to Spanish speakers (Marcus and Flannery 1978; Reeck 1982:371; Rendón 1969:123–124; Smith Stark 2001, 2003; Whitecotton 1990; Whitecotton and Whitecotton 1993).

While most scholars agree that Córdova used diacritical marks to indicate the tones he heard, we are not sure which marks go with which tones. It was, in fact, not until the late nineteenth century that professional linguists themselves developed conventions to mark different kinds of tones. It seems likely that Córdova would have tried to be consistent in his use of marks, and that he was distinguishing tone as well as dialect variation among informants in different communities. Unfortunately, he left us no guide to follow.

The Relevance of Tone Pairs and Homonyms to Ancient Zapotec Writing

One of the interesting aspects of tone languages is that puns can sometimes be based on slight differences in sound or tone. Languages can have *homonym pairs*, words that sound alike but mean different things. Examples in English include pear, pair, and pare; feet and feat; and bear and bare.

Homonyms (soundalikes and tone pairs) facilitate *rebus writing*: for example, a picture of a bee + a picture of a leaf can stand for the word "belief." In a language such as Zapotec, two words might be differentiated by tone alone. I can testify that today's speakers of Mitla Zapotec are quite fond of tone puns, especially those in which an innocuous word and an obscenity are differentiated only by tone.

One of the interesting features of tone puns and homonym pairs is that when applied to hieroglyphic writing, they allowed one to use the picture of an easily depicted object to convey something that is difficult to depict. I have already suggested that in Zapotec, a human thumb (*yobi*) could be used as the hieroglyph for "first-born son," precisely because they are homonyms or soundalike words (Córdova [1578b]1886:213–214; Marcus 1983f; Miller 1995).

In Valley Zapotec, the words for "flower," "stone," "fire," "hill," "cliff," and "rain" are homonyms. In the Isthmus of Tehuantepec, the Juchitecos use tone to differentiate "fish" from "snake" and "he became." They also use tone to differentiate "kernel," "cactus," "dry," and "frog" from one another (Radin 1925:31). Some tone pairs share a semantic relationship; for example, Merrill (2008:110) gives *guba* as the word for both "steam" and "sky."

Here are a few examples of near-homonyms and tone pairs in sixteenth-century Zapotec:

Bee = fog, turtle
Peni =footprint, step, person, people
Pell, pella = sister, fish, star, snake, he became
Guie = flower, hill, cliff, stone, fire, rain
Le = speech, patio, tube, prayer
Beñe = mud, crocodile
Beche = brother, jaguar
Cotí/gotí= bag, death, deceased person

The last term listed (*cotí* or *gotí*) can be linked to the bag glyph, shown on Zapotec monuments as early as 500 BC. That bag glyph can, in turn, be linked to the Zapotec word for "death" or "deceased person" (Figure 5.4).

Caso (1928) was very close to the correct interpretation when he concluded that the bag glyph meant "end." Had he consulted Córdova's ([1578a]1942) dictionary and seen that bag and death were homonyms, he might have suggested that the bag glyph meant "end of life," rather than just "the end." (Appropriately enough, Caso's 1928 book has the bag glyph stamped into its back cover to signify the end of the book.)

From their painted codices, we know that Mixtec scribes employed rebus principles to write place names, such as the Mixtec town of Chiyocanu. While this town is best known by its Nahuatl name (Teozacoalco), the Mixtec town of Chiyocanu once served as an important dynastic seat. According to the sixteenth-century friar Antonio de los Reyes ([1593]1976:89) the Mixtec name, Chiyocanu, meant "great platform" or "big foundation." Since the word "great" or "big" was difficult to depict, Mixtec scribes elected to draw a bent platform to stand for great platform, since the Mixtec word for "bent" was a homonym for "great." In Figure 5.5, we see a small man bending a platform (Caso 1949; M. E. Smith 1973a:57–58).

A second example of rebus writing comes from the Mixtec town of Yodzo Cahi, whose Nahuatl name is Yanhuitlán. The Mixtec words Yodzo Cahi mean "wide plain" or "broad valley." Because *yodzo* could also mean "large feather," the Mixtec scribes decided to paint a picture of a platform of large feathers, knowing that Mixtec speakers could read those large feathers as *yodzo* (Caso 1949, 1977, 1979; M. E. Smith 1973a:63).

If a much larger sample of sixteenth-century Zapotec codices existed, we should expect to find equivalent soundalike examples of rebus writing. Unfortunately, the limited corpus of Zapotec codices falls far short of that for the Mixtec. Even without much evidence, a number of scholars during the last 100 years have surmised that Zapotec writing should feature examples of near homonyms and soundalike rebus writing (e.g., Batres 1902; Caso 1928; Marcus 1976b). This was once the case with Maya writing as well (e.g., Brinton 1870, 1886; Houston 1984; Thomas 1893; Whorf 1933). Zapotec writing was probably a mixed system, a logosyllabic system (Caso 1928:65; Marcus 1976c, 1992a, 2006a) with homonyms and rebus principles playing a role. Obviously, much more evidence will be needed to show the role of phoneticism and homonyms in Zapotec writing.

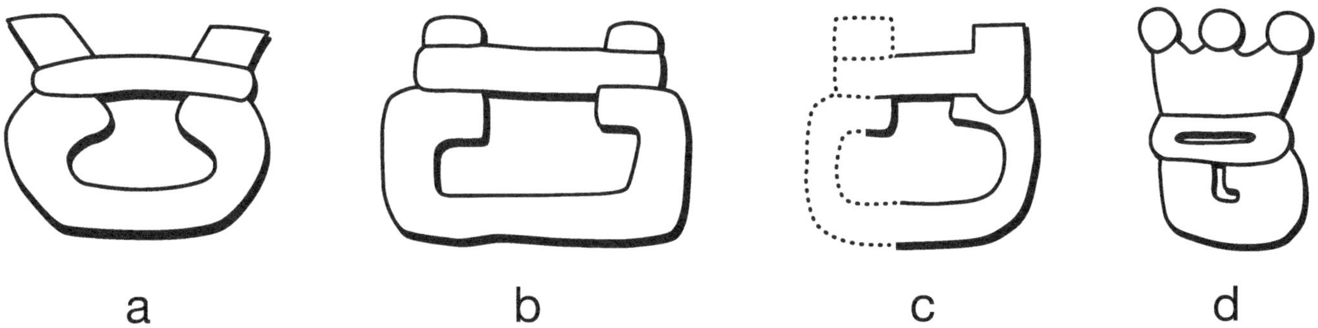

Figure 5.4. The "bag" glyph is an example of rebus writing. The Zapotec selected the bag to signify "deceased" and "death" because the word *cotí* meant "bag" as well as "dead." This is only one case in which the Zapotec used an easily drawn item to stand in for a more abstract concept. As one might expect, the bag glyph was often included in funerary texts, carved on tomb lintels, or painted in murals. It also appeared in nonfunerary contexts—for example, as the final hieroglyph in a column of text. (*a*) Monument D-55, Monte Albán; (*b*) Stela 14, Monte Albán; (*c*) Stela 15, Monte Albán; (*d*) Stela 5, Cerro de la Campana. See also Figure 8.75, where the earliest known tomb mural includes a bag glyph on the back wall of the main chamber in association with the name of the deceased. Drawing by John Klausmeyer.

Zapotec as a Monosyllabic-Isolating Language

Early linguists such as Angulo and Freeland (1935:4) believed that the Zapotec family of languages shared "a certain morphological structure [which] ... may roughly be called the 'monosyllabic-isolating type'." For them, the terms "monosyllabic" and "isolating" are descriptive terms, with monosyllabism referring to whether or not a word is a single syllable and isolatism referring to morphology. The latter denotes a structure in which a sentence is composed of separate words, each of which stands entirely by itself and is not susceptible to changes in form or meaning (Angulo and Freeland 1935:4).

The principal exception to the monosyllabic-isolating character of Zapotec would be the presence of temporal prefixes (Angulo and Freeland 1935:13). Angulo (1926a:133) has argued that Zapotec and other Otomanguean languages were undergoing change during the early twentieth century, moving from monosyllabism to polysyllabism and from "isolatism" to "affixation." As a result, some, but not all, linguists regard the present-day Zapotec language as agglutinative (cf. Pickett et al. 1988:141).

Word Order

Having examined the importance of tones, homonyms, and monosyllables, our next topic is Zapotec word order. This is a key subject, because word order often bears the burden of showing the relationship between subject and object. Speaking of Zapotec, Angulo (1926a:46) says: "In this type of language they [subjects and objects] are all straight, bare monosyllables, and their *relation* to each other and to the action is indicated by their position, by *order*."

The most common word order for Zapotec sentences in the twentieth century was **Verb + Subject + Object (VSO).**

A variant would be **Verb + Subject-Pronoun + Object-Pronoun**.

Much less common is **Subject + Verb + Object (SVO)**.

The word order SVO is common in English (e.g., "Oliver opened the book"), but it is not common in Zapotec (Angulo and Freeland 1935:10).

Since we expect many sentences written on ancient Zapotec monuments to have been declarative statements, we should look closely at their structure. In contemporary Zapotec, the typical word order of intransitive declarative sentences is: **Time + Verb + Subject + Purpose.** A twentieth-century example (Pickett 1967:303) would be *después la gu dinde nezucele laaka por terreno,* "later or afterward + fought + Nezuchele + for land."

On the other hand, the typical word order of Zapotec transitive declarative sentences is **Time + Verb + Subject + Object.** For example, *chi gulaki sti dyuzi giji layun gulaki be diija za* // day + set up + God + world + set up + he + language + Zapotec; or "When God made the world, he also made the Zapotec language."

From 1956 to 1958 Dow Robinson (1963) studied Coatlán Zapotec, a language spoken by 650 inhabitants in the village of Santa María Coatlán, 35 km southwest of Miahuatlán. Robinson considered Miahuatlán Zapotec and Coatlán Zapotec to be mutually unintelligible. He focused on three characteristics of Coatlán Zapotec: its contrastive fortis and lenis consonants, the fact that a heavy semantic load was carried by tone, and the complicated structure of its verbs. He found three phonemic tone levels (low, mid, and high) and three contrastive tone glides. For

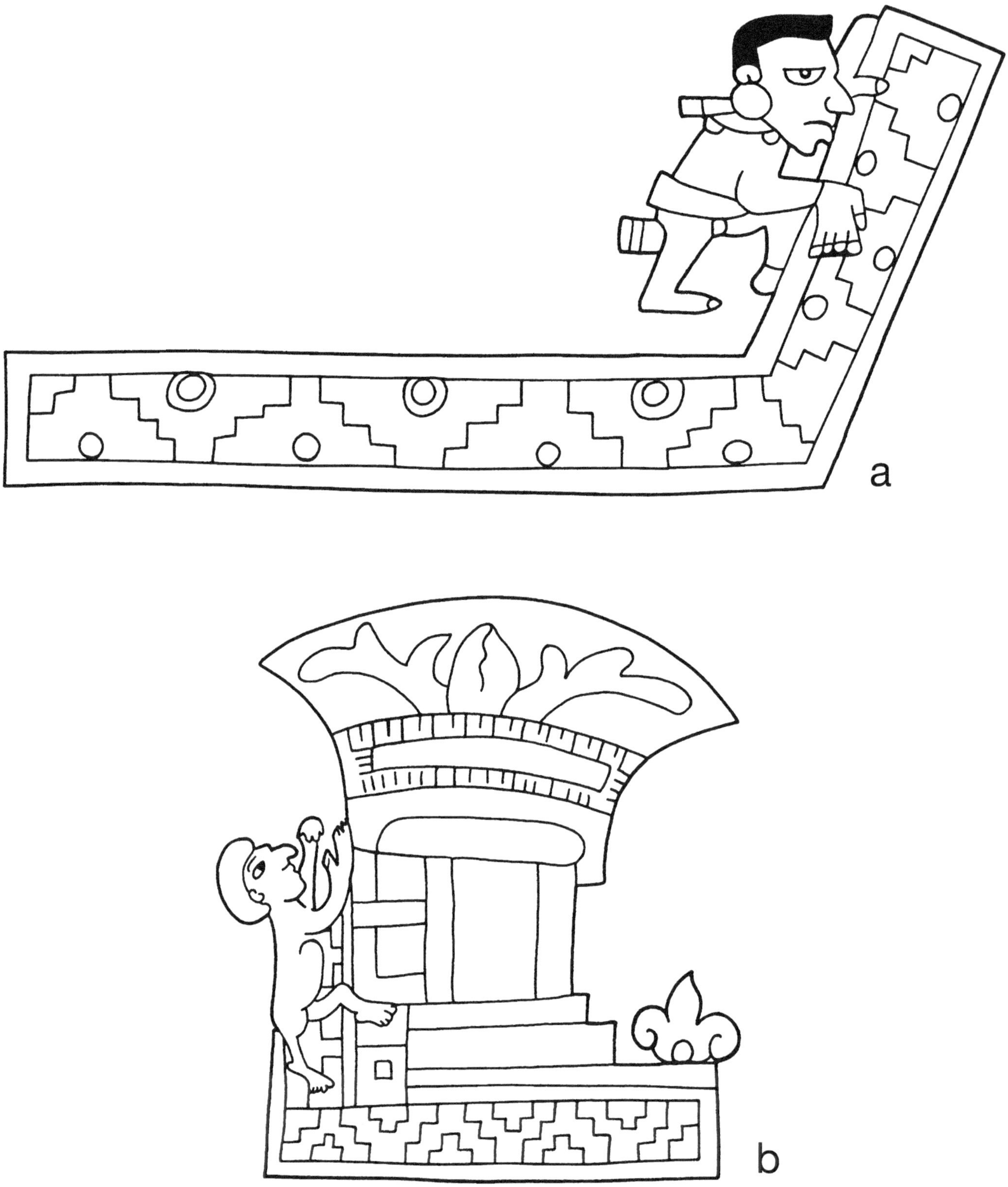

Figure 5.5. The Mixtec town of Teozacoalco presents us with a good example of rebus writing. Teozacoalco's Mixtec name, Chiyocanu, meant "great platform." Since "great platform" and "bent platform" had virtually the same sound in Mixtec, the scribe could draw a man bending a platform to represent Chiyocanu (*a*, from Codex Bodley 15; *b*, from the 1580 Mapa de Teozacoalco) (Caso 1949; Corona Núñez 1964, vol. 2: Lám. XV; Marcus 1992a: Fig. 3.14; M. E. Smith 1973a). Drawing by John Klausmeyer.

example, *bèé'* has a slow rising glide and means "turtle"; when it has a mid-low, slow-falling glide (*beè'*) it means "fog." A "cloud turtle" or "fog turtle" (*bèé' beè'*) seems to be depicted in the upper register of a carved stone from Noriega (Figure 5.6), and may refer to a remote ancestor wearing the carapace of a turtle, a being that possessed the ability to sacrifice creatures and fly among the clouds.

Most importantly, all the sentences in Coatlán Zapotec recovered by Robinson present the verb first, to wit:

(1) verb;
(2) verb + subject;
(3) verb + object;
(4) verb + subject + object;
(5) verb + subject + location.

Zapotec Word Order in Noun Phrases

Another feature of the contemporary Zapotec languages is that they place the descriptive word after the main element. To say "palm-thatched house," the Zapotec say "house," then "palm-thatched" (*yo'o ziña*, "house" + "palm thatch"). For "cloth napkin," they say *lari geta*, "cloth" + "tortilla." For "person who speaks a foreign language," the Zapotec say *binni dija subi*, "person" + "language" + "foreign."

"Bark" becomes *gidi ladi yaga*, "skin" + "body" + "tree." "Little black dog" is *biku wiini yaase*, "dog" + "little" + "black." "Moustache" is *gica rua*, "hair" + "mouth." "Big brother" is *bice naro*, "brother" + "big." As linguist Yasugi (1995:156) puts it, "Otomanguean languages are almost purely head-modifier," meaning that nouns come first, modifiers second. We should therefore look for this word order in the ancient hieroglyphic texts.

Scarcity of Prepositions

Another feature of contemporary Zapotec is that noun phrases rarely include prepositions. To say "tears," the Zapotec say *nisa lu* or "water" + "eye." To say "roof" the Zapotec say "head" + "house." To say "entrance to the town" the Zapotec say "head" + "town."

We have already seen that to say "bark," the Zapotec string three nouns together (*gidi ladi yaga*, "skin" + "body" + "tree"). No prepositions are involved (such as skin "of"), nor articles (such as "the" tree), nor possessive terms (such as "its" skin). We should therefore expect such "noun strings" or "noun sequences" to appear in ancient hieroglyphic texts as compound signs, or as separate main signs in a column.

Ethnohistoric documents indicate that sixteenth-century Zapotec also featured a main word (a head noun) followed by qualifiers. To say "mother" or "woman with child," the sixteenth-century Zapotec said *peni cozaana*, "person" + "engendered child" (Córdova [1578a]1942).

For "young girl" the Zapotec said *peni chapa*, "person" + "young." For "temple" they said *yoho pèe*, "house" + "vital force." A "dry year" was *yza cobaa*, "year" + "dry"; a "rainy year" was *yza quie* "year" + "rainy." "Sweet fruit" was *nocuana naaxi*, "fruit" + "sweet"; "sour fruit" was *nocuana nayy*, "fruit" + "sour." Note that no prepositions or possessives are used in any of these constructions.

Use of an Affix to Mark the Category "Animal"

Most Otomanguean languages use a special prefix with terms for animals. In Mixtec, for example, the prefix *ti* is used; *ti-aka* is "fish," *ti-dhitci* is "tadpole" and *ti-dha* is "bird." In Zapotec, according to Angulo and Freeland (1935:13), this animal prefix is not detachable from the term. A morpheme is the minimal unit of meaning in a language. For example, in Sierra Zapotec the animal prefix *mb-* would be a "true morpheme, i.e. a semantic unit that lost its autonomy" (some linguists would call it a "bound morpheme").

Many Valley Zapotec towns used the prefix *pe-* (*be*), *pèe-* or *pi-* (*bi*) as their animal classifier. Examples of animals that have such an initial syllable are "bat" (*piguite ziña*), "armadillo" (*bigupi*), and "snake" (*benda*). Animals were also grouped by the Valley Zapotec into larger categories such as fierce animals (*beche* or *peche*); toads and frogs (*peeche*); and fish, snakes, and worms (*pella*) (Marcus and Flannery 1978:64–67). Examples of fierce animals would include *pechetào* ("jaguar"), *peche piaha* ("puma"), and *peche peeza* ("gray fox"). Examples of *pella* would include *pellayoo* ("earthworm"), *pellaxangale* ("eel"), *pellatoxo* ("rattlesnake"), and *pellayooniça* ("water snake").

All Zapotec words for human beings (*peni, bini, binni, peeni*) share the "animal" prefix. In addition, *bi*, *pe*, *pèe*, or *pi* could stand alone as a free morpheme, defined as "wind," "breath," "life," or "vital force" (Marcus and Flannery 1978:57–58). Córdova's sixteenth-century dictionary defines *pèe* or *pi* as ánima, *lo que da vida*. It was the vital force that made all things move, distinguishing nonliving matter from living. As a result, the ancient Zapotec also used *pèe, pe,* or *pi* to begin their terms for such things as the 260-day sacred calendar (*piye*) or the effervescent foam (*pichina*) atop a cup of pulque or chocolate; these were all items they considered to be alive.

The Limited Use of Affixes

Zapotec languages generally lack affixes, which are defined as morphemes attached to the beginning (prefix) or end (suffix) of a root. In this case an affix is considered a dependent morpheme, while the root is an independent morpheme.

The fact that the Zapotec language uses relatively few affixes is something to bear in mind when we examine ancient

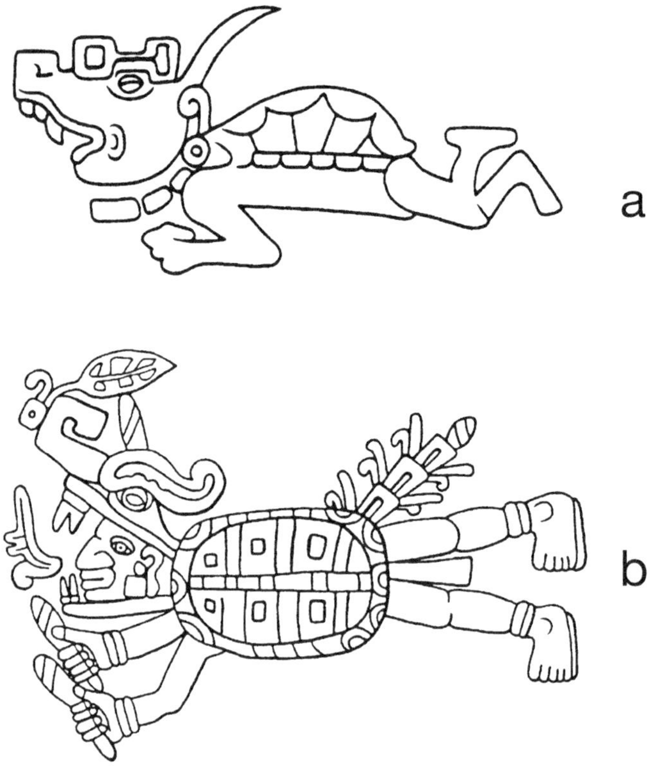

Figure 5.6. These flying creatures with turtle carapaces, called *yahui* by the Mixtec and *xicàni* by the Zapotec, have been considered sorcerers, wizards, sacrificers, and mediators who could fly back and forth between ancestors and descendants. They were believed to have participated in sacrifices, divining, and impersonating deities (Augsburger 2003; Caso 1966:324; Hermann Lejarazu 2009; Marcus 1992a: Figs. 9.8, 9.13; M. E. Smith 1973a, 1973b; Urcid 2005). Drawing by John Klausmeyer.

hieroglyphic texts. The use of few affixes constitutes a major difference between Zapotec and Maya writing; Maya texts were very rich in affixes (prefixes, suffixes, and infixes), which added everything from tense to adjectives or pronouns or phonetic complements. Some examples include *u b'a* (his image); *ah* (he of) and *ix* (she of) (male and female agentive prefixes) (Marcus 1992a:211; Roys 1940).

The Creation of Plurals

Ca was used in the creation of plurals. For example, *ti yoho* meant "a house," while *ca yoho* meant "houses." *Ca zigi* meant "chins." In these examples "*ca*" was considered a separate word, rather than a prefix (Angulo and Freeland 1935:12).

The Creation of Abstract Nouns

To create an abstract noun, the sixteenth-century Zapotec used *quela* before another word. For example, *naguichi* was used to refer to a white object; placing *quela* before the term converted it to *quela naguichi*, an abstract term that can be translated as "whiteness." Other examples abound. The term *bitoo* meant "great spirit"; *quela bitoo* meant "divinity." The adjective *cotí* meant "dead"; *quela cotí* meant "death." The noun *xini* meant "offspring"; *quela xini* meant "kinship." The noun *beni* meant "people"; *quela beniati* meant "mankind."

Possession

The prefix *x* or *xh* could express ownership. Thus *yoo* meant "house," but *xyoo* would be "the house of" or "his house." *Yaala* meant "copal," but *xyaala* would be "the copal of" or "his copal." *Sh* (or š) could also be used for "its" or "his/her." In the Mayan languages "*u*" plays a similar role, as in "*u b'ah*" ("his portrait," "his image").

Zapotec Syllable Structures

Four syllable structures were common in Zapotec languages:

consonant + vowel (CV),
consonant + vowel + consonant (CVC),
consonant + consonant + vowel (CCV); and
consonant + consonant + consonant + vowel (CCCV).

Past Participles and Past Tenses

The sixteenth-century Zapotec used a prefix, *ni*, to create past participles. For example, "a thing that has died" was called *nicooti*; a person that "was born" was *nicolle.* Hieroglyphs that may correspond to *nicolle* and *nicooti* (some dictionaries give *niguti*) appeared on Stela 5 from Cerro de la Campana (see Figure 4.4).

The opportunity to implement rebus principles presented itself because *ni* could refer to "foot" as well as "it" and "his," and could also be used to create past participles and past tense. The syllable "*co*" also occurs in Caso's "Jaws of the Sky," a symbol that seemingly referred to *cozaana*, which commences with "*co*"; unfortunately, we have too few occurrences of these hieroglyphic compounds to confirm this tentative reading of "co."

The Application of Human Body Terms to Other Objects

Like the Maya, the Zapotec used body terms to refer to parts of other objects. For example, the inside of a house was called the "stomach" or "belly"; the roof was the "head"; an area below the house was the "foot"; an area above was the "eye"; the rear was the "back" or "shoulder" of the house (MacLaury 1989; Swadesh 1949). The term "ears" was applied to the corners of the house, while "mouth" referred to the doorway.

Similar terms for house parts were used by the Maya of Zinacantán (Vogt 1969). The Tzotzil Maya of the Chiapas highlands used similar words to describe mountains. Thus, *yok* (*y* = "its" + *ok* = "foot") could refer to a house foundation or to the foot of a mountain. *Sc'ut* ("its stomach") referred either to the midpoint of a mountainside or to a midpoint in the wall of a house. *Scikin* ("its ear") referred to the "corners" of both mountains and houses. *Shol* ("its head") was used for the top of a house or the summit of a mountain (Vogt 1976:58).

Zapotec speakers in Ayoquezco, Oaxaca, also used body part terms to label the parts of a hill (MacLaury 1989:120). For example, the hill's summit was its "head"; its sides were its "ribs"; its front, its "face"; its rear, its "back"; and its base, its "foot." In Juchitán, Oaxaca, body part terms were also used to describe the parts of a basket—the bottom of a basket was its buttocks; the wall of the basket was its side or flank; the basket rim was its mouth; and the interior of the basket was its stomach (see Pérez Báez 2011:949).

Using Comparative and Historical Data on Zapotec Languages to Advance Decipherment

This brief overview of Zapotec languages has provided us with at least five general principles that might be useful in deciphering ancient Zapotec hieroglyphic texts:

(1) Zapotec is a verb-initial language

(2) typical sentence construction is time + verb + subject + object

(3) homonyms are numerous and important

(4) prepositions are not common

(5) all Otomanguean languages are head-modifying or head-marking languages (e.g., nouns precede adjectives)

Given that the verb is often the first word in a Zapotec sentence, we should find this same construction in hieroglyphic texts. We should look for clauses or sentences of three types: (1) independent declarative clauses; (2) a declarative clause plus a dependent clause; and (3) compound sentences, formed by stringing together two or more declarative clauses. Such compound sentences are common in today's spoken Zapotec, but the word "and" (which would link them in English) is optional in Zapotec. Given the brevity of most ancient Zapotec texts, we might expect that independent declarative clauses were used most frequently, rather than compound sentences.

As soon as we look for hieroglyphic sentences with the construction **Time + Verb + Subject**, we begin to find possible examples. Let us now look at three such texts. The first two examples were carved around AD 500. Our third example was probably carved around AD 700–800.

Example 1: Tentative interpretation of Stela 3, Monte Albán (Figure 5.7):

Time +	Verb +	Subject
[in the] Year 10M	**was captured**	**a man named 12D (12 Reed)**

Example 2: Tentative interpretation of Stela 6, Monte Albán (Figure 5.8):

Time +	Verb +	Subject
[in the] Year 10 Deer	**was captured**	**a man named 2S**

Example 3: Tentative interpretation of Lápida 1 from the Museo Nacional de Antropología (Figure 5.9):

Time +	Verb +	Subject
Year 8N	**received offerings**	**apical ancestor + 6 married couples**

A renewed focus on word order will be one of the productive paths that future epigraphers could take to accelerate the decipherment of Zapotec texts—especially texts from AD 400–800, when several examples of time + verb + subject are evident.

Figure 5.7. The text on Stela 3 of Monte Albán seems to exhibit typical Zapotec word order: Time + Verb + Subject (the unit of time = Year 10M; the verb = was captured; and the subject who endured that capture = a man named 12 Reed). One possible reading would be “In the Year 10M was captured a man named 12 Reed.” Drawing by Mark Orsen.

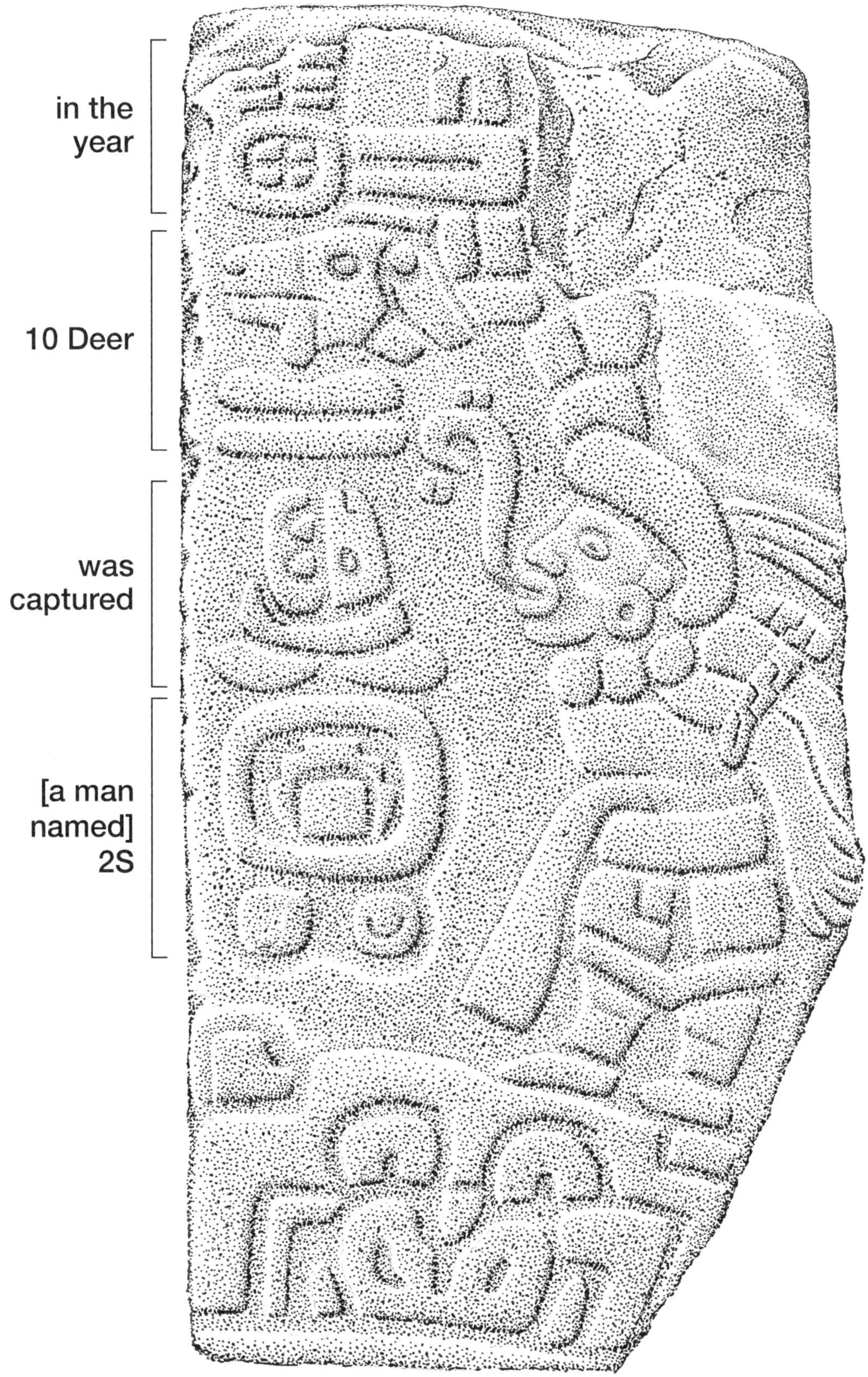

Figure 5.8. The text on Stela 6 of Monte Albán seems to exhibit typical Zapotec word order: Time + Verb + Subject. One possible reading would be "In the Year 10 Deer was captured a man named 2S." Drawing by Mark Orsen.

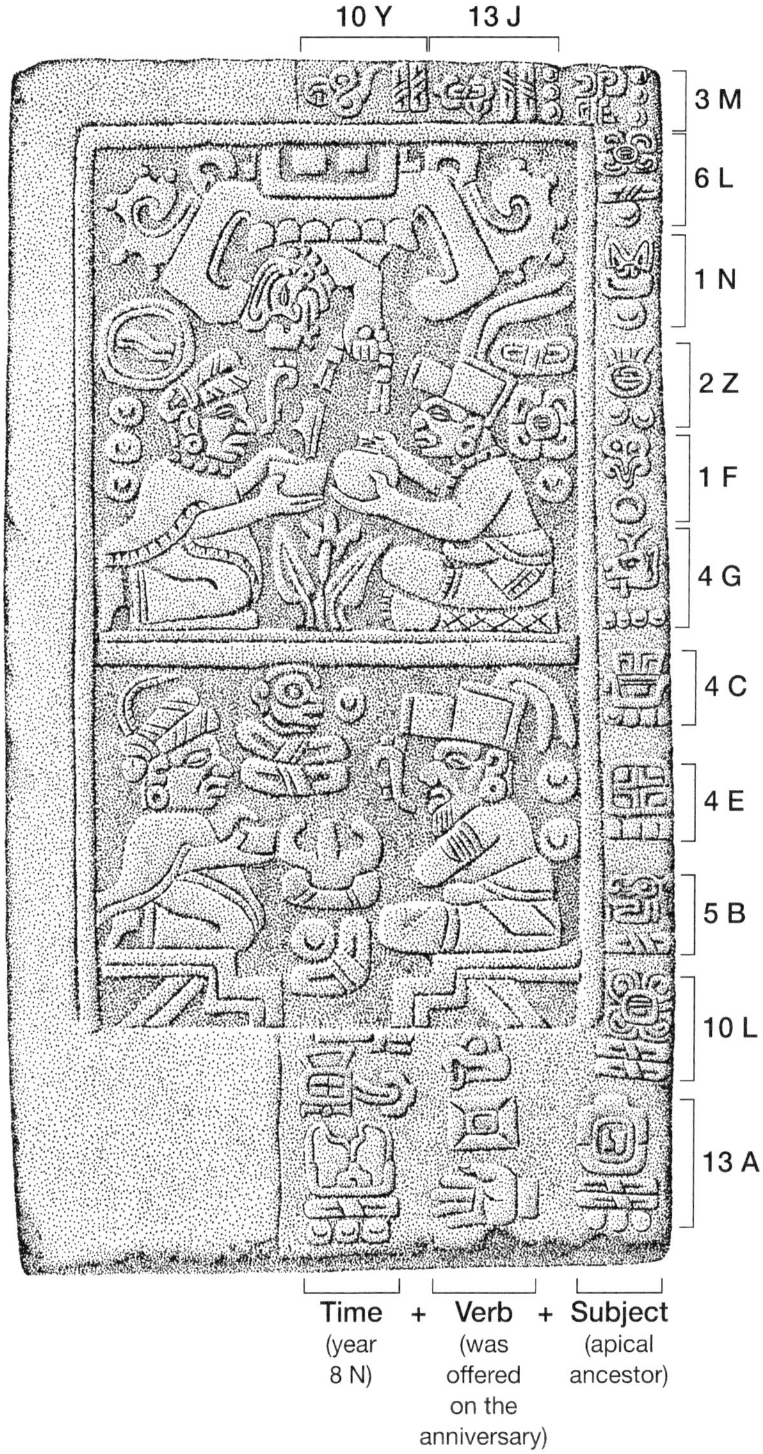

Figure 5.9. The hieroglyphic text on Lápida 1 (see Caso 1928: Fig. 81) begins at the bottom, ascends the right edge of the stone, and ends at the top. One possible reading is: "In the Year 8N + was offered [sacrificed birds?] on the anniversary [of the interment of an apical ancestor] named 13A + six possible marital pairs." The marital pairs were 10L + 5B, 4E + 4C, 4G + 1F, 2Z + 1N, 6L + 3M, and 13J + 10Y. The last four names are of particular interest. As noted by Caso, the names 6L and 3M appear not only in the column of hieroglyphs, but also in the upper register of the monument, where they label the man and woman depicted. The last two names, 13J and 10Y (13 Maize and 10 Serpent, respectively), may refer to the offspring of the couple in the upper register or to another marital pair (see also Figure 16.4). Drawing by Mark Orsen and John Klausmeyer.

Part II

The Emergence of Zapotec Writing

6

The Emergence of Zapotec Writing

The two oldest carved stones so far discovered in the Valley of Oaxaca come from San José Mogote and date to the San José phase (1150–850 BC). These stones were associated with Structure 2, a masonry platform 10 m wide and 1 m high (Figures 6.1, 6.2). Monument 1 seems to depict a feline and Monument 2 a raptorial bird (Figures 6.3, 6.4). Both carved stones had likely fallen from a wall of Structure 2.

The effort expended to build Structures 1 and 2 reflected San José Mogote's ability to organize labor on a regional scale, since some construction materials had been brought from a distance of five kilometers or more (Flannery and Marcus 2015:60–67). Given the diverse kinds of stone used to build Structures 1 and 2, it is possible that work gangs in nearby satellite communities brought construction materials to San José Mogote. Some work gangs brought volcanic tuff from nearby outcrops; others brought planoconvex adobes; still others brought basketloads of black alluvial soil, red piedmont soil, or gray-green volcanic soil. Limestone and travertine—raw materials foreign to the site—were transported from quarries farther away.

It is worth noting that San José Mogote did not actually need to import stone from elsewhere, since the site was located on its own inexhaustible source of volcanic tuff; almost certainly, it was the manpower that San José Mogote wanted to control. This ability to call on men from subordinate villages served to demonstrate that San José Mogote's leaders had some control over a wide area of the valley. As Schortman and Urban (1992:3) have said, "the goal of all elites is to control the labor and surplus production of as many subordinates as possible."

Chiefly Cycling

San José Mogote was the dominant chiefly center in the Etla arm of the valley during the San José phase (Flannery and Marcus 2012:232–237). During the following period, the Guadalupe phase, San José Mogote developed rivals, two of which were almost certainly Huitzo and San Martín Tilcajete. By Rosario times (700–500 BC), San José Mogote's population had grown substantially, but intervillage competition continued. Daub from burned buildings—likely destroyed in raids—occurs on the surface of Rosario sites at seven times the frequency seen in earlier times (Kowalewski et al. 1989:70).

One of San José Mogote's Rosario phase accomplishments was to turn Mound 1 of the site into an acropolis, with structures that could be seen from subordinate villages (Fernández Dávila 1997). San José Mogote's major Rosario temple rested on a platform of limestone blocks, many weighing half a ton. This limestone was brought from Matadamas, on the opposite side of

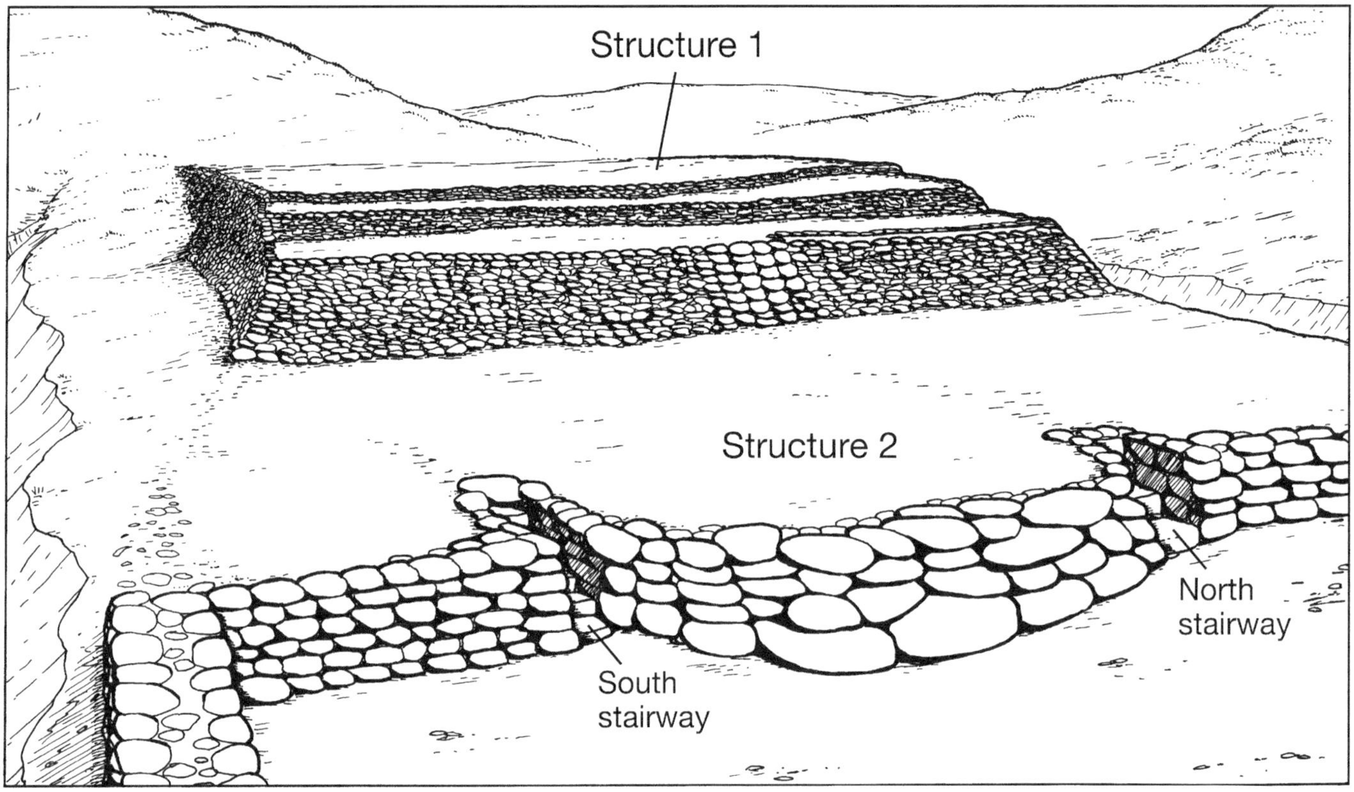

Figure 6.1. Artist's reconstruction of Structures 1 and 2 at San José Mogote, showing the stone masonry platforms but not the perishable temples that once stood atop them. Drawing by David West Reynolds.

the Atoyac River. By the late Rosario phase, the platform had been enlarged twice and its orientation changed from 8 degrees west of north to true east-west. This east-west/north-south orientation was later used for the Period I structures delimiting Monte Albán's Main Plaza.

Around 600 BC San José Mogote was attacked and its main temple (Structure 28) burned. So intense was the fire that the clay surface of the temple walls was reduced to vitrified cinders. Structure 28 was never rebuilt; instead, a new temple (Structure 37) was built a few meters to the north.

Both Structures 28 and 37 sat on limestone masonry platforms, with a corridor running between them. Anyone entering the corridor had to step on Monument 3, a carved threshold of the Rosario phase that depicted a sacrificial victim, presumably a defeated rival (Flannery and Marcus 2003; Flannery and Marcus 2015:180–192; Marcus 1976c, 1983f).

Being able to tread on the body of an enemy was a powerful message that Mesoamerican leaders were happy to send. We see the Zapotec, Maya, and other Mesoamerican peoples carving monuments depicting humiliated and sacrificed captives in prone and supine positions, shown on the risers and treads of staircases as well as below the feet of standing Maya rulers (e.g., Burdick 2016; Esparza Olguín and Pérez Gutiérrez 2009; Greene et al. 1972; Marcus 1974, 1992a, 2012; Nalda 2004; Ruppert and Denison 1943; Velásquez García 2004).

A New Motif

During the Guadalupe phase (850–700 BC), a new motif—a stylized drop of blood—appeared in the Valley of Oaxaca. This symbol combined a circle (a droplet of blood) and a triangle (flowing blood). Our earliest example of this motif is a shell pendant carved in the shape of a circle and triangle (Figure 6.5). This ornament was found at Fábrica San José, a subordinate village that contributed travertine, and almost certainly labor, to the construction of public buildings at San José Mogote (Drennan 1976: Figure 78d).

The blood motif made its first known appearance during the Guadalupe phase and went on to be used for centuries, since bloodletting was a key activity in Oaxaca and elsewhere. As early as 1000 BC the villagers at San José Mogote were using several kinds of possible bloodletting implements, including stingray spines (Figure 6.6), shark teeth, and obsidian lancets (Flannery and Marcus 2005:95–96, 321).

On Monument 3 of San José Mogote, we see two Rosario phase examples of the circle + triangle motif. During the next phase, Period I of Monte Albán, this same motif was carved on the steps of Temple T at Monte Negro in the Mixteca (Acosta n.d.; Acosta and Romero 1992:32; Balkansky et al. 2004; Flannery 1983a: Figure 4.10). This blood motif was a particularly appropriate one to carve on the steps of a temple,

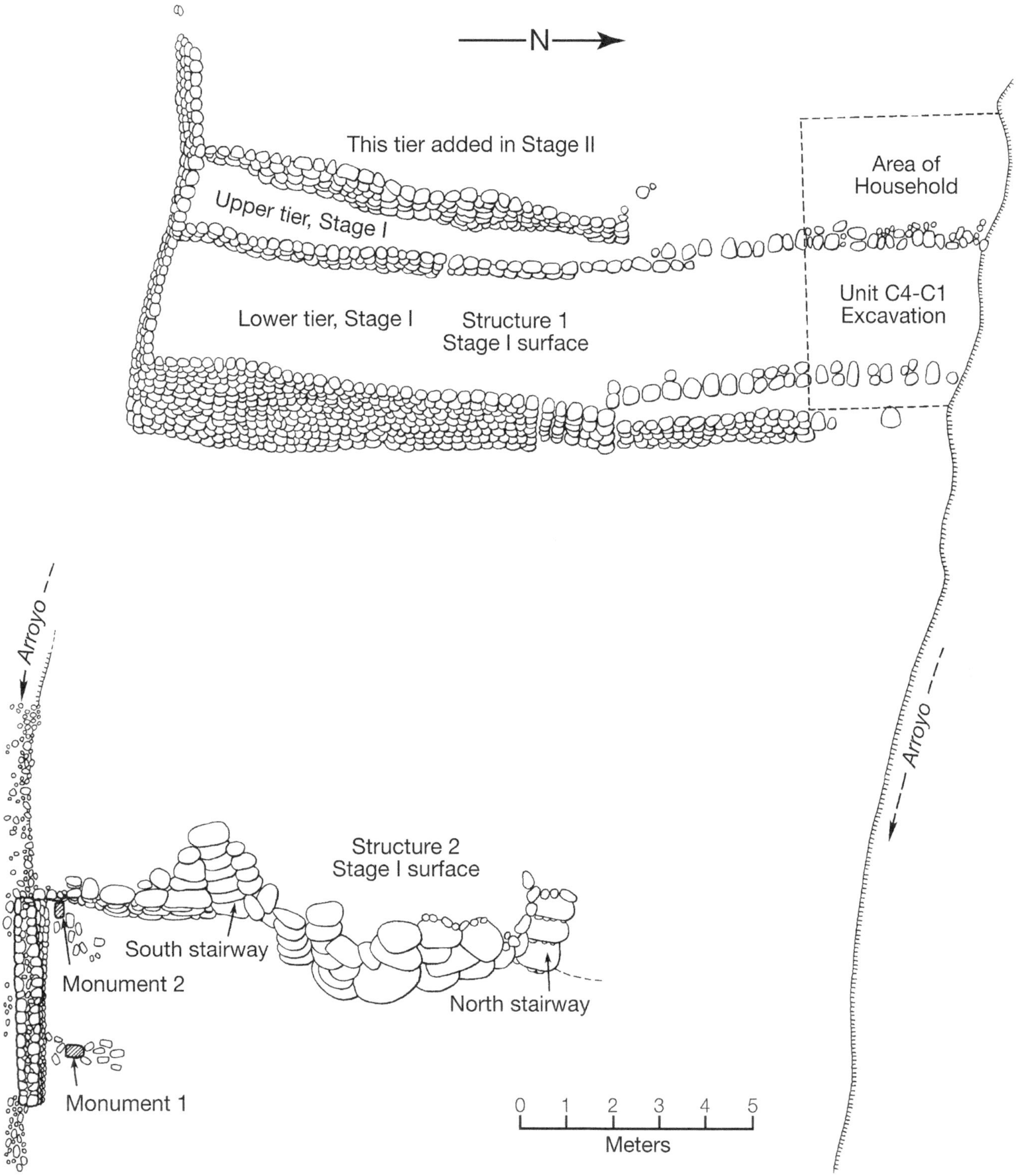

Figure 6.2. In the process of excavating Structure 2 at San José Mogote, Monuments 1 and 2 were discovered at the locations shown. Drawing by John Klausmeyer.

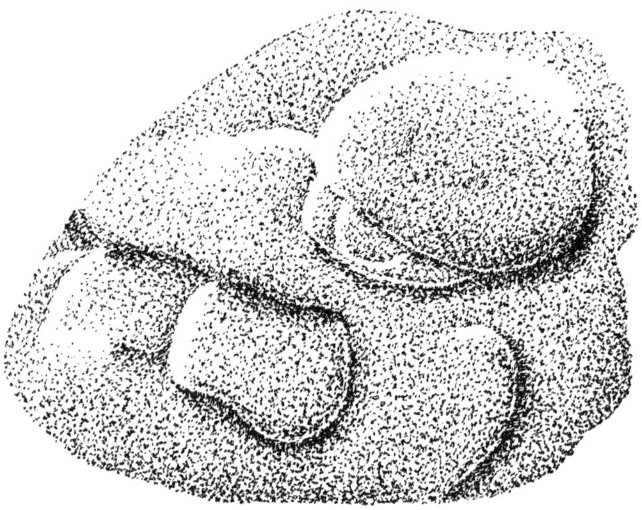

Figure 6.3. Monument 1 of San José Mogote (38 x 30 cm) dates to the San José phase (1150–850 BC). Drawing by Lois Martin.

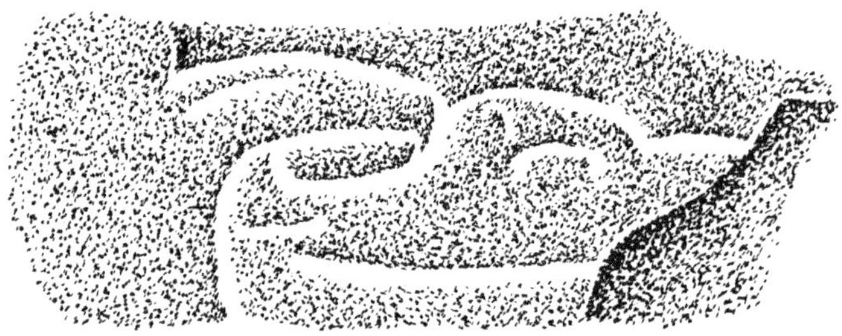

Figure 6.4. Monument 2 of San José Mogote (35 x 14 cm) dates to the San José phase (1150–850 BC). Drawing by Lois Martin.

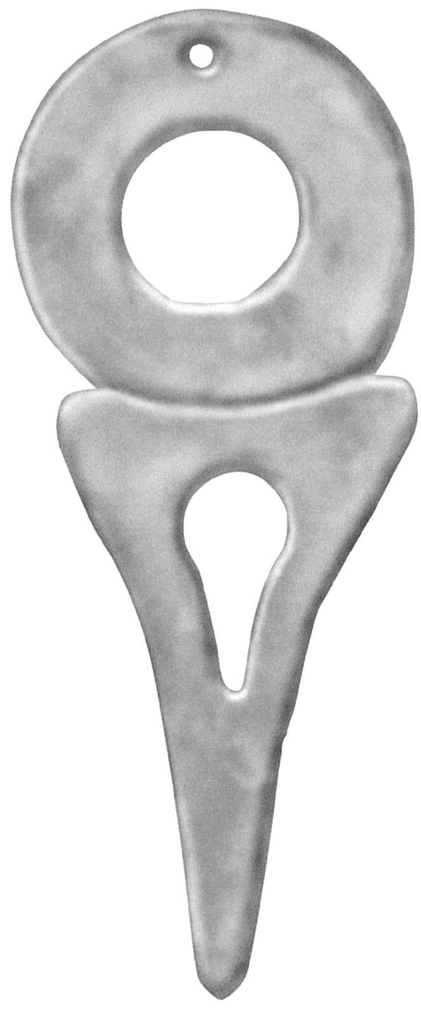

Figure 6.5. This circle + triangle shell pendant, representing a stylized drop of blood, dates to the Guadalupe phase (850–700 BC). Given the perforation at the top of the circle, this ornament may have been sewn to or suspended from another item. This pendant was found by Robert Drennan (1976: Fig. 78d) at the archaeological site of Fábrica San José. Length: 4.5 cm. Drawing by John Klausmeyer.

since bloodletting was probably one of the rituals carried out there (Figure 6.7). Monument Q-3 at Monte Albán, one of the so-called "prisoner slabs" at that site, may also display a variant of the blood motif (Figure 6.8). Over time the motif changed a bit, with the triangle becoming increasingly elongated to form a diamond shape that could include a cross or plus sign (see Chapter 12 and the "monkey + bag + blood motif" in Figures 12.17, 12.22; Sellen 2011:85–86). A necklace of the blood glyph can be seen on an urn from Monte Albán's Tomb 35.

When we look outside the State of Oaxaca, we see an example of this circle + triangle motif on a serpentine pendant from La Venta's North Pavement, located to the east of the Ceremonial Court (Drucker et al. 1959: Figure 73). On this dark green pendant (Figure 6.9) we see (1) a human head in profile, (2) a drilled eye that might have had an inlay, and (3) the circle + triangle motif. Below the gouged-out eye, we see a second motif that may also relate to flowing blood (Stocker and Spence 1973).

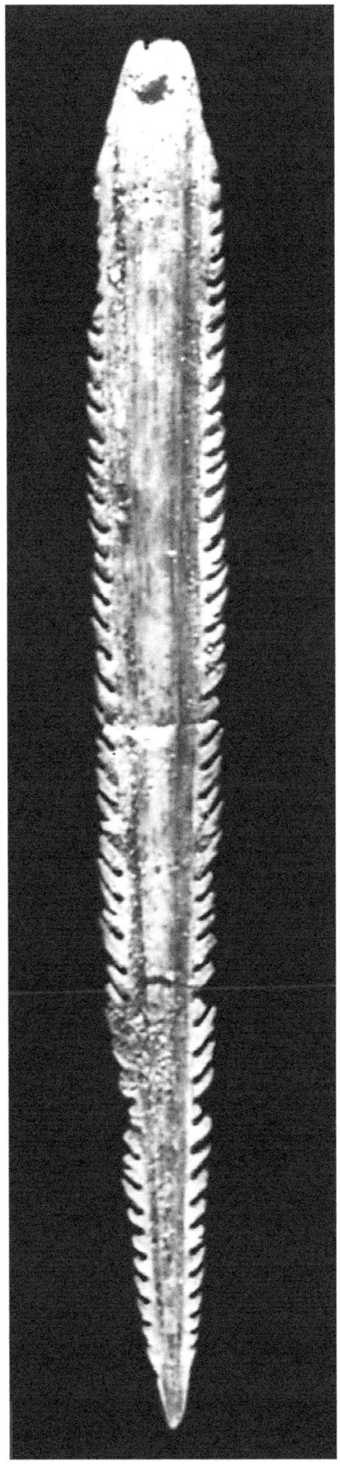

Figure 6.6. A San José phase (1150–850 BC) stingray spine found in House 17 at San José Mogote. This bloodletting tool seems to be perforated for suspension, and may have been worn around its owner's neck. Length: 9.7 cm. (See Flannery and Marcus 2005: Fig. 18.4f)

Stepping on the Body of a Human Victim

Monument 3 at San José Mogote is our earliest example of a stone set in place so that anyone entering a corridor on Mound 1 could step on the body of an enemy. This Zapotec convention was later adopted by the Maya at such sites as Yaxchilan, Tamarindito, Dos Pilas, Palenque, and Dzibanché (Figures 6.10, 6.11). Maya rulers at Calakmul, Naranjo, and elsewhere were shown standing on bound prisoners, who were sometimes squeezed into small spaces at the bases of monuments. Prisoners were also depicted on the steps of temples or palaces, in the very locations where nobles would place their feet as they were ascending or descending the steps (Burdick 2016; Flannery and Marcus 1976a; Greene et al. 1972; Marcus 1974, 1992a, 2012). Many Maya staircases depicted scantily clad prisoners, accompanied by texts that sometimes conveyed the prisoner's name, the captor's name, and the date of the capture.

At the same time that Maya rulers were commissioning prisoner staircases, the architects of Monte Albán were actively borrowing carved stones from the Prisoner Gallery of Building L (see description below), reusing them in nearby structures (Figure 6.12; Marcus 1974: Plate 9). Years ago, when Ignacio Bernal was giving me a tour of Monte Albán, he emphasized how many times certain structures had been dismantled, lamenting how the carved stones of the Prisoner Gallery had been dispersed by this activity. Sadly, the consolidation of later buildings precludes our plumbing the depths of the Main Plaza to see its overall Period I layout (Flannery and Marcus 1976a, 1983a; Marcus 2009a, 2009b; Marcus and Feinman 1998).

The Dating of Monument 3

Monument 3 of San José Mogote was sealed stratigraphically below two Rosario phase hearths (Features 18 and 19) that yielded

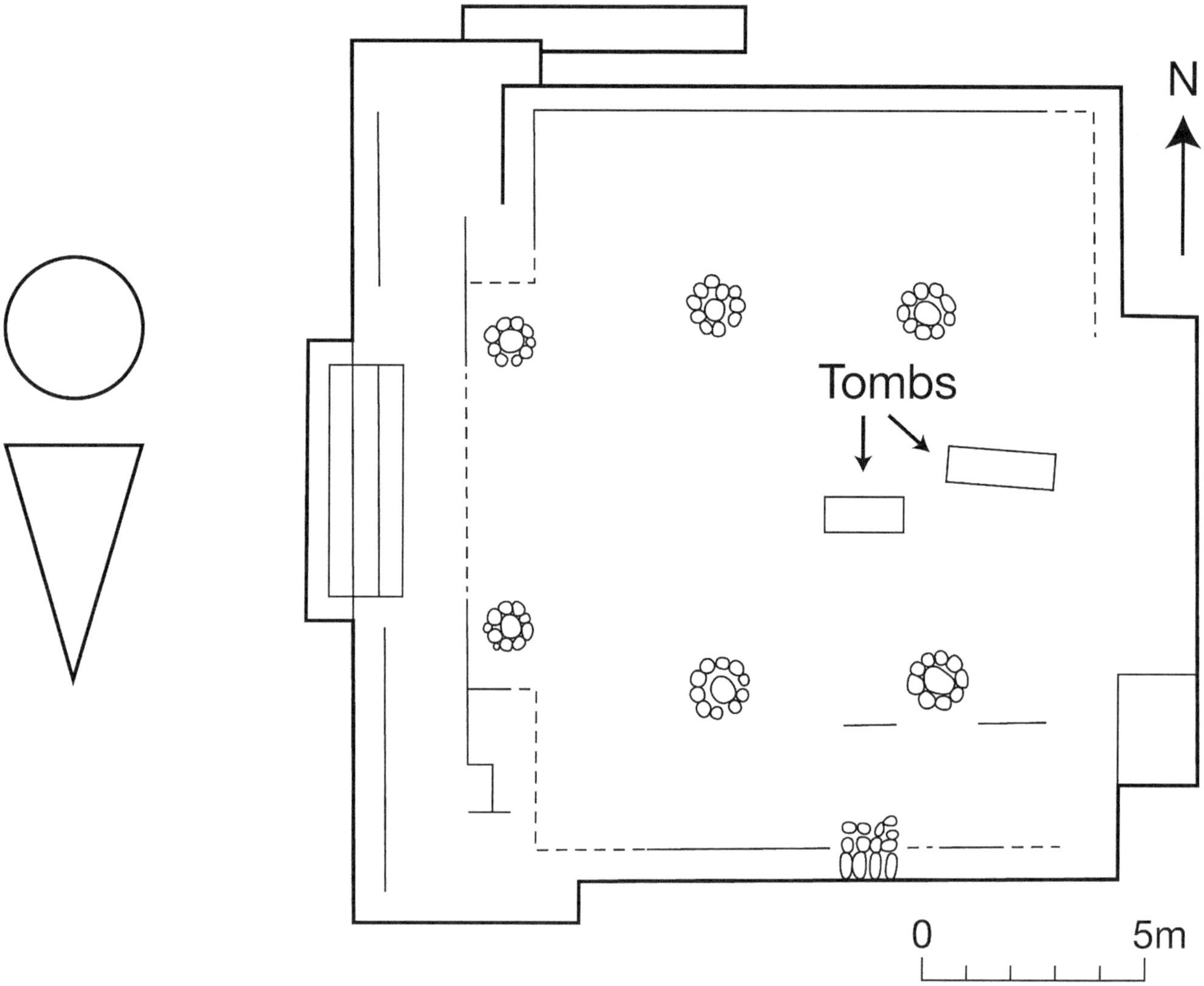

Figure 6.7. The blood motif (at left) was carved on the steps of Temple T (at right) at the archaeological site of Monte Negro, Oaxaca. (See Flannery 1983a: Fig. 4.10; Balkansky et al. 2004:38–39.) Drawing by John Klausmeyer.

datable charcoal (Flannery and Marcus 2003:11803; Flannery and Marcus 2015:180–192). Those hearth dates provided us with a *terminus ante quem* for Monument 3, showing that it was placed in its corridor prior to the end of the Rosario phase (Fernández Dávila 1997; Flannery and Marcus 2003; Flannery and Marcus 2015:180–193; Marcus 1976c, 1983f). The associated ceramics, the stratigraphy, and the radiocarbon dates of 630 BC and 560 BC for the two hearths stratigraphically above Monument 3 (Figure 6.13) do not support the speculative later dates offered by other authors (e.g., Cahn and Winter 1993). Anyone interested in a detailed account of the discovery of Monument 3 can find it in Flannery and Marcus (2015:180–193).

Before placing Monument 3 in its corridor, the Rosario phase architects arranged a layer of flat slabs that served to level and support the carved stone (Flannery and Marcus 2003; Flannery and Marcus 2015:180–193) (Figures 6.14, 6.15). All the sherds found with these slabs, with Monument 3 itself, and between Monument 3 and the two overlying hearths belonged to Rosario (or earlier) times. No attempt to argue that Monument 3 was used in an earlier phase building is supported by the currently available evidence. In sum, the stratigraphy of Monument 3, its associated ceramics, its *terminus ante quem* radiocarbon dates, and its Middle Formative circle + triangle blood motif all place it in the Rosario phase.

What Messages Were Conveyed by Monument 3?

The sacrificed captive on Monument 3 is shown stripped of his clothing and sprawled on the ground, with his eyes closed and his mouth open. On his chest is a trilobal scroll depicting blood streaming from a chest cavity. A broad ribbon of blood leads from

Figure 6.8. Monument Q-3 (located south of the main stairway in Building Q at Monte Albán) shows a possible variant of the blood motif; in this case, it consists of a droplet and two ribbons of flowing blood. This motif appears on the chest of this sacrificial victim (Acosta 1974: Fig. 31, at the top; García Moll et al. 1986, Stone 466: Lám. 171; Scott 1978, Part II: Catalogue). Drawing by John Klausmeyer.

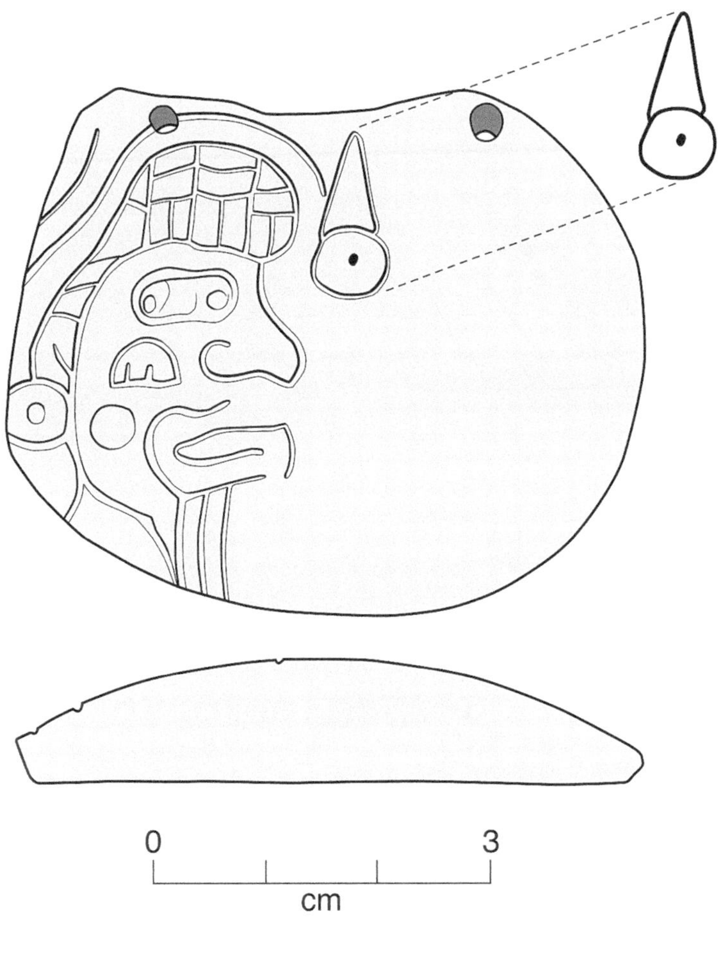

Figure 6.9. This serpentinite pendant from La Venta (Tabasco) also shows the circle + triangle blood motif (redrawn from Drucker et al. 1959: Fig. 73; see also Stocker and Spence 1973). Drawing by John Klausmeyer.

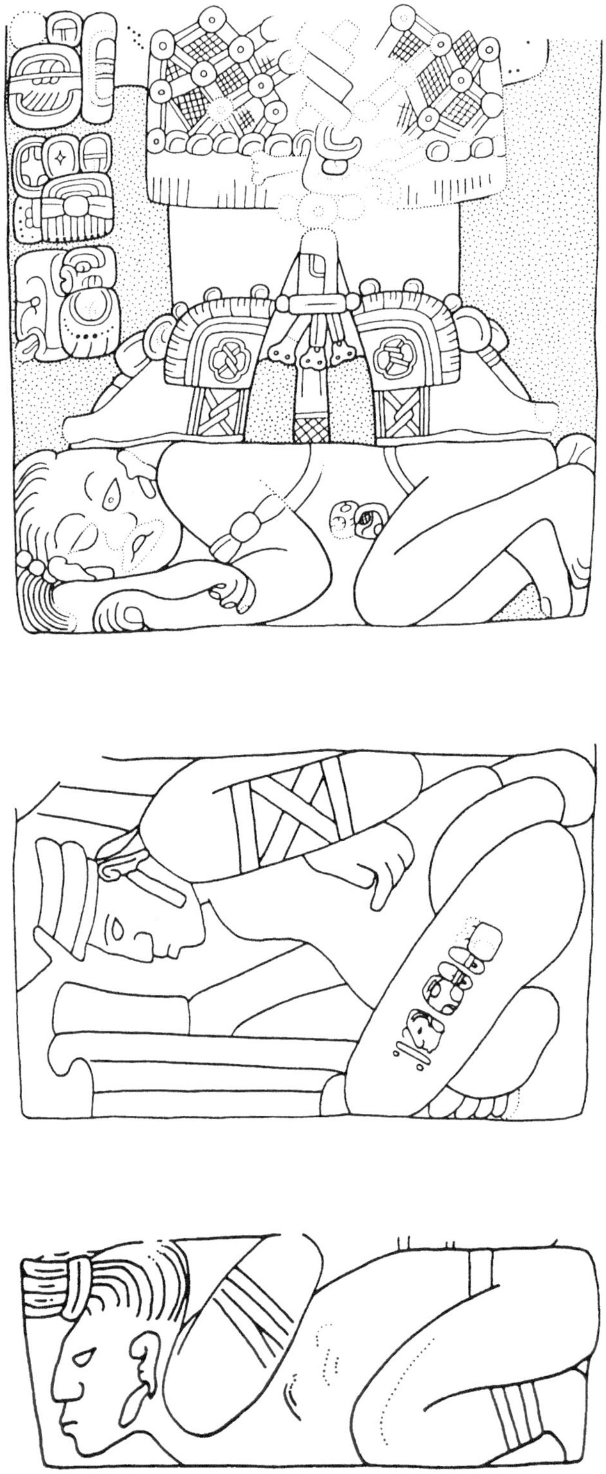

a

b

c

Figure 6.10. Maya royalty were often shown standing on the bodies of prisoners at Naranjo, Guatemala. Some of these victims (*a*, *b*) have hieroglyphs on their thighs or torsos, while others probably had such glyphs but they are now too eroded to tell (*c*). (See Graham and von Euw 1975.) Drawing by John Klausmeyer.

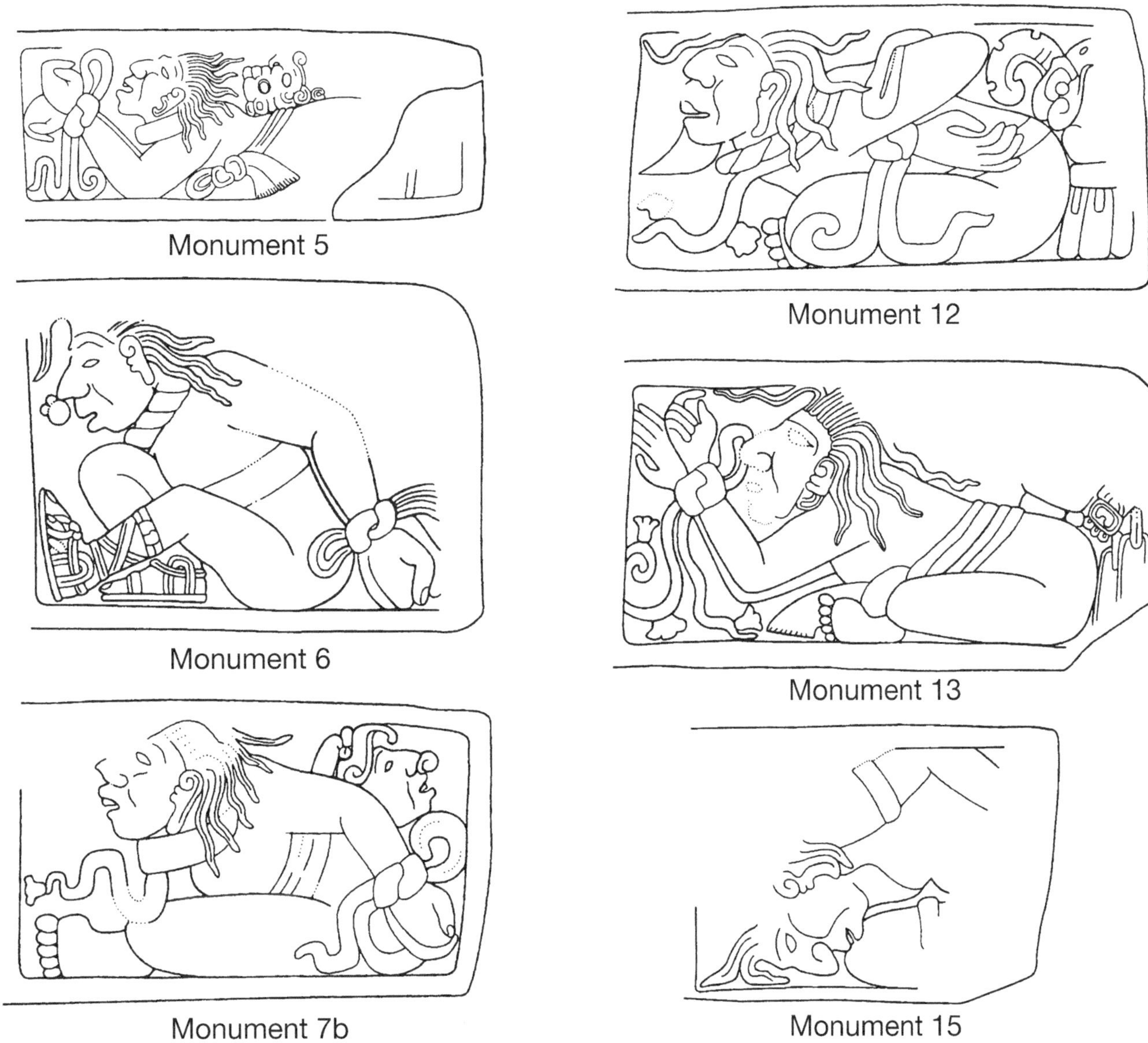

Figure 6.11. These Maya prisoners at Dzibanché, Mexico, were carved on the risers of stairs. Most are shown with their wrists tied with cords. The associated hieroglyphs (see Nalda 2004 and Velásquez García 2004) provide details on the dates of their capture and possibly the names of their captors. Redrawn by John Klausmeyer from Marcus 2012: Figs. 4.5, 4.6.

his chest to the edge of the stone, ending in two examples of the circle + triangle motif. The triangle in this case represents blood dripping down the riser of the threshold (Figure 6.16).

Between the feet of the victim are two hieroglyphs: Caso's (1928) Glyph L plus a dot for the number "one." This is a date in the 260-day calendar. In this context, 1L seems to be the victim's calendric name rather than the date of his capture.

Monument 3 provides us with the oldest Zapotec hieroglyph known so far, as well as the first carving of a sacrificial victim in the Valley of Oaxaca. We should not be surprised to find that this early Zapotec monument displays a sacrificed captive. Some 60 years ago, in speaking of the carved slabs in Building L at Monte Albán, Coe (1962:95) noted that "the distorted pose of the limbs, the open mouth and closed eyes indicate that these are corpses, undoubtedly chiefs or kings slain by the earliest rulers of Monte Albán." The word "chiefs" is still appropriate, since the Rosario phase antedates state formation and the victim on Monument 3 can be no more than a chief. The fact that his name was given reminds us of the Maori practice of naming a battle after a defeated rival chief. The Maori noble Te Rangi Hiroa once

Figure 6.12. Carved stones depicting slain captives were reused in a Building L stairway at Monte Albán (Marcus 1974: Plate 9). The lower step measures .88 x .35 m.

said, "No matter how great the casualty list after an engagement, if there were no chiefs killed, there was nothing to talk about. If there was no chiefly name to connect the engagement with… the battle was without a name" (Buck 1949:400).

In other words, Monument 3 at San José Mogote suggests that at least one motivation for the initial appearance of Zapotec writing was the need to give victory a name by specifying the name of a defeated rival chief. The message of Monument 3 may have been, "Our chief captured Lord 1L and sacrificed him; now we invite you to tread on his corpse. Behave yourself, or the same could happen to you."

The Move to Monte Albán

At around 500 BC, the leaders of San José Mogote decided to move from their vulnerable valley floor location to the top of a defensible mountain not far to the south. The founding population of this new site might have been 2000 people: 1000 from San José Mogote itself and another 1000 from its subject villages (Marcus and Flannery 1996:139). The mountain chosen lay in a buffer zone between the various arms of the valley.

Settlement pattern data suggest that people from the southern half of the Etla subvalley contributed significantly to the creation of Oaxaca's first urban center. From this defensible mountain stronghold—known today as Monte Albán—the relocated elite directed a centuries-long war against their rivals in the Valle Grande and Tlacolula arms of the valley. One of the first public buildings erected at Monte Albán— Building L—featured about 300 carved stones depicting sacrificial victims.

Propaganda Displays and the Messages They Convey: The Building L Prisoner Gallery

The victims depicted on Monte Albán's Building L (sometimes called L-sub, or the substructure of Building L) were among

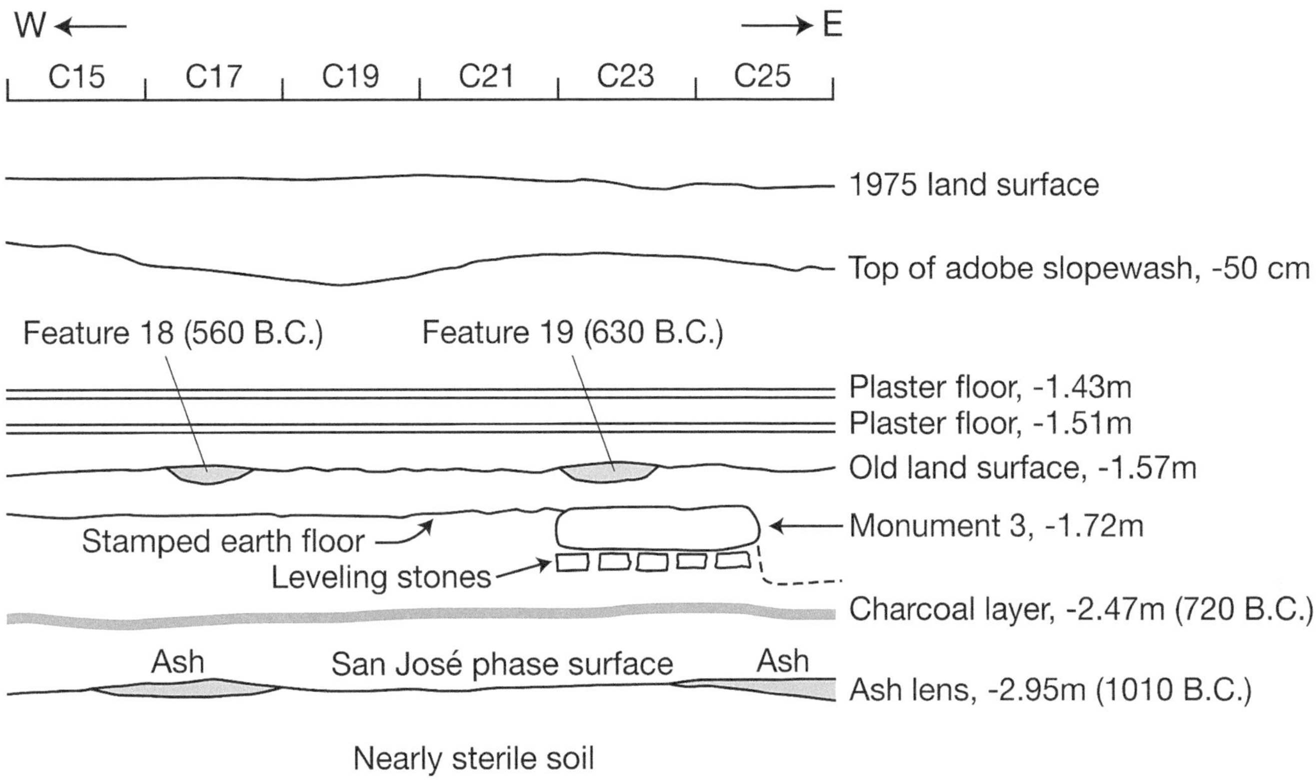

Figure 6.13. Monument 3 at San José Mogote was found above a charcoal layer with an uncalibrated radiocarbon date of 720 BC and stratigraphically below an old land surface with two hearths yielding dates of 630 and 560 BC (see Flannery and Marcus 2015: Figs. 9.16, 9.17).

the earliest Zapotec monuments reported by nineteenth-century explorers. At that time most travelers were unaware of the role warfare had played in the rise of the state, so they mistakenly called the awkwardly sprawled figures *danzantes* ("dancers"). To use this label, of course, they had to ignore their nudity, their genital mutilation, their blood scrolls, and the occasional examples of decapitation. It would also not have been clear to early travelers that the figures were meant to be seen as sprawled on the ground, rather than upright orthostats (Scott 1965).

During his 1806 expedition, Guillermo Dupaix ([1834]1969:108; Villagra Caleti n.d., 1939) became one of the first explorers to see Building L's east wall, which he correctly called a *galería*. Dupaix's artist illustrated five of the Building L-sub monuments (Figure 6.17) (Dupaix 1969: Vol. II, Lám. 20 [41], Figure 66 [A-E]; Flannery and Marcus 1983a:89).

Sometime around 1900, Sologuren and Belmar uncovered seven more carvings adjacent to the five drawn by Dupaix's artist. At that time no one suspected that Building L had once been home to hundreds of these carvings, since most had been removed to be reused in later buildings.

It was Leopoldo Batres (1902: Plates V-VI) who first made it clear that the gallery's original grand design for hundreds of carved stones had been carefully planned. Today the impact is greatly reduced because only four short rows remain. The slabs show that many men were nude. Some show genital mutilation. Some may have had their hearts removed, as indicated by a lozenge-shaped opening in the chest. The sacrificial victims in the lowest row (the easiest row to see) were, on average, larger than those in higher rows and more likely to be associated with hieroglyphs (near the face, or carved directly on the body).

During Period I any visitor seeing the original Prisoner Gallery would have been impressed by the hundreds of victims, by the humiliation and mutilation they had suffered, and by the careful planning evident in the multiple rows of stones (Figure 6.18). At that time, Building L-sub would have been one of the most impressive statements of military defeat and humiliation anywhere in the New World. Perhaps its only rival would have been the display of dismembered war captives in the temple at Cerro Sechín in Peru (Samaniego et al. 1985; Tello 1956) (see below).

Figure 6.14. *Lajas* or flagstones were used to level Monument 3 at San José Mogote. This carved stone served as the threshold in a corridor between two Rosario phase buildings (see Flannery and Marcus 2015: Figs. 9.16, 9.17).

Row 1 and Row 3 of Monte Albán's Building L contained large vertical monuments. Rows 2 and 4 had smaller stones arranged horizontally. The lowest row showed each victim facing north (to the viewer's right), while the third row showed each figure facing south (to the viewer's left) (Figure 6.18). Having nothing with which to compare them, early European explorers called the vertical figures in Rows 1 and 3 "dancers" and the horizontal figures in Rows 2 and 4 "swimmers."

After the prisoner staircases of the Maya region had become known, however, Coe and others realized that the Building L display conveyed a similar message—i.e., prisoners and captives displayed in prone, supine, and contorted positions, enemies shown nearly nude with their headdresses and earspools removed. Such prisoner galleries would serve to impress loyal supporters, to intimidate enemies, and to express political authority and legitimacy. It is worth noting that Building L-sub antedates Maya prisoner staircases by hundreds of years (Marcus 1974), and is our oldest example of such a display.

Had the substructure of Building L at Monte Albán been left as it was during Period I, we would know the position and overall arrangement of the ca. 300 carved stones. Unfortunately for us, later architects had an insatiable need to remove stones from the substructure of Building L and use them in buildings all around Monte Albán's Main Plaza. In the act of reusing them, Monte Albán's architects sometimes placed the carved surface upside down, plastered it over, or even left it facing inward so that it could not be seen.

One of the most appropriate acts of reuse was to put some of the horizontal figures from Rows 2 and 4 (the so-called *nadadores* or "swimmers") into a nearby staircase (Marcus 1974; Scott 1965, 1978). This reuse allowed anyone climbing the steps to tread on the carved bodies of vanquished enemies, much the way the Maya did with their prisoner staircases. This theme recurred at the later site of Cacaxtla, Tlaxcala, where emaciated and skeletonized prisoners painted on the treads received the humiliation of being trod upon by anyone ascending the steps (Brittenham 2015; Foncerrada de Molina 1980, 1993) (Figure 6.19).

Creating a Narrative by Grouping Stones in Architectural Programs

Dupaix's, Batres', and Caso's explorations of Monte Albán all made it clear that the rulers of Monte Albán tended to commission

Figure 6.15. Reconstruction drawing of the corridor between Structure 19 (at left) and Structure 14 (at right) at San José Mogote, as it may have looked ca. 600 BC during the Rosario phase. One can clearly see the two examples of the circle + triangle motif at the front edge of the stone. The circle (blood droplet) is on the tread surface and the triangles (the flowing blood) descend the riser. Drawing by John Klausmeyer. See also Color Plate I, this volume.

Figure 6.16. Monument 3 at San José Mogote features a captive who has had his heart removed. The blood was shown flowing from his chest (on the wide surface of the stone) to the east edge of the stone and down the side. The ribbon of blood ends in two examples of the circle + triangle blood motif (see Figure 6.5). The glyphs between the victim's feet convey his calendric name, suggesting that he may have been a captive of some importance. Drawing by Mark Orsen.

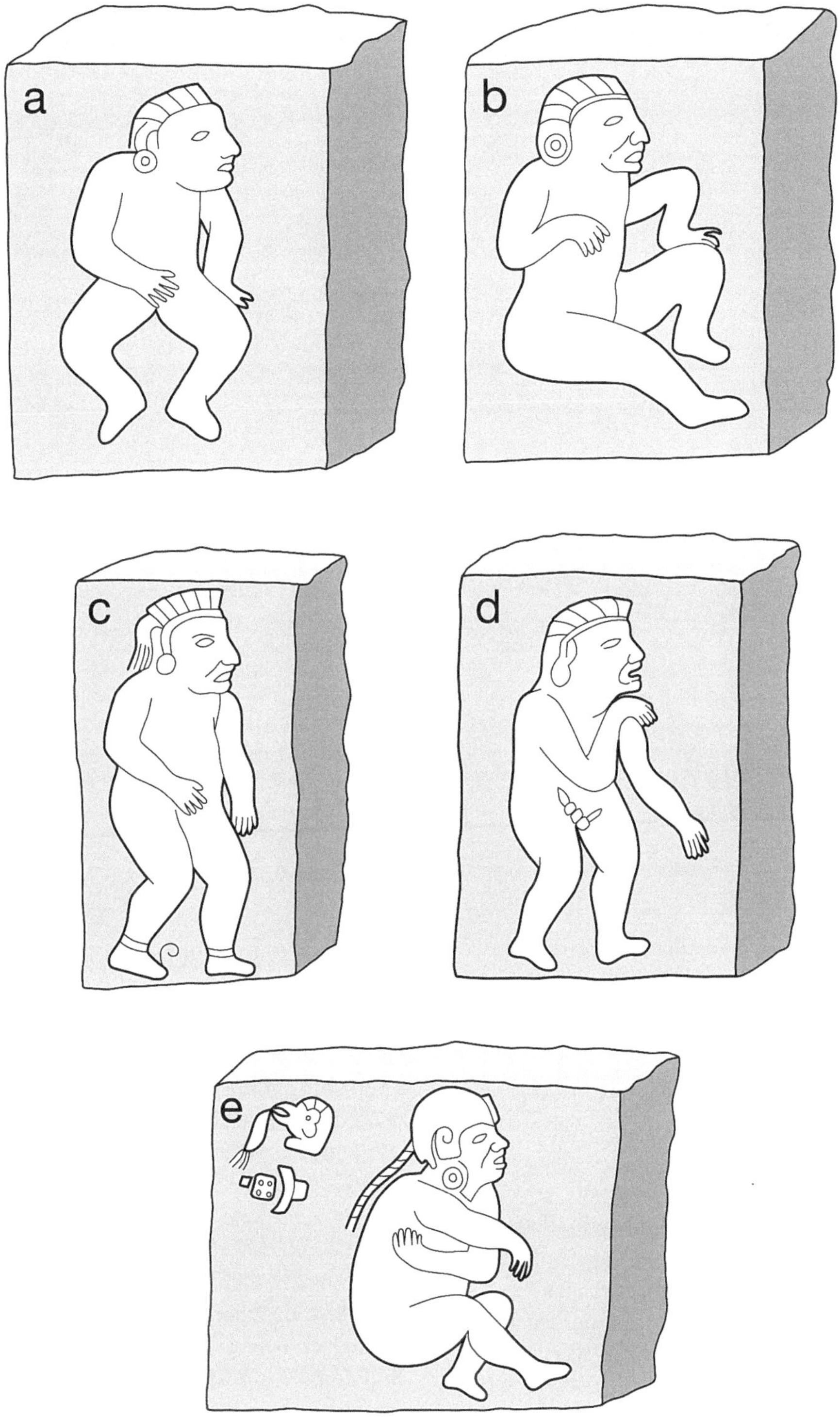

Figure 6.17. An 1806 expedition discovered these five carvings of sacrificed prisoners in the substructure of Building L, Monte Albán (adapted by John Klausmeyer from Alcina Franch 1969; Dupaix 1969: Vol. II, Lám. 20 [41], Figure 66 [A–E]).

Figure 6.18. The Prisoner Gallery at Monte Albán shows careful planning. In Row 1, the lowest, the victims face north; in Row 2, the victims are arranged horizontally; in Row 3, the victims face south; in Row 4, the victims are again horizontal. These four rows constituted a powerful narrative at ca. 500–300 BC. The boustrophedon format preceded by a millennium the comparable formats used in the Lienzo de Guevea and the Mixtec codices. Drawing by John Klausmeyer, adapted from Marcus 1992a: Fig. 11.33.

groups of carved stones to be arranged in meaningful narratives for maximal impact. Such architectural displays once graced the walls of Building L, Building J, the South Platform, and elsewhere at Monte Albán. Since such highly visible narratives were clearly intended to be seen by hundreds of commoners, they would be considered *vertical propaganda* by social scientists. This term is used to describe messages that traveled downward from nobles to commoners. Later in this book we will contrast such messages with *horizontal propaganda*, which travels between nobles.

The fact that later structures, such as Building J and the South Platform, were literally encircled with carved stones makes us wonder whether Building L was originally encircled as well. Its north, east, and south sides might have been appropriate for this.

It is significant that the theme of sprawled, sacrificed, and sometimes mutilated captives links Rosario phase San José Mogote and Period I Monte Albán. The period from 700 BC to AD 1 was a time of persistent political and military conflict, which began with rival chiefdoms and ended with the creation of a Zapotec state whose capital was Monte Albán. Once that state had been established, Monte Albán virtually monopolized hieroglyphic writing within the Valley of Oaxaca for centuries.

Cerro Sechín, Peru: An Analogue to Building L

As mentioned above, the Building L display was not unique in Nuclear America. A similar display, dating to about 1400 BC, is known from the site of Cerro Sechín in Peru's Casma Valley. There hundreds of carved stones were set in the outer wall of a temple that measured 53 m on a side (Samaniego et al. 1985; Tello 1956). Cerro Sechín outdid Monte Albán both in its number of monuments and their gruesome details (Figure 6.20). Cerro Sechín's 400 carved stones displayed mutilated, quartered, and disemboweled victims. On some slabs we see human heads with blood flowing from beneath eyelids after the eyeballs had been plucked; on others we see the intestines, arms, and legs removed from corpses. On still others we see trophy heads stacked one atop another in a kind of Andean skull rack.

Both Monte Albán and Cerro Sechín evidently decided that the impact would be far greater if hundreds of carvings were displayed. Sheer numbers could sow fear and send a message. It is possible, in fact, that such massive displays of carnage were typical of chiefly societies, where terror tactics were needed

Figure 6.19. This stair step at Cacaxtla (Tlaxcala) was painted on two surfaces: (1) the riser likely revealed the names of subject towns; (2) the tread depicted starved prisoners. Drawing by John Klausmeyer.

precisely because formal standing armies did not yet exist (Marcus 1974). In later periods, Monte Albán chose other themes; never again did it display victims of war on such a scale. The Zapotec need for a major display of military propaganda and success in raiding took place very early in the long process that led to state formation.

The Numbering System Used to Label Monte Albán Monuments

Before going any further in my description of the Period I monuments, I think a few comments about the numbering system are in order. Carved monuments were given numbers (e.g., Monument 41) by Villagra and Caso. Later, capital letters were added—for example, converting Stone 41 to Stone J-41 to show that the stone was in the wall of Structure J. Capital letters such as D, E, J, I, and N were added to refer to buildings on Monte Albán's Main Plaza (Figure 6.21).

By preserving Villagra's and Caso's monument numbers and by adding a letter as a prefix, John Scott was able both to keep Caso's original numbers and also to indicate the building where each stone was currently located.

At about the same time that Scott was working to retain Caso's numbering system, Louise Wiltraud Zehnder (1977) was completely renumbering ca. 400 stones. García Moll et al. (1986) then went one step further; they renumbered every single carved surface at Monte Albán—a total of 522 surfaces. That number is higher because some monuments had two, three, or four carved surfaces. García Moll et al.'s choice not to retain Scott's labeling system was particularly unfortunate, since one of the strengths of Scott's system was that it tied carved stones to buildings.

To reduce future confusion, in this book I provide for every monument all the numbers assigned by Caso, Villagra, Scott, Zehnder, and García Moll et al. I was particularly determined to preserve Caso's original labels, since we have had almost a century of publications that refer to them. Unfortunately, I found some stones that had never been numbered. I was forced to number them, and to differentiate my numbers from all the other extant systems, I inserted a zero (e.g., J-013, J-014, J-015) (Marcus 1972).

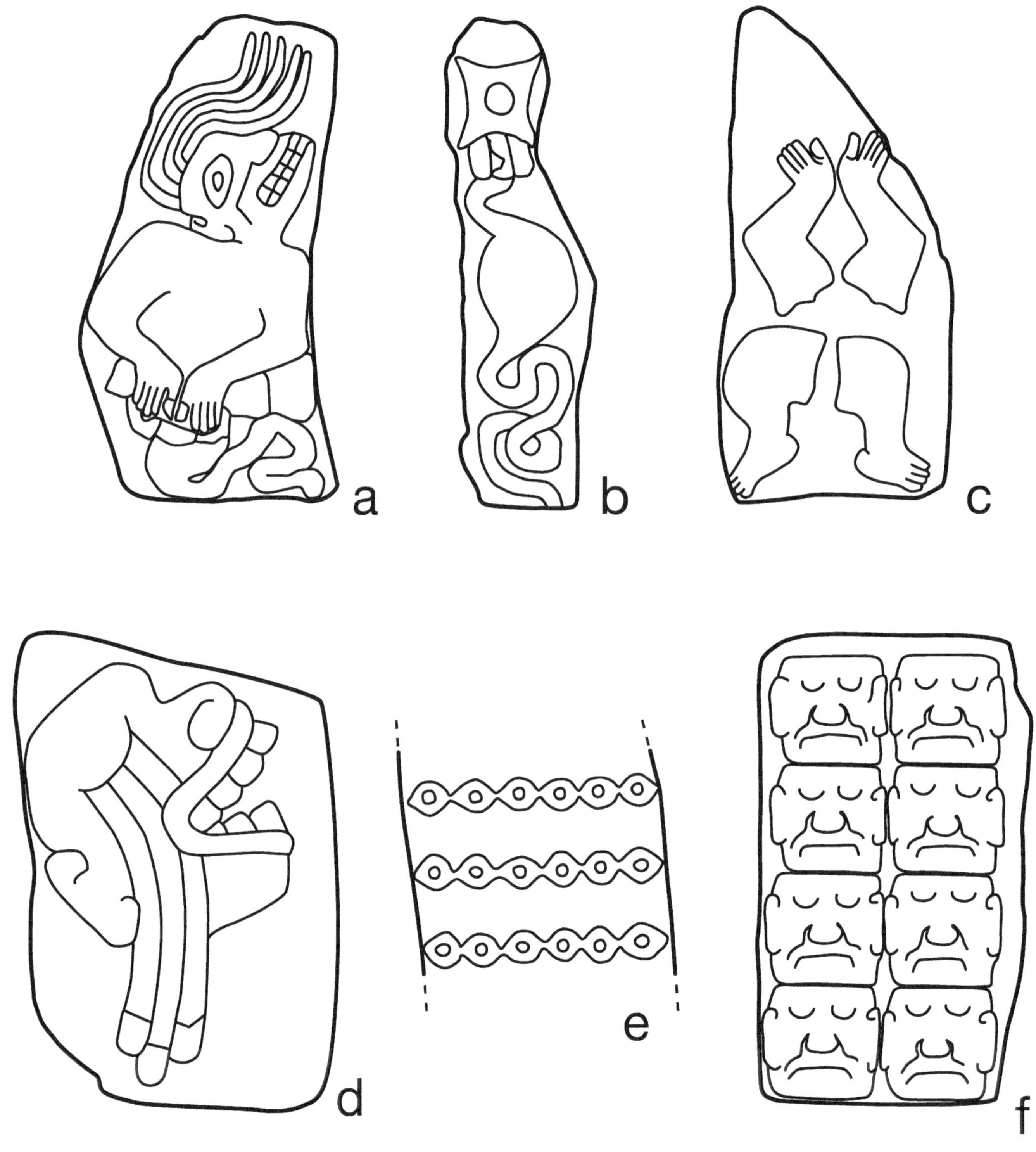

Figure 6.20. Cerro Sechín, in the Casma Valley of Peru, shows the gruesome treatment that war captives endured. Among the 400 depictions carved in stone are: *(a)* a man cut in half, with his internal organs spilling out; *(b)* internal organs; *(c)* arms and legs chopped off; *(d)* blood flowing from below the eyelid, presumably where an eye had been gouged out; *(e)* three rows of eyeballs, six per row; and *(f)* stacks of heads taken as trophies, reminiscent of a Mesoamerican *tzompantli* (Samaniego et al. 1985; Tello 1956). Drawings by Kay Clahassey and John Klausmeyer.

What was the Length of the Building L Walls?

The best-preserved rows of the Building L Prisoner Gallery average about one stone per meter. Given that the Prisoner Gallery appears to have had four rows, each meter of wall might have held four carved stones (one above another). That means that the 300 known stones would have required roughly 80 meters of wall. If the north, east, and south walls of Building L were all about 27 m in length (as the east wall appears to be), 300 stones could have been displayed without using the west wall. Unfortunately, the building was so modified in later periods that this issue may never be fully settled.

Heart Removal

The depiction of heart removal on Monument 3 is more evident than that of any Building L stone. The stone carvers at Monte Albán may have indicated heart removal simply by creating a lozenge-shaped opening in the chest. Although they could be interpreted as ornaments, I suspect that these lozenges may be openings into the chest cavity.

Examples of Building L carvings with lozenge-shaped elements on the chest include stones D-88, D-116, J-73, N-3, N-19, N-28, and N-28A in John Scott's system (Figure 6.22).

Genital Mutilation

Genital mutilation was more commonly depicted than heart removal. Scrolls of blood flowing from the groin area are seen on at least 50 slabs (e.g., Monuments D-3, D-5, D-10, D12, D-17, D-20, D-26, D-47, D-48, D-54, D-55, D-56, D-57, D-63, D-66, D-74, D-118, D-119, D-131, E-1, I-1, I-3, J-46, J-70, J-89, J-94, J-100, and N-8) (see Scott 1978). Many of the individuals accompanied by hieroglyphic captions seem to have been mutilated (Figure 6.23), and I suspect that the victims associated with hieroglyphic captions were among the most important captives.

One important prisoner who does *not* show evidence of genital mutilation is the one shown on Monument M-19 (Figure 6.24), a stone discovered by Batres (1902) in front of Structure M. Caso (1947: Figure 25) called M-19 the "Danzante del Museo," because it went on to be displayed in the Museo Nacional de Antropología in Mexico City. The hieroglyphs associated with this individual include "hand-grasping-arrow" + "animal head." Since no numerals are included, this cannot be a calendric name, although it could be a nickname. Among the many potential readings of this phrase is the possibility that it is a verb + subject, to wit, "was captured" + "jaguar."

Decapitation

At least four of the Building L slabs display severed heads; these are Monuments J-112, D-78, D-123, and one fragment found in the group called Siete Venado (drawings by Agustín Villagra). Other possible examples include Monuments D-91, D-112, and M-17. I call attention to a hieroglyph that occurs on six of these monuments (D-78, D-86, D-91, D-112, D-123, and J-112), raising the possibility that this glyph may have something to do with decapitation (Figure 6.25).

Monument J-112 (Figure 6.25b) clearly shows a severed head with a tripartite stream of blood descending from the neck. In front of the victim's mouth is an elaborate speech scroll, sometimes called a song scroll (Caso 1947: Figure 32; Scott 1978; Villagra n.d.). This stone was reused in a tunnel in Building J; Monument M-17 (38 x 35 x 40 cm) was also reused, in the patio between Buildings M and O.

Humbling the Victim by Removing His Ear Ornaments

The lowest row of the Building L Prisoner Gallery likely featured some of the most important prisoners (Caso 1947: Lámina I). Their importance is indicated in several ways: their stones are among the largest in the gallery; they often have hieroglyphs associated with them; and some of the men depicted were allowed to retain their large earspools, a sign of high status (see Monuments D-1, D-2, D-3, D-4, D-5, D-6, D-7, and D-8, pages 87–90).

Other captives were treated differently; their earspools had been removed and other items had been inserted in their earlobes. In some cases it appears that cloth or paper strips, feathers, or other perishable items were the objects inserted (see, for example, Monuments D-11, J-46, and N-21).

This treatment of high-status captives was later emulated by the Maya. For example, monuments at Toniná (ca. AD 720) and Palenque (AD 700) show noble prisoners who have cloth strips or other materials inserted into their earlobes, taking the place of the ear ornaments that had been removed by their captors. The act of removing high-status ornaments and replacing them with perishable materials is one of many behaviors designed to humiliate noble prisoners, and it is significant that Monte Albán displayed this behavior hundreds of years before the Maya did.

Carving Glyphs on the Captive's Body

Placing hieroglyphs directly on a captive's body is another Zapotec convention that can be seen in the Building L Prisoner Gallery—for example, on Monuments D-55, D-59, E-1, J-89, and M-4. This practice was later emulated by the Maya. For example, hieroglyphs can be seen on the bodies of captives displayed in Maya prisoner staircases, lintels, and stelae at several sites, such

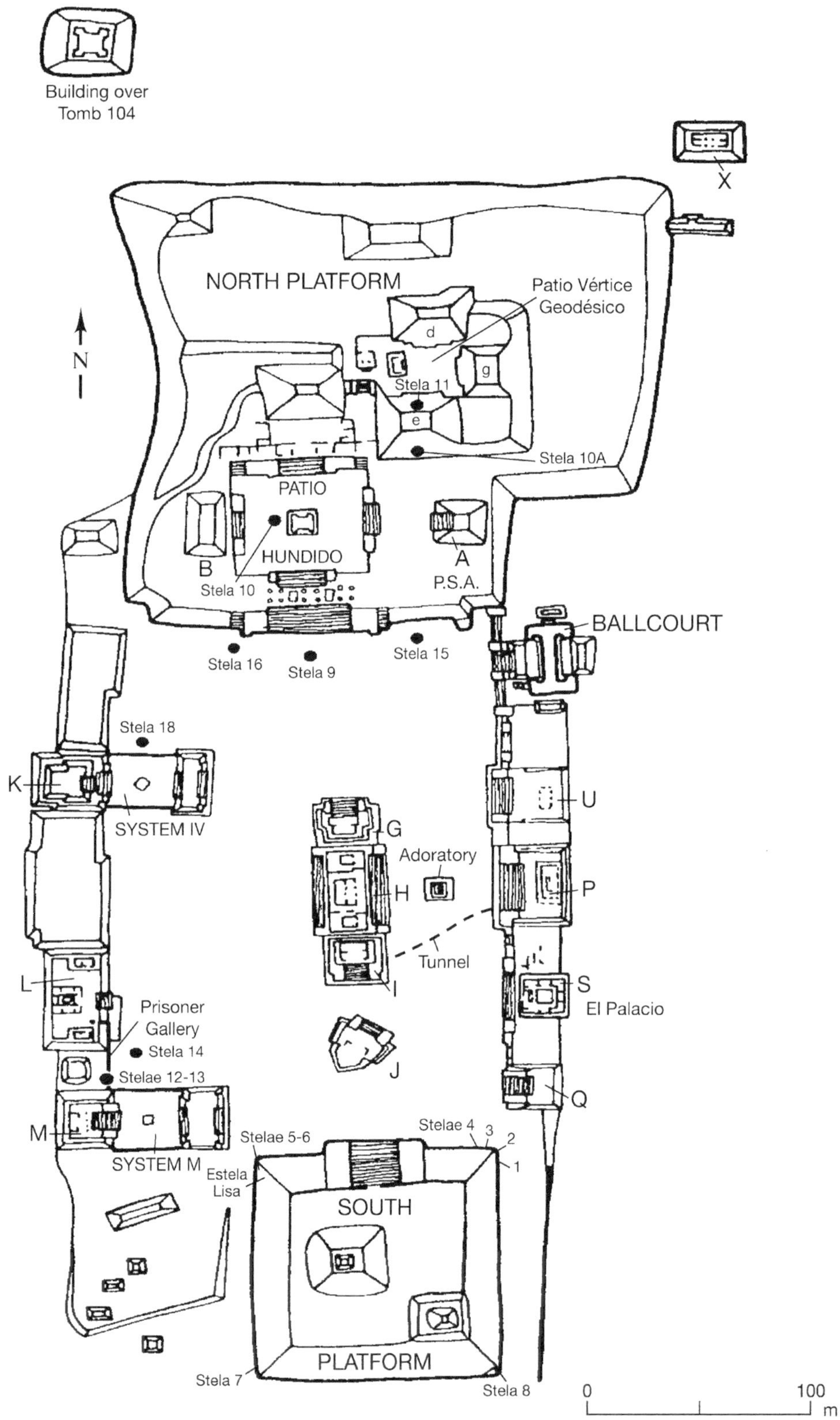

Figure 6.21. The Main Plaza at Monte Albán, showing the locations of Buildings L and M in the southwestern corner (see Marcus and Flannery 1996:176–177).

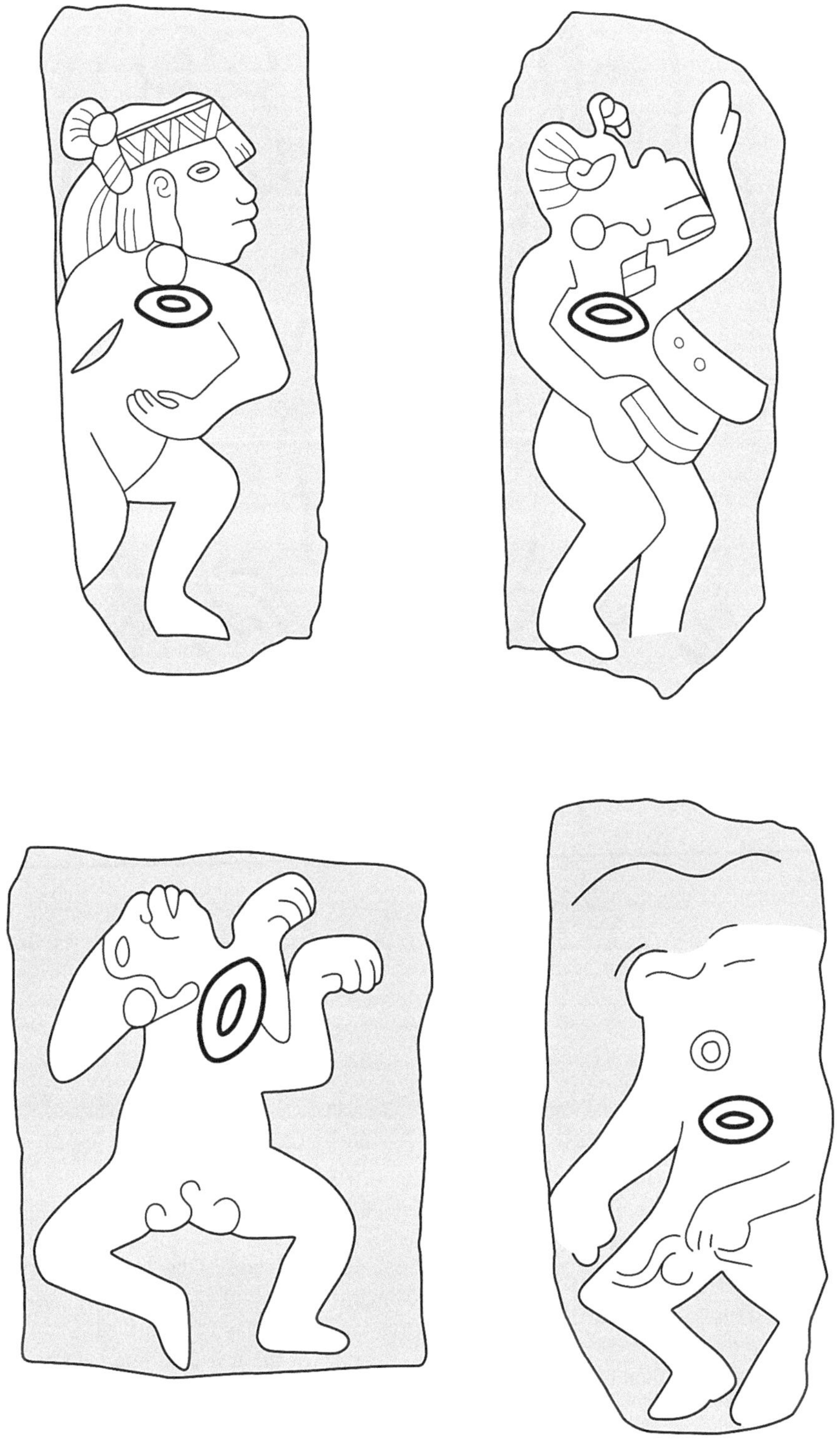

Figure 6.22. Some victims in the Building L Prisoner Gallery have an oval or lozenge-shaped motif on their chests, which may represent the openings through which their hearts had been removed. (Had these motifs been pendants or ornaments, I would have expected to see strings or cords leading to them.) Drawing by John Klausmeyer.

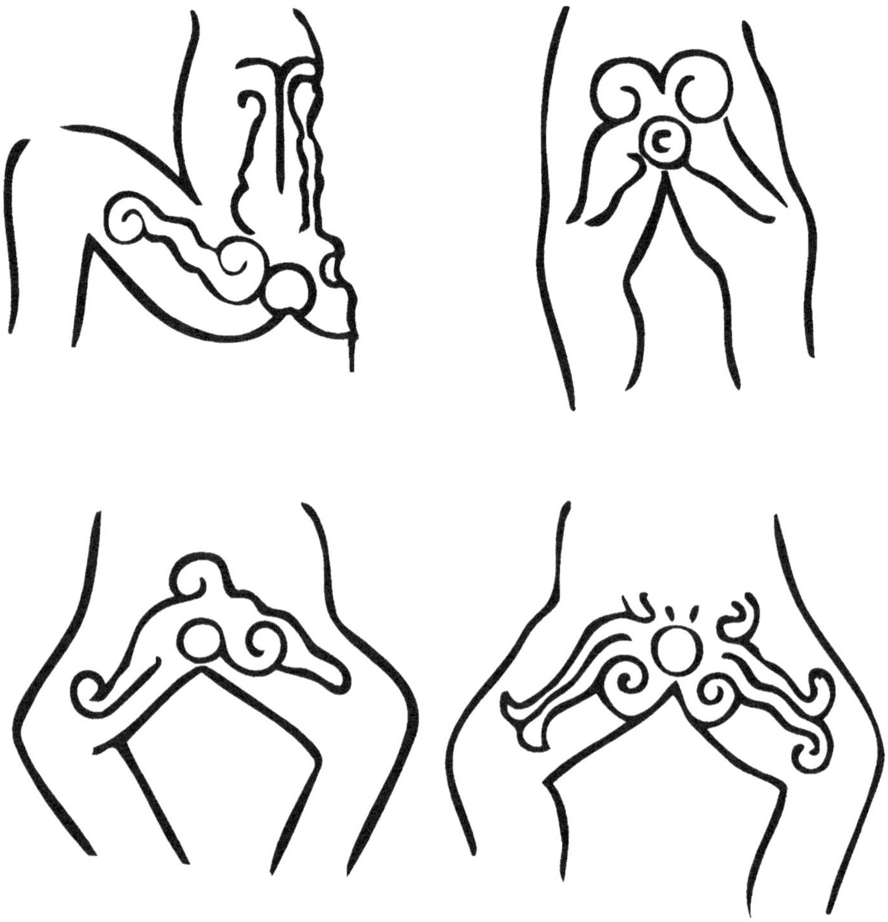

Figure 6.23. Here we see four of the many carved stones from the Prisoner Gallery of Building L-sub that reveal genital mutilation. Wavy lines and scrolls symbolize blood flow from the groin area. Redrawn by John Klausmeyer from Caso 1947: Fig. 31.

as Yaxchilan, Palenque, Toniná, Naranjo, and Piedras Negras (e.g., Greene et al. 1972; Marcus 1974: Plate 5; Marcus 2000).

Carving hieroglyphs on the depiction of a captive's body may have been one way to establish credit for taking a prisoner, almost an act of branding one's possession. This use of hieroglyphs by the Zapotec during the Middle Formative anticipates the Classic-era Maya practice of placing hieroglyphs on prisoners' bodies. Some Maya rulers, in fact, referred to themselves as "the Captor of X"—for example, on Lintel 8 at Yaxchilan (see Figure 2.6).

Labeling and Captioning

An alternative to placing a captive's name on the image of his body was to provide a hieroglyphic name, a descriptive caption, or a label nearby. This Zapotec practice began with Monument 3 at San José Mogote and continued with the Building L gallery, primarily on the stones in the lowest row.

Monument 3 at San José Mogote used a day sign + number as a name. The short texts accompanying the victims on Building L, however, rarely include bars, dots, or day signs from the 260-day calendar. This lack of day signs requires an explanation, especially since it is likely that most of the individuals depicted had been named for the day of their birth.

One of the few Building L slabs that does include bars and dots is Monument D-40 (Caso 1947: Figure 37). On this slab, the hieroglyph for 6 Water appears above the victim's hand (Caso 1947: Figure 17); on the victim's face are additional bars and a dot (see page 93). Yet another glyph on Monument D-40 resembles one seen on a serpentinite pendant from La Venta, a site contemporary with Period I of Monte Albán (see Figure 6.9).

As for the Prisoner Gallery monuments with noncalendric captions, there are several possibilities. Some of these captions

Figure 6.24. The so-called Danzante del Museo (Monument M-19) shows one of the few nude prisoners from Building L-sub who did not suffer genital mutilation. *a* shows an in-the-field sketch; *b* shows Mark Orsen's finished drawing. This victim's name may be given in the short hieroglyphic column in front of his face (162 x 56 x 30 cm).

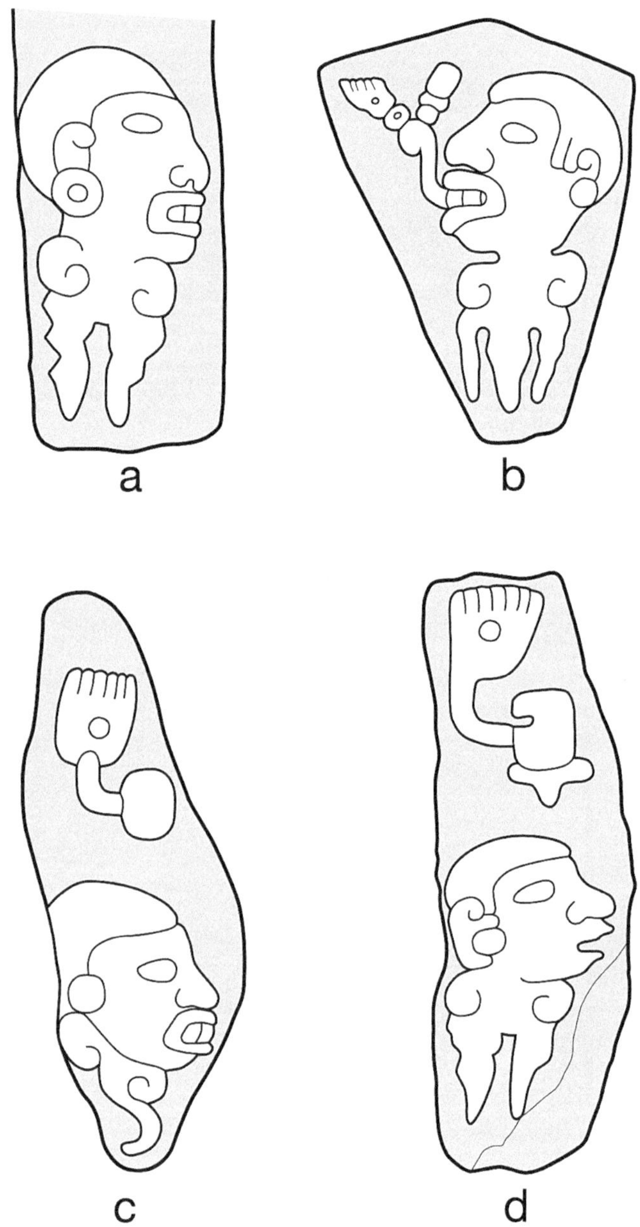

Figure 6.25. A few of the Building L prisoners were decapitated; here we see blood flowing from the heads of victims. These four stones were likely displayed in the substructure of Building L before being reused in Structure D, Structure J, and the zone south of Building M called Siete Venado. Note that *b*, *c*, and *d* are associated with similar hieroglyphs. See also Figure 6.42 where a similar glyph occurs. (*a* is a stone from Siete Venado; *b* is J-112; *c* is D-123; *d* is D-78.) Adapted by John Klausmeyer from Caso 1947: Fig. 32; García Moll et al. 1986: Lám. 14, 139, 141, 142, 382, 389; Scott 1978, Vol. II; Villagra's 1939 field drawings.

could be names that were not drawn from the 260-day calendar, perhaps because they were from a foreign ethnic group. A second possibility is that their captions could be nicknames like those found in later contexts, such as Tomb 105 of Monte Albán.

The Hieroglyphic Texts of Period I

Some Period I hieroglyphic texts are arranged in columns, which allow us to infer word order. Some of these texts accompany prisoners—for example, on Monument D-55, where three glyphs appear in front of the captive's face and five more in a column that runs from his chest to his lower legs. Other Period I monuments, such as Stelae 12, 13, 14, 15, and 17, display texts that are unaccompanied by images. Such monuments are described as featuring "pure texts."

When hieroglyphs are arranged in a column, the reading order is either from bottom to top or top to bottom. Bottom-to-top readings are indicated when a sign that customarily begins texts (such as a year sign or year bearer) appears at the bottom of a column. Stela 17 at Monte Albán, for example, includes a year sign and year bearer in the lower left corner of the monument (Caso 1947: Figure 15), which suggests a bottom-to-top reading order. In contrast, Stela 12 of Monte Albán opens with a year sign and year bearer as its uppermost glyph, suggesting that this text should be read from top to bottom (Caso 1947: Figure 10). Like so many early writing systems, the reading order and sign arrangement had yet to be standardized.

The Inventory of Period I Signs

About four dozen signs, excluding bars and dots, are known from Period I (see Caso 1928, 1947, 1965a, 1965b). These signs appear both in captions associated with images and in stand-alone "pure texts." Some signs occur only once in our current sample, making it difficult to determine their meaning. In contrast, many Maya signs occur scores of times (or even hundreds of times), which not only facilitates trial readings but also allows all-important confirmations.

In the pages that follow, we will look at both short captions (usually two to six glyphs) and the longer texts of Stelae 12, 13, 15, and 17. Before we begin, however, let us look at some of the more common signs, to see to what extent we can interpret them by comparing them to later Zapotec hieroglyphic texts and sixteenth-century Zapotec vocabularies.

Some of the Common Period I Hieroglyphs

When making an inventory of all the hieroglyphs on the Building L prisoner stones, one sees that many signs occur only once, with only a handful of signs appearing frequently (Caso 1928, 1947). These recurring glyphs are a good place to begin analysis, so let us look at one of them.

The so-called "rattle" or atlatl (spearthrower) glyph occurs on at least nine Period I slabs (Monuments D-2, D-6, D-8, D-22, D-86, D-130, E-1, J-80, and M-2; see John Scott's 1978 catalogue). This glyph (Figure 6.26) also appears during Period II on 13 of the so-called "conquest slabs" in Monte Albán's Building J (Buigues 1993; Caso 1947; Fahmel Beyer 2000; Marcus 1992a: Figures 11.35–11.36; Whittaker 1982). After Period II ended, this glyph became scarce; its decline suggests either that (1) another sign took its place or (2) the content of later texts did not require that glyph.

On the prisoner slabs of Period I, the atlatl sign is sometimes the last hieroglyph in a phrase. It is not associated with bars and dots, and has no apparent relationship to the calendar. Could the atlatl glyph be a nickname, or is it part of a descriptive phrase? Might it describe the victim as a rival captured in battle, or as a sacrificial victim? Keeping our mind open to several possibilities, let us look at some prisoner and sacrifice terms from sixteenth-century Zapotec.

Córdova's 1578 dictionary supplies several entries related to prisoners and sacrifice. The Zapotec called sacrificed prisoners of war *totétea guij, tiquíxea quij,* and *cotí* (Córdova [1578a]1942:367v). (Recall that in Chapter 4 we saw that the Zapotec word *cotí* or *gotí* could mean both "bag" and "a dead person," and probably referred to the latter on Building L.)

The Zapotec word *guij* or *quij* meant "object of sacrifice." A "sacrificed person" was a *peni guij*. A *peni cociyo* was a "person" (sacrificed to) "lightning" and a *peni quij cociyo* was a "person" + "object of sacrifice" + "lightning." "Object of sacrifice" is a possible meaning for the atlatl glyph, since the atlatl often seems to be the last glyph in the descriptive phrases associated with sacrificial victims in the Prisoner Gallery during Period I. On the other hand, during Period II this same hieroglyph appears on 13 slabs set in Building J and seems to serve another function. One possibility is that the atlatl glyph was used for its sound value—in other words, like the word for *yobi*, which meant "first-born son" and "thumb." It appears that *guij* and *quij* could mean either "object of sacrifice" or "hill." "Object of sacrifice" would be a plausible word for the Building L captives, while "hill" would be a useful word for the Building J place names (see Chapter 8). To give one example, let us look at Monument J-20 (see page 171) of Building J, which refers to "Hill of the Coyote." Reading from bottom to top we see "*guij/quij* + coyote." That reading would match the word order in spoken Zapotec.

Another recurring glyph is the "bag" sign already mentioned. It occurs, for example, in a column of glyphs near the captive depicted on Monument D-55 (see Figure 6.38). This stone has one column of glyphs near the captive's face that may provide his nickname (Caso 1947: Figure 16). The column consists of two animal heads and the "bag" or "dead man" glyph; on the body of the victim, we see additional glyphs. The longest text begins near the victim's chin with the Year 3E, followed by a face glyph similar to one in Column 2 of Stela 17 (see below). That column continues with two glyphs between the captive's legs. In this case,

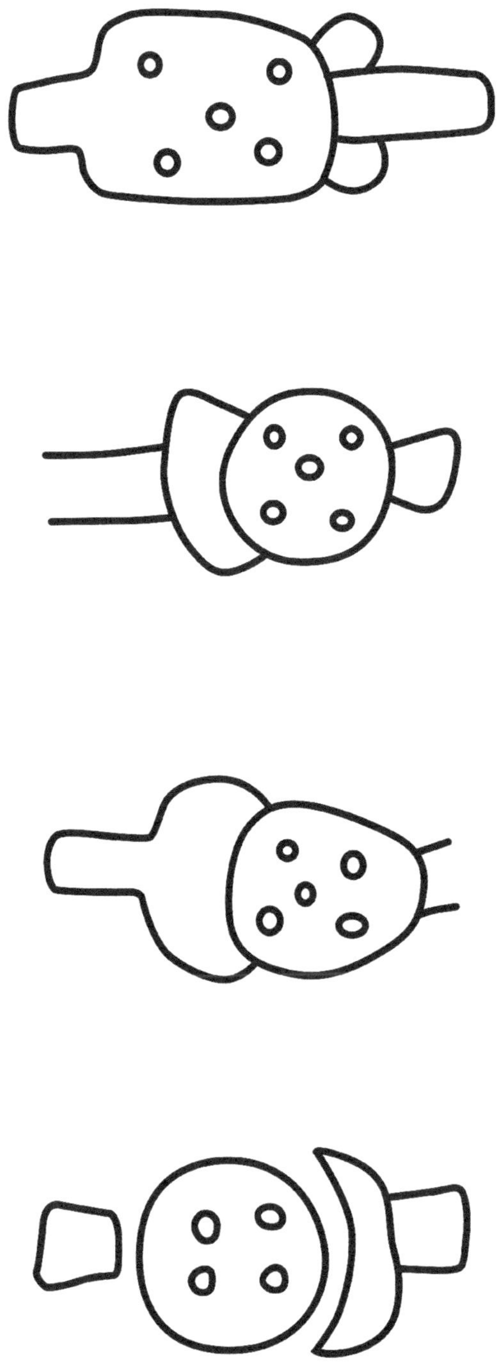

Figure 6.26. The so-called rattle or atlatl glyph appeared on Prisoner Gallery monuments in the lowest row. This sign may have been pronounced *guij,* which could mean "object of sacrifice" (this chapter) or "hill" (see Chapter 8). Drawing by John Klausmeyer.

Year 3E may be the year of this individual's capture and death, as suggested by the bag glyph.

A Sample of Prisoner Slabs Carved During Period I

Let us now look at a sample of prisoner slabs from Period I. We will begin with the most elaborate examples, all located in the lowest row of Building L's substructure.

Monument D-1 (100 x 152 x 54 cm) (Caso's Stone 1, Scott's D-1, Zehnder's L-1, García Moll et al.'s 251). D-1 is the southernmost stone in the lowest row in Building L, situated between Monuments D-2 and D-70 (Figure 6.27). This captive, like the others in the lowest row, faces north. The D-1 individual has a large earspool, prominent teeth, and a tuft of hair over his forehead. A few scrolls on his thighs indicate the blood resulting from genital mutilation.

Monument D-2 (118 x 160 x 39 cm) (Caso's Stone 2, Scott's D-2, Zehnder's L-2, García Moll et al.'s 252). This stone stands between Monuments D-1 and D-3 (Figure 6.28). Caso's illustration (1947: Figure 1) shows a hieroglyphic caption in front of the victim's face. The first glyph is not clear, but the second—the "rattle" or atlatl sign—has been discussed above. The captive sports a prominent ear ornament.

What has drawn the most attention on many of these captive depictions are the closed eye, lack of clothing, the hairdo, and body position. The body appears to be sprawled on the ground, with the left arm awkwardly bent and rubbery.

Monument D-3 (104 x 190 cm) (Caso's Stone 38-3, Scott's D-3, Zehnder's L-3, García Moll et al.'s 253). This stone (Figure 6.29) is located between Monuments D-2 and D-4. A two-glyph label, which appears in front of the captive's face, may include an animal head with a bar beneath it (a possible calendric name?). The figure has blood scrolls on his right thigh. Unlike most of the captives, this victim seems to have footwear, with a decorative ball attached to each foot (or front of the ankle). This stone is heavily eroded, with the uppermost layers spalling off, so that some of the details are not clear, such as the hieroglyph above the possible bar.

Monument D-4 (131 x 58 cm) (Caso's Stone 4, Scott's D-4, Zehnder's L-4, García Moll et al.'s 254). This stone (Figure 6.30) is set between Monuments D-3 and D-5. Like the victim on Monument D-3, this man wears possible footwear (or a band around the ankle, with balls attached). He has a large fall of hair that begins above his earspool and descends to his right shoulder (Caso 1947: Figure 2).

Scott (1978: Catalogue) notes that Monuments D-1 through D-4 were still *in situ* when Batres (1902) saw the east face of Building L's substructure. Inserted into the east façade were a few other stones that seem to have been used elsewhere before being incorporated into the gallery, since some stones were set with their carved surfaces facing inward and would not have been visible.

Monument D-5 (62 x 138 cm) (Caso's Stone 5, Scott's D-5, Zehnder's L-5, García Moll et al.'s 255). This stone (Figure 6.31), set in the lowest row of the gallery, is located between Monuments D-4 and D-6 (Caso 1947: Figure 2). The figure has a prominent earspool and a hairdo similar to that on Monument D-2. Like the victims on D-2 and D-3, this man has a short text in front of his face, consisting of two or three eroded glyphs.

A few blood scrolls associated with genital mutilation can be seen on D-5. Proof that these Building L figures were meant to be seen as lying on the ground comes from the direction the blood is flowing; that is, some blood flows from the genital region to his abdomen. The blood could not have moved in this way if he were standing, since it would have to flow upward.

Monument D-6 (101 x 173 cm) (Caso's Stone 38-6, Scott's D-6, Zehnder's L-6, García Moll et al.'s 256). This stone (Figure 6.32) is set between Monuments D-5 and D-7 (Caso 1947: Figure 3). The figure has a prominent earspool and an unusual hairdo, one that features bangs and a long braid that hangs down his back. A similar braid appears on Monument N-16 (Scott 1978).

A caption of two hieroglyphs appears behind the prisoner's head. The first glyph—possibly his name or nickname—consists of a compound sign (bird + fish?). The second glyph is the atlatl sign, whose possible meaning as object of sacrifice has been discussed above.

Monument D-7 (96 x 141 cm) (Caso's Stone 7, Scott's D-7, Zehnder's L-7, García Moll et al.'s 257). This stone (Figure 6.33) is set between Monuments D-6 and D-8 (Caso 1947: Figure 3). The captive on it has a prominent earspool and a hairdo similar to that of Monument D-8. No hieroglyphic caption is discernible.

Monument D-8 (90 x 134 cm) (Caso's Stone 39-8, Scott's D-8, Zehnder's L-8, García Moll et al.'s 258). This stone (Figure 6.34) is located between Monuments D-7 and D-9 (Caso 1947: Figure 4; Caso 1965a:932, Figure 1a). This captive has a prominent earspool and an unusual necklace, which may feature jade elements. Two hieroglyphs appear in front of the victim's mouth. The first glyph is a human head with a left hand touching its cheek; the second sign is the same atlatl glyph seen on Monuments D-2 and D-6.

Monument D-9 (75 x 147 cm) (Caso's Stone 39-9, Scott's D-9, Zehnder's L-9, García Moll et al.'s 259). This stone is located in the lowest row of the gallery; the captive is shown with his legs akimbo and his eyes tightly closed in death. No hieroglyphic caption is given.

Monument D-10 (136 x 74 x 25+ cm) (Caso's Stone 10, Scott's D-10, Zehnder's L-10, García Moll et al.'s 264). This prisoner slab appears in Row 3 of the gallery, facing south (i.e. to the viewer's left). At the center of the captive's torso we see blood scrolls flowing from the genital area toward the abdomen, as in the case of D-5.

Monument D-11 (60 x 128 cm) (Caso's Stone 11, Scott's D-11, Zehnder's L-11, García Moll et al.'s 265). This stone, which is also in Row 3 of the gallery (Caso 1947: Figure 5), depicts an individual with perhaps three cloth strips pulled through his perforated earlobe. This substitution of cloth for earspools reminds

Figure 6.27. Monument D-1, set between Monuments D-70 and D-2, is in the lowest row of the Building L Prisoner Gallery. This victim is nude and has groin scrolls. Drawing by John Klausmeyer.

Figure 6.28. Monument D-2, set between Monuments D-1 and D-3 in the lowest row of the Prisoner Gallery, shows a slain captive with a rubbery left arm, large earspool, closed eye, and two hieroglyphs (including the rattle or atlatl sign) in front of his face. Drawing by John Klausmeyer.

us of how many Maya prisoners were depicted (see above). The tuft of hair at the back of this captive's head is similar to that on Monument D-12.

Monument D-12 (69 x 153 cm) (Caso's Stone 12, Scott's D-12, Zehnder's L-12, García Moll et al.'s 266). This stone (Figure 6.35) is set in Row 3 of the gallery. The captive displays genital blood scrolls, some of which flow toward his abdomen, similar to those on Monument D-10, reinforcing the fact that he is meant to be seen as sprawled on the ground (Caso 1947: Figure 6). He sports a large earspool and distinctive hair tufts at the front and back of his head.

Monuments D-13, D-14, D-15, D-17, and D-18. These five slabs, found in Rows 2 and 4 of the gallery, tend to be narrower than those in Rows 1 and 3, and the human figures are shown in horizontal positions. (D-16 does not display a sacrificial victim, and may therefore be a stone that was reused in the Prisoner Gallery.)

Monument D-22 (59 x 65 cm) (Caso's Stone 22, Scott's D-22, Zehnder's L-23, García Moll et al.'s 274). This slab (Figure 6.36) is set at the base of the south cheekpiece of the Building L staircase; it occupies the southwest corner, right next to Monument D-21 (Scott 1978). This monument bears two hieroglyphs that are similar to those on D-3, D-5, and other monuments.

Monuments D-24, D-25, D-26, D-27, D-28, D-29, D-30, D-31, D-34, D-35, D-38, D-39. These monument fragments are all likely to have come from Rows 2 and 4 of the gallery, but were not found *in situ*. A few of the captives have belts, loincloths, or headgear.

Monument D-40 (57 x 31 x 52 cm) (Caso's Stone 40, Scott's D-40, Zehnder's L-40, García Moll et al.'s 292). This stone (Figure 6.37) was reused as the second step of a platform extending east from Mound L; it was set directly above Monument

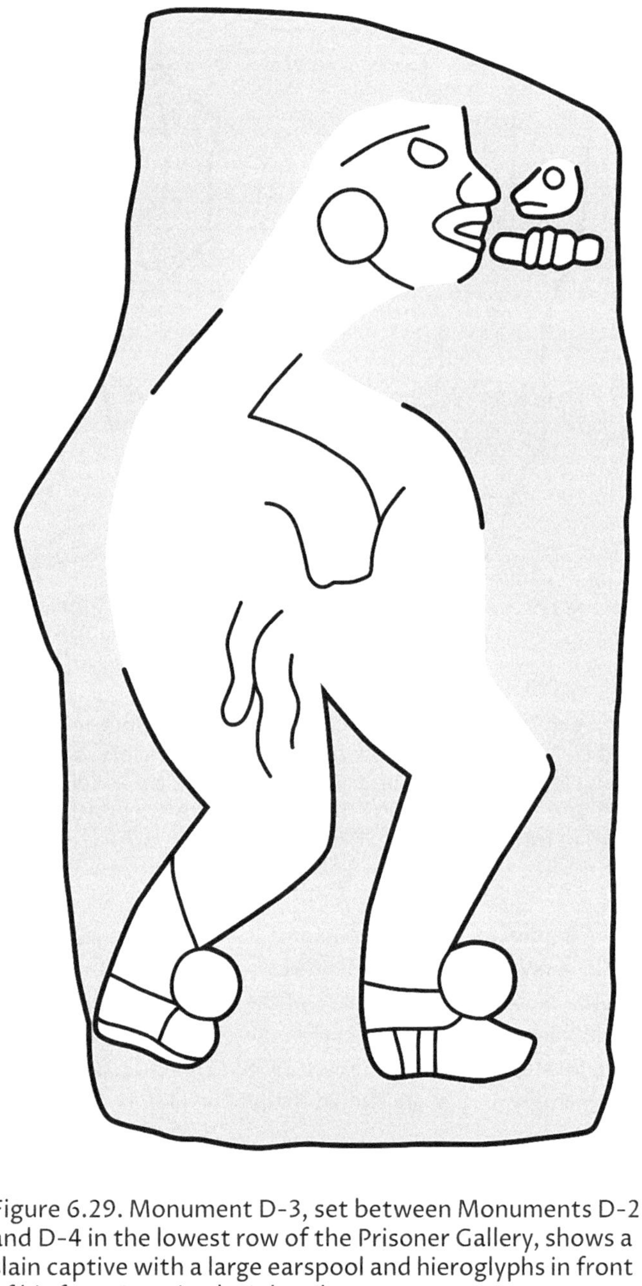

Figure 6.29. Monument D-3, set between Monuments D-2 and D-4 in the lowest row of the Prisoner Gallery, shows a slain captive with a large earspool and hieroglyphs in front of his face. Drawing by John Klausmeyer.

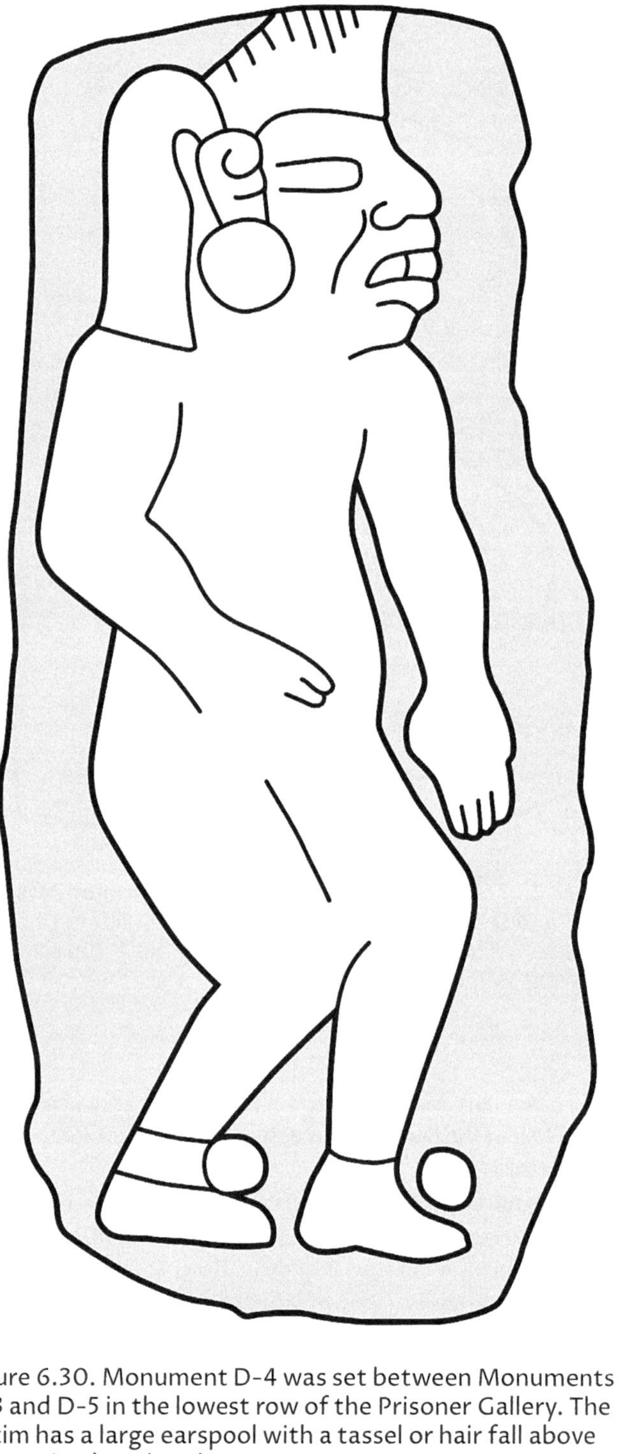

Figure 6.30. Monument D-4 was set between Monuments D-3 and D-5 in the lowest row of the Prisoner Gallery. The victim has a large earspool with a tassel or hair fall above it. Drawing by John Klausmeyer.

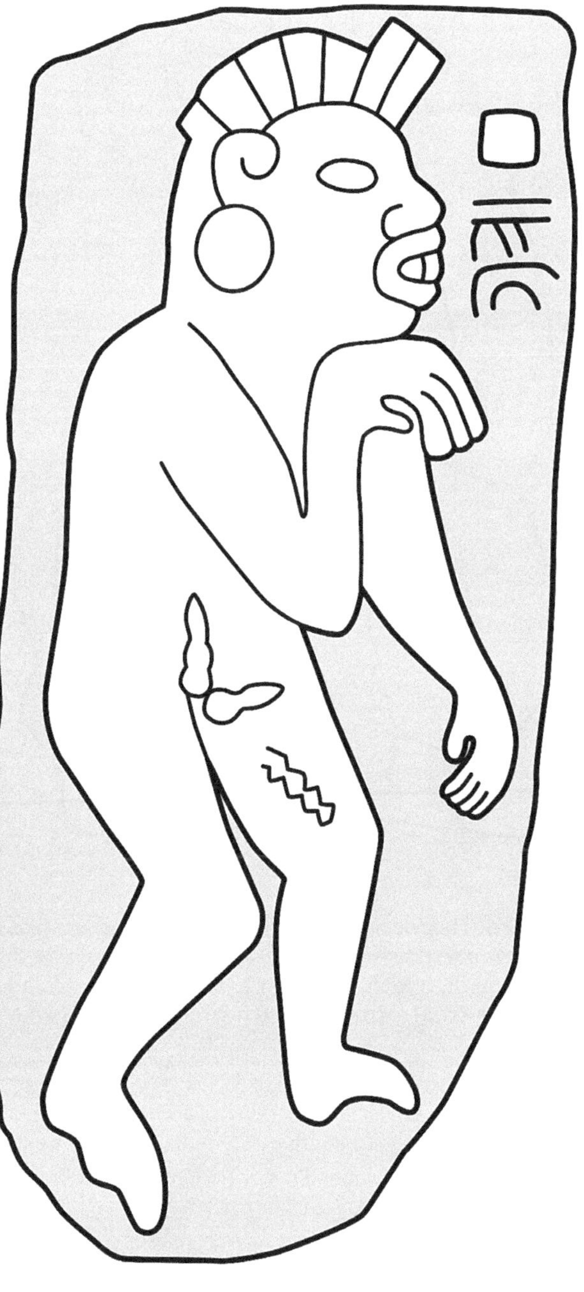

Figure 6.31. Monument D-5 was set between Monuments D-4 and D-6 in the lowest row of the Prisoner Gallery. The position of the victim's arms reinforces the fact that these slain captives were to be seen as sprawled on the ground. There are glyphs near his face and blood scrolls near his groin (Scott 1965, 1978). Drawing by John Klausmeyer.

Figure 6.32. Monument D-6 was set between Monuments D-5 and D-7 in the lowest row of the Prisoner Gallery. A long braid extends down his back, and a few hieroglyphs (including the atlatl sign) appear behind his head. Drawing by John Klausmeyer.

Figure 6.33. Monument D-7 was set between Monuments D-6 and D-8 in the lowest row of the Prisoner Gallery. Unlike Monument D-6, this stone includes no hieroglyphs. Drawing by John Klausmeyer.

Figure 6.34. This victim on Monument D-8 has not had his necklace or earspools removed. The two hieroglyphs shown are a human face with a hand touching its left cheek and below it the atlatl sign. Adapted from Caso 1947: Fig. 4.

D-30. The captive has glyphs on his face. Above his left hand is the sign for 6 Water. Unlike many of the bas-relief monuments I have already discussed, Monument D-40 was executed in a different style (see Caso 1947: Figure 37). Both the incised lines and the treatment of the hair are distinctive.

Monument D-42 (131 x 38 x 37 cm) (Caso's Stone 42, Scott's D-42, Zehnder's L-43, García Moll et al.'s 295). This stone was reused as the third step of a platform extending to the east of Mound L; it was found resting above Monument D-38. The captive has a knotted rope or cloth around his neck and wears a possible nose ornament.

Monument D-45 (44 x 55 x 31 cm) (Caso's stone 45, Scott's D-45; Zehnder's L-47; García Moll et al.'s 298). This stone was in Building L, south of the main stairway next to the tunnel entrance, in the second row. The figure's limbs are in very awkward positions (Villagra Caleti 1939; Caso 1947: Figure 9).

Monument D-47 (75 x 131 cm) (Caso's Stone 47, Scott's D-47, Zehnder's L-45, García Moll et al.'s 296). This slab, found out of context, shows a captive with prominent teeth and the blood scrolls resulting from genital mutilation.

Monument D-48 (125 x 166 x 52 cm) (Caso's Stone 48, Scott's D-48, Zehnder's GL-6, García Moll et al.'s 311). The captive on this stone has a possible beard or goatee, a feature seen also on Monuments D-68, D-72, D-73, D-80, J-61, N-10, and N-15. Some of the monuments listed above may have been carved by the same artisan, since they form a coherent subset in style.

Monument D-55 (90 x 140 x 57 cm) (Caso's Stone 55, Scott's D-55, Zehnder's GL-3, García Moll et al.'s 306; drawn by Villagra at Monte Albán). This important prisoner is associated with perhaps eight hieroglyphs—three in front of his face, three more on his body, and two more between his legs (Figure 6.38). As noted earlier, the text on his chest (the Year 3E, followed by a peculiar little man with headband and a buccal mask) is especially interesting, because another head with a buccal mask appears in Column 2 of Stela 17 (Caso 1947: Figures 15, 16).

The Year 3E may be a reference to the year of this victim's capture. The three glyphs in front of his face may be his name or nickname; the third glyph may be an early variant of the "bag" glyph and could signify "dead man." The glyphs between the captive's legs have yet to be interpreted convincingly, but the repetition of a "foot glyph" immediately below the blood scroll may signify a repeated phonetic element. This prisoner has a hairdo with bangs and a rear tuft of hair; he also wears a large earspool.

Monument D-56 (103 x 118 x 45 cm) (Caso's Stone 56, Scott's D-56, Zehnder's GL-1, García Moll et al.'s 303). This captive has a front tuft and a long fall of hair down the right side. He has the blood scrolls associated with genital mutilation.

Monument D-57 (76 x 127 x 57 cm) (Caso's Stone 57, Villagra's piedra 57, Scott's D-57, Zehnder's GL-2A, García Moll et al.'s 304). The captive on this stone (Figure 6.39) has a pair of glyphs in front of his face, and perhaps two or three hieroglyphs behind his head; some of the signs may provide his nickname. The final glyph behind his head may be the "bag" glyph, referring to him as "dead."

The captive wears a large earspool; his eyes are closed and his upper teeth exposed. He has a tuft of hair above his forehead and a longer fall of hair on the right side of his face, near the earspool. He also displays the blood scrolls associated with genital mutilation.

Monument D-59 (125 x 63 cm) (Caso's Stone 59, Scott's D-59, Zehnder's GL-4, García Moll et al.'s 308). On this stone (Figure 6.40) the captive's name seems to be written on his body. We see two glyphs on his chest that may have been read "Skull Water" (Glyphs H + Z or *lana niça*). It is not clear whether the two elements on his head are tufts of hair or decorative elements on a cap.

Monument D-63 (56 x 106 x 23 cm) (Caso's Stone 63, Scott's D-63, Zehnder's GL-18-57A-57B, García Moll et al.'s 325). This fragment shows a masked figure wearing an elaborate headdress with cloth elements (or perhaps a tassel). The captive has two glyphs near his right elbow, probably supplying his name or nickname; one glyph appears to be the head of a jaguar. Blood scrolls are prominent on this captive, with some blood flowing toward his abdomen and some across his inner thigh.

Monument D-74 (64 x 130 x 90 cm) (Caso's Stone 74, Scott's D-74, Zehnder's GL-12, García Moll et al.'s 317). The captive on this slab (Figure 6.41) is unusual in having a series of five circles on his upper left arm, possibly tattoos. Blood scrolls are present, with some blood flowing toward his abdomen and some flowing to his inner thigh.

Monument D-130 (51 x 36 x 37 cm) (Scott's D-130, Zehnder's GL-74, García Moll et al.'s 382). Although fragmentary, this stone preserves three key hieroglyphs (Figure 6.42). One glyph is similar to that associated with the severed heads on Monuments D-78 and D-123 (see Figure 6.25). The other two glyphs are the atlatl sign and a large disk with punctations. This may be a reference to sacrifice by decapitation.

Monument E-1 (65 x 117 x 41 cm) (Scott's E-1, Zehnder's N-53, García Moll et al.'s 220). The captive on this slab (Figure 6.43) has short hieroglyphic texts in front of his face and on his chest. The glyphs on his chest appear to provide his name or nickname; those in front of his face may refer to blood as an offering.

Monument E-2 (113 x 52 x 8 cm) (Caso's Stela 20, Scott's E-2, Zehnder's N-51, García Moll et al.'s 218). This slab (Figure 6.44) is unusual because the individual is still wearing his loincloth and an impressive necklace, likely of jade beads. The fact that his finery was not removed and his genitals not mutilated set him apart from other individuals we have seen. Equally unusual is the fact that he displays a speech scroll (this does not mean that he is alive, since a speech scroll can occur with a severed head, as on Monument J-112).

This person's calendric name is given as 10N (or perhaps 12N). The style of the bars and Glyph N suggest that this sculpture is much later than those set in the Prisoner Gallery of Building L-sub. This stone was found near Monte Albán's Vértice Geodésico on the North Platform.

Monument I-1 (92 x 56 cm) (Scott's I-1, Zehnder's I-1, García Moll et al.'s 158). This captive slab was found reused in the west façade of Mound I. The figure's headgear includes an unusual helmet. His name is three glyphs long—possibly the number 1 + Water + an animal. He is wearing a possible buccal mask and shows genital mutilation.

Monument J-46 (98 x 144 x 46 cm) (Caso's Stone 46, Scott's J-46, Zehnder's J-27, García Moll et al.'s 111). This prisoner slab (Figure 6.45), found reused in Building J between Monuments J-124 and J-100, features two glyphs—Caso's Glyph J plus a possible building decorated with step frets. The captive's earspool has been removed, and in the open hole there is a feather or tassel, similar to the one found in the earlobe of the captive on Monument N-21. Blood scrolls flow toward his abdomen and thighs.

Monument J-74 (42 x 116 cm) (Caso's Stone 74, Scott's J-74, Zehnder's J-57, García Moll et al.'s 13). This slab shows a captive with his left arm raised. Near his head is a hieroglyph that might be his nickname.

Monument J-89 (51 x 118 x 71 cm) (Caso's Stone 89, Scott's J-89, Zehnder's J-93, García Moll et al.'s 119). This slab shows a man with hieroglyphs on his chest and blood scrolls that flow toward his abdomen and thighs.

Monument J-100 (96 x 152 x 15 cm) (Caso's Stone 100, Scott's J-100, Zehnder's J-28, García Moll et al.'s 112). This captive (Figure 6.46) has small circles on his left shoulder and upper arm; these markings, which may be tattoos, are similar to those on Monument D-74. We also see a tassel or braid that may

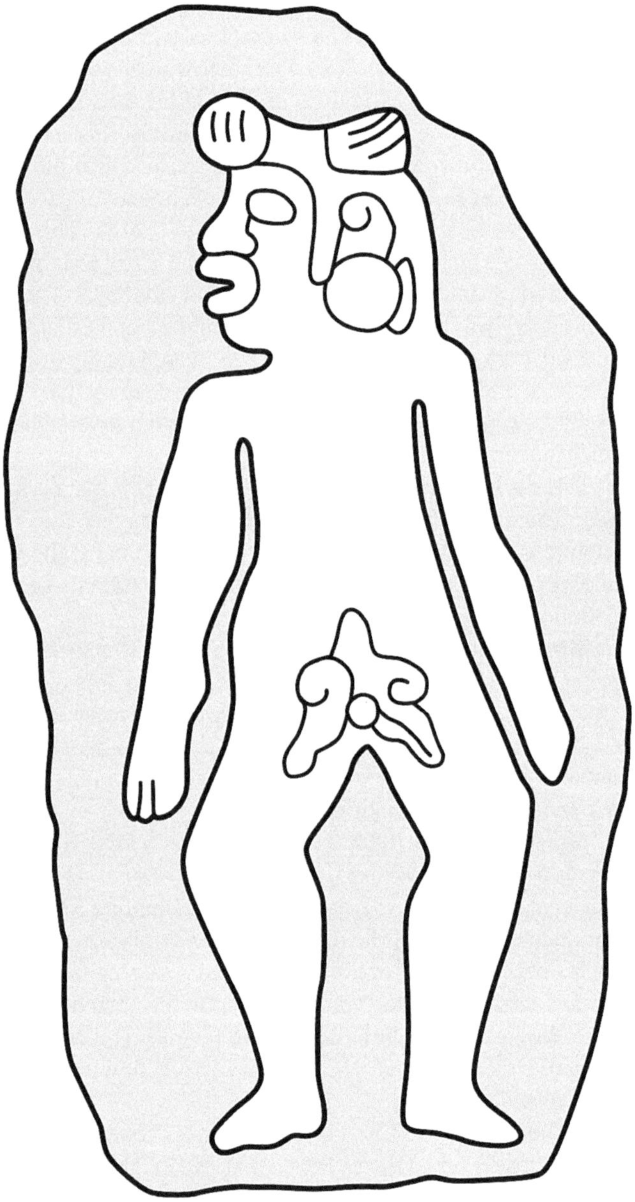

Figure 6.35. Monument D-12 was set in Row 3 of the Prisoner Gallery, and like all the victims in this row, the captive faces south. Genital mutilation is shown. Adapted by John Klausmeyer from Caso 1947: Fig. 6.

Figure 6.36. Monument D-22 was found near the Mound L staircase and Monument D-21 (Caso 1947: Fig. 7). It is not clear whether the symbol on the victim's chest represents a hole for heart removal or something else. Two hieroglyphs appear next to his chest. Drawing by John Klausmeyer.

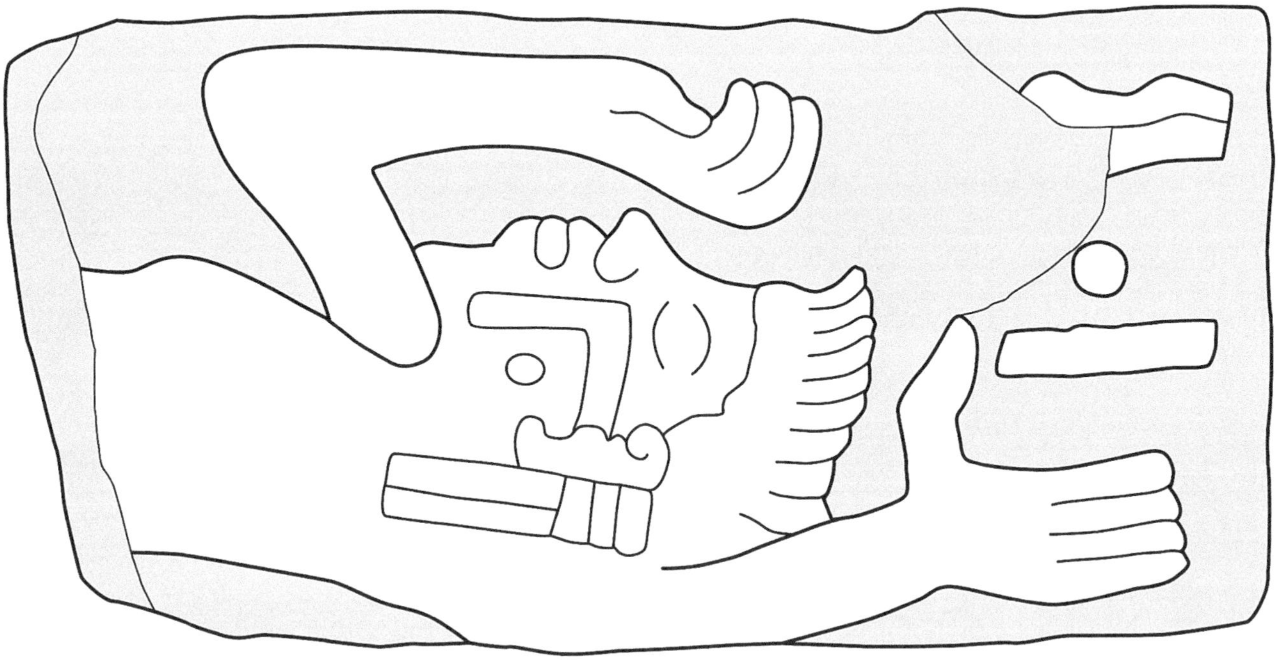

Figure 6.37. Monument D-40, forming the second step of the platform to the east of Building L, was found directly above Monument D-30. This fragment shows the upper body of a slain captive with bars and a dot on the face, as well as a bar, a dot, and a possible water sign near his left hand. This victim's name might have been 6 Water. Drawing by John Klausmeyer.

have been hanging from this captive's hairdo. Large blood scrolls flow toward his abdomen and thighs.

Monument K-9 (62 x 42 cm) (Scott's K-9). This captive has apparently been stripped of his clothing, but retains an impressive necklace of what are probably jade beads.

Monument M-1 (151 x 63 x 30 cm) (Caso's Stone 1, Scott's M-1, Zehnder's M-19, 20; García Moll et al.'s 420). The hieroglyphic name of this captive is given in front of his face.

Monument M-2 (111 x 145 x 35 cm) (Caso's Stone 2, Scott's M-2, Zehnder's M-3, García Moll et al.'s 402). This prisoner slab, although eroded, includes a short text. The best preserved of the hieroglyphs is the atlatl sign in front of the captive's face.

Monument M-4 (49 x 110 x 80 cm) (Caso's Stone 4, Scott's M-4, Zehnder's M-4, García Moll et al.'s 403). This slab (Figure 6.47) shows a captive with hieroglyphs on his chest and a series of blood scrolls where his genitals used to be.

Monument N-28 (43 x 107 x 42 cm) (Caso's Stone 28, Scott's N-28, Zehnder's N-15B, García Moll et al.'s 211). This captive (Figure 6.48) features a possible hole or two in his chest, through which his heart was probably removed. His headdress is unique among prisoner depictions.

Monument N-28A (102 x 42 cm) (Scott's N-28A). This captive (Figure 6.49) has a hole in his chest, through which his heart was probably removed. His left arm is raised and his right hand may hold something.

Monument Q-3 (31 x 102 cm) (García Moll et al.'s 466). This fragment shows only the lower portion of a captive; he apparently has a belt or similar garment tied around him in the shape of a scroll. Of particular interest is the motif on the victim's chest (see Figure 6.7), which is somewhat similar to the circle-and-triangle "blood motif"—a symbol used at Fábrica San José during the Guadalupe phase and at San José Mogote during the Rosario phase (see Figures 6.5, 6.9) (Acosta 1974: Figure 31).

Monument Q-7 (33 x 34 x 40 cm) (Scott's Q-7). This stone, now in the Museo de las Culturas de Oaxaca, shows only a head and an upraised hand and finger.

Monument S-10 (173 x 38 cm) (Caso's Stone 10, Scott's S-10, Zehnder's S-16, García Moll et al.'s 444). This prisoner slab (Figure 6.50) was reused in the South Platform. The captive, lying on his back, has a transverse mark and circle on his face and a hieroglyph above his right hand (Caso 1947: Figure 35).

The Carving Styles of the Prisoner Slabs

Caso (1947:17–19), the first investigator to classify the carving styles of the Building L slabs, divided them into two types. His Type 1, which he considered "classic" and perhaps older in date, depicts the victims' hands without fingernails and their feet without toenails; gives them thick lips and prominent teeth;

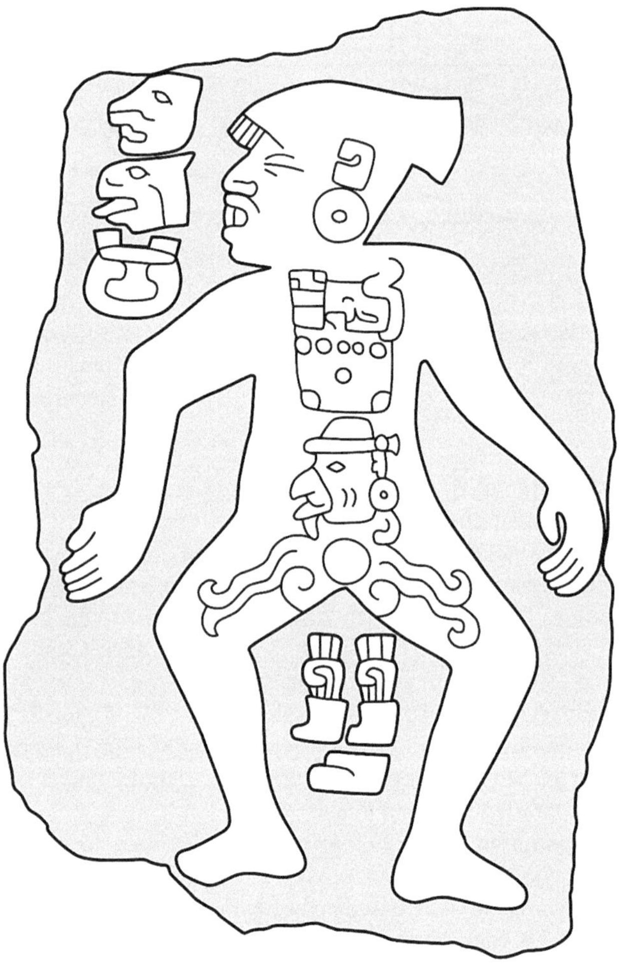

Figure 6.38. Monument D-55—set between Monument D-57 and Stela 15—shows a victim with one column of hieroglyphs extending from his neck to below his knees, and three more hieroglyphs in front of his face. Genital mutilation is suggested. Part of the hieroglyphic text on this stone is repeated on Stela 17. Drawing by John Klausmeyer.

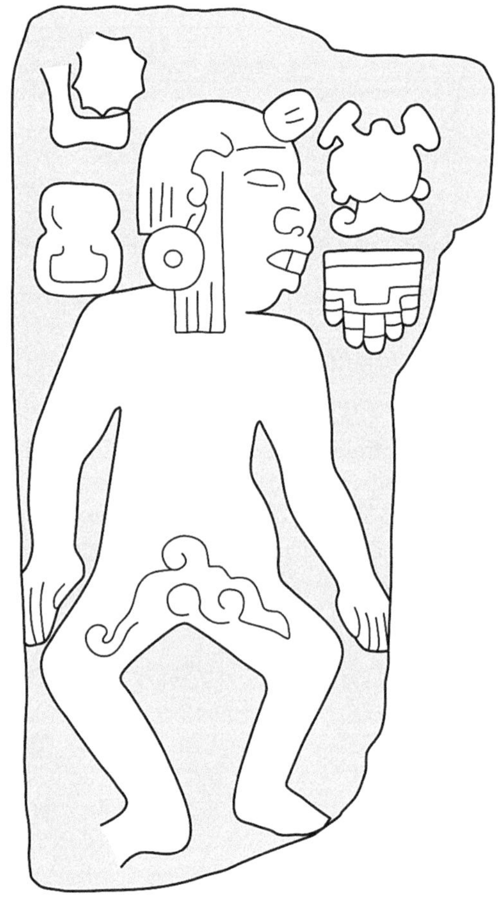

Figure 6.39. Monument D-57 shows a victim with two glyphs in front of his face and a few behind his head. Blood scrolls reveal genital mutilation. Drawing by John Klausmeyer.

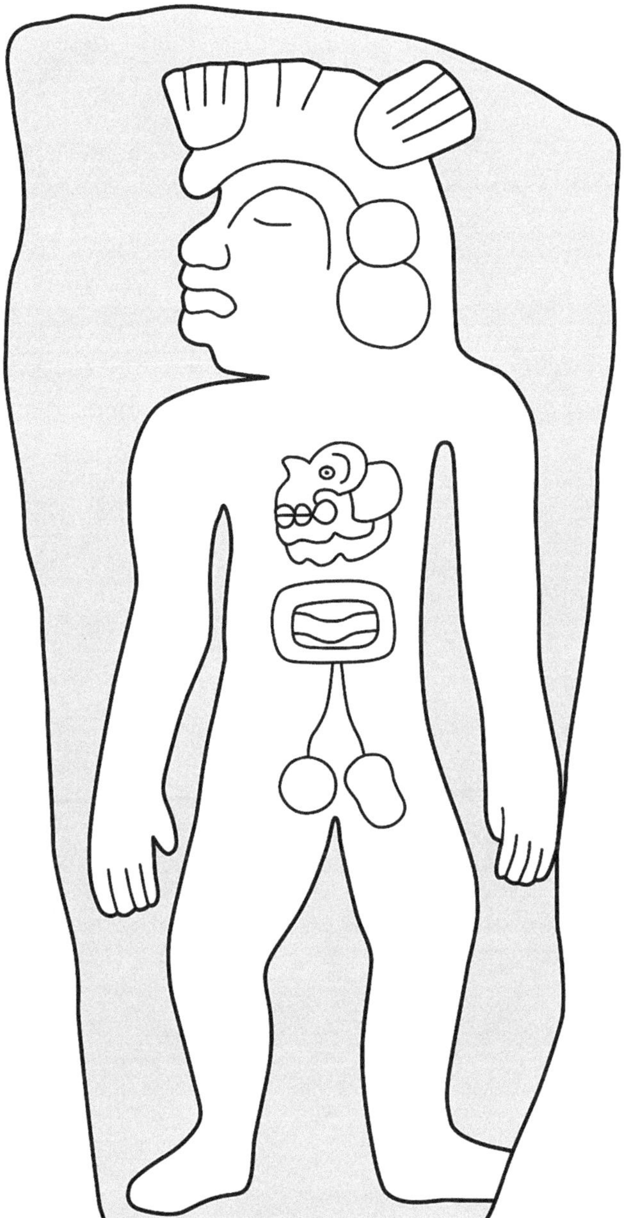

Figure 6.40. Monument D-59 shows a victim with two tufts of hair or ornaments on his head and two hieroglyphs on his chest. He faces south, like the stones in Row 3 of the Prisoner Gallery. Drawing by John Klausmeyer.

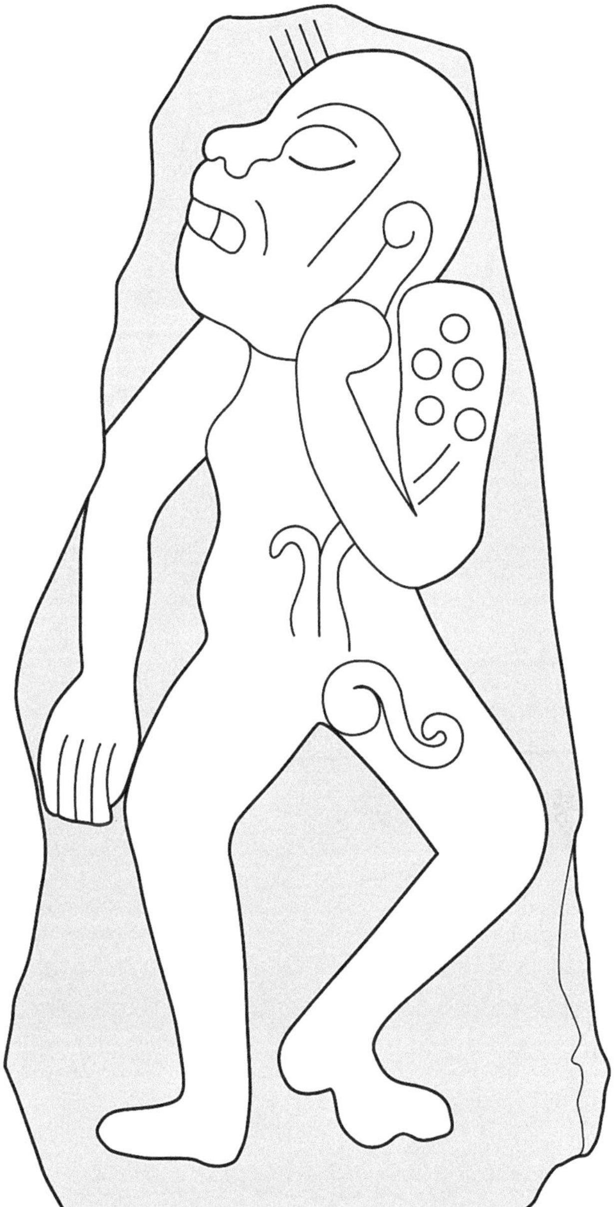

Figure 6.41. Monument D-74 shows a victim with blood scrolls on his groin and five circles on his upper left arm that may indicate tattoos. Drawing by John Klausmeyer.

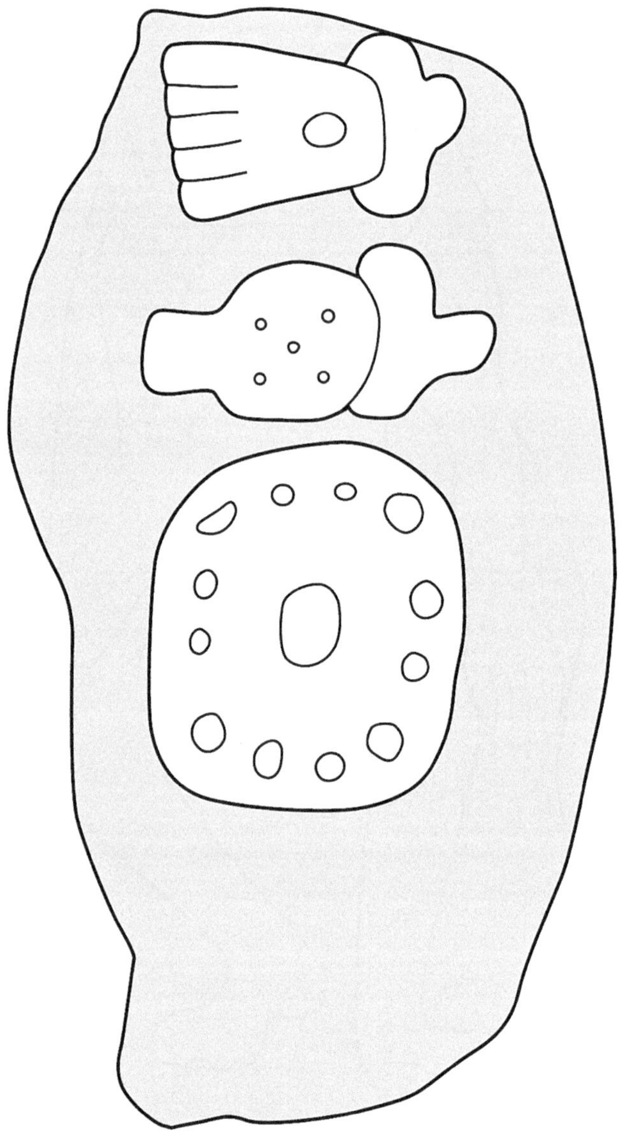

Figure 6.42. Monument D-130 bears three hieroglyphs that may be associated with decapitation and death. These glyphs can be compared with those shown in Figure 6.25. Drawing by John Klausmeyer.

Figure 6.43. The victim shown in Monument E-1 (found reused in Building E) has blood scrolls on his groin and short columns of glyphs on his chest (three hieroglyphs) and in front of his face (three hieroglyphs). Drawing by Mark Orsen.

Figure 6.44. Monument E-2, once called Stela 20, was found near the Vértice Geodésico on the North Platform of Monte Albán. Although Scott (1978) included this carved stone in his study of Period I monuments, the style both of the figure and the calendric glyphs (10N or 12N) suggest that this monument postdated by centuries the Building L substructure. Drawing by Mark Orsen.

and delineates the body by an outer line that is wide and deep, creating a bas-relief.

Caso's Type 2, which he considered more recent in date, includes slabs that are incised rather than carved in low relief; shows the captives' bodies as long and lean, rather than stocky; emphasizes the toenail on the big toe and the arches of the foot; depicts the lips as thin; and does not show teeth. An example can be found in Figure 6.50.

Although Caso suggested that these two styles may have been produced at different times, let us consider an alternative explanation. Assuming that the formidable task of carving ca. 300 stones for Building L had to be completed in a short period of time, several artisans would have been needed to shoulder the heavy work load. The simultaneous effort of multiple teams of stone carvers could explain the stylistic differences.

The Earliest Record of Accession

In addition to prisoner carvings, Period I of Monte Albán gives us our first pure texts in Zapotec hieroglyphs. These are Stelae 12, 13, 14, 15, and 17.

Stelae 12 and 13 were found at the south end of the Prisoner Gallery, in the east façade of the substructure of Building L (Figure 6.51). These earliest Zapotec stelae feature year signs, year bearers, day signs, bars and dots, and noncalendric glyphs. Some of the latter appear to be homonyms or near-homonyms that would make sense only if the hieroglyphs were created by speakers of Zapotec.

What was the motivation for carving these early columns of text? Stela 12, on the left, seems to record a Period I accession to office, carved centuries before the earliest Maya royal accessions were recorded in stone.

Stela 12

Although there are multiple ways to interpret the Stela 12 text, my tentative reading would be: "In the Year 4M [a man named] 8 Water, a first-born son, was seated in office." The fact that we cannot rule out alternative readings shows how much work remains to be done with Zapotec texts.

If this text does indeed record an accession to office, Stela 12 and the associated Building L prisoner carvings could establish several precedents. It could mean, for example, that (1) the sacrifice of captives was a prerequisite to being seated in office; that (2) the display of such captives was appropriate for the face of a public building; and that (3) birth order was taken into account in Period I, just as it was with later Zapotec leaders. What we do not

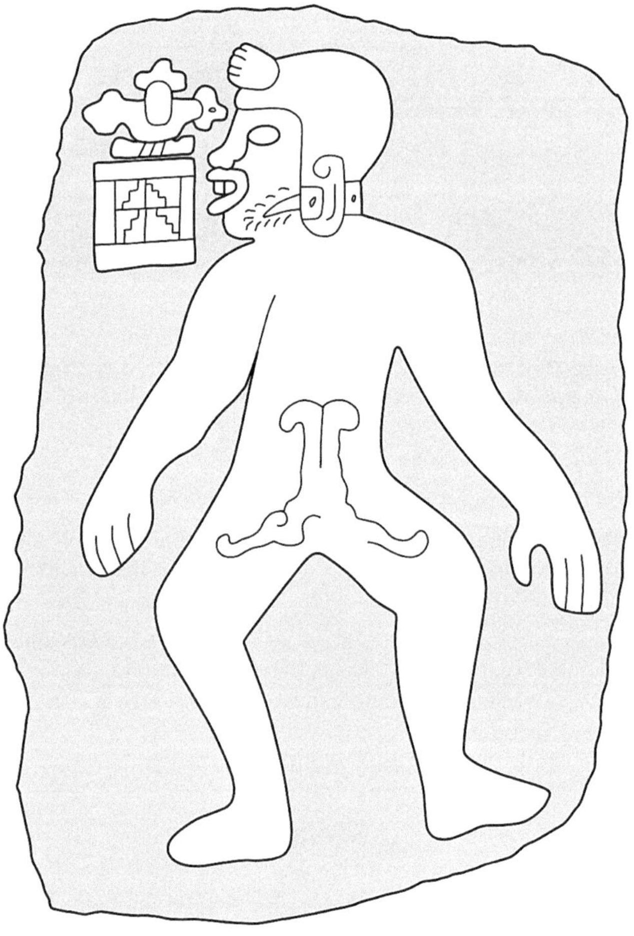

Figure 6.45. Monument J-46, found reused in Building J, shows a mutilated prisoner associated with a hieroglyphic caption that combines Glyph J + a possible building with step frets. Instead of a jade ear ornament he seems to have a feather or other perishable item inserted in his earlobe, not unlike some Maya prisoners whose jade ornaments had been removed and replaced by cloth or other perishable material (Caso 1947: Fig. 27). Drawing by John Klausmeyer.

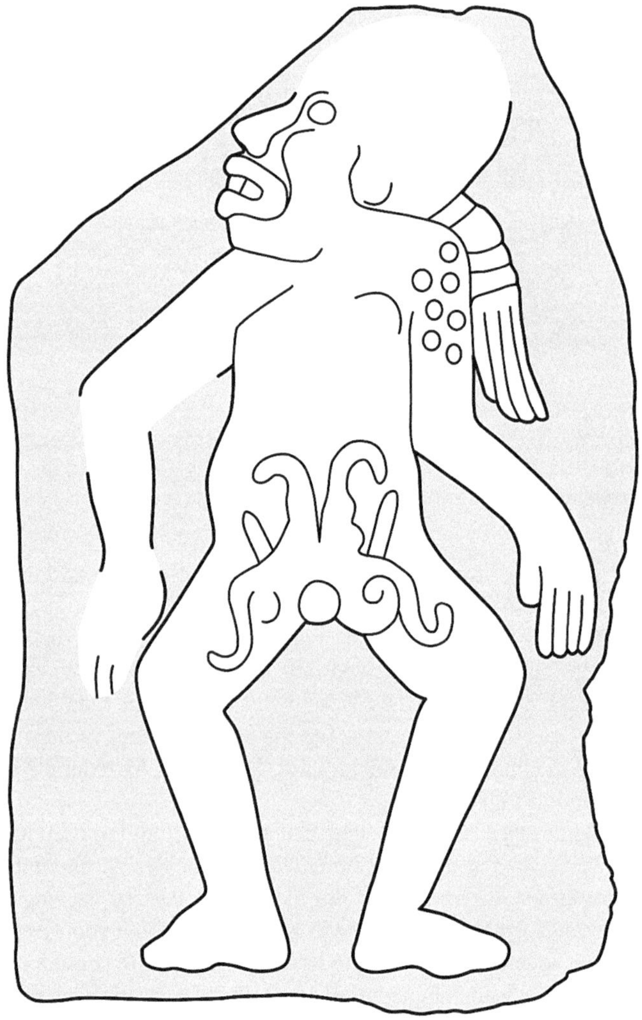

Figure 6.46. Monument J-100 shows a genitally mutilated prisoner who, like the captive on Monument D-74 (see Figure 6.41), has seven circles on his upper left shoulder. Drawing by John Klausmeyer.

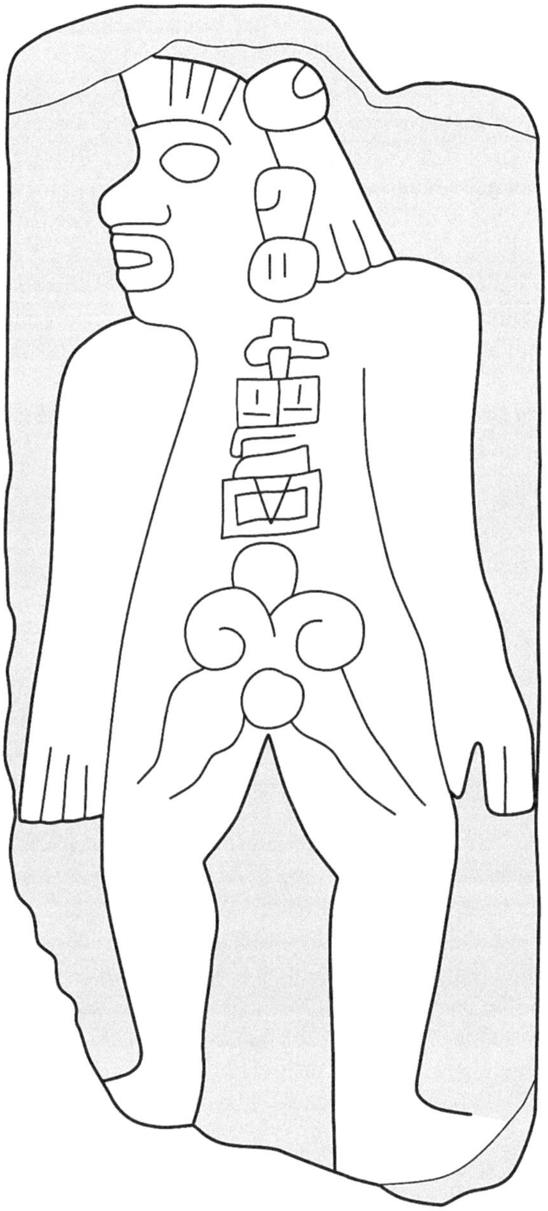

Figure 6.47. Monument M-4 was found on the east side of Building M. The victim shows genital mutilation, and we see a short column of hieroglyphs on his chest. Drawing by John Klausmeyer.

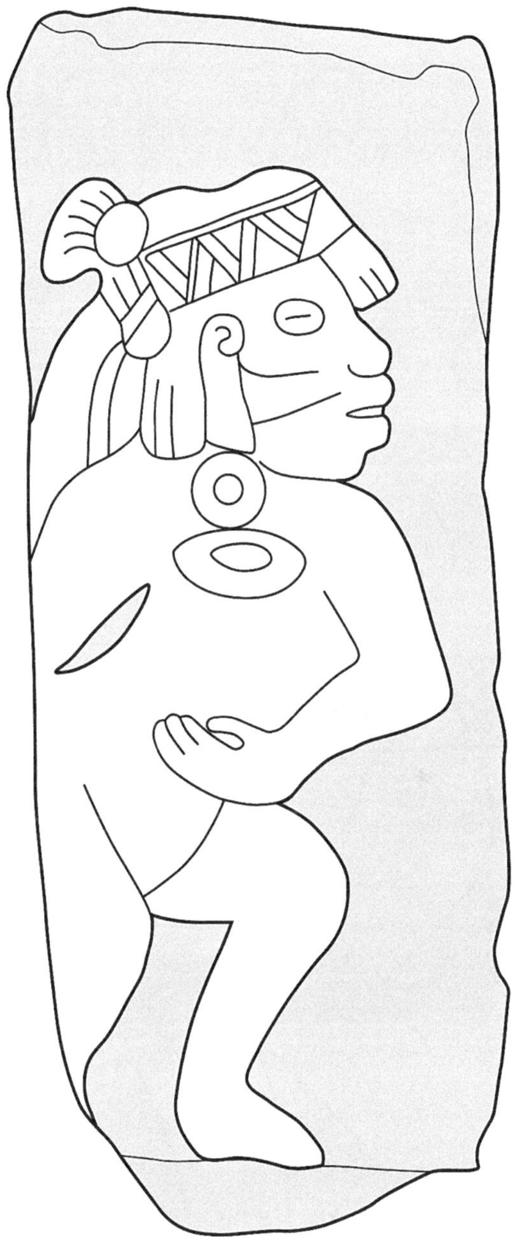

Figure 6.48. Monument N-28 shows a victim with a circle and a lozenge-shaped element on his chest. His cap and decorated headband are unusual. Drawing by John Klausmeyer.

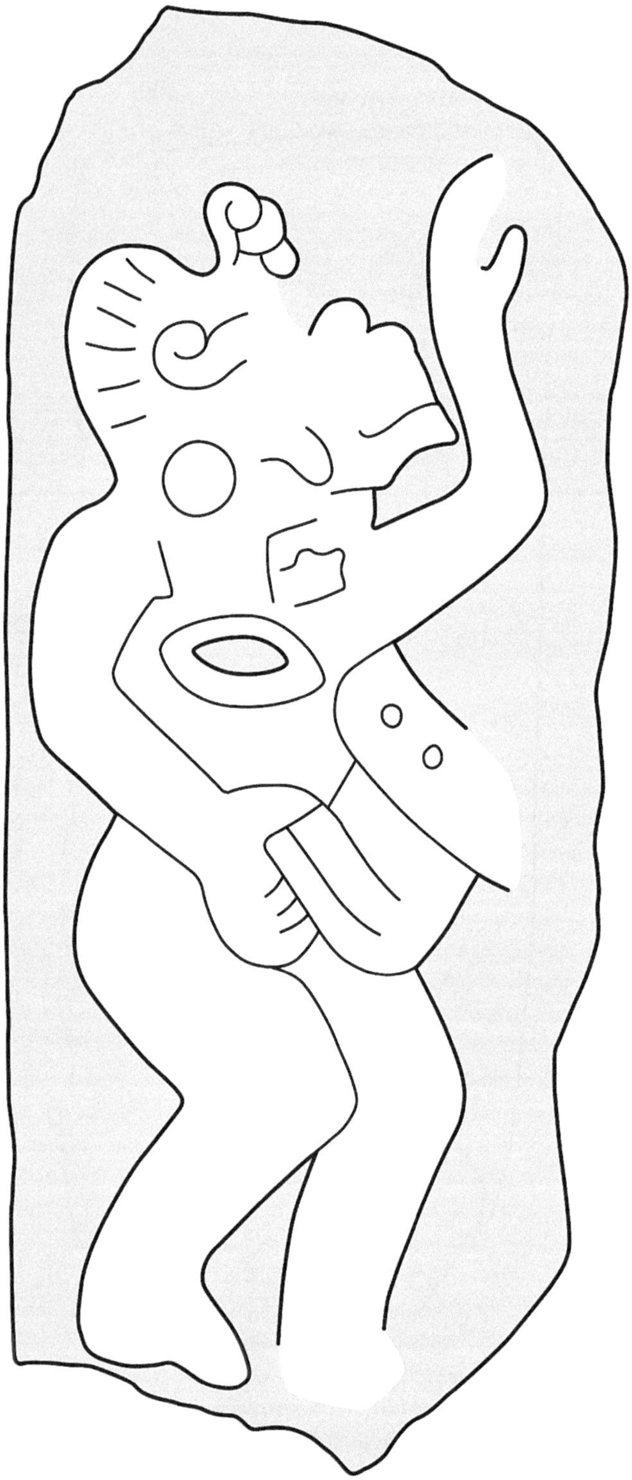

Figure 6.49. The sprawled victim on Monument N-28A has a lozenge-shaped element on his chest, like the one on Monument N-28. Such elements may represent openings for heart removal. Drawing by John Klausmeyer.

know is whether the accession of 8 Water was typical, or whether his need to show 300 slain captives was an overcompensation for dubious credentials.

At the least, Stela 12 establishes a precedent for later accessions to power. Monte Albán's South Platform, for example, featured a later inauguration at which a Period III ruler oversaw a procession of prisoners (see Chapter 9). These South Platform prisoners were probably destined to be sacrificed, as were those in Building L.

Situating Stela 12 and the Building L prisoners in a framework that provides a precedent for the later South Platform slabs helps us to understand more about both eras. Although there are important differences between the two accession programs (for example, the South Platform stelae featured prominent prisoners dressed in full animal costumes, alive but with their arms bound behind their backs, while the Building L façade featured mostly dead captives who had suffered heart removal, genital mutilation, or decapitation), the display of prisoners to legitimize the taking of office appears to have had real time depth in Oaxaca. We will return to some of these issues in Chapter 9, when we discuss the inauguration of the individual displayed on Stela 1 in the South Platform.

Stela 13

Stela 13 (Figures 6.51, 6.52) was set next to Stela 12. It, too, has four hieroglyphs in a column (B1-4), also read from top to bottom. Caso (1928:95; Caso 1969) designated the uppermost sign Glyph B, "Jaguar." Although the element above this jaguar head is similar to a year sign headband, I would suggest that it is not a year sign. My reasoning is as follows: if it were a year sign, we would expect to see it accompanied by one of the four year bearers (that is, the hieroglyphs E, M, G, and N; see Caso 1928: Figure 59 and Caso 1947: Figure 11).

Below the jaguar head on Stela 13 are two apparent bars, suggesting that this sign could be read as 10 Jaguar. (We cannot rule out the possibility that these signs are human digits rather than bars, thus representing the number two. This calendric sign would then be 2 Jaguar, which could refer either to a date or a name.) The second sign below it may be the verb "seized." The third sign looks to be Glyph 1P. Caso regarded this glyph as a day sign—and it might be—but given the index finger below it, an alternative reading would be the Zapotec word *tini*, which can mean both "index finger" and "second-born son."

The final (lowermost) hieroglyph on Stela 13 is 4W, which probably has calendric significance. Although Caso (1928:95) originally suggested that Glyph W was a day sign, he later decided that it was a month sign (Caso 1947:29). The reason Caso changed his mind was that he found Glyph W in other contexts with numbers higher than 13, which suggests that it recorded months or lunar cycles (see discussion in Urcid 2001:250–273).

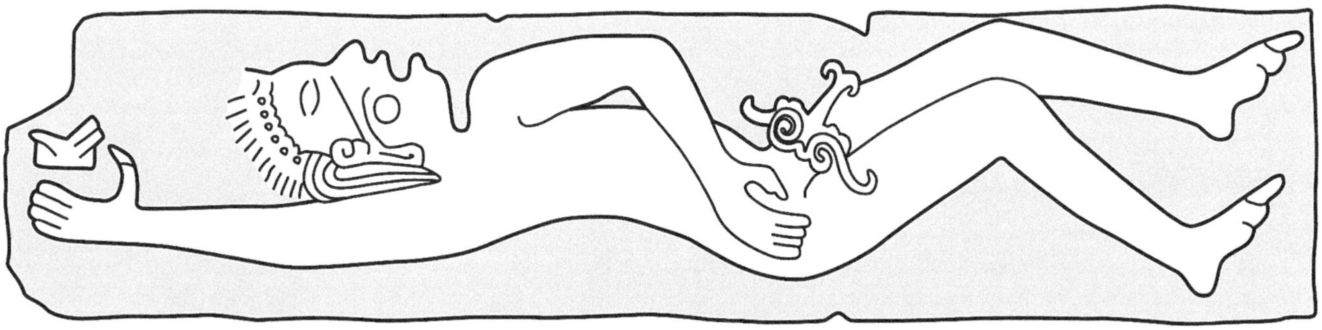

Figure 6.50. Monument S-10 was reused in the South Platform at Monte Albán. We see a hieroglyph above the victim's right hand and elaborate blood scrolls issuing from his groin. This carving is an example of Caso's Type 2, a style that features long arms and legs as well as a prominent nail on the thumb and on the big toe. Drawing by John Klausmeyer.

Stela 14

Stela 14 was found out of context and is incomplete. It shows a column of hieroglyphs (Caso 1947: Figure 20). Glyph 1 may be a structure, perhaps a temple or house (not reconstructed or shown in Figure 6.53). Glyph 2 depicts two heads facing each other (see Caso 1947: Figure 19, lowest row). Glyph 3's meaning is unknown. Glyph 4 is likely the bag or "dead man" glyph. This text may record the death of an individual, but its overall decipherment and glyph-by-glyph meaning have yet to be determined.

Stela 15

This stela fragment (Figure 6.54) presents two incomplete columns of text (Caso 1947: Figure 14), as follows.

Left column: Glyph 1 is eroded. Glyph 2 is a compound sign, featuring a jaguar head above a lower torso. Glyph 3 looks to be a hand supporting an object and is possibly a verb. Glyph 4's meaning is unknown. Glyph 5 is the bag or "death" glyph.

Right column: Caso identified the first glyph as the day sign Glyph O, but it could be interpreted as 10P or 2P. Glyph 2 is 14W. Glyph 3 is a possible hill sign with a subfix. If this text's content and word order required the bag glyph to be the final hieroglyph in the text, we would then infer that the right column was read before the left.

What is of some interest in early writing systems, whether in the Old World or the New, is the overall lack of standardization, and these Period I texts at Monte Albán are no different. They seem to demonstrate the flexibility and lack of standardization in reading order and the arrangement of columns (e.g., Stela 12 was read from top to bottom; Stela 17 was probably read from bottom to top; and Stela 15, possibly right to left).

Stela 17

This stela fragment, found out of context (Figure 6.55), includes a year sign and year bearer in its lower left corner (Caso 1947: Figure 15). Such year signs often begin columns of hieroglyphs, which suggests that this text (unlike those on Stelae 12 and 13) might have been read from bottom to top.

The Stela 17 fragment consists of two columns of text, with three signs in the left column and five on the right. This asymmetry indicates that each column was read separately.

Left column:The lowest glyph consists of the year sign with the year bearer 12E. The glyph above it is the day sign 10Z (10 Water). At the top is a head facing downward, which may signal a dead person. This column might be read, "In the Year 12E [a man named] 10 Water died."

Right column: What we notice most are the last two glyphs in the column, which look like a pair of signs that we saw on Monument D-55: the Year 3E above the depiction of an odd little man with a headband and buccal mask (see Figure 6.38; see also Caso 1947: Figure 16). Above the year sign is a sign associated with the number 18 (3 bars and 3 dots). Finally, we see a profile head with two digits below the head. This sign was designated Glyph O by Caso (1928), but given the contexts in which it occurs, it may refer to birth-order position: perhaps *tini* or second-born son.

It is unusual to see the same phrase on two Zapotec monuments—in this case Stela 17 and Monument D-55 (see Figure 6.38). In both cases, the Year 3E is associated with a little man sporting a headband. This headband is similar to those later associated with accession to high office among the Maya and Aztec (see Chapter 13). I wish I knew exactly what event occurred in the Year 3E—one that was important enough to be mentioned on two monuments.

Figure 6.51. In this 1930s photograph of Stelae 12 and 13, we see Raúl Haneine (at left) and Jorge R. Acosta (at right). This all-glyphic text was located at the south end of the Prisoner Gallery at Monte Albán. Courtesy of Ignacio Bernal.

Figure 6.52. Stelae 12 and 13 are located at the south end of the Building L Prisoner Gallery at Monte Albán (see Figure 6.51). The text on Stela 12 consists of four hieroglyphs, arranged in a column. This text must have been read from top to bottom, since the uppermost glyph (A1) is the Zapotec year sign, resting above a cartouche enclosing the day sign M; four dots occur below the cartouche. This combination of glyphs stands for a year that began with the day 4 Lightning. Since this year bearer would repeat itself every 52 years, we cannot place this year in absolute time as we can with Maya Long Count dates. The second hieroglyph (A2)—a human hand with the thumb extended—may constitute our oldest example of Mesomerican rebus writing, since the Zapotec word *yobi* meant both "thumb" and "first-born son." The third hieroglyph (A3) has been interpreted by Justeson (1986) as "seated in office." The last hieroglyph (A4) is the day sign 8 Water. In this location 8 Water would be the subject of the phrase, i.e., the name of a person. Although there are other ways to interpret this text, my tentative reading would be: "In the Year 4 Lightning [a man named] 8 Water, a first-born son, was seated in office." The fact that we cannot rule out alternative readings shows how much work remains to be done with Zapotec texts. Stela 13 (B1-4) is read from top to bottom. Caso (1928:95; Caso 1965a: Figs. 2, 3) designated the uppermost sign (B1) Jaguar. Below it are two apparent bars, suggesting that this sign could be read as 10 Jaguar (although we cannot rule out the possibility that these signs are human digits rather than bars, representing the number two). The second sign (B2), which shows a hand grasping an object, may be the verb "seized." B3 looks to be the glyph 1P. Caso regarded this glyph as a day sign, but given the index finger below it, an alternative reading would be the Zapotec word *tini*, which can mean both "index finger" and "second-born son." The final glyph (B4) is 4W, which probably has calendric significance. A tentative reading would be: "[Lord] 10 Jaguar was seized by the second-born son during the 4th month (4th lunar cycle)." To be sure, other plausible interpretations cannot be ruled out. Drawing by Mark Orsen.

Figure 6.53. Monte Albán's Stela 14 is a fragment that was found out of context. It shows glyphs in a column. The paired glyphs at the top depict two heads facing each other (Caso 1947: Fig. 19, lowest row). The lowest glyph is likely the bag or "dead person" glyph (*peni cotí*). This text may record the death of an individual, but its glyph-by-glyph decipherment has yet to be accomplished. Drawing by John Klausmeyer.

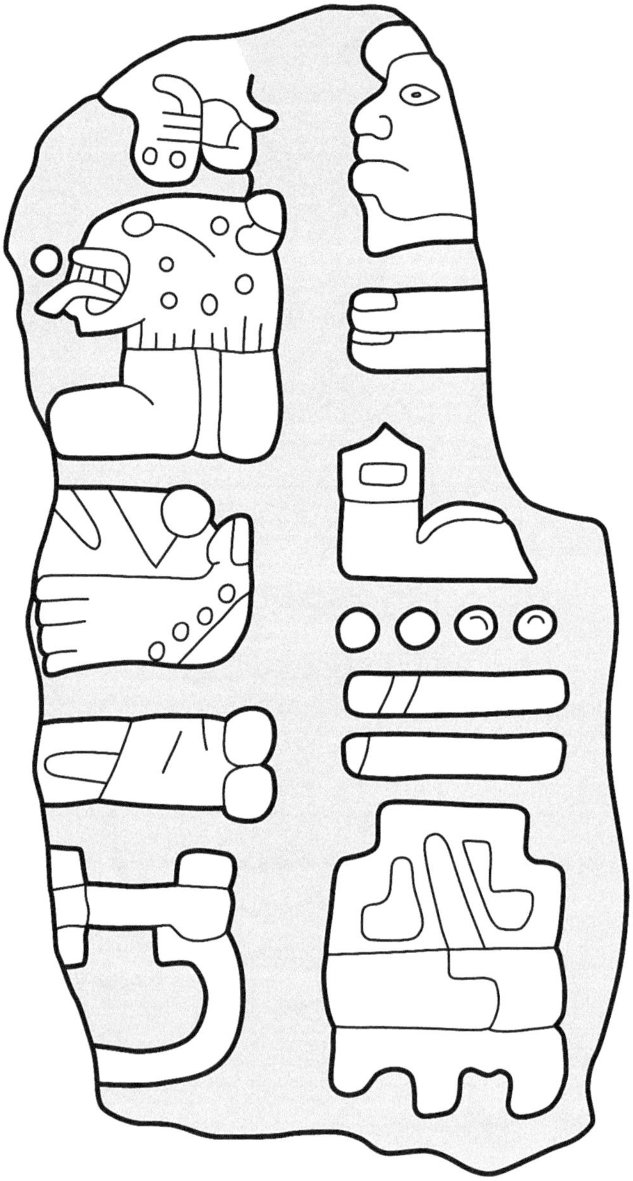

Figure 6.54. Stela 15 at Monte Albán (Caso 1947: Fig. 14) presents two columns of text, as follows. In the left column, Glyph 1 is eroded; Glyph 2 is a compound sign featuring a jaguar head above a human torso; Glyph 3, which looks to be a hand supporting an object, is a possible verb; Glyph 4's meaning is unknown; and Glyph 5 is the bag or "death" glyph. In the right column, Caso identified the first glyph as the day sign Monkey (Glyph O) and two fingers; Glyph 2 is 14W; and Glyph 3 is a possible hill sign with a subfix. If the bag glyph at the end of the left column ended the entire message carved here, it is possible that the right column was read first. Drawing by John Klausmeyer.

Figure 6.55. This stela fragment from Monte Albán is called Stela 17. The text is probably read from left to right and from bottom to top, since we see a year sign and year bearer (Caso 1947: Fig. 15) at lower left. The text begins with the year bearer 12E, moves on to the day sign 10Z (10 Water), and ends with a human head facing down (perhaps signifying dead person). This left column might be read, "In the Year 12E [a man named] 10 Water died." If we begin the right column at the bottom, we see a little head with a headband wearing a buccal mask and then the year 3E. These final two glyphs—3E + the little head with headband—are of particular interest because they are also shown on the chest of the captive in Figure 6.38. Above that pair of glyphs (3E and head with headband) is a sign associated with the number 18. At the top of the right column we see a profile head above two fingers. Drawing by John Klausmeyer.

Naming as a Catalyst for the Appearance of Writing

Chiefly societies in highland Mexican valleys engaged in many kinds of social, economic, political, and military activities. Raiding, captive-taking, and ritual sacrifice were often featured in their art. Indeed, I am struck by the frequency with which chiefly societies selected militaristic themes for their art.

Zapotec chiefs chose to depict hundreds of sacrificial victims, adding hieroglyphic captions to label important captives who may have been seen as rivals (Marcus 1974, 1992a). Monte Albán was not alone in commissioning monuments that displayed massacred rivals. Andean chiefly societies, such as the one at Cerro Sechín, made it even more gruesome—commissioning 400 carved stones, some of which show eyeballs gouged out, stacks of skulls, and intestines hanging from their bisected and dismembered bodies.

What did the Zapotec and Andean societies of this period have in common? They were both experiencing the chiefly competition out of which the first expansionist kingdoms would emerge (Feinman and Marcus 1998; Flannery and Marcus 1976a, 2012; Marcus and Flannery 1996; Sherman et al. 2010; Spencer 2019; Spencer and Redmond 2001a, 2004a, 2005, 2006). By depicting massive displays of mutilated enemies, self-aggrandizing leaders in both Mexico and Peru were using terror tactics to discourage their rivals from interfering in their quest for tribute, land, and subordinates. They let potential enemies know that the same treatment would be coming their way if they were taken prisoner. By using terror propaganda, they hoped to discourage resistance.

In the ethnography of bellicose chiefly societies like the Maori, we learn the agenda behind this kind of art. Maori craftsmen told anthropologists that the goal was to imbue their work with *wehi* (fear), *wana* (authority), and *ihi* (power) (Mead 1985:23). The best Maori wood carvers were men of high rank; in fact, one of the qualities associated with rank was knowledge of carving, a skill used to decorate chiefs' houses, canoes, and war clubs. Carving was performed by high-ranking families, by men of senior descent—people closest to the gods and the bearers of political authority. It was considered a sacred activity that linked the community as a whole to its gods and ancestors, putting the community in touch with supernatural sources of power.

The Maori went further; they named important structures, posts, and statues. The act of naming accomplished many things. It denoted ownership, personalized and animated objects, and connected living descendants with their ancestors. What the Maori lacked was a writing system to make permanent those names. Writing was the next step.

Zapotec writing arose in the context of chiefly competition and it quickly became one more strategy used by chiefs. The Zapotec monument carver went beyond the Maori to name vanquished rivals and to record in stone the accession of the victor to high office.

7

Reuse and Recycling of Carved Stones

In view of the large number of carved stones from Building L-sub that were reused in other settings, this would seem to be an appropriate point in the book to discuss recycling.

When a building and its façade of carved stones were designed as an integrated architectural program, that overall arrangement conveyed a narrative that could only be understood when all the carved stones were still in place. When such buildings were later dismantled, it became difficult or impossible to determine the stones' original arrangement and meaning.

Cities occupied for more than a millennium often witnessed the renovation of old buildings and the construction of new ones. Each generation of architects was tempted to take a shortcut in procuring construction material, so they removed stones from earlier buildings. Sometimes they reused them without modification, and sometimes they carved new images on previously unused surfaces.

It was much less work to remove stones from an adjacent building than to travel to a quarry to cut new stones and transport them to the building site. There is ample evidence from many cities, including Monte Albán, Dainzú, Tikal, Calakmul, and Xochicalco, that carved stones were moved from one place to another, then recarved, displayed, hidden, or buried (e.g., W. R. Coe 1967, 1990; Folan et al. 1995; Jones and Satterthwaite 1982; Just 2005; Marcus 1974, 1992a, 2012; Martin 2000, 2003; Sáenz 1961, 1964, 1968).

Temple platforms became taller and larger over time as new additions were superimposed on them. There were periodic flurries of construction at populous cities, whether the activity took place in Tikal's North Acropolis or Monte Albán's North Platform.

Some stones were recarved multiple times (Figure 7.1). The door of Tomb 104 at Monte Albán, for example, was carved at least three times (Caso 1938). The first carving was on the edge, and would only be seen when the stone was used as a lintel (Figure 7.1a). Later, one of its plain surfaces was carved so that the stone could serve as a tomb door (Figure 7.1b). This hieroglyphic text was arranged vertically. Later, the door was flipped over and carved on a third side. This third and final carving was arranged so that it faced the tomb interior, and this time it was displayed horizontally (Figure 7.1c) (see Caso 1938: Figures 94, 95).

Since the slabs from Building L numbered about 300 and were highly accessible, it is not surprising that they were reused in so many buildings around the Main Plaza at Monte Albán. Prisoner slabs were reused in Building M; in the North Platform (Buildings "d" and "e," as well as the Vértice Geodésico); along the central spine of the Main Plaza (Buildings I and J); along the east side of the plaza (in the ballcourt, in Buildings P and Q, and in the Building S palace); along the west side of the plaza (System IV, Tomb 128, Buildings N and O); in the South Platform; and in Siete Venado, a group of buildings south of the South Platform (Figure 7.2; see also Figure 6.21).

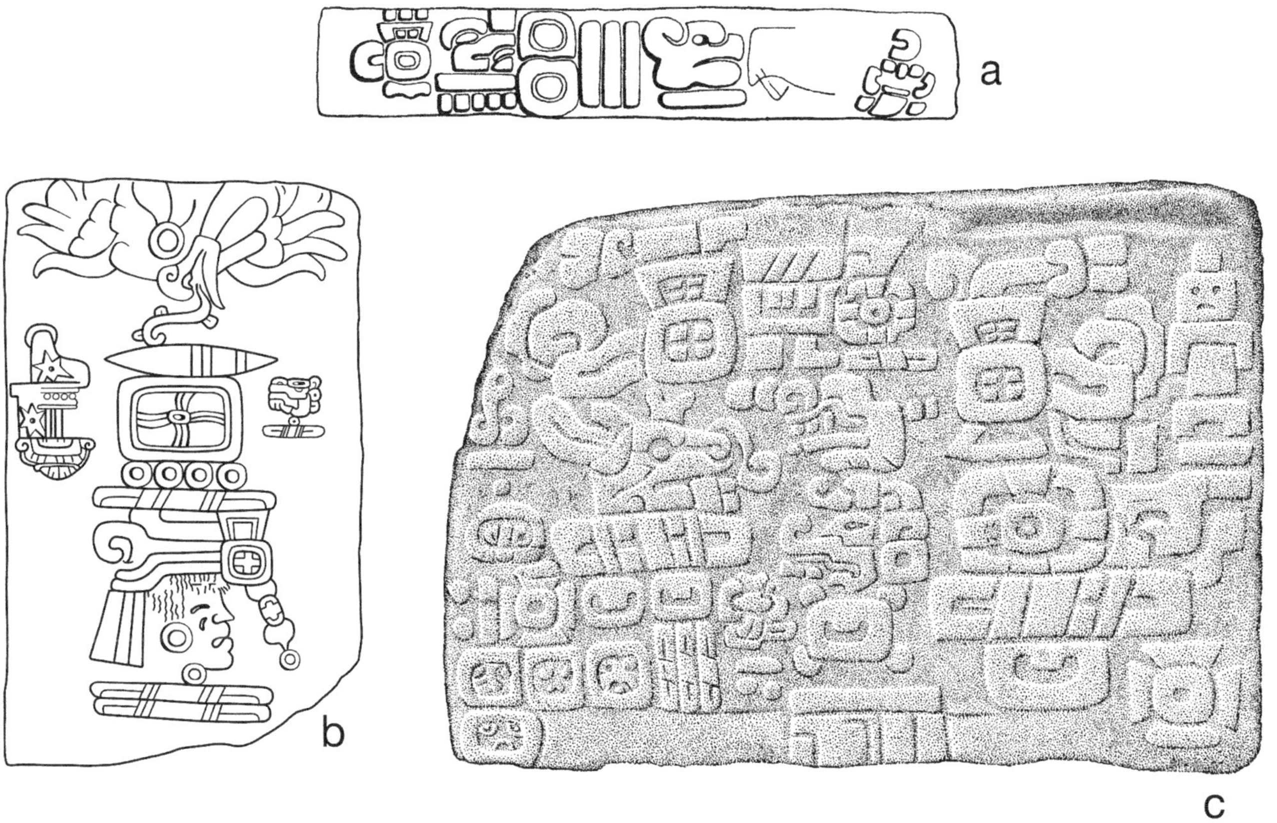

Figure 7.1. The door stone of Tomb 104 at Monte Albán is an example of a monument that was recarved and recycled. (*a*) This narrow edge, when positioned as a lintel, would have been visible to visitors. (*b*) After the stone had served as a lintel, it was carved on this second surface and used as the tomb door. (*c*) Finally, the stone was carved on a third surface, one that faced the interior of the tomb and could only be seen by the deceased (see Caso 1938: Figs. 94, 95).

Figure 7.2. An artist's conception of Monte Albán's Main Plaza showing Building S (the palace), the North Platform, the South Platform and other places mentioned in this chapter. Drawing by John Klausmeyer.

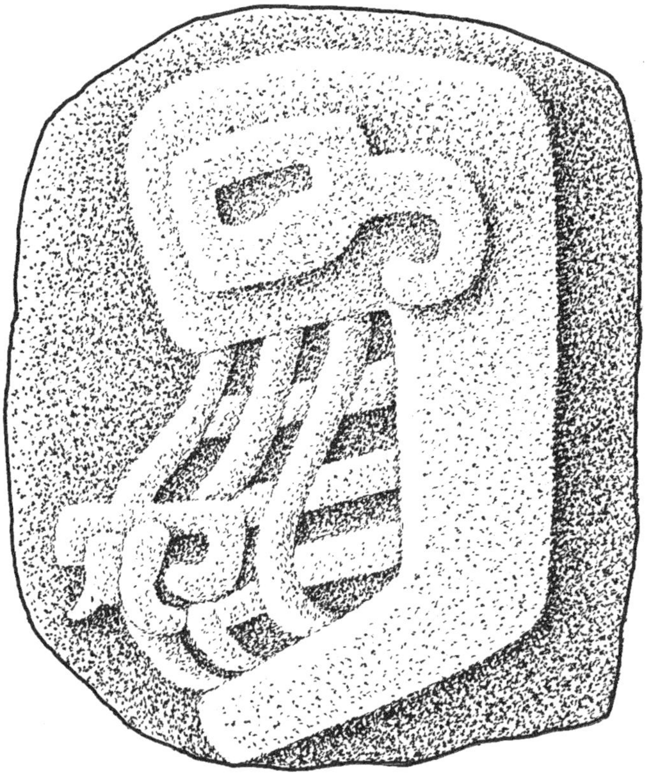

Figure 7.3. This relatively small and portable stone (40 x 33 cm), found on the North Platform at Monte Albán, shows a helmet with a grill or faceguard. This helmet is so similar to carvings at Dainzú that one might wonder whether this stone was brought from Dainzú to Monte Albán, or someone at Monte Albán copied it after seeing the carved boulders near the summit of the hill at Dainzú (see Chapter 8; see also Bernal and Seuffert 1979: Fig. 51; Caso 1969: Fig. 8; Scott 1978; Taube and Zender 2009: Fig. 7.4).

Challenges in Dating and Interpreting Out-of-Context Monuments

Many carved monuments at Monte Albán and other sites in Oaxaca were removed from their original settings. Slabs that had once been carefully arranged in Building L were reused elsewhere. When Caso (1947) and Scott (1978) studied the prisoner slabs, they noted that more than one carving technique had been used—some were bas-reliefs, some were incised, and some used other styles (see Chapter 6). They noted that the bas-reliefs occurred in Building L's first row. Given that most of the incised slabs were reused in later structures around the Main Plaza, it was difficult to determine whether all (or only some) of the incised slabs were coeval with the bas-relief sculptures still set in the lowest row of the gallery. Early on I suspected that the stylistic difference was not necessarily chronological, but may have resulted from the fact that multiple gangs of artisans needed to produce 300 prisoner carvings and to do so rapidly (see Chapter 6).

Although it is challenging to understand any narrative after the carved stones have been moved, visitors to the Main Plaza assume that even the reused stones were carved at Monte Albán itself. That is probably true, but one carved stone found in the North Platform could be an exception. That stone is reminiscent of the gladiators carved at Dainzú (a site near Tlacolula), who wore helmets with grills or faceguards (Figure 7.3) (see also Baudez 2011; Bernal 1967, 1968, 1973; Bernal and Oliveros 1988; Bernal and Seuffert 1973, 1979; Caso 1969: Figure 8; Oliveros 1997; Orr 1997, 2001, 2003; Scott 1978: Part II, N-33; Taube and Zender 2009).

It is notable that Stela 4 at Monte Albán was recarved. Its final resting place was the base of the South Platform, where it was set upright as an orthostat. Stela 4 had likely been used twice previously. It was probably carved on one of its narrow sides first and displayed in Building L; later, it was carved on one of its wide sides and perhaps displayed on the South Platform. Finally, it was re-set near the northeast corner of the South Platform. The reason this is likely is that on the narrow side of Stela 4, we see the incised and elongated figure of a captive that probably once graced Building L, along with similar stones (Figure 7.4). On a wider side of Stela 4, however, we see the carving of a warrior with a rope in his right hand and a lance in his left (Marcus 1992a: Figure 11.44).

Even more challenging than analyzing the reused monuments at Monte Albán is trying to analyze those monuments

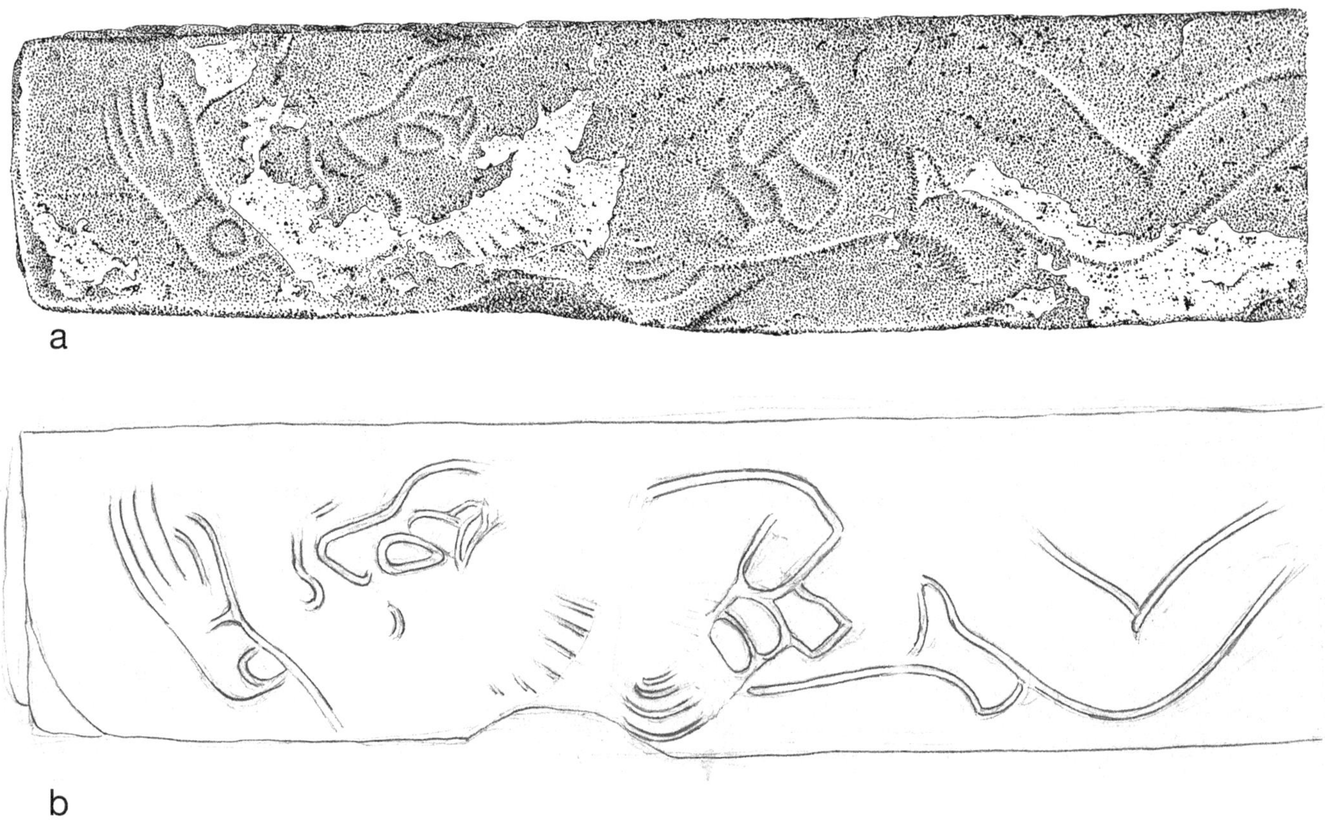

Figure 7.4. Two surfaces of Stela 4 at Monte Albán were carved on different occasions. The first carved surface is shown here in *a* and *b*: *a* is the finished drawing and *b* is Mark Orsen's in-the-field sketch. This carved surface shows a sacrificed captive like those in the Prisoner Gallery. The second surface, which was carved at a much later date, was displayed in the South Platform (see Chapter 9).

without provenience—for example, those no longer at actual archaeological sites (Figures 7.5–7.12). When nineteenth- and twentieth-century Oaxaca farmers encountered carved stones, they often hauled them to a local church, museum, residence, or other location. Scholars were then forced to speculate about the date of the carved stone as well as its original context (e.g., ballcourt, temple, platform façade, tomb, palace) and provenience (which archaeological site and which mound) (e.g., Bernal and Seuffert 1973; Caso 1928: Figures 92, 93, 94; Seler 1904b: Figures 69, 70).

Seler (1904b:298), for example, believed that a series of carved stones currently at Teotitlán del Valle (see Chapter 15) were once associated with buildings like the Period V structures at Mitla:

> nothing remains to-day [sic] of the magnificent buildings of the Zapotec Teotitlan del valle [sic], but portions of the ancient buildings, stone mosaics with geometric designs of the fashion of those of Mitla and fragments of reliefs are here and there found embedded in the walls of houses and churches in Teotitlan, as well as in those of the neighboring Macuilxochic.

While giving me a tour of Teotitlán del Valle, Ignacio Bernal suggested that some of the carved stones might well be earlier than Period V, all the while lamenting the fact that these monuments were no longer *in situ*. Although a Period V date seems likely—since the carvings show similarities to the stucco figures in Zaachila's Period V tombs—we cannot rule out an earlier date than Period V.

Once a stone has been removed from its stratigraphic context, it is difficult to date. Scholars often start by assessing its style. Style-dating can be a useful exercise, especially when a monument can be compared to others that are securely anchored by Long Count dates (e.g., Marcus 1984; Proskouriakoff 1950). Unlike the Maya, however, the Zapotec did not record Long Count dates calculated from a base date.

Had the Zapotec used a base date, we might be able to place out-of-context monuments in absolute time. Nevertheless, some scholars continue to date Zapotec stones by the style of the hieroglyphs and images. This procedure is unfortunately not reliable, since styles change at different rates and vary from region to region in the Valley of Oaxaca. The popularity and

Figure 7.5. This monument at Monte Albán (called P-2 by Scott 1978 and Stone 472 by García Moll et al. 1986: Lám. 177) was set in the palace called Building S. Given the plaster that was still evident near the base of the door jamb where this stone was set, it is possible that this monument was completely covered with plaster when it was reused as construction material. This stone (now broken) shows a crouching jaguar at upper left. In the upper right is the eroded name which may be read as 4 Chilla (4CC). The lower half of the stone combines a stairway and an animal figure; such a combination may specify a public building related to the crocodilian creature the Zapotec called Chilla. 63 x 62 x 36.5 cm.

staying power of certain themes and monument styles—as with pottery styles—varied from place to place (Flannery and Marcus 1994, 2005).

We can suggest some of the reasons why the Zapotec recycled stones:

(1) some carved stones lost their meaning and importance over time, and came to be seen as convenient, pre-cut stones for new constructions;

(2) other carved stones were removed from sight because they no longer met the political agendas of incoming rulers;

(3) old carvings might be reused because they were imbued with positive and sacred connotations;

(4) some carved stones were regarded as direct links to earlier reigns, helping to establish genealogical continuity (although archaeologists regard ancient reuse as a hindrance to contextual analysis, the Zapotec may have regarded reused stones as a link to earlier golden eras and an excellent way to re-sanctify a building);

(5) stones modified by carving may have been regarded as animate, as living and sacred items worth preserving; and

(6) some monuments may have been recarved to update their message (examples to be discussed in later chapters include the Tomb 104 door and the South Platform stelae).

In spite of the limitations inherent in analyzing stones recycled in secondary and tertiary contexts, there are ways to glean information about their original meaning and context. By measuring a reused stone, one can make an educated guess about whether it was designed as a lintel, a jamb, a step, a door, or a stela. From the layout, content, iconography, and measurements, we can sometimes infer its earlier use.

Motivations for Commissioning New Sculptures

Every ruler who commissioned new monuments with hieroglyphs had a message to convey or an event worth commemorating. From all the possible themes a ruler could record, he selected some and omitted others. His monuments could include recent events,

Figure 7.6. This unprovenienced genealogical register may have been carved at El Palmillo. In the lower register is a probable marital pair named Lady 10 Deer and Lord 1N or 6N. In the upper register we see a marital pair named Lady 3L and Lord 1 (possibly 1 Monkey). Both women seem to hold baskets, while the men seem to offer copal or rubber balls for burning in the brazier between each couple (Marcus 2008b: Fig. XIII.1). At the top of the monument is the Jaws of the Sky motif with associated leaves. Descending from the jaws is a masked ancestor who seems to offer a string of beads. Height: 51 cm. (Catalog # 30.3/1211-12, the American Museum of Natural History, New York.)

Figure 7.7 (left). This genealogical register was called "Lápida 2" of the Museo Nacional de Antropología by Alfonso Caso (1928: Fig. 82; see also Dieseldorff 1933: Abb. 91; Paddock 1966b: Plate 283). In the upper register we see the Jaws of the Sky; above that we see possible tobacco leaves and T-shaped "figuras almenadas" that Caso interpreted as clouds. At left in the upper register is a woman named 1 Deer who presents a vessel to the man named 2 Serpent. The lower register seems to show another pair, but given the break in the stone (at left) we can see only the name of the man on the right, which might be interpreted as 6 Jaguar. 55 x 31 x 4 cm.

Figure 7.8 (below). Two views of a San Lorenzo Cacaotepec monument: *a* shows an in-the-field sketch; *b* shows the finished drawing. We see a reference to 3 + a skull and a series of scrolls and eyes. This fragment was reused and incorporated into a twentieth-century building. Drawing by Mark Orsen.

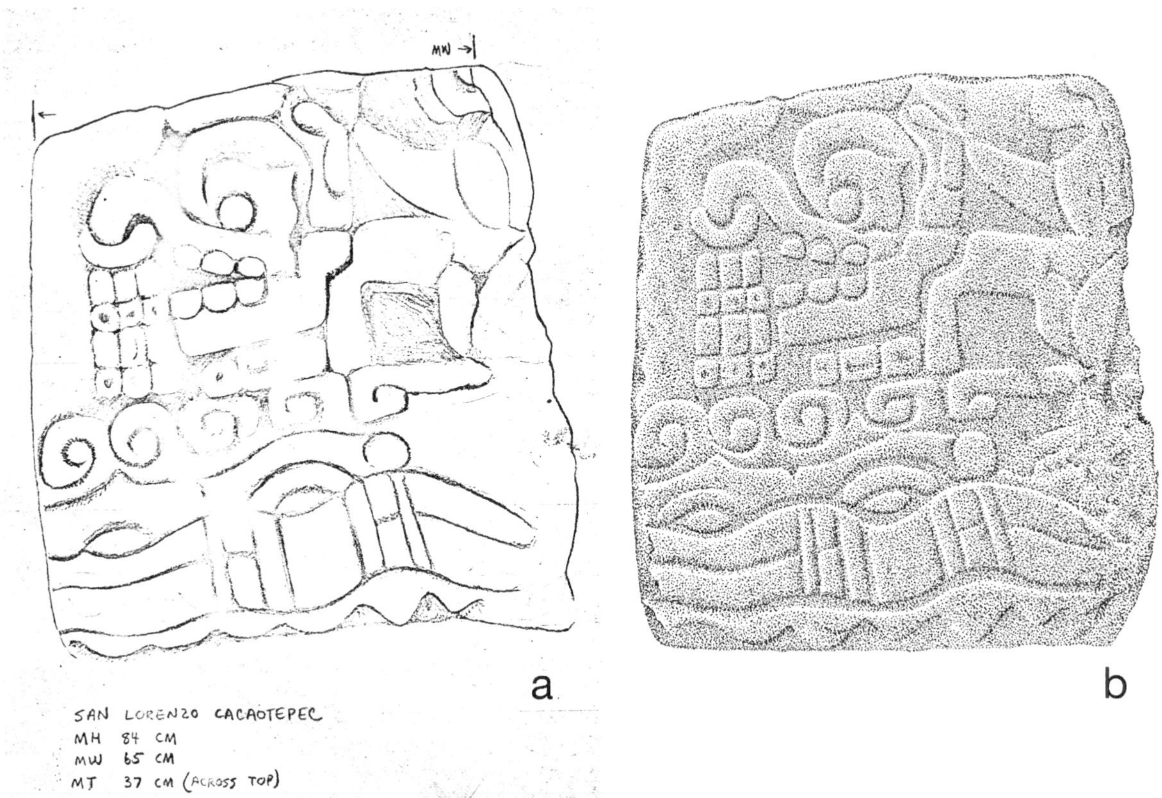

Figure 7.9. This unprovenienced fragment seems to show two people performing a ritual below a simplified version of the Jaws of the Sky. The woman (at left) faces a figure that is likely a man seated cross-legged; we can see his feathered headdress and speech scroll. A trilobal element seems to float between their outstretched hands. This is an in-the-field sketch by Mark Orsen.

Figure 7.10. This unprovenienced monument shows a bird on the roof of a structure (drawing by Mark Orsen; see also Bernal and Méndez 1974: Fig. 25). It has been housed in the Frissell Museum of Zapotec Art in Mitla for at least 50 years.

Figure 7.11. This monument was one of several carved stones commissioned to form a narrative that was probably once displayed across the façade of a Period V building at Teotitlán del Valle (see Chapter 17) (see also Seler 1904b; Rickards 1910). This in-the-field sketch was drawn by Mark Orsen.

Figure 7.12. This monument was labeled Stone 23 by Bernal and Seuffert (1973:19-20). It is currently set in the wall of the *campanario de la iglesia* at Macuilxóchitl. Since this monument was carved on two sides, both surfaces can only be seen when the stone is displayed in the corner of a building, as shown here. On one carved surface (at right) we see 6 Jaguar; on the other (at left) a year sign. Width: 0.95 m. Arranged by John Klausmeyer.

revisionist history, or exaggeration. No politician, whether in antiquity or in modern times, chose to emphasize his failures. He chose to present successes and, when necessary, embellished the truth to place himself in the best possible light. In speaking of the Classic Maya, for example, Martin and Grube (2008:123) note that Maya rulers engaged in "the usual boasting and self-aggrandizement."

That ancient rulers were not always committed to full factual accuracy should not be shocking to today's historians or political scientists. For their part, art historians long ago noted that some of the pharaohs of ancient Egypt were depicted many times greater than life-size, and frequently referred to themselves as gods; in contrast, war captives alongside these giant pharaohs were shown as tiny figures (see Figures 2.3–2.4). Such artistic license was effective because its overall goal was to show the political power that pharaohs had over ordinary men.

In addition to such artistic license, ancient rulers exaggerated their accomplishments. Many claimed exotic origins or divine descent—especially usurpers and those not in direct line of succession (Marcus 1992 a, b, c). The result is that Mesoamerican sculpture and writing—whether Maya, Mixtec, or Aztec—was a mixture of history and myth, accuracy and exaggeration designed to influence different audiences. The texts were the rulers' version of history. Recarving and recycling the monuments of earlier rulers were often part of revising that history.

Part III

The Spread of Writing after the Formation of the Monte Albán State

8

State Formation and Territorial Expansion

The Aztec and the Inca, two of the New World's largest empires, both evolved from preexisting states (Bauer 2004; Berdan et al. 1996, 2003; Flannery and Marcus 2012; Rostworowski and Morris 1999; Smith and Berdan 2003; Townsend 1992). They were the end result of four or five generations of prehispanic states, each learning from and relying on previously established templates. We have eyewitness descriptions of the Aztec and Inca, but neither can tell us how the first state in the region formed. The state centered at Monte Albán can, since it was a first-generation state.

Like other first-generation states, the Monte Albán state arose in the context of competing rank societies whose chiefs possessed no template for a kingdom. Detecting this new social type from the archaeological record can be a challenge because its features do not appear all at once, but sequentially. We often detect a state only after most (or all) of its features have coalesced. Nevertheless, significant progress has been made over the last 50 years in developing a set of criteria to demonstrate that a state has emerged. One criterion was established in southwestern Iran, where Wright and Johnson (1975) showed that the first state had a four-tiered administrative hierarchy whose upper three tiers had administrative functions. This four-tiered hierarchy emerged when one of a group of competing rank societies succeeded in subjugating its rivals, each of which already had a three-tiered hierarchy. These hierarchies were discovered by (1) conducting full-coverage survey, (2) constructing a histogram of site sizes in hectares, and (3) plotting the four modes of site size (one city at the top; then several towns; then a series of large villages; then a large number of small villages). Administrative artifacts such as seal impressions in clay (created when containers of commodities were sealed by officials) were found at sites of all sizes; the seals from which the impressions were made occurred mainly at the cities and towns where the administrators lived.

Johnson (1972, 1973) showed that some Early Dynastic cities in Iraq had regularly spaced lattices of lower-order sites around the higher-order administrative cities and towns. Early Maya states also had site-size hierarchies with hexagonal lattices of secondary sites that formed around the capitals to which they were subordinate (e.g., Marcus 1973, 1976d, 2008a, 2008b, 2012). Billman (1999) and Wilson (1988) showed that four-tiered hierarchies appeared in Peru's Moche and Santa valleys, respectively, during the first stages of state formation.

In the Valley of Oaxaca, Kowalewski et al.'s (1989) full-coverage survey has revealed a four-tiered site-size hierarchy as well as lattices of regularly spaced subordinate centers by the first century AD (Marcus and Flannery 1996:173–175). A complementary approach was taken by Charles Spencer (1998), who adapted an equation from the literature on predation to develop a mathematical model for state formation. Spencer showed that early state formation, of necessity, required territorial expansion. Spencer and Redmond (2004a) then provided archaeological evidence for the step-by-step creation of the early Zapotec state, bringing Zapotec state formation in line with other cases of first-generation states (e.g., Algaze 1993a, 1993b; Flannery 1998; Flannery and Marcus 2012; Marcus 1998b, 2008a).

The Oaxaca Case

Between 600 and 500 BC the Valley of Oaxaca was divided among at least three chiefdoms, with their paramount centers at San José Mogote, Yegüih, and San Martín Tilcajete (Figure 8.1). Rivalry among these centers was intense, with San José Mogote having to recover from having its major temple burned. Perhaps in response, San José Mogote carved a stone monument (Monument 3) that depicted a sacrificed rival. That chiefly rival was important enough to have his hieroglyphic name appear on his monument (see Chapter 6). Early scholars like V. Gordon Childe (1950) never imagined that writing could *precede* the first state by 600 years, as was the case with Monument 3 of San José Mogote.

At roughly 500 BC perhaps 2000 people from San José Mogote and its satellite villages moved to a more defensible location—the summit of a 400 meter-high mountain now called Monte Albán (Blanton 1978, 1983; Flannery and Marcus 2003; Spencer and Redmond 2003, 2004a, 2004b, 2006). Between 500 and 300 BC nearly a third of the valley's population lived at Monte Albán; many of them had come from San José Mogote and the Etla subvalley.

Less than a day's journey to the south of Monte Albán lay Tilcajete, a major rival. Tilcajete's response to the founding of Monte Albán was to double its size (from 25 ha to 52.8 ha); its elite laid out a ceremonial plaza with an astronomical orientation deliberately chosen to contrast with Monte Albán's (Redmond and Spencer 2013, 2017; Spencer and Redmond 2004a, 2004b, 2005). At roughly 330 BC Tilcajete was attacked by Monte Albán. Tilcajete refused to capitulate; instead, it attracted supporters and grew to 71.5 ha. Its leaders moved its ceremonial center to a more defensible ridge, defiantly retaining the same astronomical orientation and investing in the construction of defensive walls. In response to Tilcajete's behavior, Monte Albán concentrated thousands of farmers, artisans, and warriors in 155 satellite villages.

Not long after 300 BC, Monte Albán aimed its predatory campaign elsewhere, conquering less-powerful polities such as those in Cuicatlán (Spencer 1982, 1990, 1998; Spencer and Redmond 1997, 2001a). At roughly 30 BC Monte Albán attacked Tilcajete again, burning its ruler's palatial residence and temple. Tilcajete did not recover from this attack; it was abandoned. Then, on a mountaintop near Tilcajete, the victorious rulers of Monte Albán installed an administrative center that would be subordinate to them (Elson 2007). This new center shared Monte Albán's astronomical orientation.

What resulted from this victory over Tilcajete (and other sites) was a Zapotec state with a king, a queen, architects, scribes, full-time priests, and other specialized personnel. Accompanying the appearance of the palace, temple, ballcourt, and state-sponsored institutions, we see territorial expansion, the spread of Monte Albán's Period Ic and II graywares, shifts in settlement location in subjugated regions, and even the use of terror tactics (Redmond 1983; Sherman et al. 2010; Spencer et al. 2008). Such territorial expansion, warfare, and captive taking were vital components of the earliest state formation (e.g., R. McC. Adams 1966; Adams and Nissen 1972; Algaze 1993a, 1993b; Carneiro 1970; González Licón 2003; Hirth and Angulo Villaseñor 1981; Marcus 1976a, 1992c, 2008a, 2012; Marcus and Flannery 1996; Redmond 1983; Spencer 1982, 1998, 2007, 2009, 2010, 2019; Spencer and Redmond 2003, 2004a, 2006; Spencer et al. 2008).

Hirth and Angulo Villaseñor (1981:135) note a similar expansion of Teotihuacán, another first-generation state. Its expansion led to a pan-Mesoamerican network aimed at controlling key resources. Teotihuacán initially expanded into areas occupied by less hierarchical societies, but the diversity of these societies probably made it difficult for Teotihuacán to consolidate them into a cohesive bureaucratic system (Hirth and Angulo Villaseñor 1981:149).

With state emergence in Oaxaca the use of Zapotec hieroglyphs increased, as did the number of different hieroglyphs. At this time Monte Albán had a near-monopoly on writing and was one of the few sites that used place signs; indeed, Monte Albán displayed most of their place signs in Building J. The co-evolution of the Zapotec state and the appearance of so many new place names clustered in one building are noteworthy. During Period II (1 BC–AD 250), the Zapotec state extended its influence throughout the Valley of Oaxaca and beyond (Balkansky 1997, 1998a, 1998b, 1999, 2002; Brockington et al. 1974; Feinman and Nicholas 1990, 1993; Gaxiola 1976; Redmond 1983; Redmond and Spencer 1983, 2006; Spencer 1982, 1990, 1998, 2003, 2007, 2009, 2010, 2019; Spencer and Redmond 1997, 2001a, 2003, 2004a, 2006; Spencer et al. 2008).

The influence of the new state and its capital took many forms. Valley of Oaxaca pottery was traded to and emulated by people living outside the valley; in at least one subjugated region, a skull rack was set up by Monte Albán to terrorize the local population; and it is likely that tribute was exacted and prisoners taken (Flannery and Marcus 2012; Hirth and Angulo Villaseñor 1981; Joyce 1991, 2003, 2013, 2014; Joyce et al. 2006; Marcus 1976a, 1980; Marcus and Flannery 1996; Redmond and Spencer 2006; Spencer 1982; Spencer and Redmond 1997; Workinger and Joyce 2009; Zeitlin and Joyce 1999).

State Expansion and the Increased Use of the Hill Sign on Building J

Among other things, state formation required territorial expansion to increase the number of followers and laborers (e.g., Algaze

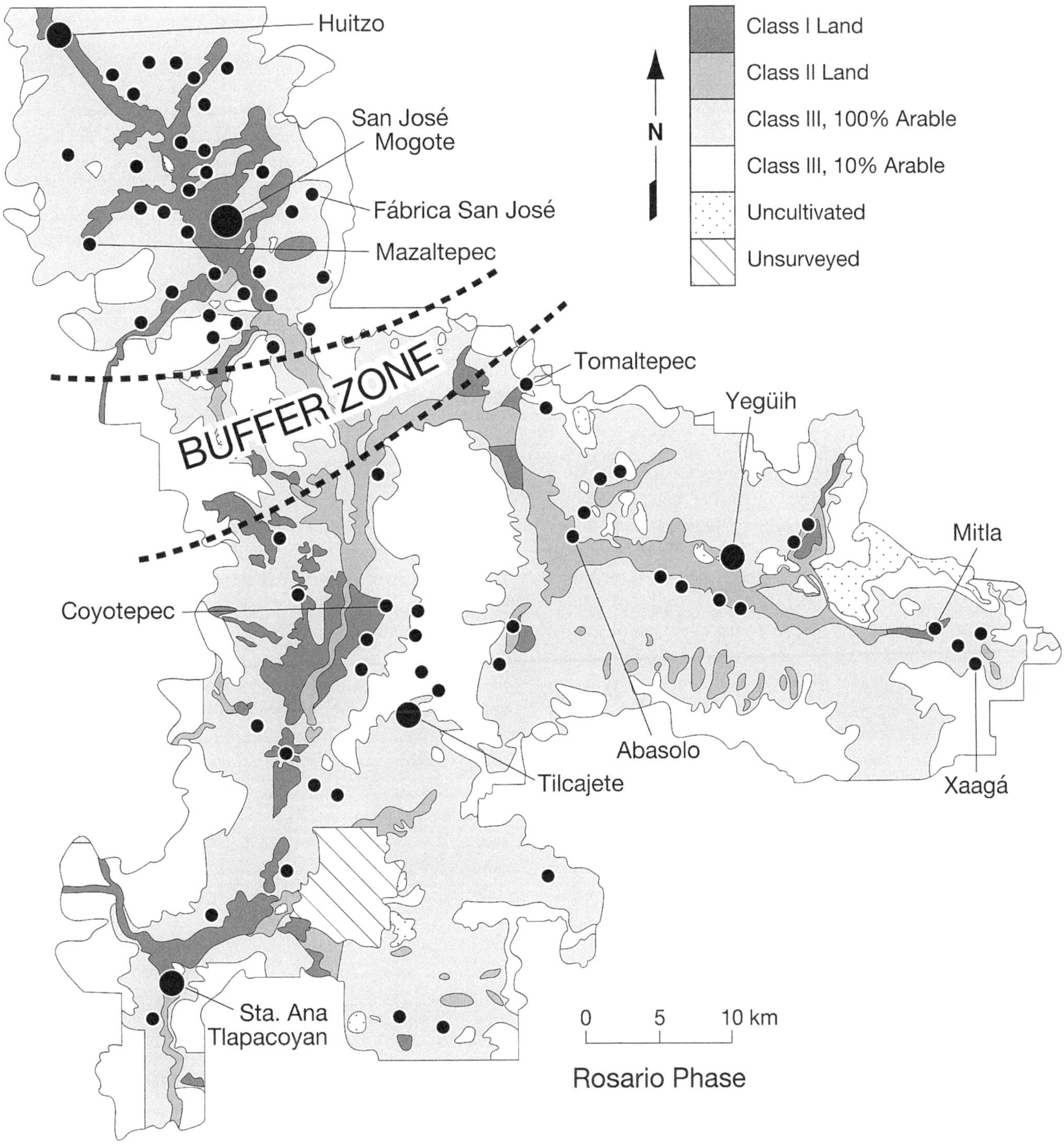

Figure 8.1. Between 600 and 500 BC the Valley of Oaxaca was divided among at least three chiefdoms, whose paramount centers were located at San José Mogote, Yegüih, and San Martín Tilcajete. Rivalry among these three centers was so intense that a buffer zone existed between them. Drawing by John Klausmeyer.

1993a, 1993b; Marcus 1992c; Marcus and Flannery 1996; Spencer 1998). Those groups could construct standardized buildings to house state personnel and supply nonlocal resources to foment additional expansion by Monte Albán. The subjugation of peoples and towns elevated Monte Albán to the top of what became a four-tiered administrative hierarchy.

Ethnic groups outside the valley—those smaller and less powerful—actually proved easier to subjugate than Monte Albán's major rivals within the Valley of Oaxaca (e.g., Spencer 1990, 2007, 2010; Spencer and Redmond 1997). By AD 200 the Monte Albán state had achieved some degree of hegemony over people outside the Valley of Oaxaca, but the area controlled was not a contiguous bloc; there were unincorporated pockets of resistance. Too little excavation has been conducted at Tier 2 and Tier 3 sites—both inside and outside the Valley of Oaxaca—to assess how specific places reacted to Monte Albán's imperialism.

The leaders of the Zapotec state lived at Monte Albán, and over time they supervised specialized personnel, including architects, artists, and stone carvers who created impressive building façades with carved stones. Columns of Period II hieroglyphs, especially from Building J of Monte Albán, tended to be longer than those seen earlier on Building L.

Caso (1947, 1965a, 1965b) was the first to study Building J's slabs, which he called *lápidas de conquista* ("conquest slabs") because each supplied the name of a subjugated place. Since Caso's 1947 pioneering study, others have offered divergent interpretations. I have viewed the Building J slabs as (1) recording subjugated places, some of which lie at the limits of Monte Albán's territorial control, and (2) presenting two types of subject polities—some that resisted and were incorporated by force, and others that submitted peacefully or diplomatically. Urcid and Joyce (2014) have suggested that the Building J slabs refer to individuals or to neighborhoods within Monte Albán; and Carter (2017) has noted that the Building J texts have not been fully deciphered. I continue to agree with Caso and others that they are conquest slabs, since (1) the heads of defeated lords are shown upside down with closed eye, a convention for dead individuals; (2) the city of Xochicalco in Morelos produced a similar list of subjugated polities; and (3) the later Maya, Mixtec, and Aztec recorded the places they subjugated. Those facts make Building J an example of a widespread process, rather than a phenomenon unique to Monte Albán.

It should be noted that Zapotec writing was confined to the Valley of Oaxaca during Period I. With territorial expansion during Period II, Zapotec writing began to appear at other sites within the valley as well as sites outside the valley (Caso and Gamio 1961; Gaxiola 1976; Marcus 1983h, 2002). In other words, the spread of writing co-occurred with state expansion, following the appearance of the earliest palace and king, the emergence of specialized personnel, and a fourth level in the political hierarchy. By plotting on a map several attributes—monuments with Zapotec hieroglyphs, Monte Albán-style pottery (both locally made and imported), Oaxaca-style tombs, daub from burned houses, and the use of terror tactics—we can begin to see the extent of Zapotec influence on communities outside the valley.

Challenges in Identifying Place Names

Documenting subordination has been easier in the Maya area than the Zapotec area because subordinate sites (e.g., Tier 2 and Tier 3) mentioned the names of the Maya rulers to whom they owed allegiance (Marcus 1976d). In turn, some of the Maya rulers at Tier 1 sites mentioned the names of lords they defeated (e.g., Berlin 1958; Marcus 1973, 1974, 1976d, 1992a, 1992b, 2012; Martin and Grube 2008). The presence of Maya "emblem glyphs" (which combine the title "divine lord" with a site name) in the texts of both Tier 1 *and* Tier 2 sites facilitates the identification of hegemonic relationships. We currently know the emblem glyphs of a few dozen Maya sites, including Palenque, Tikal, Calakmul, Copán, Quiriguá, Seibal, Caracol, Naranjo, Yaxchilan, Piedras Negras, and Toniná. Confirming subjugation, of course, requires multiple lines of evidence; simply stated, epigraphy is not enough (Feinman and Marcus 1998; Marcus 2008a, Marcus and Flannery 1996).

In the Maya region, lords at Tier 2 sites reported that they were serving kings who administered Tier 1 sites. For example, at AD 655 the ruler of Dos Pilas (Tier 2) asserted that he owed allegiance to, and was subordinate to, the ruler of Calakmul (Tier 1). Other Maya lords claimed that they were installed in office (at their Tier 2 site) by a Tier 1 king. The Maya area is exceptional in having abundant hieroglyphic data from Tier 2 and Tier 3 communities. In contrast, many claims made by the Aztec king of Tenochtitlán regarding which towns were subject to him have yet to be fully confirmed, simply because we lack hieroglyphic texts from the subject towns and provinces.

Oaxaca presents formidable challenges to reconstructing such hierarchies and hegemonies. Of the many issues, I would emphasize the following five: (1) The Zapotec lacked the Long Count, so we do not have exact dates to document decade by decade changes in hierarchies. (2) The hieroglyphic name of Monte Albán is not known, although there are several viable candidates. (3) Monte Albán had a virtual monopoly on the use of Zapotec writing during Periods I and II, which means that few subordinate sites could have mentioned Monte Albán on their monuments. (4) Smaller sites in Oaxaca (e.g., Tier 2, 3, or 4 sites) rarely used place names, even in later times such as Period IIIb–IV. (5) Many of Oaxaca's current town names were imposed by the Spaniards or the Aztec, and are not the names the Zapotec would have used during Periods I and II.

Had subordinate sites in the State of Oaxaca recorded their own Zapotec names *and* recorded the name of the capital (Monte Albán), our work would be much easier. Unfortunately, we have to employ other methods to detect the timing and nature of each province's incorporation into the Zapotec state (e.g., Redmond 1983; Redmond and Spencer 1983; Spencer and Redmond 2001a, 2001b, 2003; Spencer et al. 2008). Evidence for incorporation might include (1) deciphering the names of the polities mentioned on Building J; (2) documenting which polities received an influx of Valley of Oaxaca graywares during Period Ic/II, or began to produce local imitations of Caso et al.'s (1967) Type G-12 and other Monte Albán pottery types; and (3) evidence of burning, violent attacks, terror tactics, and defensive features such as ditches, palisades, and walls (e.g., Marcus and Flannery 1996:205; Redmond 1983, 1994; Spencer 1982, 2007, 2009; Spencer and Redmond 1997, 2005, 2006; Spencer et al. 2008).

Evidence of violence can take the form of burned temples and palaces, skull racks, trophy skulls, mass graves, and burned palisades. Evidence of emulation or placement of a colony of nonlocal people might include the construction of houses and tombs that echo the style of the conquering society, or the sudden appearance of numerous imported vessels (e.g., Pareyón Moreno 1960). Multiple lines of evidence are what every archaeologist needs in order to confirm the names of both the superordinate and subordinate center.

Evidence of violent takeover is often the most compelling evidence, but the duration of any period of subjugation is very difficult to determine without texts that supply Long Count dates. Extensive excavations at Tier 2 and 3 sites often reveal circumstantial evidence of incorporation, resistance, emulation, and cooperation (Marcus 1992a, 1992b; Spencer and Redmond 2006). Not every subject town or province, however, had to be subdued by force. Some provinces were simply colonized, while others were incorporated via marriage alliances or political accords (e.g., Balkansky 2002; Feinman and Marcus 1998; Feinman and Nicholas 1990, 1993; Flannery and Marcus 2012; Marcus and Flannery 1996).

The place glyphs on Building J seem to record two pathways to incorporating subjects—by peaceful means or by military takeover. Building J slabs that include an inverted human head below the hill sign probably imply a defeated rival (Caso 1947). Slabs that lack an inverted head may imply that some means other than military conquest brought about incorporation. Examples of such alternatives abound in Mexico. In speaking of the Aztec Empire, for example, Isaac (1983:129) notes that nonbelligerent communities were permitted to submit peacefully as tributaries, while rebellious communities were attacked ferociously and repeatedly.

Building J at Monte Albán

Building J is shaped like an arrowhead (Figure 8.2). Its alignment does not follow the north-south orientation of the other buildings in the Main Plaza, which convey a sense of symmetry, planning, and order. Caso (1947:20) was among the first to call attention to this unusual orientation, noting that Building J was oriented NE-SW.

Caso (1938:11) assumed that Building J's unusual alignment had something to do with its function (Figure 8.3). He noted that while all the other buildings nearby had their axes oriented toward the cardinal points, Mound J had its stairway facing northeast, with the back of the structure ending in a point. Building J also had tunnels that penetrated the structure. Based on these attributes, Caso (1938:10) suggested that Building J might have been used for astronomical observations. Building J was, in fact, labeled an "Observatory" on the Monte Albán map in the *Handbook of Middle American Indians* (Acosta 1965:815). Unusual structures in other parts of Mesoamerica have typically been called observatories based on their orientation (e.g., Aveni and Linsley 1972; Dow 1967; Fuson 1969; Macgowan 1945; Marquina 1951, 1964; Peeler and Winter 1992, 1995).

Labeling Building J an observatory continued for decades prior to any testing of that assertion. In January 1971, Anthony Aveni and Robert Linsley mapped Building J and concluded that "an observer looking out of the doorway of the temple atop Mound J would have been able to view Capella rising directly in front of him. Capella was unique among the bright stars at this time since it underwent heliacal rising on or about the same day as the sun underwent the first of 2 annual passages through the zenith of Monte Albán" (Aveni and Linsley 1972:529). They went on to say, "If the deliberate disorientation of the front of Mound J relative to the other buildings at Monte Albán was astronomically motivated, we regard the phenomenon of the heliacal rising of Capella on the day of the passage of the sun as a possible cause for that motivation." Aveni and Linsley presented this explanation as no more than one possibility, since the building's orientation might have nothing to do with the stars. In addition, the correlation with Capella was based on an old, uncalibrated radiocarbon date of 275 BC, a date that now seems far too early for Period II.

Aveni and Linsley found no astronomical significance for the tunnels in Building J, despite Marquina's (1951) assumption that a tunnel could have served as a viewing location. Since most temples at Monte Albán were oriented east-west, an alternative explanation for Building J's alignment is that it was a *secular* building—one that tells us more about territorial expansion than astronomy.

The Incised Slabs of Building J

In contrast to the bas-relief slabs of Period I, some Period II slabs were incised. Both Periods I and II featured columns of hieroglyphs, but those of Period II were often longer and included several new signs.

Caso (1947:21–28) was the first to call the Building J stones *lápidas de conquista* or "conquest slabs." He suggested that (1) each slab commemorated the name of a place conquered by Monte Albán and (2) all the slabs naming the conquered places were originally displayed in Building J. (Various construction stages of Building J included reused slabs depicting slain sacrificial victims, presumably "borrowed" from Building L, suggesting that the Building L Prisoner Gallery narrative was no longer important enough to keep intact.) Many Building J slabs are eroded, with approximately 40 of the conquest slabs in good shape and another

a

b

Figure 8.2. Here we see two views of Building J, an arrowhead-shaped building located in Monte Albán's Main Plaza. (*a*) This is how Building J looked in the 1930s, when many stones had fallen from its walls; from this photo we can appreciate what a huge challenge Caso faced in his efforts to reconstruct the building. (*b*) This is how Building J looked in the 1980s, after Caso had incorporated many of the loose stones he encountered. The consolidated building, however, did not absorb all. Many of the Building J stones still lie nearby. (*a*, courtesy of Ignacio Bernal; *b*, photo by the author)

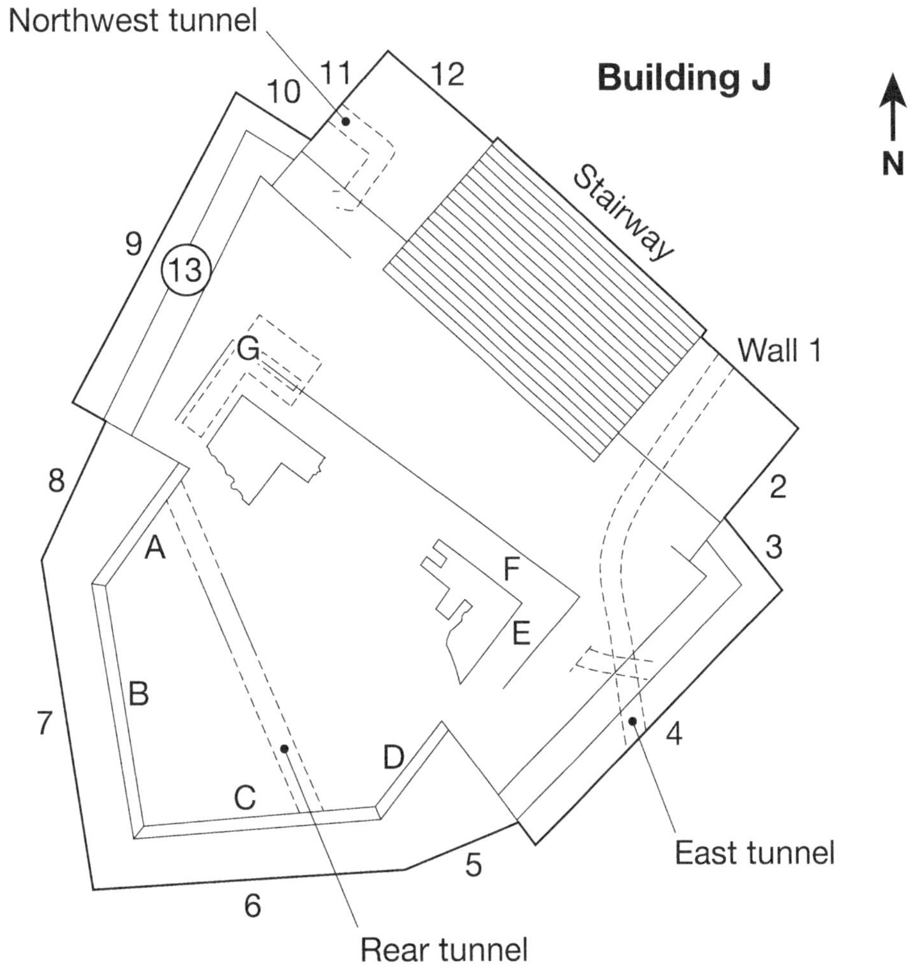

Figure 8.3. This plan reveals how unusual Building J was in its alignment, tunnels, and multiple walls and construction stages. The numbers 1–13 label the walls at the plaza level; the letters A–G label the upper walls. Caso (1947:20–21) was the first to emphasize Building J's complex construction history, noting that only the stones at the lowest level seemed to be *in situ*. He recognized that many stones from Building L had been incorporated into Building J's different construction stages. He was the first to note that most of the Period II stones in Building J were "conquest slabs" commemorating places that Monte Albán claimed to have subjugated. Adapted by John Klausmeyer from Mark Orsen's field plan.

20 or so in more fragmentary and eroded condition. This estimate gives us a total of more than 60 that once formed a narrative program on the walls of Building J.

It is worth noting that while Monte Albán was the first Mesoamerican city to display a list of subject places, it was not the last. The Pyramid of the Plumed Serpent at Xochicalco (discussed below) seems to display a similar list of tribute-paying provinces (Berlo 1989; Hirth 1989). Xochicalco, however, did not distinguish between those that were subdued by force and those that were not.

Does the fact that Building J featured subjugated places mean that it had no astronomical function? Not necessarily. Consider that in Mesoamerica, war and its timing were often affected by heavenly bodies. This was the case, for example, with the Maya (Freidel et al. 1993; Schele and Freidel 1990). The Maya closely followed the movement of the planet Venus, and some of their military battles were timed to coincide with various phases of the planet's cycle. Thus war and astronomy were not unrelated (e.g., Freidel et al. 1993; Lounsbury 1978, 1988; Thompson 1950).

Building J's Analogy with Xochicalco (AD 600–900)

An interesting analogy with Monte Albán's Building J is provided by the Pyramid of the Plumed Serpent at Xochicalco. The latter building has been interpreted as a war memorial, depicting warriors with shields and darts and listing provinces that paid tribute to Xochicalco (Figure 8.4). Hirth (1989:73) views the carved friezes

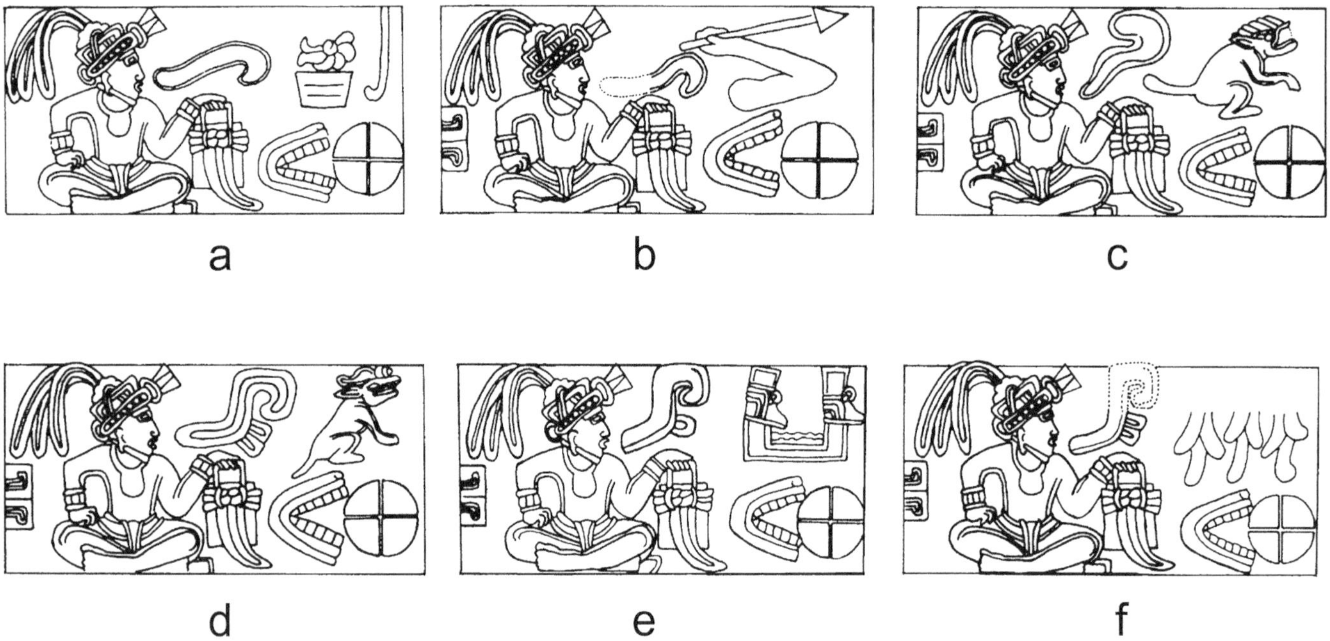

Figure 8.4. The building called the Pyramid of the Plumed Serpent at Xochicalco displays a series of friezes that show evidence of militarism, place names, and tribute. Its militaristic iconography included twelve armed warriors on the upper walls, and below them (as shown here) a series of seated figures, each associated with a place name and a tribute glyph. At least seven of the twenty-eight Xochicalco toponyms are identifiable. The six places illustrated here are *a*, Xochitopilan; *b*, Miacatlan; *c*, Cuetzpalan; *d*, Coyoacan; *e*, Panohuayan; and *f*, a place too eroded to interpret. Below each place name are two hieroglyphs interpreted by Hirth as tribute—a jaw biting a circle that may represent a disk of chocolate. Drawing by John Klausmeyer.

on the pyramid as a demonstration that Xochicalco's militarism was intended to create a tribute-paying conquest state. Toponyms on the building suggest that Xochicalco's conquest domain extended from Morelos north into the Ajusco Mountains (on the border of the Basin of Mexico) as well as south and west to the Mixteca Baja and the Balsas Depression. Hirth (1989) and Berlo (1989) have interpreted two of the place glyphs as Tlamacazapa (Figure 8.5a) and Panohuayan (Figure 8.5b). Accompanying the place glyphs is Xochicalco's symbol for tribute, which consists of human upper and lower jaws biting a circular disk of chocolate; incisions divide the disk into quadrants (see Berlo 1989; Hirth 1989). Similar disks of chocolate are still made in Mexico.

Militaristic iconography at Xochicalco included twelve armed warriors on the upper walls of the Pyramid of the Plumed Serpent. Below them was a series of seated figures, each associated with a place name and the tribute glyph. Seven of the twenty-eight toponyms (including the two already mentioned) can be identified (Berlo 1989; Hirth 1989). Six of these appeared on the north wall, where nineteenth-century photographs show the original façade to have been well preserved (Peñafiel 1890).

The Pyramid of the Plumed Serpent at Xochicalco was built at least six centuries after Building J at Monte Albán. Nevertheless, these two public buildings display similar types of vertical political propaganda. Both Monte Albán and Xochicalco were built on fortified hills that had to be modified to create terraces, plazas, and monumental buildings. Both cities were interested in recording military successes, listing subject provinces, and making declarations about the extent of their territory. Monte Albán seemingly distinguished between military and political incorporation; Xochicalco made it clear that tribute was involved (Hirth 1989).

The Creation of Architectural Programs

Like the hundreds of carved stones that once formed the Prisoner Gallery of Building L, Building J's conquest slabs were once arranged to create an impressive display. All the Building J slabs are similar in style; those that include inverted heads show all the heads facing the same direction (Figure 8.6). In other words, the slabs display the kind of overall planning that also went into the Building L gallery, where prisoners in the same row all faced the same direction. The principal difference between the two buildings is that the emphasis had shifted from naming defeated individuals (Period I) to naming subjugated places (Period II).

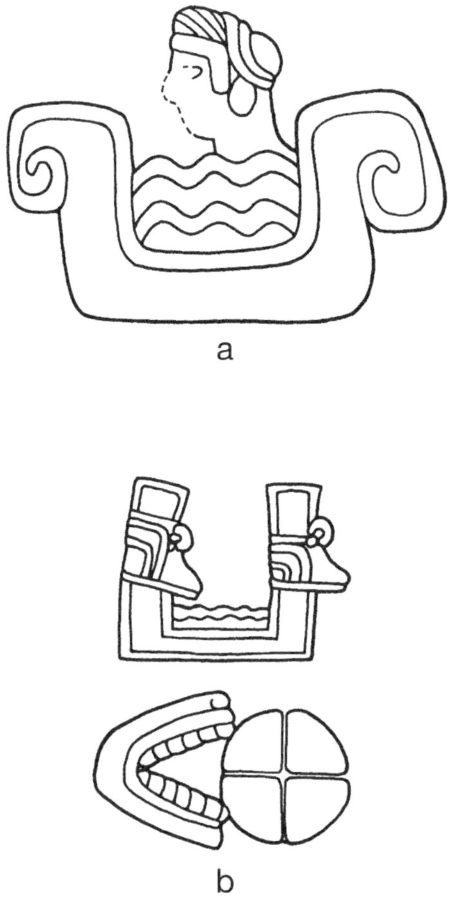

Figure 8.5. Here we see two of the twenty-eight subjugated places listed on the Pyramid of the Plumed Serpent at Xochicalco. Kenneth Hirth and Janet Berlo have interpreted these two place glyphs as (a) Tlamacazapa and (b) Panohuayan. Accompanying the Panohuayan place glyph is the symbol for tribute—a human jaw biting a circle divided into quadrants. Drawing by John Klausmeyer.

This is a change we might expect as a result of the evolution from early state formation to imperial expansion.

The Components of a Conquest Slab

Caso (1947:21) was the first to identify the four principal components of a conquest slab:

First, a stereotyped hill sign meaning "hill of" or "place of";

Second, one or more glyphs above the hill sign that specified the place name;

Third (on some slabs), an inverted human head that symbolized the leader of a defeated locality;

Fourth (on some slabs), hieroglyphs including a year sign, a year bearer, and noncalendric glyphs.

The inverted human heads all face the same direction and have their eyes closed, suggesting that they are deceased. Each upside-down head wears a unique hairstyle, headdress, or cap; this may link that deceased leader to a specific region. Many of the heads also display distinctive facial paint or tattoos.

In other words, places that had to be subdued by conquest were identified in two ways: *in writing*, by the hieroglyphs located above the hill sign, and *iconographically*, by the distinctive headgear, hairdo, and facial markings on the upside-down head.

Because the conquest slabs share a similar layout and were incised in the same style, it follows that they were originally grouped as part of one large display. At the top of Building J is an edifice that Caso (1947) called a temple, but he was unsure whether that structure dated to the same era as the conquest slabs. The available data suggest that it postdated the carving of the conquest slabs.

The Hill Sign

Let us now look at the "hill" or "place" sign. It includes (1) two vertical projections that resemble the arms of a cactus, (2) notches or incised lines at the base of each projection, (3) two or three diagonal lines in the interior of the hill sign, and (4) paired circles or figure eights to either side of the diagonal lines (Figure 8.7).

Although the hill sign made its first appearance in Period I (Stela 15, last sign in the right column), it did not become common until Period II. There it became a geographical referent, although it is not always clear whether it refers to a natural landmark, a town, or an entire province, or serves as a locative determinative

Figure 8.6. The 25 heads shown here were all carved on Building J conquest slabs at Monte Albán, where they were displayed upside down below the hill sign. It is noteworthy that all heads face the same direction, suggesting that all the slabs originally formed a planned narrative. Caso (1947:27) identified three major elements on conquest slabs: (1) upside-down heads (shown here); (2) hill signs (signifying "place of"); and (3) place specifiers (above the hill sign). He noted that the eye was usually closed (*el ojo del muerto*), signifying that the local lord was dead. Caso noted that each head differed in hairdo, headgear, or facial markings. Like the hundreds of carved stones that once formed Building L's Prisoner Gallery, the Building J conquest slabs were arranged to create an impressive display. The principal difference between Building L and Building J was that the emphasis had shifted from naming defeated individuals (Rosario and Period I) to naming subjugated places (Period II). This is a change one might expect as a result of the evolution from incipient state to expansionist empire. Drawing by John Klausmeyer.

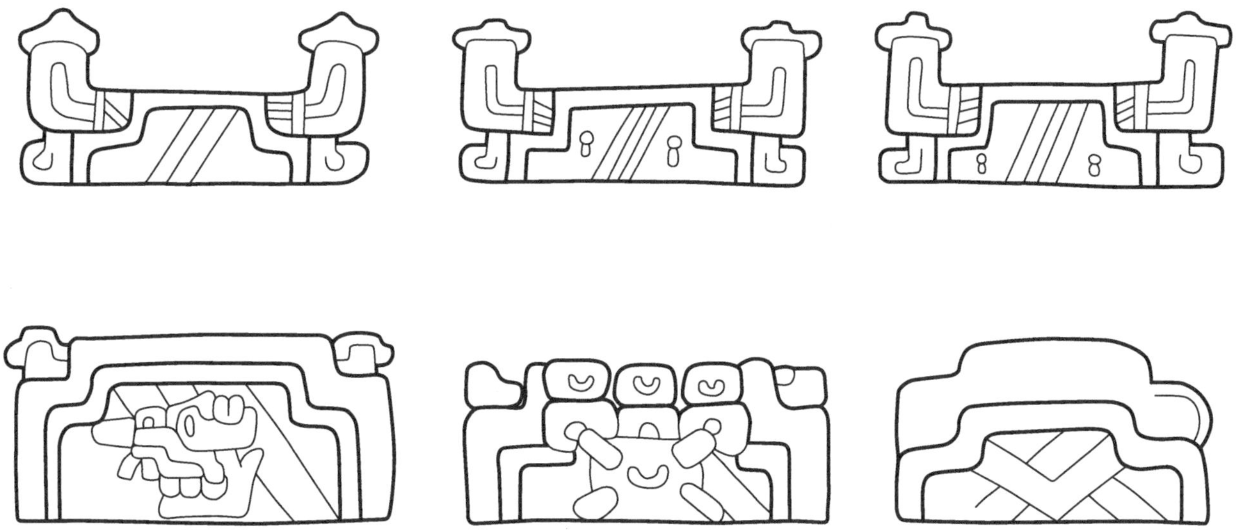

Figure 8.7. The Zapotec had multiple terms for "hill," including *tani, dani, gui,* and **gui?ya. Tani* often referred to an individual mountain, while *gui* and the proto-Zapotec **gui?ya* usually referred to hills, cliffs, or mountain ranges. These six hill signs are of two types: the upper row shows three generic hill signs; the lower row shows three hill signs that have "place-specifiers" or "place names" incorporated into the interior of the hill. As shown in the upper row, the hill sign usually included (1) two vertical projections that resembled the arms of an organ cactus, (2) notches or incised lines at the base of each projection, (3) two or three diagonal lines in the interior of the generic hill sign, and (4) paired circles or figure eights to either side of the diagonal lines. In some cases these figure eights appear to be droplets, either of water or blood. Drawing by John Klausmeyer.

(Caso 1947; Kirchhoff et al. 1976; Marcus 1992a: Ch. 6; Marcus 2005, 2006a; Peñafiel 1885; M. E. Smith 1973a).

How Was the Hill Sign Pronounced?

Zapotec terms for "hill" included *dani, tani, gui,* and **gui?ya. Tani* (sometimes given as *taani, daani, dani,* or *daan*) often refers to an individual mountain that serves as a landmark. *Gui* and **gui?ya* usually refer to hills, cliffs, or ranges of mountains. (The term **gui?ya* carries an asterisk to show that it has been reconstructed as a proto-Zapotec word [Fernández de Miranda 1995]).

As for how the hill sign might have functioned, I see at least three possibilities: it could have been pronounced (1) *tani/dani* or (2) *gui?ya/guij* or (3) not pronounced at all in the event that it served as a *determinative*, indicating that a geographical place was being referenced.

The use of a hill sign as a geographical referent was common in Mesoamerica. The Nahuatl *tepetl/tepec*, the Mixtec *yucu*, and the Mayan *witz* all played important roles in their respective writing systems. One Maya toponym—*hix witz* or "Jaguar Hill"—is a possible counterpart to the Zapotec toponym *Tani Gui Beche.*

The Rattle or Atlatl Sign

At least 13 of the slabs on Building J included the rattle or atlatl sign discussed earlier. Caso himself (1947:25, Figure 62) estimated that this sign occurred on 24% of the Period II slabs. I have suggested that on the Building L prisoner slabs, the atlatl sign might have been pronounced *gui*, identifying the victim as an object of sacrifice (see Figure 6.26). It is less clear how the atlatl sign functioned on the Building J conquest slabs. We do not know whether it (1) identified a place as having been captured in war or (2) was simply a phonetic complement, reinforcing the *gui* sound for "hill," "stone," and "cliff."

Sixteenth-Century Landmarks, Place Signs, and Maps

For the Zapotec we have an invaluable sixteenth-century source that provides us with a map, hill signs, and place names that are analogous to Building J's hill signs. That source is the Lienzo de Guevea, and it shows the hill signs and landmarks used as the boundaries of a Zapotec polity in Colonial times (Figures 8.8, 8.9).

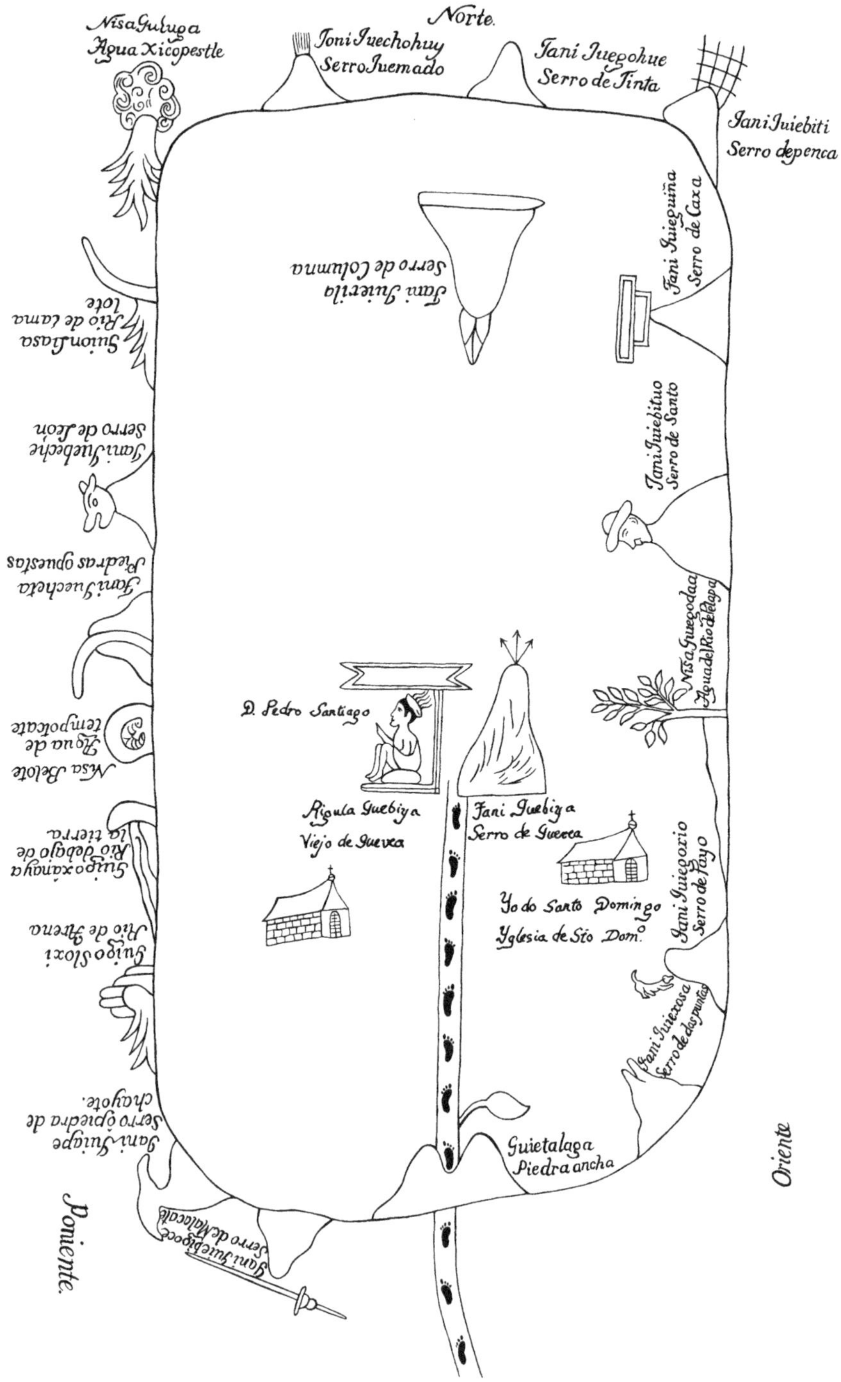

Figure 8.8. Here we see the upper half of the Lienzo de Guevea, which was painted in AD 1540. The lienzo was named after Santiago Guevea de Humboldt, a town 30 km north of the Tehuantepec River. Like the Building J conquest slabs at Monte Albán, which provided hill signs and place specifiers, this half of the lienzo was a map showing the natural landmarks that delimited the territory claimed by the Zapotec rulers. Place names that delimited the Guevea territory included mountains (*tani*), rivers (*guego, guigo*), streams (*nisa*), or stony cliffs (*guie*). Within the oval we see a man seated inside a temple. The gloss refers to him as don Pedro Santiago, *rigula* or "Viejo of Guevea." Behind him is the hill sign for Guevea, designated Tani Guebiya or Serro [sic] de Guevea. On the east side of the lienzo we see Nisa Guiegodaa or Agua del Río de Petapa. One can still find the Río Petapa not far from two contemporary villages named Santo Domingo Petapa and Santa María Petapa. Some place names included both *tani* (hill) and *gui* (stone). When both words were used, *tani* usually preceded *gui* (see Covarrubias 1946; Parsons 1936; Schmieder 1930; Seler 1906, 1986; Stubblefield and Stubblefield 1991). Drawing by John Klausmeyer.

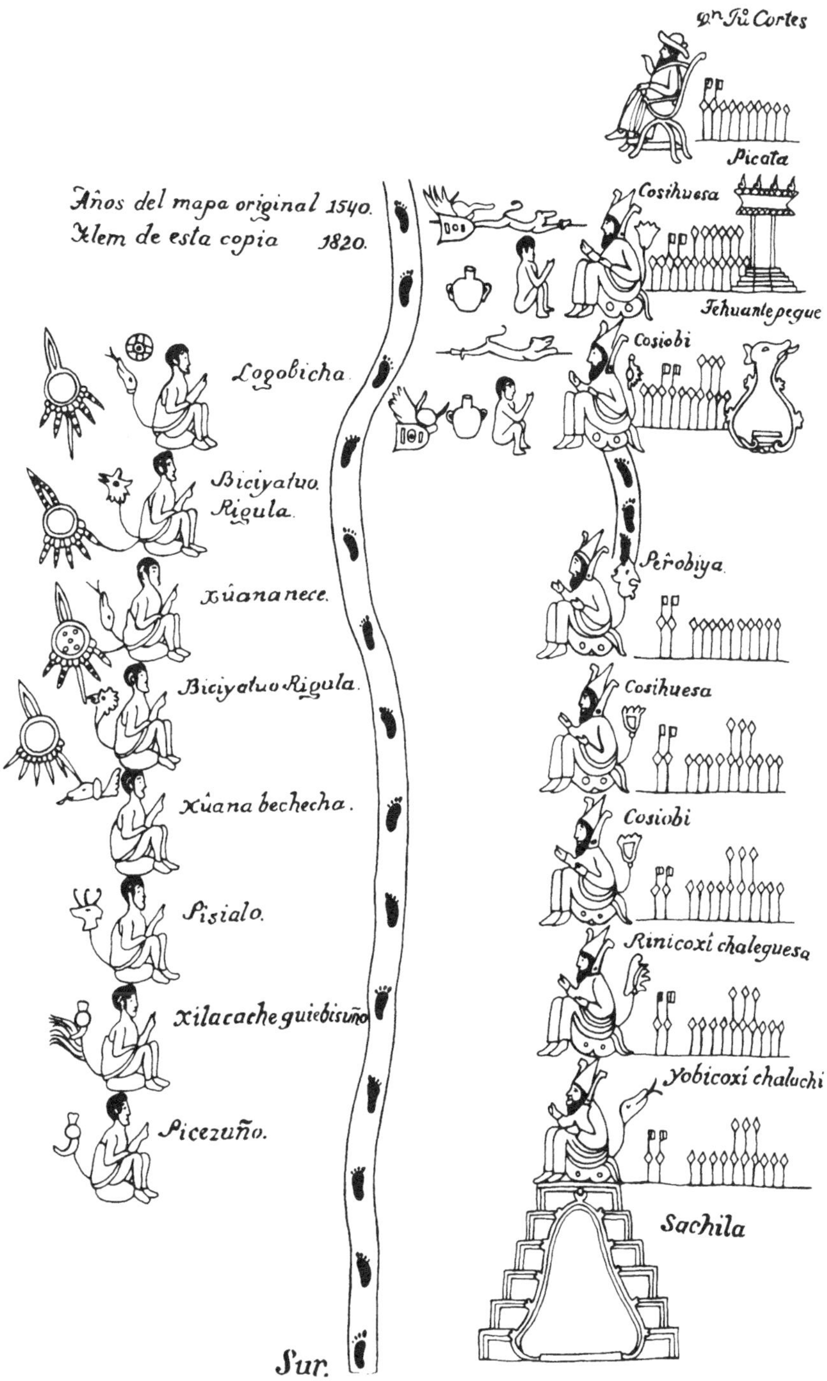

Figure 8.9. The lower half of the Lienzo de Guevea provides a list of the coquìs who ruled at Zaachila before they moved to Tehuantepec. Reading from bottom to top we see the place name for Zaachila (Sachila [sic]) and above it the coquìs who ruled Zaachila before they moved to Tehuantepec. The column of individuals at left are the *xoànas* or nobles of the subject town of Guevea, who were paying tribute to the Zapotec rulers now administering from Tehuantepec. Drawing by John Klausmeyer.

The original lienzo, painted in AD 1540, is now lost; fortunately, during the eighteenth and nineteenth centuries additional copies (called A and B) were painted (Marcus 2005; Oudijk and Jansen 1998, 2000; Paddock 1983f; Seler 1906, 1986).

The lienzo is named for Santiago Guevea de Humboldt, a town about 30 km north of the Tehuantepec River in southeastern Oaxaca. The document is divided into two parts: a map in the upper half that shows the natural landmarks delimiting the territory of Guevea, and a lower half that gives the genealogical relationships of the Zapotec rulers and the tribute they received. It is the upper half of the lienzo, with its cartographic data, that is of relevance here.

A passage on Copy B of the lienzo states, "By direction of the King of Spain and Mexico, 19 mountains have been placed as landmarks. On the first of June in the year 1540." To paraphrase the remaining Spanish text,

> To study this map and the division or boundaries of the land of the indigenous people of the town of Santiago Guevea with more clarity, look for the number 1 on the Peak named Cerro de Malacate in Spanish, and right there the line that encircles said land ends with number 18 at the *paraje* named Cerro de Chayote; each place or *paraje's* name is given in three languages…Mexicano [Nahuatl], Zapoteco, and Spanish. (Seler 1906, 1986)

Each landmark delimiting Guevea's realm is referred to as a *tepetl-mojón* (*tepetl* = hill, *mojón* = boundary marker). These place names referred to natural landmarks that delimited Guevea's territorial boundaries. Such landmarks included the terms for mountain (*tani*), river (*guego, guigo*), stream (*nisa*), or stony cliff (*guie*).

The upper half of the lienzo has an oval perimeter, with some landmarks placed inside the perimeter line, others outside. I suspect that these two sets of places—some inside and some outside the line—were originally intended to be read in zigzag or *boustrophedon* fashion (Marcus 2005). Similar toponyms are arranged that way in the Mixtec codices called Selden and Nuttall (see Caso 1964b, 1977, 1979; Jansen and Pérez Jiménez 2011; Nuttall 1975; M. E. Smith 1973a). Independently, Oudijk and Jansen (1998, 2000) have arrived at the same conclusion, i.e. that Zapotec artists had taken a codex with place signs arranged in boustrophedon layout and converted it to a European-style map with an oval layout.

Inside the oval map of place names on the upper half of the lienzo is a man seated inside a temple. The gloss refers to him as don Pedro Santiago, *rigula* or Viejo of Guevea, evidently the local ruler of Guevea. Behind him is the hill sign for Guevea, designated Tani Guebiya or Serro [sic] de Guevea.

The Boundaries of the Guevea Polity

Now let us compare the Lienzo de Guevea to a modern map of Oaxaca, in hopes of finding the key mountains and rivers used as landmarks. On the southern edge of the lienzo is a hill glossed as Guietalaga or Piedra Ancha. A road passing between its two peaks displays precolumbian-style footprints leading north to the town of Guevea. These two peaks may correspond to Cerro El Comal and Cordón Indio Dormido on today's maps.

In the southeastern corner of the lienzo is a place called Hill of Lightning, Serro [sic] de Rayo in Spanish and Tani Guiegoxio (*Quie Cociyo*) in Zapotec. Copy A of the lienzo shows a dog next to this hill. In comparing this Zapotec version to Maya and Aztec depictions of Lightning, Seler (1906, 1986) concluded that dogs were sometimes used to represent lightning and might be shown plunging toward earth. No modern map shows a Hill of Lightning southeast of Guevea, but some do have a "Río de los Perros" in that location. (If Seler's hunch is correct, the dogs may be an indirect reference to Lightning—but I have my doubts.)

In the upper right corner of the lienzo is a hill with the Spanish gloss Serro [sic] de Penca. On Copy A, the Zapotec version is given as Tani Guiebiti or Tani Guiebili; on Copy B, it is Dani Chiba Beago. Neither Zapotec gloss seems to refer to the *penca* or fleshy stem of the agave. On one modern map, however, we find a hill named Cerro de Penca some 25 km northeast of Guevea; this might be the place referred to in the lienzo.

On the east side of the lienzo we see the Zapotec gloss Nisa Guiegodaa (Copy A) or Guegodaa (Copy B). The Spanish version is Agua del Río de Petapa. Nisa Guigodaa (*nisa* = water, *guigo* = river, *daa* = mat) can be translated "Water [Tributary] of the River of the Mat." The Nahuatl gloss for this same river in Copy B is Petlapan, which can be translated "On the Water of the Mat." Seler (1906) suggests that this name could be a description of the river itself, calling it as still and level and smooth as a mat. One can still find a Río Petapa on various maps, and not far away are two villages: Santo Domingo Petapa and Santa María Petapa. Thus, the Río Petapa seems to have retained its name for centuries and still constitutes the eastern boundary of the Guevea polity.

Of the seven places on the west side of the lienzo, five refer to bodies of water and two to hills. One of the two hills is Serro [sic] de León in Spanish, and Tani Guebeche or Tani Que Peche in Zapotec. *Beche* or *peche* is the Zapotec word for "fierce animal" and can refer to either the puma or jaguar (Córdova [1578a]1942; Marcus and Flannery 1978). On Copy A of the lienzo the artist painted a yellow feline without spots, possibly a puma. Modern maps of Oaxaca do show a hill named Cerro León, and even a nearby river named Río León. Both the hill and river are northwest of Santiago Guevea, in a location similar to that of Serro [sic] de León on the lienzo.

Just below Serro [sic] de León on the lienzo is a landmark named Tani Quechela or Tani Guechela (Zapotec), glossed Piedras Opuestas in Spanish. The term *piedras opuestas* may refer to a pair of mountains found just south of Cerro León on modern maps. Today the western mountain of the pair is not labeled, but its eastern companion is called Cerro Centinela.

Another landmark on the west side of the lienzo is glossed Río de Arena in Spanish and Guigo Lloxi in Zapotec (Copy

A). Copy B of the lienzo also includes the Spanish gloss Río de Arena. A modern tributary of the Tehuantepec River, called Río Arenal, may be the River of Sand mentioned on both Copies A and B. This river is located west of Guevea, just as shown on the lienzo.

Another river on the lienzo is glossed Agua Xicapestle in Spanish/Nahuatl, and either Nisa Guiaga or Nisa Quiapa (Copy A) or Niza Lovaa (Copy B) in Zapotec. All these glosses can be translated "Water [tributary] of the Gourd Vessel." A hill named Cerro Jilapextla or Cerro Jicalpestle can be found west of Guevea on modern maps. Both of today's names are derived from the sixteenth-century Nahuatl word *xicalpeztli*.

Along the northern limits of Guevea's realm, the lienzo shows places called Tani Quechohuy or Burnt Hill and Tani Guegohue or Serro [sic] de Tinta. The modern town of San Juan Guichicovi is located in this area today.

One other landmark of the lienzo is an upside-down hill sign associated with various Zapotec names (Tani Guixila, Tani Guiecila, Tani Gueexilla) and the Spanish name Serro [sic] de Columna; the element on top of the hill glyph may represent three stone columns or peaks. One can, in fact, find a hill north of Guevea that is called Cerro Tres Picos on today's maps.

Unfortunately, we cannot locate all 18 Lienzo de Guevea landmarks on any modern map. We are, nevertheless, able to determine the approximate boundaries of the polity.

The Toponyms in the Lienzo de Guevea

We have seen that some places in the Lienzo de Guevea incorporated two terms: *tani* (hill) and *gui* (stone). When both were used, *tani* usually preceded *gui*. We can still find this word sequence today, as, for example, in the Tehuantepec landmark Dani Gui Beche or "Hill of the Jaguar" (Covarrubias 1946: map).

Examples of place names in the lienzo that combine *tani* and *guie* include:

Tani Guie Bigoce, "Hill of the Spindle Whorl"
Tani Guie Xosa, "Hill of the Peaks"
Tani Guie Goxio, "Hill of Lightning"
Tani Guie Bituo, "Hill of the Spirit or Vital Force"
Tani Guie Guiña, "Hill of the Box or Trunk"
Tani Gue Cheta, "Hill on Opposite Sides"
Tani Gue Beche, "Hill of the Jaguar"
Tani Guie Biti, "Hill of the Penca"
Tani Gui Ape, "Hill of the Chayote"

Other places in the lienzo begin with one of the two Zapotec terms for hill, either *tani* or *guiya*. Other Oaxaca places whose names begin with *gui* or *gui ya* are as follows:

Guije Zeechi, Santa Inés Yatzeche
Gui Ande, Santa Catarina
Gui Joo, Tlapacoya
Guia Loo, Santa Cruz
Guia Ta, Ixtaltepec
Guie Niza, Altepeques
Guie Beezia, Ixtlán
Guia Bere, Totolapa
Guie Zij, Tehuantepec

The word *gui* is still used today in the Tlacolula region to refer to mountains, hills, villages, and towns (Covarrubias 1946; Parsons 1936; Schmieder 1930; Stubblefield and Stubblefield 1991). A few examples are:

Gui huijxh, Macuilxóchitl
Gui binii, a mountain to the south of Tlacolula
Gui dolaii, a sacred mountain north of Mitla
Gui gaa, a mountain south of Mitla, now called Nueve Puntas
Gui gajl, Zempoaltepetl
Gui gojn, Santa María Zoquitlán
Gui gotz, a mountain northwest of Mitla
Gui run, a mountain east of Mitla
Gui sie, Tehuantepec
Guilá Naquitz, a white cliff 4 km northwest of Mitla
Guila siuaa, north of Xaaga
Gui lee, the stone fort or fortaleza
Guiengola, "old stone," a mountain near Tehuantepec
Xaqui ya, at the foot of the Hill?
Xi guiiaa, Teotitlán del Valle

Other Zapotec Geographical Terms

Other Zapotec words featured in place names include "plain" (*lachi, lache*), "field" (*guela, queela, guehl*), and "river" (*guego*).

Lachi occurs in the following place names: Lachitao (Great or Big Plain), Lachi guirag (Plain of Ocotes), Lochitia (Santa María Albarradas), Lechiyela ("plain" + hollow" or Ixtepeji), Lachi china (Plain of the Deer), Lads-ro (Great Plain), and Lachi goloo (Plain of the Monkey).

Guela occurs in Guelatao (Big Field) and Guelavía, while *guego* (river) appears in Guego loo gueche (San Pedro Zimatlán), Guego chooni (Ayoquesco), Guego bere (Totolapilla), Guego Tee (Nejapa, or River of Ash), and Guego Taa (Petapa or Mat River).

The Zapotec term for "tree" (*yaga, yag, ya*) is used in some place names, such as Yavesía (*ya* = tree; *vesia* = eagle), Yahuiche (*ya* = tree, *huich* = fig?), Yagalaxi (*yaga* = tree; *laxi* = thin), and Yaganiza (*yaga* = tree; *niza* = water) (e.g., Bradomín [1955]1980; Schmieder 1930).

The term for "water" (*niza, nisa, nis*) also appears in place names, such as Nis-ya-yagsín ("Spring of the Oak Wood") (Schmieder 1930:39). These examples provide a sample of place names that incorporate tree and water, but it is not clear whether any of these terms occur in the place signs of Building J.

The Many Problems in Deciphering Building J Place Names

Thanks to Caso, for more than 80 years we have known that the Building J slabs featured a "hill" or place sign plus one or more glyphs that seemingly specified the name of the place. Sadly, only a handful can be matched to places in the State of Oaxaca today, and that match must remain tentative. An obvious problem is that remarkably few places retain the same name for millennia. There are some unusual instances—like Yaxha in the Maya region—where a place can be shown to have retained its name for more than two millennia (see Justeson 1975; Stuart 1985; Villagutierre Soto-Mayor [1701]1983).

There are many reasons why a site does not retain its name. We have cases of cultural and linguistic domination; state expansion and conquest; political and economic domination; instances in which populations migrated and displaced others; and cases of marriage alliances that introduced new languages. Long-term interaction occurred between Zapotec, Cuicatec, Chinantec, and Mixtec speakers. Some places that formerly had Zapotec names came to have Nahuatl or Spanish names. Only when the Nahuatl name is a direct translation of the Zapotec name do we have any chance of identifying a place on Building J.

Another obvious problem is that the place names given on Building J are likely Zapotec, and may not be the way that subjugated and non-Zapotec speakers referred to their own towns. In the Maya region, we are fortunate that some place names are mentioned dozens of times by both Maya capitals and their Maya subjects, rather than only once as on Building J (e.g., Berlin 1958; Marcus 1973, 1976d; Martin and Grube 2008).

While the hill sign and the geographical specifier are standard elements on Building J, the inverted human head below the hill sign is not. Some Building J slabs have it, others do not. A plausible reason, already mentioned, is that not all the provinces of the expanding Zapotec state needed to be incorporated by force. For example, when sparsely populated regions such as Sola de Vega were incorporated, no conquest was necessary; the Zapotec simply sent in colonists (Balkansky 2002). Other regions, such as Ejutla, seem to have joined Monte Albán's hegemony peacefully, perhaps through political or royal marriage alliance (Feinman and Nicholas 1990, 1993, 1995). Only regions that resisted a Zapotec takeover, such as Cuicatlán, had to be subdued by force (Spencer and Redmond 1997). It is those regions, we believe, whose place names and hill signs were given an inverted head.

What Building J Looks Like Today

When Caso (1947) began his excavations, he found evidence that Building J had been partially looted and many of its carved stones were no longer in their original positions. (Indeed, during the Colonial era the building had survived an attempt to blow it up with gunpowder.) Today the building is so consolidated and reconstructed that tourists would never suspect how damaged it once was.

Caso also noted that Building J had been renovated various times in antiquity. During those renovations and alterations, the ancient architects added stones taken from other structures in the Main Plaza. Many Building L stones had been incorporated into Building J during Period II, and during Period IIIa some of these were covered over with layers of stucco, hiding their carvings from view.

When Caso began work on Building J, he felt that only the slabs in the lowest row were still in place (see Figure 8.3). Many had been removed, making it difficult for Caso and Acosta to determine their original placement. After working to consolidate the surviving walls of Building J, they found that there was no room to accommodate all the carved slabs lying around; in fact, one can still see carved stones lying on the ground just to the west of Building J. Many of these leftover stones remained unlabeled until later investigators came along and assigned numbers to them.

Too Many Numbering Systems?

Caso (1947) was the first to assign numbers to the carved stones of Building J. I have maintained Caso's original numbers not only because his numbers have priority, but also because they have appeared in so many publications over the last six decades. Since there was no need to change them, most scholars have retained Caso's numbers. Unfortunately, Caso did not number all of the carved stones. For my study I needed a way to refer to these unnumbered stones. I decided to use a letter (such as "J" for Building J) and a zero before the number, so that my designations could not be confused with Caso's. The stones that I numbered became J-01, J-02, and so on (Marcus 1972).

A few years after I began working on the Building J stones, Louise Wiltraud Zehnder (1977) wrote a thesis in which she gave her own set of numbers to the stones already numbered by Caso. Shortly thereafter, John F. Scott (1978) produced a study in which he retained most of Caso's numbers. Still later, García Moll et al. (1986) arrived in Oaxaca and renumbered most of the carved stones, i.e. retaining almost none of Caso's original numbers.

These alternative numbering schemes can be quite confusing; two examples should suffice. Caso's Lápida 41 is Scott's Monument J-41, but that same monument was called Stone 47 by García Moll et al. (1986). Scott's J-41, of course, is not the same stone that Zehnder called J-41, and to make matters worse, her J-41 is García Moll et al.'s Stone 80.

To help the reader navigate this maze, I list all the alternative numbers in my discussion of each stone. We will proceed around Building J wall by wall, so that visitors to the site will be able to use this chapter as a general guide to the location of every carved stone in the building.

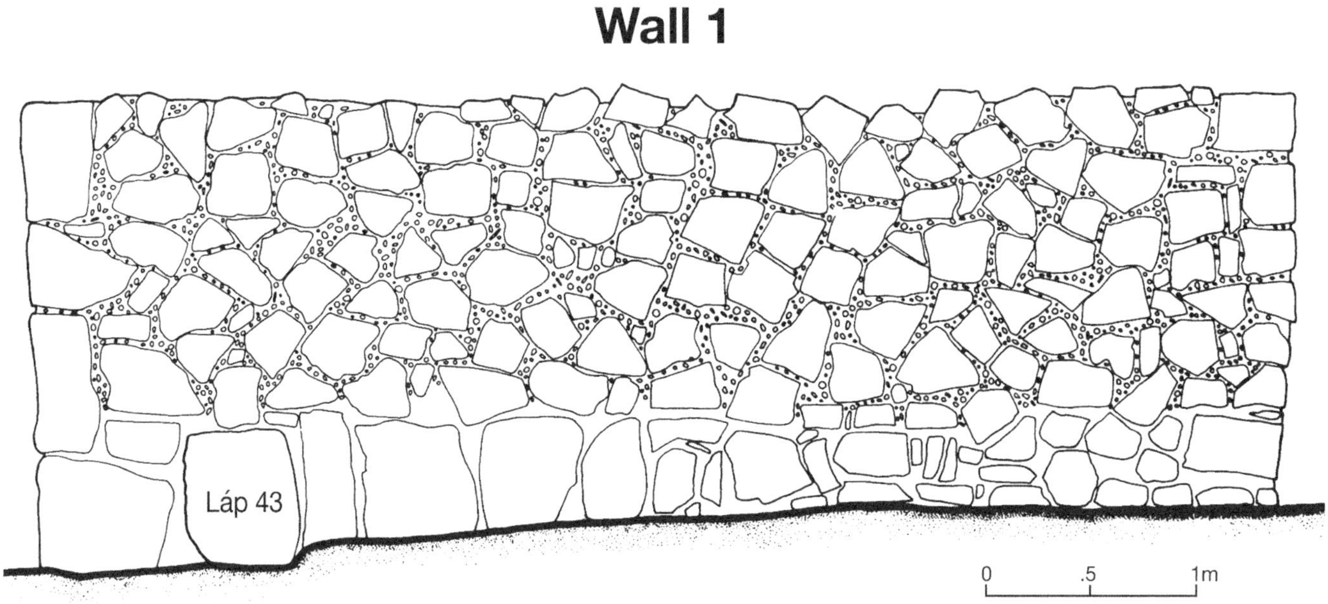

Figure 8.10. This simplified drawing of Wall 1 of Building J at Monte Albán shows the location of Lápida 43 (see García Moll et al. 1986). Drawing by John Klausmeyer.

Wall 1 (Figure 8.10)

Lápida 43 (58 x 51 cm) (Caso's Lápida 43; Zehnder's J-85; García Moll et al.'s Stone 37). This stone (Caso 1947: Figure 48) has a place sign with two of the principal components defined by Caso—the hill sign and the elements above it that specify the name. The latter elements are a basin of water or a canal with maize tassels. In earlier publications (Marcus 1976a, 1980, 1992a), I suggested that this place sign referred to the Miahuatlán region. According to Martínez Gracida (1883:72), Miahuatlán can be translated as "place of the corn tassels"; the Zapotec name for this place, *Pelopeniza*, can be translated "in the water of the maize tassels," "among the maize cobs," or "among the spikes of grain" (Figure 8.11). Another Nahuatl name—Miahuapan—can be translated "in the canal of the maize tassels." This identification may take time to confirm because no corresponding place signs have been found on monuments in the Miahuatlán area.

There is no inverted head below the hill sign on Lápida 43. This lack of an upside-down head may suggest that military force was unnecessary to ensure the subjugation of Miahuatlán, a place known to have been colonized by Monte Albán during Period II (Marcus and Flannery 1996).

The Valley of Miahuatlán, located 30 km south of Ejutla, lies on the route to the Pacific Ocean. By Period II a cluster of seven sites had emerged near the main river, with the largest of these dominating the region. Surveys by Donald Brockington (1973) and Charles Markman (1981) showed that the Miahuatlán region had been sparsely occupied before the Zapotec state formed. After the Zapotec state arose, the ceramics in the Miahuatlán Valley came to look like those of Monte Albán.

Wall 2 (Figure 8.12)

In this wall we see three stones (J-85, J-86, and J-87) that depict slain captives (García Moll et al. 1986: Láminas 16, 211). Most scholars consider these stones to have been removed from the Building L Prisoner Gallery and reused in Building J. It is puzzling that Scott (1978: Figure 22, lowermost right corner and see J-85 through J-87 in Part II: Catalogue) described these three stones as "*in situ*"; perhaps he meant that the stones were in the wall, as opposed to lying loose near the building.

Stone J-85 (70 x 58 cm) (Caso's stone 85; Scott's J-85; Zehnder's J-84; García Moll et al.'s Stone 36). This slain captive is flat on his back. Scott (1978) describes this stone's carving style as "fourth row or earlier?," indicating that he knew it was borrowed from Row 4 of the Building L gallery. He also noted that the stone is set upside down in Building J, additional evidence that it had been reused.

Stone J-86 (123 x 54 cm) (Caso's stone 86; Scott's J-86; Zehnder's J-83, García Moll et al.'s Stone 35). Scott describes this sprawling figure as located on the "base of southeast cheekpiece, Mound J stair, in situ, between J-87 and J-85" (Scott 1978, Vol. II). It, too, is borrowed from Building L.

Figure 8.11. Lápida 43's place sign has two of the three components that Caso defined—the hill sign + elements above the hill sign that specify the place name. The latter elements appear to be a canal or basin with maize tassels. This sign may have referred to the Miahuatlán region, since both its Zapotec and Nahuatl names mean "in the water of the maize tassels." The Zapotec name *Pelopeniza* has been translated as "in the water of the maize tassels" or "among the maize spikes." No inverted head appears below the hill sign, and this lack of an upside-down head may suggest that military force was unnecessary to ensure the flow of tribute from Miahuatlán. This site and region are known to have been colonized by Monte Albán during Period II. Drawing by Jane Mariouw.

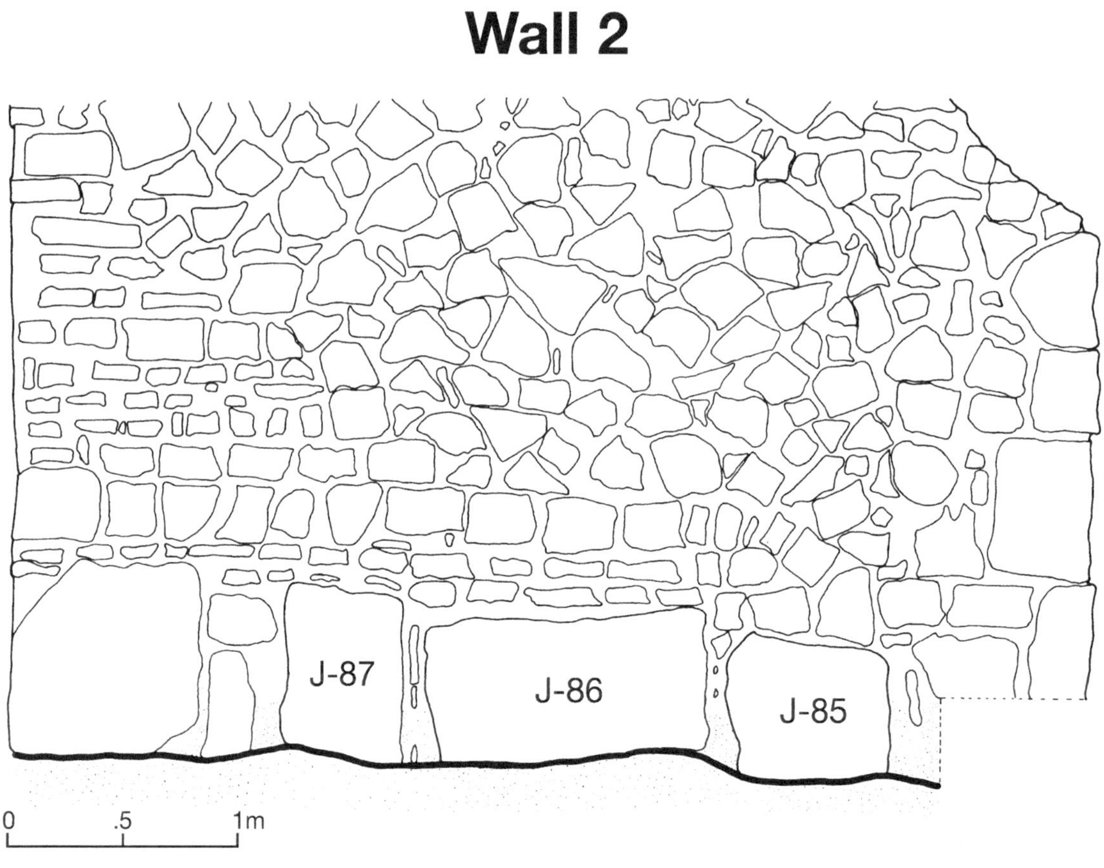

Figure 8.12. In Wall 2 of Building J we see three carved stones (J-85, J-86, and J-87) that depicted slain captives (García Moll et al. 1986: Láminas 16, 211). These stones had been removed from the Building L Prisoner Gallery and reused in Building J. Scott (1978, Part II: Catalogue) noted that J-85 was set upside down in Building J, additional evidence that it had been reused. Drawing by John Klausmeyer.

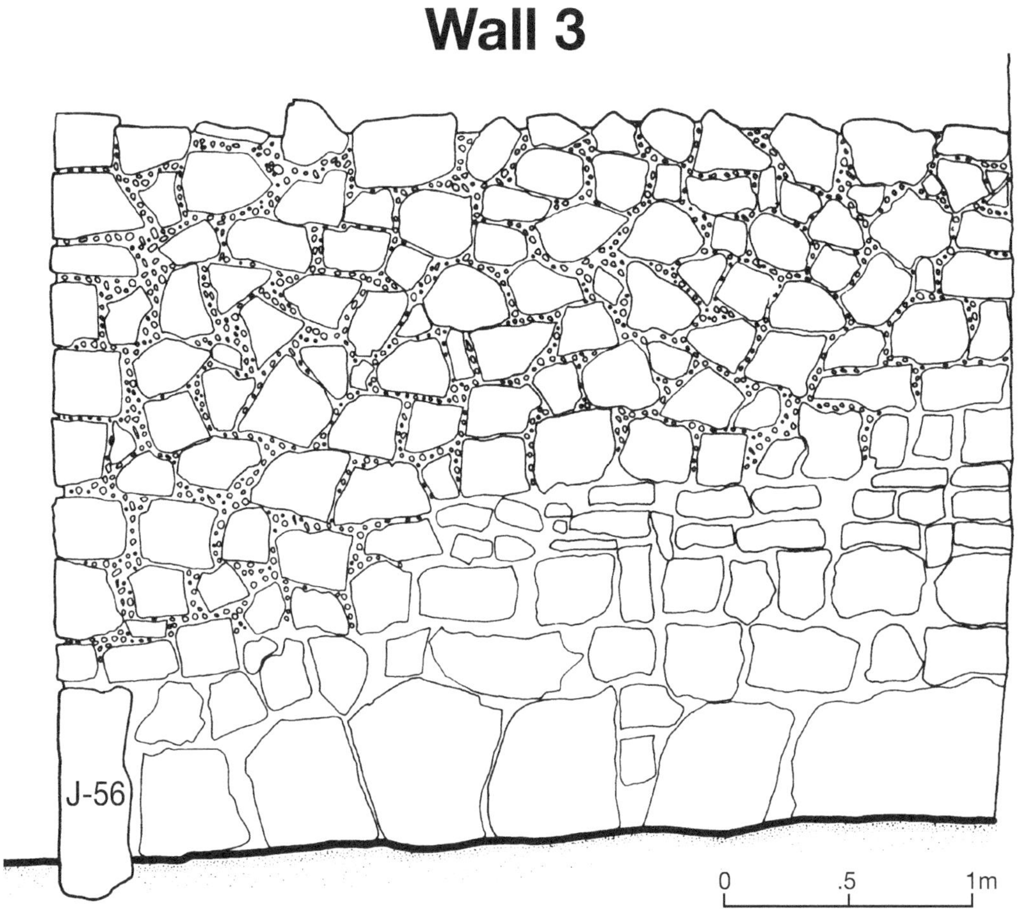

Figure 8.13. In Wall 3 of Building J was Monument J-56, another stone clearly borrowed from Building L (see also García Moll et al. 1986). Drawing by John Klausmeyer.

Stone J-87 (54 x 70 cm) (Caso's stone 87; Scott's J-87; Zehnder's J-82, García Moll et al.'s Stone 34). The arms and legs of this slain captive are flung out, making it appear that this victim was lying on his back. He also seems to have a hole in his chest, from which his heart may have been removed. Stone J-87, too, is a reused Building L monument.

Wall 3 (Figure 8.13)

Stone J-56 (92 x 27 cm) (Caso's Stone 56; Scott's J-56; Zehnder's J-24; García Moll et al.'s stone 33). This reused Building L stone shows a prone figure facing right, wearing a large earspool and possible nose ornament.

Wall 4 (Figure 8.14)

Stone 92 (32 x 50 cm) (Caso's Stone 92; Zehnder's J-23; Scott's J-99; García Moll et al.'s Stone 19). Here we see the lower body of a sacrificial victim displayed originally in the Prisoner Gallery of Building L.

Wall 6 (Figure 8.15)

Lápida 47 (87 x 82 cm) (Caso's Lápida 47; Zehnder's J-1; García Moll et al.'s Stone 18). This is a typical Building J conquest slab with three elements: an inverted head, a hill sign, and a compound name above the hill (Caso 1947: Figure 62). The inverted head likely signifies military conquest, and the archaeological record supports this interpretation (Figure 8.16).

Above the standard hill sign we see a human head with a decorated speech scroll, likely signifying "The Place of Song." Below the head is a sign that may have been pronounced *gui* in Zapotec. In earlier publications (Marcus 1976a, 1980), I have suggested that this place sign refers to the Cañada de Cuicatlán, an important route linking the Valley of Oaxaca and the Tehuacán Valley (see Chapter 9).

The Cuicatlán Cañada has been systematically surveyed by Elsa Redmond (1983; Redmond and Spencer 1983). Excavations there by Spencer and Redmond (1997) brought to light communities that were either overthrown by the Zapotec or annexed and later punished for rebellion. These data fit well with the fact that Lápida 47 has an inverted head. Prior to its conquest by Monte Albán, the Cuicatlán region displayed ceramics unlike

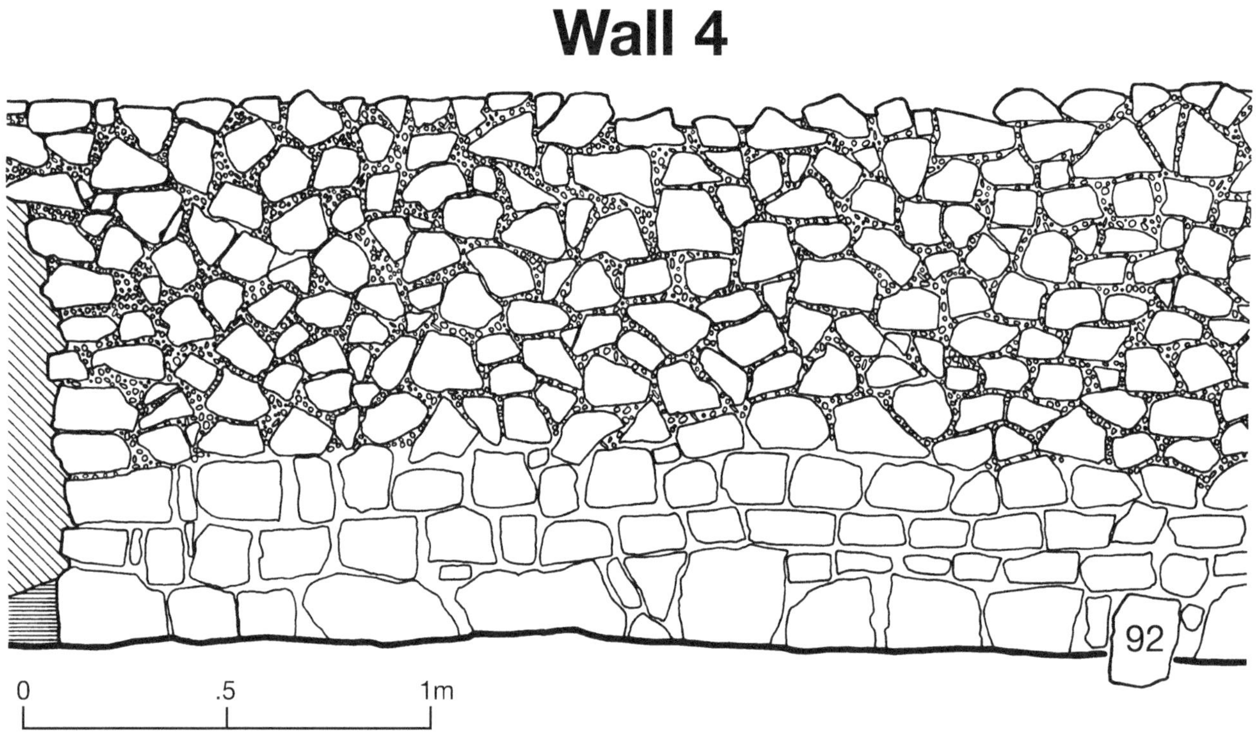

Figure 8.14. In Wall 4 of Building J was Stone 92, a slain captive originally displayed in the Prisoner Gallery of Building L (see also García Moll et al. 1986). Drawing by John Klausmeyer.

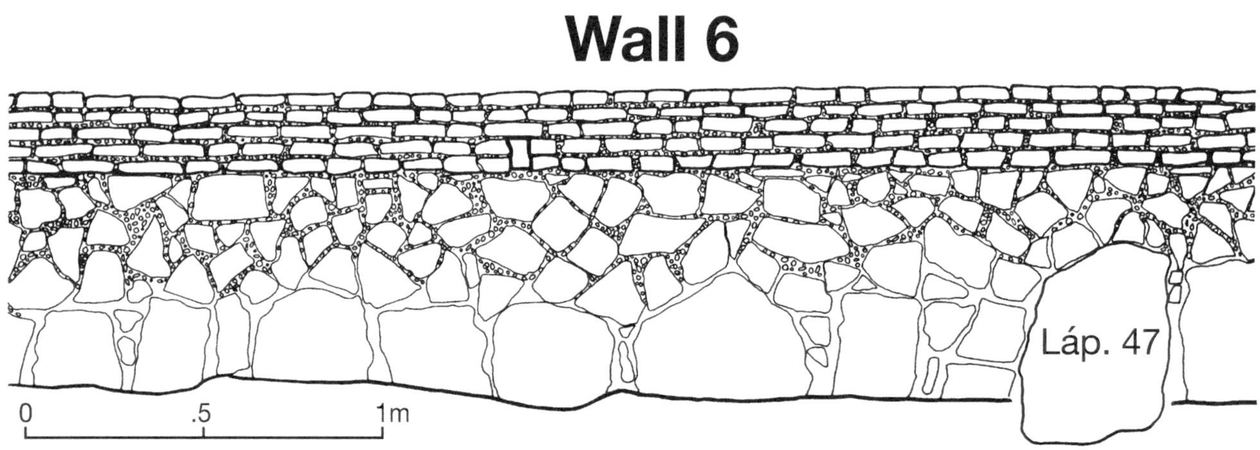

Figure 8.15. In Wall 6 of Building J was Lápida 47 (see García Moll et al. 1986). Drawing by John Klausmeyer.

Figure 8.16. Lápida 47 is a typical Building J conquest slab with three elements: an inverted head below the hill, a hill sign above the inverted head, and a place-specifier (or name) above the hill (Caso 1947: Fig. 62). The inverted head likely signifies conquest, and the archaeological record supports this interpretation. The name specifier is a human head with a decorated speech scroll, likely signifying "The Place of Song." (Below the head is the atlatl sign, which may have been pronounced *gui* in Zapotec.) In earlier publications I suggested that this place sign referred to the Cañada de Cuicatlán. Excavations by Spencer and Redmond (1997) brought to light communities that were either overthrown by the Zapotec or annexed and later punished for rebellion. Their data fit well with the fact that Lápida 47 has an inverted head. Like the Miahuatlán area, which had different ceramic types prior to its conquest, the Cuicatlán region displayed ceramics unlike those in the Valley of Oaxaca prior to its conquest. Drawing by Jane Mariouw.

those in the Valley of Oaxaca. Eventually, however, Cuicatlán's communities had "abundant pottery showing close stylistic affinity to that of Monte Albán II in the Valley of Oaxaca" (Redmond and Spencer 1983:119).

This stylistic change in ceramics was accompanied by the building of an actual fortress at Quiotepec, which lies on a natural river ford leading to the Tehuacán Valley. The fortress, which featured pottery and noble tombs in Valley of Oaxaca style, possessed defensive walls, large public buildings, and a plaza through which travelers would have to pass. North of the Quiotepec Fortress, Redmond and Spencer found a seven-kilometer-wide, unoccupied buffer zone (see Figure 8.1). To the north of this buffer zone the surface pottery reflected the influence of Tehuacán, rather than Monte Albán.

The Fortress of Quiotepec would seem to mark the northernmost expansion of the Zapotec state administered from Monte Albán. With a fortress guarding the northern Cañada de Cuicatlán, Monte Albán effectively prevented southward expansion by rival kingdoms in Puebla, Tlaxcala, or the Basin of Mexico.

To the south of the Fortress of Quiotepec, Spencer and Redmond (1997) found an archaeological site named La Coyotera, a community that appears to have been burned and punished for resisting Zapotec control. The Zapotec conquerors burned La Coyotera and moved its population to a piedmont ridge nearby, creating a three-hectare community with public buildings.

In front of the largest pyramid there, Spencer and Redmond found an actual skull rack that contained 61 human skulls aligned in rows. This kind of skull rack was called *yàgabetoo* by the Zapotec and *tzompantli* by the later Aztec. Such displays of severed heads were widespread in Mesoamerica, serving to discourage subject people from rebelling or refusing to pay their tribute (Figure 8.17).

Figure 8.17. To the south of the Fortress of Quiotepec in the Cuicatlán Cañada, Charles Spencer and Elsa Redmond found an archaeological site named La Coyotera, a community that appears to have been burned and punished for resisting Zapotec control. Its Zapotec conquerors moved La Coyotera's population to a piedmont ridge nearby, creating a three-hectare community with public buildings. In front of the largest pyramid, Spencer and Redmond found an actual skull rack that contained 61 human skulls aligned in rows. Here we see an artist's reconstruction of this skull rack, which the Zapotec called *yàgabetoo* and the Aztec called *tzompantli*. Such displays of decapitated heads were widespread in Mesoamerica, serving to discourage subject people from rebelling. The archaeological evidence for a Zapotec conquest strengthens the tentative interpretation of the name-specifier on Lápida 47 as Cuicatlán or "Place of Song" (redrawn by John Klausmeyer from Spencer 1982: Fig. 5.12).

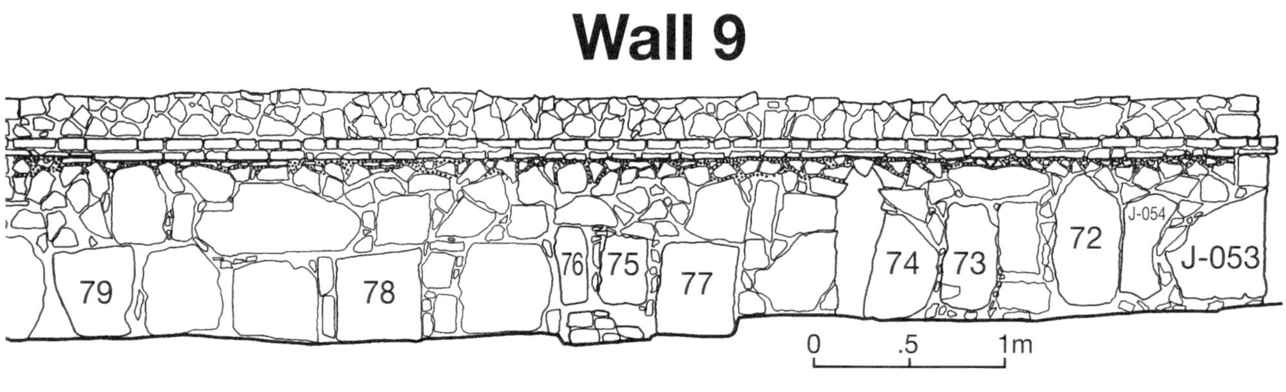

Figure 8.18. Set in Wall 9 of Building J there were ten carved stones (Stones 72–79, J-053, and J-054), all of which appear to have been borrowed from Building L (see García Moll et al. 1986). Drawing by John Klausmeyer.

Wall 9 (Figure 8.18)

Almost all the stones in this wall appear to have been borrowed from Building L.

Monument J-053 (103 x 73 cm) (Marcus' J-053; Zehnder's J-53; García Moll et al.'s stone 17). This carved stone is completely eroded.

Monument J-054 (181 x 47 cm) (Marcus' J-054; Zehnder's J-54; García Moll et al.'s Stone 16). This is only a fragment of a carved stone.

Stone 72 (173 x 70 cm) (Caso's Stone 72; Scott's J-72; Zehnder's J-55; García Moll et al.'s Stone 15). This slab shows the outline of a dead prisoner facing toward the viewer's right. His right arm hangs fairly straight and his left arm is akimbo, with its hand resting on his hip and thigh.

Stone 73 (98 x 53 cm) (Caso's Stone 73; Scott's J-73; Zehnder's J-56; García Moll et al.'s Stone 14). This stone shows a prisoner lying on his back or side, with his right arm on his body and his left arm outstretched in front of him. Of great interest is the oval element on his chest, which may depict the place where a sacrificer reached in to remove the heart.

Stone 74 (100 x 44 cm) (Caso's Stone 74; Scott's J-74; Zehnder's J-57; García Moll et al.'s Stone 13). This slab shows a prisoner with a foreshortened upper body. His right arm crosses his abdomen while his left arm is bent, pointing toward the edge of the stone. A brief label composed of two hieroglyphs—a plus-shaped element and a possible pectoral or necklace—may represent his noncalendric nickname.

Stone 77 (62 x 79 cm) (Caso's Stone 77; Scott's J-77; Zehnder's J-58; García Moll et al.'s Stone 12). This slab shows a victim wearing a helmet-like headdress or elaborate hairdo. His arm is outstretched.

Stone 75 (49 x 71 cm) (Caso's Stone 75; Scott's J-75; Zehnder's J-59; García Moll et al.'s Stone 11). The prisoner on this slab is in an awkward position, with closed eyes and rubbery limbs.

Stone 76 (34 x 83 cm) (Caso's Stone 76; Scott's J-76; Zehnder's J-60; García Moll et al.'s Stone 10). This largely eroded slab shows the outlines of a horizontal prisoner's head and torso.

Stone 78 (85 x 78 cm) (Caso's Stone 78; Scott's J-78; Zehnder's J-61; García Moll et al.'s Stone 9). This prisoner is shown sprawling, with his legs apart.

Stone 79 (83 x 71 cm) (Caso's Stone 79; Zehnder's J-62; García Moll et al.'s Stone 8). On this largely eroded slab, the outstretched arms of the prisoner stand out.

Wall 10 (Figure 8.19)

Monument J-80 (23 x 40 cm) Caso's Stone 80; Zehnder's J-63; Scott's J-80; García Moll et al.'s Stone 7) [García Moll et al. 1986: Lám. 6]. On this slab, the atlatl sign appears above the head of a prisoner with his arms reaching up.

Wall 11 (Figure 8.20)

Lápida 42 (63 x 53 cm) (Caso's Lápida 42; Zehnder's J-89; García Moll et al.'s Stone 3). This conquest slab (Figure 8.21) bears a cluster of glyphs above a hill sign. At the top is a crossed band enclosed by a frame; below is a possible sign for "knot" or "smoke;" and still lower is a basin-shaped sign (Caso 1947: Figure 47). In the interior of the hill sign are the usual diagonal lines with small circles on either side.

No inverted head appears below the hill sign, suggesting that this place was not subjugated by force.

Lápida 81 (31 x 10 cm) (Caso's Lápida 81; Zehnder's J-88; García Moll et al.'s Stone 2). This conquest slab has only a small fragment of a hill sign, showing just one of its upright projections.

Monument J-54 (50 x 96 cm) (Caso's Stone 54; Zehnder's J-87; Scott's J-54; García Moll et al.'s Stone 1). This stone, borrowed from Building L, shows a prisoner in an awkward position, with elaborate headgear and possible ties or knots below his chin.

The Northwest Tunnel

Stone 115 (93 x 63 cm) (Caso's stone 115; Zehnder's J-110: Scott's J-115; García moll et al.'s stone 4). The prisoner on this stone, borrowed from Building L, faces to the viewer's right and wears a prominent earspool.

Stone 116 (132 x 85 cm) (Caso's stone 116; Zehnder's J-111: Scott's J-116; García moll et al.'s stone 5). This Building L monument resembles Stone 115.

Monument J-029 (81 x 55 cm) (Marcus' J-029; Zehnder's J-112; García moll et al.'s stone 6). This conquest slab has a hieroglyph similar to one at the site of Caballito Blanco in the Tlacolula region (discussed later in this chapter).

Wall 12 (Figure 8.22)

Monument J-55 (46 x 66 cm) (Caso's stone 55; Scott's J-55; Zehnder's J-86; García Moll et al.'s Stone 38). The prisoner on this stone, borrowed from Building L, displays a lozenge-shaped opening where his heart may have been removed.

Wall 13 (Figure 8.23)

Stone 70 (36 x 99 x 55 cm) (Caso's Stone 70, Zehnder's J-70; Scott's J-70; Garcia Moll et al.'s Stone 40). This reused Building L stone shows the victim's left arm crossing over his torso as well as blood scrolls in his groin area. The nail of the big toe is prominently shown on each foot. The more delicate style of carving seen on this slab and the emphasis placed on

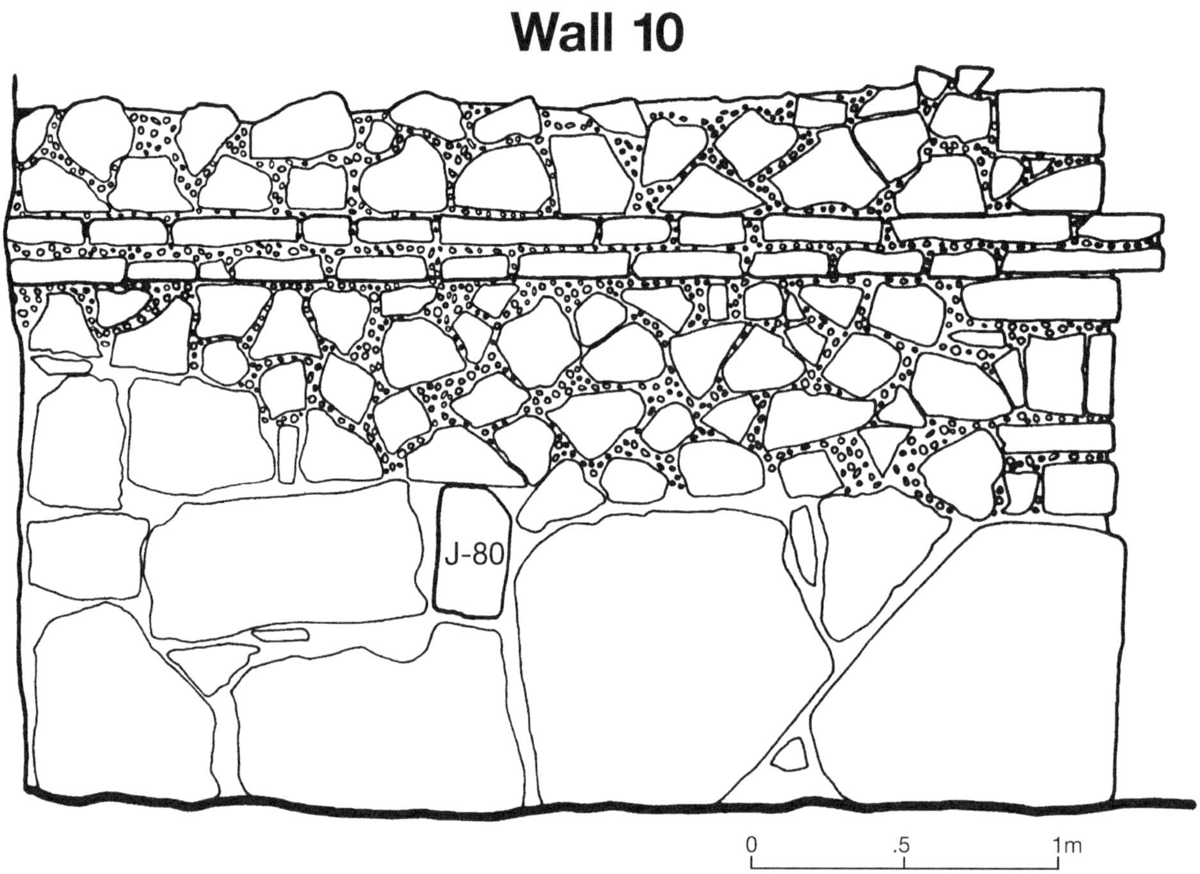

Figure 8.19. Set in Wall 10 of Building J is Monument J-80, another carved stone borrowed from Building L (García Moll et al. 1986: Lámina 6). Drawing by John Klausmeyer.

the nail of the victim's big toe are regarded by Scott (1978) as being attributes of a later style than that displayed by the slabs found *in situ* in Building L. The difference in style, however, may simply reflect the fact that multiple sculptors and work gangs were commissioned to produce the hundreds of prisoner carvings originally placed in Building L.

Stone 41 (80 x 130 x 57 cm) (Caso's Stone 41, Zehnder's J-80; Scott's J-41; Garcia Moll et al.'s Stone 47). This monument (Figure 8.24) is located above Caso's Stone 70, near the top of Building J and on its northwest side (Caso 1947: Figure 23). We see a standing figure who wears a cape, a large earspool, and a mask that may represent Lightning. Above his left hand is the head of a jaguar. Behind the figure's right leg are two hieroglyphs, a hill sign and a compound glyph.

On the figure's body are hieroglyphs. The trident or flowing blood sign seems particularly important here, since it occurs both on the chest and as the second glyph below the right hand.

This monument was originally called "Danzante 41" by Caso (1947: Figure 23), but the individual portrayed is not a Building L-style nude captive. We do not know whether Stone 41 actually goes with Building J or was borrowed from elsewhere, but his costume suggests he was participating in rites involving the offering of blood.

Stone 120 (59 x 90 cm) (Caso's Stone 120; Zehnder's J-69; Scott's J-120; García Moll et al.'s Stone 41). This reused Building L stone shows the highly eroded figure of a captive.

Lápida 40 (107 x 152 cm) (Caso's Lápida 40; Zehnder's J-79; García Moll et al.'s Stone 48). The inverted head below the hill sign on this conquest slab (Figure 8.25) has a hair bun in the rear and a possible pair of feathers on the front of the headdress. The glyph above the hill sign resembles a pectoral.

Monument J-69 (97 x 71 cm) (Caso's Stone 69; Zehnder's J-68; Scott's J-69; García Moll et al.'s Stone 42). This highly eroded outline of a Building L prisoner shows the shoulders, torso, and upper legs.

Monument J-68 (75 x 78 cm) (Caso's Stone 68; Scott's J-68; Zehnder's J-67; García Moll et al.'s Stone 43). This borrowed Building L stone shows a prisoner with his legs splayed awkwardly. His earspool and hairdo are intact.

Monument J-61 (120 x 87 cm) (Caso's stone 61; Scott's J-61; Zehnder's J-66; García Moll et al.'s Stone 44). The captive on this borrowed Building L stone is one of a series

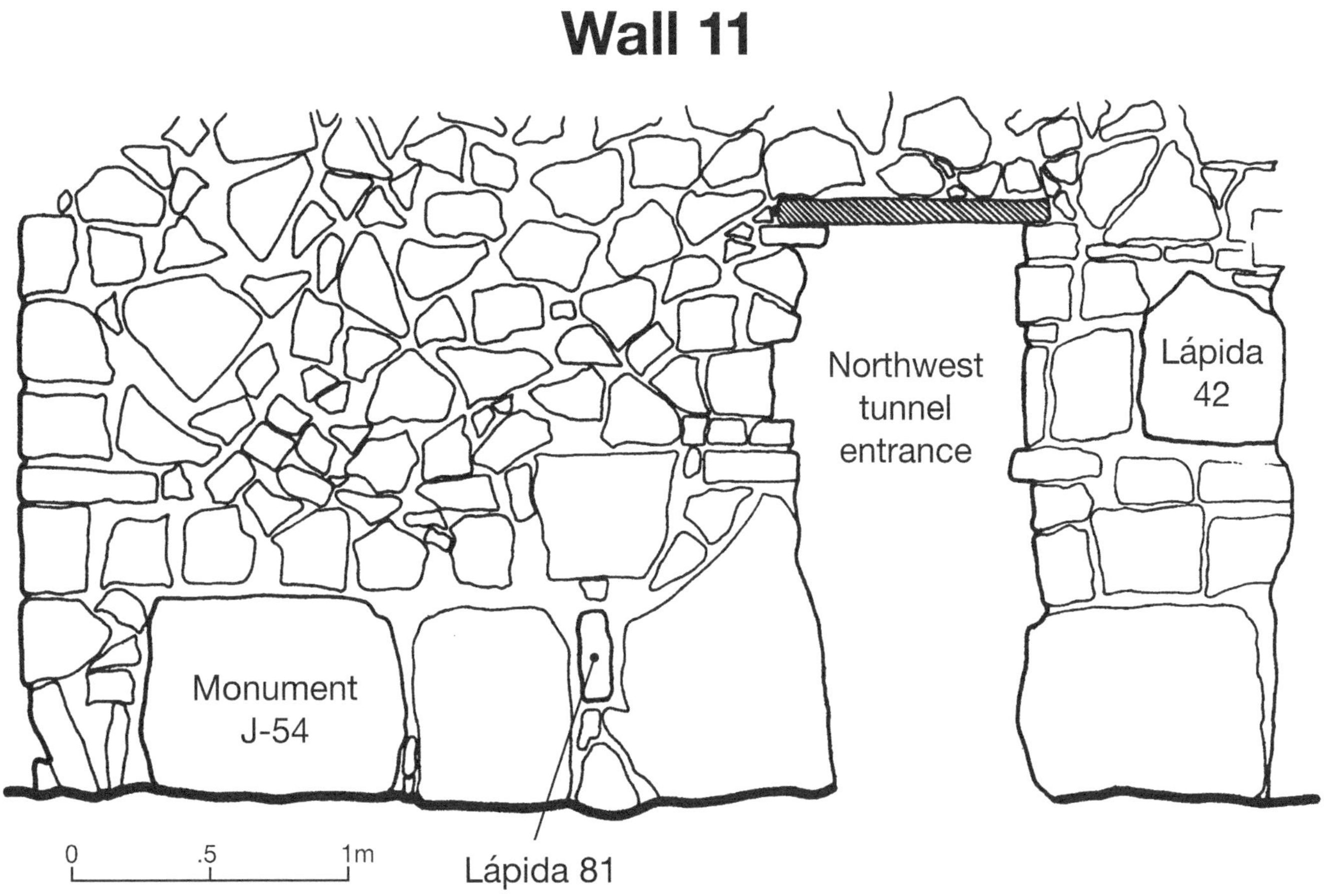

Figure 8.20. Set in Wall 11 of Building J is a narrow fragment, Lápida 81, which shows just one of the upright projections of a hill sign. Monument J-54, borrowed from Building L, shows a captive in an awkward position, with elaborate headgear and possible ties or knots below his chin (García Moll et al. 1986). Drawing by John Klausmeyer.

Figure 8.21. Lápida 42 on Building J (see Figure 8.20 for location) has no inverted head below the hill sign, suggesting that this place was not subjugated by force. Drawing by Jane Mariouw.

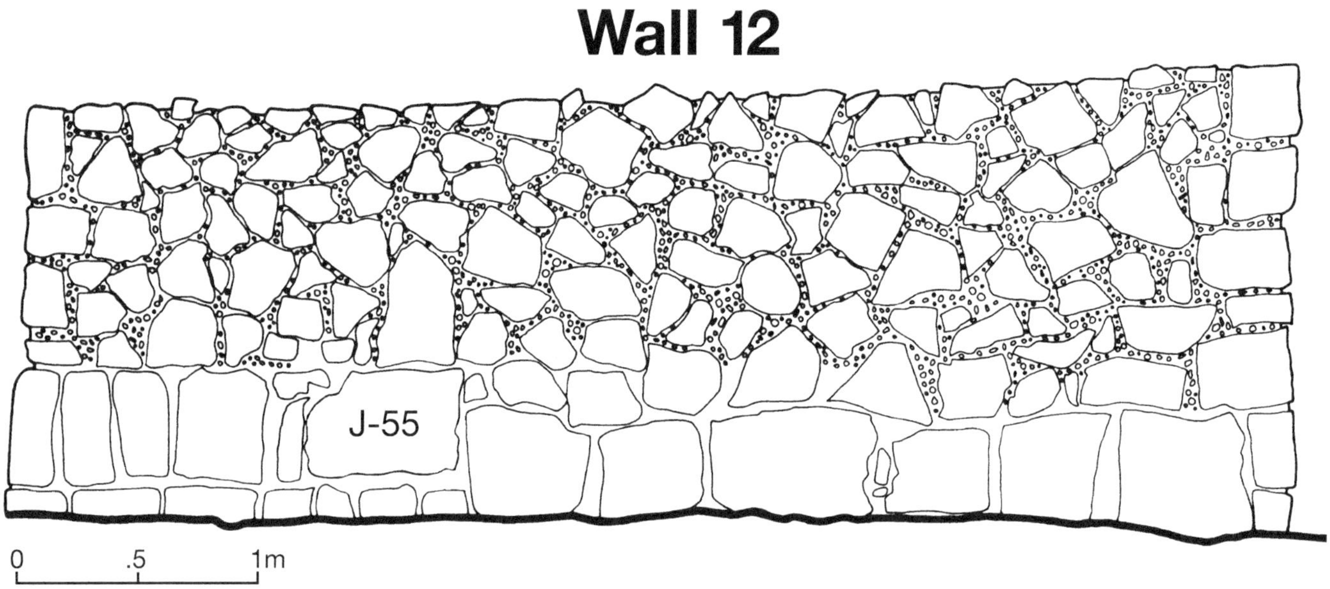

Figure 8.22. Set in Wall 12 of Building J is Monument J-55, a stone borrowed from Building L (García Moll et al. 1986). Drawing by John Klausmeyer.

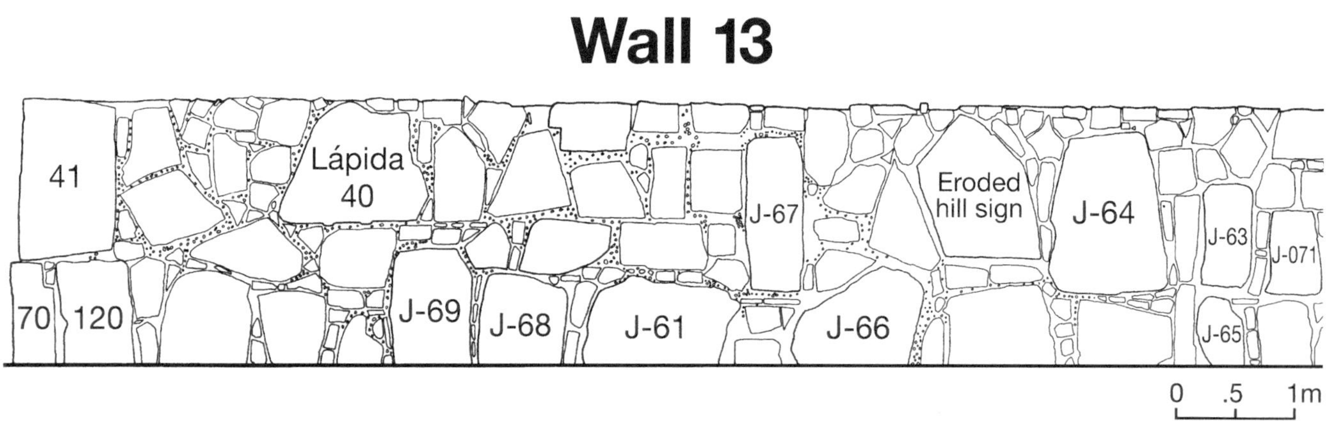

Figure 8.23. Wall 13 on Building J contains both conquest slabs and reused stones with slain captives borrowed from Building L (e.g., Stone 70) (García Moll et al. 1986). Drawing by John Klausmeyer.

Figure 8.24. Stone J-41 was located near the top of Building J (Caso 1947: Fig. 23). We see a standing figure who wears a cape and a mask that may represent *Cociyo* or Lightning. Above his left hand is the head of a jaguar, which may represent the individual's noncalendric nickname. Behind the figure's right leg are two hieroglyphs—a hill sign and a possible compound glyph. These two hieroglyphs seem to be placed on the inside of his cape. This placement is reminiscent of some Classic Maya monuments (e.g., Stela 9 at Calakmul), where hieroglyphs are placed on clothing, such as the hem of a woman's skirt (Marcus 1987:162–163). On this figure's body are hieroglyphic elements on the chest, below the right hand, and in front of the right hand. The trident element (possibly representing flowing blood) seems particularly important, since it occurs both on the chest and as the second glyph below the right hand. On top of the figure's feet are balls similar to those worn by the captives on Monuments D-3 and D-4 (see Figs. 6.29, 6.30). This monument was originally called "Danzante 41" by Caso (1947: Fig. 23), but the individual is clearly not a Building L naked prisoner; he was neither stripped of his attire nor made to suffer the loss of his heart or genitals. He seems to be a *Cociyo* impersonator participating in a ritual, and the placement of his feet may even suggest he danced as part of this ritual. Drawn by Jane Mariouw.

Figure 8.25. Lápida 40 on Building J has an inverted head below the hill sign. The head features a hair bun and a possible pair of feathers on the front of the headdress. Some facial marking is evident on his face. The place name specifier above the hill sign resembles a pectoral, but it has so far not been linked to the name of any archaeological site. Drawing by Jane Mariouw.

of "bearded hulks" (my nickname for a distinctive subset of prisoners). Other "bearded hulks" can be seen on Monuments D-68, D-72, D72A, D-73A, D-80, D-80A, N-10, and N-15.

Monument J-67 (130 x 48 cm) (Caso's Stone 67; Scott's J-67; Zehnder's J-75; García Moll et al.'s Stone 52). The captive on this borrowed Building L stone faces to the viewer's left. His left arm is foreshortened and held against his chest.

Monument J-66 (112 x 86 cm) (Caso's Stone 66; Scott's J-66; Zehnder's J-65; García Moll et al.'s Stone 45). On this borrowed Building L stone, only the bare outlines of a prisoner are present.

Monument J-64 (104 x 136 cm) (Caso's Stone 64; Zehnder's J-73; Scott's J-64; García Moll et al.'s Stone 54). The sprawled captive on this borrowed Building L stone appears to have suffered genital mutilation.

Monument J-63 (41 x 92 cm) (Caso's Stone 63; Zehnder's J-72; Scott's J-63; García Moll et al.'s Stone 55). This borrowed captive stone has a hieroglyph in front of the victim's face, possibly his noncalendric nickname.

Monument J-65 (40 x 72 cm) (Caso's stone 65; Zehnder's J-64; García Moll et al.'s Stone 46). This borrowed Building L prisoner figure is highly eroded.

Monument J-071 (74 x 52 cm) (Marcus' J-071; Zehnder's J-71; García Moll et al.'s Stone 56). This conquest slab bears a hill sign with an inverted head; the specific place name is eroded.

East Tunnel (Figure 8.26)

Lápida 102 (73 x 64 cm) (Caso's Lápida 102; Zehnder's J-103; García Moll et al.'s Stone 26). Preserved on this fragment of a conquest slab is a tiny portion of a hill sign, showing only the top of one of the upward projections.

Lápida 103 (77 x 92 cm) (Caso's Lápida 103; Zehnder's J-102; García Moll et al.'s Stone 25). This conquest slab (Figure 8.27) has the usual hill sign with its interior diagonal lines. Below it is an inverted head that has its cheek decorated with wavy lines, descending from a curved line; an earspool incised with crossed bands; and a unique headdress with what seem to be feathers and a bird head attached to it.

Lápida 104 (94 x 160 cm) (Caso's Lápida 104; Zehnder's J-101; García Moll et al.'s Stone 24). This conquest slab (Figure 8.28) has a hill sign with an inverted head below it. Unfortunately, the specific place glyph above the hill sign is badly eroded. The inverted head is eroded as well, but its headdress seems to have borne a long, loose plant or cloth element.

Lápida 105 (66 x 23 cm) (Caso's Lápida 105; Zehnder's J-100; García Moll et al.'s Stone 23). This carved stone shows fragments of two elements: (1) what seems to be the top of one upright arm of a hill sign; and (2) what appears to be part of a year sign (Figure 8.29).

Lápida 106 (67 x 109 cm) (Caso's Lápida 106; Zehnder's J-99; García Moll et al.'s Stone 22). This conquest slab (Figure 8.30) is better preserved than most, perhaps because it was set in the wall of the East Tunnel and thus protected from the elements (Caso 1947: Figure 50-A).

We see the usual hill sign, a compound place sign above it, an elaborate inverted head below, and a column of two hieroglyphs to the left. The compound place name includes a hand grasping an object.

One of the most impressive parts of the carving is the headdress worn by the upside-down head. The incised cross-hatching may signify that the headdress incorporated braided bundles of hair or similar material. Above the cartouche is a motif that may represent smoke.

Lápida 107 (89 x 96 cm) (Caso's Lápida 107; Zehnder's J-98; García Moll et al.'s Stone 21). This conquest slab (Figure 8.31) shows a hill sign lacking an inverted head. The elements above the hill sign have yet to be identified.

Lápida 108 (90 x 102 cm) (Caso's Lápida 108; Zehnder's J-97; García Moll et al.'s Stone 20). This large conquest slab shows a hill sign with an inverted head below it. Only the right half of the hill sign is preserved.

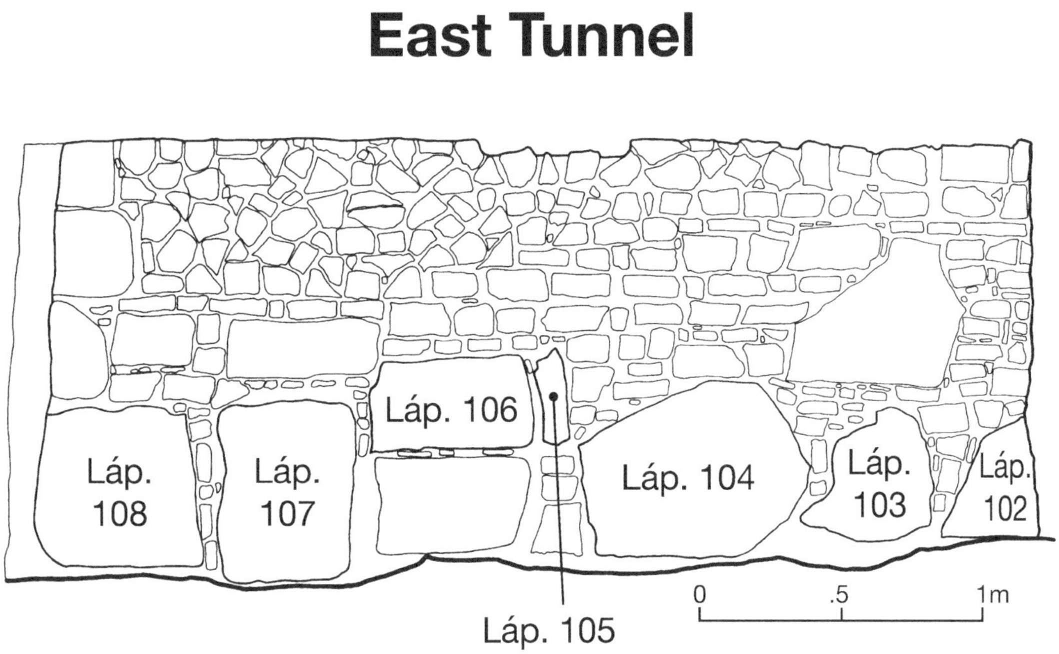

Figure 8.26. Seven carved stones are set in the East Tunnel of Building J. Lápida 102 displays a tiny portion of a hill sign. Lápida 103 has a hill sign with an inverted head. Lápida 104 has a hill sign with an inverted head below it. Lápida 105 shows what seems to be the top of one upright arm of a hill sign and what appears to be part of a year sign. Lápida 106 is one of the most elaborate, better preserved than most of the others (Caso 1947: Figure 50-A). We see the usual hill sign, a compound place sign above it, an elaborate inverted head below, a column of two hieroglyphs to the left, and a single hieroglyph immediately below the inverted head. One of the most impressive parts of the carving is the headdress worn by the upside-down head. The incised cross-hatching may signify that the headdress incorporated braided bundles of hair or similar material. Lápida 107 shows a hill sign without an inverted head. Lápida 108 shows a hill sign with an inverted head below it (see García Moll et al. 1986). Drawing by John Klausmeyer.

Figure 8.27. Lápida 103 on Building J has a hill sign with interior diagonal lines. Below it is an inverted head that has its cheek decorated with three incised lines, descending from a curved line; an earspool with crossed bands; and a unique headdress with what seem to be feathers and a bird head attached to the front of it. Drawing by Jane Mariouw.

Figure 8.28. Lápida 104 on Building J has a hill sign with an inverted head below it. Unfortunately, the place-specifying glyph above the hill sign is badly eroded. The inverted head is eroded as well, but its headdress seems to have borne a long plant or cloth element and crossed bands inside a circular ornament. Drawing by Jane Mariouw.

Figure 8.29. Lápida 105 on Building J shows two elements: (1) at upper left is what seems to be the top of one upright arm of a hill sign; and (2) at lower right is what appears to be part of a year sign. Drawing by Jane Mariouw.

Monuments J-115 and J-116. Both Monuments J-115 and J-116 are borrowed Building L stones, depicting naked prisoners with rubbery, awkwardly positioned bodies, closed eyes, and open mouths. Both individuals face toward the observer's right and wear circular ear ornaments.

Stone J-109 (one fragment measures 72 x 20 cm; another, 30 x 69 cm) (Caso's Stone 109; Zehnder's J-104 and J-108; Scott's J-109; García Moll et al.'s Stone 27). This borrowed Building L stone is now broken in two, near the waist of the prisoner; the upper body is on one slab and the lower body on the other. His body was evidently sprawled full length on his back, with arms at his side and legs apart.

Monument J-110 (46 x 73 cm) (Caso's Stone 110; Zehnder's J-105; Scott's J-110; García Moll et al.'s Stone 28). This borrowed Building L stone shows a prisoner with closed eyes, his right arm dangling down.

Monument J-111 (52 x 45 cm) (Caso's Stone 111; Zehnder's J-106; Scott's J-111; García Moll et al.'s Stone 29). This fragmentary Building L stone shows only the head and shoulders of the prisoner. We see his closed eye, earspool, and open mouth.

Monument J-112 (75 x 69 cm) (Caso's Stone 112; Zehnder's J-107; Scott's J-112; García Moll et al.'s Stone 30). This borrowed Building L stone shows blood flowing from a severed head (see Figure 6.25). Although decapitation was not commonly depicted at Monte Albán, it was a widespread terror tactic used by ancient leaders to intimidate their enemies. The three-pronged flow of blood is a convention seen on other monuments.

Lápida 114 (96 x 90 cm) (Caso's Lápida 114; Zehnder's J-109; García Moll et al.'s Stone 32). Only the hill sign is preserved on this conquest slab; there is no evidence for an inverted head below it, nor any place-specifying elements above it.

Wall A (Figure 8.32)

Many Period II conquest slabs are found in Walls A-D (see Figure 8.3), which form the triangular projection that gives Building J its arrowhead shape.

Monument J-040 (127 x 62 cm) (Marcus' J-040; Zehnder's J-40; García Moll et al.'s Stone 57). An incised hill sign and an oval glyph above it are all that can be detected on this conquest slab.

Lápida 3 (153 x 111 cm) (Caso's Lápida 3; Zehnder's J-39; García Moll et al.'s Stone 58). This conquest slab (Figure 8.33) features all three components of a defeated place: the hill sign, the specific element above it that supplies the place name, and the inverted head below. Above the hill sign is a chile pepper plant, plus a second element that may have been pronounced *guehl* (field) or *xan* ("below or at the base of").

I have suggested that Chiltepec (a locality between the Valley of Oaxaca and the Pacific Coast) may have been the name of this subjugated place. I also considered Chilixtlahuaca, "plain of the chiles," as well as San Jacinto Chilateca, "where chiles abound."

Figure 8.30. Lápida 106 on Building J is one of the most elaborate of the conquest slabs. It is better preserved than most of the others, perhaps because it was set into the wall of the East Tunnel and thus protected from the elements (Caso 1947: Fig. 50-A). We see the usual hill sign; a compound place-specifier above it; an elaborate inverted head below. We also see a column of two hieroglyphs to the left and a single hieroglyph immediately below the inverted head. The compound place name above the hill sign includes two or three elements, including a hand grasping an object. One of the most impressive parts of the carving is the headdress worn by the upside-down head. Projecting from the headdress is what appears to be a weapon with inset obsidian triangles. The two-glyph column on the left consists of an unusual hieroglyph, followed by 2W. Below the inverted head is the hieroglyph for 2 Maize (2J). Drawing by Jane Mariouw.

Figure 8.31. Lápida 107 on Building J shows a hill sign with no inverted head below it. The place-specifying elements above the hill sign have yet to be identified. Drawing by Jane Mariouw.

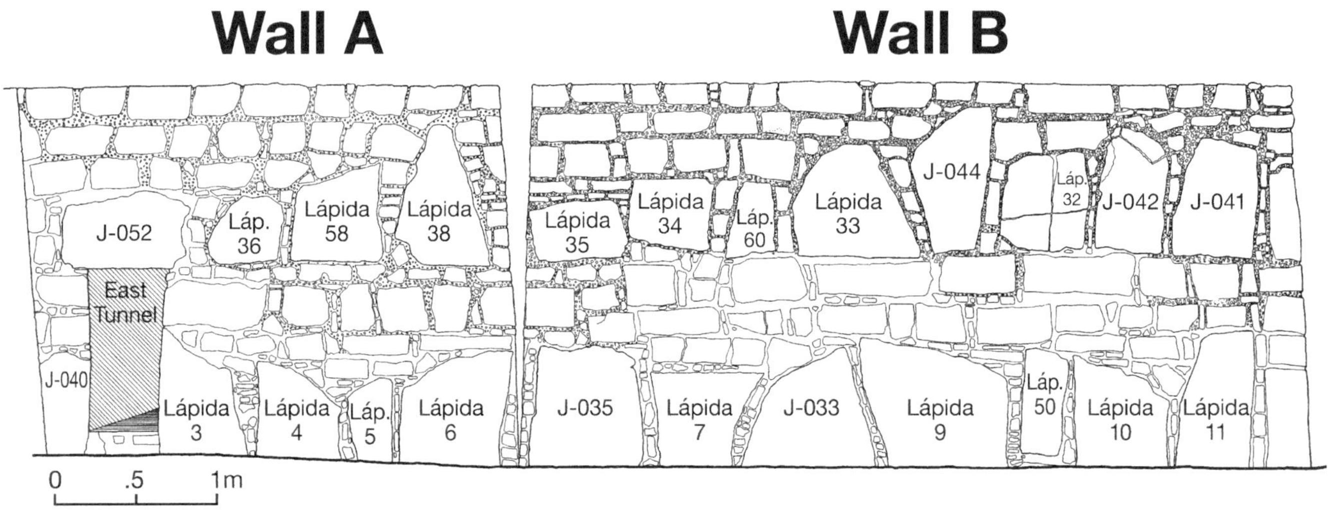

Figure 8.32. Walls A and B of Building J include a large number of Period II conquest slabs (see Figure 8.3 for the location of Walls A and B; see also García Moll et al. 1986). Drawing by John Klausmeyer.

These names are Nahuatl, so we can only hope that the Nahuatl names are translations of the original Zapotec place names (see Bradomín [1955]1980:56, 102, 129, 198). All three of these places should be surveyed to see whether Period II pottery is present.

Lápida 4 (121 x 108 cm) (Caso's Lápida 4; Zehnder's J-38; García Moll et al.'s Stone 59). This conquest slab, like Lápida 3, has three elements: (1) a hill sign; (2) a place-specifying glyph depicting a stone structure with crossed bands inside its doorway, three decorative circles just below its roof, and five circles pecked into its base; and (3) an inverted head with horizontal lines above and below the eye (Figure 8.34) (Caso 1947: Figure 41).

On the assumption that the stone structure is a palace, Santo Domingo Teipan, "palace" and San Juan Teitipac, "toward the stone palace," are two possibilities. Alfredo Chavero is cited by Bradomín ([1955]1980:184), who has this to say about Teitipac:

> diremos que tenían otro lugar de descanso llamado Zeetobá, que eso significa la palabra que servía para enterrar a los grandes señores que no eran reyes. Estaba en un lugar (Teitipac) llamado Keuékijezá, que quiere decir: "palacio de piedra", porque, según el cronista, se edificó sobre una grandísima losa.

I am not sure whether the crossed-bands motif in the doorway of the building adds semantic or phonetic value, but it may help to reinforce the reading of this place name as "stone palace."

Lápida 5 (105 x 57 cm) (Figure 8.35) (Caso's Lápida 5; Zehnder's J-37; García Moll et al.'s Stone 60). This is another conquest slab with all three elements: the hill sign, the glyphs above the hill sign, and the inverted head. The hill sign has three diagonal interior lines (running from top right to bottom left) and no circles. The specifier is a compound with two elements: a possible necklace and, below it, a possible pectoral.

Lápida 6 (141 x 136 cm) (Figure 8.36) (Caso's Lápida 6; Zehnder's J-36; García Moll et al.'s Stone 61). This conquest slab bears four elements. The place-specifying glyph above the hill sign is not clear. Below the hill sign we see an inverted head with a folded-over braid of hair and a folded-over cloth. The fourth element below the hill sign is 7 Owl (7 Night), which could either be the calendric name of the lord whose inverted head is shown or the date of his defeat.

Monument J-052 (95 x 160 cm) (Marcus' J-052; Zehnder's J-52; García Moll et al.'s Stone 62). This conquest slab displays three elements: a hill sign, a largely eroded glyph that once specified the place name, and the lower half of an inverted head. This slab was set into the wall just above the tunnel entrance.

Lápida 36 (85 x 93 cm) (Caso's Lápida 36; Zehnder's J-51; García Moll et al.'s Stone 63). This conquest slab has three components: a hill sign, a somewhat eroded place-specifying glyph, and an inverted human head.

Lápida 58 (126 x 119 cm) (Caso's Lápida 58; Zehnder's J-50; García Moll et al.'s Stone 64). This conquest slab is quite eroded, but we can see part of the inverted head and the feathers or ornaments that formed part of its headdress. We see only the lower right portion of the hill sign. The place-specifying glyphs above the hill sign are missing except for a few lines.

Figure 8.33. Lápida 3 on Building J features the three components of a defeated place: the hill sign, the specific element above it that supplies the place name, and the inverted head. Above the hill sign is a chile pepper plant, plus a second element that may be a phonetic complement. I have suggested that Chiltepec (a locality between the Valley of Oaxaca and the Pacific Coast) may have been the name of this subjugated place. However, I also considered Chilixtlahuaca, "plain of the chiles," as well as San Jacinto Chilateca, "where chiles abound." Unfortunately, all these names are Nahuatl, so we can only hope that those names were translations of the original Zapotec place names (see Bradomín [1955]1980:56, 102, 129, 198). (All three of these places should be surveyed to see whether Monte Albán Period II pottery is present.) The inverted head below the hill sign has a transverse stripe extending from the top of the nose to the jaw. The pillbox hat is distinctive and would have reinforced the place name by signifying the ethnic group or region. Drawing by Jane Mariouw.

Figure 8.34. Lápida 4 on Building J has all three elements: (1) a hill sign; (2) a place-specifying glyph depicting a stone structure with crossed bands inside its doorway, three decorative circles just below its roof, and five circles pecked into its base; and (3) an inverted head with horizontal lines above and below the eye. On the assumption that the stone structure is a palace, two possible places would be Santo Domingo Teipan, "palace," and San Juan Teitipac, "toward the stone palace." Drawing by Jane Mariouw.

Figure 8.35. Lápida 5 on Building J has the hill sign, the place-specifying glyphs above the hill sign, and the inverted head. The hill sign has three diagonal interior lines but no droplets or circles. The specific place glyph is a compound with two elements: a possible necklace, and below it, a possible pectoral. The inverted head has a diagonal stripe extending from above the nose to below the ear. Its headgear includes a frisbee-like cap with dangling ornaments or strips of cloth. Drawing by Jane Mariouw.

Figure 8.36. Lápida 6 on Building J has four elements; the place-specifying glyph above the hill sign is not clear. Below the hill sign we see an inverted head with a folded-over braid of hair and a folded cloth. The fourth element (below the hill sign) seems to be 7 Owl/Night, which could either be (1) the calendric name of the deceased lord whose inverted head is shown or (2) the date of his defeat. Drawing by Jane Mariouw.

Figure 8.37. Lápida 38 on Building J refers to a place that has a similar name to that on Lápida 35. The place-specifying glyph consists of a rectangular object above the atlatl sign. The inverted head has a hair bun or spherical element at the rear; a prominent strap seems to fasten the headgear to the individual's hair. Drawing by Jane Mariouw.

Lápida 38 (165 x 123 cm) (Caso's Lápida 38; Zehnder's J-49; García Moll et al.'s Stone 65). This conquest slab (Figure 8.37) refers to a place that is similar to the one on Lápida 35 (see below). The place-specifying glyph consists of a rectangular object and the atlatl sign. The inverted head has a hair bun or spherical element at the rear.

Wall B (see Figure 8.32)

Lápida 35 (74 x 125 cm) (Caso's Lápida 35; Zehnder's J-48; García Moll et al. Stone 73). This conquest slab (Figure 8.38) displays three elements: the hill sign, a place-specifying compound above the hill sign, and an inverted head below it. The compound includes the atlatl sign.

Such a place name might have been read *tani* + *gui* (hill sign + atlatl) or *gui* (with the *gui* of atlatl and the *gui* of rocky hill simply reinforcing each other). Note that this place name is similar to the one on Lápida 38.

Lápida 34 (90 x 105 cm) (Caso's Lápida 34; Zehnder's J-47; García Moll et al.'s Stone 74). This conquest slab (Figure 8.39) displays three components: the hill sign, the head of a jackrabbit, and an inverted head with its hair in a knot above the forehead. "Hill of the Jackrabbit" would be Tepetochtepec in Nahuatl and *Tani Bi'lana* or *Tani Pillana* in Zapotec.

Lápida 60 (81 x 95 cm) (Caso's Lápida 60; Zehnder's J-46; García Moll et al.'s Stone 75). This conquest slab (Figure 8.40) features a hill sign plus two elements that form a compound place name. These elements consist of a bean-like sign above an unknown glyph. Oaxaca does have places whose

Figure 8.38. Lápida 35 on Building J displays three elements: the hill sign, a place-specifying compound above the hill sign, and an inverted head below it. The compound includes the atlatl sign, attached to a rectangular element with diagonal lines inside it. Such a place name might have been read *tani* + *gui* (hill sign + atlatl) or *gui* (with the *gui* of atlatl and the *gui* of rocky hill simply reinforcing each other). Note that this place name is similar to the one on Lápida 38, which is set nearby in Wall A (see Figure 8.37). The inverted heads are also similar. Drawing by Jane Mariouw.

Figure 8.39. Lápida 34 on Building J displays three components: the hill sign, the head of a jackrabbit, and an inverted head with its hair tied in a knot above the forehead. One translation of "Hill of the Jackrabbit" might be Tepetochtepec in Nahuatl and *Tani Bi'lana* or *Tani Pillana* in Zapotec. We have yet to locate a place with this name that also has Monte Albán Period II ceramics. Drawing by Jane Mariouw.

names incorporate the term for "beans," such as Lachi Bishá, but the evidence here is not sufficient to specify a place. If Lápida 60 ever had an inverted head below the hill sign, it is now gone.

Lápida 33 (145 x 154 cm) (Caso's Lápida 33; Zehnder's J-45; García Moll et al.'s Stone 76). This conquest slab (Figure 8.41) displays the hill sign, a compound place name above it, and an inverted human head below it. The hill sign has diagonal lines in its center, but lacks the figure eights frequently seen to either side of those lines. The elements comprising the compound name include the atlatl and a possible grasshopper. A vertical line (possibly depicting paint) passes through the eye of the inverted head, then curves to connect with the nose.

Monument J-044 (180 x 100 cm) (Marcus' J-044; Zehnder's J-44 and García Moll et al.'s Stone 77). This stone has suffered exfoliation, which unfortunately means that most of the incised lines are gone.

Lápida 32 (122 x 112 cm) (Caso's Lápida 32; Zehnder's J-43; García Moll et al.'s Stone 78). This conquest slab (Figure 8.42) features the hill sign, a place-specifying glyph above it, and an inverted head with a possible tattoo below it. The place-specifying glyph is a human face pierced by a lance. I have suggested that this glyph may refer to Sosola, "The Place of the Pierced Face."

There is a place called Sosola today in the nearby Mixteca Alta. There Robert Drennan (1983:111) found that the "ceramic affinities at this time period (Late and Terminal Formative) are clearly with the Valley of Oaxaca rather than with Nochixtlán, and suggest Zapotec expansion."

Monument J-042 (158 x 85 cm) (Marcus' J-042; Zehnder's J-42; García Moll et al.'s Stone 79). This slab is heavily weathered.

Monument J-041 (117 x 145 cm) (Marcus' J-041; Zehnder's J-41; García Moll et al.'s Stone 80). This conquest slab was labeled J-41 by Zehnder, which created some confusion, since both Caso and Scott had assigned that number to other carved stones. I designated this stone J-041 rather than pick yet another number. Since only the left half of a hill sign can be identified, the problem may be moot.

Monument J-035 (152 x 151 cm) (Marcus' J-035; Zehnder's J-35; García Moll et al.'s Stone 66). The carving has spalled off this slab.

Lápida 7 (120 x 146 cm) (Caso's Lápida 7; Zehnder's J-34; García Moll et al.'s Stone 67). This conquest slab (Figure 8.43) displays four elements: (1) the hill sign; (2) a compound place name above it; (3) an inverted head below it; and (4) a date. The compound place name consists of a hand grasping an element, a trilobal element, and two flower-like or maize kernel projections. Such tripartite compound signs were probably read phonetically, as Caso (1947) once suggested; other hand-grasping glyphs can be found on Lápidas 13, 14, 21, and 106. As for the date, it consists of an 8 (one bar and three dots) and a day sign.

Monument J-033 (146 x 165 cm) (Marcus's J-033; Zehnder's J-33; García Moll et al.'s Stone 68). This slab is very eroded.

Figure 8.40. Lápida 60 on Building J features a hill sign plus two elements that form a compound place name. These elements consist of a bean-like sign above an unknown glyph. Oaxaca does have places whose names incorporate the term for "beans," such as Lachi Bishá, but the evidence here is not sufficient to specify a place. If Lápida 60 had once had an inverted head below the hill sign, it is now too eroded to study. Drawing by Jane Mariouw.

Figure 8.41. Lápida 33 on Building J displays the hill sign, a compound place name above it, and an inverted human head below it. The hill sign has diagonal lines in its interior, but lacks the circles or droplets frequently seen on either side of those lines. The elements comprising the compound name include the atlatl and a possible grasshopper. A vertical line passes through the eye of the inverted head, then curves to connect with the nose; a knot is tied in the forelock, similar to the one on Lápida 34 (Figure 8.39). Drawing by Jane Mariouw.

Figure 8.42. Lápida 32 on Building J features the hill sign, a place-specifying glyph above it, and an inverted head. The place-specifying glyph is a human face whose cheek has been pierced by a lance. I have suggested that this glyph may refer to Sosola, "The Place of the Pierced Face." There is a place called Sosola where Robert Drennan (1983:111) found that the "ceramic affinities at this time period (Late and Terminal Formative) are clearly with the Valley of Oaxaca rather than with Nochixtlán, and suggest Zapotec expansion." Drawing by Jane Mariouw.

Lápida 9 (157 x 195 cm) (Caso's Lápida 9; Zehnder's J-32; García Moll et al.'s Stone 69). This conquest slab (Figure 8.44) displays the hill sign, a place name, and a date. There seems to have been an inverted head below the hill sign, but it is now eroded. The two elements above the hill sign include (1) a plant (?) and (2) a box-like element which may be the sign for "field" (*guehl* or *gehl* in Zapotec). There are many Zapotec place names that include "field"—for example, *Guehl ze'e*, "milpa de elotes" or "field of corn" (Zúñiga 1982:65, 130).

Lápida 50 (133 x 55 cm) (Caso's Lápida 50; Zehnder's J-31; García Moll et al.'s Stone 70). This conquest slab (Figure 8.45) features a hill sign with two place-specifying elements above it. One element is an unidentified object, while the other appears to be the sign for water (*nis* or *nisa* in Zapotec). The date 11 Water (11Z) occurs on the slab.

Lápida 10 (138 x 125 cm) (Caso's Lápida 10; Zehnder's J-30; García Moll et al.'s Stone 71). The layout of this conquest slab (Figure 8.46) is similar to that of Lápidas 12, 13, and 16. The year sign and year bearer on the right side of the stone (Caso 1947: Figure 42) can be read as the Year 6E. To the left of the hill sign is 8W. Below the place name is a possible 12B.

The place-specifying glyph above the hill sign is a heron or similar bird. The inverted head has a beard, a scroll that curls up and ends behind the mouth, and a diagonal line that extends from below the ear up to the top of the nose. The associated headgear may include cloth strips, some of which dangle free while others appear to be tied together.

Lápida 11 (175 x 95 cm) (Caso's Lápida 11; Zehnder's J-29; García Moll et al.'s Stone 72). This conquest slab (Figure 8.47) displays the hill sign, a compound place name, and an inverted head. The place name includes crossed bands and a box like that of Lápida 43, which may stand for *guehl/guela*, "field."

Wall C (Figure 8.48)

Lápida 12 (148 x 133 cm) (Caso's Lápida 12; Zehnder's J-2; García Moll et al.'s Stone 81). This complex slab (Figure 8.49) displays multiple components: (1) a hill sign whose interior is largely eroded, but whose upward arms are well preserved; (2) place-specifying glyphs above the hill sign; (3) an inverted head; (4) a year sign (at far right) containing the number 12; (5) the hieroglyphs 2 + Monkey (below the place name); and (6) two glyphs, the lower of which appears to be an upside-down Glyph W.

Lápida 13 (191 x 198 cm) (Caso's Lápida 13; Zehnder's J-3; García Moll et al.'s Stone 82). This slab (Figure 8.50) is similar in layout to Lápida 12. The year sign appears to the right of the centrally situated place glyph; a two-glyph column appears on the left side of the stone, with its lower element being a Glyph W; and a day sign is centered below the place glyph. The hill sign has diagonal lines within it and two figure eights to either side. The element below the hill sign is not an inverted head.

Lápida 14 (190 x 158 cm) (Caso's Lápida 14; Zehnder's J-4; García Moll et al.'s Stone 83). This conquest slab (Figure 8.51) is notable for its columns of text. A year sign + year bearer

Figure 8.43. Lápida 7 on Building J displays four elements: (1) the hill sign; (2) a compound place name above it; (3) an inverted head below it; and (4) a date. The compound place name consists of a hand grasping an element, a trilobal element that some interpret as a heart, and two projections similar to stylized maize kernels. Such compound signs were probably read phonetically, as Caso (1947) once suggested. Other hand-grasping glyphs can be found on Lápidas 13, 14, 21, and 106, as well as on Stela 12 (Chapter 6, Figure 6.52). Drawing by Jane Mariouw.

Figure 8.44. Lápida 9 on Building J displays the hill sign, the place name, and a date. There are traces of an inverted head below the hill sign, but it is now eroded. The two elements above the hill sign include (1) a plant (?) and (2) a box-like element, which may be the sign for "field" (*guehl* or *gehl* in Zapotec). (There are many Zapotec place names that include "field," including *Guehl ze'e* or "field of corn" [Zúñiga 1982:65, 130]). As for the date, it consists of the number 6 or 11 and a possible day sign for Maize (Glyph J). Drawing by Jane Mariouw.

Figure 8.45. Lápida 50 on Building J features a hill sign with place-specifying elements above it. One element has a comb-like end; the other appears to be the sign for water (*nis* or *nisa* in Zapotec). The date 11 Water (11Z) occurs below the hill sign. There is no inverted human head below the hill sign, suggesting that this place joined Monte Albán's sphere peacefully. Drawing by Jane Mariouw.

Figure 8.46. Lápida 10 on Building J is similar to Lápidas 12, 13, and 16 in having all three elements plus hieroglyphs. There is a year sign at right (6E) and 8W at left. In the 1930s, Caso could see 8 + Glyph W (1947: Fig. 42, page 75), and although my artists in the 1970s could just see a few faint lines, those lines did fit the outline of a Glyph W. Below the place name is a day sign, possibly 12B, which may be either the calendric name of the defeated lord or the date the place was conquered. The place-specifying glyph above the hill sign is a heron or similar bird. The inverted head has chin hair, a scroll that curls up and ends behind the mouth, and a diagonal stripe that extends from below the ear to the top of the nose. The associated headgear may include cloth strips, some of which dangle while others appear to be tied together. The latter feature reminds us of Lápida 5 (see Figure 8.35). Drawing by Jane Mariouw.

Figure 8.47. Lápida 11 on Building J displays the hill sign, a compound place name, and an inverted head. The place name includes two elements: (1) crossed bands and (2) a box like that of Lápida 43, which may stand for the Zapotec word *guehl/guela*, which means “field.” Only a possible earspool of the inverted head below the hill sign can be detected. Drawing by Jane Mariouw.

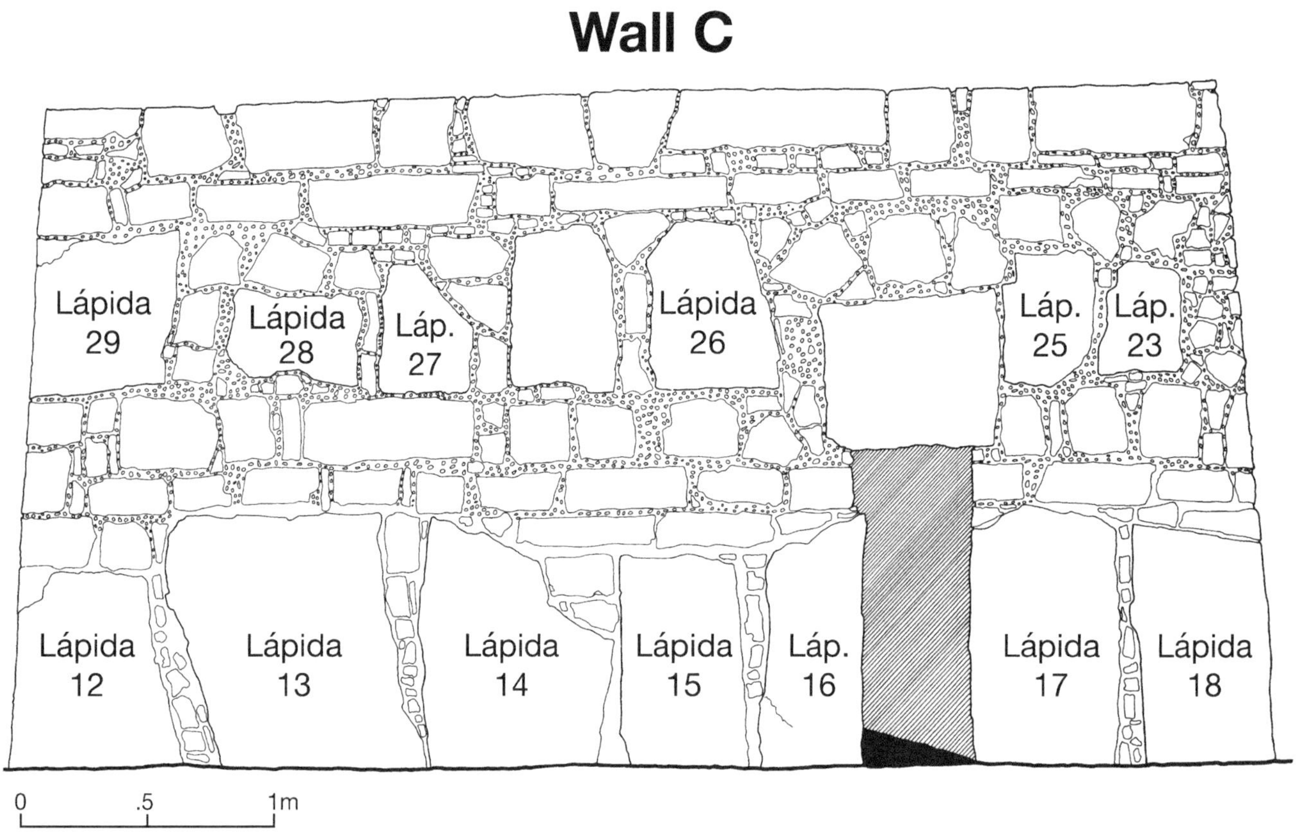

Figure 8.48. Wall C of Building J featured 13 carved stones (Lápidas 12–18, 23, and 23–29). See also Figure 8.3. Drawing by John Klausmeyer.

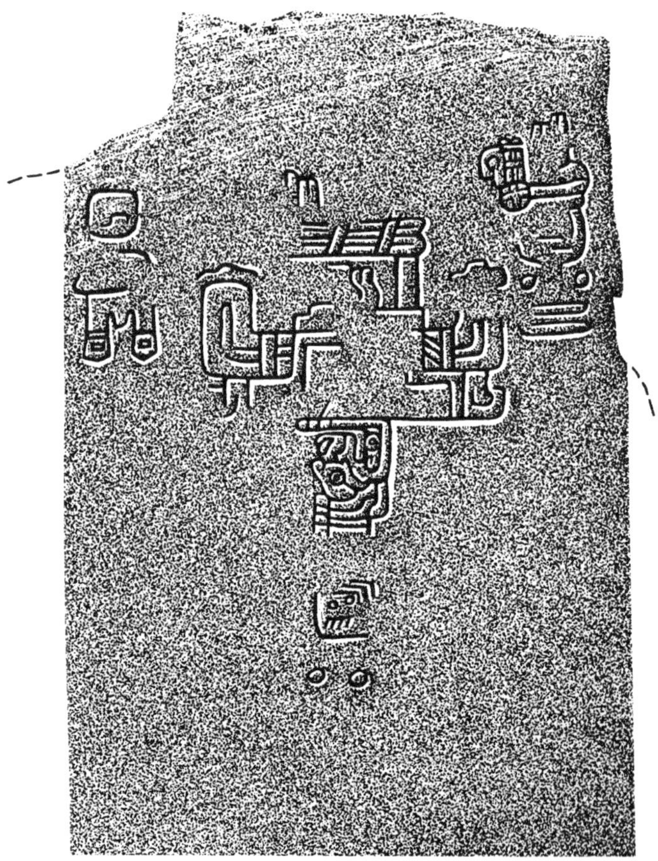

Figure 8.49. Lápida 12 on Building J displays six components: (1) a hill sign whose interior is largely eroded, but whose upward arms are well preserved; (2) place-specifying glyphs above the hill sign; (3) an inverted head; (4) a year sign (at far right) containing the number 12; (5) a day sign (below the place name and inverted head) that may be 2 Monkey; and (6) two glyphs (at far left), the lower of which appears to be an upside-down Glyph W. Drawing by Jane Mariouw.

Figure 8.50. Lápida 13 on Building J is similar in layout to Lápida 12 (Figure 8.49). A column of text appears on the left side of the monument, with two glyphs: 5P and 15W. A day sign (7 + ?) is centered at the bottom of this stone. The year sign (at far right) seems to designate the Year 3M. The hill sign has diagonal lines within it and two figure eights to either side. The element below the hill sign is not an inverted head. The glyphs above the hill sign form a place-specifying compound; included are three or four elements, the lowest of which is a hand grasping an object. Drawing by Jane Mariouw.

Figure 8.51. Lápida 14 is notable for displaying some of the longest columns of texts on Building J. We see a year sign + year bearer (6E) at the top center of the stone; that 6E appears above the compound place-specifying sign. Below we see a day sign with the number 11. Since these dates bracket the place sign, it seems likely that they date Monte Albán's takeover of that place; nevertheless, no inverted head is shown. There are three columns of hieroglyphs: (1) at upper left we see perhaps a dozen small glyphs, plus one large glyph compound at the end of the far left column; and (2) a single column of four glyphs at the right edge of the stone. Although the upper text includes both calendric (e.g., 2CC, 8A, 10P) and noncalendric glyphs, it is the calendric signs (i.e., those with bars and dots) that have received the most attention. One hieroglyph that occurs four times in this text—Caso's Glyph W—is of particular interest, because in other texts it occurs with numbers greater than 13. Because day signs cannot be associated with a number exceeding 13, Caso interpreted Glyph W as a month sign. Drawing by Jane Mariouw.

Figure 8.52. Lápida 15 on Building J features the usual hill sign, a compound place-specifier above it, an inverted head below it, and a text near the inverted head. The hill sign has the usual interior diagonal lines, but lacks the circles that often flank them. The compound place-specifier includes three or four elements that combine to form the place name. Reading from bottom to top, we see (1) a rectangular element filled with bead-like circles; (2) a bean-shaped element; and (3) what may be a flower. These elements may have been read phonetically. The inverted head on this slab has a tied element as its ear ornament and a bejeweled feather or other element projecting from the top of the headgear. To the right of the inverted head we see a year sign + Glyph 5E (according to Caso). Directly below the inverted head is another date (possibly 5 Knot or 5A). At the left are two hieroglyphs: an inverted Glyph W with an eroded sign above it. (Note that year signs were placed below the hill sign and near the right edge, on this slab and on Lápida 16). Drawing by Jane Mariouw.

(6E) appear above the compound place sign; a day sign with the number 11 appears below.

The long text on this slab is divided into two parts: (1) a text at upper left with perhaps a dozen small glyphs, plus a large glyph compound at the end of the left-hand column; and (2) a single column of four glyphs at right. Although the text includes both calendric and noncalendric glyphs, it is the calendric signs that have received the most attention.

One hieroglyph that occurs four times—Glyph W—is of particular interest, because this monument should be one of the keys in its decipherment. One clue is that in other texts, Glyph W occurs with numbers greater than 13, i.e. more than a day in the 260-day calendar can have (see Caso 1947, 1967; Urcid 2001; Whittaker 1982).

Lápida 15 (160 x 98 cm) (Caso's Lápida 15; Zehnder's J-5; García Moll et al.'s Stone 84). This slab (Figure 8.52) features the hill sign, a place-specifier sign above it, an inverted head below it, and a text below the place-specifier. The hill sign has the usual interior diagonal lines. The compound place-specifier includes three or four elements that combine to form the place name. Reading from bottom to top, we see (1) a rectangular element filled with bead-like circles; (2) a bean-shaped element; and (3) a possible plant.

The inverted head on this slab has a tied element as its ear ornament and a bejeweled feather or other element projecting from the top of its headgear. A hieroglyphic text begins at the right, where we see a year sign that Caso regarded as Glyph 5E. (Note that year signs were also placed below the hill sign and near the right edge of the slab on Lápida 16 [see below]). Below the inverted head is another date. At the left are two more hieroglyphs, including an inverted Glyph W.

Lápida 16 (185 x 76 cm) (Caso's Lápida 16; Zehnder's J-6; García Moll et al.'s Stone 85). This conquest slab (Figure 8.53) features a place sign in the upper center of the stone, a year sign on the right, and a column of three glyphs on the left; the latter column includes an upside-down Glyph W. There is also an inverted head with a few dots on its cheek and tight-fitting headgear.

Above the hill sign is a compound place-specifier consisting of a three-pronged element like a plant or crown, and a thin base or platform with five pecked circles (the latter is reminiscent of the base of the stone structure in the place-specifier on Lápida 4). On the right we see the Year 8M. At left we see an animal head (?), the upside-down Glyph W, and another sign (possibly Monkey or Glyph O) bearing the coefficient 13, although it looks like 18 (Caso 1947: Lámina 66).

Lápida 17 (193 x 114 cm) (Caso's Lápida 17; Zehnder's J-7; García Moll et al.'s Stone 86). This slab is largely eroded, but we can see traces of the two vertical projections of the hill sign, equally faint traces of the elements comprising the specific name of the place, and an inverted head.

Lápida 18 (177 x 107 cm) (Caso's Lápida 18; Zehnder's J-8; García Moll et al.'s Stone 87). This conquest slab (Figure 8.54) displays the hill sign, a tripartite place name, an inverted head, and an associated hieroglyphic date. The hill sign has the three

Figure 8.53. Lápida 16 on Building J features a place sign, a year sign (lower right), and a column of three glyphs to the left; the latter column includes an animal head, an upside-down Glyph W, and possibly 13 Monkey (13O), even though it almost looks like 18O. The inverted head has a few dots on its cheek. Above the hill sign is a compound place-specifier consisting of a three-pronged element like a crown, and a thin base or platform with five pecked circles (the latter is reminiscent of the base of the stone structure in the place-specifier on Lápida 4). On the right, we see the Year 8M (see Caso 1947: Fig. 45, Lámina 66). Drawing by Jane Mariouw.

Figure 8.54. Lápida 18 on Building J displays the hill sign, a compound place name, an inverted head, and an associated hieroglyphic date. The hill sign has the diagnostic diagonal lines and paired figure eights. The tripartite place-specifier includes (from bottom to top) an element that is also seen on Lápida 3; a possible head; and two pennants. Below the head is a day sign with 11 as its coefficient, associated with a possible Glyph B (11B). The inverted head has a knotted hairdo and a bejeweled element projecting from the top of its headgear (like the one on Lápida 15). This inverted head has distinctive markings. See also Figure 8.27. Drawing by Jane Mariouw.

Figure 8.55. Although Lápida 23 on Building J has no columns of hieroglyphs, it does include two of the typical elements: the hill sign and a place-specifier above it. The hill sign has diagonal lines in the interior, but lacks the usual paired circles. The place-specifier—which includes only one element: the head of a jaguar or ocelot—might have been pronounced *Gui Beche, Tani Gui Beche*, or *Tani Beche* in Zapotec. A hill with the Zapotec name Dani Gui Beche lies in the Isthmus of Tehuantepec (Covarrubias 1946: map). A town with the Nahuatl name Ocelotepec lies southeast of the Valley of Oaxaca. The Nahuatl name for Tehuantepec is also composed of the words *tehuan/tecuani*, "jaguar," and *tepetl/tepec*, "hill"; it is possible that this might be a Nahuatl translation of the original Zapotec name. Of special note is the fact that this slab has no inverted head, suggesting that this community accepted Monte Albán's expansion peacefully. Drawing by Jane Mariouw.

expected diagonal lines and paired figure eights. The tripartite place name includes (from bottom to top): an element that is also seen on Lápida 3, an unknown element, and two pennants. The inverted head has a knotted hairdo and a bejeweled element on a feather projecting from the top of its headgear. A curved line extends from the cheek to the side of the nose; wiggly lines descend from a line below the eye.

Lápida 23 (72 x 85 cm) (Caso's Lápida 23; Zehnder's J-19; García Moll et al.'s Stone 95). On this slab (Figure 8.55) we see two of the typical elements: the hill sign and a place-specifier above it. The hill sign has diagonal lines in the interior, but lacks the usual paired figure eights. The place-specifier—which includes only one element, the head of a jaguar or ocelot—might have been pronounced *Gui Beche, Tani Gui Beche,* or *Tani Beche* in Zapotec.

A hill with the Zapotec name Dani Gui Beche lies in the Isthmus of Tehuantepec (Covarrubias 1946: map). A town with the Nahuatl name Ocelotepec lies southeast of the Valley of Oaxaca (Marcus 1980, 1992a, 1992c).

The Nahuatl name for Tehuantepec is composed of the words *tehuan/tecuani*, "jaguar," and *tepetl/tepec*, "hill"; it is possible that the Nahuatl name is a translation of the original Zapotec name. (It is not clear what distinction, if any, the Zapotec made between a jaguar and an ocelot.)

Lápida 25 (100 x 70 cm) (Caso's Lápida 25; Zehnder's J-18; García Moll et al.'s Stone 94). This conquest slab (Figure 8.56) features a hill sign; a place-specifier combining a dumbbell-shaped object with a sign that has lines descending from it; an inverted head with a vertical line passing through its eye and curving to touch its nose; and a bejeweled feather projecting from its headgear.

Lápida 26 (120 x 99 cm) (Caso's Lápida 26; Zehnder's J-16; García Moll et al.'s Stone 92). This conquest slab (Figure 8.57) displays three components: (1) a hill sign whose internal diagonal lines have no paired figure eights flanking them; (2) a place-specifier resembling male genitalia; and (3) an inverted head with a vertical line passing through its eye and a bejeweled feather projecting from the rear of its headgear.

Lápida 27 (93 x 76 cm) (Caso's Lápida 27; Zehnder's J-14; García Moll et al.'s Stone 90). This conquest slab (Figure 8.58) is heavily damaged, but we can see part of a hill sign with its two arms and a couple of diagonal lines in its interior. The specifier above the hill sign appears to include wavy lines, similar to the sign for water. Below the hill sign is an inverted head with its hair (or cloth headgear) drawn forward and tied with a cord.

Lápida 28 (74 x 106 cm) (Caso's Lápida 28; Zehnder's J-13; García Moll et al.'s Stone 89). This conquest slab (Figure 8.59) features three components: (1) a hill sign with shorter diagonal lines at the base of its arms and longer diagonal lines in its interior; (2) a compound place name, seemingly depicting plant tassels or feathers above an implement with a handle; and (3) an inverted head with a vertical line behind the eye and a curving line below the eye.

Lápida 29 (118 x 115 cm) (Caso's Lápida 29; Zehnder's J-12; García Moll et al.'s Stone 88). This slab (Figure 8.60)

Figure 8.56. Lápida 25 on Building J features a hill sign; a place-specifier combining a dumbbell-shaped object with a sign that has lines descending from it; an inverted head with a vertical line passing through its eye and curving to touch its nose; and a bejeweled feather or other element projecting from the front of its headgear (like those on Lápidas 15 and 18). Drawing by Jane Mariouw.

Figure 8.57. Lápida 26 on Building J displays three components: (1) a hill sign whose internal diagonal lines have no paired circles flanking them; (2) a place-specifier resembling male genitalia; and (3) an inverted head with a vertical line passing through its eye. This head has a bejeweled feather projecting from the rear of its headgear; it also may have an animal head projecting from the front. Drawing by Jane Mariouw.

Figure 8.58. Lápida 27 on Building J is heavily weathered, but we can see part of a hill sign with its two arms and a couple of diagonal lines in its interior. The place-specifier above the hill sign appears to include wavy lines, similar to the glyph for water. Drawing by Jane Mariouw.

Figure 8.59. Lápida 28 on Building J features three components: (1) a hill sign with shorter diagonal lines at the base of its arms and longer diagonal lines in its interior; (2) a compound place-specifier, seemingly depicting feathers or plant tassels above an implement with a handle; and (3) an inverted head with a vertical line behind the eye and a curving line below the eye, accompanied by two short vertical lines. A bundle composed of hair and cloth seems to be tied together and allowed to flop down over the brow of the inverted head. Drawing by Jane Mariouw.

Figure 8.60. Lápida 29 on Building J displays a hill sign with the usual diagonal lines and pair of figure eights. Among the place-specifying elements above the hill sign is a human head. Below the hill sign is an inverted head with tied cords and a wrapped, bun-like element; the two ends of the cord dangle in front of his face. An incised line extends across the cheek. Drawing by Jane Mariouw.

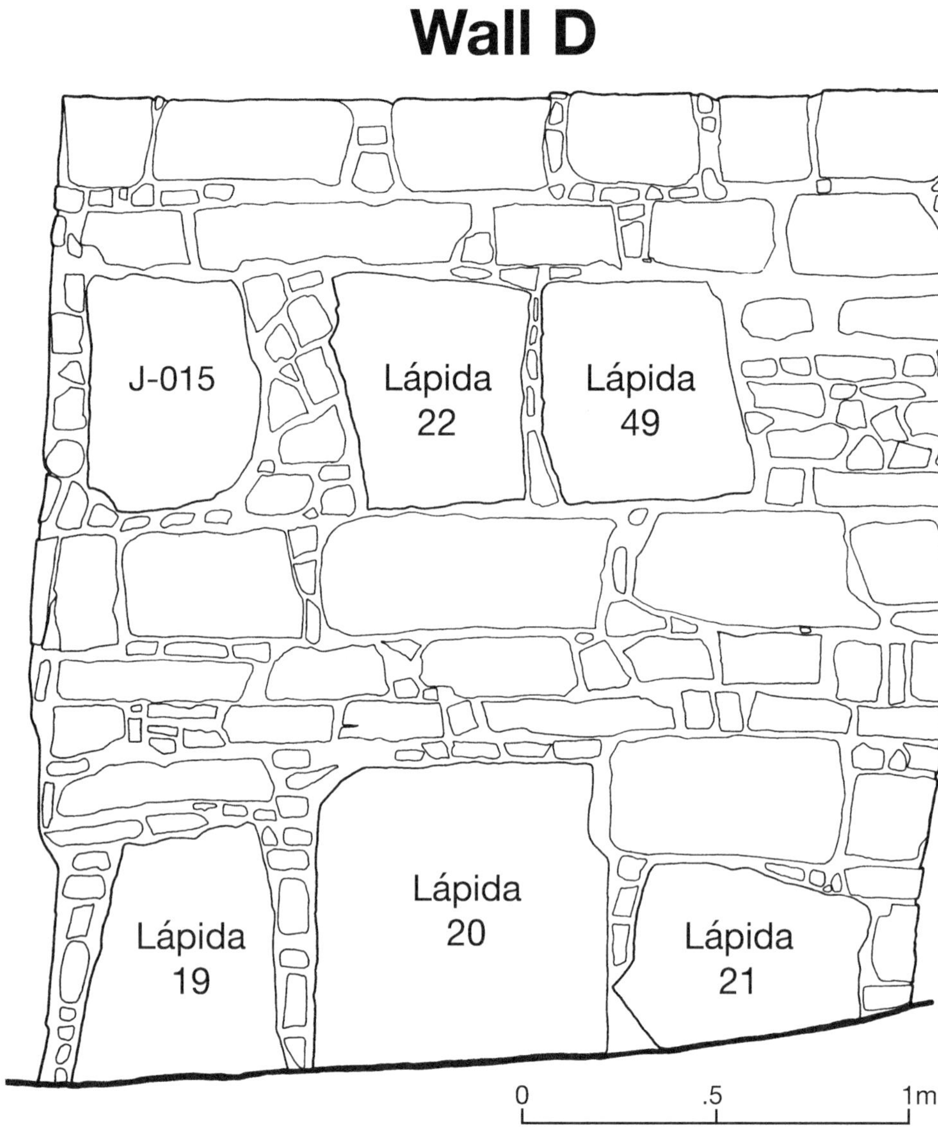

Figure 8.61. Wall D of Building J features six carved stones (Lápidas 19, 20, 21, 22, 49 and J-015). Drawing by John Klausmeyer.

displays a hill sign with the usual diagonal lines and paired figure eights. Among the place-specifying elements above the hill sign is a human head. Below the hill sign is an inverted head with tied cords and a wrapped, bun-like element; the two ends of the cord dangle.

Wall D (Figure 8.61)

Lápida 19 (124 x 105 cm) (Caso's Lápida 19; Zehnder's J-9; García Moll et al.'s Stone 96). Only the left half of a hill sign is preserved on this conquest slab. The element above the hill sign includes the atlatl sign. Only traces of the incisions can be seen below the hill sign.

Lápida 20 (148 x 158 cm) (Caso's Lápida 20; Zehnder's J-10; García Moll et al.'s Stone 97). This slab (Figure 8.62) displays the hill sign, the place-specifying glyphs, and an inverted head. The main elements in the place-specifier are many small dots, an atlatl, and the head of what appears to be a coyote. It is possible that the atlatl sign reinforced the sound *gui*, so that the place would be pronounced *Gui Gheu*, "Hill of the Coyote," rather than simply "Place of the Coyote."

Lápida 21 (97 x 130 cm) (Caso's Lápida 21; Zehnder's J-11; García Moll et al.'s Stone 98). This conquest slab (Figure 8.63) features the three main components: hill sign, place-specifier, and inverted head. The hill sign has three diagonal lines flanked by figure eights. The compound element above the hill sign includes a hand grasping a tool, as if in the act of carving or working a stone; it may refer to a place called *Quiegolani*, "peña tajada," or *Guiegolani*, "piedra tajada" (Martínez Gracida 1883:96). The inverted head has wavy lines descending from below the eye; its headgear resembles a bundle of cloth or hair pulled through a ring.

J-015 (125 x 88 cm) (Marcus' J-015; Zehnder's J-20; García Moll et al.'s Stone 99). On this slab we see only a highly eroded hill sign.

Lápida 22 (125 x 108 cm) (Caso's Lápida 22; Zehnder's J-21; García Moll et al.'s Stone 100). This conquest slab (Figure 8.64) features a hill sign, a compound place-specifier, and an inverted head. The hill sign has three diagonal lines, and one of its upward arms is eroded. The place-specifier is composed of an atlatl sign and a possible headband.

Lápida 49 (112 x 108 cm) (Caso's Lápida 49; Zehnder's J-22; García Moll et al.'s Stone 101). This conquest slab (Figure 8.65) has the hill sign, place-specifier, and inverted head. The place-specifier includes the atlatl sign and a possible glyph for smoke, with the atlatl sign possibly reinforcing the *gui* sound. It may represent the place *Iya Ceni*, "Smoke Hill" (Zúñiga 1982:56) or "Fire Hill."

Figure 8.62. Lápida 20 on Building J displays the hill sign, the place-specifying glyphs, and an inverted head. The main elements in the place-specifier are an atlatl and the head of what appears to be a fox or coyote. It is possible that the atlatl sign reinforced the sound *gui*, so that the place would be pronounced *Gui Gheu*, "Hill of the Coyote." The Nahuatl version would be Coyotepec, and one of the places with this name is a nearby town in the Valle Grande. Drawing by Jane Mariouw.

Wall E (Figure 8.66)

Stone 124 (159 x 64 cm) (Caso's Stone 124; Zehnder's J-26; Scott's J-124; García Moll et al.'s Stone 110). This stone,

Figure 8.63. Lápida 21 on Building J features three main components: a hill sign, a place-specifier, and an inverted head. The hill sign has three diagonal lines flanked by figure eights. The compound element above the hill sign includes a hand grasping a tool, as if in the act of carving or working stone; it may refer to a place called Quiegolani or Guiegolani, "piedra tajada." Drawing by Jane Mariouw.

Figure 8.64. Lápida 22 on Building J features a hill sign, a compound place-specifier, and an inverted head. The hill sign has three diagonal lines, and one of its upward arms is eroded. The place-specifier is composed of an atlatl sign and a possible headband or cord with beads. The inverted head has tight-fitting headgear and a very large ear ornament. Drawing by Jane Mariouw.

Figure 8.65. Lápida 49 on Building J has the hill sign, place-specifier, and inverted head. The place-specifier includes the atlatl sign and a possible glyph for smoke, with the atlatl possibly reinforcing the *gui* sound. This place may be *Iya Ceni*, "Smoke Hill" (Zúñiga 1982:56) or "Fire Hill." The inverted head has a knot on its forelock like many others. Drawing by Jane Mariouw.

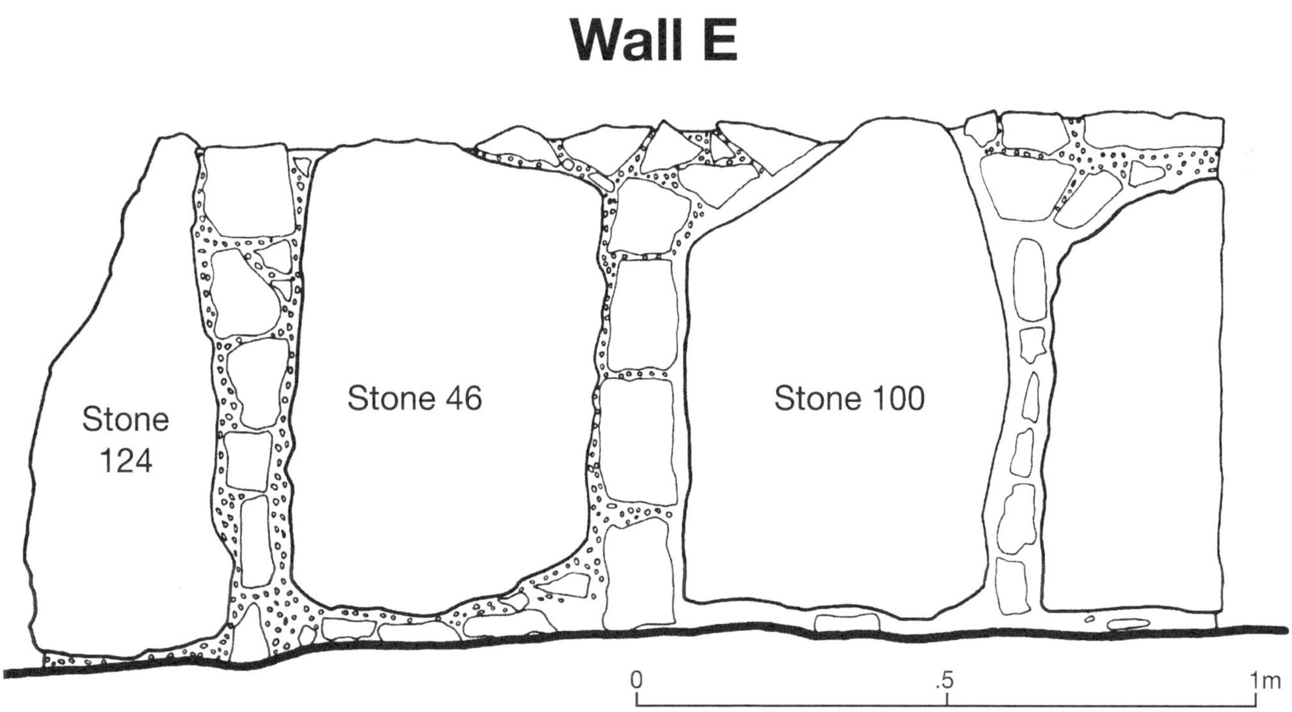

Figure 8.66. Wall E of Building J features three carved stones. Stone 124 shows a mutilated prisoner with blood scrolls. Stone 46 features two glyphs—Caso's Glyph J and a possible building with step-fret motifs. The captive's earspool has been removed, replaced by a feather tassel similar to the one found in the earlobe of the captive on Monument N-21. Blood scrolls flow toward his abdomen and thighs. Stone 100 shows a captive with small circles on his left shoulder and upper arm (perhaps like those shown on Monument D-74). Drawing by John Klausmeyer.

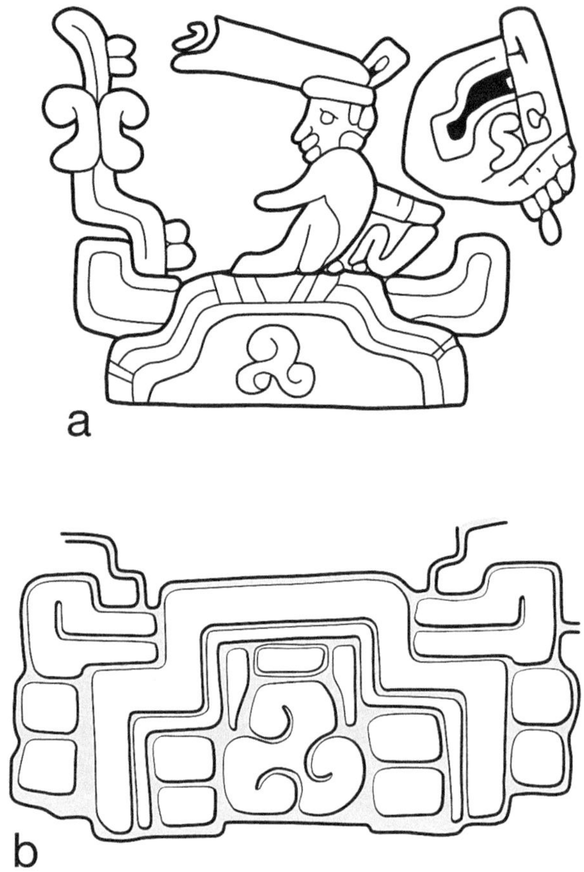

Figure 8.67. "Place of the Heart" or "Place of Sacrifice" are two possible names for the entire city of Monte Albán or specific locations within it. (*a*) from Stela 8 at Monte Albán. (*b*) from Lápida 44 of Building J at Monte Albán (Acosta 1958–1959; Caso 1947: Fig. 49). Drawing by John Klausmeyer.

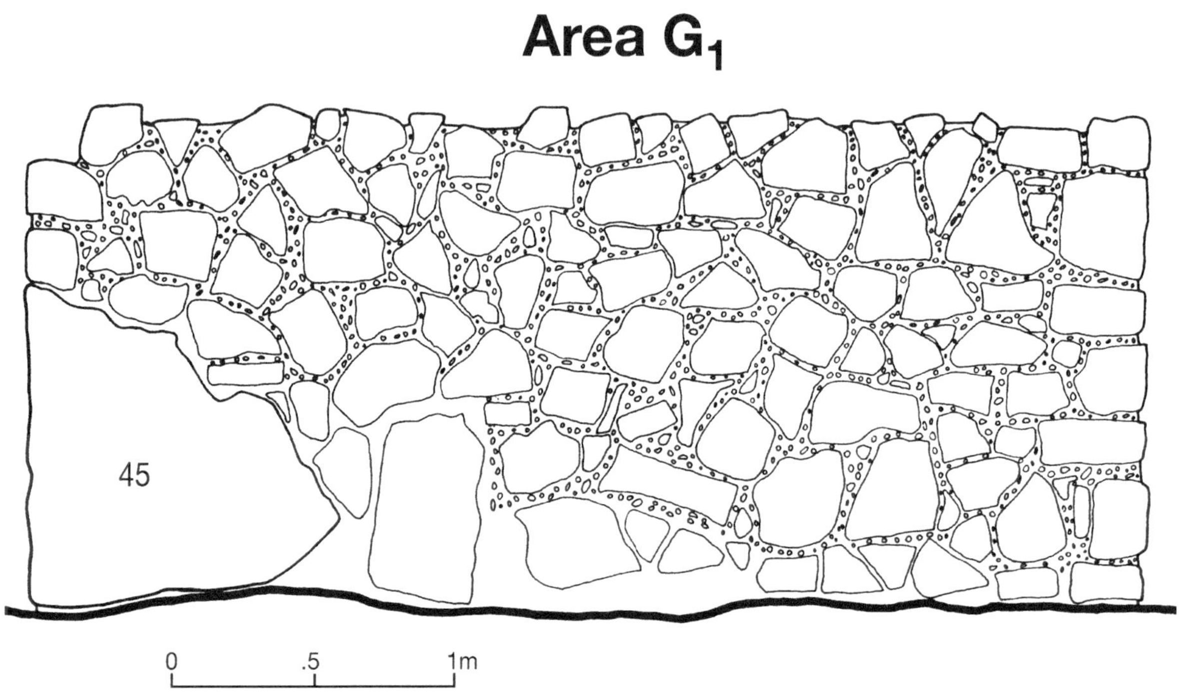

Figure 8.68. Wall G_1 of Building J features Stone 45 (García Moll et al. 1986). Drawing by John Klausmeyer.

obviously borrowed from Building L, shows a mutilated prisoner with blood scrolls in his groin area and above the waist.

Stone 46 (98 x 144 x 46 cm) (Caso's stone 46; Zehnder's J-27; Scott's J-46; García Moll et al.'s Stone 111). This reused Building L stone, found between Monuments J-124 and J-100, features two glyphs—Caso's Glyph J plus a possible building with greca motifs. The captive's earspool has been removed, and in the open hole there is a feather tassel, similar to the one found in the earlobe of the captive on Monument N-21. Blood scrolls flow toward his abdomen and thighs.

Stone 100 (96 x 151 x 24 cm) (Caso's stone 100; Zehnder's J-28; Scott's J-100; García Moll et al.'s Stone 112). This reused Building L slab shows a captive with small circles on his left shoulder and upper arm (perhaps tattoos like those shown on Monument D-74). We see a tassel or braid hanging from his hairdo. Blood scrolls flow toward his abdomen and thighs.

Lápida 44 (55 x 59 x 33 cm) (Caso's Lápida 44; Zehnder's J-90; García Moll et al.'s Stone 109). On this conquest slab we see a hill sign with the three-scroll or trilobal motif, which has been interpreted "place of the heart" or "place of sacrifice" (Figure 8.67).

Wall F

This wall contains a reused Building L stone (Scott's J-101), which is discussed in Chapter 6.

Wall G_1 (Figure 8.68)

Stone 45 (110 x 109 x 46 cm) (Caso's Stone 45, Zehnder's J-92-A; Scott's J-45; Garcia Moll et al.'s stone 117). This carved stone (Figure 8.69) appears at the base of the northeast wall in the structure set atop Building J. We see a short man (facing to the viewer's left), holding what appears to be a staff of office and wearing a headdress with an unusual element projecting from its back.

Figure 8.69. Stone 45 appears at the base of the northeast wall of the structure set atop Building J (Wall G_1). To the right of the hill sign we see a standing man holding what appears to be a staff of office; he is wearing a headdress with an unusual element projecting from it. The place-specifier consists of four dots above the hill sign. There also seems to be a number 1 and five dots below the hill. Drawing by Jane Mariouw.

Wall G_2 (Figure 8.70)

Lápida 97 (70 x 69 cm) (Caso's Lápida 97; García Moll et al.'s Stone 107). The hill sign on this conquest slab has the atlatl sign above it, but the rest of the place-specifier is missing. This stone did not have an inverted head below the hill sign.

Lápida 91 (66 x 108 cm) (Caso's Lápida 91; García Moll et al.'s Stone 106). This conquest slab is very similar to Lápida 97, featuring an atlatl sign but no inverted head.

Stones Lying on the Ground to the West of Building J (Figure 8.71)

As I mentioned earlier, Caso faced the formidable challenge of consolidating Building J. He was unable to determine where all

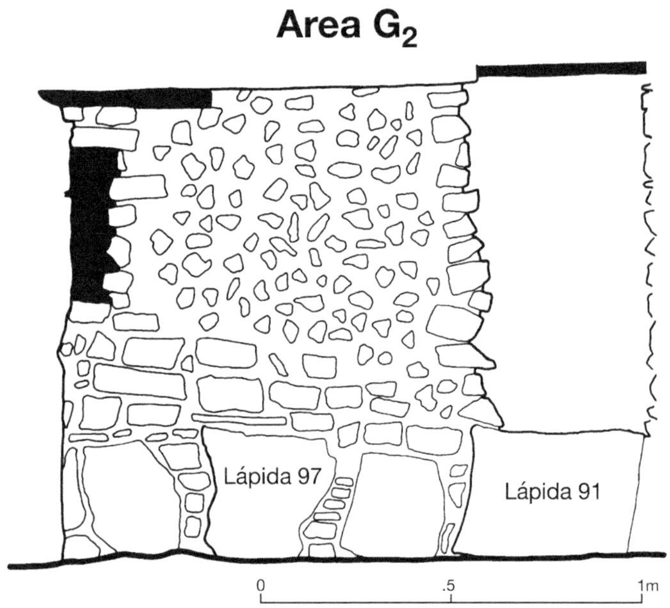

Figure 8.70. Area G_2 of Building J has two carved stones called Lápidas 91 and 97 (García Moll et al. 1986). Drawing by John Klausmeyer.

the carved stones had originally been positioned in Building J and found he could not accommodate every stone he recovered. Many of the leftover slabs were still lying to the west of Building J when I arrived in Oaxaca.

Monument 52 (56 x 54 x 55 cm) (Caso's stone 52; Zehnder's J-115; Scott's J-52; García Moll et al.'s Stone 121). This is a reused prisoner stone from Building L.

J-01 (39 x 50 x 44 cm) (Marcus' J-01; García Moll et al.'s Stone 120). This is only a fragment of a conquest slab, showing the hill sign and nothing else.

J-02 (37x 24 cm) (Marcus' J-02; García Moll et al.'s Stone 122). Only a human foot is visible on this fragment.

Lápida 51 (80 x 80 cm) (Caso's Lápida 51; García Moll et al.'s 123). This stone, borrowed from Building L, shows the figure of a naked prisoner, now quite eroded.

J-03 (42 x 22 cm) (Marcus' J-03; García Moll et al.'s 124). A fragment of prisoner stone borrowed from Building L, showing only an arm.

J-04 (79 x 69 x 56 cm) (Marcus' J-04; García Moll et al.'s 125). A conquest slab showing only a hill sign, with no place-specifier surviving above it and no inverted head below it.

Stone 130 (50 x 27 x 48) (Caso's Stone 130; Zehnder's J-124; Scott's J-133; García Moll et al.'s Stone 126). This stone is now so eroded that it is difficult to discern any details.

Lápida 57 (80 x 125 x 48 cm) (Caso's Lápida 57; García Moll et al.'s Stone 127). This conquest slab (Figure 8.72) is now broken in such a way that we cannot see whether or not it once had an inverted head below the hill sign. In earlier publications (Marcus 1976a, 1980) I suggested that this monument referred to a "Hill of the Bird," which might correspond to present-day Tututepec. I considered other possible places because Hill of the Bird might have been a common name. Since then, additional research strengthens the possibility that Tututepec may be the place involved.

It is notable that Tututepec was called "Hill of the Bird" in Nahuatl, Mixtec, Zapotec, and Spanish. At the base of the hill with this name—on the Río San Francisco, some 20 to 30 kilometers from the Pacific Coast of Oaxaca—lies the important site of San Francisco Arriba. This site's pottery resembles that of Monte Albán during Periods I and II (De Cicco and Brockington 1956).

This evidence for Monte Albán-style pottery on the Pacific Coastal plain reinforces Monte Albán's claim (made on Lápida 57) that Tututepec was one of its subject provinces. Unfortunately, owing to the fact that this conquest slab is broken precisely where any inverted head would be, we do not know whether Monte Albán was claiming conquest of the Tututepec region or merely diplomatic and political annexation.

Some distance to the southeast of San Francisco Arriba, Joyce (2003) and Workinger and Joyce (2009) have surveyed an area of 200 km^2 near the mouth of the Río Verde. While this survey is too far from Tututepec to shed light on how the "Hill of the Bird" was incorporated into the expansionist Zapotec empire, even the area they surveyed felt the impact of Monte Albán. The mouth of the Río Verde was sparsely populated before 500 BC, but the number of communities increased there between 400 and 100 BC, and some 278 burnished gray sherds described as "identical in both appearance and mineralogy to [Monte Albán I] pottery from the Valley of Oaxaca" (Joyce 1991) have been found there.

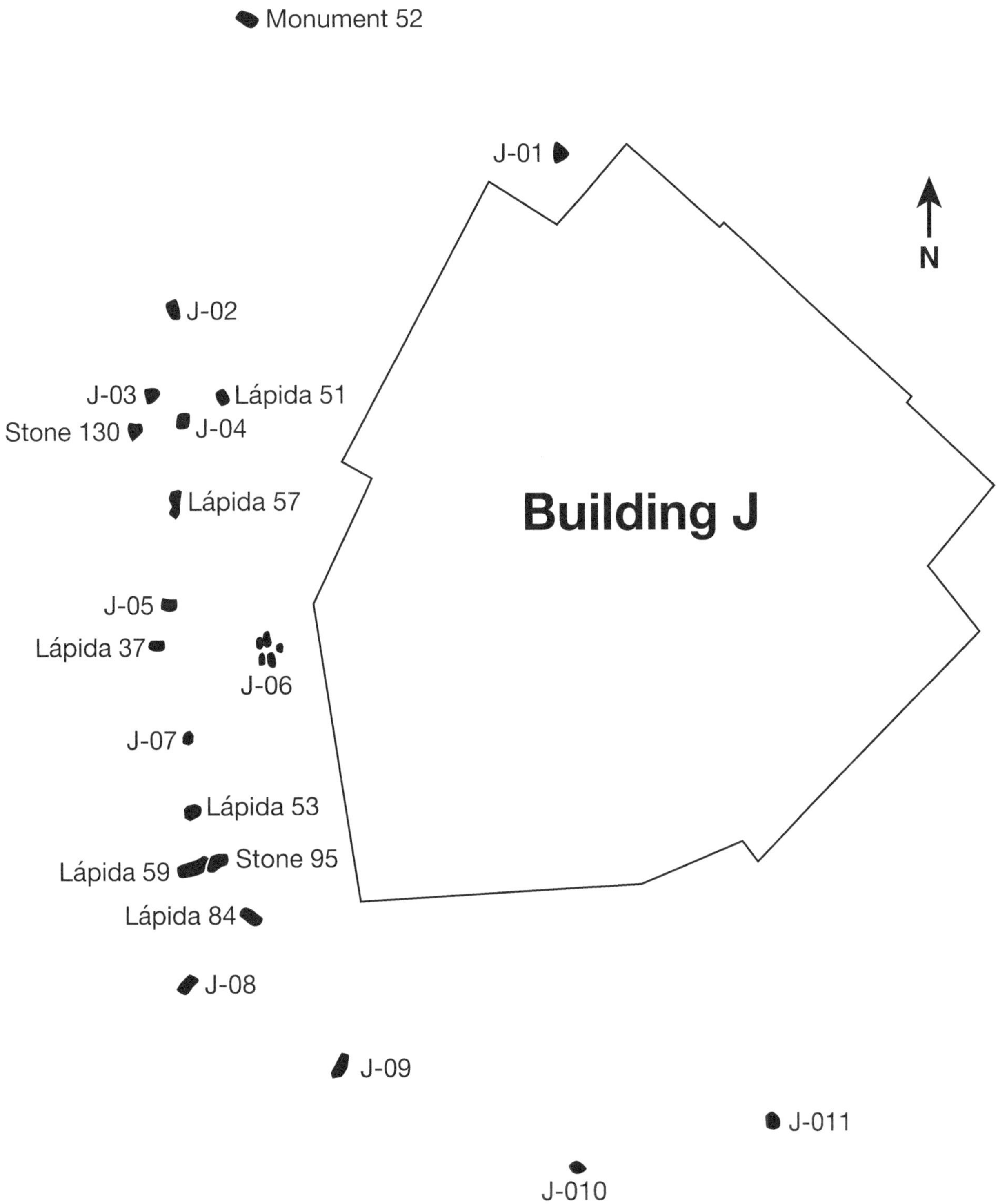

Figure 8.71. This plan, which was drawn in 1975, shows the location of the loose stones lying on the ground to the west and south of Building J (see also Figures 8.2b, 8.10). Adapted by John Klausmeyer from original drawings by Lois Martin and Mark Orsen.

Figure 8.72. Lápida 57 of Building J, left on the ground to the west of Building J, is now broken in such a way that we cannot be sure that the element below the hill sign was an upside-down head. Above the hill sign is a bird and possibly two atlatl darts. I suggested that it might refer to Tututepec, but I considered several other places because "Hill of the Bird" might have been a common place name. At the base of the hill now called Tututepec lies San Francisco Arriba, whose pottery resembles that of Monte Albán during Periods I and II. The appearance of such pottery on the Pacific Coast plain reinforces Monte Albán's claim on Lápida 57 that Tututepec was one of its subject provinces. Near the mouth of the Río Verde, at some distance to the southeast, an area has been surveyed and even this area revealed the impact of Monte Albán. Some 278 burnished gray sherds were described as "identical in both appearance and mineralogy to [Monte Albán I] pottery from the Valley of Oaxaca" (Joyce 1991). The fact that Monte Albán-style graywares linked the Pacific Coast to the Valley of Oaxaca at precisely this time is significant, because it was exactly the moment that the Valley Zapotec were colonizing places like Sola de Vega (Balkansky 1997, 2002). During the peak of Monte Albán's expansion, settlements on the Río Verde increased in number and used both imports and imitations of Period Ic–II pottery. Drawing by Jane Mariouw.

Figure 8.73. Lápida 84 (Stone 135), found lying near Building J, has a hill sign and an inverted head, but is so damaged that it is difficult to make out the details of the place-specifier and upside-down head. Drawing by Jane Mariouw.

The bulk of these imported graywares were found in relatively high-status residential areas, suggesting ties between elite Río Verde families and the Valley of Oaxaca.

The fact that Monte Albán style graywares linked the Pacific Coast to the Valley of Oaxaca at precisely this time is significant, because it comes at exactly the moment that the Valley Zapotec were colonizing places like Sola de Vega on their way to the Pacific piedmont (Balkansky 1997, 2002). From 100 BC to AD 200 (the peak of Monte Albán's political expansion), settlements on the Río Verde increased in number, featuring both imports and imitations of Period Ic–II pottery. Just as significantly, by AD 200, similarities between the ceramics of the Río Verde area and the Valley of Oaxaca decreased.

J-05 (82 x 100 x 53 cm) (Marcus' J-05; García Moll et al.'s 128). This conquest slab displays a hill sign with an inverted head below it. The latter has a bow or knot above its forehead.

Lápida 37 (47 x 70 x 45 cm) (Caso's Lápida 37; García Moll et al.'s Stone 129). Most of the carved portion of this conquest slab is missing; what remains are a bar-like element and six possible rectangular beads.

J-06 (110 x 155 cm) (Marcus' J-06; García Moll et al.'s 130). A largely eroded carved stone, broken into three pieces.

J-07 (52 x 32 x 36 cm) (Marcus' J-07; García Moll et al.'s 131). A conquest slab with only part of the hill sign preserved.

Lápida 53 (54 x 49 x 42 cm) (Caso's Lápida 53; García Moll et al.'s Stone 132). A conquest slab with a hill sign and an inverted head, so damaged that it is difficult to discern details of the place specifier above the hill (Figure 8.73).

Lápida 59 (52 x 79 x 40 cm) (Caso's Lápida 59; García Moll et al.'s Stone 134). A fragment of conquest slab, preserving only three large bead-like elements above an atlatl sign.

Stone 95 (61 x 52 x 55) (Caso's stone 95; Zehnder's J-114; Scott's J-95; García Moll et al.'s 133). A carved stone that is highly eroded.

Lápida 84 (63 x 112 x 51 cm) (Caso's Lápida 84; García Moll et al.'s Stone 135). A conquest slab that has a hill sign and an inverted head below it. The place-specifier above the hill sign is not well preserved.

J-08 (115 x 110 cm) (Marcus' J-08; García Moll et al.'s 136). This is a slab preserving only a highly eroded hill sign.

J-09 (48 x 17 cm) (Marcus' J-09; García Moll et al.'s 137). This is a slab preserving only a fragment of the hill sign.

J-010 (71 x 47 x 43 cm) (Marcus' J-010; García Moll et al.'s 140). A badly broken conquest slab. All we can see is that it once had a hill sign and an inverted head.

J-011 (45 x 55 cm) (Marcus' J-011; García Moll et al.'s 148). A piece of conquest slab showing only a fragment of hill sign.

The Meaning of the Inverted Heads

Although Caso coined the term *lápidas de conquista* for the Building J slabs, it seems possible that not all the places listed on the building would have required actual military conquest (see Figure 8.6). This would explain why some slabs do not display the inverted heads of defeated leaders. The slabs lacking inverted heads may refer to places incorporated into Monte Albán's polity by more peaceful means, such as political treaties and marriage alliances.

At least forty stones have an inverted head below the hill sign. Included are Lápidas 1, 3, 4, 5, 6, 7, 10, 15, 16, 17, 18, 19, 20, 21, 22, 25, 26, 27, 28, 29, 32, 33, 34, 35, 36, 38, 40, 47, 49, 51, 53, 54, 57, 58, 62, 82, 83, 84, 103, and 106. Those 40 examples constitute about 75% of the reasonably well preserved slabs. Among them were places tentatively identified as Chiltepec, Cuicatlán, and Sosola. Conquest has been confirmed archaeologically at Cuicatlán (Spencer and Redmond 1997), but no comprehensive excavations have been done at Chiltepec and Sosola.

At least 13 stones do not have inverted heads. Included are Caso's Lápidas 23, 42, 43, 50, 59, 91, 96, 97, 98, 99, 107, 114, and 122. Among those places were Miahuatlán and Ocelotepec. A number of the places seemingly incorporated by peaceful means lie between Monte Albán and the Pacific Coast, and that region almost certainly includes communities that benefited from being part of Monte Albán's economic network. For example, Ejutla

Figure 8.74. Here we see one of the box-shaped pottery vessels with lids from Building H at Monte Albán. On the side of the box are depictions of water and stylized maize kernels (Caso and Bernal 1952:22, 25, 30; Caso et al. 1967: Lámina XII; Sellen 2011; see also Color Plate V, this volume). Drawing by John Klausmeyer.

(for which we have no conquest slab) seems to have become a supplier of marine shell and mica to Monte Albán (Feinman and Nicholas 1990, 1993; Manzanilla et al. 2017).

Many of the Building J conquest slabs are simply too fragmentary or eroded to show whether or not an inverted head was present below the hill sign. Included are Lápidas 8, 9, 11, 24, 31, 48, 60, and 132. One of those places, as discussed earlier, was Tututepec.

There are also a few unusual conquest slabs that have something other than a human head attached to the underside of the hill. Lápida 12, for example, has an inverted animal head, while Lápidas 13 and 14 have possible glyphs.

Other Period II Monuments

Stela 18 (507 x 164 x 60 cm) (García Moll et al. 1986: Lámina 103; Monuments 249 and 250).

Freestanding stelae are rare at Monte Albán; one example from Period II is noteworthy for its height and location. Southwest of Monte Albán's North Platform and north of its System IV, Caso found Stela 18, a monument whose carving style and positioning of hieroglyphs are similar to those of other Period II monuments. On one side of this imposing stela are two hieroglyphs, one associated with the number 5 and the other with the number 2. On the opposite side are two hieroglyphs, neither associated with a number. This stela's height of 5 m would have made its text highly visible from a distance. It was likely an example of vertical propaganda, which makes it all the more disappointing that its damaged text cannot be read.

Period II Vessels with Hieroglyphs from Building H, Monte Albán

In Offering 4 of Building H at Monte Albán, Caso et al. (1967) found a series of fabulous ceramic boxes with lids. Each box is roughly half a meter tall (Figure 8.74).

On the side of each box is the hieroglyph for water as well as stylized symbols that represent maize kernels (Caso and Bernal 1952:22, 25, 30; Caso et al. 1967: Lámina XII). Water was intimately associated with *Cociyo*, the embodiment of Rain and Lightning, as emphasized by Caso et al. (1967) and others (e.g., Flannery and Marcus 1976b; Marcus 1999b, 2006c; Marcus and Flannery 1996; Sandstrom 1991; Sellen 2002, 2011; Taube 1996).

The Painted Walls of Tomb 72, Monte Albán

Our earliest evidence for Zapotec hieroglyphs in tomb murals occurs in Period II. In Tomb 72 at Monte Albán, Caso (1965b:864–865) found hieroglyphs inside rectangular frames, painted in two tones of red (Figure 8.75).

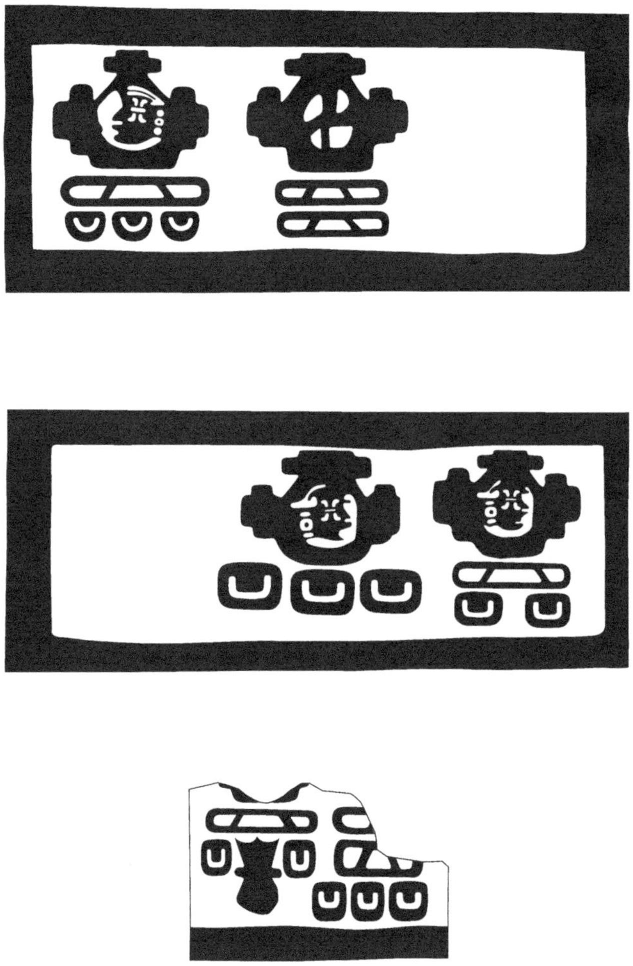

Figure 8.75. This mural in Tomb 72 is the earliest known at Monte Albán. It supplies names and dates, possibly including the names of noble couples. On the south wall (top) was a pair of names, 8Ñ and 10J, possibly a marital pair. These calendar signs were placed inside elaborate cartouches with three projections, similar to the shapes associated with maize or Glyph J. On the north wall (middle) were two calendar signs (possibly 3Ñ and 7Ñ) that may correspond to the names of another noble couple. On the west wall (bottom) we see more numerical coefficients (7 and 13), but the day signs are largely effaced. The day sign that begins with 7 seems to be associated with the bag glyph (Caso 1935, 1965b: Fig. 25; Lombardo de Ruiz 2008:91; Miller 1995). Two striking aspects of Tomb 72 are the large size of its calendar signs and the lack of any accompanying scenes. I suspect that the north and south walls recorded the names of noble couples. Since the rear (or west) wall displayed the bag, or "dead" glyph, this wall might have featured (1) the death date of the tomb's most important occupant and (2) an apical ancestor's name, which included the numeral 13. This kind of all-glyphic tomb mural is unusual for the Zapotec, but there are precedents in stone (e.g., during Period I we saw all-glyphic Stelae 12, 13, 14, and 17). Drawing by John Klausmeyer.

Figure 8.76. The Scribe of Cuilapan was not found during a legal excavation, so little is known about its original context. During Period II, Cuilapan was probably in the second tier of the Zapotec state hierarchy, and this Period II ceramic sculpture of a young lord was evidently produced there. He has two hieroglyphs, one on his headdress and one on his chest. I suspect that the glyphs on his chest supply his own name, 13Q. The name on his headdress—13 Water—may be his father's name, or that of a more distant ancestor from whom he inherited his right to rule. Drawing by John Klausmeyer.

On the north wall of Tomb 72 were two large calendar signs (possibly 3Ñ and 7Ñ) that may correspond to the names of a noble couple. On the south wall was another pair of names, 8Ñ and 10J. These calendar signs were placed inside elaborate cartouches with three projections, similar to those that appear with Glyph J.

On the west wall we see more numerical coefficients (13 and 7), but the day signs are largely effaced. The day sign that begins with 7 seems to be associated with the bag glyph (Caso 1935; see also Lombardo de Ruiz 2008:91 and Miller 1995).

Two striking aspects of Tomb 72 are (1) the large size of its calendar signs and (2) the lack of any accompanying scenes or depictions of individuals. I suspect that the north and south walls recorded the names of noble couples. My suggestion that these hieroglyphs give the names of two noble couples would be strengthened if two male and two female skeletons had been identified by biological anthropologists, or if some of the burial vessels also displayed the hieroglyphic names 8Ñ + 10J and 3Ñ + 7Ñ. Caso (1965b:864) offered different interpretations of the hieroglyphs, including the reading of the Ñ glyphs as Glyph L.

Since the rear wall displays the bag or "dead man" sign, this wall might have featured (1) the death date of the tomb's most important occupant and/or (2) an apical ancestor's name that included the numeral 13. The all-glyphic tomb mural is unusual for the Zapotec, but there are precedents that were carved in stone. Examples of all-glyphic texts from Period I include Stelae 12, 13, 14, and 17 (Caso 1928).

The Ceramic Sculpture Called the "Scribe of Cuilapan"

Cuilapan was one of the earliest villages in the Valley of Oaxaca, founded by 1150 BC. During Period II, Cuilapan (only 7 km southwest of Monte Albán) was probably in the second tier of the Zapotec state hierarchy. Cuilapan increased in prominence as Monte Albán began to decline.

Cuilapan has produced a Period II ceramic sculpture that depicts *not* a scribe (as its colloquial name implies), but rather a young Zapotec lord (Figure 8.76). This youth bears two hieroglyphs, one on his headdress and one on his chest, both of which are numbers + day signs. I suspect that the calendar glyphs on his chest supply his name, 13Q. The calendric name on his headdress—13 Water—may be his father's name, or that of a more distant ancestor from whom he inherited his right to rule. Caso and Bernal (1952:337) illustrated a second sculpture bearing the calendric name 13 Water on his headdress. Assuming that this repetition of the name is not simply a coincidence, this object may be a second depiction of this same young lord.

The "Scribe of Cuilapan" was unfortunately not found by legal excavation, so little is known about its context.

Period II Carved Stones in the Tlacolula Region: Mound O at Caballito Blanco

The unusual arrowhead shape of Monte Albán's Building J seems to be replicated by Mound O at Caballito Blanco in the Tlacolula arm of the valley. Mound O, however, is smaller and has a different orientation. Paddock (1966b:126), nevertheless, noted that the orientations of Building J at Monte Albán and Structure O at Caballito Blanco were similar *relative to other buildings* at their respective sites; it is only their absolute orientations that are not the same (Paddock 1983e).

At present these are the only arrowhead-shaped buildings known from the Valley of Oaxaca, and both were built during Period II. The fact that no one has found a convincing astronomical function for Structure O likely weakens the astronomical argument for Building J as well.

The Period II Hieroglyphs at Caballito Blanco

Carved cliff faces are rare in Oaxaca; one of the few places we see them is at the mesa-top site of Caballito Blanco, where Howard Leigh (personal communication, 1973) found a series of hieroglyphs (Figure 8.77). Since the ruins of Caballito Blanco apparently date to Period II, Leigh assigned the cliff carvings to that same time period. In support of Leigh's dating, it should be noted that the position of the numbers (with the dots appearing above the bars) is consistent with a Period II date.

Some of the cliff carvings are isolated hieroglyphs. One of these glyphs is noteworthy because it occurs three times at Caballito Blanco; two times it is associated with the number 9 and once with the number 10 (Figure 8.77a and c); this glyph appears to be an early form of Glyph C. There is also a circular glyph associated with the number 4 (Figure 8.77b).

One carving is a column of glyphs (Figure 8.77d); most of the glyphs are similar to those known from the site of Monte Albán. The column begins with a year sign and possibly ends with the name of a person. At the top of the column we see the year sign and the year bearer, possibly a version of Glyph E followed by a bar; together they may have been read as Year 5E. What follows is a square with four circles in it, then a flower and plant element, and a horizontal figure eight; the latter is similar to a hieroglyph that appears in the name clause of one of the women in the Tomb 105 mural at Monte Albán (Chapter 9). Finally we see a knotted cord above a curved bar, followed by 7 Jaguar.

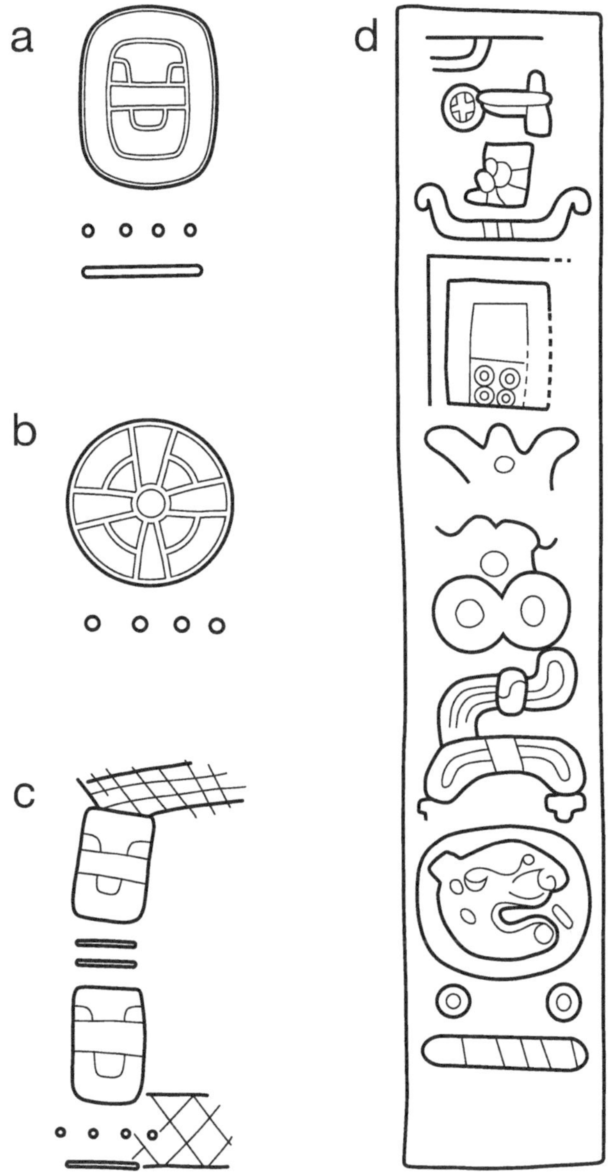

Figure 8.77. These hieroglyphs were found on the cliffs of Caballito Blanco, located in the Tlacolula region. Petroglyphs are rare in the Valley of Oaxaca. Since the ruins of Caballito Blanco date to Period II, it is likely that the cliff carvings date to that same time period. One part of the cliff has a column of glyphs (*d*). One of the Caballito Blanco hieroglyphs that occurs three times is an early form of Glyph C: two times associated with the number 9 (*a* and *c*) and once with the number 10 (*c*). There is also a circular glyph associated with the number 4 (*b*). The column of glyphs (*d*) begins with a year sign (possibly 5E) and ends with a likely personal name (7B?). Drawing by Howard Leigh.

Other Period II Carved Stones in the Tlacolula Region

It is significant that during Period I, the site of Monte Albán had an apparent monopoly on hieroglyphic writing. That monopoly ended in Period II, perhaps because the entire Valley of Oaxaca was now under Monte Albán's political control and there was less reason to restrict writing.

During Period II the central region of the valley saw the number of settlements dramatically shrink from 155 to 23, presumably because Monte Albán no longer needed to concentrate thousands of farmers, warriors, and craftsmen within 15 km of the city. The capital could now count on the support of its second-tier administrative centers and allow them to erect monuments. To be sure, Monte Albán was still at the top of the settlement hierarchy, with an estimated population of 14,000 to 15,000. However, six of its Tier 2 centers now had populations of 970 to 1950 and had their own palaces and temples.

Dainzú

One of the Tier 2 towns of Period II was Dainzú, in the Tlacolula arm of the valley. Dainzú, whose estimated population was 1000 people during Period II, constructed impressive buildings against the base of a defensible hill, and Complex A was one of these. We should note, however, that Dainzú had no main plaza laid out in imitation of Monte Albán's. This fact provides a contrast to the Tier 2 site of San José Mogote, in the Etla arm of the valley.

When Ignacio Bernal and Lorenzo Gamio discovered Dainzú during their surveys in the 1960s, their attention was drawn to a partially exposed carved stone (Stone 1) that stood in the southwest corner of the building they had designated Complex A. To determine the date of the stone, they made a test pit to recover the associated ceramics. That limited excavation in 1966 led to the discovery of additional carved stones, all of which encouraged Bernal to excavate Complex A in its entirety. Bernal invited Arturo Oliveros to join him as co-director, and together they excavated Dainzú from 1966 to 1973 (Bernal and Oliveros 1988).

Complex A, which measures 54 x 42 m, was built against a natural hill, obviating the need to construct a back wall (Bernal 1967:8). According to Bernal and Oliveros (1988), Complex A was begun in Period Ic and reached its maximum size in Period II (Figure 8.78).

My own interest in Dainzú was piqued in the summers of 1972 and 1973 when Bernal and Oliveros led me up the hill behind Complex A to see 50 carvings of decapitated heads (Figure 8.79). These heads were wearing helmets with face guards. Together the 50 carvings, which appear on naturally occurring boulders, are referred to as the Tzompantli Group (Bernal and Seuffert 1979). That label is apt, since the carvings of decapitated heads sent a message similar to that conveyed by a skull rack or *tzompantli*. Unlike the usual *tzompantli*, however, these heads are seemingly linked to the Mesoamerican use of stone balls, *manoplas*, and knuckledusters as weapons (e.g., Taube and Zender 2009; see also Berger 2011; Borhegyi 1961, 1967; Clune 1963; Orr 2003; Taladoire 2003). The heads are believed to be from combatants who protected themselves by wearing helmets with faceguards. The Zapotec term for *manoplas* combines hand, hammer, and war.

During my tour, Bernal and Oliveros showed me the Wall of Sacrifice, a carved rock face 1.70 m high. On that rock face is a helmeted person (either well-padded or corpulent) standing on a hill sign or toponym (Figure 8.80). This individual points his weapon at a similarly attired foe who is lying on his back with his left leg in the air, presumably after having been wounded or killed (Bernal and Seuffert 1979: Figure 45). This Wall of Sacrifice is the closest thing we have to an "action scene" at Dainzú—that is, a confrontation between a victor (at left) and a loser (at right).

Unlike the Wall of Sacrifice, most Dainzú carved stones depict the aftermath of confrontation—that is, they show the wounded or dead lying on the ground, or as scattered body parts (e.g., hearts [Stone 83]; a severed arm still holding a stone ball [Stone 86]; or helmeted heads grouped on hillside boulders [see Figure 8.79]). Such dismemberment of victims was a common theme in Peru from Cerro Sechín times to the Moche state (Donnan 1988; Quilter 2002; Samaniego et al. 1985), but it was shown much less frequently in Zapotec art.

I was struck by how many decapitated heads were depicted on the hillside at Dainzú. I began to suspect that their placement on the hill—which contrasts with the intact corpses depicted in Complex A—might suggest that the rite of decapitation took place on the summit of that hill. I later learned that Bernal and Seuffert (1979) had found steps carved into the hillside, perhaps enabling the decapitators and their victims to ascend to the summit.

More than 100 carved stones have been discovered at Dainzú, and at least seven display Zapotec glyphs (Stones 1, 3, 45, 46, 52, 63, and 65). In addition to the Tzompantli Group and the Wall of Sacrifice, a substantial number of carvings were used (or reused) in Complex A of Dainzú (Figures 8.81, 8.82). Some of the men depicted have impressive masks, helmets, and faceguards; some do not. Some of the Dainzú figures hold two stone balls; some hold one ball; some hold nothing. This brings to mind an urn from Monte Albán's Tomb 58, where we also see an individual holding a ball in one hand and a trophy head in the other, while wearing a series of human maxillae around his neck. Given the co-occurrence of a ball, a trophy head, and human maxillae, we recognized the possibility that the stone he holds in his hand was used as a weapon.

In the 1960s and 1970s, many scholars regarded the Dainzú figures as "ballplayers" (e.g., Bernal 1967, 1968, 1973; Bernal and Oliveros 1988; Bernal and Seuffert 1979). An entirely new view of Complex A began to appear in the 1990s, however, when Heather Orr interpreted the figures as participants in a scripted set of behaviors, whose ultimate goal was decapitation (Baudez 2011; Orr 1997, 2001, 2003). Since then there has been considerable discussion of these individuals as participants in warfare (Berger 2011), in mock battles (Baudez 2011; Orr 1997), or gladiators who used stone balls as weapons (Taube and Zender 2009:162). These new interpretations offer an explanation for one of the "ballplayer" theory's major flaws—there was no ballcourt at Dainzú during Period II (Marcus and Flannery 1990).

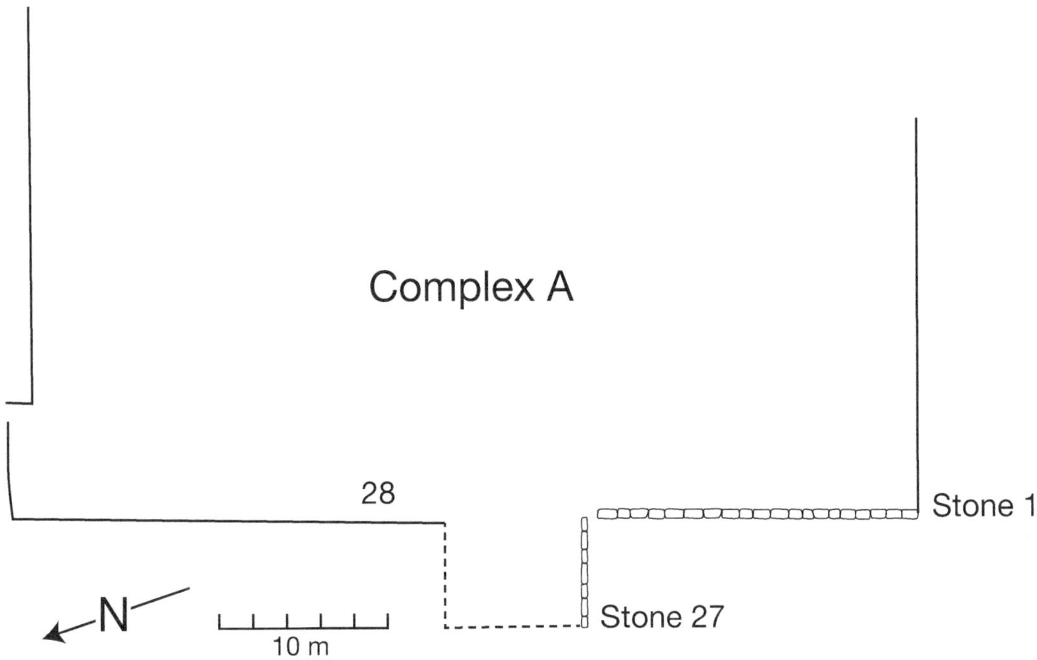

Figure 8.78. Here we see a simplified plan of Complex A at Dainzú, one of the Tier 2 towns of Period II in the Tlacolula arm of the valley. Dainzú, whose estimated population was 1000 people during this era, constructed this impressive building against the base of a defensible hill. Four dozen stones were found in its façade. When Ignacio Bernal and Lorenzo Gamio discovered Dainzú during their survey in the 1960s, their attention was drawn to the partially exposed Stone 1 in the corner of Complex A. To determine the date of the stone, they made a test pit to recover the associated ceramics. That limited excavation in 1966 led to the discovery of additional carved stones, all of which encouraged Bernal to excavate Complex A in its entirety. Bernal invited Arturo Oliveros to join him as co-director, and together they excavated Dainzú from 1966 to 1973. Complex A, which measures 54 x 42 m, was built in three stages or terraces, similar to Buildings L and J at Monte Albán. According to Bernal and Oliveros (1988), the construction of Complex A was begun in Period Ic and reached its maximum size in Period II. Drawing by John Klausmeyer.

Figure 8.79. On the boulders near the summit of the hill behind Complex A at Dainzú were the depictions of 50 helmets and faceguards, many with a scroll ruff at the base of the helmet. These carvings are referred to as the Tzompantli Group (Bernal and Seuffert 1979: Pl. 41). That label is apt, since the carvings of decapitated heads sent a message similar to that conveyed by a skull rack or *tzompantli*. Unlike the usual *tzompantli*, however, these heads are linked to activities and individuals, both here and elsewhere, that involve stone balls, *manoplas*, and knuckledusters. Adapted from Bernal and Seuffert by John Klausmeyer.

Figure 8.80. This Dainzú scene shows a victor standing on a platform or toponym while holding a ball in his right hand and a sword or dagger in his left. The victim lies on his back (at right). Both participants wear helmets with faceguards. Redrawn from Bernal and Seuffert (1979) by John Klausmeyer. Height: 1.70 m.

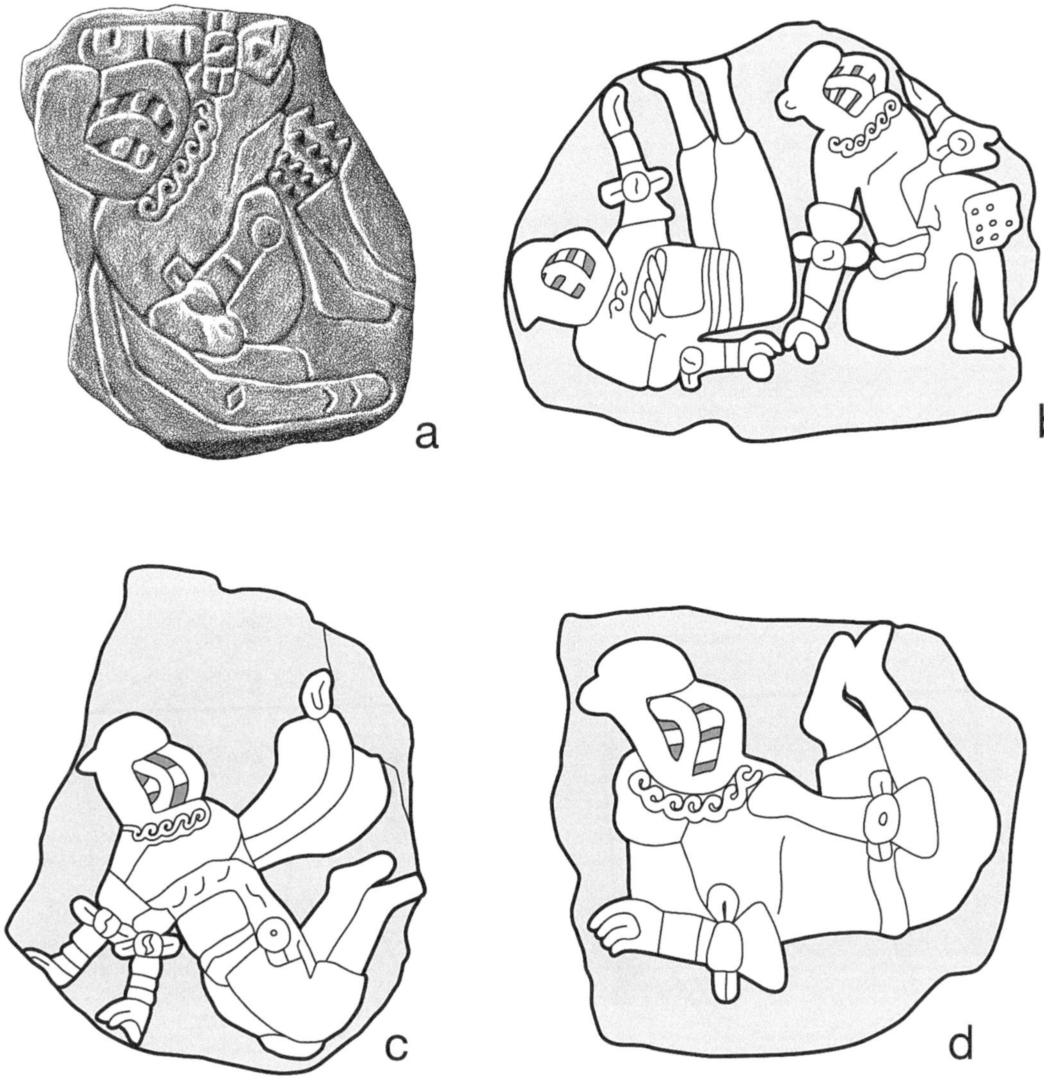

Figure 8.81. Monuments at Dainzú depict men wearing padded suits, helmets, and faceguards: *a*, Stone 19 (.70 x .55 m); *b*, Stone 23 (1.28 x 1.50 m); *c*, Stone 39 (1.11 x .95 m); and *d*, Stone 17 (.69 x .72 m). (See Bernal and Seuffert 1979: Plates 15, 18, 28, and 13). Drawings by John Klausmeyer.

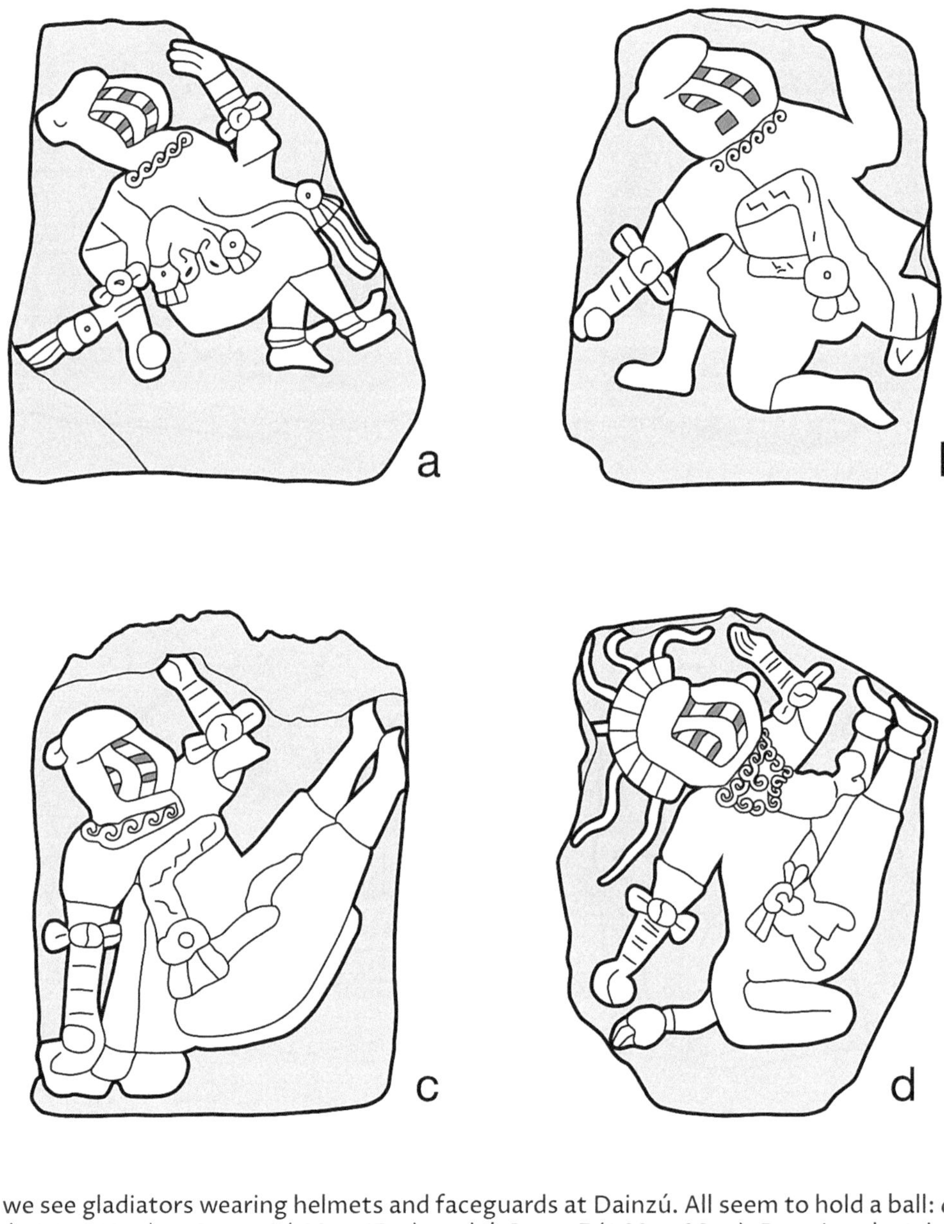

Figure 8.82. Here we see gladiators wearing helmets and faceguards at Dainzú. All seem to hold a ball: *a*, Stone 11 (.98 x .78 m); *b*, Stone 6 (1.06 x .69 m); *c*, Stone 4 (.83 x .67 m); and *d*, Stone 7 (1.23 x .89 m). Drawings by John Klausmeyer.

Mock Battle or Real War?

The Dainzú case provides us with the opportunity to counter two common but unwarranted assumptions. One is the false dichotomy of secular vs. ritual war, with the former regarded as serious and the latter as having few consequences. The second unwarranted assumption is the notion that real war is unscripted while ritual warfare is scripted. A significant paper taking up this theme is that by Arkush and Stanish (2005), who emphasize that so-called "ritual battles" often led to the procurement of sacrificial victims. They note that some archaeologists mistakenly see "ritualization" and "lethal warfare" as mutually exclusive. The more limited loss of life associated with scripted rites (such as procuring prisoners for sacrifice) can, and often did, coexist with all-out unscripted warfare. In fact, secular warfare among the Inca, Moche, Aztec, Maya, and other groups often included an array of rituals (Arkush and Stanish 2005; Carman 1999; Hassig 1988; Marcus 2000; Morris and von Hagen 2011; Schele and Freidel 1990).

As Arkush and Stanish point out, warfare at any scale can be ritualized, and when it is, what do anthropologists gain by using labels such as "ritual battle" or "ritual combat"? The Aztec, for example, conducted both all-out wars and "flower wars." The latter were formalized and prearranged, and allowed combatants to obtain training; flower wars also provided opportunities for warriors to gain personal prestige by taking captives for sacrifice (Hassig 1988).

Arkush and Stanish argue that "contained" or "festive" forms of battle occur primarily under the umbrella of an organized state. Trophy-taking, decapitation, and heart sacrifice are the kinds of activities that were surrounded by ritualized behaviors (see Moser 1973). Individuals performing these sacrificial rites usually wore special garb, including masks that allowed them to hide their identity and assume the role of a deity (Donnan 1988; Hvidtfeldt 1958).

In 2011 Baudez proposed a new way of looking at the Dainzú monuments, one that makes good anthropological sense. His approach allows us to see thematic relationships between the Dainzú carvings and the Building L mutilated captives at Monte Albán. The reconstruction of the events at Dainzú commences with genuine combat and ends with the ritual sacrifice of the prisoners taken. For Baudez, the story begins with the combatants depicted on the carved stones of Complex A. They are not typical "warriors," since they wear masks and helmets with faceguards and usually carry stone balls rather than atlatls or spears. Instead of men playing ball, Baudez views the figures as combatants whose goal was to decapitate the losers. The story then shifts to the more than four dozen severed heads on the hillside, victims that were analogous to the slain captives of Monte Albán's Building L. In fact, it is possible that many of the figures represent previously obtained captives, who had been dressed as gladiators so that they could participate in the sacrificial ritual.

Baudez (2011) calls attention to the diversity of markings on the helmets—some have a hook-like element, others have a *Cociyo* mask, others have feline ears, and still others have S-shaped volutes. Baudez (2011:26) believes that these helmet decorations identified different groups or teams of combatants.

Helmeted figures are almost completely restricted to Dainzú, with two exceptions—a carved stone from the North Platform of Monte Albán (Caso 1969: Figure 8) and a group of figures in the murals of Tomb 5 at Cerro de la Campana (see Chapter 12). The Monte Albán stone shows a decapitated head wearing a Dainzú-style helmet with a grill or faceguard (see Figure 7.3). This Monte Albán carving of a helmet (34 x 42 x 12 cm) strongly resembles those depicted on the Tzompantli Group at Dainzú. Whether the stone was carved at Monte Albán or brought from Dainzú is unknown.

Like the prisoner slabs of Building L at Monte Albán, the carved stones at Dainzú show many more victims than victors. The display, in other words, emphasizes the outcome, and features losers more often than it celebrates the victors.

Period II Hieroglyphs at Dainzú

Although 100 carvings are known from Dainzú, very few include hieroglyphs. An exception is Stone 1—an orthostat standing 1.80 m in height—now set into a corner of Complex A (Figure 8.83). Stone 1 shows a helmeted individual associated with a hieroglyphic name (Bernal 1967:10–11).

Among the other monuments bearing hieroglyphs are Stone 45 (Glyph 6C), Stone 46 (Glyph E), Stone 63 (Glyph 5E), and Stone 65 (Glyphs 2T and 10E). Most of the hieroglyphs seem to be labels supplying the names of individuals, although it is possible that some calendar signs are dates (Figure 8.84). Other signs include hills (see Stone 85 and the Wall of Sacrifice at Dainzú).

Bernal and Seuffert (1973:7) regarded the carved stones from three sites near the center of the Tlacolula arm (Tlacochahuaya, Macuilxóchitl, and Dainzú) as constituting a "regional substyle with certain characteristics of their own." Bernal and others have recorded several dozen stones from those sites, including 11 carved stones from Tlacochahuaya alone.

A Tentative Sequence of Events at Dainzú

If we accept Baudez's (2011) interpretation of the Dainzú carvings, we can suggest a sequence of events: combat, the taking of prisoners, the dressing of the prisoners as gladiators, and the ritual decapitation of the latter on the summit of the hill behind Complex A. A tentative sequence of events would be as follows:

(1) Captives are taken during a battle.
(2) Captives are brought to Dainzú.

Figure 8.83. Dainzú's Stone 1, set in the corner of Complex A, is the only monument showing an individual facing north (Bernal and Seuffert 1979: Plate 2). Although 100 carvings are known from Dainzú, few include hieroglyphs. An exception is Stone 1, an orthostat standing 1.80 m in height, which shows a helmeted individual associated with a hieroglyph that may be his calendric name (Bernal 1967:10-11). Drawing by John Klausmeyer.

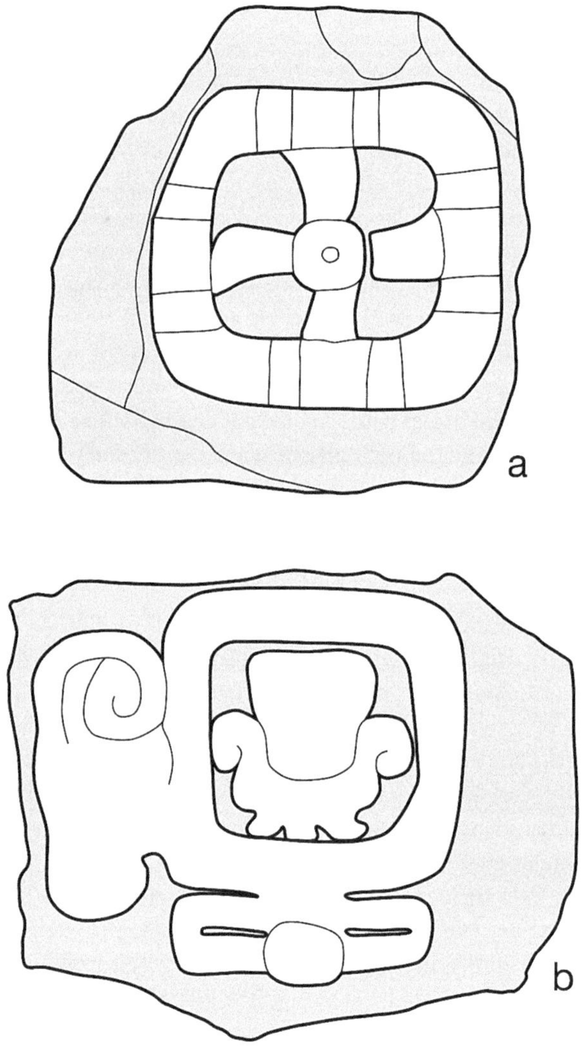

Figure 8.84. Although not prone to using columns of text, Dainzú did use isolated hieroglyphs to specify the names of individuals. *a*, Stone 46 with Glyph E (1.14 x 1.18 m); *b*, Stone 45 with Glyph 6C (0.64 x .90 m) (see Bernal and Seuffert 1979; Bernal and Oliveros 1988). Among the other monuments bearing hieroglyphs were Stone 63 (with Glyph 5E) and Stone 65 (with Glyphs 2T and 10E; see Bernal and Oliveros 1988: Fotos 39c, 39d). Most of the hieroglyphs seem to be labels supplying the names of individuals, although it is possible that some day signs were dates. Drawing by John Klausmeyer.

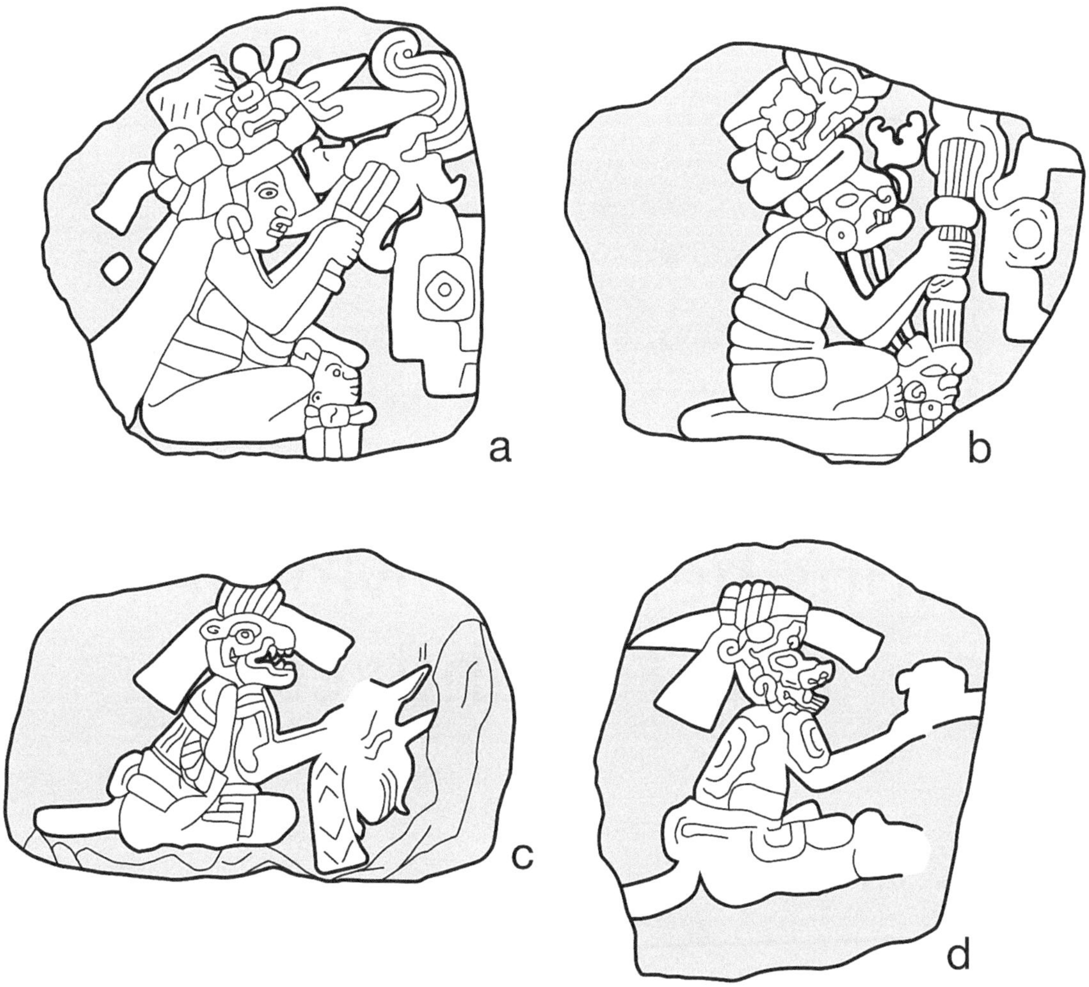

Figure 8.85. Some of the seated figures at Dainzú wear jaguar costumes: *a*, Stone 40 (1.18 x 1.25 m); *b*, Stone 50 (1.02 x 1.27 m); *c*, Stone 44 (1.32 x .71 m); and *d*, Stone 38 (1.09 x 1.05 m). Redrawn by John Klausmeyer from Bernal and Seuffert 1979: Plates 32–35.

(3) Captives are dressed as gladiators (Team A).

(4) Team B, a group of Dainzú warriors, is dressed as gladiators.

(5) After a ritualized confrontation, the captives (Team A) are taken to the top of the hill to be sacrificed.

(6) The following series of monuments are carved:

(a) Boulders carved to depict helmeted heads or stylized human hearts (Bernal and Oliveros 1988: Photos 34, 35a, 35b, 35c; Stones 48, 49, 54, 55, and 83);

(b) Victors depicted on Stones 1 and 3;

(c) Victims shown sprawling;

(d) Seated figures (called "Gods of the Ball Game" by Bernal and Seuffert [1979]) were carved on Stones 38, 40, 44, and 50 (Figure 8.85). Obviously, in Baudez's (2011) and Taube and Zender's (2009) scenario, these figures would have nothing to do with the ball game; they may be priests or officials supervising the ritual.

Battles, Conquest, and Sacrificial Victims as Major Themes in Periods I and II

There can be little doubt that two of the major reasons for carving stone monuments during Periods I and II were to celebrate victory and depict sacrificed captives. Approximately 300 depictions of slain captives once appeared on Building L at Monte Albán. More than 50 slabs showing subjugated or tribute-paying places appeared on Building J, and more than half of these had inverted human heads, implying military conquest. With the establishment of the Monte Albán II state, ritualized warfare and the decapitation of victims were celebrated in stone at Dainzú, a Tier 2 administrative center.

Supplying the hieroglyphic names of important individuals was a major incentive for Zapotec writing during Periods I and II at Monte Albán. The hilltop boulders at Dainzú show dozens of helmeted and decapitated heads, but no hieroglyphic names are associated with them. The cornerstone in Complex A may, however, supply the name of at least one victor.

9

Relations between Monte Albán and Teotihuacán

Monte Albán was, to be sure, not the only expansionist first-generation state of its era. Approximately 500 km to the north lay Teotihuacán, the capital of a rival state. During Period IIIa, Monte Albán's monuments and artifacts give us insight into its relationship with Teotihuacán.

Teotihuacán was perhaps the most populous city in ancient Mexico, and between AD 100 and 300 it was extending its influence to the south. Inevitably it encountered the Zapotec, who were expanding to the north. At the north end of the Cuicatlán Cañada, these two expansionist states created a buffer zone (Figure 9.1) that prevented hostilities along the border (Redmond 1983; Redmond and Spencer 1983; Spencer 1982, 1998, 2007; Spencer and Redmond 1997, 2001a, 2001b, 2003, 2004a, 2004b, 2005, 2006).

By AD 200–500 Teotihuacán was engaged in trading goods with far-flung Maya cities such as Kaminaljuyú and Tikal (e.g., Braswell 2003; Kidder et al. 1946; Marcus 1998b, 2003a; C. Millon 1973, 1988; Proskouriakoff 1993; White et al. 2000, 2004). Many other sites of this era, however, show little or no evidence of interaction with Teotihuacán. Some of these differences may be due to sampling bias, but it now appears that large sites and regional capitals were the principal targets for interaction with Teotihuacanos.

Teotihuacán was distinct from most cities of this era in having wards of foreigners. In the eastern sector of the city was a Merchants' Barrio, with circular residences and pottery from the Gulf Coast and the Maya region (Diehl and Berlo 1989; Manzanilla 2009; R. Millon 1973a, 1973b, 1981, 1992; Rattray 1993, 2001; Spence 1989, 1992, 1996, 2004; White et al. 2004). In another ward were Michoacanos, who buried their dead in cist tombs and maintained the same funerary practices they had used in their West Mexican homeland. In the western part of the city were people from Oaxaca, who used typical Zapotec tombs and funerary urns.

We do not know the number of Zapotecs who lived in Teotihuacán's Oaxaca Barrio, since only a small part of that ward has been excavated (Croissier 2007; Paddock 1983c; Rattray 1993; Spence 1989, 1992, 1996, 2004). One estimate is that 600 Zapotecs were living at Teotihuacán (e.g., Palomares Rodríguez 2013). New evidence suggests that over time, some of these Zapotec families relocated to new settlements in Hidalgo (Holt Mehta 2018).

Monte Albán does not appear to have had colonies of foreigners, but occasionally it hosted visitors from Teotihuacán bearing gifts.

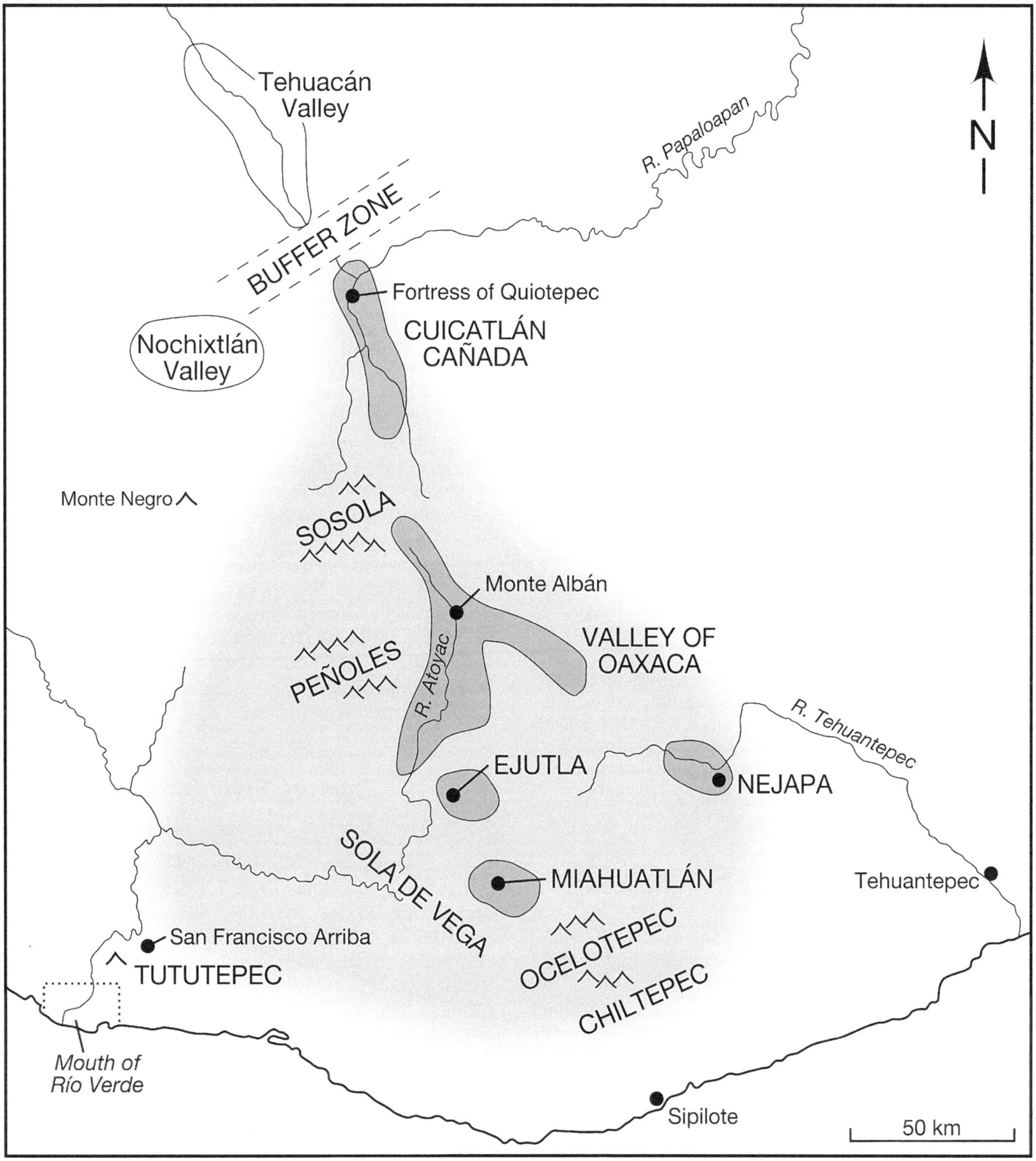

Figure 9.1. During Period II a buffer zone separated Tehuacán and Cuicatlán, preventing expansionist Teotihuacán and expansionist Monte Albán from infringing on each other's sphere of influence. Adapted from Marcus and Flannery (1996) by John Klausmeyer.

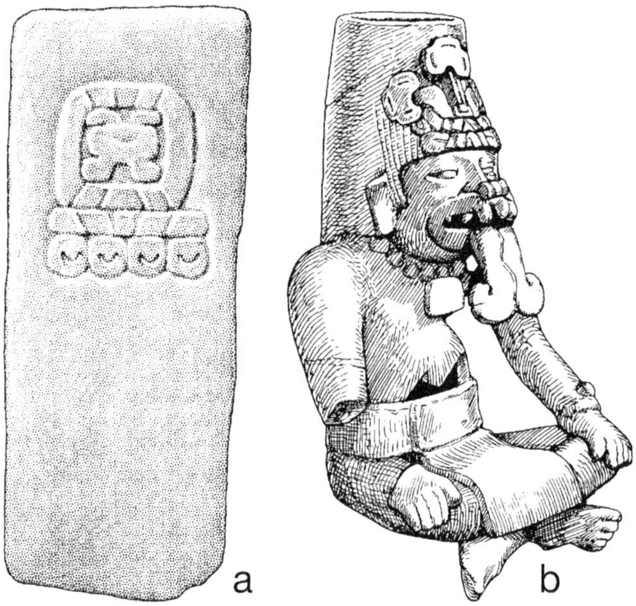

Figure 9.2. The Oaxaca Barrio at Teotihuacán produced (*a*) a tomb jamb carved with the Zapotec hieroglyph 9 + L (9 Motion or 9 Eye) and (*b*) a Zapotec urn with the hieroglyph 8 + J (8 Maize) displayed above the face. The Zapotecs living at Teotihuacán continued to bury their dead and to honor their ancestors much as they had in Oaxaca. Drawing by John Klausmeyer.

The Oaxaca Barrio at Teotihuacán

The Oaxaca Barrio, perhaps 1 to 2 hectares in extent, lies three kilometers west of the Ciudadela at Teotihuacán. Our best guess is that the resident Zapotecs, some of whom were nobles, had two roles: (1) they served as diplomatic ambassadors, and (2) they facilitated interregional trade.

In Teotihuacán the Zapotecs lived in Teotihuacán-style compounds, but they continued to import Period II vessels made of Oaxaca clays. To augment that imported pottery, they used local Basin of Mexico clays to replicate Zapotec vessels (e.g., incense burners, urns, bowls, and large basins or *apaxtles*) (Paddock 1983c:170; Rattray 1993). In addition to using vessels made on both Basin of Mexico clays and Valley of Oaxaca clays, the occupants of the Oaxaca Barrio used Thin Orange pottery imported from San Juan Ixcaquixtla, Puebla. Thin Orange vessels, especially ring-base hemispherical bowls, were used throughout the Oaxaca Barrio and often placed in tombs and caches. Their abundance in the barrio suggests to some scholars that the Zapotecs may have been middlemen in the distribution of Thin Orange (e.g., Rattray 1990a, 1990b, 1993; Rattray and Harbottle 1992; Spence 1989).

To the north of Teotihuacán were the sites of Acoculco, El Tesoro, and Chingú in Hidalgo. Their ceramic assemblages were similar to that known from Teotihuacán's Oaxaca Barrio (Crespo and Mastache 1981; Díaz Oyarzábal 1980, 1981; Hernández Reyes 1990, 1994; Holt Mehta 2018; Paddock 1983c; Rattray 1990a, 1990b, 1993; Smith and Lind 2005:173). This appearance of Period II Oaxaca-style pottery in the state of Hidalgo was unexpected, especially for those scholars who had assumed that Teotihuacán was the only city that had foreign enclaves. Holt Mehta (2018) suggests that Chingú, considered a Teotihuacán administrative center in Hidalgo, had Zapotec residents living in their own separate ward, replicating the pattern at Teotihuacán. El Tesoro, she believes, was an actual Zapotec community in Hidalgo, not simply an enclave (Holt Mehta 2018:132).

Holt Mehta suggests that these Zapotec families moved to Hidalgo from Teotihuacán's Oaxaca Barrio and continued to maintain ties both to Teotihuacán and the Valley of Oaxaca. One possibility is that the transplanted Zapotec may have been involved in importing mica and cochineal from Oaxaca and Thin Orange bowls from Puebla. Still another scenario is presented by Crespo and Mastache (1981), who note the existence of extensive lime deposits in southern Hidalgo. They suggest that Zapotec families from the Oaxaca Barrio at Teotihuacán came to Hidalgo to collect lime for Teotihuacán, where it was used to make plaster (Torres Rodríguez et al. 1999). At present we lack the data to decide between these scenarios.

Zapotec-Style Tombs

Residents of the Oaxaca Barrio at Teotihuacán buried their dead in Oaxaca-style tombs (R. Millon 1973a:42–44; Palomares Rodríguez 2013; Rattray 1993, 2001; Spence 1989, 1992; Urcid 2003b). On one carved tomb jamb we see the Zapotec hieroglyph 9L, perhaps the name of the deceased (Figure 9.2a). Other burials in the barrio contained Zapotec-style vessels, including (1) urns that honored ancestors associated with Lightning, Rain, and Maize; (2) urns that show humans and ancestors impersonating supernatural beings; and (3) urns that honor important individuals such as 8 Maize (see Figure 9.2b), 2 Water, and 2 Lightning.

The Zapotec residing at Teotihuacán buried their dead in the same way they had been doing in Oaxaca, and evidently beliefs about their ancestors were slow to change, even in the face of upheaval and resettlement. The Zapotec placed hieroglyphs on stone and clay to memorialize their ancestors and to communicate with supernatural forces like Lightning. Parenthetically, I note that these are not the only Zapotec-style tombs known from sites outside Oaxaca; Smith and Lind (2005) discuss three others. One is at the fortified site of Chimalacatlán in southern Morelos, where Müller (1948) found pottery that looked like that made in the Valley of Oaxaca. Upon looking at the pottery, Caso said that it resembled Period I and II pottery that he had recovered in tombs at Monte Albán. Noguera (1940) reported two additional Oaxaca-style tombs in the Tehuacán Valley.

Stable oxygen isotopes from the Oaxaca Barrio skeletons tell a story similar to that of the artifacts—that is, that there was ongoing interaction between Oaxaca and the Central Mexican highlands. White et al. (2004) conclude that throughout the occupation of the Oaxaca Barrio at Teotihuacán, new waves of Oaxaca immigrants augmented the initial group. These new immigrants continued to circulate among various highland settlements, actively participating in an extensive exchange network.

Thus—rather than supporting a simple dyadic model in which Teotihuacán and Monte Albán were the only exchange partners—the analyses of both material culture and stable oxygen isotopes show that there was a diaspora from Oaxaca to several sites in the central highlands (Spence 2004). White et al. (2004:385) have even suggested that many of the secondary burials in the Oaxaca Barrio were deceased relatives that had been transported from Oaxaca to Teotihuacán, perhaps as mummy bundles.

Offerings in Building I at Monte Albán

Both depictions of Teotihuacanos and gifts from Teotihuacán have been found at Monte Albán. One possible cache of gifts from Teotihuacán was found beneath a temple on Building I, a structure located along the central spine of Monte Albán's Main Plaza. In the cache Caso (1938) found a locally made urn of a man impersonating *Cociyo* by wearing a buccal mask; he had his hands on his knees and wore a necklace of large beads. Inside the *Cociyo* urn were 24 greenstone figurines that Caso (1965d:901–902) considered to be imports from Teotihuacán. One of the functions of such a gift was presumably to confirm that representatives from Teotihuacán were in attendance at a ceremony. In some instances, to be sure, we cannot rule out down-the-line exchange nor local emulation of Teotihuacán-style ceramics.

In the same cache, Caso found a large beaker incised with the name 3 Maize (3J) (Figure 9.3). This beaker contained two shells and a jade figure (Caso and Bernal 1965: Figure 7). There are at least four possible explanations for this offering: (1) a Zapotec noble named 3 Maize (Caso and Bernal 1965: Figure 14b) was honored by the dedicatory cache; (2) 3 Maize was an ancestor whose name was invoked when the temple was dedicated; (3) the beaker marks the postmortem apotheosis of 3 Maize into *Cociyo*; or (4) 3 Maize refers to a day of significance such as the dedication of the building. By drinking from this beaker, a person could honor the event or the metamorphosed 3 Maize.

Figure 9.3. This beaker, probably used for drinking pulque or chocolate, bears the hieroglyphic designation 3J (3 Maize). The beaker contained a jade figure and two shells when it was discovered in a dedicatory cache beneath one of the floors of Building I at Monte Albán. Drawing by John Klausmeyer.

The Lápida de Bazán from Monte Albán

Evidence of Teotihuacanos visiting Monte Albán is also suggested by the text and iconography on a beautifully incised travertine slab found in 1936 on Mound X, to the east of Monte Albán's North Platform (Caso 1938: Figure 25). Caso named this slab the "Lápida de Bazán" to honor Martín Bazán, the man who discovered it.

This slab was probably exhibited in, or associated with, a temple on Mound X (Caso 1965b:855–856). The left side of the slab (Figure 9.4) depicts a man dressed as a Teotihuacano, holding a pouch of copal. To the right is a Zapotec dressed in a jaguar costume. Each man stands on a hill sign that contains a date or day name. Based on these hieroglyphs, Caso suggested that the Teotihuacano was named 8E and the Zapotec 3E.

Figure 9.4. This stone is called the Lápida de Bazán. It was associated with Mound X, a temple to the east of the North Platform at Monte Albán. On the left we see a Teotihuacano and on the right a jaguar-costumed Zapotec. They stand on hill signs with hieroglyphs embedded inside the hills; Caso suggested that the Teotihuacano was named 8E and the Zapotec was named 3E. Each man is associated with a column of hieroglyphs. Of special note are the hieroglyphs at A6 and B4 that allude to the city of Teotihuacán. At A6 we see the Tassel Headdress that Clara Millon (1973) associated with Teotihuacán ambassadors and long-distance traders. At B4 we see the hieroglyph for the Teotihuacán sandal, which can be compared to that worn by the Teotihuacano at left. Note that the Teotihuacano is carrying a pouch—this is in contrast to some Teotihuacanos depicted on Maya monuments, who carry weapons. It is possible that this scene commemorates rituals conducted by a Teotihuacán ambassador and a Zapotec ruler. Drawing by Mark Orsen.

Each man is also associated with a column of hieroglyphs. The columns of text allude to Teotihuacán twice: once by a Teotihuacán-style ambassadorial headdress (called the "Tassel Headdress" by Clara Millon 1973) in Column A, Glyph 6, and once by a foot that wears a Teotihuacán-style sandal (Column B, Glyph 4). Travel is indicated by footprints at A7 and B6, and flowery speech may be indicated by the scrolls issuing from a head at A5. At A8 we see a Zapotec-style incense burner. At A4 a hand holds a single bean, such as those used during divination. Do these signs—"Tassel Headdress" and "hand with bean"—serve as pictograms that refer to activities carried out by the Teotihuacano and his Zapotec host, or should they be read phonetically? (See also Aztec and Mixtec writing; e.g., Anders et al. 1992a, 1992b; Caso 1977, 1979; Dibble 1940, 1955, 1971; Nicholson 1973; Smith 1973a.)

Other hieroglyphs on the *lápida* include hand gestures similar to "verbs of action" in the Maya writing system (e.g., Schele 1982). It is likely, as Caso (1947) suggested, that these Zapotec signs were verbs. While we cannot phonetically transcribe the 16 hieroglyphs on the Lápida de Bazán, the two columns of text appear to be a permanent record in stone of rituals conducted by a Teotihuacán ambassador and a Zapotec ruler. Such rituals probably helped to maintain peaceful relations between the two cities and ensured the flow of products between them. As discussed above, it is possible that mica and cochineal were two of the items exported from Oaxaca to Teotihuacán.

Teotihuacán Gifts Found on the North Platform at Monte Albán

Monte Albán's North Platform was built over the course of hundreds of years, and its excavation yielded a sequence of deeply nested structures. What we see today is the final stage—a set of temples, residences, interior patios, and a sunken court.

When tourists walk around the consolidated structures on the summit of the North Platform, they sense how restricted the access to this area would have been for commoners. Based on a traffic flow study, Blanton (1978:61–63) showed that one particular patio was the least accessible place in the city. If privacy was a major concern of the royal family and members of the court, the North Platform would have been the perfect place to conduct activities without being seen.

The North Platform has a majestic staircase, some 38 m wide. Upon reaching the top of the stairway, one passes through a portico with massive columns that probably supported a roof. From this portico one can look down into a sunken court, a 60 x 60 m area, where various rituals could be conducted. This court was so deep (4 m) that only those standing on the edge of the court could have seen the rites performed there.

Walking to the northeast sector of the North Platform, one sees three temples—Structures d, e, and g—surrounding the least accessible patio in the city. This patio is probably where members of the royal family conducted important rites. Such privacy was valued by royal families and court personnel because it set them and their rituals apart from those conducted even by lesser nobles.

Excavations on the North Platform yielded important items, including Thin Orange pottery and Teotihuacán-style cylindrical tripod vessels. Although some of these vessels appear to have been imported from Teotihuacán, others were locally made imitations of Teotihuacán wares. One locally made type, made on a yellowish clay, was called Type A3 by Caso et al. (1967); the end product was pottery that looks like Ixcaquixtla Thin Orange. Thus Monte Albán both received and emulated the pottery of the Central Mexican highlands.

One greenstone statue from Monte Albán's North Platform may be another import, given its stylistic similarity to statues made at Teotihuacán. Since this North Platform statue was broken and redeposited (it was found next to the wall of a platform designated Vértice Geodésico-East; see Martínez López 1994: Figure 20), we cannot say much about its original function or context at Monte Albán.

An unknown number of items on the North Platform may have been actual gifts from Teotihuacanos to Monte Albán rulers. Other objects, formerly thought to be imports from Teotihuacán, have turned out to be locally made imitations. The process of emulation is worth exploring in greater depth, simply because Teotihuacán-style items may have been highly valued and may have carried meanings for Zapotec nobles that we have yet to determine.

Just east of the North Platform, González Licón (2003) found evidence of mica cutting. The mining of mica was very ancient in the Valley of Oaxaca, going back to at least 1150 BC. The earliest villages, including San José Mogote, were involved in cutting and trimming mica into geometric shapes (e.g., Flannery and Marcus 2005:87–88, 249). González Licón found additional evidence for mica processing in a refuse pile southeast of the most private patio in the Vértice Geodésico. It dated to AD 200 ± 70 years, overlapping in time with the occupation of the Oaxaca Barrio at Teotihuacán.

At least three types of mica are abundant in the Precambrian metamorphic rocks that run for 70 km along the west side of the Valley of Oaxaca. The type of mica most commonly found on Monte Albán's North Platform is biotite, which is usually brown to black in color.

What did the Zapotec do with all of this mica? Locally, mica was cut into different shapes to adorn large incense burners for local use. Oaxaca mica was also exported to Teotihuacán, where it was cut into different geometric shapes (circles, triangles, rectangles) and used to cover the walls and floors of elite residential compounds.

An amazing discovery made by Pedro Armillas showed that mica was used to pave the entire floor in the interior patio of a building some 300 m southwest of the Pyramid of the Sun at Teotihuacán (Figures 9.5, 9.6). Given its delicate nature, Armillas (1944) suggested that the entire mica floor in the Viking Group may have been considered a large ritual offering. Armillas found evidence that the walls, too, had been covered with mica. In a recent article, Manzanilla et al. (2017) note that 90% of the

Figure 9.5. In the 1940s Pedro Armillas discovered that mica was sometimes used to pave the entire floor of an interior patio at Teotihuacán. Here we see the uppermost mica floor that he found in the Viking Group, ca. 300 m southwest of the Pyramid of the Sun. Given mica's friable and delicate nature, Armillas (1944) suggested that the entire floor could be considered a ritual offering. Chemical analyses show that the mica was imported from Oaxaca. Courtesy of Pedro Armillas.

mica found at Teotihuacán comes from the Viking Group and the Xalla Palace, two compounds tied to the governing elite. That mica has now been tied to Oaxaca, and much of it came from a source near Ejutla (Feinman and Nicholas 1990, 1993; Manzanilla et al. 2017).

Teotihuacán's Role in Rituals Associated with Monte Albán's South Platform

Many ritual activities were associated with Monte Albán's South Platform. Here I will discuss only three: (1) the placing of dedicatory offerings at the corners of the platform; (2) the carving of stones to show a procession of possible Teotihuacán visitors; and (3) the carving of stones to commemorate the inauguration of a Monte Albán ruler in Period IIIa. The precise amount of time that elapsed between these events is not known, but it seems significant that they were recorded on the South Platform.

The first major description of the South Platform was that of Guillermo Dupaix, who based it on his 1806 visit (Alcina Franch 1969). Although this building has been in the literature for more than a century (Batres 1902), little was known about the dedicatory caches and inaugural rites that took place there until the mapping and excavations conducted by Caso (1928) and Acosta (1958–1959, 1965). As with so many buildings at Monte Albán, the South Platform witnessed multiple renovations and expansions, as well as the display of recarved and reused stones. Additional excavation of the South Platform could bring to light more carved stones that once formed part of an ancient narrative.

Figure 9.6. This photo shows multiple superimposed mica floors in the Viking Group at Teotihuacán (see also Figure 9.5). Courtesy of Pedro Armillas.

Dedicatory Offerings below the South Platform

While excavating the South Platform, Jorge Acosta came upon offering boxes and cached items below three of its corners (Figure 9.7). Each offering box contained 10 *Spondylus* shells (5 *Spondylus princeps*, 5 *Spondylus calcifer*), 10 tent olive shells (*Oliva porphyria*), and 7 jade beads. Two of the offering boxes also contained spouted vessels assignable to Period IIIa (Acosta 1958–1959:27). This distribution of items among the offering boxes suggests that an effort was made to divide the offerings as evenly as possible.

These South Platform offerings continue a long Oaxaca tradition of placing offerings at the corners of a structure (e.g., as seen in the patio of Middle Formative Structure 28 at San José Mogote; see Flannery and Marcus 2015:153). Such Oaxaca offering boxes also anticipated the later Aztec offering boxes that variously honored the four quadrants of the earth, four cosmogonic eras, or four aspects of rain. Inside some of the stone dedicatory boxes of the Templo Mayor, for example, the Aztec placed four miniature serpents, four staffs, four drums, and four flutes (Gaida 2011; López Luján 2012:39).

Carved Stones Set into the Base of the South Platform

Above the offering boxes just described, the South Platform displayed carved stones, some of which depict apparent visitors from Teotihuacán (Figure 9.8). These visitors are named on the edges of Stelae 1, 7, 8, and the so-called Estela Lisa (Caso

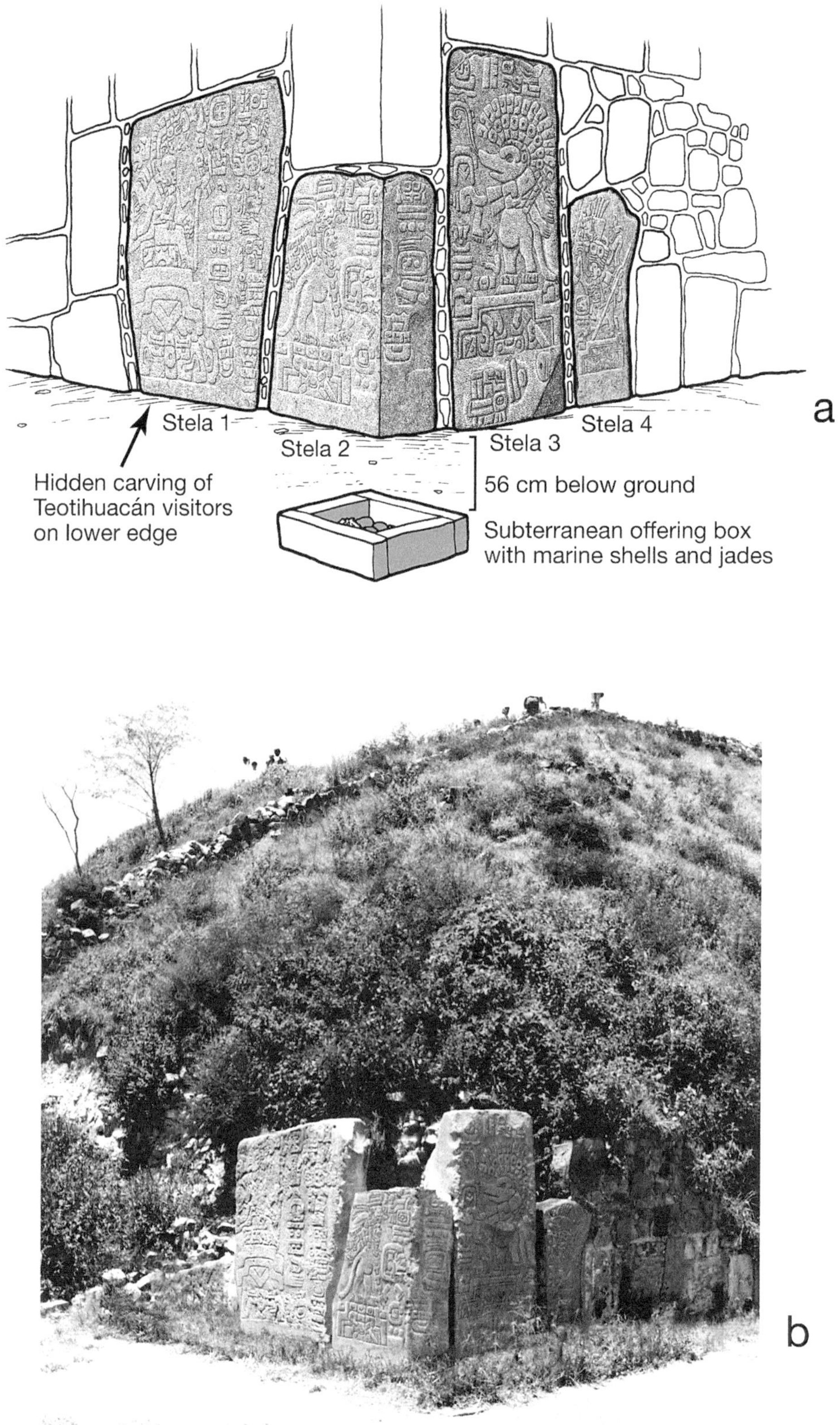

Figure 9.7. While excavating the South Platform at Monte Albán, Jorge Acosta (1958–1959) found offering boxes below three of its corners. In *a* we see the location of the offering box below the northeast corner; it contained 10 *Spondylus* shells, 10 tent olive shells, 1 spouted vessel assignable to Period IIIa, and 7 jade beads. In *b* we see Stelae 1–4 and the South Platform before it underwent additional excavation and consolidation. Drawing by John Klausmeyer, from a photograph courtesy of Ignacio Bernal.

1965b:856). Each visitor wore the Tassel Headdress, an item of apparel that Clara Millon (1973) has associated with Teotihuacán ambassadors who traveled long distances, including trips from Teotihuacán to Kaminaljuyú. Each visitor also carries a bag of incense; none of them carry the spearthrowers, darts, and shields that some Teotihuacanos carried when visiting Tikal and other Maya sites (Braswell 2003; Marcus 2003a). Rather, the men holding incense pouches at Monte Albán are similar to those depicted on the so-called Calpulalpan bowl from Las Colinas in Tlaxcala (Linné 1942: Figures 170–174).

Visitors Attending the Dedication of the South Platform

The Estela Lisa, or "plain stela" (Figure 9.8), documents a procession of men—from left to right, they are named 13 Knot, 9 Monkey, 1 Owl, and 6 Chilla. Next comes the sign Hill of 1 + (?) and a seated individual, a man named 13N who is elaborately attired. Lord 13N seems to be receiving the visitors. We also see a Teotihuacán-style temple, a set of footprints that may signify "travel," and a person who may be a traveler or ambassador.

On Stela 1, the visitors carved on the stone's upper and lower edges predate the carving of the stone's front face. On the upper edge are three well-preserved compartments; there is evidence that other compartments are now missing. The first compartment contains one large sign: a bar and a full-frontal glyph that may express the name 5 Jaguar (5B). The next compartment has calendar signs (perhaps 7 Rabbit) and noncalendric signs (a bundled item and a possible headdress with elements that might specify the name of a place). The third compartment includes the Glyph 5 Rain (5C), as well as Glyph E and other elements that appear to supply noncalendric information.

On the underside of Stela 1 we see more compartments (Figure 9.8). The first compartment is missing; the second includes a large cartouche followed by 13 Knot (the same name we saw on the Estela Lisa). The next compartment includes 3C. The following compartment includes 9 Monkey, plus the same Teotihuacán-style temple and set of footprints we saw on the Estela Lisa (von Winning 1947).

The edge of Stela 7 (Figure 9.8) displays men named 8N, 5E, and 12H (Marcus 1983d: Figure 6.5). The upper edge has large compartments that are similar to those on the edge of Stela 1.

On the bottom of Stela 8 we see compartments with incense burners (Figure 9.8). In the first compartment we see the Glyph 8N; the next compartment includes 5E, then 12H, all of which can be matched with the names on Stela 7. In the last compartment we see a figure seated on a hill with a triple spiral or heart symbol in its interior (see Neys and von Winning 1946).

The top edge of Stela 8 shows an initial compartment—now largely missing—followed by a compartment with a plant + Glyphs 6CC/6J and a compound sign that includes Glyph J (maize) + spiral scroll (heart) + three elements. The next compartment includes Lightning (M), possibly 1M, and 3 + Hill.

What can we say about these individuals? It appears that 6 Chilla (6 CC), 1 Owl/Night (1F), 9 Monkey (9O), 13 Knot (13A), 8N, 5E, and 12H were all participants in a procession that led to the burning of incense at a ceremony involving the South Platform. After that event, these stones were carved to provide a permanent record of the ceremony and the distinguished visitors who had traveled so far to participate in it. The Tassel Headdress and Teotihuacán-style temples and sandals hint at the place from which the visitors came.

The Scenes on the South Platform Stelae

One of the strategies a new ruler could use—especially if he were not in the direct line to rule—was to exaggerate his military prowess (Marcus 1974, 1994). Commissioning carved stones that show him reviewing a procession of bound captives would be an example of powerful propaganda.

Set in the base of the South Platform is a series of slabs depicting just such captives, each shown with his arms tied behind his back. These captives and others were probably destined to be sacrificed during the inaugural rites of the ruler depicted on Stela 1 (see below).

Eight of these slabs had been carved on their faces and displayed in the corners of the South Platform. Six of the eight (Stelae 2, 3, 5, 6, 7, and 8) depict captives standing on hill signs that may indicate their place of origin (Caso 1928; Marcus 1980, 1992a, 1994). The other two stones, featuring elegantly dressed individuals wielding lances, probably depict victorious Zapotec lords.

Stela 1

When originally discovered, Stela 1 was set upright in the northeast corner of the South Platform. Because earlier carvings depicting Teotihuacán visitors were on its upper and lower edges, later stone carvers turned to the still unused face of the stone (2.05 x 2.13 m) (Caso 1928: Figure 26; Rickards 1910:110 bis). On this surface they carved a ruler on a magnificent throne, sitting on a cushion covered by a jaguar pelt (Figure 9.9).

The ruler on Stela 1 wears a jaguar costume and an elaborate feather headdress. The latter seems to include an abbreviated version of the supernatural being shown at the base of the throne. The ruler also holds a lance with flapping ribbons, presumably a symbol of his military role. The hieroglyphs on Stela 1 have not been translated, but tentative interpretations can be offered. The text includes as many as three year signs and year bearers. Urcid (2001:378) has suggested that the time span covered 60 years.

In the first column the initial hieroglyph is a year sign that can be read either as the completion of Year 13E or the beginning of Year 1E. An event in that year seems to be linked to the verb that follows. We then see the calendric sign 7A and the compound

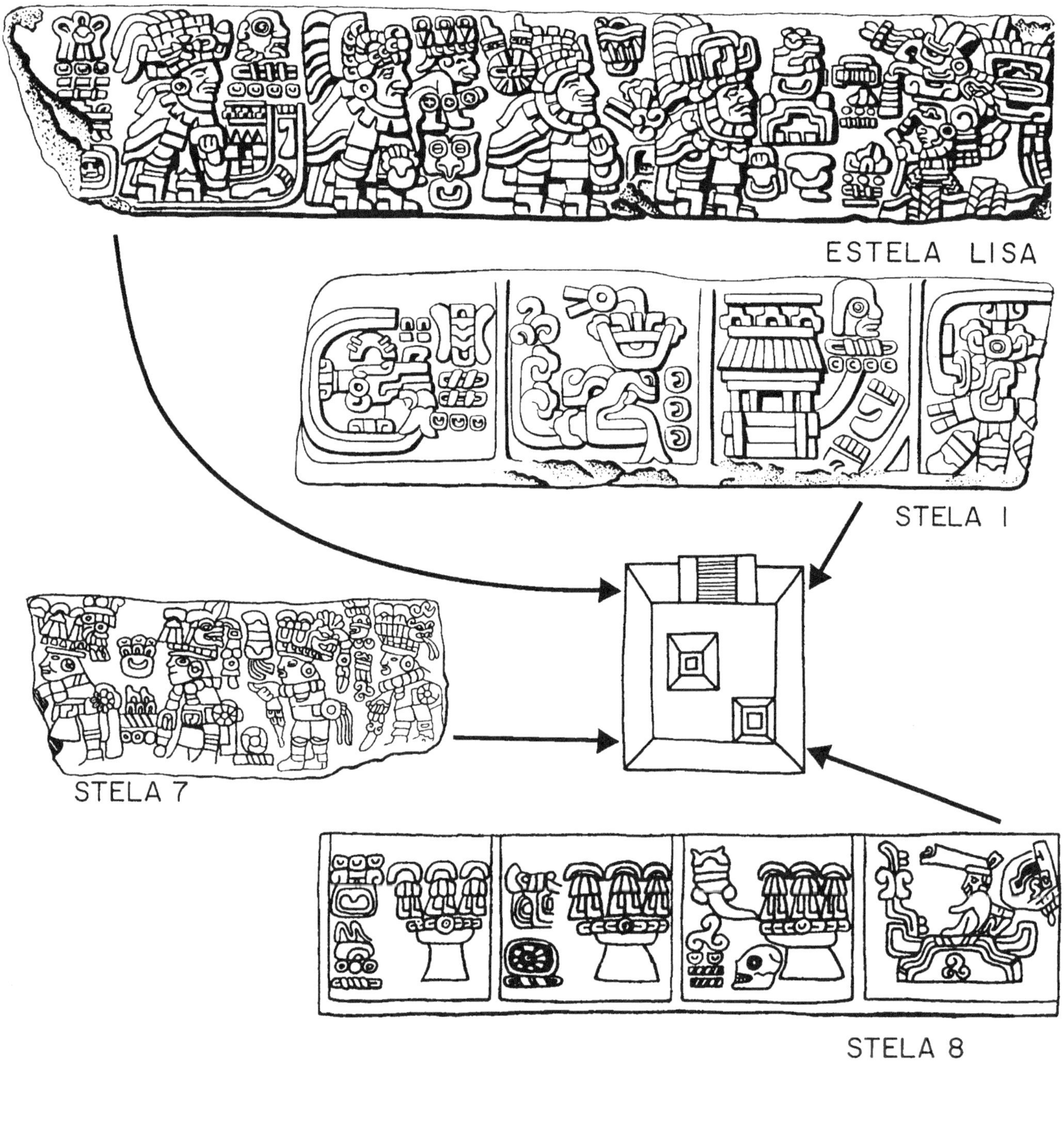

Figure 9.8. On these stelae the Tassel Headdresses, copal pouches, and incense burners suggest that we are seeing Teotihuacán visitors who came to Monte Albán to participate in a ritual at the South Platform. The Estela Lisa and Stela 1 were found at the front (north) corners of the platform, while Stelae 7 and 8 were found at the rear (south) corners. Much of the information on the Estela Lisa is repeated on Stela 1; similarly, much of the information on Stela 7 is repeated on Stela 8 (Acosta 1958–1959).

Figure 9.9. When discovered, Stela 1 was set in the northeast corner of the South Platform at Monte Albán (see Figure 9.7). Earlier carvings depicting Teotihuacán visitors were featured on its upper and lower edges (Figure 9.8). Later, the carvers turned this stone over to create on its wide face a new scene, one that commemorated a newly inaugurated ruler. They then set Stela 1 into the base of the South Platform, along with other stelae depicting bound prisoners; the ruler was positioned as if he were reviewing the latter in single-file procession. Drawing by Mark Orsen.

sign, which may document an important event in the life of a person named 7A. The first column of hieroglyphs ends with the bag glyph, indicating completion or death. We cannot be sure in this case whether 7A was the name of the person on the throne or someone involved with him in some way. If 7A refers to the individual on the throne, he must have received a new name—possibly 12 Jaguar or 13 Owl—at the time of his inauguration. I mention this because the acquisition of a new name during inauguration was a fairly widespread practice in Mesoamerica.

The second column begins with the Year 8E, followed by a series of hieroglyphs. Then we see another year sign and year bearer that can be read as the Year 5E. The logogram that follows seems to be a place sign, followed by the name 8 Water. The final sign is once again the bag glyph.

What are we to make of Stela 1? The iconographic content seems clear: a new ruler has taken the throne. Our eyes focus on the trappings of his office—the headdress, the jaguar costume, the lance, the jaguar pelt cushion, the immense throne, and the hill sign. Since the symbols of office, especially the cushion and throne, take up so much space on the face of Stela 1, the underlying message may have been "Focus on the office of kingship, rather than the person."

By placing Stela 1 into the base of the South Platform along with other stelae that depict prisoners, the ruler would have been positioned to review prisoners in single-file procession. Each of these prisoners appears on the face of monuments that were recarved and reset into the walls of the South Platform. Now let us turn to the prisoners.

Stela 2

The captive on Stela 2 is dressed in a jaguar costume, with his arms tied behind his back (Figure 9.10a). Note that an unfinished version of this same individual (3 Knot) had been carved on the back of this stela (Figure 9.10b). Figure 9.10b provides us with an unusual opportunity to see an abandoned effort at carving (see also Marcus 1992a: Figure 11.39b). The version on the back was left unfinished because the stone carver had not allowed enough room for all the hieroglyphs he planned to include. Specifically, the hill sign on the back of the monument filled the entire width of the stone, leaving too little room for the footprints that were to be inserted between the second and fourth glyphs. Such errors may have been relatively rare, and in this case did not lead to a discarding of the stone. Since this slab otherwise met all desired specifications, the carver simply decided to turn the stone upside down and start over, carving the same scene on the opposite side. One interesting note about the unfinished back of Stela 2: the one glyph that *was* finished was the name of the prisoner, 3 Knot.

The column of hieroglyphs on the front of Stela 2 begins with the Year 13E (Caso 1928: Figures 27, 28). The position of the three dots—*below* the two bars—is typical of Period IIIa. (The bars are straight and undecorated instead of bent with diagonal lines or bindings, as so often happened during Period IIIb–IV.) Below the Year 13E are three signs: a large cartouche framing a jaguar; footprints pointing down; and then Glyph 3A. If Stela 1's opening date is confirmed as Year 13E, that would mean that the texts on both Stelae 1 and 2 probably opened with the same year.

As noted in an earlier chapter (Chapter 5) on the Otomanguean languages, typical Zapotec word order is usually VSO (verb, subject, object). Stela 2 opens with a temporal designation, the Year 13E. The second sign seems to be a logogram for "traveled," which is associated with the jaguar-costumed figure by combining a cartouche + jaguar + footprints. Given typical Zapotec word order, we would next expect to see the prisoner mentioned; his name is indeed given as 3 Knot. Thus we might read this short clause as follows: "In the Year 13E was brought [the jaguar-costumed prisoner named] 3 Knot." From whence was he brought? If we could identify the town on whose glyph 3 Knot stands, we might be able to say more about this prisoner and the distance he was forced to travel to get to Monte Albán.

The hieroglyphic text then continues on the *side* of Stela 2 (Figure 9.10c). The text at this point is damaged (Caso 1928: Figure 30; Urcid 2003a: Figure 8). The next surviving glyph is the name 13 Owl, followed by a composite sign that may refer to an accession. Once again, the bag glyph closes the text.

Since Stela 6 (Figure 9.10d) also mentions a person named 13 Owl, we wonder who he was. Did 13 Owl accede to the throne himself, or was 13 Owl a noble warrior who brought the jaguar-costumed captive (3 Knot) to Monte Albán, thereby delivering him to the ruler depicted on Stela 1?

The possibility considered above, to be sure, raises the question of whether the Zapotec would actually place a noble warrior's name on a monument to honor his taking of a prisoner. As it happens, their Maya contemporaries did just that. Figure 9.11 shows a Maya monument, dating to AD 783, on which a stone carver created such a scene. He depicted a throne with steps leading up to it, thereby establishing the different levels upon which participants could stand according to their positions in the political hierarchy. In the upper level we see Itzamnaaj B'ahlam, the ruler of Yaxchilan, seated on his throne. In the middle level is Aj Chak Maax, a subordinate lord and warrior, who rests his right knee on one step and his left foot on a lower step. In the lowest level we see three elite prisoners whom Aj Chak Maax has captured. The hieroglyphic text tells us that Aj Chak Maax has dressed the prisoners for their ceremonial presentation to the ruler. Aj Chak Maax has replaced the prisoners' jade ear ornaments with strips of cloth and bound their upper arms with rope; he has, however, let them continue to wear some of the trappings of elite status, such as headdresses and necklaces.

We have already seen another Maya monument, Lintel 8 of Yaxchilan, which features captive taking by a noble warrior (see Figure 2.6, Chapter 2). On the right is Bird Jaguar, ruler of Yaxchilan, taking a prisoner named Jeweled Skull (Proskouriakoff 1963, 1964). To the left is a subordinate ruler, or *b'aah sajal*, who is also taking a prisoner. This noble warrior is named K'an Tok Wayib, and the text refers to him as the "Captor of Ko'te' ajaw," referring to the prisoner who kneels before him. These two Maya

Figure 9.10. Stela 2 (*a–c*), re-set in the northeast corner of Monte Albán's South Platform, depicts a jaguar-costumed prisoner with his arms bound behind his back; his name was 3 Knot (3A). At *a* we see the front of Stela 2. At *b* we see the back of Stela 2; this side was carved first, but the carving was abandoned when the sculptor discovered that he had left no room to insert the footprints. At *c* we see a third side of Stela 2, which mentions 13 Owl at the top. One side of Stela 6 also mentions 13 Owl (*d*). We are not sure who 13 Owl was. Two possibilities are (1) that he was the ruler on Stela 1 or (2) that he was a noble warrior who delivered prisoners for the inauguration of the ruler on Stela 1 (see Figure 9.9). Drawings by Mark Orsen.

Figure 9.11. Maya monuments sometimes depicted subordinate lords delivering prisoners to their superiors. In the lowest level of this Yaxchilan monument (Level 3) are three prisoners who are named by hieroglyphs; they were presumably elite, since their names were considered worth mentioning and their jade earspools had been replaced by strips of paper or cloth. These captives were taken by the subordinate lord Aj Chak Maax in AD 783. Aj Chak Maax is shown on Level 2, resting his right knee on one step as he faces his superior. At the top (Level 1) is the Yaxchilan ruler seated on his throne. It is possible that the Zapotec noble named 13 Owl (Figure 9.10) played the same role as Aj Chak Maax. Redrawn by John Klausmeyer from Marcus 2006b: Fig. 11.2.

cases show that it is far from implausible that a noble warrior who delivers important captives might be featured on a stela.

Stela 3

Stela 3 (see Figure 5.7, Chapter 5) depicts a prisoner wearing an elaborate animal costume. There has been considerable speculation about whether this costume depicts a coyote, an opossum, or some other animal (Marcus 1992a: Figure 11.40). Like other captives displayed on the South Platform, this one has his arms bound behind his back.

The text on Stela 3 begins with the Year 10M, followed by the "fish" glyph, a possible hill sign, a shell + footprint compound, and the name 12 Reed (or 12 Flower, according to Caso). We see a knot sign that seems to reinforce the depiction of knots tied around the prisoner's ankles.

One possible interpretation of this text is "the prisoner named 12 Reed was [led or traveled] to his end." Below the hill sign is an upside-down year sign 11M (the Year 11 Lightning).

Stela 4

The man depicted on Stela 4 (Figure 9.12) is either a ruler or another noble warrior. In the latter case, he may have conquered a rival town or provided an important captive for his ruler.

The Stela 4 warrior appears to be named 8 Deer. He is shown in elaborate attire, possibly with a trophy head on his chest. His magnificent headdress includes elements like Lightning or Jaguar. He carries a lance in his left hand and in his right hand a doubled-over cord, likely the kind carried into combat and used to tie prisoners. The way 8 Deer's lance is thrust into the hill sign is similar to the iconographic convention used by the Postclassic Mixtec to indicate "conquest" or "conquered place" (Caso 1965c, 1977, 1979; M. Smith 1973a).

Figure 9.12. The front of Stela 4 at Monte Albán features a Zapotec warrior named 8 Deer (8G), who may have captured prisoners for the inauguration of the ruler on Stela 1. Drawing by Mark Orsen.

Stela 5

Stela 5 (Figure 9.13) displays a captive named 8P. In the manner of Stela 3, this monument shows an upside-down year sign, a year bearer, and a fish, all placed below a hill sign. The year is given as 5 Deer.

Since Stelae 3 and 5 both have an inverted year sign and fish below the hill sign, we may surmise that that date was either the year of their capture or their sacrifice. The meaning of the fish glyph is not known, but one interpretation favored by Terry Kaufman and Javier Urcid is "captor." A reading of "was captured" would fit the context here, since the fish glyph often occurs immediately following the date (i.e., in the position where one would expect a verb).

Thus the text on this monument might have been read: "In the Year 5 Deer" + "was captured and was led or traveled" + "the man named 8P."

Figure 9.13. The lower half of Stela 5 at Monte Albán shows a captive named 8P. His arms were bound behind his back (top left), as were those of other prisoners displayed on the South Platform. Drawing by Mark Orsen.

Stela 6

On the front of Stela 6 (see Figure 5.8, Chapter 5) is a text that can be read "In the Year 10 Deer was captured a man named 2S." The captive named 2S (2 + a hieroglyph depicting the tail of a rattlesnake associated with "turtle-man" or *xicàni*) does not wear an animal costume. His arms are bound behind his back. He is associated with a speech scroll—as are the prisoners depicted on Stelae 3 and 8—and stands on a place sign that has yet to be linked to an actual locality.

The text on the left side of the monument (Caso 1928: Figure 40) begins with a year sign and year bearer that can be read as the Year 1 Deer (Figure 9.10d). We then see three hieroglyphs—a probable verb whose principal sign might be a seated torso, possibly meaning "seated in office"; the subject of the clause, a man named 13 Owl; then a horizontal rendering of the "fish glyph." We might interpret this text as "In the Year 1 Deer, 13 Owl was seated in office" (a reference to the ruler on Stela 1). It is not clear why the fish glyph is recorded here, although (following Kaufman and Urcid) it may have served the same role as the Maya hieroglyphic term, "captor."

Stela 7

This monument is broken, with only the lower half well preserved. A bound figure is shown standing on a hill sign that has yet to be associated with a specific place.

Stela 8

Stela 8 (Figure 9.14) shows a bound captive who is barefoot. Unlike the prisoners in elaborate animal costumes, this man wears only a loincloth. He is associated with a large speech scroll.

Although the text is brief, the sculptor uses a large hieroglyph—3 Maize (3J)—to emphasize the name of this captive. Below his name we see the bag glyph, which in this context may indicate that he ended up dead (see Figure 5.4, Chapter 5).

The hill sign and the personal name of the captive are large and impressive. The hill sign contains three elements—a human face + Glyph M + a mandible. Unfortunately, the hometown of this prisoner has not been identified.

This monument brings to half a dozen the number of South Platform stelae whose front faces depict bound captives. One possible explanation is that (like the later Aztec kings) a Zapotec ruler of Period IIIa needed to demonstrate military prowess by displaying captives for sacrifice at his inauguration (Caso 1928; Marcus 1976a, 1976d, 1994; Townsend 1987).

The Mound II Carved Stone at Monte Albán

Mound II, on the east side of Monte Albán's Main Plaza, was the location of another Period IIIa monument (Figure 9.15). The Mound II stone shares some features with those re-set around the base of the South Platform (Alcina Franch 1993: Figure 243; Caso 1965b:857, Figure 17; Urcid 2011). It shows a man in full jaguar costume, unbound and clearly not a captive. His name is 11 Rain (11C), and he wears a disk or mirror on his chest. At the far right of the slab we see the Year 13 Deer (13G).

The most eye-catching feature of this monument appears at the far left, where we see the still-articulated rattles of a snake; this unusual artistic convention emanates from the man's mouth. I can think of no other example in which we see 20+ rattlesnake rattles emanating from the mouth of a costumed figure. We can only wonder if this symbolizes a specific kind of menacing speech.

Figure 9.14. Stela 8 shows 3 Maize, a bound captive, whose name (3 + Glyph J) is emphasized by its large size. Drawing by Mark Orsen.

Figure 9.15. This monument was found on Mound II on the east side of the Main Plaza at Monte Albán. I suspect that it may once have been displayed elsewhere—perhaps on the South Platform—because it shows a figure dressed in an animal costume that is similar to those featured there. The man on this monument is named 11 Rain (hieroglyphs in front of him), and he is associated with the Year 13 Deer (hieroglyphs behind him). The text may record an accession to office; a possible “seated in office” sign occurs at the base of the long string of rattlesnake rattles (at left). Drawing by Mark Orsen.

(An analogy might be the Mixtec use of obsidian knives on a speech scroll to indicate "cutting words.")

At the lower left of the scene we see a possible accession or "seated in office" sign. Unfortunately, we do not know whether the reference is to 11 Rain's accession or someone else's.

Comparing Zapotec Accessions to Those of Other States

The stelae of Monte Albán's South Platform, even in their re-set condition, suggest three features of Zapotec inaugurations: (1) monuments showing the ruler enthroned; (2) dedicatory caches placed beneath the corners of an important building; and (3) monuments showing bound captives destined for sacrifice.

Human sacrifice was an important component of inaugurations for many Mesoamerican states. For example, on Stela 11 at Piedras Negras, a Maya ruler is shown sitting on his throne at the top of a stairway while the body of a sacrificial victim lies at the bottom of the stairway. The sacrificial victim has had his heart removed, and his precious blood is symbolized by a bundle of long (quetzal?) feathers rising from his open chest (Marcus 1994:259).

By studying the inaugural rites conducted in a number of societies, Hocart (1927) isolated 26 practices, including (1) sacrificing human victims; (2) giving a new name to the king; (3) providing regalia, such as a scepter or staff; (4) seating the ruler-elect on a throne; (5) crowning the latter; and (6) having participants impersonate gods by wearing masks and special garb (Caso and Bernal 1952: Figures 420–421).

Inaugurations could also be protracted, multistage affairs. For example, Aztec inaugurations have been divided into four stages: (1) Separation and Retreat, (2) Investiture and Coronation, (3) a Coronation War, and (4) Confirmation (Townsend 1987). Since the data from Monte Albán's South Platform accord well with some aspects of Townsend's Stages 2 and 3, let us look more closely at those two stages in Aztec inaugurations. Stage 2 began with the Aztec ruler's enthronement, which involved placing a special headdress on his head and transporting him to the main Aztec temple, where he assumed his eagle/ocelot throne. Following coronation, the Aztec ruler sacrificed quail and offered his own blood. Stage 3 entailed military expeditions led by the new ruler. Before he could be considered in control of his office, however, the new ruler had to demonstrate that he could obtain prisoners to be sacrificed at his confirmation ceremony, which included the dedication of a temple. The Aztec ruler also showed military prowess by re-subjugating rebellious towns and taking captives. The defeated rulers of these towns were then required to attend his confirmation and temple dedication.

The final three components of Ahuitzotl's AD 1487 inauguration, for example, were (1) dedicating the Temple of Huitzilopochtli in Tenochtitlán; (2) commissioning a Dedication Stone that recorded that event; and (3) sacrificing the captives taken by him during his Coronation War (Alvarado Tezozómoc 1944:330; Townsend 1987; Umberger 1987:422).

Kingship was an institution that had to look stable and enduring, even when the dynastic line was broken. When a usurper took the throne, he often needed to take dramatic steps to conceal the fact that the dynastic line had been interrupted. For example, in ancient Burma, we learn from Aung-Thwin (1983:81–85) that at least eight of the nine kings of the Pagan Dynasty (AD 1000–1200) were not in direct line, and had to go to great lengths to establish their legitimacy. They did so by staging spectacular inaugural ceremonies, which sometimes included a parade of humiliated captives. We wonder if this might have been the case with the ruler on Stela 1 at Monte Albán, whose massive display of legitimacy was unique for Period IIIa. If every other ruler of that period had needed such a display, we would have many more Period IIIa monuments to study.

Consider, in addition, the huge throne featured on Stela 1, which contrasts with the smaller hill signs associated with other rulers. The deliberate reuse of monuments whose edges show Teotihuacán visitors may have added to the Stela 1 ruler's legitimacy. We note that other Mesoamerican rulers in need of legitimization might also be guilty of such overkill. One possible example is Stela 22 from Naranjo, where we see a Maya ruler sitting on an immense throne. He is said to have taken the throne at age five and claimed to have achieved several military victories at that tender age, as unlikely as that seems.

Period IIIa Tombs with Writing and Iconography

Like their inaugurations, Zapotec royal funerals could also be protracted, multistage affairs. Funerary rites often benefited the rulers' descendants by creating powerful horizontal propaganda about their ancestors.

The nobles at Monte Albán constructed even more impressive tombs than the Oaxaca ambassadors at Teotihuacán. As time passed, the Zapotec elite invested more and more effort in painting polychrome murals in their family tombs. Such murals began to display a new motif, Caso's "Fauces del Cielo" (Jaws of the Sky), which referred to the semidivine ancestors of "people of noble lineage" [*tija coquì*] (Caso 1928, 1965b; Marcus 1980, 1992a, 2002). A venerated ancestor was often shown descending from the Jaws of the Sky; he might be associated with a hieroglyphic name, a bird, leaves, a string of jade beads, or other unidentified items (Figure 9.16).

Polychrome murals sometimes showed ancestors walking single file to the back of the tomb to greet an apical ancestor; at other times a mural showed marital pairs entering and exiting the tomb. The main concerns of tomb murals thus seem to have been to (1) assert an unbroken line of descent from an apical ancestor and (2) provide the names of marital couples and their descendants (Fuente 2008; Miller 1995).

The tombs of Period IIIa nobles were more elaborate than those of their predecessors. We see hieroglyphic texts carved on

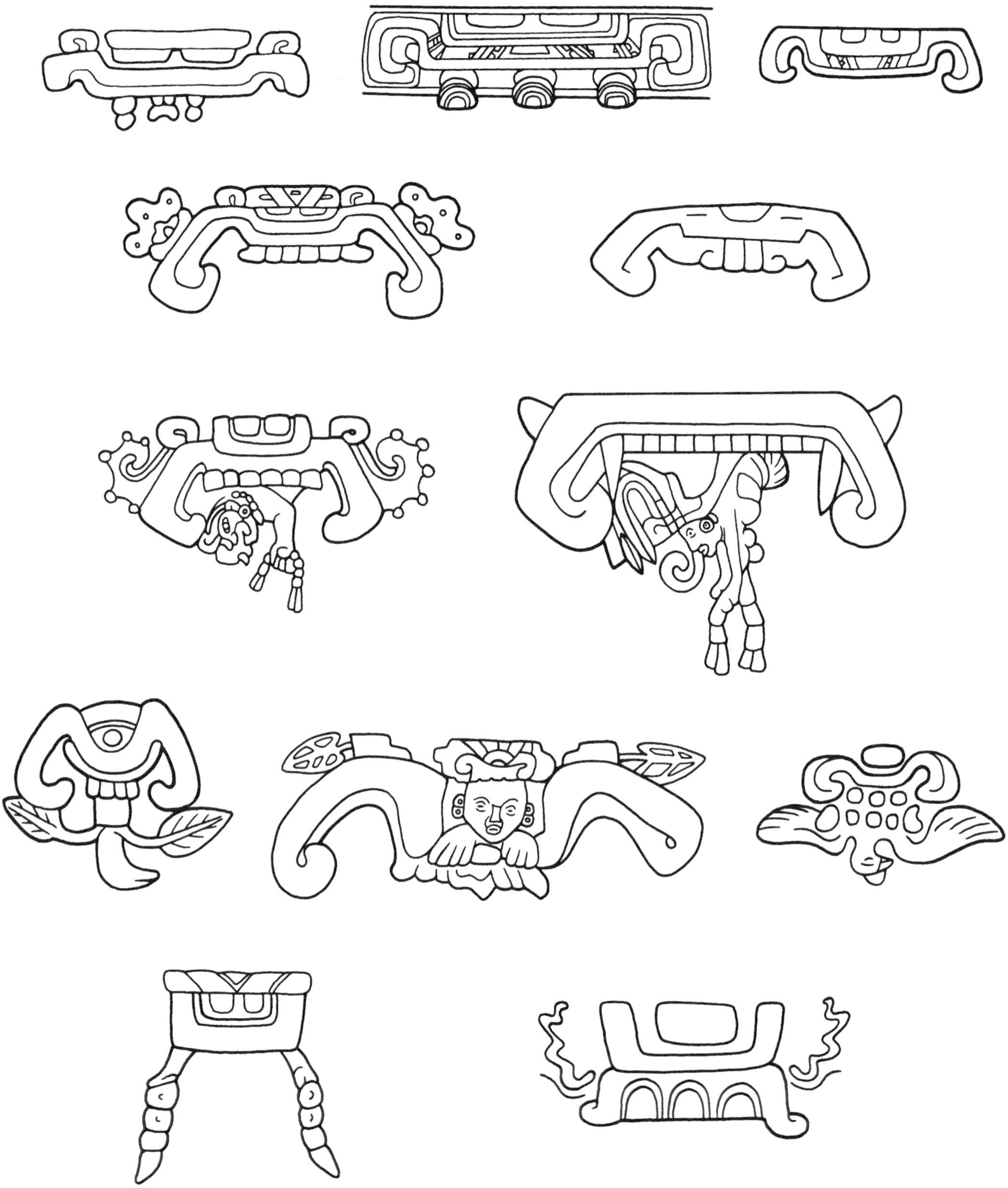

Figure 9.16. Here we see multiple examples of the Jaws of the Sky, a motif identified by Caso (1928). This motif often appears at the top of a monument, above the heads of noble couples; thus it is linked to people of noble lineage (*tija coquì*). Descending from the Jaws of the Sky we often see a human figure or a series of ritual objects, including strands of jade beads, leaves, or birds. See also Balkansky 2002. Redrawn by John Klausmeyer from Marcus 2002: Fig. 7.22.

tomb jambs, lintels, and doors, or added to the murals painted on the stucco walls of the main chamber. Many of these tombs can be seen in the elite residential neighborhood just north of the North Platform at Monte Albán. Some texts may well have been commissioned by the descendants of the tomb's occupants, eager to validate their status. As a result, many Period IIIa tombs became multigenerational family mausolea, remaining accessible so that new offerings could be added to the antechamber and new family members could be added to the main chamber. Often when new corpses were added, the skeletons of earlier occupants were simply shoved to the back of the tomb.

To understand the mortuary practices of some Period IIIa nobles, I will begin by looking at three of the most famous sepulchers at Monte Albán—Tombs 103, 104, and 105.

Ancestor Veneration in Tomb Murals

Although earlier Monte Albán tombs, such as Tomb 72, had murals, the Period IIIa tombs made more extensive use of wall space and utilized more colors. These polychrome tributes and the ongoing performance of rites at the tomb entrance helped the elite to maintain communication between the living and the dead.

Both Caso and Acosta have described Period IIIa tombs as "veritable ossuaries," given the number of individuals placed in them. At least one tomb literally replicated the layout of the palace where the nobles had resided when they were alive (Miller 1995; see Tomb 5 of Cerro de la Campana in Chapter 12). In those cases where a tomb lay beneath an elite residence, it was usually reached by a stairway descending from an interior patio (Caso 1938; Flannery 1983c, 1998). Thus entry and exit from the family tomb could be witnessed both by those living in the palace and the guests invited to attend the funerary rites.

The tomb entrance was often closed with a rectangular stone that could be moved to one side when reentry was desired. Such stone doors, often carved with hieroglyphic texts, ensured that the tomb could be reopened to receive new offerings or the recently deceased.

Communicating with the ancestors has great time depth in Oaxaca. As early as 1400 BC, Oaxaca's families were creating clay figurines to provide a venue for the spirits of their ancestors (Marcus 1998a, 2006c, 2007, 2019; Meissner et al. 2013). Some of the earliest Formative figurines depicted human ancestors; others depicted individuals impersonating supernatural beings by wearing masks and other paraphernalia. The rituals conducted in early Zapotec households allowed their ancestors to witness events taking place in the lives of their descendants. These ancestors were asked by their descendants to intercede on their behalf when communicating with remote apical ancestors and supernatural forces such as Lightning (Flannery and Marcus 1976b; Marcus 1998a; Marcus and Flannery 1978, 1994).

The metamorphosis of an elite human into Lightning was displayed in a miniature adobe tomb, placed below the Structure 35 temple at San José Mogote during Period II (Marcus and Flannery 1996:186–188). A kneeling figure with a jade necklace and earspools (probably a deceased noble) was buried in the miniature tomb along with a sacrificed quail; on the tomb's roof, the metamorphosis of the noble into a flying *Cociyo* figure was witnessed by four clay sculptures depicting Lightning's allies: Clouds, Rain, Hail, and Wind. With the escalation of social stratification during Period II, such rites of elite metamorphosis acquired a new purpose: reinforcing the different postmortem destinies of elites and commoners. The funerals of the privileged class attracted nobles from near and far. People came to burn incense, offer food and drink, and utter the name of the deceased. In front of some tombs, the attendees placed offerings, burned incense, and arranged spectacular urns (Caso and Bernal 1952; Saville 1904).

Like the clay figurines made by the earliest villagers in the valley, some Zapotec funerary urns depicted human ancestors. Others showed humans impersonating supernaturals by wearing full-face or buccal masks, along with special headdresses and elaborate necklaces. Still other urns displayed deified ancestors who had metamorphosed into creatures with special abilities, such as flight (Flannery and Marcus 2015:266–270).

Well past the Spanish Conquest, the Zapotec elite continued to venerate their ancestors, referring to them as *peni coniyto* (ancestors) and *pixozacolatono* (ancestors in one's lineage) (Córdova [1578a]1942:29v). The writings of many sixteenth-century friars show that they did not understand ancestor veneration, but rather confused it with the Classical pantheons of Greek and Roman gods (Balsalobre [1656]1892; Córdova [1578a]1942; W. Cruz 1935, 1936, 1946; Marcus 1978, 1983b, 1992a).

This confusion becomes apparent in the lists of "gods" compiled by the Spaniards after they visited each town. When one examines these lists, three clues emerge. First, the so-called "deities" were notably different for each Zapotec town. Our second clue is that the terms *coquì* (male ruler) and *xonàxi* (female ruler) appear in many of the names of the alleged "deities." The use of such terms shows that these were actually venerated lords and ladies. In some cases, the Spaniards recorded the names of a husband-wife dynastic founder couple and assumed that they were deities. The fact that many founder couples had names taken from the 260-day calendar is our third clue that they were venerated ancestors.

In sixteenth-century documents (Espíndola [1580]1905a, 1905b; *Relaciones geográficas* 1579–1581), for example, we read of a male-female pair—Benelaba and Xonàxi Belachina—who were still being venerated. To honor their memory, the Zapotec in Coatlán sacrificed dogs, turkeys, quails, and war captives. The man's name—Benelaba—can be translated as 7 Rabbit, while the woman's name—Xonàxi Belachina— can be translated as Lady 3 Deer. It is likely that these were the names of a founder couple whose memory was maintained by conducting commemorative rites, including human and animal sacrifices. Other cases of venerated male and female rulers abound; Coquì Bila was venerated in Macuilxóchitl, Coquì Cehuiyo in Tlacolula, and

Coquì Huani in Tlalixtac de Cabrera. In Mitla, a woman named Xonàxi Quecuya was the object of veneration.

Such veneration of a founder couple occurred as early as Period IIIa. At Monte Albán and elsewhere in the valley, a primordial couple named 1 Jaguar (1B) and 2 Maize (2J) were often honored by having their names carved on drinking beakers (Figure 9.17). These carved beakers were sometimes left as offerings in temples and tombs (Seler 1991:196).

At Monte Albán, the tombs of many nobles were built before the palace itself. Heavy masonry construction and bedrock locations ensured that such tombs would not collapse under the weight of the buildings above. Above Tombs 104 and 105 at Monte Albán, the Zapotec constructed Period IIIa palaces complete with plastered patios, L-shaped corner rooms, and curtain walls. The descendants of the deceased continued to live in the palace so that they could make offerings to the deceased below.

We have some hints, from elsewhere in Mesoamerica, about how long funerary rituals could last. On some Maya stone monuments, for example, the hieroglyphs record not only the ruler's death date but also his burial date; those two dates are sometimes separated by months (as at Toniná) or years (as at Piedras Negras). Such evidence forces us to think about (1) where the corpse was kept between the date of death and the date of interment; (2) whether or not the corpse was converted into a bundle that was carried to various localities; (3) what rites were performed during that time interval; and (4) what rules determined the appropriate day to put the funerary bundle into a tomb. Substantial periods of time devoted to the transport and display of mortuary bundles are known for many groups, including the Mixtec, Maya, and Aztec (e.g., del Castillo 2001; Freidel and Guenter 2006; Hermann Lejarazu 2009; Jansen and Pérez Jiménez 2011; M. E. Smith 1973a; Stenzel 1968–1970).

In addition to having protracted rites leading up to the final interment, the Maya and Zapotec also honored their ancestors on important anniversaries. I have suggested that one Zapotec hieroglyph—the Maltese cross—referred to anniversaries, and that the number associated with the Maltese cross (Caso's Glyph I [1928:35]) might have specified on which anniversary (e.g., the seventh) offerings were made. On such anniversaries new offerings were made, and red pigment might be sprinkled over the dry bones.

Multiple Messages of the Period IIIa Tombs

Some Period IIIa tombs have murals painted on the walls of the main chamber; others have hieroglyphs on the door; still others contain ceramic effigy urns depicting deities, metamorphosed individuals, or royal ancestors. A few tombs have all three.

The most elaborate Period IIIa tombs consisted of a main chamber with wall niches, an antechamber, a movable stone door, and an access stairway. Even when the tomb itself was sealed, the stairway might be left accessible, usually reached from an opening in the palace's interior patio. As in the case of Monte Albán's Tomb 104, the original carvings on the door stone could be changed over time, with the names of new individuals added (see Figure 7.1, Chapter 7).

The practice of decorating tomb chambers with murals actually began in Period Ic or II; Tomb 72 at Monte Albán is an example. Period IIIa tombs had more extensive murals and used a broader range of colors. The hieroglyphs in those murals could supply the names of the tomb's original occupants, their ancestors, and even relatives added later. Many Zapotec tombs contained urns which made reference to *Cociyo*, or Lightning, while others had urns depicting royal ancestors who, after death, had metamorphosed and gone to live in the sky. The full story of any tomb must be pieced together by looking at the multiple messages of its murals, the carvings on its door stone, and the iconography of its funerary urns.

Tomb 104 of Monte Albán

Our tour of Tomb 104 begins with its elaborate façade and the large urn above its doorway. The urn depicts a person whose calendric name was 5E, possibly the name of the original tomb occupant (Caso 1938: Figure 92; Miller 1995:112–115). The name 5E is mentioned not only on the interior face of the door stone (Figure 7.1c), but also on the rear wall of the tomb. The polychrome mural on the wall of the main chamber names the relatives of 5E and links him to an apical ancestor, 10 Lao, whose name occurs on the rear wall (Caso 1938:77; Marcus 1983d: Figure 5.9; Marcus 1992a:283).

Tomb 104 contains five niches—one on the north wall, one on the south wall, and three along the rear (or east) wall. One large niche in the center of the rear wall actually intrudes into the painted name 10 Lao; two other rear-wall niches flank the larger one (Caso 1938: Plano 17). At the time of the tomb's discovery, four of the five niches still contained ceramic offerings.

The mural in the main chamber (Figure 9.18) shows a series of nobles facing the rear wall. The man painted on the south wall is wearing sandals; his peaked hat and headdress are distinctive. He holds a bag in one hand, while his other hand stretches out toward a box painted red, white, and green. His outstretched hand (and that of his counterpart on the north wall) extends to the tomb's side niches, where offerings of pottery had been placed.

Above the niche on the south wall is the painting of a box, on top of which we see a yellow bird with a corn kernel in its beak. Nearby is a second box, this one accompanied by the calendric names 2 Lightning (2M) and 10 Serpent (10Y). These hieroglyphic names may refer to a marital pair. The fact that the name 10Y is painted immediately above the box may mean that through that individual, lineage continuity was maintained. All the figures in Tomb 104 (including the yellow bird) are shown facing the ancestor on the back wall.

Figure 9.17. Paired drinking vessels honoring a primordial Zapotec founder couple named Lord 1 Jaguar (at left) and Lady 2 Maize (at right). Drawing by John Klausmeyer.

Interpreting the Boxes Depicted in Tomb 104

We know that sacred offering boxes were used in a variety of rituals throughout Mesoamerica, including building dedications, inaugurations, funerals, and rites that asserted continuity from a lineage founder or apical ancestor (e.g., Ayala 2002; Burgoa 1674[1934]; Freidel and Guenter 2006; Guernsey and Reilly 2006; Hermann Lejarazu 2008; Stenzel 1968–1970).

Manuscripts in the Archivo General de Indias (Sevilla, #882-16) describe sacred boxes kept by Zapotec lineages, and they discuss the ways lineage descendants sacrificed to the *cabezas de [sus] abuelos* (Alcina Franch 1993:114–116). If the term "*cabezas*" in this phrase refers to depictions of ancestors' heads, the painting of 10 Lao on the back wall of Tomb 104 may be an example, and the two boxes painted on the walls may have contained perishable offerings given to lineage heads or marital pairs. Sixteenth-century texts indicate that both perishable items (such as maize or feathers) and nonperishables (such as stone statues and figurines) could be placed inside the boxes. Even the tomb niches could be regarded as sacred boxes, because they provided a rectangular space where items could be stored. When tombs were reopened, attendees sometimes emptied the niches and placed the bones of former occupants there.

Associated with the wall niches in Tomb 104 are streaks of cinnabar, which drew the attention of Caso (1938:82). These finger-width vertical streaks occur either above or inside the niche and may be the result of mourners having placed their pigment-stained fingers there, to confirm that they witnessed the funeral and the placement of new offerings in the niches. On the north wall (or right side) of Tomb 104 is another pair of day names and numbers: 10 Owl and 10/13 *Cociyo*. These hieroglyphs may refer to another marital pair. Nearby we see the hieroglyph 1Ñ (a day name that also appears on the interior surface of the tomb's door), accompanied by a noncalendric sign that may represent plant parts and a heart. This hieroglyphic compound may be a title or a nickname associated with the person named 1Ñ.

On the same wall we see a young individual extending his hand toward the wall niche. This is the same gesture we saw associated with an individual on the south wall of the tomb (near the doorway). These two individuals near the tomb entrance

Figure 9.18. The polychrome murals of Monte Albán's Tomb 104 cover the back wall (at center) and side walls (left and right). This tomb had five niches (shown as stippled), with three of them located along the back wall; at the time of discovery, four of the niches still had offerings in them. The niche at the center of the back wall interrupts the hieroglyph naming an apical ancestor (10 Lao); above we see the Jaws of the Sky. In the upper left portion of the back wall we also see Glyph 5E, which might be the name of the tomb's principal occupant. The individuals painted on the side walls face the back of the tomb, paying their respects to the apical ancestor and the principal occupant of the tomb. Drawing by John Klausmeyer.

extend their arms to the niche while holding a copal bag. Since these individuals are unaccompanied by hieroglyphic names they may not be ancestors, but rather unnamed participants in the funeral ceremony.

The Door of Tomb 104

The door stone of Tomb 104 is beautifully carved not only on its interior and exterior surfaces but also along its edge, albeit in three different styles (see Figure 7.1, Chapter 7).

Caso (1938:76) was the first epigrapher to argue that this door stone had been recarved and reused. The hieroglyphs on the edge of the stone would only have been seen when it was positioned as a lintel. Reading from left to right, this edge (or lintel) text might be read: Year 9 Lightning (9M), 15 units [perhaps 15 balls of copal]; 5B (5 Jaguar); an unknown item that looks like a leaf; and a bag.

This carved edge, as well as the exterior of the tomb door, fails to refer to any of the hieroglyphic names in the tomb murals. Caso therefore concluded that the carving on the exterior of the door stone bore no relationship to the individual buried in the main chamber. In contrast, the obverse (the interior carved surface of the door) did repeat hieroglyphs painted in the tomb murals. Caso thus inferred that the interior surface of the door was contemporaneous with the painting of the tomb mural and contained related subject matter.

Such reuse of carved stones was characteristic of Monte Albán. Rarely, however, do we have evidence for a single stone being reused three times—first as a lintel, second as a door stone whose exterior hieroglyphic text could be read when the stone was vertical, and third as a door stone carved on the opposite side.

The interior surface of the door stone was the key to Caso's interpretation. Pointing to similarities between the hieroglyphs painted in the tomb's mural and the hieroglyphs carved on the interior surface of the door stone, Caso argued that the two were contemporary. Indeed, both the murals and the interior surface of the door supply the names of ancestors and depict the sacred boxes associated with the hieroglyphs 1Ñ and 5E.

On the interior surface of the door stone we see a prominent year sign—Year 7G (7 Deer)—and several other glyphs, including 6Y (6 Serpent); 7I (7 Maltese cross); the number 15, associated with four balls of what may be copal or rubber; and the number 7, possibly associated with bags of tobacco. The glyph 7I may refer to the seventh anniversary of the interment, perhaps involving rites organized by an individual named 6Y. For his part, 6Y may be a descendant eager to honor his ascendant generations—a father (5E); his grandparents (2 Lightning and 10 Serpent); his great grandparents (10 Owl and 10 [or 13] *Cociyo*); his great-great-grandfather (1Ñ), and a remote lineage founder or apical ancestor, 10 Lao.

In the center of the door stone we see an abbreviated version of the Jaws of the Sky, but here the motif appears to have been given feet—possibly meaning either "descending from the sky" (was born) or "ascending to the sky" (has died). If in this context the sign constitutes a verb, it should be followed by the subject of a clause; in this case that subject appears to be a person named 5E. This interpretation is reinforced by a footprint ascending to the sky. (Another instance where this glyphic compound appears as a verb is on Stela 5 in Tomb 5 at Cerro de la Campana; see Chapter 12.)

In the case of the Tomb 104 door, the footprint above 5E helps us decide between "was born" and "has died." In Zapotec the word *peni* or *pèni* can mean footprint, step, or person. The Tomb 104 footprint is directed toward the top of the stone, suggesting that 7 Deer was the year of 5E's death—in other words, his ascension to the Jaws of the Sky.

Let us turn now to the calendric names of what may be 5E's ancestors. The name 6Y (at far left) appears to connect the deceased (5E) to his grandmother (2M) and his great-great-grandfather (1Ñ, shown with a mouth mask and topknot). These relatives, in turn, seem to be linked to the Year 11E. The name 1Ñ appears above a sacred box at the bottom of the carved stone; this name, 1Ñ, also appears above the boxlike niche on the north wall of the tomb. Note that the Ñ glyph was not included in Caso's 1928 classification of hieroglyphs (Caso and Bernal 1952:107), because at that time he simply had too few examples to warrant giving it a separate letter. All that changed in the 1930s, when Caso, Martín Bazán, and Jorge Acosta discovered both the Period IIIa monuments in the South Platform and the murals in Tombs 103 and 104.

The Year 11E on the door of Tomb 104 is huge, filling about a third of the door. A possible reason for its size could lie in the importance of the ancestor who died in that year. The Year 11E is linked to key mortuary hieroglyphs (e.g., the hieroglyph of a stone statue and the Maltese cross). I have already suggested that the Maltese cross may be associated with an important anniversary of death or interment.

Córdova's ([1578a]1942:189v) Zapotec dictionary includes the word *lohuaa*, "statue, bundle, and image." The stone statue glyph depicted on the door stone of Tomb 104 may be an example of *lohuaa*. We will see that similar hieroglyphs showing stiff statues appear on other Zapotec tomb lintels, such as Lintel 3 at Xoxocotlán (see Chapter 14), where the figure appears above a Maltese cross (Martínez Gracida 1910: Lámina 45, Tomo II).

The Zapotec Maltese cross is often associated with a number. On the door stone of Tomb 104, it is associated with the number 7 on the left side of the door; on the right side, the Maltese cross has no associated number.

We have seen that the inner face of the door and the murals of Tomb 104 share elements, including the name of the tomb's principal occupant. His name—5E—can be found on the back wall near the name of his apical ancestor, 10 Lao. Being linked to an apical ancestor is a concern that goes back to the chiefly societies of the Early Formative (Flannery and Marcus 1976b; Marcus 1976c, 1989a, 2008a). The artists of Period IIIa were able to emphasize this concern in polychrome murals.

The name 1Ñ appears at the base of the door stone above a probable sacred box; it also occurs above the boxlike niche in the north wall of the tomb chamber. It is worth noting that the idea of a sacred box containing ancestor memorabilia had a long history among the Zapotec. Such boxes were called *quiña* in Zapotec, *tepetlacalli* in Nahuatl, and *petacas* or *petaquillas* in sixteenth-century Spanish. Oudijk (2000:164) refers to a number of Zapotec lineage founders who were venerated by their descendants after death. In the Genealogy of Quialoo, for example, one Zapotec ruler stated that if he had an ancestral *petaca* in his possession "it would legitimize his position as ruler." Some *petacas* held cloth, paper, feathers, maize, or even stone statues.

Other sixteenth-century documents show the ways that Zapotec nobles used sacred *petacas* to legitimize their descent (Oudijk 2000:164). Such customs, to be sure, were not limited to the Zapotec. Throughout much of Mesoamerica, sacred boxes or bundles were used in a wide array of ceremonies. Passing such a sacred object on to the next person in line reinforced genealogical continuity and its associated rights. It is therefore no surprise that Tomb 104 would depict at least two boxes.

Tomb 105

The palace associated with Tomb 105 was one of those built only after the architects had excavated a royal tomb into bedrock (Figure 9.19). That residence, built on the path leading to a neighborhood now called El Plumaje, had the plan of a Zapotec palace or *quehui*, with a central patio surrounded by several large rooms. In the center of the patio was an offering box similar to those found below the corners of the South Platform; it contained Period III *floreros* and small ollas, rectangular vessels, and an obsidian knife. Under the western room of the palace was a small urn depicting *Cociyo* and a jade figurine in Teotihuacán style (Caso 1938:84).

Below the eastern room of the palace was Tomb 105; enormous stones comprised its roof. To reach the tomb from the patio one descended four steps. The tomb entrance was low, but once inside one could stand or walk around because the ceiling was 2 m high.

In the back of the tomb Caso found fragments of stone columns, the partial remains of a human skeleton, and a fragment of worked bone. With the exception of these partial skeletal remains the tomb was empty, suggesting that the principal occupant may have been removed. Indeed, both the position of the door stone and the well-preserved stucco over the antechamber led Caso to conclude that the final sealing of the tomb had occurred only after the family had taken the contents elsewhere.

Two marital pairs are featured in the murals of Tomb 105 (Caso 1938: Láminas III and IV). On the south door jamb we see the first couple: a man named 2 Jaguar and a woman named 1 Deer. The man is elderly and wears a high turban of jaguar skin; the woman wears an elaborate headdress. The north jamb is not well preserved, making it difficult to read the names of the second couple. In any event, the entrance to Tomb 105 was flanked by two couples, in effect greeting those who came to the tomb (Miller 1995:91).

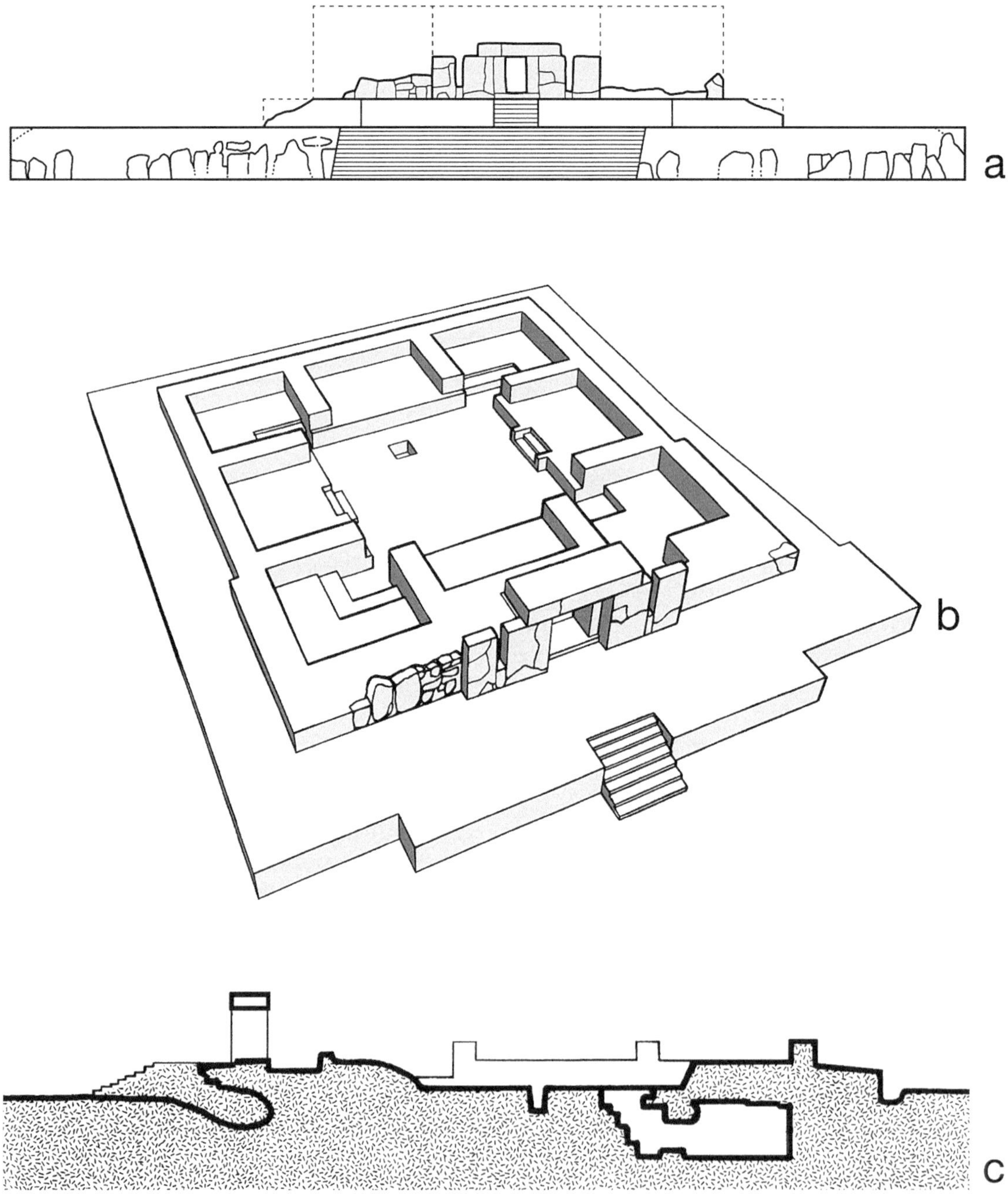

Figure 9.19. Three views of the palace above Tomb 105 at Monte Albán: (*a*) the façade of the palace; (*b*) the ground plan of the palace; and (*c*) a cross-section, showing that the tomb was excavated into bedrock before the palace was built. Redrawn by John Klausmeyer from Marcus and Flannery 1996: Figs. 248, 249.

Figure 9.20. The mural in the main chamber of Monte Albán's Tomb 105 shows a procession of marital pairs exiting the tomb. Here (from left to right) we see two of these elaborately attired couples: a woman (7E + nickname) followed by a man who is probably her husband (1E + nickname), then a woman named 1 Water followed by her probable husband (8 Knot). The giant Jaws of the Sky motif (at the top) serves as an umbrella above all four nobles. Drawing by John Klausmeyer.

The main chamber of the tomb shows a procession of marital pairs exiting the chamber (Figure 9.20). By showing these couples departing the tomb, the painters may have intended to indicate that we are dealing with living relatives, in contrast to the deceased individuals mentioned in Tomb 104.

Beneath the Jaws of the Sky—which begins at the door and proceeds to the niches—we see the following couples painted on the north wall of Tomb 105: a woman (7E) with a cluster of tied cloth, knotted hair, and feathers; a man named 1E (or 4E) + Q + 3J (3 Maize); a woman named 1 Water + Maize + 3 Hill; and a man named 8 Knot + E + J (Figure 9.20).

The prominent circle around the eye of the man whose names include 3 Maize is a symbol frequently linked to military prowess, especially in Central Mexican warriors. It was used, in addition, by Maya lords who wanted to be credited with military prowess—for example, Yax K'uk' Mo'o, the dynastic founder of Copán (Braswell 2003; Sharer et al. 1999). Ruler 2 of Piedras Negras also had himself portrayed with a circle around the eye, implying that he had the same military skills as a Central Mexican warrior. In other words, the circle does not necessarily identify its bearer as being ethnically Central Mexican; it merely identifies someone who compares his military skills to those of a warrior from that region.

In the case of the man on the north wall of Tomb 105, scholars are still debating whether the eye circle here alludes to Teotihuacán warriors or the Central Mexican deity Tlaloc (Miller 1973: Figures 129, 132).

Each man in the north wall mural carries a lance in his right hand and a bag in his left. The women in the same mural wear elaborate headdresses, each as distinctive as her hieroglyphic name. The men wear sandals; the women are barefoot.

Painted on the south wall of Tomb 105, beneath the Jaws of the Sky, is a procession of two more couples: a man named 3 Monkey, a woman named 4B (4 Jaguar), a man named 4M (4 Lightning), and a woman named 12 Monkey (Caso 1938: Lámina III). As was the case with the north wall, each individual in this procession bears a distinctive hieroglyphic name and headdress. The names can be as simple as a day in the 260-day calendar or as complex as a compound (a nickname + a 260-day calendar name). In the case of the nicknames, they may have been needed in order to distinguish between nobles born on the same day. The headdresses may signify differences in rank, role, or office.

Each man carries a bag in his right hand and seems to be divining with maize kernels, throwing these items out with his left hand. We do not know whether the fact that the artist portrayed four kernels is deliberate or coincidental. Several individuals in this south wall procession seem to be elderly.

Considering both tomb walls, it appears that we are dealing with a total of nine couples who had some relationship to an apical ancestor—13 Monkey—whose name was centrally located on the back wall. However, Miller (1995:101) has pointed out that during one of the three (or more) repaintings of this mural, one male was actually changed to a female; this altered the "male-female organization in the tomb iconography." Miller's close examination revealed that in this case, a skirt was painted over a male loincloth. We do not know why this change was made, but it may have to do with changes in relatives or in-laws over time.

Because the murals of this tomb were repainted three or more times, it has become difficult to read every hieroglyph and to separate the uppermost layer from those below. Caso (1938:91) counted at least three different layers on the back wall, where the repainting is most evident. When Miller restudied the murals 50 years later, he noted that "unfortunately, all three layers are visible in various parts of the wall, producing a most confused impression" (Miller 1995:101).

To summarize: the murals of Period IIIa provide important information about Zapotec nobles, their funerals, and their concern with genealogy and legitimization. The increased use of the Jaws of the Sky motif (five times in Tomb 105 alone) is consistent with the Zapotec taking still greater interest in honoring their noble ancestors (Marcus 1983d:143, 2002). The fact that husband-wife couples were depicted below the Jaws of the Sky suggests that descent was reckoned through both maternal and paternal lines, which is consistent with Zapotec kinship (Spores and Flannery 1983).

This Zapotec emphasis on marital pairs and co-rulership, already evident in Period IIIa, continued well into the seventeenth century and is evident in the Mixtec codices (Caso 1977, 1979; M. E. Smith 1973a). The same was not characteristic of Maya monuments, which tended to emphasize male rulers. Although we rarely see a Maya ruler depicted next to his wife, we sometimes learn about their wives when the latter were more highly ranked or came from more important cities (e.g., Marcus 1973, 1976d, 1987, 1992a; Martin and Grube 2008).

Thus the Zapotec murals of Period IIIa remind us that co-rulership and bilateral inheritance were distinctively Otomanguean. During the sixteenth century, both Zapotec and Mixtec kinship was of the Hawai'ian type, which combines bilateral descent with rank differences (Spores and Flannery 1983).

A Period IIIa Tomb from the Site of Dainzú

Monte Albán was not the only site to construct elegant tombs during Period IIIa. Tomb 7 at Dainzú, a second-tier administrative center in the Tlacolula arm of the valley, is an example (Oliveros 1997). Tomb 7 was located on the first terrace of the third construction phase of Complex B at Dainzú.

To enter Tomb 7, one had to pass between the forelegs of a jaguar carved on the tomb jambs (Bernal and Oliveros 1988: Lámina 12); on the lintel we see the jaguar's magnificent head and shoulders (Figure 9.21).

Tomb 7 was deep (2.89 m), high (2.03 m), and wide (1.40 m). A megalithic construction with an antechamber and main chamber, Tomb 7's roof consisted of four large stones. A small niche, high on the west wall of the antechamber, contained clay tubing thought by the excavators to be a "psychoduct," allowing the spirit of the deceased to leave and reenter at will.

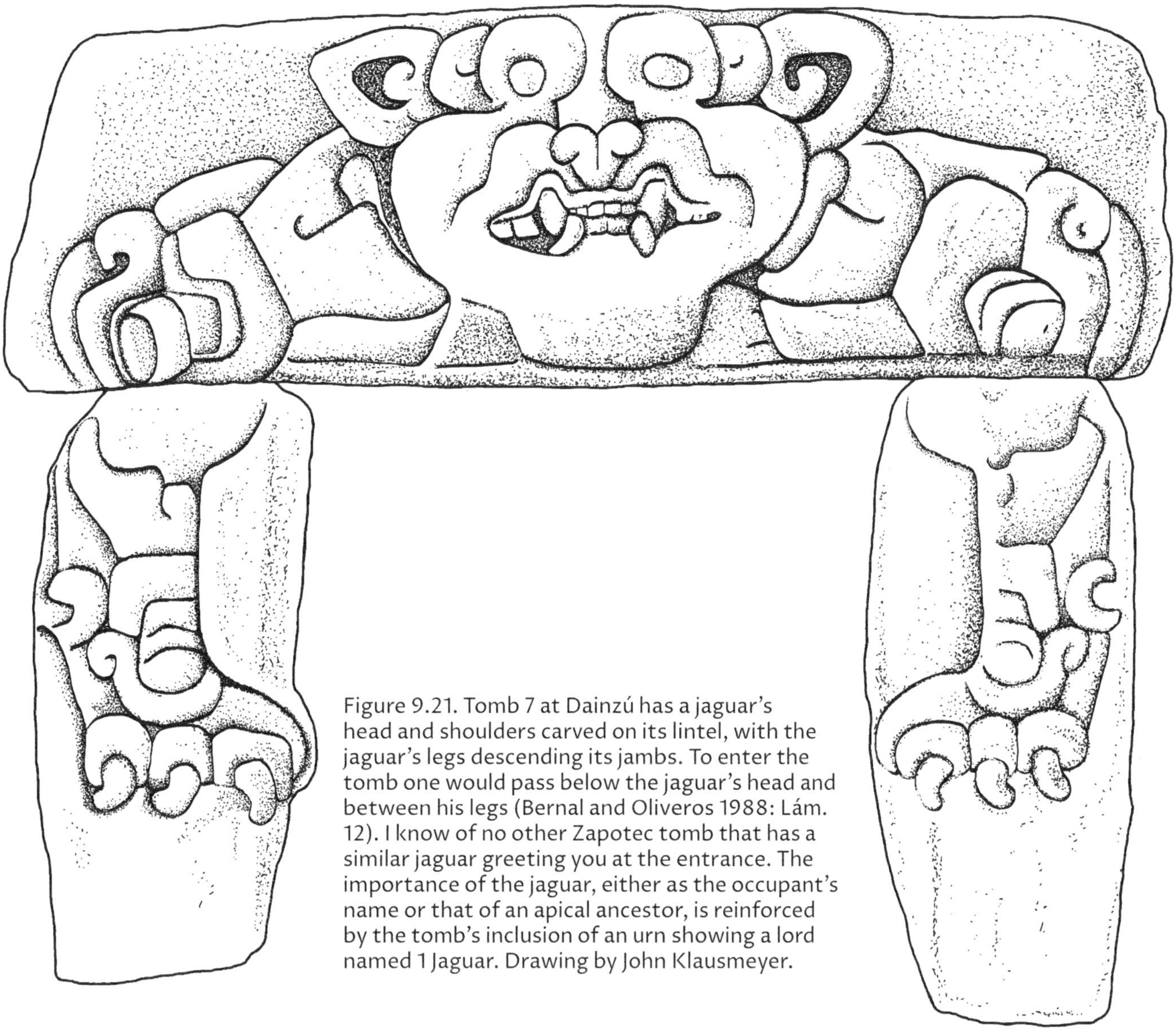

Figure 9.21. Tomb 7 at Dainzú has a jaguar's head and shoulders carved on its lintel, with the jaguar's legs descending its jambs. To enter the tomb one would pass below the jaguar's head and between his legs (Bernal and Oliveros 1988: Lám. 12). I know of no other Zapotec tomb that has a similar jaguar greeting you at the entrance. The importance of the jaguar, either as the occupant's name or that of an apical ancestor, is reinforced by the tomb's inclusion of an urn showing a lord named 1 Jaguar. Drawing by John Klausmeyer.

The tomb's most impressive feature is the carved jaguar, which may have been intended to guard the tomb; unfortunately, it failed to deter looters from reopening the tomb and turning the lintel around. Bernal and Oliveros (1988: Lámina 12) were able to restore the lintel to its original position by rotating it 180 degrees. Among the items not removed by looters was a cinnabar-covered urn depicting an individual named 1 Jaguar (Figure 9.22). This urn may refer to the tomb occupant or to the male member of the legendary Zapotec founder couple, Lord 1 Jaguar and Lady 2 Maize (see Figure 9.17).

The looters broke nearly all the whole vessels in the tomb, scattered the bones, and filled the chamber with material from a nearby structure. Bernal (1976) was able to separate the Tomb 7 items into two lots: those that went with the original interment and those from later periods. The first lot contained the 1 Jaguar urn. In the second lot were three objects, one of which was a stone ball depicting a heart.

Before moving on to Period IIIb–IV and the appearance of "genealogical registers," we will next discuss how Zapotec nobles at newly autonomous Tier 2 sites sought to increase their status and construct elaborate mortuary shrines to their ancestors.

Figure 9.22. An urn from Tomb 7 at Dainzú, depicting a noble named 1 Jaguar (Bernal 1976). His name can be seen between his knees. Drawing by Kay Clahassey.

10

How Noble Families Changed the Political Landscape during Period IIIb–IV

The period AD 600–900 witnessed many sociopolitical changes. Prior to AD 600, the Zapotec capital had enjoyed a near monopoly of hieroglyphic writing. That situation ended in Period IIIb–IV, when the nobles at Tier 2 towns began to use writing to further their own political agendas.

One of the interests of those nobles was to record their genealogies. To do so they created the **genealogical register**, a stone monument featuring two or three compartments. These compartments usually presented marital pairs from different generations (see, for example, Figures 7.6 and 7.7). Another goal of the Tier 2 nobles was to record the names of participants in important rituals held in private, rather than public, settings.

During Period IIIb–IV, a number of former Tier 2 communities appear to have gained political prominence by forging horizontal alliances with other Tier 2 communities. These alliances ultimately allowed some Tier 2 towns to achieve their independence from Monte Albán. With their newly found independence, Tier 2 noble families employed skilled stone carvers to produce genealogical registers. By commissioning their own genealogical histories, Tier 2 nobles gained a major advantage, because these records could then be used to support their claims to social, economic, and political privileges.

The Growing Power of Tier 2 Towns in the Valley of Oaxaca

By AD 600, about a dozen Tier 2 towns in the Valley of Oaxaca were investing in their own political agendas. Many of these communities now considered themselves to be on a par with Monte Albán—either politically, socially, or both.

How had these formerly subordinate leaders broken the grip of Monte Albán? Based on our understanding of a number of similar cases of this phenomenon, the optimal moment for secession and coalition was when a capital's dynastic line was interrupted. Thus Tier 2 nobles saw their chance to break away when Monte Albán's dynastic line was either (1) temporarily without an heir; (2) experiencing internal chaos, such as when multiple claimants competed for the throne; (3) enduring a string of weak rulers; or (4) losing the economic support of subjects, allies, and long-distance trading partners.

If the throne of Monte Albán was vacant for any length of time, or occupied by a weak leader, Tier 2 towns could have forged coalitions that posed a threat to the capital. In turn, the rise of such Tier 2 coalitions could have hastened the decline of Monte Albán's preeminence.

Noble families that were able to forge advantageous marriage and political alliances often succeeded in elevating their status. They also gained access to skilled architects, stone masons, scribes, and sculptors. Such access often led to the construction of increasingly elaborate palatial residences at Tier 2 towns, with correspondingly impressive tombs. Indeed, some of the tombs at Tier 2 communities were now more elegant than those being constructed at Monte Albán. Among the Period IIIb–IV communities creating elaborate tombs and genealogical registers were

(1) sites in the Etla region (e.g., Reyes Etla, San Lázaro Etla, and Cerro de la Campana; see Chapter 12);

(2) sites in the Valle Grande (e.g., Cuilapan, Xoxocotlán, and Zaachila; see Chapter 14); and

(3) sites in the Tlacolula subvalley (e.g., Lambityeco and Yagul; see Chapter 15).

By the latter half of Period IIIb–IV, Monte Albán was no longer the preeminent demographic center in the valley (Feinman and Nicholas 2017:83, 88). By AD 800 Monte Albán is estimated to have lost about 22,000 inhabitants from its peak population of 30,000, and the city was no longer the powerful military and political force it had been. Jalieza in the Valle Grande, for example, covered more than five square kilometers and was now estimated to have a larger population than Monte Albán (Finsten 1983).

One can imagine a "break-away" strategy that involved four steps, as follows: (1) secede from Monte Albán's hegemony; (2) avoid reincorporation by elevating the status of one of your Tier 2 noble families; (3) forge a larger polity by adding political allies, loyal neighbors, and noble spouses from multiple towns; and (4) commission genealogical registers to legitimize your noble descent (Marcus 1976a, 1992a, 1992c).

Founding a New Polity

Founding a new polity was a challenge for Tier 2 noble families because they needed sufficient demographic strength to avoid reincorporation by Monte Albán. Noble families achieved this by attracting new trading partners and arranging new marriage alliances with nobles of equal or higher rank. To find a spouse of equal or higher rank, a noble often had to look to other towns. Multiple marriage alliances led to a web of horizontal links that helped to maintain a polity's prestige (Angulo Villaseñor 2008; Pohl 2003b; Spores 1974; Terraciano 2001).

It is likely that by Period IIIb–IV, Zapotec society already featured strata similar to those described by the sixteenth-century Spaniards. That Zapotec society was composed of two class-endogamous groups—a stratum of nobles and a stratum of commoners. Within the upper stratum were many ranks and categories of nobles, including the king (*coquitào*), his wife (*xonàxi*), and his sons or princes (*coquihualao*). The royal family spoke "palace speech" (*ticha quehui*), while nobles spoke "elegant speech" (*ticha nayacha*) (Marcus 1992a:69). From Córdova ([1578a]1942) we also learn that below the "lineage of the great lords" (*tija coquì*) were two lineages of lesser nobles: the *tija joàna* ("like *caballeros* in Spain") and *tija joanahuini* ("like *hidalgos* in Spain").

It is also clear that there were highly regarded commoners who could be appointed to important posts; such men were called *peni nacaa* or "hombre puesto en una oficina o cargo." Some rose to become *peni quela*, "hombres de autoridad." Commoners also might become a *golaba*, "lord's solicitor" or *copeeche*, "master craftsman." A commoner without a profession or office was known as a *peni late*, "hombre sin oficio u ocupación." Although the lower stratum had a variety of lineages (*tija*), the sixteenth-century Spaniards chose to focus most of their attention on noble lineages because they reminded the Spaniards of their own *señores, caballeros,* and *hidalgos*.

Genealogical Registers

Establishing legitimacy and asserting dynastic continuity—especially at times when such legitimacy and continuity could be challenged—were two of the motivations for commissioning genealogical registers. Such registers might show the parents of the current ruler as well as dynastic founders, or even an important apical ancestor. The Zapotec, to be sure, had a long history of honoring certain ancestors with carved stones, urns, and drinking vessels bearing their names. One example, already discussed, was the pair of vessels designed to honor 1 Jaguar and 2 Maize (see Figure 9.17). The names of this founder couple were invoked at multiple sites (Paddock 1966a: Figure 103; Seler 1991).

By drinking from vessels bearing the names of ancestors, an individual could be linked more directly to them. Such rituals probably involved uttering the names of these founders so that the latter were remembered. When one called out their names, the spirits of the ancestors might return to the vessel to share the beverage with a descendant. Furthermore, some royal ancestors had metamorphosed into semidivine or divine beings who could legitimize new dynastic lineages.

Period IIIb–IV carved stones depicted a wide variety of rites linked to legitimization, sanctification, and ancestor veneration (Caso 1965a, 1965b; Marcus 1980, 1983d, 1989b; Masson and Orr 1998a; Miller 1995; Rabin 1970). In contrast to earlier Zapotec monuments, however, many of these stones were designed to be seen by the few, since they were usually placed in the interior spaces of private residences or family tombs (see Chapter 11). The noble families of Tier 2 towns busily commissioned tomb doors, jambs, lintels, genealogical registers, polychrome murals, and stucco-modeled façades (Caso 1928, 1965a, 1965b; Marcus 1980:61–64, 1983c:191; Marcus 2006b, 2008b, 2009a, 2009b; Miller 1995).

Of special note is the high number of carved stones commissioned for mortuary contexts (see Chapter 11), many of which were in places of great privacy, limited space, and inaccessibility. Stones displayed inside elite residences and family tombs contrasted with earlier public displays, such as the

Prisoner Gallery on the façade of Building L, the procession of captives on the façade of the South Platform, and the architectural narrative program on the façade of Complex A at Dainzú, all of which were intended for larger audiences (Bernal 1965a, 1965b; Bernal and Oliveros 1988; Bernal and Seuffert 1979; Caso 1928, 1965b; Marcus 1980, 1992a; Scott 1978).

The earlier displays on the façades of buildings were examples of "vertical propaganda" (the communications from nobles to commoners), whereas the texts in the interior of tombs were examples of "horizontal propaganda" (nobles communicating primarily with other nobles) (e.g., Marcus 1992a, 2003b, 2006b; Miller 1995; Saville 1899; Séjourné 1960).

The term propaganda in this context refers to assertions aimed at a specific audience. As defined by Lerner (1951) and Ellul (1973), "propaganda" is a special type of art, speech, or writing designed to influence a targeted segment of society. Both Maya and Zapotec rulers used propaganda to disseminate specific messages. For example, in speaking of a Maya ruler who took the Yaxchilan throne at age 43 and had commissioned many new sculptures and buildings, Martin and Grube (2008:128) say, "Throughout these efforts there runs a single, barely concealed agenda: the relentless promotion of his own legitimacy. More than any other Maya king, his every action betrays the heavy hand of the manipulator and propagandist." For their part, Zapotec nobles of Period IIIb–IV increasingly invested in a range of strategies to increase the distance between themselves and commoners. This set of strategies would ensure their ability to retain privileges and rights.

Special Attributes Associated with Nobles

Before looking at the Period IIIb–IV monuments and tombs from each arm of the Valley of Oaxaca (Chapters 12–15), it is worth mentioning five of the alleged abilities that set nobles apart from commoners—(1) the ability to impersonate supernatural forces, (2) the ability to undergo metamorphosis, (3) the ability to fly, (4) a sacred and semidivine origin, and (5) the ability to communicate with apical ancestors.

During the Early Formative of the Valley of Oaxaca, the wearing of masks and animal costumes had been an activity in which all households in the village could participate (Flannery [ed.] 1976; Marcus 1998a, 1999a, 1999b, 2019). After the Zapotec hereditary elite emerged, however, they monopolized some of the rites formerly performed by every household. By wearing masks and animal costumes, the elite could impersonate ancestors, fantastic creatures, alter egos, and supernatural forces.

Such behaviors were widespread in Mesoamerica and well documented by the time of the Spanish Conquest. Among the Aztec, for example, the term *teixiptla* could refer to (1) living humans who wore a costume; (2) effigies made of stone, wood, or dough; or (3) masks and costumes hanging on wooden frames (Hvidtfeldt 1958; Townsend 1992). Aztec impersonators (*in ixiptla in teteo*) could represent deities, animals, Maize, Lightning, or items containing the vital force. Impersonators could be the priests who performed a sacrifice, the victims to be sacrificed, or both. At one ritual, Durán ([1581]1964:111) says: "The priests who were to perform the sacrifice stood in a long row, according to their rank. Each one of them was disguised as a god." Even the dead might be costumed as impersonators. Speaking of the wooden statue of a dead Aztec king, Durán ([1581]1964:176) says, "Over this garb he was dressed with the garments of the divinity Tlaloc so that he represented that deity. Upon his head was a crown of mixed white and green plumes. In one hand he held a shield of fine quality and in the other a stick carved in the form of Lightning, like that of Tlaloc, since he was the god of thunderbolts and rain."

By wearing masks and costumes to impersonate fantastic creatures, performers *became* those creatures during their performances. Just as contemporary actors and actresses *become* Henry VIII or Queen Victoria when dressed in costume, masked Zapotec performers became supernatural intermediaries in order to communicate directly with Lightning or their remote ancestors.

A Zapotec ruler could link himself to (or take the name of) Sun or Lightning. In addition to having the ability to impersonate (and metamorphose into) powerful natural forces, the Zapotec ruler likened his role to *Cociyo*'s—both could create rain, storms, and abundant harvests. When rulers died, they could be transformed into fantastic composite creatures. Although the promise of an afterlife as a supernatural being was seemingly restricted to nobles, all levels of society venerated near and remote ancestors and primordial ancestral couples.

Interaction with this living landscape required ritual and respect. To maintain an open line of communication, pacts of reciprocity were formed (Marcus 1974, 1978, 1983e). These reciprocal obligations ensured ongoing relationships between the living and the supernatural.

How did Zapotec nobles initiate communication with supernatural beings? There were at least four ways. One way that we have discussed was impersonation (wearing a mask and dressing in the garb and paraphernalia associated with that supernatural). A second way was consuming hallucinogens (*Datura* or jimson weed, morning glory, or *Psilocybe* mushrooms) or drinking fermented beverages such as pulque (Marcus and Flannery 1978:73–74). A third way was letting one's own blood using a stingray spine, an obsidian lancet, an *Agave* or *Opuntia* spine, or a shark tooth. A fourth way was burning copal, tobacco, paper, rubber, or other items, because the act of creating smoke served to feed the ancestors. Noble ancestors and supernatural beings were thought to enjoy the smoke, or essence, of the items that were burning.

Apical ancestors and supernatural beings, unlike their terrestrially tethered descendants, occupied the sky. Ancestors had the ability to fly like a bird, a bat, a butterfly, or a composite creature with a turtle-carapace body that could descend from the Jaws of the Sky to receive offerings, conduct sacrifices, and give advice.

Supernatural beings could display the attributes of various animals, merged to form a fantastic creature. Some supernatural

Figure 10.1. Found on the North Platform at Monte Albán, this ceramic model shows an open temple with a bird emerging from a tunnel or hidden entrance in the floor. Height: 49.5 cm. Redrawn by John Klausmeyer from Marcus and Flannery 1996:185.

beings combined the attributes of a terrestrial or marine animal (e.g., a turtle, cayman, crocodile, fish, jaguar, or snail) with a celestial animal (bird, butterfly, or bat). Given that the Zapotec regarded their noble ancestors as "cloud people" who had the ability to fly, it follows that bird impersonators could contact their ancestors.

Zapotec Alter Egos, Tonos, and Naguales

Yet another connection existed between the world of man and animal. Fray Francisco de Burgoa (1674, vol. 26:356) reported that each Zapotec was born with an animal alter ego or "double" that shared his destiny; in other words, whatever happened to the animal would also occur in the life of his human counterpart.

Twentieth-century occupants of Mitla still spoke of *laja'ben*, the Zapotec term for (1) animals that could transform themselves into other animals and (2) animals that could change into Lightning (Parsons 1936:225). When a *laja'ben* was killed, the human associated with it would also die. It is interesting that many of these alter egos were birds, animals that could fly to the heavens and return to earth.

Monte Albán has produced the remarkable ceramic sculpture of a miniature open temple with its roof supported by columns on all sides (Figure 10.1). Inside the temple, lurking in the shadow of the columns, is a giant macaw caught with its mouth open in full cry. Only half of the bird's body is visible, as if it were emerging from some hidden entrance in the floor. In fact, the Main Plaza at Monte Albán was replete with tunnels that linked temples, providing a venue from which priests dressed as giant birds could emerge dramatically. The frequency with which birds were chosen as *laja'ben* makes us wish we had more data on what the sculpture in Figure 10.1 represents (see also Paddock 1966a:118).

Like the temple in the aforementioned sculpture, Building II at Monte Albán has five pillars in the front and five in the back. It never had side walls, and was "open to the four winds" (Bernal 1985; Marcus and Flannery 1996:184–185). On the south side of this open temple, excavators found the entrance to a tunnel that would have allowed priests to enter and leave the building unseen, crossing below the eastern half of the Main Plaza to a building on the plaza's central spine.

Birds as Messengers

The Zapotec were fascinated by a wide range of flying creatures, from birds to butterflies to bats. The ability to fly gave these animals the potential to travel back and forth between the lands of the living and the dead.

One Zapotec stone model shows a bird dive-bombing inside a structure, perhaps to enter the tomb itself (see Chapter 16). The identity of this bird is not certain, but it may be a depiction of the whippoorwill (*Caprimulgus* sp.), a crepuscular bird whose haunting song gives the bird its onomatopoetic name. In his sixteenth-century dictionary, Córdova ([1578a]1942:48r) referred to an "augury bird" (*mani pijci*) whose genus is unfortunately unknown. Other birds that brought auguries and prognostications to their descendants included the *pecuicui* (a small dove raised on maize kernels?), the *tama* (owl), the *huija* (?), and the *piguiñilana* ("black bird"), perhaps a crow (Córdova [1578a]1942:151r).

Various birds were associated with the Jaws of the Sky motif on Zapotec monuments of this period. While the artistic representations are not completely naturalistic, some appear to be quails (*pechi*) or doves (*peete*). These birds are usually shown descending from the Jaws of the Sky or flying near the motif. Stela 5 at Cerro de la Campana seems to depict the sacrifice of three quails by the relatives of the deceased (Chapter 12).

Such use of birds is reminiscent of monuments in Chiapas and Guatemala, which also show descending bird-men or men impersonating birds. Between 200 BC and AD 250, several Izapa monuments depicted humans impersonating birds (e.g., Altar 3, Stela 4) or half-human/half-bird figures (e.g., Stela 2, Altar 20, Stela 4). Kaminaljuyú's Stela 11 shows figures masked as birds descending from a "sky band" (Guernsey 2006; Norman 1973, 1976; Quirarte 1973, 1977, 1981; Virginia Smith 1984; Strauss 2018) (Figure 10.2).

These monuments suggest that the Izapa elite might have impersonated birds in order to approach supernatural beings. Norman (1976:136) views birds as heavenly intermediaries as well. Sometimes an individual is shown holding a pole that leads like a ladder to the sky, where a metamorphosed ancestor bird sits (e.g., Izapa Stela 25). Izapa's Altar 3 (Norman 1976: Figure 5.5) shows a bird impersonator, a messenger morphing into a bird. There may be analogies among the Zapotec (Navarijo Ornelas 2008). Having a close relationship with birds and supernaturals allowed the elite to further distance itself from commoners.

Many of these attributes of Zapotec nobles were increasingly embellished during Period IIIb–IV. These special abilities helped to aggrandize the nobles at former Tier 2 communities, aiding them in their attempt to achieve independence from, and parity with, the ruling lineages at Monte Albán. It is also clear that the Tier 2 nobles were most interested in convincing other nobles of their legitimacy and noble descent, an agenda that increased the use of horizontal propaganda relative to vertical propaganda.

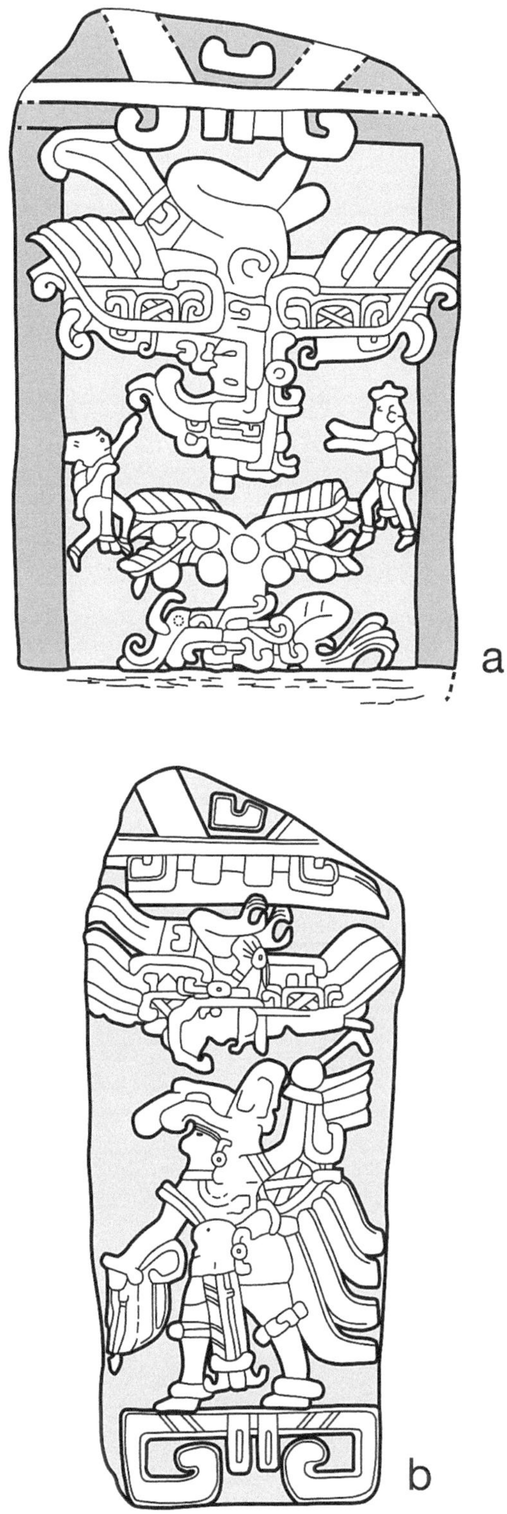

Figure 10.2. Two monuments from Izapa, Chiapas, that show men descending from the sky. These "bird-men" are either metamorphosed creatures or humans impersonating birds. *a*, Stela 2; *b*, Stela 4. (See Stirling 1943: Plates 49 and 51 and Norman 1976: Figs. 3.3, 3.5.) Drawing by John Klausmeyer.

Part IV

Funerary Rituals and Family Shrines

11

The Tomb as a Context for Decipherment

Many Period IIIb–IV monuments (AD 600–900) were commissioned for mortuary contexts. I once wondered why such a shift occurred at this time, especially since so many earlier monuments had been displayed publicly on building façades. I eventually came to realize that such contexts met the emergent needs of the noble lineages at Tier 2 towns (Chapter 10). Mortuary settings allowed noble families to exclude commoners from participation, inviting only fellow nobles to take part in funerary rituals designed to reinforce their genealogical right to rule.

During funerary rites at Tier 2 towns, the Zapotec elite communicated with their ancestors by burning incense, making offerings of food and beverages, displaying objects bearing their ancestors' names, placing sumptuary goods in wall niches, and adding new corpses to the family crypt (Marcus and Flannery 1994). The most elegant Zapotec tombs had more than one chamber, polychrome murals, multiple individuals identified by their hieroglyphic names, and numerous marital pairs (Caso 1938; Méndez Martínez 1988; Middleton et al. 1998; Miller 1995). A well-known example of a family crypt is Tomb 6 at Lambityeco, which had been opened six times (Lind 2003; Lind and Urcid 1983, 2010).

Deciphering Tomb Texts

Anyone entering an elaborate Zapotec tomb would expect to see hieroglyphs painted on tomb walls and carved on stone lintels, doors, and door jambs. Such texts provided the same kinds of information that we often see on marble slabs in today's family crypts:

(1) the name of the deceased
(2) the birthdate of the deceased
(3) the date of death
(4) names of the deceased's ancestors, and/or
(5) names of the deceased's descendants

The Zapotec, of course, were not alone in providing such information. Two other ancient societies with hieroglyphic texts—the Egyptians and the Maya—provide us with analogous examples.

An Egyptian Example

Egyptian kings were concerned with being remembered. They believed that having their names carved in stone meant eternal life. Commoners' names, in contrast, were generally not recorded, and their afterlife was considered unimportant to society as a whole.

The Tomb of Tutankhamun

The most famous Egyptian tomb is that of Tutankhamun, the so-called "boy king," who died in 1323 BC after a reign of only nine years. His tomb was opened on November 26, 1922, by Howard Carter, and since that day Tutankhamun has been the subject of hundreds of articles and books—largely because his tomb contained so many splendid items (e.g., Carter and Mace 1923; Desroches-Noblecourt 1978; Edwards 1976; Reeves 1990).

Even though his tomb had been richly stocked with thousands of objects (including gold, silver, ebony, and ivory), Tutankhamun was actually a weak king who had been the pawn of competitive factions. One source says: "Where Akhenaten [Tutankhamun's predecessor] had been strong, Tutankhamun was weak: behind the gold mask of the all-powerful god-ruler is the face of a vulnerable and manipulated little boy, a mere cipher for the deeds and aspirations of others" (Reeves 1990:14).

For more than 3000 years Tutankhamun's mummy lay in the Valley of the Kings, in a tomb cut into limestone bedrock. The tomb of Tutankhamun was similar to some of the most elaborate Zapotec tombs because it had more than one room: an antechamber, a burial chamber, an annex, and a room called "the treasury" (Figure 11.1). Those four rooms were filled with bejeweled thrones, shrines, chests, trunks, boxes, and statues, many of which bear hieroglyphs that supply the name of the owner or specify the contents (Černý 1965). Such treasure would transform the weak boy king into the Sun God (Desroches-Noblecourt 1978:245).

Like many Zapotec ritual structures, Tutankhamun's tomb was oriented east-west. To enter his tomb one faced west and descended 16 steps, reaching an eight-meter-long corridor that led to the antechamber (7.8 x 3.5 m). The latter was a room containing a jumble of chests, statues, chairs, beds, and even disassembled chariots (Carter and Mace 1923). A number of the items in this room depicted the pharaoh's enemies; even the upper surface of the sole of the pharaoh's sandals was decorated with the image of a bound captive. The message was: "With every step he took, King Tutankhamun was crushing enemies under his feet"; it was a message that would also resonate with the ancient Zapotec and Maya.

North of the antechamber and a meter lower was the burial chamber (4.0 x 6.3 m). Cut into each of the four walls of this room was a niche (a feature known from many Zapotec tombs as well). Each niche in Tutankhamun's burial chamber contained a "magic brick," that is, a pedestal support for the statue of a deity. It was in this burial chamber that Howard Carter found Tutankhamun's mummy lying inside a nested set of coffins, which in turn were placed inside spectacular gold and silver shrines.

To the east of the burial chamber was a room called the treasury (3.8 x 4.7 m), which did in fact include signs of wealth—chests of drawers, jewel cases, a gold shrine, miniature boats, and two mummified fetuses. To the west of the antechamber was the annex (4.3 x 2.6 m), a storage room for oils and unguents, meats, and wine.

On various objects in the tomb were written the hieroglyphic name and titles of Tutankhamun. With minor variations the titles were those used by every Egyptian king, to wit, the ruler's Horus name; his *nebty* name (He whose laws are good, who pacifies the Two Lands); his Golden Falcon name; his *prenomen* (King of Upper and Lower Egypt); and his *nomen* (Son of the Sun). The *prenomen* and *nomen* were placed within cartouches or oval rings, a convention that later helped Champollion and others deduce that cartouches contained royal names.

Not all the objects in the tomb belonged to Tutankhamun. Some bore the names of other kings and relatives, including his wife Ankhensenamun. Other objects had been carved for his predecessors, Akhenaten, Tutmosis III, and Nefernefruaten. Perhaps the most touching and personal of all the items were those that bore the names of Tutankhamun's half-sisters, Meritaten and Meketaten, and their grandmother. Inside a miniature coffin bearing the name of his grandmother—Queen Tiye—was a plaited lock of her hair, since traced to her by DNA analysis.

Why did Egyptian kings have multiple rooms in their tombs (Figure 11.1)? One reason, presumably, was to store all the things needed in the afterlife—food and beverages, clothes and belongings, thrones, chests of drawers, beds and footstools, and statues of the servants that would continue to wait on the ruler. Another reason for multiple rooms was to replicate the layout of a palace, so that the deceased would live in familiar spaces forever. In addition, the presence of murals showing the king hunting, fishing, and engaged in his favorite activities ensured that the deceased would continue those activities in the afterlife.

In Tutankhamun's tomb were many utilitarian ceramic vessels, including dishes, cups, and jars. Of the 50 jars, 26 had once contained wine, and the inscriptions indicated that some held "wine of good quality," while others contained "sweet wine" and others "pomegranate wine" (Černý 1965). Different kinds of bread were included as well as dates, *dom*-palm fruits, bunches of onions and garlic, jars of honey, and boxes of meat such as ox tongues, sheep ribs, and the breasts of geese and ducks. Some baskets contained emmer wheat (*Triticum dicoccum*) or barley (*Hordeum vulgare*).

Tutankhamun's tomb honored not only the boy king but also other members of his family. In this regard it reminds us of a number of Period IIIb–IV Zapotec tombs.

Maya Tombs (muknalob) and Texts (tz'ibob)

In the green forests of Chiapas lies Palenque, the site of one of the most famous Maya tombs. Like King Tutankhamun's, this tomb was opulent and cut out of the limestone bedrock. Unlike Tutankhamun's, however, it was set below a temple (Figure 11.2).

While excavating Palenque's Temple of the Inscriptions, archaeologist Alberto Ruz (1973) noted that one stone in the floor had a series of finger-sized holes. Upon inserting his fingers, he was able to lift the stone. At first he saw only rubble. In the course of removing the rubble he found a step, then several more, then a landing, a change of direction, and another stairway.

Over a four-year period, Ruz and his crew cleared all the steps, and at the base of the stairway they found the remains of four sacrificial victims. Beyond the victims lay the tomb's stone door. Ruz had found the tomb of K'inich Janaab' Pakal, which had been sealed since his death in AD 683. Ruz peered inside the tomb on June 15, 1952, much as Howard Carter had done 30 years earlier when he opened the tomb of Tutankhamun.

Upon entering the tomb, Ruz saw a stone sarcophagus whose sides were elaborately carved with human figures and hieroglyphs. The tomb's enormous lid had a text on its front edge that supplied the dates of K'inich Janaab' Pakal's birth and death (Figure 11.3). The syntax of the text on the sarcophagus lid text is (Date + Verb) + (Date + Verb) + (Subject). It begins with the ruler's date of birth, followed by the date of his death, his name and title and a phrase meaning "under the auspices of the ancestors."

To be specific, we can read the front edge of the tomb lid as follows: On March 23, AD 603, he was born; on August 28, AD 683, after 80 years, he died (Lounsbury 1974). Then the text gives the subject (K'inich Janaab' Pakal) and his title (Lord of Palenque). He is then said to be "entering the realm of his ancestors who dwell in the White Bone House of the Snake" (Schele and Freidel 1990).

On the sides of the sarcophagus are depictions of K'inich Janaab' Pakal's parents and his predecessors in office, each identified by name. On the upper surface of the sarcophagus lid is a depiction of K'inich Janaab' Pakal in the act of metamorphosing into a Maize Deity. He is ready to pass through the open jaws of Sak Bak Nakan (White Bone House of the Snake). (Note how reminiscent this passage through open jaws is to the Zapotec concept of the Jaws of the Sky, an opening from which noble ancestors could descend with ritual items.)

K'inich Janaab' Pakal may have been given such an elaborate tomb because he was the founder of a new dynasty. Later rulers used him to legitimize their claims to the throne by referring to his birth and death dates (e.g., Berlin 1959, 1977; Schele and Mathews 1999). In fact, they used those dates as starting points, reckoning time in years since K'inich Janaab' Pakal's reign much as Christians reckon years since the birth of Christ.

Janaab' Pakal's tomb is not the only Maya example of this phenomenon. At the site of Río Azul in northeastern Guatemala, R. E. W. Adams salvaged a series of tombs dating to the fifth century AD. Tomb 12 had the hieroglyph for "East" painted on the east wall of the tomb, the hieroglyph for "West" on the west wall, and so on (R. E. W. Adams 1999: Figures 3-15, 3-16; Coggins 1988; Hall 1984, 1986, 1989). Included on the east wall was a hieroglyphic text with the following word order:

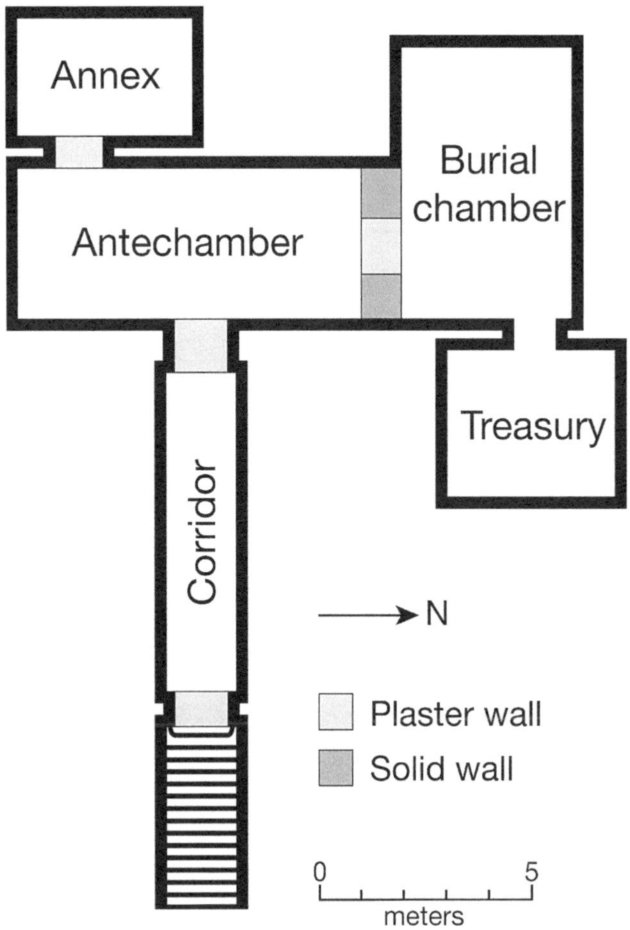

Figure 11.1. A long corridor led down to the multi-chambered tomb of Egypt's King Tutankhamun. Redrawn by John Klausmeyer from Edwards 1976:13 and Reeves 1990:71.

Figure 11.2. Deep inside the Temple of the Inscriptions at Palenque (Chiapas, Mexico), Alberto Ruz found the tomb of the Maya ruler K'inich Janaab' Pakal. The staircase to his tomb begins inside the temple and leads down through the pyramid's interior. Adapted by John Klausmeyer from Sharer 1994: Fig. 5.31.

AD 449 + the verb *mucah,* "was buried" + "6 Sky, Lord of Río Azul" (Figure 11.4)

This sentence construction (date + verb + subject + title) is the same as that seen on some Zapotec tombs, for example the one at Cerro de la Campana described in Chapter 12.

Zapotec Tombs (quie paa, "stone tomb")

Unlike K'inich Janaab' Pakal, who was buried beneath a huge temple, Zapotec rulers were more often buried beneath residences. Such a location ensured that the surviving inhabitants of the residence could continue to leave offerings at tombs constructed below interior patios and even, in some cases, have their own remains added to those of the original occupant. Entombment thus did not prevent deceased Zapotec nobles from ritually interacting with their descendants.

When possible, the Zapotec elite excavated their tombs into bedrock, just as the Maya did for K'inich Janaab' Pakal and the Egyptians did for Tutankhamun. Unlike most Maya tombs, however—which were built to house a single ruler—Zapotec tombs often received marital pairs and served as multigenerational mausolea for multiple marital pairs.

Many Zapotec tombs were left open to facilitate the addition of new corpses. Others had a door that could be moved to the side whenever people wanted to reenter the tomb. One of the best-known examples of a multigenerational mausoleum is Tomb 6 at Lambityeco (see Chapter 15). This tomb had been placed beneath an impressive palace (Figure 11.5). Over the tomb entrance were the portraits of an ancestral husband-wife pair, whose faces were beautifully modeled in stucco (Figure 11.6). In front of these portraits the excavators found small vessels and offerings, some of which depicted Lightning.

Such exterior friezes served multiple purposes: (1) keeping the names of noble couples and royal ancestors alive; (2) providing a location for periodic offerings and ancestor veneration; and (3) legitimizing the claims and privileges of descendants.

Continuity in dynastic lines was shown in the friezes of Tomb 6 by depicting each first-born son brandishing the femur of his father, as well as by providing the names of each ancestral marital pair. The femur of the founder was held by his son; in turn, that son's femur was held by *his* son (e.g., Lind and Urcid

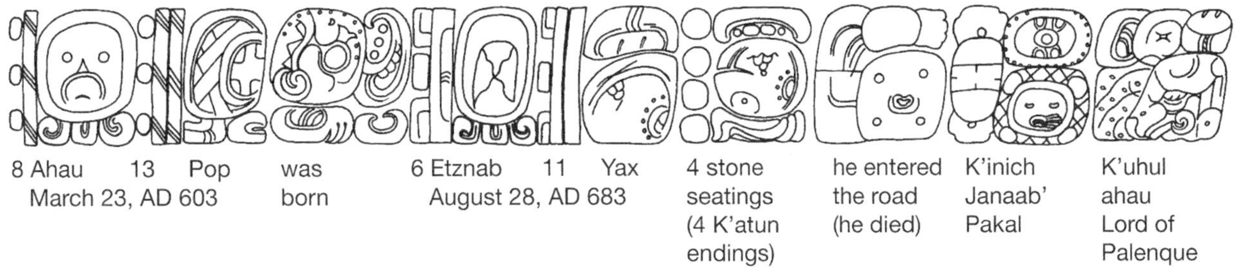

Figure 11.3. Carved on the front edge of a multi-ton sarcophagus lid, this text reveals the birth date and death date of K'inich Janaab' Pakal, a Maya ruler of Palenque. Redrawn by John Klausmeyer from Robertson 1983.

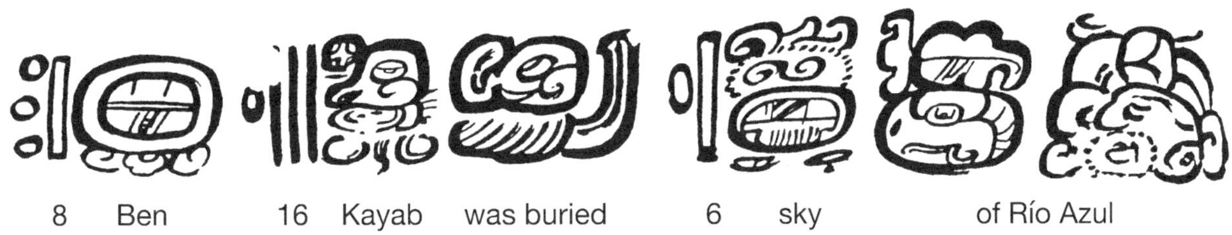

Figure 11.4. Lord 6 Sky's burial date is painted on the east wall of Tomb 12 at Río Azul, a Maya site located in the northeast corner of Guatemala. Redrawn by John Klausmeyer from Coggins 1988: Fig. 3-15.

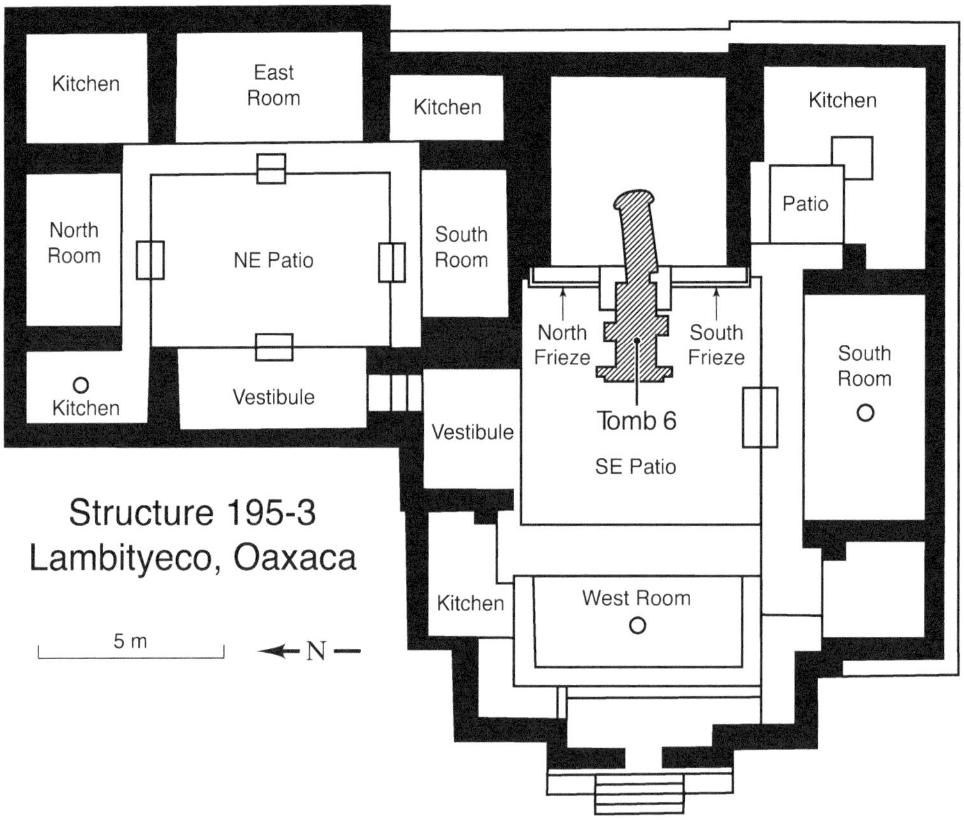

Figure 11.5. Tomb 6 at Lambityeco lay beneath the east room of a palace that featured two interior patios. Redrawn by Kay Clahassey and John Klausmeyer from Lind and Urcid 1983: Fig. 3.

1983; Marcus 2006b; Miller 1995; Rabin 1970). These scenes of femur brandishing were not mere symbolism; nine of the twelve expected femora from the six skeletons in Tomb 6 were missing. We do not know where the femora were stored between rituals, but it appears that there were occasions when a ruler's femur was brought out and displayed publicly.

The friezes of Tomb 6 and the curated femora made the case that an unbroken line of descendants had emerged from a founding couple. By supplying their predecessors' names, the Zapotec ensured that their ancestors would live forever, much as the Egyptians and Maya had.

Comparing the Zapotec and the Merina

Most of the elaborate Egyptian and Maya tombs contained one primary individual, e.g., the pharaoh or divine king. The elaborate tombs of the Zapotec, in contrast, often served as mausolea for several family members. In this respect the Zapotec resembled the Merina of Madagascar, for whom the ideology of descent centered on the family tomb.

Merina tombs stood for kinship and moral obligations; thus the Merina expended much more effort on tomb construction than they did on house construction (Bloch 1971). For the Merina, the funeral itself was not as important as the *famadihanas*, which were commemorative rites held at least two years after the funeral. The date for the *famadihanas* was selected as much as a year in advance, and involved many more people than could attend the funeral. For example, one of the *famadihanas* was attended by 500 people (Bloch 1971:148).

These memorial services involved expenses second only to the cost of building the tomb. The single major expense was food, some of which was taken home by the guests. The night before the main ceremony of the *famadihana,* several relatives of the dead went to the tomb and stood on the roof to "call the dead," addressing the spirits of those whose bodies they would exhume the next day. The senior person in the family called the spirits by addressing the hills with a short cry, calling the deceaseds' names and inviting them to rejoin their bodies. They even offered the spirits rum and honey.

Bloch (1971:154–156) says that around midday of the following day the relatives convened to go to the family tomb with all the guests. Only when accompanied by others would anyone

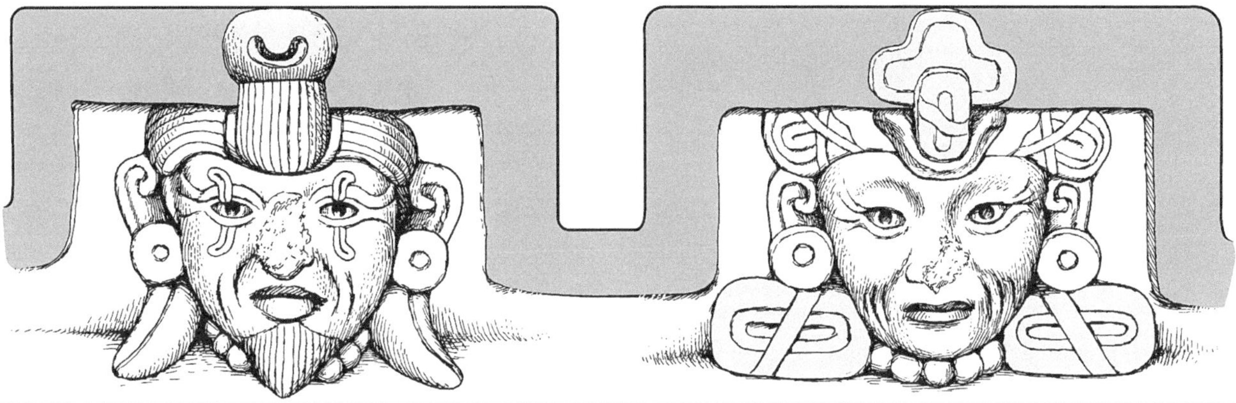

Figure 11.6. The marital pair Lord 1Ñ and Lady 10J were modeled in stucco and displayed on the exterior of Tomb 6 at Lambityeco in the Tlacolula arm of the Valley of Oaxaca. Redrawn from Marcus 2009b: Fig. 7 and Lind and Urcid 2010.

approach a tomb; the rest of the time the Merina expressed dread about going near it.

All the guests formed a single-file line to walk to the tomb, where the young men dug out a trapdoor to expose the stairs leading down to the sepulcher. Throughout this digging, the men found small amulets in the earth, pulled them out, and saved them so that they could replace them later when the hole was refilled. Finally, the massive tomb door was revealed and the head of the family opened the door, entered the tomb, and sprinkled the skeletons with medicine and rum. The medicine was said to be both protection for the living and a gift to the dead. Once the skeletons to be honored by removal from the tomb had been selected, they were wrapped in linen because their original red burial cloth had decayed.

Safely wrapped again, the bodies were taken out of the tomb and each was bundled in a papyrus mat. The bodies were then hoisted onto the shoulders of their relatives, who danced with them. Neighbors and friends stood at a distance and watched the dance. Next, the bundles were placed on the laps of female relatives, who sat on the ground while the oldest man in the family recounted the deeds of the deceased.

The Merina distinguished four categories of the dead, from "most recently deceased" to "longest deceased." The first category was the most honored, because they had not been touched since their funeral. They were wrapped in many red cloths when removed from the tomb. Those deceased longer were removed from the tomb to be danced with, but received fewer red cloths. Still older remains were not removed from the tomb, but received one red cloth. Finally, the longest deceased were not personally remembered, and when they were wrapped it took place inside the tomb.

All these commemorative rites resulted in a reorganization of the tomb's contents—the new corpses were put in favored positions, while the long dead were moved to less favored locations. Once all the corpses had been returned to the tomb, their relatives entered to take note of the location of the dead to whom they were related; they were urged to remember where each was placed, in preparation for the next occasion (Bloch 1971:159). Note that the Zapotec also moved old skeletons aside to make way for the new.

While different in detail from Zapotec mausoleum rituals, these Merina practices were analogous in the sense that they were based on a proverb, *Velona iray trano, maty iray fasana*, "Those who live in one house should be buried in one tomb" (Bloch 1971:165)—a proverb with which the Zapotec of Period IIIb–IV would have agreed.

One other Merina practice is of relevance here. The Merina occasionally had to create a new tomb, an action that required that some of the dead from an old tomb be moved to the new. "This action obviously stresses the importance of continuity of a kinship group through time" (Bloch 1971:166). Bloch (1971:167) went on to emphasize that the idea of "corporateness" is a concept that could only exist in relationship to tombs: Merina kinship relied on relatives having a common ancestor in an ascending generation.

The Role of Tomb Texts

The tomb—whether Egyptian, Maya, or Zapotec—is an ideal place to start the process of hieroglyphic decipherment, simply because the names of the deceased and his or her relatives are so often given. Tomb texts also tend to be well preserved, because they have been protected from the elements. It is worth noting that many Egyptian pharaohs were buried on the west side of the Nile, far from their former palaces on the east side. In the case of the Zapotec, many tombs were placed below the floor of the very palace in which the ruler had lived.

As we have seen, one reason for the texts in Zapotec tombs was the need for their descendants to base their claims of authority on their genealogical relationship to the deceased. We have also seen that some Zapotec rulers underwent a metamorphosis after death, serving as intermediaries between their descendants and the great life forces such as Lightning. This was not unlike the process the ancient Greeks called *euhemerism*, whereby extraordinary leaders became culture heroes; some culture heroes became deified or semidivine ancestors; and some deified ancestors were treated as if they were actual deities or gods (Cruz 1935, 1936; Henestrosa 1936; Marcus 1992a:261, 442; Parsons 1936; Royce 2011). Perhaps one of the best Zapotec examples of euhemerism is the primordial couple Lord 1 Jaguar and Lady 2 Maize (see Chapter 9).

Period IIIb Mortuary Contexts

As we will see in the pages that follow, Period IIIb in Oaxaca saw an investment in larger crypts designed to contain the remains of multiple family members. Relatives reopened these tombs both on anniversaries and when they wanted to add new corpses. The tomb was an ideal place for the display of genealogical data—the names of marital pairs, dynastic founders, and ancestors. A genealogical register was the ideal monument for this display.

This practice stood in contrast to the Maya and the Egyptians, who usually emphasized one person—the king—and did so by creating all-male king lists. For example, the Maya carved Altar Q at Copán to show that 16 kings had ruled that city; no queens were mentioned. Similarly, Egypt's Royal King List at Abydos featured 76 males, intentionally omitting female rulers such as Hatshepsut (Marcus 2001b).

In the next four chapters I discuss monuments from each arm of the valley that were (for the most part) carved between AD 600 and 900. Many of these monuments were commissioned for mortuary contexts, and hieroglyphic texts were displayed on tomb doors, lintels, jambs, and wall slabs. We see occasional stelae from this period, but they were the exception rather than the rule.

12

Monuments of the Etla Region

In the northern arm of the Valley of Oaxaca, only a few sites have yielded hieroglyphic texts dating to AD 600–900 (Figure 12.1). This scarcity may be due partly to sampling bias and partly to the fact that so many Period IIIb–IV monuments were designed for tombs rather than the façades of buildings. When more Period IIIb–IV towns have been excavated, I expect to see more hieroglyphic texts from this arm of the valley.

Three of the principal sites that have yielded IIIb–IV texts are Reyes Etla, San Lázaro Etla, and Cerro de la Campana.

Cerro de la Campana

On the hill called Cerro de la Campana, Enrique Méndez Martínez (1988) found a remarkable tomb with hieroglyphic texts, polychrome murals, painted lintels, carved stones, and stucco sculptures. Although apical ancestors and genealogical records had been featured in previously discovered tombs, Cerro de la Campana's Tomb 5 was by far the most elaborate.

Cerro de la Campana and Cerro de la Cantera are two hills that lie between the modern towns of San Pablo Huitzo and Santiago Suchilquitongo. These hills form part of the extensive archaeological zone of Suchilquitongo, which has an occupational history spanning the Formative, Classic, and Postclassic. The Valley of Oaxaca Settlement Pattern Project estimates that by Early Classic times (AD 250–600), Suchilquitongo had 16 mounds and a population of 1789 people (Kowalewski et al. 1989:227). By Late Classic times (AD 600–900), the number of mounds had doubled (to 33) and the population is estimated at 4000 (Kowalewski et al. 1989:227–229, 260).

Tomb 5 of Cerro de la Campana was excavated into bedrock, some five meters below the palace where we presume the deceased had once lived. This tomb, which served as a "palace of the dead," was a scale model of a palace with rooms arrayed around a central interior patio (Miller 1995:166) (Figure 12.2). Its contents call to mind a commentary accompanying the Codex Telleriano-Remensis, which reads, "The Mixtec, Zapotec, and Mixe people honored their dead in a way almost like the Spaniards, for they built a tomb covered in black and placed much food around it. .... And after the bodies had been eaten away, they unearthed the bones from the tomb and put them in ossuaries made of mortar in the patios of their temples" (Quiñones Keber 1995:254).

Tomb 5 at Cerro de la Campana had (1) multiple rooms (outer and inner vestibules, a sunken patio, a West Room and an East Room situated to either side of the patio, and a principal burial chamber); (2) hieroglyphic texts that supplied the names of nobles and associated year dates; (3) two entablatures with stone and stucco sculptures—one displayed above the tomb entrance and one above the entrance to the burial chamber; (4) ten rectangular pillars displaying men dressed in jaguar costumes, accompanied by women who may have been their wives; (5) five lintels, two of which had painted hieroglyphic texts; (6) polychrome murals

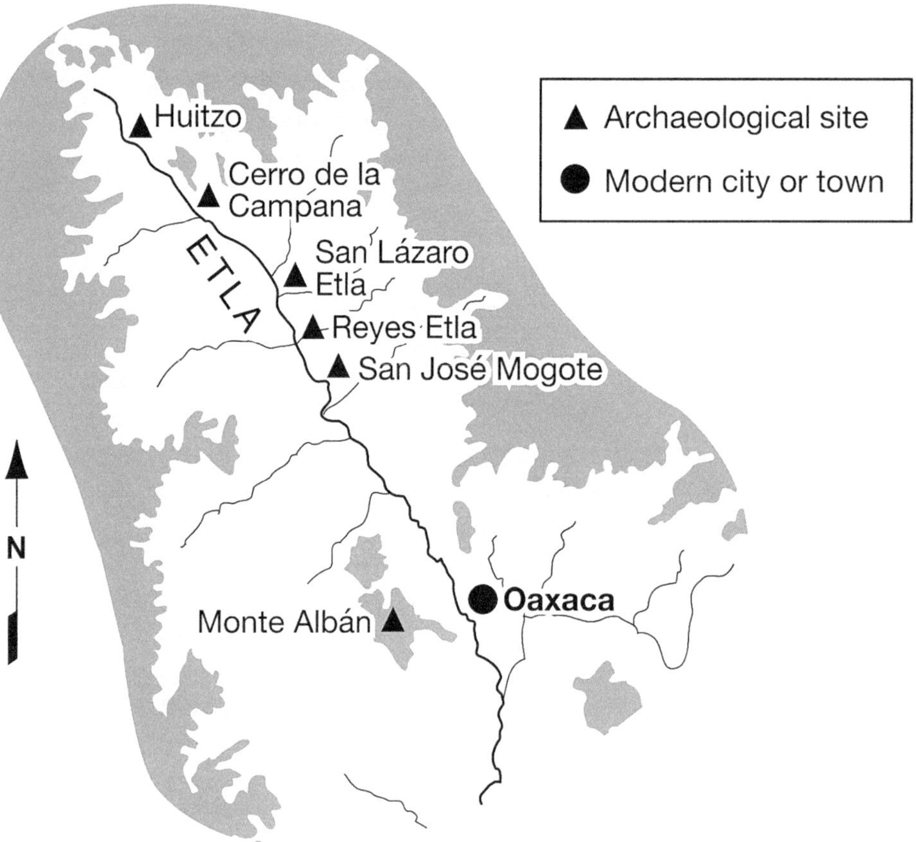

Figure 12.1. Map of the northern arm of the Valley of Oaxaca, showing the location of Huitzo, Cerro de la Campana, San Lázaro Etla, Reyes Etla, San José Mogote, and Monte Albán. Drawing by John Klausmeyer, adapted from "Mapa de las Localidades del Valle de Oaxaca" by Cecil R. Welte.

depicting more than 80 individuals; and (7) a carved stone (added during a late tomb reopening) that supplied the genealogy of Lord 12 Monkey.

If I had to pick one dominant theme of the Tomb 5 murals, it would be paying homage to mortuary bundles. Just as our own deceased presidents lie in state while government officials, military officers, and relatives pay their respects, the Tomb 5 murals indicate that five Zapotec nobles were honored by a procession of dozens of people who approached their funerary bundles, bringing offerings and burning incense.

These five Zapotec nobles had evidently been wrapped in cloth and propped up in wooden crates or boxes. We are immediately struck by how similar this practice is to the treatment of later Mixtec rulers (Figure 12.3). The Mixtec placed such wooden crates over hot ash to smoke the body (see Anders et al. 1992a:236; Caso 1977, 1979; Duncan et al. 2008; Nuttall 1902, 1975; M. E. Smith 1973a; Seler 1960, 1991). For example, on page 4 of the Codex Nuttall we see the bundled corpses of Lord 4 Motion and Lord 7 Flower enclosed in crate-like armature (Figure 12.3b).

At least two tombs at Kaminaljuyú show us that some Maya communities also placed the principal tomb occupant in a wooden box (Kidder et al. 1946:56, 68–69). For example, Tombs A-III and B-I at that site revealed the remains of individuals seated in wooden funerary boxes (Figure 12.4). When A. V. Kidder returned from excavating these tombs in 1936, J. Eric S. Thompson called his attention to a passage in fray Román y Zamora's sixteenth-century account of burial practices in Alta Verapaz:

> They placed the corpse in a public place while awaiting the arrival of the chiefs and vassals. It was in a seated position, for thus were the inhabitants of this province buried, and they dressed it in rich and precious clothing, which everyone, according to their rank, used to collect as soon as he [the deceased] began to grow old so that they should be placed on his shoulders when he died and should be buried with them. When the day of the interment came… they covered him with many mantles, and they placed him, well wrapped up in them, in a large box of wood or stone so that he filled it when squatting on his haunches, for that was their usual manner of sitting. (Kidder et al. 1946:89; Thompson 1939:283–284)

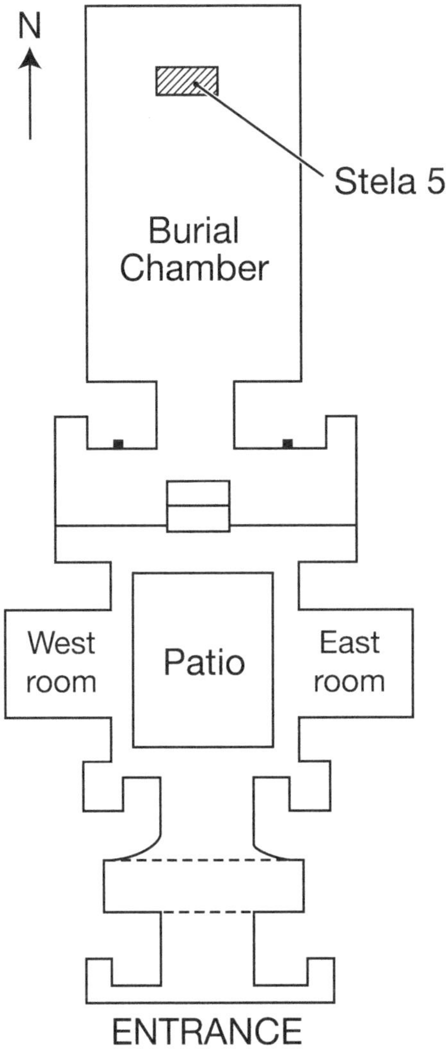

Figure 12.2. Plan of Tomb 5 at Cerro de la Campana, the only Zapotec tomb known so far that convincingly exhibits the plan of a palace. Note also the location of Stela 5, a monument introduced into the back of the tomb during one of a series of reentries. Adapted by John Klausmeyer from Miller 1995: Fig. 54.

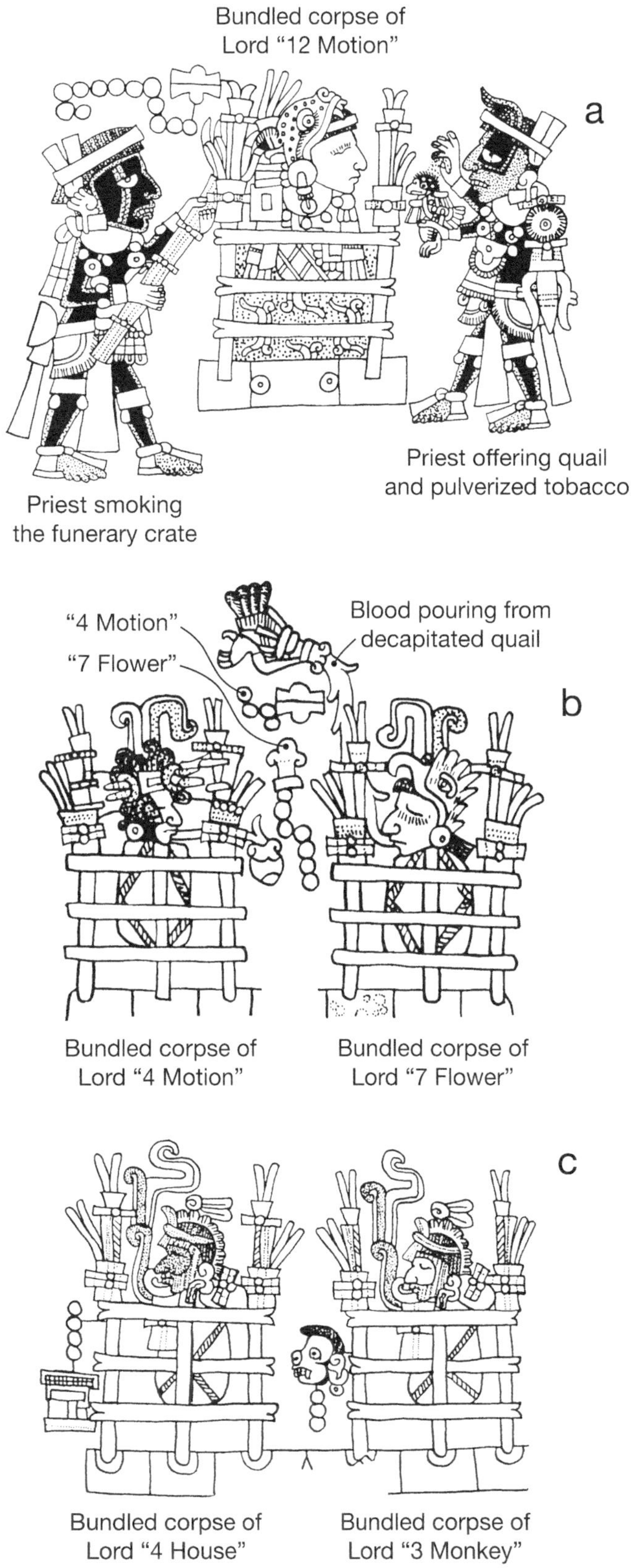

Figure 12.3 (right). Funerary bundles of Mixtec lords, as shown in the codices. (*a*) Lord 12 Motion's bundled corpse was suspended in a crate-like frame and set above a fire that would dry and smoke his body. The priest at right offers the corpse pulverized tobacco and a quail, while the priest at left holds a torch near the funerary crate. (*b*) The bundled corpses of Lord 4 Motion and Lord 7 Flower receive the blood and heart of a decapitated quail (the latter is shown to the left of the dots in the name 7 Flower, against the crate of 4 Motion). (*c*) Lords 4 House and 3 Monkey are suspended in wooden crates and accompanied by billowing smoke, presumably from a fire below them (see Anders et al. 1992a; Duncan et al. 2008). Drawing by John Klausmeyer.

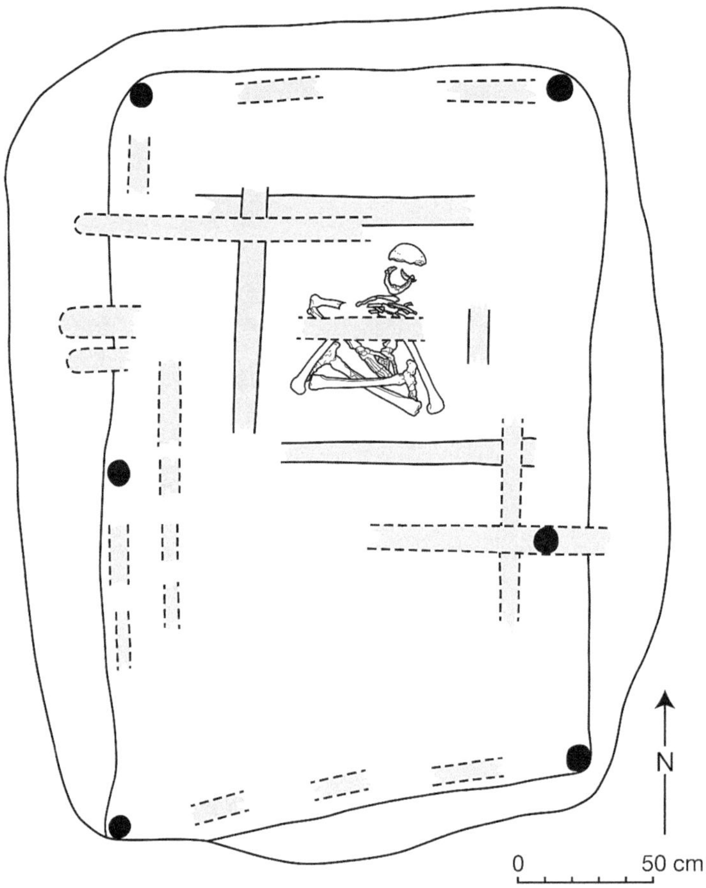

Figure 12.4. The principal occupant of Tomb A-III at the Maya site of Kaminaljuyú was seated cross-legged in a funerary crate. He was also associated with a wooden conveyance, probably a litter that transported him from place to place. The shaded areas indicate the traces of wooden slats. Redrawn by John Klausmeyer from Kidder et al. 1946: Fig. 23.

Kidder et al. (1946:89) go on to say:

> A "coffin or box" capable of accommodating a corpse seated cross-legged and "well wrapped in many mantles" would have been large enough to allow the upper part of the body to slump freely, and such a box would have been sufficiently strong to protect its contents, even more effectively than the bulkiest wrappings, from the pressure of the fill while decay was taking place.

Zapotec Funerary Boxes and Ancestor Bundles

The Zapotec term for a wooden funerary litter is mentioned in the sixteenth-century dictionary of Juan de Córdova, who refers to a *yága pelágati xòbapeni coti* ("litter of the dead") and to a *yàga quiña* ("wood box"). The initial word "*yaga*" specifies that this item was made of wood (Córdova [1578a]1942:28v). The reference is likely to a portable funerary crate, which allowed the bundled corpse to be carried from place to place.

As we will see, carved stones at both San Lázaro Etla and Cerro de la Campana depict funerary boxes with revered ancestors propped up in them (e.g., Caso 1928; Fahmel Beyer 2005a, 2005b; Fuente 2008; Seler 1991).

The Murals of Tomb 5

The Tomb 5 murals at Cerro de la Campana depict more than 80 people, including men holding spears, gladiators wearing helmets with faceguards, finely dressed women, warriors wearing jaguar costumes, and priests wearing the flayed skin of sacrificial victims (Figure 12.5). These attendees are walking in single file to pay their respects to the bundled bodies of nobles propped up in wooden boxes (Berger 2011; Lombardo de Ruiz 2008; Miller

Figure 12.5. In the polychrome murals of Tomb 5 at Cerro de la Campana, we see nobles wearing different headdresses and clothing, forming a procession as they pass by corpses propped up in wooden crates. Among those attending the funeral were: (*a*) warriors wearing helmets with faceguards, carrying *manoplas* in their right hands; (*b*) men carrying staffs and spears; and (*c*) priests wearing the yellow flayed skin of sacrificial victims. Redrawn by John Klausmeyer from Miller 1995: Figs. 76, 77, 80; Lombardo de Ruiz 2008.

Figure 12.6. The stucco sculpture of a possible apical ancestor named 10 Chilla (10 Crocodile) was displayed over the entrance to Tomb 5 at Cerro de la Campana. Redrawn by John Klausmeyer after Miller 1995: Figs. 52, 55, and Plate 29.

1995: Plates 44 and 45; Taladoire 2003; Urcid 2008). Although the preservation of the Tomb 5 murals is variable, they appear to show four wooden crates containing funerary bundles—two on the back wall of the main funerary chamber, one on the wall of the East Room, and one on the wall of the West Room (see Figure 12.2). A fifth crate is depicted on the stela that was added to the back of the burial chamber of Tomb 5 during one of the reentries.

It appears that the Tomb 5 murals, sculptures, and carved pillars were all planned by the Zapotec to form a coherent narrative; thus, we need to take a holistic approach to understand the message. Such an approach encourages us to think about the dominant theme as well as the intended audience (e.g., Fash 1991; Fash and Fash 1996; Fash et al. 1992; Gendrop 1998; Kowalski 1999; Miller 1995; Proskouriakoff 1946; Schele and Mathews 1999).

After the initial commissioning of texts and murals to memorialize these royal ancestors, multiple generations of Zapotec nobles evidently entered Tomb 5 at Cerro de la Campana to conduct commemorative rituals. The excavators suggest that the tomb was reopened from two to ten times. Mortuary rituals clearly included the burning of incense (since incense burners were held by individuals depicted to either side of the mortuary bundles), offering of goods (as depicted), and the singing of songs (as suggested by speech scrolls and musicians).

Entering Tomb 5

To reach Tomb 5, one had to descend nine steps that led from the patio floor of the palace to the top of an 80-cm-high wall delimiting the tomb's outer vestibule. Visitors then had to pass through a 1.37-m-high doorway to an inner vestibule, where they found a tiny sunken patio (1.5 x 1.7 m). From there visitors climbed three steps to enter the doorway (1.00 x 1.38 m) of the main burial chamber (2 x 4 m), which rested on a one-meter-high platform rising above the level of the sunken patio. Even though Tomb 5 is the most elaborate of its era, earlier examples

Figure 12.7. The stucco sculpture of a possible apical ancestor named 11 Monkey was displayed over the door leading to the main burial chamber of Tomb 5, Cerro de la Campana. Redrawn by John Klausmeyer after Miller 1995: Figs. 67, 68, and Plate 34.

such as Monte Albán's Tombs 104 and 105 may have served as inspirations. None of those earlier tombs, however, had the layout of a miniature palace with an interior sunken patio.

Above the outermost entrance to Tomb 5 was the impressive figure of a crocodile with a bird's head in its mouth, accompanied by the numeral ten (Figure 12.6). This stone and stucco image may refer to an apical ancestor named 10 Crocodile (10 Chilla) (see Miller 1995: Plate 29).

The tomb murals are divided into three registers, with the upper two registers showing people standing in line to enter the interior of the tomb. The lowest register is only 15 cm high and features green volutes on a red background (Miller 1995).

In both the West Room and the East Room, the murals show individuals flanking a funerary box. The East Room mural also shows priests wearing the yellowed skin of flayed individuals (see Figure 12.5c). This wearing of the victim's skin is not without precedent, since priests wearing the facial skin of sacrificial victims had been depicted on ceramic urns recovered from tombs at Monte Albán (Caso and Bernal 1952:249–257).

A second huge sculpture of stone and stucco appears above the entrance to the main burial chamber. It is a monkey wearing a jaguar helmet, accompanied by the numeral 11 (Figure 12.7). In all likelihood, 11 Monkey was another apical ancestor (Miller 1995: Plate 34).

Along the back wall of the main burial chamber were painted two wooden crates containing funerary bundles. These two deceased individuals sport the most elaborate headdresses and bird masks seen in the tomb (Figure 12.8). They may be a marital pair to whom the descendants of multiple generations paid respects, perhaps analogous to the way the Period IIIa primordial couple named 1 Jaguar (1B) + 2 Maize (2J) was honored.

The magnificence of Tomb 5 is indicative not only of its occupants' high status, but also that of their living heirs (Marcus 1992b, 2003b). Rites made in the presence of mortuary bundles allowed relatives to commune directly with the bodies of their ancestors in ways reminiscent of the Merina of Madagascar, who also entered family tombs to interact with (and often rearrange) the bodies of the deceased (see Chapter 10).

Figure 12.8. The mural on the back wall of Tomb 5 at Cerro de la Campana featured two richly attired mummy bundles that faced each other. A wall niche can be seen between them. Both corpses were shown propped up in wooden crates. They wore elaborate headdresses with feathers, leaves, and bird masks. These two individuals seem to have been the most important of the four deceased individuals in the murals. Redrawn by John Klausmeyer after Miller 1995: Plate 44; Lombardo de Ruiz 2008:132.

Stela 5

One feature that was not part of the original Tomb 5 was Stela 5. That carved stone was added during one of the tomb's reopenings, perhaps on an anniversary of the original interment (Marcus 2003b, 2006b; Miller 1991, 1995).

Stela 5 (82 cm tall) is divided into two registers (Figure 12.9). In the upper register, we see Lord 13 Monkey (13O) on the right propped up in a wooden crate, showing that he is a mortuary bundle (see Color Plate VIII). He presumably participated posthumously in events with his descendants, who are shown making bird sacrifices in his honor. The lower register, to be discussed below, features the relatives of Lord 13 Monkey, who are shown holding the items they use to perform bird sacrifices.

The funerary bundle of Lord 13 Monkey was the primary focus of Stela 5, just as the four other funerary bundles had been the focus of the painted murals in the same tomb. Lord 13 Monkey was apparently being transformed into a supernatural being who could make animal and human sacrifices. We will see in Chapter 17 that this ability was shared with the "flying turtle" or *yahui/ xicàni* shown on the back wall of a later tomb at Zaachila (see also Figure 5.6) (Caso 1966; Gallegos 1963, 1964; Hermann Lejarazu 2009; Paddock 1966b; Pohl 1994; M. E. Smith 1973b; Urcid 2005).

When deceased lords were depicted as metamorphosed beings, it was often their own offspring who commissioned these depictions. For example, the sarcophagus lid at Palenque shows the Maya ruler K'inich Janaab' Pakal being transformed into the Maize Deity. In K'inich Janaab' Pakal's case, it was his son K'inich Kan Bahlam who commissioned the lid; in the case of the Zapotec ruler 13 Monkey, it was also his descendants who commissioned Stela 5 (Miller 1991, 1995; see endnote 2).

Lord 13 Monkey's relatives reinforced their position in the noble lineage by featuring themselves on the sides of Stela 5 (see Figure 12.9). One text featured Lord 12 Monkey, the son of Lord 13 Monkey. The other side text featured Lady 12N (see Figure 4.4, Chapter 4). It is significant that both of the side texts display prototypic Zapotec syntax (time + verb + subject). Helping us interpret those parallel texts are the later "name clauses" that appear in sixteenth-century Zapotec documents. These documents show us that the names of Zapotec nobles could include as many as five elements—nickname, calendar name, birth-order position, status term, and hometown.

While the syntax of the Stela 5 clauses generally conforms to the structure of sixteenth-century Zapotec name clauses, there are a few aspects that require comment. Many sixteenth-century clauses give the individual's birth-order position *before* his

Figure 12.9. Stela 5 at Cerro de la Campana was carved on four surfaces—the top, sides, and front face. The front face had two registers. In the upper register we see Lord 13 Monkey (propped up in his funerary crate) and his son 12 Monkey, sitting in front of him. In the lower register we see Lady 12N and Lord 11A, both of whom have made bird sacrifices to honor 13 Monkey. On the left edge is a text that discusses Lady 12N (see the drawing in Figure 4.4 and Color Plate VIII). Drawing by John Klausmeyer from Miller 1995: Figs. 81–85.

calendar name, while the clauses on Stela 5 give the calendar name before the birth-order position (see Figure 4.4, Chapter 4). While this order is not common, I can point to one similar case: the sixteenth-century Etla Genealogy, in which the individual's calendric name was given before his birth order (Whitecotton 1990, 2003).

Sacrificing Birds to Honor Ancestors

The lower register of Stela 5 shows a marital pair, Lady 12N and Lord 11A, performing bird sacrifices. In the upper register of the stela this same ritual had been carried out by 12 Monkey, who sits immediately in front of 13 Monkey's funerary bundle (Figure 12.10; see also Color Plate VIII).

Sacrificing birds at funerals had a long history in Oaxaca. Feature 96 of San José Mogote, a ritual scene of burial and metamorphosis created during Period II, included a sacrificed quail (Flannery and Marcus 2005, 2015; Marcus and Flannery 1994, 1996). In addition, in the Mixtec codices we see bird sacrifice being performed by priests standing next to the funerary crates holding the bundled corpses of their rulers (see Figure 12.3).

Reentry into Zapotec Tombs

By removing the door of a tomb, descendants could enter to add new offerings or insert the bodies of newly deceased relatives (Middleton et al. 1998). On such occasions the visitors might also repaint the tomb murals, adding either the names of the newly deceased relatives or the date of reentry. Reentry often occurred on the anniversary of the original interment, and it could include placing new offerings in the tomb.

One of the hieroglyphs that commonly occurs in mortuary settings is Caso's Glyph I—the Maltese cross—which sometimes is accompanied by a number and the depiction of a deceased person's head. I have already suggested that this Maltese cross may refer to offerings made to the deceased on the anniversary of his original interment.

The Maltese cross appears three times in Tomb 5 at Cerro de la Campana. One occurrence is on Stela 5, where the Maltese cross is associated with the date 7N and the head of a deceased person.

The second instance of a Maltese cross is found in a painted text in the tomb. This text seems to imply that on Day 3L, a commemorative rite was conducted on the third anniversary of the interment, in the Year 2E, by a descendant named 10 Serpent, who burned incense at the funerary bundles of two marital pairs named 7 Rain (7C) + 3 Crocodile (3 CC) and 9 Water (9Z) + 5E (Figure 12.11, top text).

In the third case the Maltese cross is painted on another lintel, where it is accompanied by a death's head and 3 bars + 5 fingers, perhaps signifying the number 20 (Miller 1995: Figure 74); whether they are actually bars or some other item (such as cloth) is not clear. One of the possible interpretations of this text would be "On the twentieth anniversary of 13 Monkey's death, which occurred on the day 7N in the Year 11N, his son 12 Monkey conducted commemorative rites in his father's memory" (Figure 12.11, bottom text). If this is accurate, 12 Monkey must have died shortly thereafter, as recorded on the side of Stela 5.

Final Thoughts on Tomb 5

The elegance of Tomb 5 at Cerro de la Campana could be explained in at least two ways. Either (1) we have underestimated the power and prestige of the families administering secondary centers, or (2) such families were compelled to expend great effort to legitimize their position and newly acquired status. In either case, Tomb 5 supports the argument that when Monte Albán was in decline, secondary centers began to command greater manpower and had access to highly skilled scribes, painters, and stone carvers. As a result, many secondary centers went on to produce some of the finest funerary art and hieroglyphic texts ever commissioned in the valley (Lombardo de Ruiz 2008; Miller 1995).

Reyes Etla

Another key site of Period IIIb–IV in the northern arm of the valley was Reyes Etla. Its mounds were impressive in number, height, and volume (Figure 12.12). Kowalewski et al. (1989:270) report that the east mound of a four-mound group at the center of the site stands more than 20 m high and may contain 14,000 m^3 of construction fill.

A series of tombs have been uncovered at Reyes Etla, some of which yielded carved jambs (Marcus and Flannery 1996:216). The individuals on one pair of jambs were named 5 Reed and 8 Reed. These two male figures stand on generic hill signs that do not seem to contain specific town names. Above both figures are the Jaws of the Sky, suggesting they are of noble descent. Both figures are in jaguar costumes and feather headdresses; they carry staffs of office and possible copal bags (Figure 12.13*a*). The individuals depicted are similar to some of the figures shown on tomb jambs attributed to Suchilquitongo by Bernal and Méndez (1974) (Figure 12.13*b*) and on the jambs and pillars of Tomb 5 at Cerro de la Campana (Miller 1995).

Another sculpture from Reyes Etla was found in the site's ballcourt (Figure 12.14). It was carved in the round and is similar to other sculptures found in ballcourts at other sites, including Zaachila, Yagul, Lambityeco, and Sola de Vega (Balkansky 2002; Berlin 1946, 1951, 1957; Feinman and Nicholas 2016b, 2017; Marcus 2002). Such carved-in-the-round sculptures are often considered to represent serpents or crocodilian creatures; a few may be related to the creatures with upturned snouts called *xicàni* (necromancers, wizards, or sacrificers) (Augsburger 2003; Córdova [1578a]1942; Hermann Lejarazu 2009; M. E. Smith 1973b). Many such stones may originally have been associated with ballcourts, and some of them may have been tenoned (Figure 12.15).

Figure 12.10. The upper register on the face of Stela 5 shows Lord 12 Monkey (at left) and his father, Lord 13 Monkey (at right). This stela, which was not part of the original interment, was introduced during one of the reentry episodes. On that same occasion—judging from its similar message—a lintel was painted with a similar hieroglyphic text. Drawing by John Klausmeyer and Kay Clahassey.

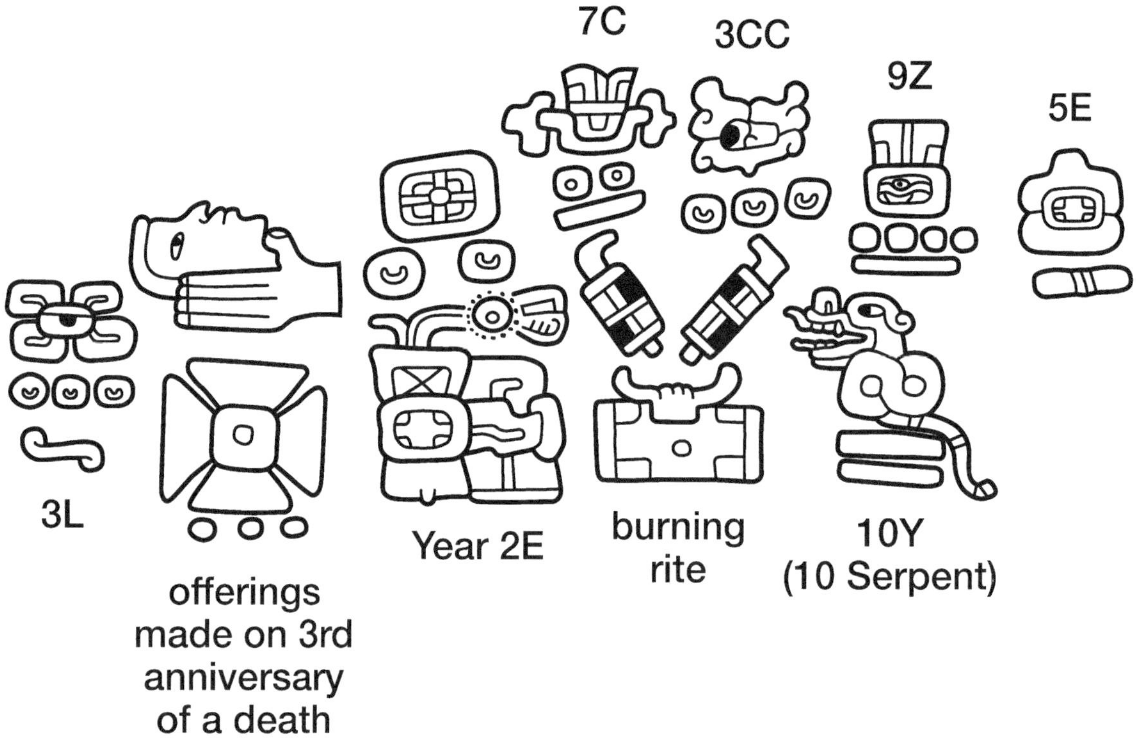

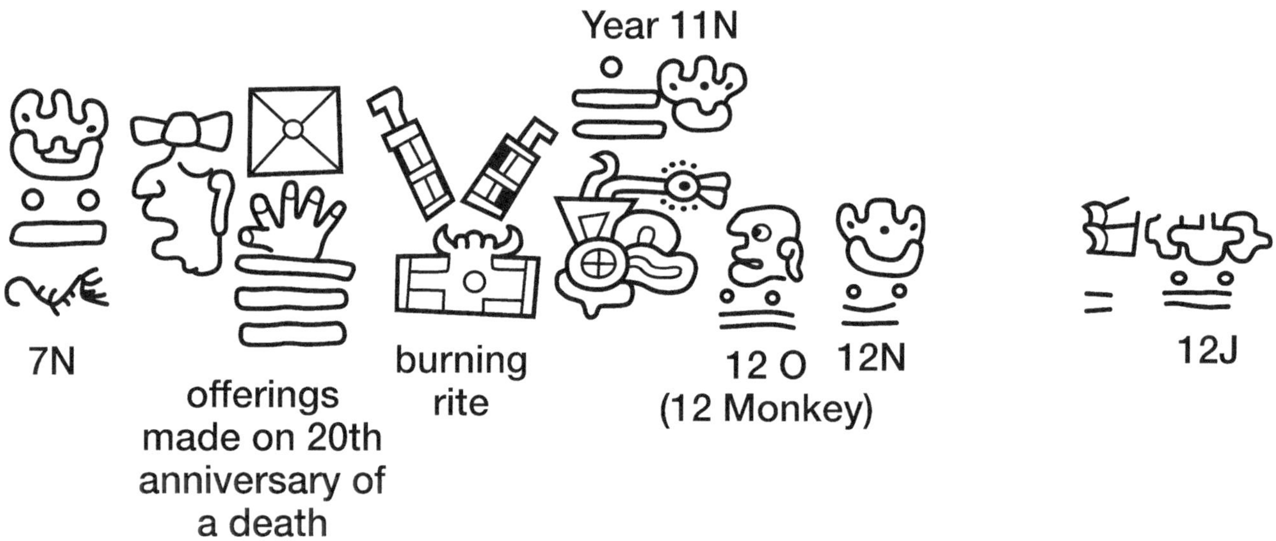

Figure 12.11. These hieroglyphic texts were painted on two different occasions on the lintels of Tomb 5 at Cerro de la Campana. Arthur Miller (1995:183–185) suggests that the text (at the top) was painted first, while the other lintel text (at the bottom) was painted during one of the later reentries into the tomb. Reinforcing Miller's interpretation is the fact that the lower text repeats much of the information carved on Stela 5, a monument introduced into the tomb during a reentry episode (see Figures 12.9, 12.10). Redrawn by John Klausmeyer from Díaz Castro 2008:493; Miller 1995: Fig. 74, Plate 35.

Figure 12.12. Map of the site of Reyes Etla, showing the location of the ballcourt where a carved stone was found. Map by Dudley Varner.

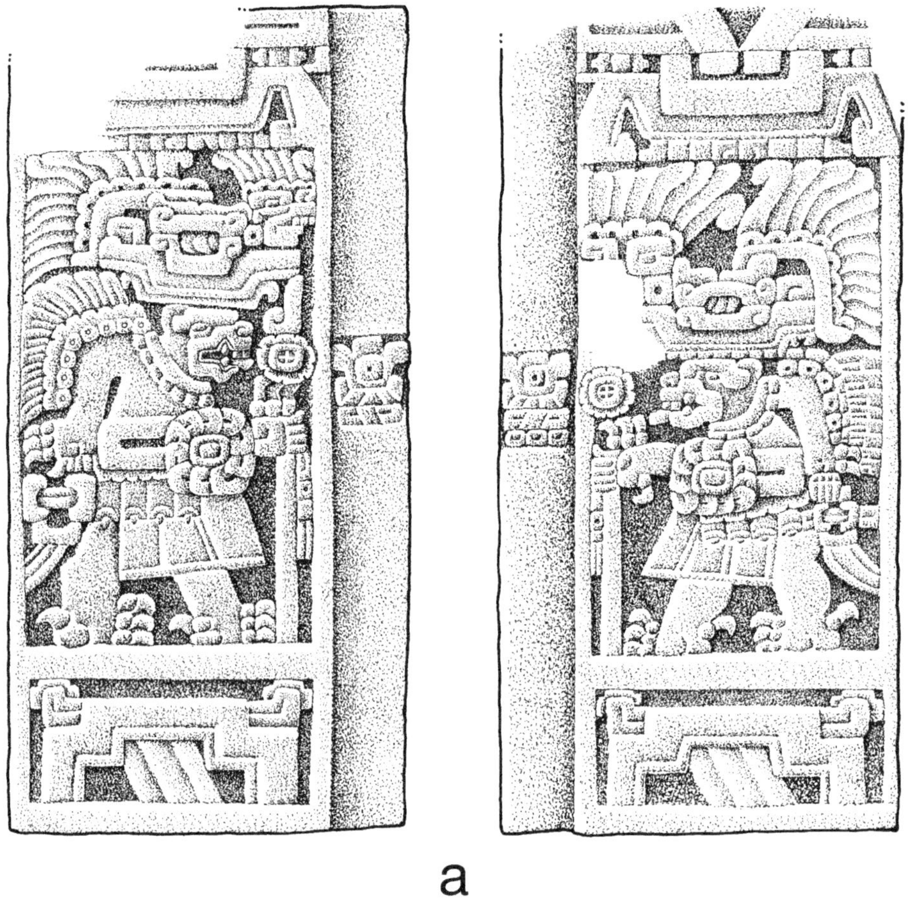

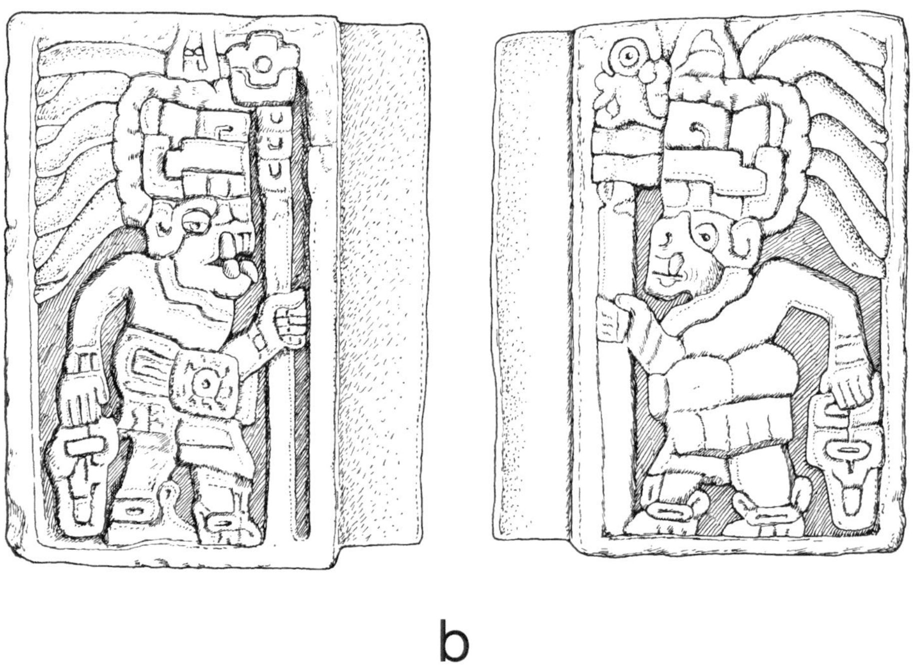

Figure 12.13. The Etla subvalley has produced numerous pairs of door jambs, likely designed to have flanked the entrances to tombs. (*a*) These jambs from Reyes Etla show men dressed in jaguar costumes, standing on generic hill signs. At the left is 5 Reed; at the right we see 8 Reed. (*b*) These jambs, now housed in Mitla, are believed to have been brought from Suchilquitongo (see Bernal and Méndez 1974: Figs. 1, 2). The names of the two jaguar-costumed individuals seem to be embedded in the top of their staffs. On the left we see a man named 3 Reed; on the right we see 10 Monkey. *a* was drawn by Mark Orsen; *b* was drawn by Rubén Méndez.

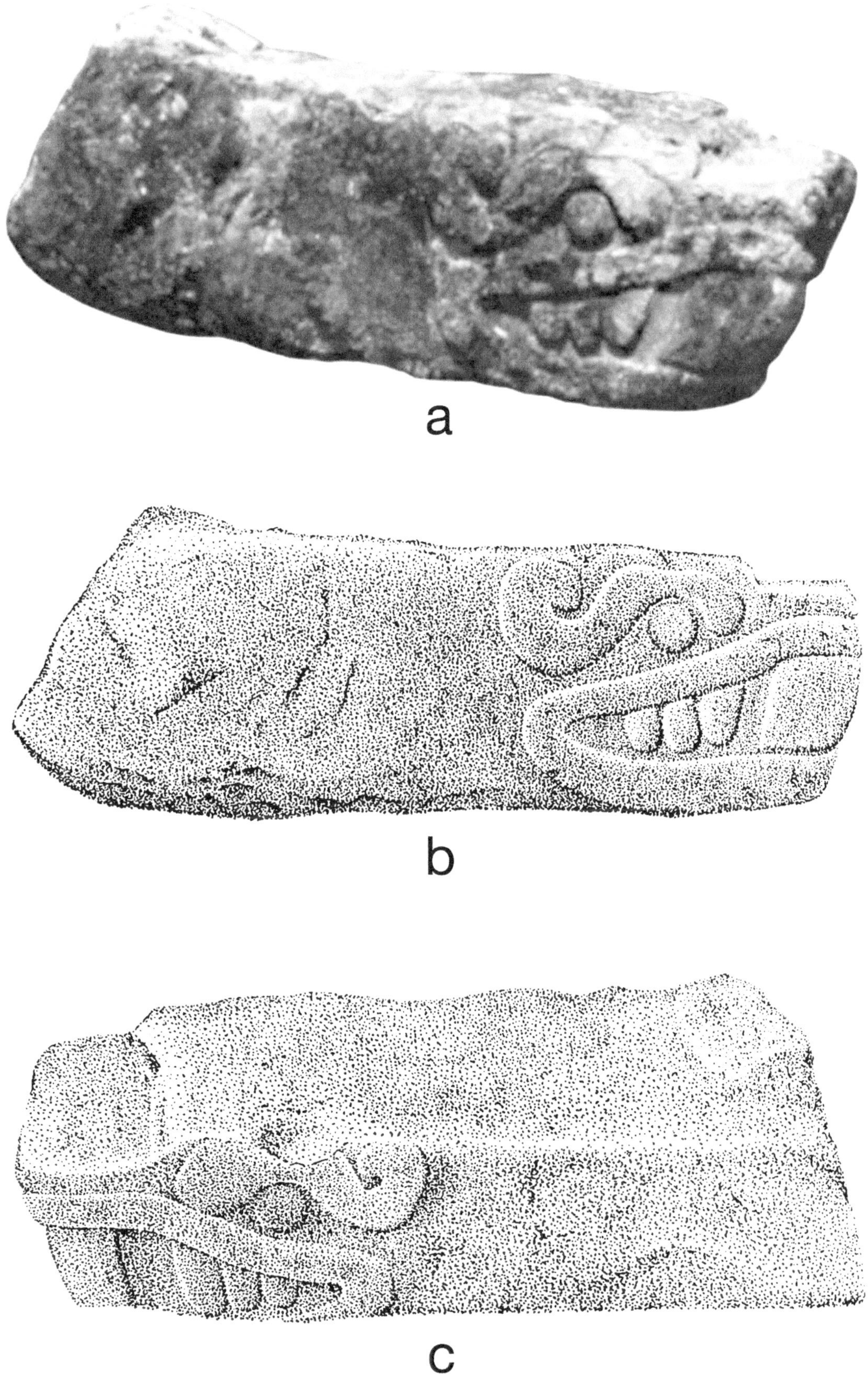

Figure 12.14. Three views of the same carved stone found in the ballcourt at Reyes Etla (see Figure 12.12). Of its 1.9 m length, only 0.79 m was carved; the uncarved portion would likely have been tenoned into one of the ballcourt walls. The photo in *a* was taken in 1974; *b* and *c* were drawn by Mark Orsen.

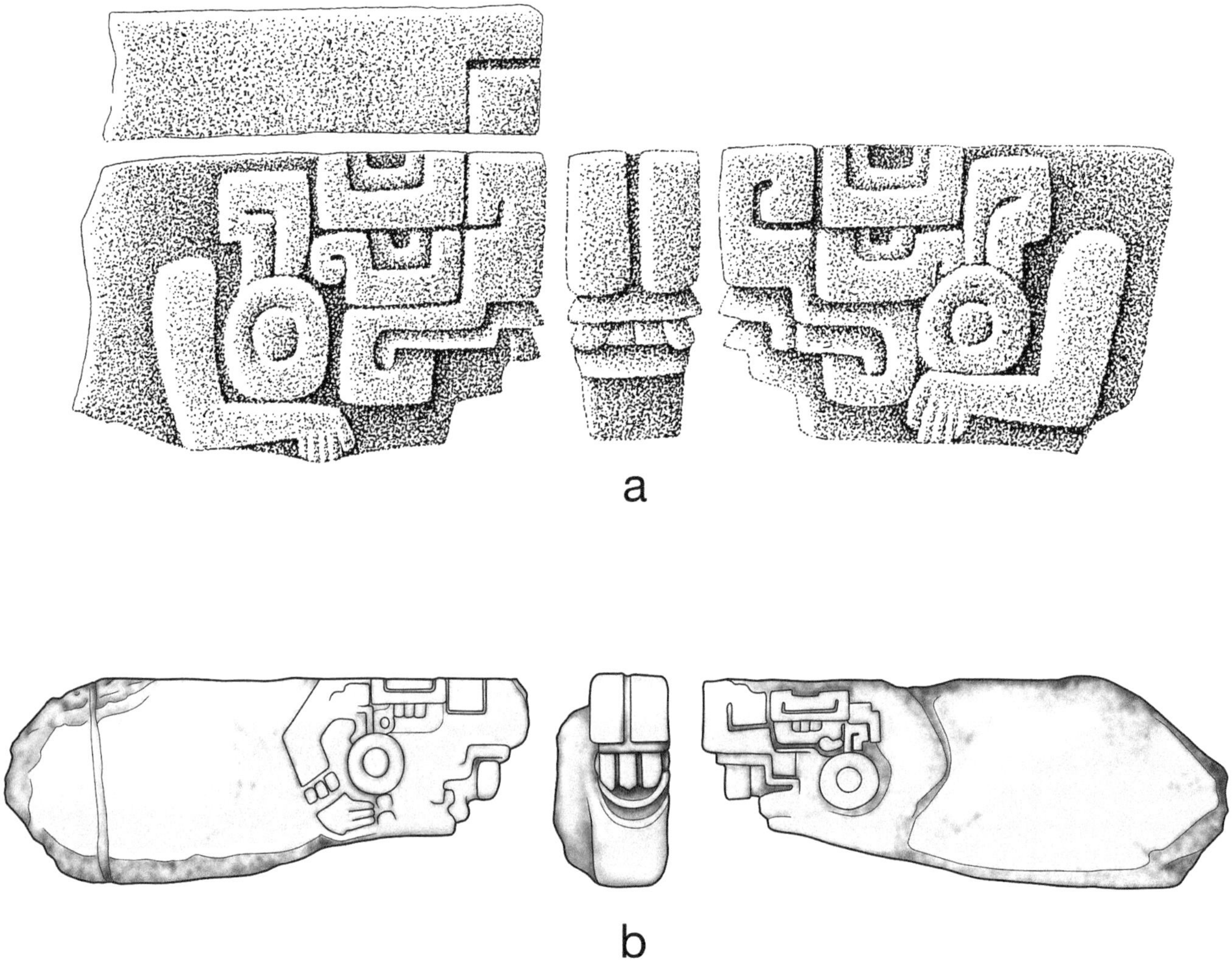

Figure 12.15. These carved stones were found in the Tlacolula region. (*a*) This stone, found in the Yagul ballcourt during excavations, might have been tenoned into a wall; it combines the arms of a human with the head of a reptile with an upturned snout. Such a creature has been linked to transformation, metamorphosis, sacrifice, divination, and wizardry. 1.25 m x 0.80 m. (*b*) Found during excavations at Lambityeco by Gary Feinman and Linda Nicholas, who suggest that it was originally the balustrade of a stairway on Mound 170. Note the crocodile head as well as the human arm and bracelet. *a*, drawing by Mark Orsen; *b*, redrawn by John Klausmeyer from Feinman and Nicholas 2019: Fig. 14.5.

San Lázaro Etla

In the 1850s, eight carved stones (Monuments E-1 through E-8) were discovered at "San Lázaro Zautla," a town known today as San Lázaro Etla. These carved stones of San Lázaro Etla (not surprisingly) show similarities to those of Reyes Etla to the south and Suchilquitongo to the north.

Years after their discovery, considerable confusion arose about the context and provenience of these San Lázaro Etla monuments. Three scholars—Manuel Martínez Gracida, Jesús Galindo y Villa, and Caecilie Seler—correctly reported that these carved stones were from the Etla subvalley. Eduard Seler, however, mistakenly attributed six of the eight carved stones to Tlacolula (Seler 1960: Abb. 98a and 98b; Seler 1991).

The eight monuments were originally published by Baron Johann Wilhelm von Müller (1864) and Martínez Gracida (1883). Two were later published by Caecilie Seler (1900: Tafel VIII); five were published by Eduard Seler (1960: Abb. 94–98); and Caso (1928: Figures 88–91) published four of them.

Given their similarities, it seems likely that these San Lázaro Etla monuments were all commissioned within a relatively short period of time. When I first saw the stones in the 1970s, I concluded that all probably came from the same site because (1) they were similar in style and format; (2) some were clearly paired tomb jambs (that is, individuals facing each other from opposite sides of a doorway); (3) most early sources (e.g., Martínez Gracida, Caecilie Seler, and Galindo y Villa) attributed them to Etla; and (4) they seemed to depict corpses propped up in wooden crates. In the 1990s, Ferdinand Anders et al. (1992a:236) independently came to the same conclusion.

Anders et al. dismissed Eduard Seler's statement that some of the stones were from Tlacolula, and emphasized that Martínez Gracida (1883) had said that five of the stones were in "San Lázaro Zautla" in June of 1857. Additional support for this position came from Eduard Seler himself, who said that he had seen one of the carved stones set in the wall of a building in the modern town of Etla. I thus consider San Lázaro Etla the most likely provenience.

San Lázaro Monument E-1

This stone (Figure 12.16), called Lápida 8 by Caso, was published as Figure 88 in his 1928 book (Caso 1928:189). Earlier illustrations were published by von Müller (1864: Vol. II, Figure 5) and Eduard Seler (1960: Vol. II, 359, Figure 97).

Caso (1928:115) gave the stone's measurements as 80 x 65 cm. Its original height was once greater, since the base of the stone is now missing. Caso (1928:116) interpreted the seated person on Monument E-1 as an elderly male, because Zapotec stone carvers often depicted the elderly by showing wrinkles around the chin, as is the case with this individual. Such a wrinkled face was called *tinoñilaoa* in Zapotec (Córdova [1578a]1942:72r).

The elderly man on Monument E-1 is seated in a wooden funerary crate, which Caso (1928:116) calls an *angarilla*, a term in Spanish meaning litter, crate, or bin. Based on similar depictions in Cerro de la Campana's Tomb 5 and in the Mixtec codices, I believe that this funerary crate was the kind used to transport mummy bundles from place to place, allowing them to be honored and approached by different individuals before burial.

The base of the carved stone is now missing, making it impossible to see whether the crate was originally placed on a hill sign. The presence of a hill sign immediately below a funerary litter is characteristic of several jambs from the Etla arm, and would seem to indicate that the funerary crate was displayed at a "place" or "hill," without specifying *which* place or hill.

The elderly man on Monument E-1 has a speech scroll with two elements attached, a Zapotec convention for elegant speech. He holds a pouch of the type used for copal incense. He wears an elaborate headdress composed of an animal with an upturned snout and the characteristics of a crocodile, along with many long feathers, and the head of a monkey atop a second pouch (behind the old man's head). He wears a necklace, probably of jade beads. His cloak is noteworthy for the three or four large disks affixed to it.

To the left of the elderly man we see a short hieroglyphic text. In the upper left corner is a bent bar designating the number 5; immediately below is the day sign Glyph E, and below Glyph E are three dots representing the number 3 (Caso 1928:116). Taken together, these signs were identified as 8E by Caso. In the lower left corner of the stone is another bent bar with a dot above it, signifying the number 6, and it is associated with the blood motif.

San Lázaro Monument E-2

Monument E-2 measures 95 x 39 cm (Figure 12.17). This carved stone displays many of the same elements we saw on Monument E-1: a man propped up in a funerary crate wearing an elaborate and distinctive headdress. The headdress includes an animal with upturned snout, long feathers, crocodile eyes, and a monkey head atop a pouch and the circle + triangle blood motif (Caso 1928:117, 190; Galindo y Villa 1905:223, Note 40; E. Seler 1960: Vol. II, 359, Figure 95). The headdress on this man is similar to that worn by the deceased Lord 13 Monkey in the top register of Stela 5 at Cerro de la Campana.

The man on Monument E-2 has large earspools, a necklace, and the same cloak decorated with large disks that we saw on Monument E-1. His funerary crate has a horizontal scroll. At San Lázaro Etla, the motifs on the side of the wooden crate vary—some, including this one, bear a horizontal scroll (Monuments E-2, E-3), while others bear a woven mat (Monuments E-4, E-6, E-7). What this variation in motifs signifies is not clear. The mat may refer to royal authority in general, but the meaning of the scroll in this context is not clear.

Caso (1928:117) noted that the seated figures on Monuments E-1 and E-2 were dressed in nearly identical ways. There are,

Figure 12.16. San Lázaro Etla's Monument E-1 shares many features with the stones shown in Figures 12.17–12.23, suggesting that all eight monuments were commissioned in a relatively short period of time. Of great interest is the fact that all eight stones show a bundled corpse propped up in a wooden crate. Given this stone's width (ca. 65 cm), it was likely a tomb door. The hieroglyphs on Monument E-1 seem to supply the man's calendric name, 8E (given in front of his face) and possibly his nickname "6 + blood motif" (given in the lower left corner). Another distinctive trait shared by some of the San Lázaro Etla stones is a cloak bearing three or four large disks. Like other figures from San Lázaro Etla, the corpse wears a headdress featuring a reptile related to the *yahui* or *xicàni*, a powerful sacrificer associated with wizardry, metamorphosis, and deity impersonation. Note also the monkey head + triangular bag that hang from the back of his headdress. Adapted from Seler 1991 by John Klausmeyer.

however, some differences: (1) the figure on Monument E-2 is depicted without wrinkles and (2) the hieroglyphs differ from those on E-1.

The hieroglyphic text on Monument E-2 is short (see Figure 12.17). At the upper left we see the sign for Serpent (Glyph Y), which has been interpreted as Serpent by Caso (1928:117–118). Note that there appear to be at least two dots and possibly a bent bar in front of the upturned snout headdress. If those dots and the bar were combined with the Glyph Y above, we might interpret this individual's name as 7 Serpent.

Since the dimensions of this stone correspond closely to those of tomb jambs in the Valley of Oaxaca during this period, it seems likely that Monument E-2 was a jamb (see discussion below).

San Lázaro Monument E-3

Monument E-3 was probably a tomb jamb and likely paired with Monument E-2 or one of the other jambs to be discussed below. Caso gave the monument's dimensions as 1.0 x 0.40 m. The photograph of this carved stone appears as Figure 90 in Caso (1928) (see von Müller's Figure 2).

Caso (1928:118) believed that the person on Monument E-3 (Figure 12.18) was the same as that depicted on Monuments E-1 and E-2. His principal reason was that this individual was shown wearing the same cloak with large disks on it. However, the person on Monument E-3 does not wear the identical headdress, does not have wrinkles like the figure on Monument E-1, and is not associated with the same hieroglyphic text (which probably constitutes part of the individual's personal name).

The hieroglyphs on Monument E-3 are carved above the feather headdress. They include two bars and three dots, giving us the number 13, but the associated hieroglyph above the number is not clear. This combination of 13 + (an eroded sign) was probably the name of the corpse propped up in the funerary crate. In Eduard Seler's drawing (Seler 1960: Figure 96), we see another unassociated dot or two floating in front of the feathers in the headdress. This suggests that additional areas of sculpture once existed at the top and bottom of this damaged jamb.

Figure 12.17. Monument E-2 from San Lázaro Etla depicts a corpse propped up in a funerary crate. The name associated with the corpse may be 2 Serpent (or possibly 7 Serpent). At the base of the carving we see a generic hill sign. This man displays the same reptilian *yahui* or *xicàni* headdress and the same "monkey + bag + blood motif" that we saw in Figure 12.16. He also has three disks on his cloak. This monument appears to have been a jamb, given its shape and its width of 39 cm. This monument was called Lápida 9 by Caso (1928:190). See also Seler 1991: Fig. 95. Drawing by John Klausmeyer.

Figure 12.18. The shape of Monument E-3 from San Lázaro Etla suggests that it was a jamb. The calendric name, which Seler (1991: Fig. 96) could not see well enough to draw, includes a number that might be 13. The corpse has three disks on its cloak and a speech scroll issuing from the mouth. Drawing by John Klausmeyer.

Figure 12.19. Monument E-4 from San Lázaro Etla, which was probably used as a jamb, features a woman whose funerary crate is decorated with the mat motif. At the bottom of the stone we see a generic hill sign. Behind the woman's head we see a Maltese cross, often used to signal anniversary offerings. At the upper left we see 7 Serpent (7Y), which may be her name (see Caso 1928: Fig. 91; Seler 1991: Fig. 94). Drawing by Mark Orsen.

San Lázaro Monument E-4

This monument is probably another tomb jamb, and in this case a woman is clearly depicted. A photograph of this monument appears as Figure 91 in Caso (1928:192; see also Caecilie Seler 1900: Plate VIII, lower left; E. Seler 1960: Figure 94; von Müller 1864, Vol. II: Figure 1). Caso (1928:118) gives the stone's measurements as 1.20 m in height and 0.45 m in width (Figure 12.19).

This woman is shown wearing a huipil and skirt; her hair is in braids doubled over and tied above her head; and she is kneeling. In Zapotec monuments, these characteristics typically indicate a woman. She kneels within a funerary crate above a hill sign. What sets this stone apart from the E-1, E-2, and E-3 monuments is the motif on the side of the crate; in this case it is the mat motif.

Behind the woman's head is the Maltese cross that Caso (1928:119) designated Glyph I. This is a sign often associated not only with mortuary contexts, but also with commemorative offerings marking an anniversary of the deceased, perhaps timed to coincide with the date of his or her interment. In this case, no numerals are associated with the cross.

As Caso (1928:35) noted, Glyph I could occur with numbers from 2 to 9, but sometimes occurred without any numeral. We have already noted the presence of this cross in many anniversaries, sometimes accompanied by the sacrifice of birds. For example, Glyph I was sometimes associated with an open hand, a human head with the mouth open and eye closed, or a stiff stone figure or statuette, all of which seem to be associated with the act of making offerings to ancestors and commemorating the anniversary of interments.

Glyph I could occur on tomb lintels (e.g., Cuilapan, Xoxocotlán, Yagul, Zaachila, and Cerro de la Campana); on tomb jambs (San Lázaro Etla); on stelae and tomb doors (e.g., Stela 9 and Tomb 104, Monte Albán); in tomb murals (Monte Albán); and in genealogical registers (e.g., Cerro de la Campana and Zaachila).

Immediately above the woman's head on Monument E-4 is a large serpent with a bifid tongue. Still higher up on the stone we see two dots and a bar, plus an eroded sign. Caso (1928:119) read this set of hieroglyphs as 7E and interpreted it as a year bearer. I think it is more likely that 7Y or 7 Serpent was the name of this woman.

San Lázaro Monument E-5

This carved stone is known only from a drawing published by von Müller (1864: Vol. II, Figure 3), and is reproduced here as Figure 12.20. Unfortunately, its current whereabouts are unknown.

Monument E-5 appears to have been another tomb jamb, probably placed to the right of the entrance. It depicts an individual propped up in a wooden funerary box like those seen on other Etla monuments. This deceased person is associated with a feathered headdress and a speech scroll.

Figure 12.20. Monument E-5 from San Lázaro Etla is known only from a nineteenth-century drawing by von Müller (1864, Vol II: Fig. 3). Redrawn by John Klausmeyer.

Figure 12.21. Monument E-6 from San Lázaro Etla shares many of the elements we have seen on other San Lázaro Etla monuments. This elderly man's name seems to be either 5 Owl or 7 Owl (see Caso 1965b: Fig. 23). The corpse has a trophy head suspended from his neck, an attribute shared with Monument E-7. His funerary crate is decorated with the mat motif, like those on Monuments E-4 and E-7. He also has three disks on his cloak. This tomb jamb may have been paired with the one in Figure 12.19. Drawing by Mark Orsen.

San Lázaro Monument E-6

A photograph of this monument was published by Caso (1965b: Figure 23), who referred to it simply as "Stone at Etla." During the years 1972 to 1975, this monument was on display at the Oaxaca Regional Museum, and at that time I arranged to have it drawn by Lois Martin (see Figure 12.21).

This stone shares many elements with the other San Lázaro Etla monuments, including the funerary box. It may be one of the carved stones seen by von Müller in 1857; however, he states that he "selected [only] five of the carved stone slabs to sketch and measure" (von Müller 1864: Vol. II, 252; translated by M. Dembo).

Monument E-6 appears to be another tomb jamb. It depicts an elderly man who resembles the individuals on Monuments E-1, E-2, and E-7. He has the monkey + pouch + blood motif attached to the back of his headdress. His headdress features the upturned snout. On his chest we see a possible mask or trophy head suspended with a cord from his neck. His cloak is decorated with three large disks that resemble those on the aforementioned stones, but his associated hieroglyphic text is different. On the upper left corner of the monument we see the glyph for the day sign "Owl" with a bar below it; this compound was presumably read 5 Owl or 7 Owl (or Night).

The old man on Monument E-6 faces to our left. He is seated in a funerary box with a mat motif on its side, below which we see a hill sign. This use of the mat motif, the layout of elements above and below the man, and his left-facing position all lead me to suggest that this monument may have been the right jamb of the same tomb for which Monument E-4 was the left jamb.

San Lázaro Monument E-7

Monument E-7 (Figure 12.22) is known only from a drawing published by Eduard Seler (1960: Figure 98a). He reported its provenience as "the town of Etla" where it was "used as a cornerstone in a house." Monument E-7 bears a striking resemblance to Monument E-6; the main difference is that Monument E-6 gives the hieroglyphic compound 5 Owl or 7 Owl in the upper left corner, while the upper portion of Monument E-7 is missing. As a result, all we have in the case of E-7 are two dots floating in front of the old man's face.

Monument E-7 depicts a man facing left, holding a possible incense bag and wearing a possible trophy head or mask around his neck. I say "possible incense bag" because in the Oaxaca highlands, such pouches could hold either copal or pulverized tobacco. For example, in the Codex Nuttall the bundled corpse of the Mixtec lord named 12 Motion is approached by a priest who offers him a quail and powdered tobacco (see Figure 12.3).

The man on Monument E-7 wears a cloak with the familiar three large disks seen on Monuments E-1, E-2, E-3, and E-6. When Seler saw this stone it was covered with red pigment,

Figure 12.22. Monument E-7 from San Lázaro Etla shares many of elements seen on other San Lázaro Etla monuments: the *yahui/xicàni* headdress, the monkey + bag + blood motif, the mat motif, and three disks on the cloak. The corpse also wears a trophy head, like the figure on Monument E-6. Redrawn by John Klausmeyer from Seler 1991: Fig. 98a.

perhaps similar to the pigment that covered Stela 5 at Cerro de la Campana. A strong case can be made that Monument E-7 is from San Lázaro Etla, and one could argue that both Monuments E-6 and E-7 were carved to be used as tomb jambs.

San Lázaro Monument E-8

This monument was first published by Eduard Seler (1960: Vol. II, Figure 98b), who reported its provenience as "the town of Etla." This stone might be one of those seen by von Müller (Figure 12.23).

Monument E-8 shows a figure with a speech scroll, propped up inside a wooden funerary crate. Note that this figure is set so far down inside the crate that it appears to be little more than the upper third of the bundle. This position is also seen on Monuments E-2 and E-3.

Although Monument E-8 once had a short hieroglyphic text at the top of the stone, the latter is now largely eroded. All we can see are perhaps three or four floating dots that may have been numerals linked to a hieroglyphic day sign.

Figure 12.23. The upper section of Monument E-8 from San Lázaro Etla is badly eroded. The crate at the bottom, however, is clear, as is the scroll emanating from the mouth of the corpse. Redrawn by John Klausmeyer from Seler 1991: Fig. 98b.

Implications of the Monuments from San Lázaro Etla

We have now seen eight monuments attributable to San Lázaro Etla, some of which were likely jambs that flanked the entrances to tombs. Some paired jambs almost certainly depict married couples, and one of the individuals in each pair usually has a speech scroll. Some jambs clearly depict mummy bundles or desiccated corpses propped up in wooden boxes, much like the revered ancestors depicted in the murals and stela at nearby Cerro de la Campana.

Dating the San Lázaro Etla Monuments

What do we know about San Lázaro Etla? When Ignacio Bernal surveyed the site, he found pottery on the surface that spanned the centuries from Period I to Period IIIb–IV. We now know that the site goes back still farther in time; when I visited San Lázaro, I was able to recover Early Formative sherds from beneath some of the giant pigs happily rolling in the mud near the base of the main mound. All the known monuments, however, seem to date to Period IIIb–IV.

In his field notes Ignacio Bernal says: "The site is located … to the west of the church, parallel to Highway 2a Benito Juárez. There are four large mounds, built of adobe with little rock. The tallest is 7.6 meters. There are remains of stucco and much of the surface is marked with it. The mounds on the south and north of the road probably form a plaza, but the road and houses make it impossible to say. The fourth mound is 70 m south of the easternmost mound of the first group. The mound is built of adobe with a building on top and a second building further down."

The stylistic similarities shared by the eight monuments (E-1–E-8) make it likely that all were carved during a short span of time. Not only do they share similarities with each other, but also with other carvings in Period IIIb–IV style. For example, Monuments E-1 to E-8 display bars and dots that look like those on other IIIb–IV monuments. Typical of Period IIIb were bars that had ties or bindings wrapped around them, and bars that were bent (sometimes forming 90° angles to make them fit into small spaces).

Also typical of the era were bars and dots that were not tightly spaced or closely associated; and sometimes the bar might be placed above the day sign while the dots were shown below the day sign (e.g., Figure 12.16). This period also featured day signs and/or numerals that appear to be unattached to the other parts of the text. All these characteristics are so typical of the era that Period IIIb–IV is the likely date for all eight San Lázaro monuments. Caso's position would likely be the same, since he assigned Monument E-6 to Period IIIb–IV (Caso 1965b:862).

The general theme of the San Lázaro monuments also suggests a Period IIIb–IV date. Many monuments of that era featured genealogical information and scenes of ancestor veneration (Marcus 1983c:191). The monuments that I have called genealogical registers continued this theme into Period IV (Marcus 1980:61).

The Significance of the Funerary Crate

The wooden funerary crate is one of the distinctive features of monuments in the Etla arm of the valley, although possible examples can occasionally be found elsewhere (one possible crate may appear in a tomb mural at Xoxocotlán).

I have already suggested that the funerary crate was used to display and transport the bundled corpse of a ruler or important noble. To understand the full significance of these crates, we need to look closely at how the ancient Zapotec regarded their deceased rulers.

The Zapotec were concerned with showing that nobles—unlike commoners—did not really die, but rather (1) could continue to witness events, (2) could metamorphose into a supernatural being or semidivine creature, (3) could fly into the clouds, and (4) could be petitioned to intercede on behalf of their descendants (Marcus 1983e:347–348).

A deceased noble ultimately became a "cloud ancestor," sometimes depicted as a flying supernatural with a reptilian head or a turtle's body, or wearing the mask of a creature with an upturned snout who could receive sacrificed birds and humans. Occasionally such metamorphosed figures were shown wearing a cape or lying prone, like the ceramic figure from Feature 96 at San José Mogote (Figure 12.24). Metamorphosed ancestors with upturned snouts and crocodilian attributes were depicted in Tomb 1 at Zaachila (Chapter 17), in a genealogical register from Noriega (Chapter 14), and associated with the deceased rulers at San Lázaro Etla and Cerro de la Campana (Chapter 12). Sometimes ancestors were depicted as supernatural creatures resting on their forearms, or creatures incorporated into the feathered headdresses worn by nobles, rulers, and bundled corpses (see Figures 12.10, 12.24, and 12.25).

Although there are hundreds of Zapotec carved stones, depictions of bundled corpses propped up in funerary crates are rare outside the Etla arm of the valley. Similar practices in which a dead lord is carried on a wooden litter, however, are known for the Mixtec, the Aztec, the Maya, the Inca, and others (Anders et al. 1992a, 1992b; Bauer 2004; Morris and von Hagen 2011; Rostworowski and Morris 1999; M. E. Smith 1973a). Smoked, desiccated, and mummified lords were transported from place to place in special crates so that those deceased lords could continue to participate in religious and social rites. On such occasions their funerary bundles might receive offerings such as sacrificed quail, human blood, burning incense, or fermented beverages.

It is likely that only a limited number of people (perhaps exclusively nobles) would have had access to the tomb interior. Accordingly, I suggest that the hieroglyphic texts on San Lázaro Etla's tomb walls and jambs qualify as "horizontal propaganda"—that is, texts designed to present the deceased's genealogical credentials to other nobles (Marcus 1992a:11–12). One of the major differences between the monuments and texts of Periods I and II and those of Period IIIb–IV is that the former were predominantly vertical propaganda while the latter were predominantly horizontal.

The high frequency of funerary crate depictions in the Etla region provides a contrast with the Tlacolula region during Period IIIb–IV. Rather than funerary crates, the Tlacolula region more often featured genealogical registers and friezes showing the heirs of rulers brandishing their fathers' femora (Chapter 15).

Figure 12.24. Feature 96 at San José Mogote contained an arranged scene, including a miniature tomb with evidence of a bird sacrifice and possible musical instruments. On the stone lid of the tomb we see the pottery sculpture of a flying figure, wearing a cape. The tomb occupant was a kneeling ceramic figure with a necklace, set upright in a bowl. To the left of the bowl was a bobwhite quail (*Colinus virginianus*), one of the Zapotecs' most popular birds for sacrifice. Just outside the miniature tomb lay a pair of deer antlers and a broken flute made from the limb bone of an unidentified bird. The four sculptures in the background appear to be women in masks who are witnessing the scene. The flying figure may represent the transformation of the deceased noble in the tomb; he is undergoing metamorphosis, being transformed into a "cloud person" who can join Lightning in the sky (see Flannery and Marcus 2015:266–272). Drawing by John Klausmeyer.

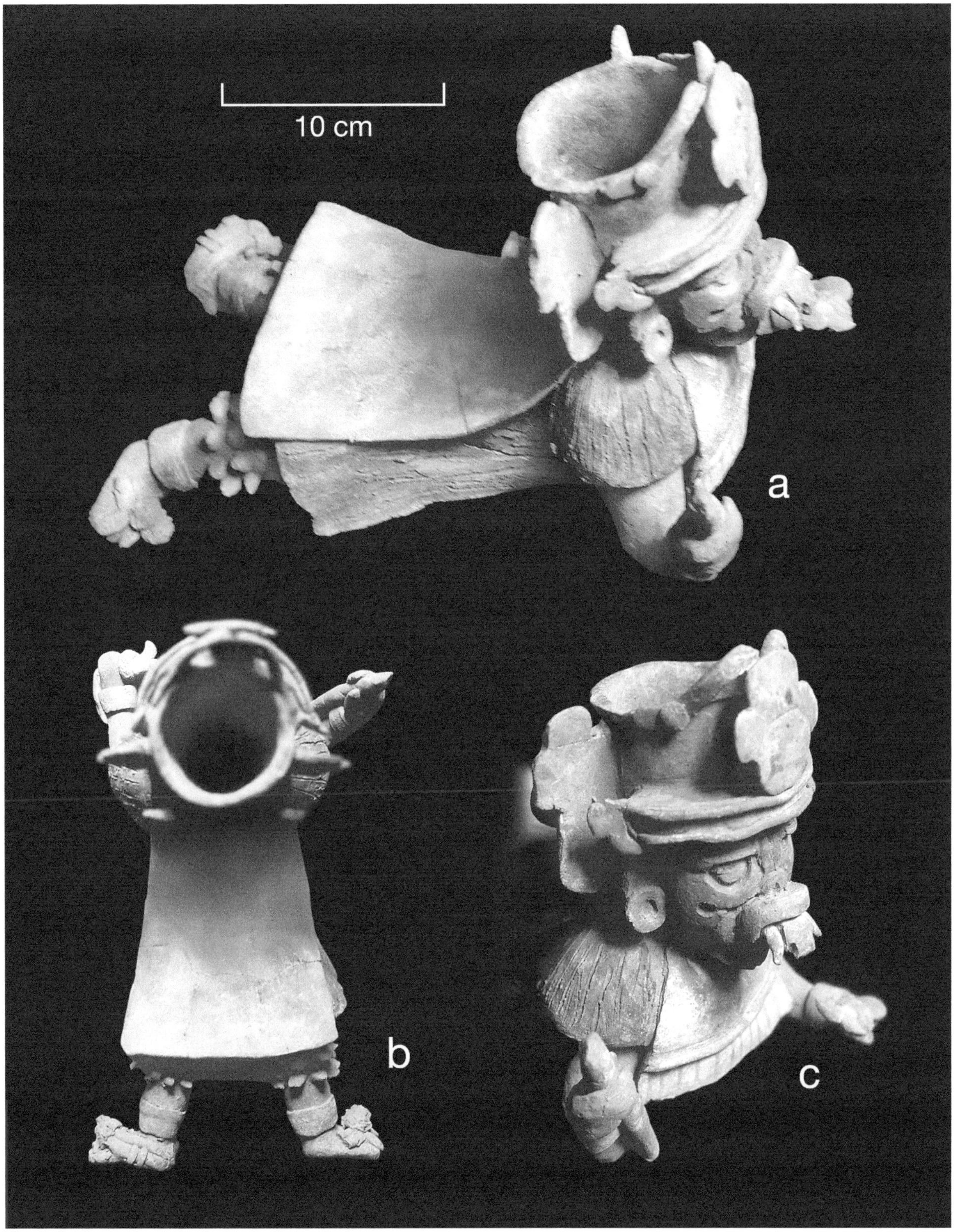

Figure 12.25. Three views of the flying figure from Feature 96 at San José Mogote: (*a*) side view; (*b*) top view showing the cylindrical receptacle on the figure's head; (*c*) three-quarter view, showing the items carried in the hands of the figure (see Flannery and Marcus 2015:267). This Period II scene anticipates by centuries the flying figures seen in later Zapotec tombs (see Chapter 17).

13

Monte Albán Monuments from AD 600 to 900

By Period IIIb the number of monuments at Monte Albán and the audience for whom they were intended had undergone a significant change. Period I saw hundreds of carved stones displayed on the exterior of Building L, bringing vertical propaganda to the public. Each period saw a decrease in this political strategy. By Period IIIb there were still fewer carved stones, and most occurred in places where only elites were likely to see them.

The North Platform was a huge acropolis that supported both roofed and unroofed spaces, a colonnaded portico, a sunken patio, temples, and the least accessible places in the city from an ekistic or "traffic flow" standpoint. In fact, the North Platform featured one of the most private courtyards at Monte Albán (Blanton 1978:61–63; Fahmel Beyer 1991; Marcus 2008b).

Unlike the South Platform, which seems to have been devoted primarily to religious activities, the North Platform had large spaces for a range of political gatherings and residential activities. Privacy was ensured not only by the impressive height of the North Platform, but also by a deeply recessed sunken patio and a small court surrounded by temples d, g, and e in the northeast sector (Figure 13.1). Few of the activities conducted on the North Platform could be seen from the Main Plaza.

True stelae were rare for any period at Monte Albán, but during Period IIIb–IV the North Platform was associated with three (Stelae 9, 10, and 10A). In earlier periods, stelae could reasonably be considered vertical propaganda. However, the location of Stelae 10 and 10A (in the restricted-access parts of the North Platform) shows that their audience was primarily the royal family and noble guests.

Stela 9

On a 1920s map of the Main Plaza (Caso 1928), Stela 9 stood in front of the North Platform, making it virtually the only Period IIIb–IV stela likely to represent vertical propaganda. This was a very tall monument (3.11 m) with the shape of an obelisk, making it the only one of its kind known from Monte Albán. Unlike most earlier carved stones at Monte Albán—which were usually incorporated into buildings as cornerstones, lintels, jambs, doors, steps, and façade slabs—Stela 9 was free-standing. Like so many Maya examples of the same period, Stela 9 was carved on all four sides (Marcus 1992a:410–411).

The front (or south side) of Stela 9 (Figure 13.2) faced the plaza and its principal figure was the frontal view of a man, likely a ruler dressed as a warrior. This man appears to be standing on a hieroglyphic name that may be interpreted as 8 Reed (8D) (Caso 1928:90). He appears to be holding doubled-over cords of the type used to bind captives. Similar cords seem to be shown on the east

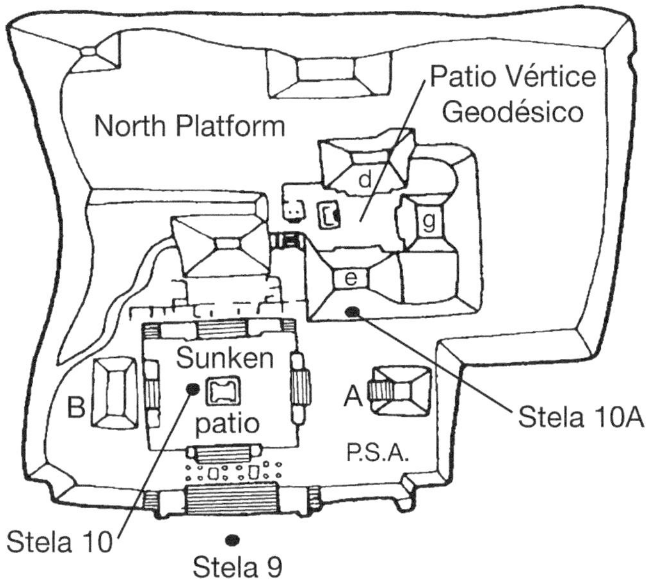

Figure 13.1. When discovered, Stelae 9, 10, and 10A were on or near Monte Albán's North Platform (see also Figure 6.21). Drawing by John Klausmeyer.

Figure 13.2. Stela 9 was found standing in front of the North Platform at Monte Albán. The south side of the stela, shown here, is the frontal view of a man named 8 Reed (8D). Drawing by Mark Orsen.

and west sides of the stela. Finally, the man on the front of Stela 9 may be wearing the headdress of a feathered serpent; an alternative possibility is that he has his head inside a feathered serpent's maw, like some of the figures depicted on stelae at Xochicalco, Chichén Itzá, Tula, and other sites (Cobean and Mastache 1995; Marcus 2001a; Tozzer 1941, 1957).

Stela 9 is unusual for Monte Albán in that it depicts only men, while so many other IIIb–IV monuments show both men and women—sometimes as marital pairs in genealogical registers, sometimes conducting rites of conjuring, bird sacrifice, divination, and ancestor veneration.

The east, north, and west sides of Stela 9 seem to form an iconographic unit, since the individuals shown on the east and west sides face the rear (or north side) of the monument (Figures 13.3, 13.4). The east side shows two men in profile view. The hieroglyphic sign 9K may be the name of the uppermost man; he stands on a possible spear. The lower figure seems to hold a cord; his name appears to be a compound of 1 Maize (1J) and 3E.

The north (or rear) side shows two men facing each other, accompanied by more than a dozen hieroglyphs. The top of the monument is eroded, but we can see a possible 4 Chilla (4CC); lower down, and in the left column, we see 3 Owl (or 3 Night). Among the other glyphs we can identify are 2J, 11D, and the Year 6 Deer (or 11 Deer).

The appearance of the Maltese cross (Caso's Glyph I) to the right of 3 Owl is noteworthy, because this hieroglyph often appears in mortuary texts. Glyph I appears twice on the rear of Stela 9. In one instance it seems to be linked to the bag glyph and not associated with any number; in the second instance it seems to be associated with the bag glyph and the number five. It is possible that the bag and Glyph I refer to the death and interment of 3 Owl. Given the Maltese cross, the 5 + Glyph I may refer to the fifth anniversary of that interment, when offerings were made in his memory (in the Year 6 or 11 Deer). To either side of Glyph 2J (2 Maize) we see two possible bag glyphs.

There is only one male figure on the west side of Stela 9 (Figure 13.3); he faces the rear of the monument. Associated with him are two columns of text. In the left column we see Glyph A, a possible mat sign, then Glyphs 2A and 7E. In the right column we see Glyphs 7D and then perhaps 7B or 2B. The end of the right column may have been left unfinished, or perhaps the hieroglyphs have been eroded away.

Stela 10

Stela 10, found in the great sunken patio of the North Platform, depicts multiple generations of nobility or royalty (Marcus 2009: Figure 24). The placing of the earlier generations at the bottom of the stela (Figure 13.5) suggests that we should read the text from bottom to top. This is the same reading order seen in a number of genealogical registers—for example, Stela 5 of Cerro de la Campana (Chapter 12) and Lápida 1 of the Museo Nacional (Caso 1928; see also Chapter 16).

At the bottom of Stela 10 we see two remote ancestors; the hieroglyphic name on the lower left may be 6E and that on the right, 10L. Above those ancestors are two seated individuals, possibly named 3E and 9D. At the very center of the stela is a seated individual, now highly eroded because this is precisely where the stone is broken.

At the top of the stela are two more individuals, both associated with the name 2J (a name that also appeared on Stela 9 in the center of the north side). Both of the individuals on Stela 10 that are named 2 Maize appear to be women.

The Year 6 Deer (6G) appears at the top of Stela 10 and may be the date that some memorial offerings were made. Caso's Glyph I—the Maltese cross—is here associated with the number 9; the bar standing for 5 appears above the Maltese cross and the four dots appear below the cross, followed by a skull. This text may be conveying the fact that the Year 6 Deer was the ninth anniversary of an important funeral.

At the very top of the carved stone is the Jaws of the Sky motif. This motif, as we have seen, is often associated with nobility and with a descending ancestor who intervenes between the living and the dead (Caso 1928; Lind 2015; Marcus 1992a; Smith Stark 2002:95–110).

The placement of Stela 10—in the sunken patio of the North Platform—would have made it invisible to commoners in the Main Plaza, making it likely that it was viewed mainly by nobles.

Stela 10A

Stela 10A may have been carved at about the same time as Stela 10, and both were set up on the North Platform, where commoner access would have been restricted. Their limited-access location and their genealogical content are what made them horizontal propaganda. Since these two monuments once stood more than 2.7 m in height, they would have been extremely visible to those occupying the North Platform. If we assume that Stelae 10 and 10A recorded the genealogical history of families residing on the North Platform, their height and their strategic placement would have been a constant reminder to their descendants.

Stela 10A rested on the steps of Temple e, an even more restricted setting than the one assigned to Stela 10. This monument was carved on two sides. The best-preserved side (Figure 13.6) displays several characteristics of a genealogical register, including (1) the Jaws of the Sky motif at the top; (2) a side spiral or scroll—a motif that serves to frame scenes of noble descent—at the upper left; (3) enough registers stacked one above another to account for three generations; and (4) the typical placement of the oldest generation at the bottom.

The aforementioned oldest generation includes two women seated on hill signs, each presumably specifying her hometown. The woman on the left has the calendric name 5 Owl (5 Night) and the nickname "Mat of Authority." We cannot link 5 Owl's hill sign to a known place.

Figure 13.3. Figures carved on the east and west sides of Stela 9 face the back (or north side) of the monument. Taken together, these three carved surfaces form a compositional unit that can be understood as a single narrative. To read this narrative, one might start on the south side (Figure 13.2), then walk in a counterclockwise direction past the east, north, and west sides. Drawing by Mark Orsen.

Figure 13.4. This three-dimensional view of Stela 9 shows how the east and north sides connect seamlessly. The text at the base of the monument was apparently never finished. The north side appears to have been the focus of attention for the individuals depicted on the west and east sides. Created by John Klausmeyer.

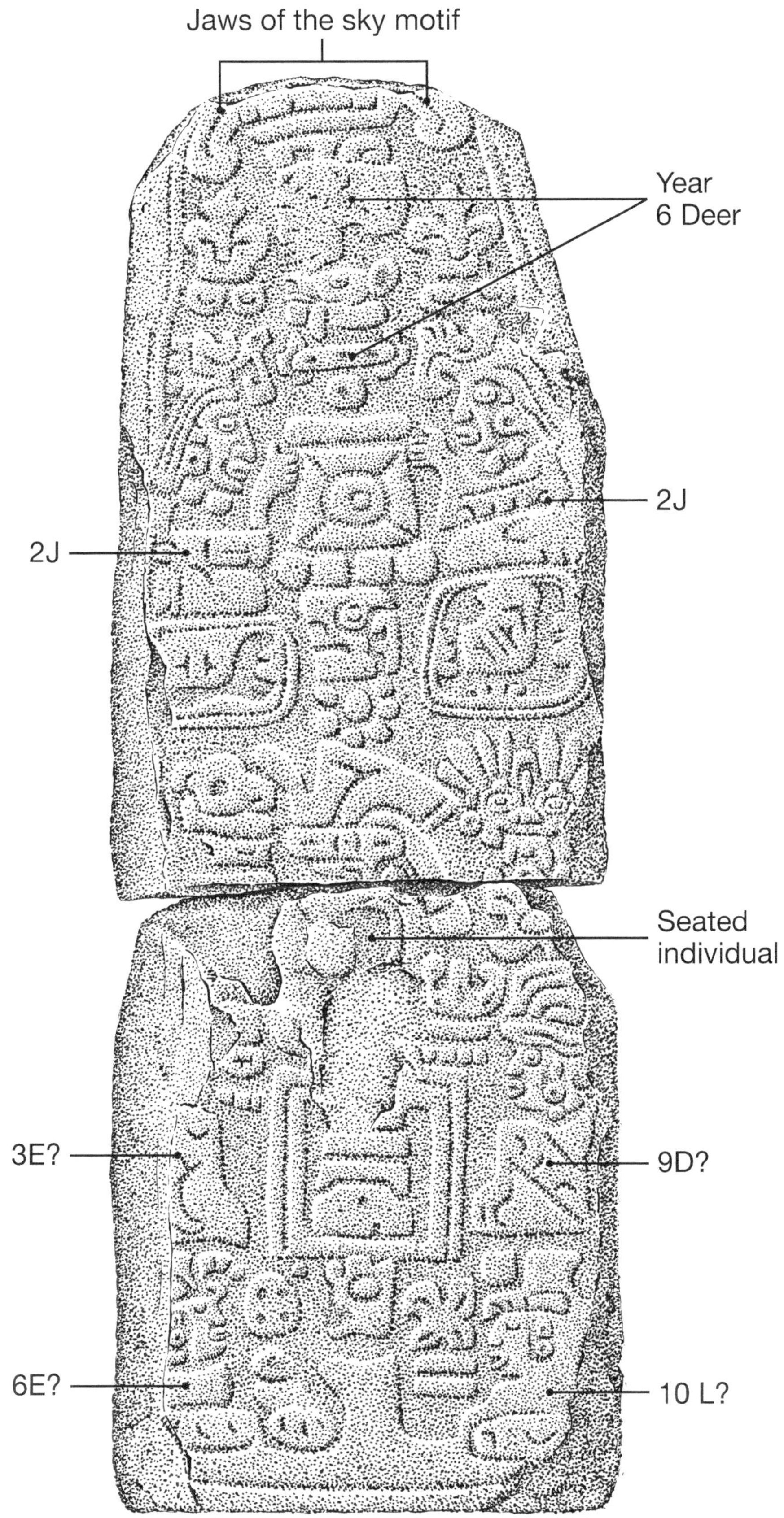

Figure 13.5. Stela 10, discovered in the sunken patio of the North Platform, once reached a height of 2.92 m but has suffered damage. Drawing by Mark Orsen.

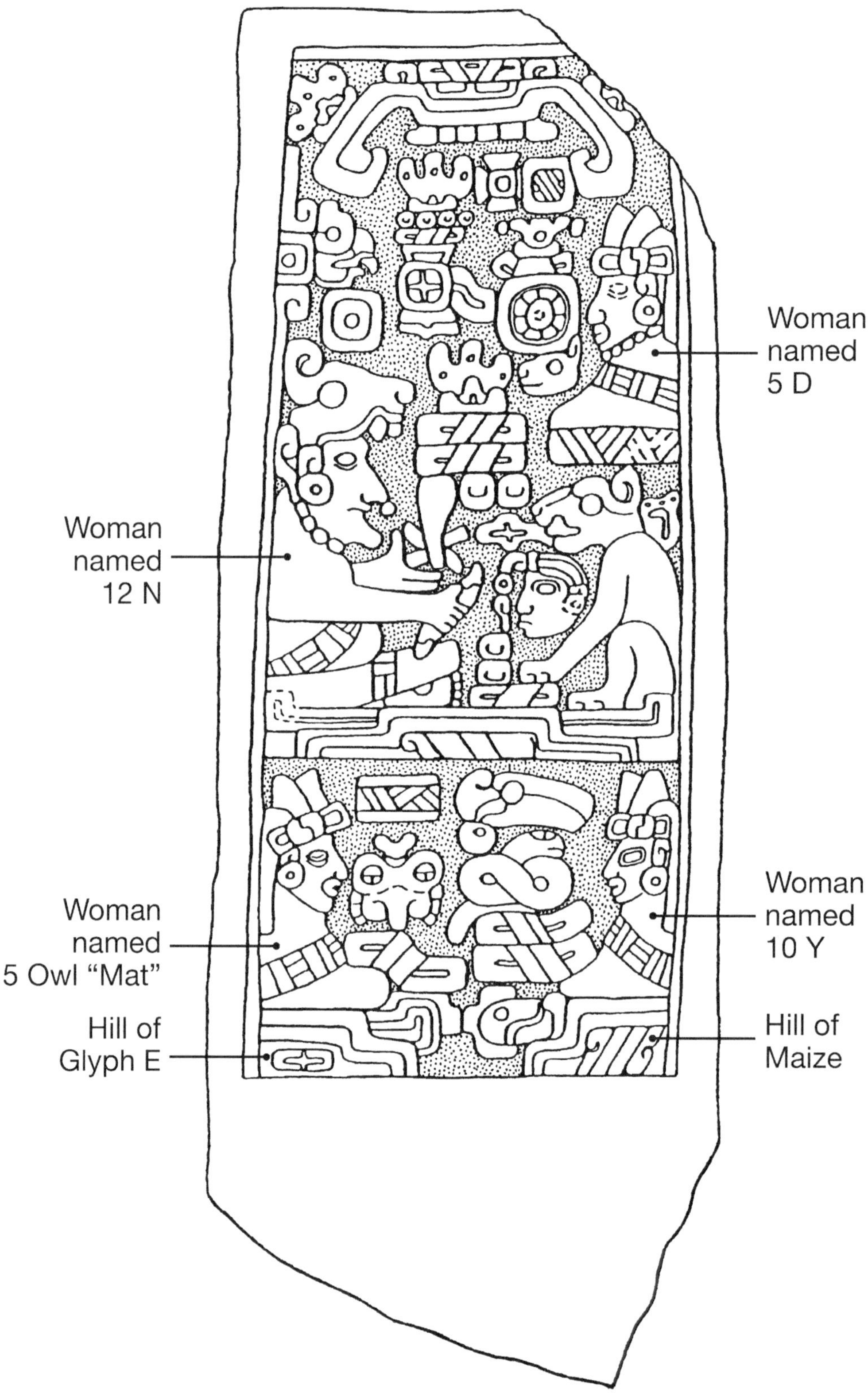

Figure 13.6. Stela 10A at Monte Albán featured at least four women. This stela was found just south of the Patio Vértice Geodésico, on the steps of Temple e (see Figure 13.1). Height: 2.76 m. Redrawn by Kay Clahassey and John Klausmeyer. See also Marcus 2008b: Fig. XII.13; Marcus 2009b: Fig. 23; Urcid et al. 1994: Fig. 20.

The woman on the right sits on a hill sign that may mean "Hill of Maize" or "Place of Maize." Her calendric name appears to be 10 Serpent (10Y), and her nickname includes the head of a bird.

Above 5 Owl and 10 Serpent we see the second generation, two people who share (i.e. sit on) the same hill sign. An old woman named 12N seems to be a key person in this register, since she is shown conducting a rite (we infer this because she is manipulating two objects, one in each hand). Lady 12N wears a prominent earspool and jade necklace; her headdress resembles the head of a deer. She faces someone who appears to be a metamorphosed lord, a person named 7Ñ (a head with the hair gathered together above the forehead). This lord seems to have been transformed into a jaguar, and emanating from his mouth is the blood motif we have seen at many sites.

The third generation on Stela 10A, shown in the uppermost register, features just one person—a seated woman with the calendric name 5 Reed (5D) and a nickname formed by two hieroglyphs. On the left edge we see the familiar frame with a scroll that defines these scenes as genealogical. To the right of the scroll is another nickname that perhaps includes a bird head.

Stela 10A also includes the year sign 9N, which, in conjunction with the Maltese cross (Glyph I), may specify a commemorative mortuary date. Clearly the Jaws of the Sky motif, the Maltese cross, the scroll along the edge of the frame, and the multiple registers all reinforce the genealogical theme of noble descent.

The Jaws of the Sky at the top of the stela displays Glyph N in a location where we often see leaves, jade beads, shells, or other motifs. The bar at the very top of the Jaws motif and the Glyph N to either side presumably refer to an apical ancestor whose name was 5N (who is named here but not depicted).

One plausible explanation for Stela 10A is that it was commissioned by Lady 5 Reed to provide her dynastic credentials. To do so she mentions at least two previous generations. She used the middle register of the stela to feature her elderly mother and deceased father—arguably a former ruler who, in death, had metamorphosed into a jaguar.

Lady 5 Reed used the lower register of the stela to honor two senior aunts or grandmothers, who apparently came to Monte Albán from two different places. This monument underscores the fact that the Zapotec reckoned descent in both male and female lines. It also calls our attention to the likelihood that during a period when Monte Albán's power may have been waning, royal or noble women were brought in from other important places.

On the opposite side of Stela 10A (not illustrated), the text seems to record the year that (1) a mortuary offering was made and (2) the ascension of an ancestor took place. The year is given as Year 13M, and a bird is associated with the year sign. A second bird is associated prominently with the Jaws of the Sky. Significantly, a series of footprints ascend both to the bird and to the Jaws of the Sky.

We see, in addition, the Maltese cross, the hieroglyph we have previously associated with commemorative offerings to the dead. We cannot be sure who is being commemorated; our only clue is a mat sign, which could refer to one individual's nickname.

Other Restricted-Access Texts

Tombs are the ideal places for horizontal propaganda (see Chapter 11). Only a small number of people, most of them nobles, could fit inside a tomb to see the murals and the underside of a lintel; and when the tomb door was carved on its inner surface, only the deceased himself (or a visitor exiting the tomb) could see the text. Such was the case with the lintels to be described below.

The Lintel of Tomb 10, Monte Albán

Tomb 10 was excavated by Alfonso Caso during the 1931–1932 field season. This Period IIIb–IV tomb had a painted lintel with hieroglyphs (Figure 13.7). The three prominent glyphs are: (1) the name of the family's apical ancestor—12N—which appears at the center of the lintel atop a sacred box; and (2) a flanking pair of glyphs (5M and 7E) that may supply the names of a man and woman buried in the tomb. More than two skeletons, however, were found in the tomb (see Caso 1932c; Caso 1965b:865), likely an indication of more than one reopening. Below the name of the apical ancestor, 12N, is the possible depiction of a sacred box like those we noted in the murals of Tombs 104 and 105 at Monte Albán.

This Tomb 10 lintel is reminiscent of those in Tomb 28 at Yagul (see Chapter 15), in which an apical ancestor is mentioned at the center of a lintel, flanked by the names of a marital pair. The painted lintel of Tomb 10 at Monte Albán shows the name of an apical ancestor at the center of the lintel, between a pair of glyphs that likely give the names of a married couple. In the case of Tomb 10, however, determining which name goes with the man and which goes with the woman is difficult to determine, since the individuals themselves are not depicted (see Caso 1965b: Figure 29).

The Lintel of Tomb 50, Monte Albán

Caso found Tomb 50 to the south of the South Platform at Monte Albán, in an area of the site called Siete Venado. The tomb's façade has been illustrated in earlier publications (Caso and Bernal 1952: Figure 122; Marquina 1951: Lámina 96).

In the center of the façade we see a front-facing bat. Flanking the bat are two hieroglyphs in rectangular boxes; included is the same glyph that sometimes appears in hill signs as two scrolls arranged diagonally.

The Tomb 50 lintel has a band of green waves or volutes painted on a red background. Previously we saw similar bands of waves on a monument at San Lorenzo Cacaotepec (see Figure 7.8, Chapter 7). Painted volutes also occur in the murals of Tombs 103 and 112 at Monte Albán, in Tomb A at Xoxocotlán, and Tomb 5 at Cerro de la Campana (Miller 1995; Seler 1991; Urcid and Sellen 2009). Some of these waves seem to have the eyes of a

Figure 13.7. This painted lintel (green on a red background) was placed above the entrance to Tomb 10 at Monte Albán. In the center we see the name of an apical ancestor (possibly 12N), seemingly sitting atop a sacred box. The flanking pair of glyphs—5M and 7E—likely provide the names of a married couple. Redrawn by John Klausmeyer from Caso 1936:234 and Caso 1965b: Fig. 29.

crocodile and the waves themselves seem to relate to the watery abode of Chilla, the Zapotec cayman or crocodile.

The Lintel of Tomb 158, Monte Albán

Tomb 158, dating to Period IIIb–IV, was discovered on a terrace to the northeast of the North Platform (Acosta 1974:76; Caso et al. 1967: Table XVI). According to Acosta and Obregón de la Parra, this tomb included a lintel carved on two surfaces: (1) on the narrow outer edge facing the visitor, and (2) on the underside (Acosta 1974: Figure 25).

The text on the outer edge refers to three individuals. To separate their hieroglyphic names, the artisan left uncarved spaces (Figure 13.8). The name in the middle is 12 Maize (12J). The outermost hieroglyph at both ends of the lintel is the bag glyph, often signifying deceased individuals.

The sequence of hieroglyphic names is 3 Reed (3D) + 12 Maize (12J) + 8 Reed (8D). This arrangement—the centrally placed name of an apical ancestor, flanked by the names of a marital pair—is similar to that on the lintels of Yagul's Tomb 28 (see Chapter 15). However, in those cases the bag glyph does not precede and follow the flanking names. Although 12 Maize might be the name of the apical ancestor, it is worth considering a second possibility: that 12 Maize is the offspring of a deceased marital pair, both of whose names are associated with the bag glyph.

To view the other carved surface of the Tomb 158 lintel—the underside—we have to assume either the position of a departing visitor or that of the deceased occupant himself (Figure 13.9). Once in this position we see a Glyph C at lower left, perhaps associated with the coefficient 3 or 4. Above is a hand grasping an unidentified object, associated with three other items. At the bottom (center) is a hill sign. At the very center of the lintel is the name 2Z (2 Water). Above we see the Year 3M (3 Lightning), and then the bag glyph at the upper right. The full reading of this important lintel has yet to be made, but its location and content both suggest that funerary rites were conducted and an ancestor was commemorated.

Figure 13.8. This carving was found on the lintel of Tomb 158 at Monte Albán. The calendric names of three individuals are shown, and to separate them the sculptor has left uncarved spaces between them. On the left, the bag glyph precedes 3 Reed; in the middle, we see 12 Maize; on the right is 8 Reed, followed by the bag glyph. Although such a glyphic arrangement (a central name + flanking names) is usually interpreted as an apical ancestor with his descendants to either side, there is at least one other possibility—that is, 3 Reed and 8 Reed may be the deceased parents of 12 Maize. I suggest this because the bag glyph begins and ends the text and is associated with 3 Reed and 8 Reed. Dimensions: 88 x 12 x 52 cm. Redrawn by John Klausmeyer from Acosta 1974: Fig. 25.

Figure 13.9. The carved underside of the Tomb 158 lintel. On the left we see Glyph C, possibly associated with the coefficient 3 or 4. At the bottom center are a hill sign and the day sign 2 Water. Above we see the year 3M (3 Lightning). Redrawn by John Klausmeyer from Acosta 1974: Fig. 25.

Figure 13.10. The edge of the lintel from Tomb 155 at Monte Albán was carved with a row of four hieroglyphs—1E, the bag glyph, 8E, and 5B. Redrawn by John Klausmeyer from Acosta 1974: Fig. 22.

Figure 13.11. The underside of the Tomb 155 lintel displayed the Year 1 Lightning (Acosta 1974: Fig. 23). In the tomb's south wall niche was another carved stone with the date 13A. Redrawn by John Klausmeyer from Acosta 1974: Fig. 21C.

The Lintel of Tomb 155, Monte Albán

Tomb 155 was exposed during the fourteenth season at Monte Albán (1945–1946) by Henri Lehmann. One of the key finds in this tomb was a lintel with hieroglyphs carved on two of its surfaces.

On the lintel's edge is the bag glyph, often used to signify death. The bag is carved between the hieroglyphic names 1E and 8E (Figure 13.10). The name of a third individual, possibly 5B, follows. The jaguar head (Glyph B) faces downward, perhaps signifying that he is deceased. We cannot determine which of the names are those of men and which are of women, since there are no images or depictions of them (Acosta 1974: Figure 23). The arrangement, however, suggests that the name of an apical ancestor (8E) is flanked by the names of a marital pair (1E and 5B).

The underside of this same lintel shows only shows a possible year sign and year bearer (Figure 13.11). This date may mark the year of interment of one or more of the principal occupants. The year seems to be 1M (1 Lightning); note that this sign could only be viewed by someone exiting the tomb or by the deceased himself (Acosta 1974: Figure 23).

Monte Albán's Investment in Art and Writing from AD 600 to 900

In this era at Monte Albán there were few examples of vertical propaganda. Gone were the massive narrative displays of hundreds of sacrificed captives. Gone were the scores of subjugated and tribute-paying towns. Now the dominant propaganda effort was to establish one's genealogical credentials by listing near, distant, and apical ancestors.

In this horizontal propaganda campaign, marital pairs and individual female ancestors played a major role. Even noble women who came to Monte Albán from other communities were featured in genealogies, making it likely that former Tier 2 centers were developing their own dynastic lineages.

14

Monuments from the Valle Grande (Zaachila-Zimatlán)

During the period from AD 600 to 900, ritual obligations, funerals, and the exchange of sumptuary goods linked noble families to each other in the Valle Grande and well beyond. Among the towns producing carved stones were Xoxocotlán, Cuilapan, Zaachila, Noriega, Santa Inés Yatzeche, and Rancho Tejas de Morelos (Figure 14.1).

Ironically, no monuments are known so far from Santo Tomás Jalieza, the largest Period IIIb–IV site in the Valle Grande. The six towns mentioned above, while smaller than Jalieza, nevertheless seem to have been ruled by prestigious noble families. Their elite residences typically consisted of multiple rooms surrounding a private interior patio; below that patio was a family crypt whose door could be moved to one side to allow relatives to reenter. The most noble of these families commissioned murals and carved stones for display in their residences and tombs. Their tombs often included references to apical ancestors and other relatives.

Xoxocotlán

About four kilometers from the base of Monte Albán lies the archaeological site of Xoxocotlán. It covers 115 hectares on prime agricultural land adjacent to the Río Atoyac. Marshall Saville's 1899 map of the site shows many mounds that can no longer be seen (Figure 14.2; see also Blanton et al. 1982:255). Some of these mounds were deliberately removed when the Oaxaca airport extended its runway. Others were gradually plowed away by farmers.

The earliest excavations at Xoxocotlán were conducted by Fernando Sologuren in 1886 and Marshall Saville in 1897–1898. These pioneers ended up providing us with the first detailed information on Zapotec funerary rites and anniversaries.

> According to early accounts regarding the customs of the Zapotecan Indians, which have been verified by the explorations of the Loubat Expeditions, their funeral ceremonies were as follows: When an important person died, the body was placed in a stone chamber, dressed, and with various personal ornaments and objects belonging to the deceased. Food and drink were placed in or near the tomb to sustain the deceased on his journey to the other world. Once a year, for four years, his friends came to the tomb and made fresh offerings of food and drink. At the expiration of this time the flesh had decayed. Sometimes then the bones were gathered together and placed in niches, but sometimes they were allowed to remain on the floor. Often they were painted red. (Saville 1904:59–60)

This passage reveals some important practices—annual visits for four years, followed by the gathering up and painting of the bones—which explain much of the archaeological data. As the years passed, anniversaries of the original interment became increasingly important. Among today's Zapotec of Tehuantepec, as in the Classic era in the Valley of Oaxaca, these anniversaries continue to be very important occasions (see Royce 2011).

Saville (1899, 1904) was one of the first to focus on the arrangement of Zapotec funerary urns in and around tombs. These urns are probably the most distinctive ceramic artifact ever made by the potters of the Valley of Oaxaca. Saville showed that the Zapotec urn was often associated with funerary rites honoring ancestors, *Cociyo*, and the realm of lightning, rain, and storms. These urns were used for rituals in other settings as well.

Urns filled some of the roles played previously by the hand-modeled figurines used for ritual scenes (Caso and Bernal 1952; Flannery and Marcus 1976b; Marcus 1998a; Marcus and Flannery 1996). Urns could be used to (1) give the spirit of an ancestor a venue to occupy; (2) display an ancestor's calendric name; (3) provide a place where offerings [e.g., liquids, jades, stone figurines] could be stored; (4) depict ancestors after they had been transformed into supernatural beings or deities; and (5) depict the deceased so that he/she could continue to be addressed and manipulated in relationship to other urns arranged in scenes.

When Saville found urns in primary context, he opened the door to a deeper understanding of Zapotec beliefs. Sologuren's and Saville's excavations at Xoxocotlán showed that

(1) urns could be arranged in rows above the tomb;

(2) urns could be placed in exterior tomb niches; and

(3) urns could be placed at tomb entrances where visitors came to eat, drink, burn incense, and conduct rites of remembrance (Figure 14.3).

One contrast between Monte Albán and Xoxocotlán was in the placement of urns. At Monte Albán, urns were usually arranged *inside* the tomb; at Xoxocotlán, urns were found lined up *outside* the tomb. For example, at Xoxocotlán, four or five urns were usually arranged in front of the tomb door or on the roof. At Cuilapan, urns were also placed outside the tomb, sometimes in an exterior niche (see below).

Mound 5 at Xoxocotlán

In Mound 5 at Xoxocotlán, Sologuren exposed a tomb he called Tomb A, located at a depth of five meters below a series of plaster floors and adobe constructions that look to have been the remains of elite residences (Batres 1888; Fahmel Beyer 2005a; Martínez Gracida 1910; Rickards 1910, 1918; Saville 1899; Seler 1960, 1991). Tomb A at Xoxocotlán lies at the same depth below its associated palace as does Tomb 5 at Cerro de la Campana (Chapter 12).

Shortly after Tomb A was opened, Eduard and Caecilie Seler were given a tour of Sologuren's excavation. They and others have published reconstruction drawings of the tomb façade (Figures

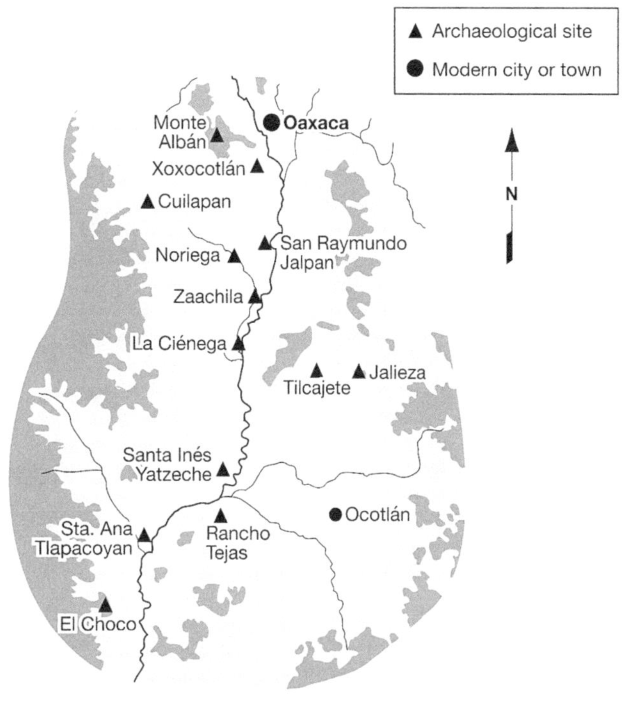

Figure 14.1. Key archaeological sites in the Valle Grande include Xoxocotlán, Cuilapan, and Zaachila. This map by John Klausmeyer was adapted from the 1970 "Mapa de las Localidades del Valle de Oaxaca" by Cecil R. Welte.

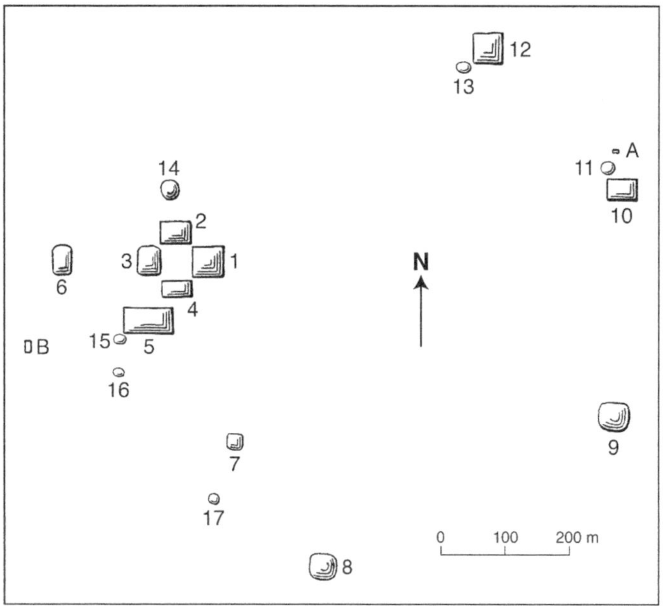

Figure 14.2. The archaeological site of Xoxocotlán lies about four kilometers from Monte Albán. In the 1890s the site covered at least 115 hectares and had many more mounds than we see today. It is fortunate that we have Marshall Saville's 1898 map, shown here, which captured the location of those mounds. Redrawn by John Klausmeyer from Saville 1899: Fig. 8.

Figure 14.3. This row of urns, found on the plaster floor in front of Tomb 1, Mound 7, Xoxocotlán, provides evidence for ritual activity conducted outside the tomb (from Saville 1899:356–357).

14.4, 14.5) (e.g., Peñafiel 1890: Plate 132; Seler 1960, 1991). Not shown in any of these drawings, however, were the five large urns that Sologuren discovered on the roof of the tomb. These urns were arranged in a row and described as being of the "box-and-cover" variety—the base being a square box and the cover a separate lid (Figure 14.6).

Most of the urn lids seem to depict men impersonating *Cociyo* (Saville 1899:353); one of these lids was published by Caso and Bernal (1952: Figure 1). On each lid the man is shown wearing a mask and elaborate feather headdress, with two ears of maize set vertically on either side of his headdress. Below the ears of maize, we see a horizontal squiggle or S-shaped curve, a motif often associated with clouds, lightning, and rain (for example, at Chalcatzingo in Morelos and at various Classic Maya sites, where this motif is referred to as *muyal*).

In the center of the band between these cloud-like sine curves is a prominent Glyph C, a hieroglyph for rain (see Leigh 1966). *Cociyo* has diagnostic elements above his eyes and a bifid tongue, as well as a nasal ornament and/or buccal mask. His arms are extended forward, palms down. Around his neck is an element that Caso and Bernal (1952) interpreted as "sprouting maize." This is plausible, since many depictions of *Cociyo* present us with a complex of iconographic elements that include lightning, clouds, rain, water, maize, and sprouting kernels. The box includes elements that refer to the earth and a crocodile.

These box-and-cover *Cociyo* urns probably constituted sumptuary goods. They occur at only a few sites and in elite contexts at Xoxocotlán, Monte Albán, and Cerro de la Campana. For example, at Monte Albán such urns were recovered in an elite residential area to the south of System M (just west of the South Platform) (Martínez López et al. 1995: Figures 43, 78c, 79). They were also found inside Tomb 5 at Cerro de la Campana (Méndez Martínez 1988).

The noble families who had access to box-and-cover *Cociyo* urns at Xoxocotlán, Monte Albán, and Cerro de la Campana were probably among the most influential of their era. Future researchers should consider studying the distribution of these urns in detail, because they seem to have been reserved for use in the most important rituals conducted by noble families.

The Façade of Tomb A at Xoxocotlán

One reconstruction drawing shows the lintel of Tomb A at Xoxocotlán painted with red volutes or scrolls (see Figure 14.4; see also Seler 1960:335, Abb. 60c and Seler 1991). Similar scrolls appear in the lowest register of the polychrome murals in Tomb 5 at Cerro de la Campana and in Tombs 103 and 112 at Monte

Figure 14.4. In his 1886 excavations in Mound 5 at Xoxocotlán, Fernando Sologuren discovered Tomb A. The tomb façade was embellished with stucco modeling and paint. At left we see the name 5 Owl and at right Glyphs M + E (unaccompanied by numerals). At the center is the depiction of a possible apical ancestor that can be compared to similarly positioned apical ancestors above the lintels of Tomb 5 at Cerro de la Campana and Tombs 3 and 4 at Cuilapan. Drawing by John Klausmeyer, adapted from Seler 1960:335, 1991: Fig. 60c and Bernal 1958:41–45.

Albán (Caso 1938: Plano No. 15). In another reconstruction drawing of the Tomb A façade (see Figure 14.5) we see a band of rectilinear, greca-like elements instead of volutes and scrolls (Peñafiel 1890: Plate 132).

Above the Tomb A lintel was a ledge decorated with stucco images and hieroglyphs. At the far left was a bar standing for the number five; then we see Glyph F, an owl, which may stand for "night," the second day of the 260-day calendar (see Figure 14.5). Caso interpreted this combination of signs as the date 5 Owl. At the center of the ledge was a front-facing composite figure—a possible metamorphosed apical ancestor (depicted as a bat-jaguar) whose hands almost touch the painted band of volutes on the lintel. Above the bat-jaguar's face was an elaborate headdress of *Cociyo*, its feathers extending well above the top of the tomb, similar to the headdress on the Tomb 190 façade at Lambityeco (see Chapter 15).

Tomb A also displayed a smaller stucco mask of *Cociyo* set inside the shelf above the lintel, probably with the name 1M (although the number one can no longer be seen). Still farther to the right we see Caso's Glyph E (shown in Peñafiel 1890: Plate 132).

Caso (1928:105) concluded that the stuccoed elements flanking the central bat-jaguar figure on the lintel included a calendar date—5F (5 Owl) in the Year 1E. If Caso is correct, that year could be the deceased's date of death or interment. Based on other Period IIIb–IV tombs, however, one can offer an alternative interpretation—5 Owl might be the name of an important person buried in this tomb, with the bat-jaguar and *Cociyo* figures serving as his divine patron and apical ancestor. The final sign, possibly 1E, may refer to 5 Owl's wife. This arrangement—a centrally placed apical ancestor flanked by the names of a marital pair—is common in this period.

The Door of Tomb A

The entrance to Tomb A was sealed with a large square stone door (Figure 14.7). Early drawings of this stone were published by Batres (1888: Lámina VI, no. 4), Martínez Gracida (1910: Vol. II, Plate 49), and Rickards (1910: Lámina 113a). A photograph was later published by Caso (1928: Figure 78).

At the top of this carved door we see the Jaws of the Sky, a motif associated with the Zapotec concept of *cozaana* or noble descent (Córdova [1578a]1942). The Tomb A door displays something akin to a trompe l'oeil, an optical illusion that can be interpreted in two ways—(1) as a single animal in full frontal view, and (2) as two profile heads facing each other. Given the animal's large size and its placement at the center of the stone,

Figure 14.5. This reconstruction drawing of the Tomb A façade at Xoxocotlán can be compared with that in Figure 14.4. This version was adapted from Peñafiel (1890: Plate 132) by John Klausmeyer.

this is likely an apical ancestor named 7 Crocodile (7 Chilla). This Xoxocotlán depiction shares a number of attributes with the stucco figure of 10 Crocodile set above the entrance to Tomb 5 at Cerro de la Campana (e.g., Miller 1995: Figure 52; Urcid 2001). Other pairs of profile heads can be seen in Zapotec art—some are shown face to face sharing a nose, as on Tomb A at Xoxocotlán and at Zaachila (see Alcina Franch 1969: Figure 109, Plate 64; Dupaix 1969; Urcid and Sellen 2009). Some are shown back to back sharing an earflare (e.g., Stela 1 at Monte Albán). These profile heads are conceptually related to the tenoned heads that are carved on three surfaces, with profile heads on either side of a three-dimensional stone with the nose on the front (or third) surface (e.g., Yagul, Zaachila, and Lambityeco; see Chapter 15). This tomb door shows an unfolded or split image of the crocodile; this same animal could also be depicted on the square bases of the box-and-cover urns and depicted on the three surfaces of a tenon.

On the Tomb A door we also see two pairs of crosses, one above another. Since these crosses or plus signs were next to the central figure's ears, Caso called them "orejeras de turquesa" (turquoise ear ornaments). Caso (1928:106) also compared the crosses to his Glyph E. I would suggest that these plus signs stand for drops of blood, because similar crosses are sometimes shown near the ears or mouths of bats, crocodiles, jaguars, and other animals (e.g., Boos 1966a, 1966b; Caso and Bernal 1952: Figures 113, 118). Sellen, too, has argued that the Middle Formative blood motif (circle + triangle) seen at Fábrica San José and San José Mogote gradually changed over time, and by the Classic period had become a circle + diamond, sometimes a circle + diamond + cross (Sellen 2011: Figures 22–23).

Finally, on the lower half of the Tomb A door we see at least three hieroglyphs that could be personal names taken from the 260-day calendar. At the left is a sign that Caso interpreted as 6M (but which looks more like 5M or 5 Lightning) (Caso 1928: Figure 18, VIII). At the center is 1C or 6C, above a disk with four sine curves or clouds. At the lower right is a sign that Caso (1928: Figure 4, VII) interpreted as 7B, but which might actually be 6M.

In Front of the Door of Tomb A

In front of the Tomb A door was an enclosure with two steps leading down into the tomb (this can be compared with the approach to Tomb 28 at Yagul in Chapter 15). The side walls of this Xoxocotlán enclosure were perpendicular to the tomb façade. Since Saville (1899:354) thought that the deposits in this enclosure were undisturbed, he paid particular attention to

Figure 14.6. Six examples of "box-and-cover" urns from three sites in the Valley of Oaxaca. These urns seem to have been sumptuary items of considerable importance. The cover or lid depicts *Cociyo* with a headdress containing Glyph C (Rain), maize cobs, and squiggles and sine curves that relate to rain and lightning in the celestial realm. On *Cociyo's* chest is a motif that Caso and Bernal (1952) and Sellen (2002) linked to maize and maize fields. The lower half of each urn bears terrestrial and aquatic motifs linked to the cayman or crocodile that the Zapotec called *chilla*. *a, b,* urns found in Tomb A, Mound 5 at Xoxocotlán; *c–e,* urns found west of the South Platform at Monte Albán; *f,* an urn found in Tomb 5 at Cerro de la Campana. Redrawn by John Klausmeyer from Caso and Bernal 1952: Figs. 1, 59 and Martínez López et al. 1995: Figs. 43, 79.

Figure 14.7. This stone served as the door of Tomb A in Mound 5 at Xoxocotlán. At the top we see the Jaws of the Sky; below that motif we see an apical ancestor named 7 Chilla. Below that apical ancestor we see 1C or 6C (1 Rain or 6 Rain). In the lower left corner of the stone is the calendric name 5M; at lower right is 6M. It is possible that 7 Chilla and 1 Rain were a founding couple, while Glyphs 5M and 6M refer to another marital pair. In the center (at the bottom of the stone) is a disk with four sine curves that in other contexts seem to refer to clouds. Drawing by Mark Orsen.

the thick accumulation of material in front of the tomb door. That deposit included "objects apparently thrown in during some ceremony; all were covered with vermilion and the earth itself was highly colored." Such a ceremony might have taken place on the anniversary of the original interment. Saville found many small vessels (bowls and cups) that could have contained beverages to be consumed during this ceremony. In addition, he found a number of incense burners. Saville discovered filed human teeth with inlays, as well as fragments of human crania, hand bones, and foot bones, all of which were covered with vermilion pigment. Twenty-six jadeite beads were also found. We have no way of knowing whether these human remains resulted from (1) the original occupants, disturbed by visitors when they created room to insert new family members, or (2) an incomplete burial newly placed in front of the tomb door.

Mound 7 at Xoxocotlán

Sologuren excavated Tomb 1 in Xoxocotlán's Mound 7. In front of the tomb he found a row of five large urns. Saville (1899:355–356) described the discovery of these urns as follows:

> About 10 feet from the end of the [large clay] tube [a possible psychoduct allowing the deceased to interact with descendants], resting directly on the cement floor at the center of the mound, were five large funeral urns, representing seated figures, placed in a row facing the west. The urn in the center has a remarkably well modeled face, undoubtedly a portrait of some ancient Zapotec personage. The two on either side are of the same general size and character, with the exception of the face which is covered with a mask in the form of a grotesque face, probably the conventionalized serpent, as the bifurcated tongue is one of the most prominent characteristics.

The urns with bifurcated tongues are, in fact, excellent examples of *Cociyo*, each with a Glyph C in his headdress (Figures 14.8, 14.9). Around the neck of each *Cociyo* hangs a pectoral or pendant with a human face, which may be a mask or the trophy head of an enemy. Four large shells rest on his breechclout. Caso and Bernal (1952:17) described these urns as follows:

> El elemento más constante en la representación del *Cocijo*, es una máscara que cubre prácticamente todas las facciones del rostro. Los ojos aparecen entre unas cejas de forma almenada, como si representaron cerros, al estilo zapoteca, en la parte superior, y otra ceja en la parte inferior, que termina en una voluta que se curva sobre la mejilla. La nariz está cubierta por una gruesa placa que se une a las cejas inferiores y por otra más delgada que se une a la máscara bucal. A veces aparece, abajo de estas dos placas, una línea, pero ya generalmente forma parte de la máscara bucal y de ella sale la lengua bífida de la serpiente. Por la parte superior, la máscara que cubre la nariz, termina a veces con dos tapones de nariz que rematan en unas cintas que se doblan formando unas volutas alrededor de la comisura de la boca.

The urn that occupies the central position in the group of five was illustrated by Caso and Bernal (1952:46, Figure 63), who described it as "Urna del Dios del Maíz." After looking at Saville's sketches, however, I consider the objects in the headdress not to be maize cobs, but rather small jaguar heads. The individual on the urn is seated on a platform with a hill sign incised into it.

In general appearance, this centrally placed urn at Xoxocotlán is similar to the one inserted into the façade of Tomb 104 at Monte Albán (Caso and Bernal 1952: Figure 72). Like the Tomb 104 urn, the Xoxocotlán urn probably depicts a historic personage, perhaps an apical ancestor or the occupant of the tomb.

On the ceramic tube (or psychoduct) outside Tomb 1, a remarkable urn depicting a woman came to light (Figure 14.10). This woman wears a feather headdress with plaited cords decorating its front (Saville 1904:56, on the right). She is shown with her arms crossed in front of her. Her earspools have the same M-shaped elements often associated with ear ornaments worn by *Cociyo*. Her *huipil* is beautifully edged with beads or shells.

Mound 8 at Xoxocotlán

Saville made a center-line trench into the western side of Xoxocotlán's Mound 8. About five meters from the start of his trench, Saville discovered the front wall of a tomb (Tomb 2) still sealed by a large stone of irregular shape. In a niche above the lintel of the tomb was an urn painted red. The stones around this urn, as well as the lintel and both sides of the doorway, were also painted red (Saville 1899: Plate 22).

Saville then began excavating another trench on the eastern side of the mound so that he could expose the back of the tomb. Here he reports finding "the largest specimen of terra-cotta ever found in America." Saville (1899:357) concluded that this enormous ceramic figure was a warrior with the head, upper torso, and right arm fallen, but lying face upward. The figure's open mouth revealed filed teeth painted white; its eyes were painted white and red. Its head was covered with a turban of feathers, and its nose was ornamented with a long cylindrical bead, attached by a string fastened at top and bottom through the septum. The figure's breast was painted red and white and ornamented with curious designs made by circular indentations. The figure wore sandals, had bells around its ankles, and had its toenails and fingernails painted white. The figure's right arm was bent in the appropriate position to grasp a spear or staff. Unfortunately, I have been unable to find a photo of this ceramic figure, said to have been "six feet tall."

Five urns were found in a row on the roof of Tomb 2, just above a series of modeled stucco figures; all five were of the box-and-lid variety. One of those urns (Figure 14.11) was a *Cociyo* figure (American Museum of Natural History #30/07101), cruder than any of those in the façade of Tomb 3 in Mound 9. This Tomb 2 *Cociyo* urn, which had a Glyph C in his feather headdress, wore an unusual necklace.

Figure 14.8. Five urns were placed in front of Tomb 1 in Mound 7 at Xoxocotlán. This urn shows *Cociyo* with a headdress that includes Glyph C, as well as stylized maize cobs. On his earspools we see motifs associated with crocodiles, lightning, and rain, and on his chest we see a mask or trophy head. Courtesy of the American Museum of Natural History, catalogue #30/06332. Height: 55.9 cm.

Figure 14.9. One of five urns found in front of Tomb 1 in Mound 7 at Xoxocotlán. It is not clear whether this urn shows *Cociyo* or a human impersonating him. On his earspools we see a motif associated with crocodiles and lightning; we also see a mask or trophy head on his chest. Courtesy of the American Museum of Natural History, catalogue #30/06333. Height: 52.07 cm.

Figure 14.10. One of five urns found in front of Tomb 1 in Mound 7 at Xoxocotlán. Unlike the urns in Figures 14.8 and 14.9, this one represents a woman. However, like the *Cociyo* figures nearby, she also has earspools decorated with symbols that relate to crocodiles, lightning, and rain. Courtesy of the American Museum of Natural History, catalogue #30/06331. Height: 39.5 cm.

Figure 14.11. This *Cociyo* urn from Tomb 2 in Mound 8 at Xoxocotlán includes a Glyph C at the center of its headdress. Courtesy of the American Museum of Natural History, catalogue #30/07101. Height: 25.4 cm.

Figure 14.12. Here we see the façade of Tomb 3 in Mound 9 at Xoxocotlán. Unlike other Xoxocotlán tombs excavated by Sologuren and Saville, this tomb had a lintel with hieroglyphs, as well as five *Cociyo* urn covers set on a shelf above the lintel. The five covers had been separated from their boxlike bases, which were thrown into a ceremonial deposit in front of the tomb door. The carved lintel gives the calendric names of 15 ancestors. Drawing by Kay Clahassey, based on photos and sketches in Marshall Saville's files at the American Museum of Natural History.

Mound 9 at Xoxocotlán

While digging in Mound 9, Saville found a third tomb that he designated Tomb 3. Just east of the center of the mound, he found a flight of stone steps leading down to a plaster floor. A meter or so in front of the lowest step was the front wall of Tomb 3, which Saville called "the most important tomb ever found in southern Mexico." His assertion was based on the presence of three primary features: (1) the five unusual urn lids set into the shelf on the entablature above the tomb entrance (Figure 14.12); (2) a hieroglyphic lintel above the tomb door, which seems to list the names of 15 ancestors; and (3) the remarkable painted murals inside the tomb.

Tomb 3

An important feature of the Tomb 3 façade at Xoxocotlán was the shelf where five *Cociyo* urns were fastened (Figures 14.12, 14.13). All these urns were painted red, and on either side of each centrally placed *Cociyo* image was a tiny stucco skull. Although these skulls were fully consistent with the theme of death, they seem only to have occurred with Tomb 3.

The *Cociyo* figures fastened to the façade were not complete urns; they were merely the lids from five box-and-lid urns (Figure 14.14). Evidently at the time the tomb was closed and its roof was covered with earth, the urn bases had been thrown into the fill in front of the tomb door. Why the bases were treated this way is unknown; however, it may be that each base once contained

Figure 14.13. The façade of Tomb 3 in Mound 9 at Xoxocotlán displayed the covers of *Cociyo* urns. Flanking the central urn, we see two stucco skulls. Below the urns is the lintel listing the names of 15 ancestors.

some liquid that was to be offered as a libation, after which the bases themselves were discarded in the fill.

Why was five a recurrent number at Xoxocotlán? *Cociyo* was often accompanied by his four assistants—hail, wind, clouds, and rain. It is possible when we see five *Cociyos*, the message was that one supreme *Cociyo* was overseeing his four assistants. Similar groups of four assistants can be found in the cosmology of other Mesoamerican groups. For example, the Maya believed in four "lightnings" or *chaakob*, each associated with a world direction and different color. The Aztec believed in four *tlaloque*, who accompanied the supreme storm-and-lightning supernatural they called Tlaloc (Marcus 2006c).

In addition to the box-like bases of *Cociyo* urns in front of the Tomb 3 door, Saville found at least seven incense burners (*sahumadores*) in the fill, as well as plates and bowls that could have been used as vessels for serving food. Let us look first at the iconography of the five lids from *Cociyo* urns. They show us that the ancient Zapotec associated lightning with rain, clouds, water, sprouting maize, ears of maize, and corn silk. Many of these attributes can be seen on the Tomb 3 *Cociyos*, whose headdresses also show nine large feathers. To either side of these feathers was an ear of maize that has been linked to the race Confite Puntiagudo/Canguil by Eubanks (1999:134–135). Around each *Cociyo*'s neck there was also a symbol that Caso and Bernal (1952) interpreted as maize or sprouting maize. Each *Cociyo* was given an extra nose ornament and a bifid tongue (Figures 14.15, 14.16, 14.17).

Figure 14.14. This box-like base, set on pedestal feet, is the lower half of a *Cociyo* urn. It was found in Section D of Mound 9 at Xoxocotlán. The central motif represents the cayman or crocodile the Zapotec called Chilla (see Glyph CC in Tables 3.1, 3.5). Courtesy of the American Museum of Natural History, catalogue #30/06339. Height: 25.4 cm.

Figure 14.15. Here we see one of the urn covers fastened to the façade of Tomb 3 in Mound 9 at Xoxocotlán. This human impersonator of *Cociyo* wears an elaborate headdress featuring Glyph C (Rain) in the center, maize cobs and squiggles for rain to either side of Glyph C, ear ornaments related to lightning, and a necklace depicting a maize field. Courtesy of the American Museum of Natural History, catalogue #30/06334. Height: 47.6 cm.

Figure 14.16. Another urn cover showing a man impersonating *Cociyo*. This urn lid was fastened to the façade of Tomb 3 in Mound 9 at Xoxocotlán. See Saville 1899:361; 1904: pp. 54, 56. Courtesy of the American Museum of Natural History, catalogue #30/06335. Height: 47 cm.

Figure 14.17. A third example of the *Cociyo* urn covers fastened to the façade of Tomb 3 in Mound 9 at Xoxocotlán (Saville 1899:362). Courtesy of the American Museum of Natural History, catalogue #30/06336. Height: 43.8 cm.

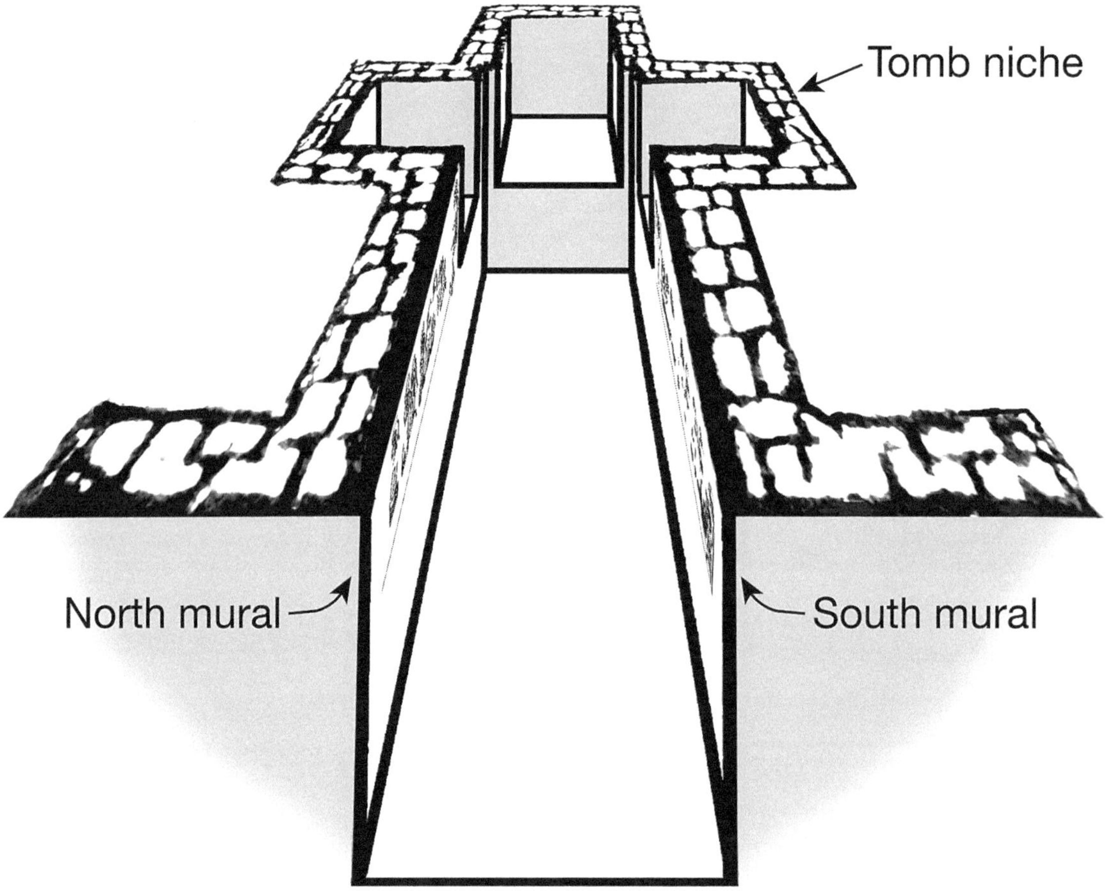

Figure 14.18. This reconstruction drawing by John Klausmeyer shows the location of the murals on the walls of Tomb 3 in Mound 9 at Xoxocotlán.

Glyph C, often associated with *Cociyo*, can be seen at the center of the headband on each urn lid. To either side of the Glyph C we see squiggly lines of appliquéd clay that run horizontally; such squiggles may have represented lightning, clouds, or running water to the Zapotec. Additional squiggly lines of appliquéd clay run vertically along the side flanges. All five lids show *Cociyo* resting his hands palm-side down.

Finally, near the eastern end of his trench, Saville found a large urn with a box-like base whose lid resembled those forming a row on the shelf of the tomb façade.

The door of Tomb 3 had been sealed with a large stone. On the floor of the tomb were several skeletons, accompanied by incense burners and vessels that could have held food. All of the niches of this tomb contained human remains, perhaps gathered up from previous interments. The bones in the main chamber were said to be a disarticulated torso and limb bones, over which crania had been placed. All the bones had been covered with red pigment, and additional pottery vessels and incense burners had been placed in front of them (Saville 1899:359).

The Murals inside Tomb 3

The north and south walls of Tomb 3 bore faded polychrome murals (Figure 14.18). Saville reports that the tomb had been reentered and repainted in antiquity, adding that:

> The walls of the chamber were formerly entirely covered with plaster, but during the lapse of centuries, probably accelerated by the action of earthquakes, the greater part had fallen off. They had been entirely covered with paintings in various bright colors, traces of which are distinctly visible. Over these bright-colored paintings a thin coating of stucco had been laid, upon which, in black outlines, were painted a series of human figures draped in flowing garments, the *tilma* of ancient Mexico. There were also complicated designs, possibly hieroglyphics. Many of the faces of the figures

Figure 14.19. This mural appears on the south wall of Tomb 3 in Mound 9 at Xoxocotlán. We see eight women facing the back wall of the tomb. Although poorly preserved, a bundled corpse is propped up in a wooden funerary crate (at far right). This drawing by John Klausmeyer was adapted from Marshall Saville's sketch.

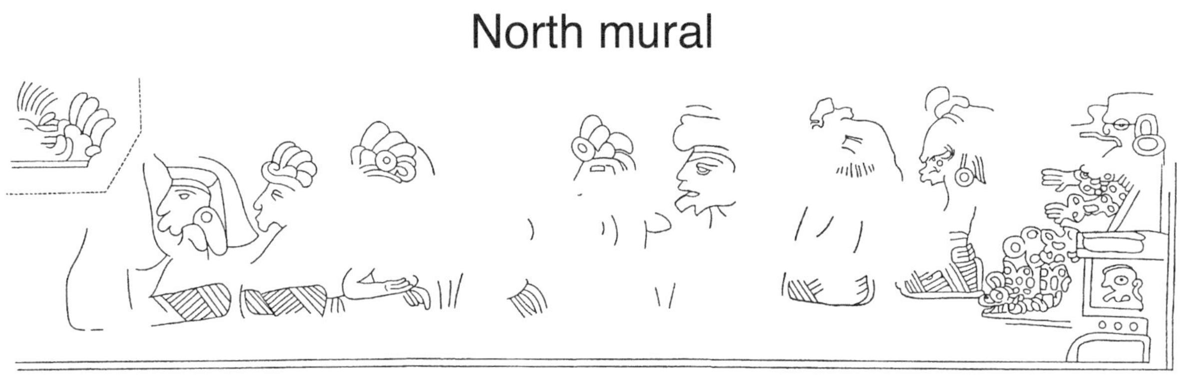

Figure 14.20. Like the south mural of Tomb 3 in Mound 9 at Xoxocotlán, this north mural shows eight seated women; here, however, they face the tomb entrance. A deceased lord, apparently named 3 Monkey, is shown propped up in a funerary crate (at far right). The way that 3 Monkey is depicted reminds us of propped-up corpses on monuments from the Etla region (see Chapter 12). This drawing by John Klausmeyer was adapted from Marshall Saville's sketch.

> were further ornamented by a thin wash of red paint. The remains of these paintings, were they complete, would be of great value in a comparative study of the old Zapotec codices (Saville 1899:359).

The south mural of Tomb 3. A visitor entering the tomb and looking at the south wall would see that all the figures painted on that wall faced the back of the tomb (Figure 14.19). The first figure in the row wore a feather headdress and a spotted feline costume; this person seemed to be seated on a "wooden chair" (possibly a funerary crate like those depicted at San Lázaro Etla and on the back wall of Tomb 5 at Cerro de la Campana; see Chapter 12).

As Saville noted, eight other figures in the south mural wore "flowing garments," apparently a *tilma* (*huipil*) or blouse associated with women. Although today it is difficult to discern the flowing garments described by Saville, each of the eight figures seems to have been kneeling in the position the Zapotec used when depicting women. In addition, each of the kneeling figures wore a scarf or cloth that was either tied around her hair or hanging from it. These women could have been relatives of the deceased, mourners at the funeral, or both.

The north mural of Tomb 3. On the north wall of the tomb was a row of painted figures who (in contrast to the south wall) faced the tomb entrance, presumably prepared to exit (Figure 14.20).

The first figure in the row was seated in a wooden crate and resembled the first figure on the south wall. His image was much better preserved than the south mural counterpart, allowing us to confirm that he was a corpse wearing a mask and (perhaps) the costume of a spotted feline. It is significant that this individual was associated with a hieroglyphic name, placed right beneath the funerary crate. His name might have been 3 Monkey.

Figure 14.21. This lintel from Tomb 3 in Mound 9 at Xoxocotlán bears one of the longest lists of ancestors the Zapotec ever recorded. The text provides a list of 15 calendric names and profile heads, presumably naming the male ancestors of the tomb's principal occupant. Original drawing by Mark Orsen.

It is not clear whether the bundled corpse in the north mural was wearing a feline costume to impersonate a jaguar, or whether he himself had metamorphosed into a jaguar. We have seen that such metamorphosis was expected by the Zapotec.

Let us turn to the other eight figures in the north mural (Figure 14.20). Their kneeling position and the presence of cloth hanging from their hair or headdresses suggest that these figures were women.

We should consider the possibility that both murals in Tomb 3 refer to the same ceremony. With the figures on the south wall facing the back of the tomb and the figures on the north wall facing the front, the artist may be implying that a procession of eight women entered the tomb to witness the interment, remained there for a while to watch the ceremony, and eventually exited. Sadly, neither mural is preserved as well as it was in Saville's day, so we cannot say much more.

Lintel 2 of Tomb 3

Immediately above the door of Tomb 3, Saville discovered Lintel 2 (1.77 x 0.67 x 0.29 m) (Figure 14.21). This carved lintel was unusual in displaying both the profile heads and the hieroglyphic names of 15 people, presumably individuals in the genealogy of the tomb's main occupant.

Lintel 2 was divided into 15 compartments, each displaying a day name + number taken from the 260-day calendar. Below each of the 15 calendric names was the profile view of a wrinkled man with a beard. The depiction of a wrinkled face is a Zapotec convention for someone from an older generation. (The Maya were known to use bearded heads to convey the same message.)

One possible reason for listing the names of 15 elderly men on this lintel is that they were important male ancestors of the tomb occupant (Marcus 1983i:150–152). Using Caso's letter designations for hieroglyphs, the 15 names can be transcribed (from left to right) as follows:

5N
5 Monkey (5O)
8 Motion/ 8 Eye (8L)
8 Maize (8J)
4 Tigre (4B?)
6 Motion/ 6 Eye (6L)
8 Water (8Z)
4 Jaguar (4B)
1 Cane (1D)
6 Jaguar (6B)
7 Owl (7F)
2E
2C
3 Deer (3G)
12E

Unfortunately, the current whereabouts of Lintel 2 are unknown. When I searched for it in the 1970s I found that Saville's trench was still open, but the lintel had been removed. Saville's plaster cast of Lintel 2 had been stored in the American Museum of Natural History for decades, but that cast has also disappeared. When I visited the late Gordon Ekholm, Curator of Mesoamerican Archaeology at that time, he suggested to me that the cast had probably disintegrated so badly over the years that the museum was forced to throw it out. We are thus left only with Saville's photograph.

The tombs of Xoxocotlán, like others that date to AD 600–900, belong to an era when Zapotec nobles were intensely

concerned with establishing their genealogical credentials (Marcus 1983c, 2006b; Urcid and Sellen 2009). Their ancestors played an enormous role in this process, so Zapotec nobles—particularly at former Tier 2 towns that were politically ascendant—focused much of their energy on communicating with those ancestors. Honoring them during funerals and on the anniversaries of their entombment were key events that took place right near the entrances to their tombs.

The tombs of Xoxocotlán show us many of the components of Zapotec funerary ritual: (1) the arrangement of offerings and urns; (2) murals depicting funeral attendees; (3) the maintenance of a cleared area in front of the tomb, where incense was burned and food consumed; (4) the fastening of urns to the tomb façade; and (5) suggestions of chanting or singing, dancing, the wearing of costumes, the burning of incense, and the sacrifice of birds and mammals. Through these and other rites, the nobles of Xoxocotlán kept alive the memory of the ancestors who legitimized their right to rule.

Lintel 3 of Xoxocotlán

Another lintel from Xoxocotlán, designated Lintel 3 (Figure 14.22), was drawn by Sabino Soriano and published by Martínez Gracida (1910, Tomo II: Lámina 45). Lintel 3's content is similar to that on other tomb lintels and doors from the site.

At the center of Lintel 3 we see the frontal view of an owl associated with the number 13. This lintel may honor an apical ancestor named 13 Owl and commemorate the anniversary of 6 Monkey's death. Reading from left to right we see the Year 10M; the apical ancestor 13 Owl; the name 6 Monkey; and finally, a cluster of signs that include the bag glyph, a possible footprint, and a human figure sitting atop a Maltese cross (Glyph I). I have already argued that the Maltese cross was associated with offerings made on anniversaries, sometimes those associated with burial events. Similar clusters of hieroglyphs referring to anniversaries occur on the door of Monte Albán's Tomb 104, as well as on a tomb door that Caso called Lápida 1 del Museo Nacional (Caso 1928: Figure 81).

Cuilapan

Cuilapan de Guerrero lies on the Río Valiente, a tributary of the Atoyac, about eight kilometers southwest of Monte Albán. This site once had many impressive buildings (Figure 14.23). A flurry of construction during Period IIIb–IV suggests that Cuilapan was becoming prominent at the very time that Monte Albán was losing power. Many of Cuilapan's 15 mounds and associated structures may have been built, modified, or refurbished at that time.

According to his field notes, Marshall Saville began excavations at Cuilapan on January 20, 1902. He produced summaries of his most important tomb and temple excavations, but was never able to publish all of his field results and artifacts. After Saville's project ended, decades of inactivity passed before Ignacio Bernal (1958) conducted excavations at Cuilapan. Bernal not only published his own results, he also included data from Saville's excavations. In the 1960s the University of Michigan mapped and surface-collected Cuilapan and was able to extend the occupational sequence back in time by recovering Early Formative pottery. Finally, in the 1970s, Blanton et al. (1982) systematically

Figure 14.22. This carved lintel from Xoxocotlán is broken, with the left portion still missing. From left to right we can read a year sign, possibly the Year 10M (10 Lightning). In the center is an owl with the number 13; it is likely that 13 Owl was the name of an apical ancestor. To the right we see the name 6 Monkey. Finally there is a cluster of signs that we have come to associate with death and funerary offerings, including a bag, a descending foot, and a statuette sitting atop the Maltese cross. These glyphs suggest that on the anniversary of 6 Monkey's death, the Zapotec made offerings to him. This Xoxocotlán lintel can be compared to the carved door from Tomb 104 at Monte Albán (see Figure 7.1b), where we see a similar cluster of signs on the right edge, including the Maltese cross and a human statuette. Redrawn by John Klausmeyer from Sabino Soriano. (See Martínez Gracida 1910: Lám. 45. Tomo II:17.)

surveyed this part of the valley and produced population estimates for each period.

Mound 1 at Cuilapan

Mound 1 occupied a central position at Cuilapan (Rickards 1910:118); it was oriented east-west and once stood 9.53 m high. Saville made two trenches in this mound, one running north-south and the other east-west.

One of Saville's trenches exposed Tomb 1, which can be dated to Period IIIb–IV (Figures 14.24, 14.25). A stairway of nine steps led from a patio floor down to Tomb 1, which had an antechamber and a main chamber.

Tomb 1 had been closed with a large stone door, and the tomb jambs appear to have been painted; the north jamb was apparently painted red and the south jamb blue. The roof was made of enormous, well-cut stones; the main chamber had one niche in its back wall, while the antechamber had niches in its side walls.

Saville (1904) mentions a number of vessels left just outside the tomb, just as we saw in the case of some Xoxocotlán tombs. Inside the tomb he found several vessels, including a 40-cm-tall urn full of ash and a 70-cm-tall urn depicting *Cociyo* with filed teeth (Bernal 1958:23; Saville 1904:58).

Lintel 1 of Tomb 1

Over the entrance to the burial chamber of Tomb 1, Saville found an enormous lintel with a hieroglyphic inscription (see Figure 14.24) (Bernal 1958:15–16; Caso 1928: Figure 75c; Rickards 1938: Plate IVC). Beginning on the left, we see a claw and a possible numeral 5 associated with the Maltese cross. (We cannot be sure whether five refers to the number of items offered or the fifth anniversary of someone's death, but the latter seems more likely.) At the center of the lintel is the Year 6E, and at the far right is the glyph 7E. If we had had more information from the artifacts or murals inside the tomb, we might be able to confirm that 7E was the name of its principal occupant.

Lápida 1 from Tomb 1

This monument was once set in the wall of Tomb 1's burial chamber (Figure 14.25) (Bernal 1958:17). Measuring 41 x 29 x 9 cm, it was apparently removed from the tomb by Saville and taken to the American Museum of Natural History, where it remains today (catalogue # 30/11172) (Bernal 1958:23; Caso 1928: Figure 80).

Lápida 1 (Figure 14.26) shows a simplified version of the Jaws of the Sky (top center), a reference to elite descent. Descending from that motif we see a strand of large beads.

The left side of the stone shows a possible marital pair, seated one behind the other on the same mat. At the far left is a woman named 2Y. Seated in front of her is a man named 2T. The right side of the stone shows a man, possibly named 11E, sitting alone on a mat. Behind him (in the upper right corner) is the hieroglyphic name 2G (2 Deer). Because no depiction accompanies the name 2 Deer, we cannot be sure what relationship that person bears to the man named 11E.

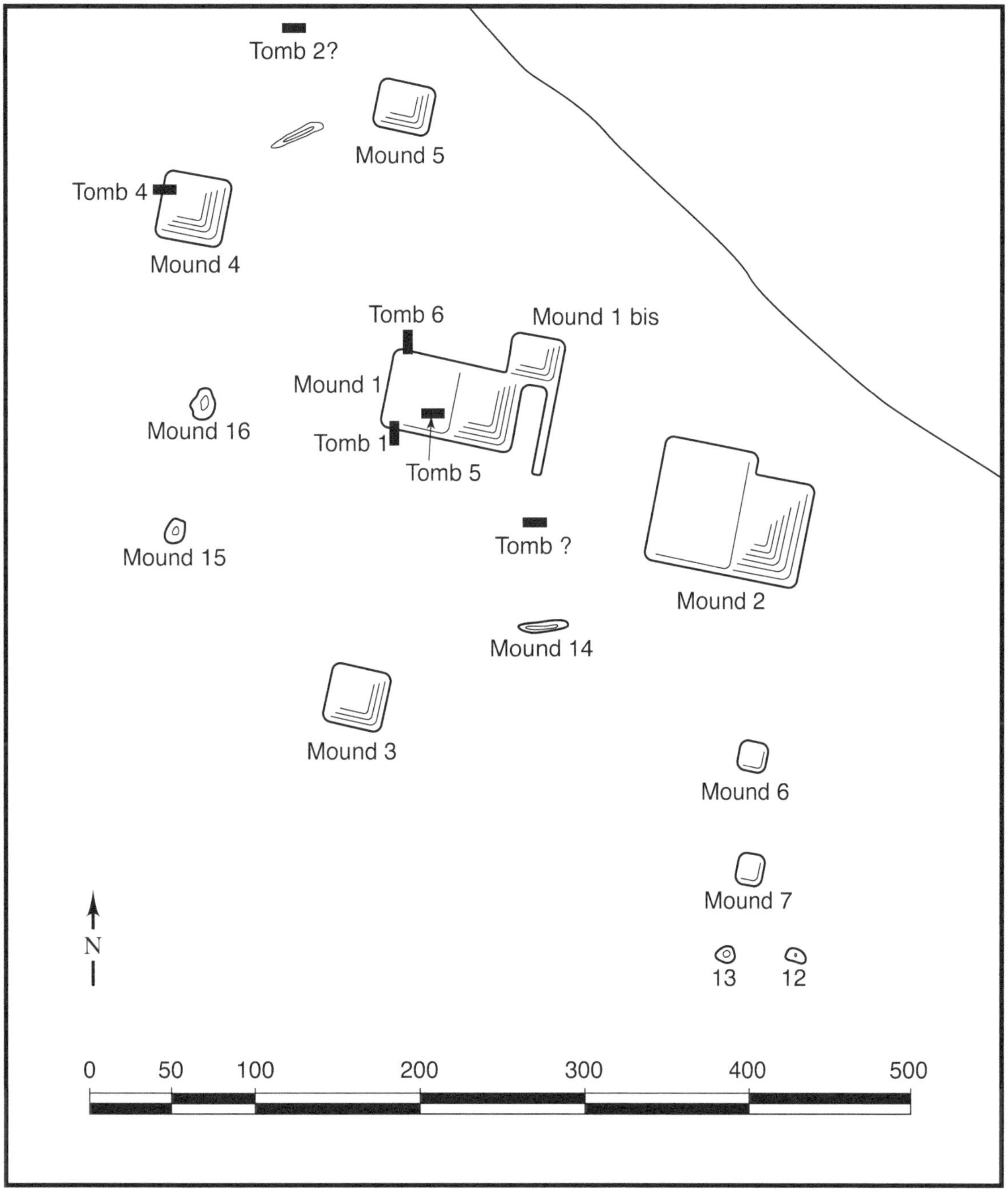

Figure 14.23. Map of the archaeological site of Cuilapan, showing notable mounds and tombs. Modified from Bernal 1958:8 by John Klausmeyer.

Figure 14.24. This enormous tomb lintel was first published by Constantine Rickards in 1910. It is now known as Lintel 1 of Tomb 1 from Mound 1 at Cuilapan (Bernal 1958: Fotos 6, 7). From left to right we see an unidentified glyph; an animal claw above a Maltese cross; the Year 6E; and finally the name 7E. One possible interpretation is "Offerings were made in the Year 6E, on the anniversary of the interment of 7E, the principal occupant of the tomb." *a*, courtesy of Ignacio Bernal; *b*, drawing by John Klausmeyer.

In the middle of the stone—below the Jaws of the Sky—we see a large Glyph E; below that is either a simplified hill sign or an altar. On this simplified sign rests a possible human head associated with a scroll, likely signifying blood or smoke. To the left of the altar/hill is a possible Glyph 1Ñ. Witnesses to the ceremony seem to be the couple on the left; they are looking at the actions being performed by the man named 11E (at right). The ritual actions may involve conjuring up the person who is symbolized by the human head on the altar.

Mound 1 *bis* at Cuilapan

This structure, more than 6 m high, was originally designated Mound 1 *bis* because it is connected to Mound 1. Saville considered Mound 1 *bis* a *teocalli* or temple. For his part, Bernal (1958:25) concluded that this mound, which lies northeast of the mound that contained Tomb 1, held the stratified remains of a sequence of structures. The earliest structure in the sequence seems to have been a temple with walls made of large adobes. This temple, which was preserved to a height of 1.22 m, had columns 3.5 m in circumference.

A few centimeters above the earliest temple in Mound 1 *bis* were stucco layers that corresponded to a second building, whose remains consisted of a small talud, an entrance, a cornice, and the start of a tablero.

Fifty-seven centimeters above this stucco—probably coincident with the destruction of the second building and the

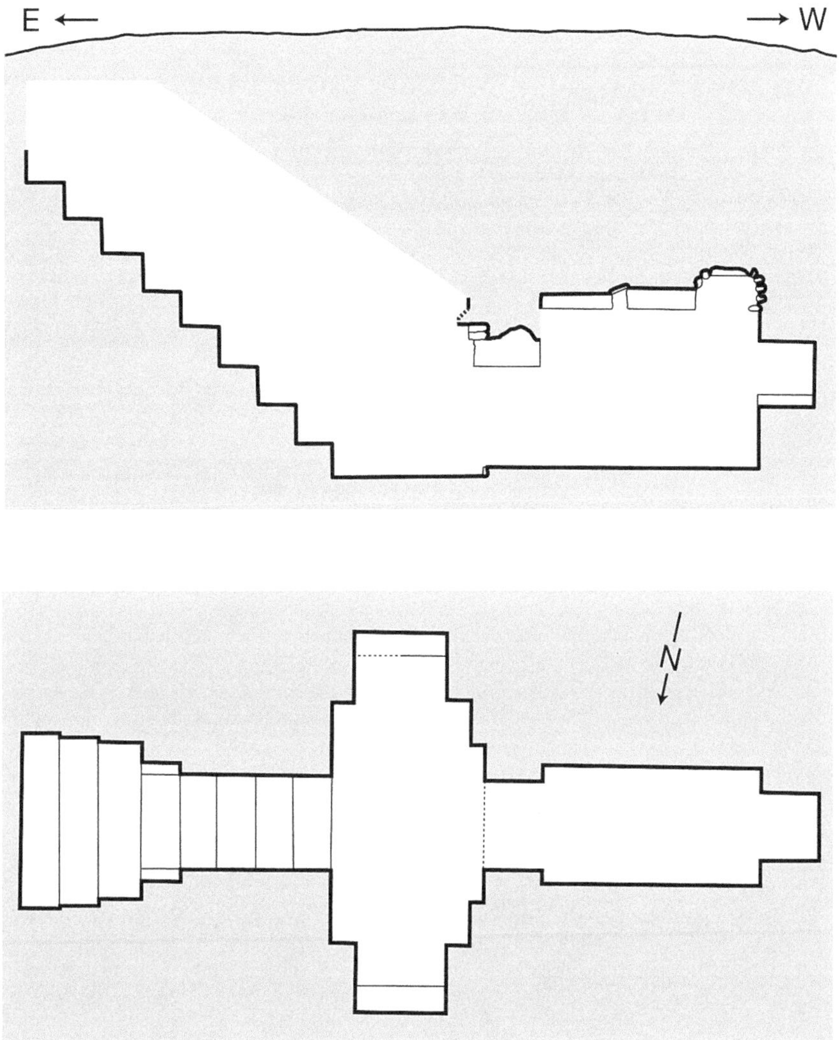

Figure 14.25. Two views of Tomb 1 in Mound 1, Cuilapan. Profile view (top); plan view (below). Modified by John Klausmeyer from Bernal 1958:11.

construction of a third—Bernal found an offering that included a sacrificed child. The child's skeleton and all associated artifacts were covered with red pigment. Encircling the child were 17 greenstone figurines, more than 400 greenstone beads of different sizes, 35 seashells perforated for suspension, and fragments of mother of pearl, obsidian, and hematite, many of which were evidently part of a disintegrated mosaic. Of all the objects found, Bernal (1958:25) considered the most interesting to be a pair of small clay disks on whose surface were glued thin pieces of polished hematite (Saville 1922:50–51, Figure 7). These glittering disks appear to have served as ear ornaments. Each has a diameter of 4.5 cm and a thickness of 3 cm. These ornaments now reside in two countries: one is in the American Museum of Natural History and the other in the Museo Nacional de Antropología in Mexico.

I mention the 17 greenstone figurines found with this child at Cuilapan because they are similar to the 24 greenstone figurines found inside a *Cociyo* urn (Caso 1938: Figure 4) in a Period IIIa dedicatory cache below Mound I on the central spine of Monte Albán's Main Plaza (Caso 1938: Figures 8–11). The 31-cm-tall figure illustrated in Bernal's report (1958: Foto 20) also came from Cuilapan.

Tombs 3 and 4 at Cuilapan

Tomb 3 of Cuilapan had a stucco figure over its doorway. Saville considered this figure to be a bat, while Bernal (1958:43) regarded it as a jaguar. Bernal noted that Tomb 3 at Cuilapan was similar

Figure 14.26. Lápida 1 was probably set into the wall of Tomb 1 in Mound 1 at Cuilapan (Bernal 1958:17). At top center we see a simplified version of the Jaws of the Sky; descending from that motif we see a strand of large beads. At the far left is a woman probably named 2 Serpent; seated in front of her is a man named 2 Rabbit. These two are seated on the same mat, and were likely a married couple. On the right side of the stone we see a second man, possibly named 11E, who is seated alone on his own mat. Behind him (in the upper right corner) is the hieroglyphic name 2G (2 Deer). Because no depiction accompanies the name 2 Deer, we cannot be sure what relationship that person bears to 11E. In the middle of the stone—below the Jaws of the Sky—we see a large Glyph E; below that glyph is either an altar or a simplified hill sign. On this sign we see a possible human head, associated with a scroll that likely signifies blood or smoke. To the left of the altar or hill is a possible Glyph 1Ñ. A tentative interpretation of this ritual scene would be as follows: The couple seated on the mat (at left) are witnesses to a ritual being performed by the man at right, and that rite may involve conjuring up the person symbolized by the human head. *a*, Courtesy of the American Museum of Natural History, catalogue # 30/11172; *b*, drawing by Mark Orsen and John Klausmeyer. Dimensions: 54 x 38 cm.

Figure 14.27. This trio of urns at Cuilapan had been placed in an exterior niche, immediately above the entrance to Tomb 5. The urn at left is Caso and Bernal's (1952) 2 Maize (2J); the urn in the middle has a Glyph C in its headdress; the urn at right is the so-called "bat god." Photo courtesy of Ignacio Bernal; see also Bernal 1958:57.

to Tomb 50 at Monte Albán (Caso and Bernal 1952: Figure 122) and Tomb 5 at Xoxocotlán (Saville 1909:153).

Tomb 4 at Cuilapan had a similar stucco figure above its door, as well as a deposit of urns in front of the tomb (Bernal 1958:52).

The Patio West of Mound 1: Tombs 5, 6, and 7 of Cuilapan

While excavating the patio of an elite residence at Cuilapan, Saville found Tombs 5–7. Tomb 5 was notable because it had an exterior niche in which three complete urns were found (Figure 14.27). These urns, which stood in a niche above the tomb door, were the first to greet visitors (Bernal 1958:57). The three urns can be identified as follows—on the left is 2 Maize (2J); in the center is an urn with Glyph C in his headdress; and on the right is Caso and Bernal's (1952) bat god.

The Noriega Monument: The Story of a Young Heir to the Throne

Before discussing the Zapotec carved stone called the "Noriega Monument," let us look briefly at some analogous Maya monuments featuring royal children. Some Maya rulers who inherited their positions while still very young were depicted on monuments,

(1) reviewing warriors, each of whom represented a different town (e.g., Panel 2, Piedras Negras);

(2) receiving a new name (e.g., Altar Q, Copán); or

(3) having a headband tied around their heads to signal that they were taking office (e.g., Temple of the Cross, Palenque).

The Maya expressions for "tying a headband"—*joyaj ti ajaw lel* and *i k'al sak huun*—are two of the many phrases associated with taking office. Some Maya texts also include both the preregnal and regnal names of a royal heir. For example, before taking office, the Palenque lord K'an Joy Chitam II was known as Ox Ch'akan Mat. At Yaxchilan, the royal heir Chel Te' became known as Shield Jaguar once he assumed the throne. Upon accession to the Piedras Negras throne in AD 687, the new king dropped his preregnal name "Puma" (Kooj), taking on the name of his honored grandfather Yo'nal Ahk. At the site of Dos Pilas, the boy heir B'alaj Chan K'awiil participated in a headband-tying ceremony at age 10; eight years passed, however, before he received the *k'awiil* scepter of office as king.

As for the Zapotec, we might expect their noble heirs to have participated in analogous rites. Among other things, we would not be surprised to find evidence for the headband ritual and the adoption of a new name when a young heir took office. In fact, the Noriega Monument shows a royal Zapotec child participating in a headband-tying rite (and possibly receiving a new name).

The multiregister Noriega Monument (Figure 14.28) presents a narrative about a boy at three stages of his life: as a newborn, as a toddler, and as a youngster (Bernal 1960; Caso 1965a:942; Easby and Scott 1970; Marcus 1980, 1983c: Figure 7.5; Paddock 1966a; Rabin 1970; Urcid 1999). Although there is a general consensus that this stone presents events in the life of an heir to the throne, there are multiple ways to interpret the details.

Years ago, while I was standing next to the Noriega Monument, archaeologist Lorenzo Gamio approached me and recounted how this stone was discovered. He said that it came from the roof of a masonry cist at "Hacienda Noriega" (also known as San Lucas Tlanichico), which lies between Cuilapan and Zaachila (Gamio 1944). Gamio said that the heavy rains of 1944 had exposed a stone construction in Bernal's Mound N (Bernal 1960), which seems to correspond to Blanton et al.'s (1982) Mound 4. Gamio also said that human bones were found in the cist, but he was not sure whether more than one individual was present.

As is often the case with Period IIIb–IV monuments, the text on the Noriega Monument is intended to be read from bottom to top (e.g., Easby and Scott 1970; Marcus 1980). In the lower register we see a marital pair—a man named 10 Water (10Z) on the left and a woman named 9 Water (9Z) on the right. Between them is a stylized version of the Jaws of the Sky with a hill sign below it. On either side of the hill is a supernatural being with an upturned snout; this same creature is seen on sculptures at Monte Albán, Zaachila, Yagul, and Lambityeco, and in the Sola Valley (e.g., Berlin 1946, 1951, 1957; Feinman and Nicholas 2016b, 2017; Marcus 2002).

The middle register of the monument features three more adults whose names include the day sign Water (i.e., 2 Water, 2 Water, and 8 Water). Although the numbers generally differ, the repetition of the day sign Water in the names of five adults in the lower and middle registers was probably not due to chance.

One of the individuals named 2 Water is a woman (at far left), who wears an elaborate headdress and mouth mask and is associated with a speech scroll. In front of her knees is an infant. We also see a seated man, holding in his hands an object that may be a human cranium (Caso 1965a: Figure 18). The name 2 Water appears for a second time; it is difficult to tell whether it applies to the man or the infant.

Still in the middle register, we next see that the child has become a toddler, sitting upright and facing a woman named 8 Water, who also wears an elaborate headdress and a mouth mask.

Finally we come to the upper register. There we see a flying turtle apical ancestor (top center), three seated adults, and the child (now a bit older), seated on a cushion and having a band tied around his head. The woman at the far right, holding a staff of office, is named 9 Deer (9G). The child is having his headband tied by a man named 1 Serpent (1Y). The woman at the far left is named 2N; she has a speech scroll in front of her mouth, as well as a bar and a dot signifying 6. The man named 1 Serpent has a speech scroll associated with the day sign Owl.

It appears that while the woman is supplying the numerical coefficient "6," the man is uttering the word "Owl." This raises the possibility that the man and woman are jointly supplying the royal heir with his new name—6 Owl (6 Night). This interpretation was originally suggested by Anne Perry (cited by Urcid 1995:222).

Who are the individuals named 2N and 1Y on this monument? Are they the priests who divined the heir's new name, or are they his parents? Without having Zapotec hieroglyphs for "mother," "father," "aunt," "uncle," or "grandparent," it is impossible to be certain. Even the name of the child, to be honest, is not certain. One possibility is that the child began life with the name 2 Water and his name was changed to 6 Owl after the headband rite.

In sum, several points can be made about the Noriega Monument:

For both the Zapotec and the Maya, the tying of the headband was an important ritual.

Both Zapotec and Maya rulers sometimes had their childhood names replaced by a new name when they took office. The taking of a new name served to mark the transition to a new office and political role.

The fact that the day name "Water" occurs in the names of five individuals on the monument seems significant enough to warrant future investigation.

Many of the details of the Noriega Monument will continue to be the subject of discussion, including the birth name of the child and the identity of all the participants in the headband ceremony.

Figure 14.28 (opposite page). This Noriega Stone (discovered at Rancho Noriega near San Lucas Tlanichico) tells the story of a boy who was the heir to the throne. We are presented with a narrative about him as an infant, a toddler, and finally a youngster participating in the headband-tying rite that marks his designation as heir to office. In the lowest register we see a marital pair—a man named 10 Water and a woman named 9 Water. Between them is a stylized version of the Jaws of the Sky, with a hill sign below it. The middle register of the monument features three more adults whose calendric names include Water (2 Water, 2 Water, and 8 Water). One of the individuals named 2 Water is a woman (at far left); in front of her is an infant. We also see a seated man and the name 2 Water, but it is difficult to tell whether the name applies to the man or the infant. Still in the middle register, we see that the child has now become a toddler, sitting upright and facing a woman named 8 Water. Finally we come to the uppermost register; there we see an apical ancestor (top center), three seated adults, and the child (now older) having a band tied around his head. The woman at the far right, holding a staff of office, is named 9 Deer. The child receives his headband from a man named 1 Serpent. The woman at the far left is named 2N; she has a speech scroll in front of her mouth, as well as a bar and a dot signifying "6." The man named 1 Serpent has a speech scroll associated with the day sign Owl. It is possible that the woman is supplying the numerical coefficient "6," while the man is uttering the word "Owl"; this raises the possibility that they jointly supplied the royal heir with a new name, 6 Owl. Drawing by Mark Orsen.

Figure 14.29. This monument was incorporated into a bridge on the Río Valiente near San Raymundo Jalpan, to the north of Zaachila. It shares attributes with two other carved stones, one from Zaachila and one from Monte Albán. In the upper portion we see two lords sitting cross-legged on an immense throne or hill. On the left is Lord 3 Maize (3J) and on the right is Lord 3 Knot (3A). Drawing by Mark Orsen.

The San Raymundo Jalpan Stone

When the Jalpan monument (Figure 14.29) first came to the attention of archaeologists, it had already been incorporated into a bridge spanning the Río Valiente. When I first saw this carved stone it was no longer in the bridge, but standing next to the entrance of the Museo de las Culturas de Oaxaca. I was immediately struck by how blocky and heavy the stone was (160 x 78 x 52 cm), which perhaps suggests that its original provenience was not far from the bridge. Oral tradition attributes it to San Raymundo Jalpan, a site located between Xoxocotlán and Zaachila (Caso and Bernal 1952:213, Figure 350-I). The monument shares attributes with two other carved stones, one from Zaachila and one from Monte Albán.

The shape, dimensions, and weight of the San Raymundo Jalpan stone suggest that it may have been a stela, and in fact it reminds us a bit of Monte Albán's Stela 1 (Chapter 9, Figure 9.9). Rather than displaying one ruler, however, the Jalpan monument depicts two lords facing each other. Each sits cross-legged on an immense throne or hill. On the left is Lord 3 Maize (3J) and on the right is Lord 3 Knot (3A). In this respect the Jalpan stone has a layout similar to a monument from Zaachila (see below), which also shows two lords seated on hills or thrones and facing each other.

Monuments from Zaachila

Like Mitla, Zaachila is one of the few sites in the Valley of Oaxaca that has been continuously occupied for more than two millennia. When Monte Albán was at its peak, Zaachila was probably one of its subjects and allies. When Monte Albán was declining in both population and political authority, Zaachila's political stature was increasing. Eventually, Zaachila supplanted Monte Albán as the Zapotec capital.

By Period V, Zaachila was a major dynastic seat and—as we will see in Chapter 17—during the thirteenth century AD and later, its royal family was linked by marriage to prominent families at Tlaxiaco, Teozacoalco, and Yanhuitlán in the Mixteca Alta (Caso 1949, 1964a, 1966; Jansen and Oudijk 1998; Oudijk 2000; Paddock 1966b; Spores 1974). These Mixtec-Zapotec marriage alliances did much to enhance the local nobility at several Valley of Oaxaca sites.

Although at least two dozen carved stones were once known from the archaeological site of Zaachila, the whereabouts of several are unknown today (e.g., Caso 1928; Paddock 1966a; Reh 1928; Rickards 1910; Vicente Cruz and Sánchez Santiago 2014).

Based on style and subject matter, many of the Zaachila stones appear to date to Period IIIb–IV and some were likely found in tombs, given that their measurements are consistent with tomb doors or lintels. Still other Zaachila stones were probably tenoned into the walls of ballcourts, and resemble other ballcourt tenons from Yagul and Lambityeco (e.g., Berlin 1946, 1951; Marcus 2002; Wicke 1957).

Figure 14.30. Caso's "Lápida 13" is one of the best-preserved monuments attributed to Zaachila, but the precise circumstances of its discovery remain unknown. At the top of the stone we see the Jaws of the Sky; descending from that motif is a metamorphosed figure who seems to be wearing a bird mask. He also has an elaborate headdress that includes a leaf and the name "12L." In his hand is an unidentified object. The scrolls and cartouche that enclose the entire scene include elements that Caso interpreted as clouds. Seated on hill signs are a woman (on the left) and a man (on the right). In front of the woman is the name 11C; in front of the man is 8N. Their likely parents are shown in the corners of Lápida 13. The woman's father is 11 Death (shown in the upper left corner); her mother is 8 Serpent (shown in the lower left corner). The man's father is 10 Knot (shown in the upper right corner); his mother's name seems to be missing. Between Lady 11C and Lord 8N is a T-shaped altar that supports a small ball, possibly copal or rubber to be burned during a ritual (see Peñafiel 1893: Pl. 61; Martínez Gracida 1910, Vol. II: Pl. 67; Caso 1928: Fig. 93). Drawing by John Klausmeyer.

Lápida 13 of Zaachila

One of the best-preserved monuments attributed to Zaachila is shown in Figure 14.30. The assignment of this 31 x 43 cm slab to Zaachila appears in Galindo y Villa (1905) and Martínez Gracida (1910: tomo II, Plate 67), but the precise circumstances of its discovery remain unknown.

According to Galindo y Villa, this monument came into Manuel Martínez Gracida's hands shortly after its discovery at Zaachila (Caso 1928:120). Caso (1928:120–121) published early photographs of the stone but added, "Ignoro en dónde se encuentra actualmente." He simply referred to this monument as "Lápida 13 de Manuel Martínez Gracida," because it had been in the latter's private collection. It evidently passed through other hands and ultimately made its way to the Smithsonian Institution, where it can be seen today.

At the top of Lápida 13 we see the Jaws of the Sky, signifying noble descent. Descending from this motif is a metamorphosed figure that is part human/part animal, perhaps wearing a mouth mask. These *yahui*-like figures ("*hechizeros,*" "*xicàni,*" or "*nilla*" according to Córdova [1578]1942:216v and Pohl 1994:67) could

Figure 14.31. On this photograph of a Zaachila monument we see Lord 13 Maize and Lord 3 Water seated on toponyms. Between them we see 7 + an eroded Maltese cross. The frequency with which this Maltese cross occurs in tombs suggests that it may have been associated with offerings made on the anniversaries of a person's death or burial. Photo by the author.

communicate with remote ancestors and conduct sacrificial rites by using quail and other birds as well as humans. Some *xicàni* had names derived from the 260-day calendar, suggesting that they were deceased rulers or dynastic founders who had undergone metamorphosis.

The figure descending from the Jaws of the Sky wears an elaborate headdress that includes a leaf and the name "12L." He also wears a mouth mask with a possible bird beak. In this down-gazing ancestor's hand is a net-like object inside a possible wooden frame, shaped a bit like a snowshoe (Caso 1928:120; Urcid 1995). A similar object was depicted on a carved stone from Santa Inés Yatzeche (see below).

The scrolls and cartouche that enclose the entire scene include elements that Caso (1928:120) interpreted as clouds. Such scrolls were often used by the Zapotec to signal that the individuals were hereditary nobles.

Seated on hill signs are a woman (on the left) and a man (on the right). In front of the woman is the day name 11C; in front of the man is 8N. (Note that Caso [1928:120] interpreted the man's name as 5D, not 8N.)

From this carved stone we learn the names of several people, including 12L—the name of the metamorphosed ancestor descending from the Jaws of the Sky. In each corner of Lápida 13 is a seated person who appears to belong to an earlier generation. The woman's father is 11 Death (11H) and is shown in the upper left corner; her mother is 8 Serpent (8Y) and is shown in the lower left corner. Her husband's parents are named on the other corners of the stone. His father's name is 10 Knot (10A), shown in the upper right corner; his mother's name is not legible.

Between the two principal, centrally placed figures—Lady 11C and Lord 8N—is a T-shaped stone altar that supports a small ball possibly of rubber or copal, apparently to be burned during a ritual. The meaning of the two birds shown (one in her feather headdress and another near the altar) are not clear, but they were apparently important to this rite.

Other Zaachila Monuments

On another Zaachila monument, shown in Figures 14.31 and 14.32, we see two figures—Lord 13 Maize and Lord 3 Water—each seated on a hill or toponym. The seated figures face each other, and between them we see footprints. Elsewhere in Mesoamerica (for example, on Stela 11 at the Maya site of Piedras Negras [Marcus 1994:257–259], such use of footprints sometimes signifies accession to the throne.

Between the two seated figures in Figures 14.31 and 14.32 we see 7I (7 + Maltese cross). As discussed already, the frequency with which this cross occurs in tombs suggests that it may have been associated with offerings made to honor the memory of a deceased ancestor or founding couple, and in this instance it may commemorate the seventh anniversary of an interment.

As Caso (1928:35) noted, the Maltese cross can occur with or without a numeral. It can also be associated with the following hieroglyphs: an open hand; a human head that appears to represent a deceased person with his mouth open and eyes closed; and a stiff stone figure. All these items suggest offerings made to the ancestors, perhaps on the anniversary of their interments.

Another Zaachila monument (Figure 14.33) was seen by Caso (1928:104) when it was set near the entrance of a twentieth-century house in the town. Given its rectangular shape and dimensions (1.51 x 1.02 m), this slab may have served as a door to a tomb of Period IIIb–IV date. The outer cartouche frame displays scrolls on all four sides. Inside the cartouche we see the hieroglyphic names of an ancestral marital pair or founding couple (Caso 1928: Figure 77). (Note that the Maya also used cartouches and quatrefoils to enclose the names and depictions of ancestors [e.g., Guernsey 2010].) The names of the ancestral pair in Figure 14.33 are Death + 4 Earthquake (H + 4E) (on the left) and 13 Monkey (13 O) (on the right). Unfortunately, this monument shows scars from the forklift used to transport it (Figure 14.33a).

The carved lintel from Zaachila shown in Figure 14.34 (180 x 66 cm) was published by Rickards (1910) and Caso (1928: Figure 75 A and B). On the underside of the lintel is a cartouche that contains the names of a marital pair, possibly 6 Monkey (6 O) and 2 or 7 Maize (2J or 7J). On the edge of the lintel we see another marital pair named 5 Jaguar and 13 Jaguar. The nickname associated with 13 Jaguar involves the Tassel Headdress, a motif known from the South Platform monuments at Monte Albán (Chapter 9). At the center of the lintel is a glyph that may allude to offerings made to an apical ancestor.

The tenon from Zaachila shown in Figure 14.35 portrays a supernatural being whose upturned snout has a brief hieroglyphic label, possibly to be read 5 Reed + a leaf (see Marcus 2002:107). This stone—carved in the round—is similar to other tenons set into the walls of ballcourts. Heinrich Berlin (1951: Figures 3, 4, 5, 6; see also Marcus 2002:105) noted that whenever such tenoned stones were found *in situ* in the Sola Valley, they were associated with ballcourts; the ballcourt at Reyes Etla had a similar tenoned stone (see Chapter 12).

The creature depicted in Figure 14.35 resembles those on monuments from Yagul, Lambityeco, Mitla, Monte Albán, Sola, and Reyes Etla (Feinman and Nicholas 2016b; Marcus 2002). A similar creature is depicted on the Noriega Monument and in Zaachila's Tomb 1, where it is modeled in stucco on the back wall (see Marcus 2002:107; Vicente Cruz and Sánchez Santiago 2014). Such creatures have been alternately identified as crocodiles (Feinman and Nicholas 2011; 2016b:114–115); turtle men (Gallegos 1978); turtle-*xiuhcoatl* sacrificers (Caso 1964b:27, 75); alter egos, *nahuales*, sacrificers, or apical ancestors who could impersonate other beings while mediating between the living and the dead; and *yahui* or *xicàni* that flew and controlled esoteric knowledge while performing black magic (e.g., Alcina Franch 1971, 1972; Augsburger 2003; Caso 1964b:27, 75; Córdova [1578a]1942:216v; Hermann Lejarazu 2009; Lupo 1999; Pohl 1994:67; M. E. Smith 1973b: Figures 2, 4; Urcid 1999:223).

The Sacristan Monument

The genealogical register shown in Figure 14.36 is mounted inside the sacristan of the church at Zaachila. This stone at Zaachila is

Figure 14.32. A drawing of the same monument seen in Figure 14.31. Between Lord 13 Maize and Lord 3 Water we see footprints. 105 x 65 x 30 cm. Drawing by Mark Orsen.

a

b

Figure 14.33. Photograph (a) and drawing (b) of a Zaachila monument. This stone, which may once have been the door to a tomb, has been difficult to study because it is not only weathered but also damaged by being moved with a forklift. Inside the nested cartouches we see the hieroglyphic names of a possible marital pair—Glyph H (death) + 3E on the left and 13 (?) Monkey on the right. (The fact that Monkey seems to be accompanied by 2 bars and 4 dots deserves a comment, since days in the 260-day calendar could not occur with numbers higher than 13; a scribal or carving error might be involved.) Drawing by Mark Orsen.

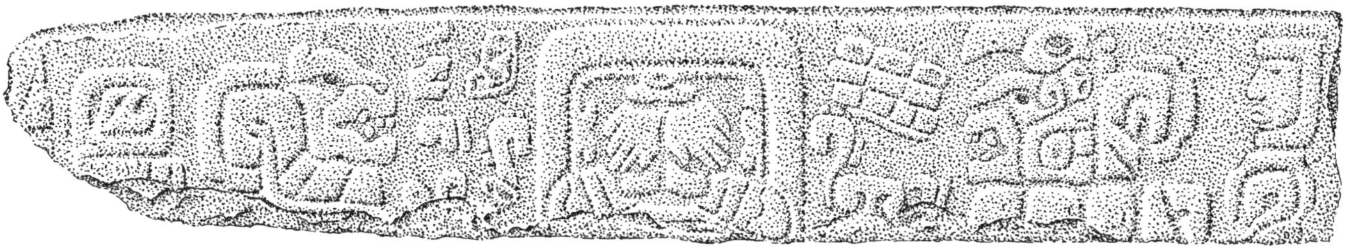

Figure 14.34. This lintel from Zaachila was carved on two surfaces. On the edge of the lintel (above) we see a marital pair named 5 Jaguar and 13 Jaguar. On the underside (below) is a cartouche containing the names of a second marital pair, possibly 6 Monkey and 2 Maize (or 7 Maize). The nickname associated with 13 Jaguar includes the Tassel Headdress, a motif known from South Platform monuments at Monte Albán (Rickards 1910:118). Dimensions: 28 x 180 x 66 cm. Drawing by Mark Orsen.

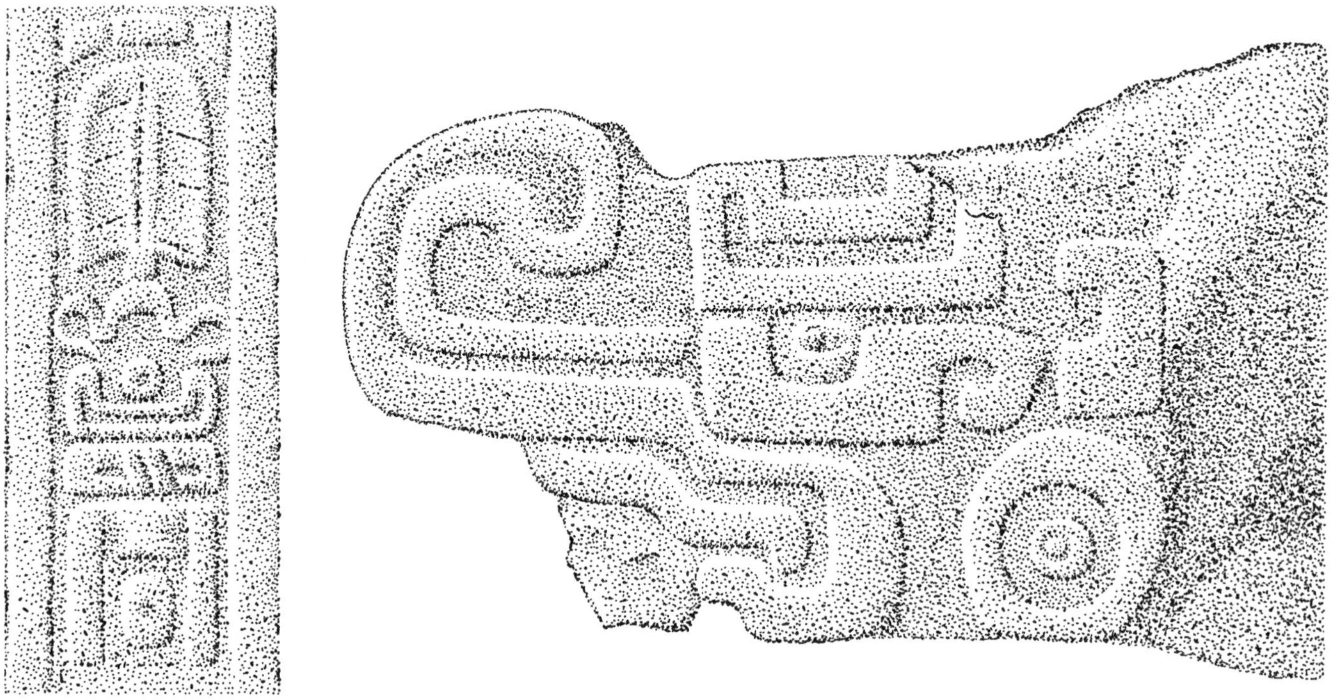

Figure 14.35. This carved tenon from Zaachila portrays a supernatural being whose upturned snout bears a short hieroglyphic caption (at left) that can be read as 5 Reed + a leaf. This carved-in-the-round stone (at right) is similar to other tenons set into the walls of ballcourts. Such creatures with upturned snouts have been identified as crocodiles (Feinman and Nicholas 2011; 2016b); as turtle men (Gallegos 1978); as turtle-*xiuhcoatl* sacrificers (Caso 1964b:27, 75); as alter egos, *nahuales*, sacrificers, or *yahui/xicàni* who could fly and conduct sacrifices; and as apical ancestors who could impersonate flying creatures while mediating between the living and the dead (e.g., Alcina Franch 1971, 1972; Augsburger 2003; Caso 1964b:27, 75; Córdova [1578a]1942:216v; Hermann Lejarazu 2009; Lupo 1999; Pohl 1994:67; M. E. Smith 1973b: Figs. 2, 4; Urcid 1999:223). Dimensions: 55 x 150 x 35 cm. Drawing by Mark Orsen.

Figure 14.36 (opposite page). Genealogical register mounted inside the sacristan of the church at Zaachila. This badly eroded monument is divided into three registers; each register shows a pair of seated individuals conducting a ritual. The uppermost register shows a figure descending from the Jaws of the Sky, holding a strand of beads; the name of this descending ancestor seems to be 6E. The person sitting on the right in each register seems to be using ritual paraphernalia, while the person on the left is merely observing the rite. In the lowest register, the figure on the left seems to be male. There are a number of ways to interpret this monument; one possibility is that the same individuals are depicted in each register, conducting three different rites in an established sequence, not unlike the sequence depicted on the Noriega Monument (Figure 14.28). A second possibility is that each register shows a different pair of individuals, all of whom are engaged in the same ritual—a rite that involved smoking and the use of drum-shaped vessels. The fact that none of the individuals are named makes it difficult to decide between these two scenarios (Marcus 2006b: Fig. 11.12; Reh 1928). Drawing by Mark Orsen.

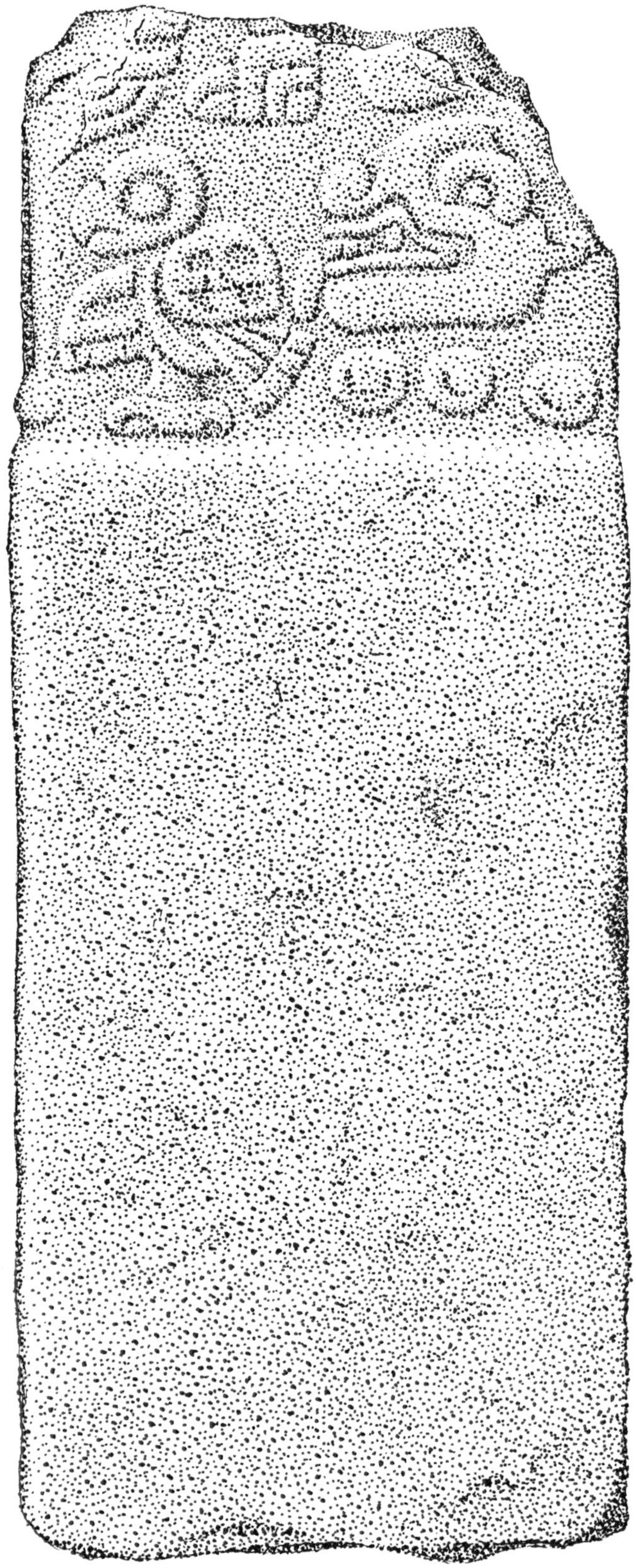

now very worn, even smooth in places, which makes the details difficult to discern. Clearly, however, the monument is divided into three registers, each showing a pair of seated individuals conducting a ritual (Marcus 2006b: Figure 11.12; Reh 1928). This monument (0.86 x 0.49 m) is similar in height to Stela 5 at Cerro de la Campana (Chapter 13).

The uppermost register shows a figure descending from the Jaws of the Sky, holding a rope or a strand of beads. The name of this descending ancestor is 6E.

The person sitting on the right in each register seems to be wearing ritual paraphernalia, while the person on the left is merely a witness observing the action. In the lowest register the figure on the left seems to be male. His arms are crossed and he does not seem to be using any paraphernalia, only watching.

There are a number of ways to interpret this monument's three registers. One possibility is that the same individuals are depicted in each register, conducting three different rites in an established sequence (not unlike the Noriega Monument). A second possibility is that each register shows a different pair of individuals, all of whom perform the same ritual. It was a rite that involved smoking and the use of two drum-like vessels. The fact that none of the individuals are associated with hieroglyphic names makes it difficult to decide between these two scenarios.

Miscellaneous Zaachila Monuments

Figure 14.37 shows a stone measuring 90 x 36 x 12 cm, with its carving limited to a bird + 3 Jaguar or 3 Monkey. Most of the stone is plain, suggesting that it might have been inserted into the wall of a building or set into the ground as a stela.

Figure 14.38 shows a statue from Zaachila that is carved in the round (110 x 55 cm). The hands of the individual are treated in a crude fashion, reminiscent of the way feet and hands were treated on later (Period V) carvings from Teotitlán del Valle (Chapter 17).

The La Ciénega Stone

According to Jesús Galindo y Villa, the circular slab shown in Figure 14.39 was found at La Ciénega, a site that lies south of Zaachila. Eduard Seler reported that he once saw this stone in Dr. Fernando Sologuren's collection. The monument measures 43 cm in diameter and 6 cm thick (see Caso 1928:113).

Figure 14.37. This monument from Zaachila measures 90 x 36 x 12 cm, with its carving limited to a Bird + 3 Jaguar. Most of the stone is uncarved, suggesting that its lower shaft might have been inserted into the wall of a building or set into the ground. Drawing by Mark Orsen.

The monument features "noble cartouches" or "ancestor cartouches" that typically encircle important Zapotec nobles and ancestors. As is typical of such cartouches, there are side scrolls halfway down the left and right sides of the slab. Caso (1928:113) and others have interpreted these scrolls as flowers. They usually appear in pairs at the edges of cartouches, with the interior contents referring to ancestors.

The woman, while holding an enigmatic object, seems to be conjuring up a metamorphosed ancestor. Conjuring one's ancestors was a widespread Mesoamerican ritual, one for which we have numerous Maya examples. On Lintel 25 at Yaxchilan, for example, Lady K'abal Xook can be seen celebrating her husband's accession to the throne in AD 681. In her hand she holds a basket with a stingray spine; a thorny cord that has been pulled through a hole in her tongue; blood-spattered papers; and the hieroglyph for bloodletting. A second vessel, shown below the conjured vision of an ancestor, holds similar bloodletting paraphernalia. Other Maya monuments show (1) an ancestor as a disembodied head, floating above the heads of his descendants (e.g., Stela 1 of El Baúl and Stela 31 of Tikal); (2) ancestors at the top of a monument, floating with arms extended (e.g., Stela 1 at Jimbal); and (3) a dead lord metamorphosed and emanating from the body of a decaying serpent (e.g., Lintel 15 at Yaxchilan).

These Maya scenes of conjuring make us wonder what object the Zapotec woman on the La Ciénega monument was holding, and whether her actions had conjured up the metamorphosed figure shown.

Let us now look at this monument in more detail. At the top we see a bird descending from an abbreviated version of the Jaws of the Sky. Nearby we see the hieroglyph 4E or 6E, which may be the name of an ancestor.

Lower down we see a marital pair sitting on a single hill sign, suggesting that they co-ruled that town. The man, at left, seems to be named 5 Owl (5F); the woman, at right, seems to be named 2E. The woman appears to be conducting a rite, while the man watches. Judging from the speech scrolls associated with the pair, I think it is possible that they were speaking or singing, and perhaps calling out the names of ancestors.

Lord 5 Owl seems to be associated with two ancestors. One is named 4 Skull (4H), shown above and behind 5 Owl; the other ancestor seems to be named 6E. Lady 2E is associated with the names of two ancestors, who seem to be named 10 O (10 Monkey) and 3H (3 Skull). The latter is shown above and behind 2E.

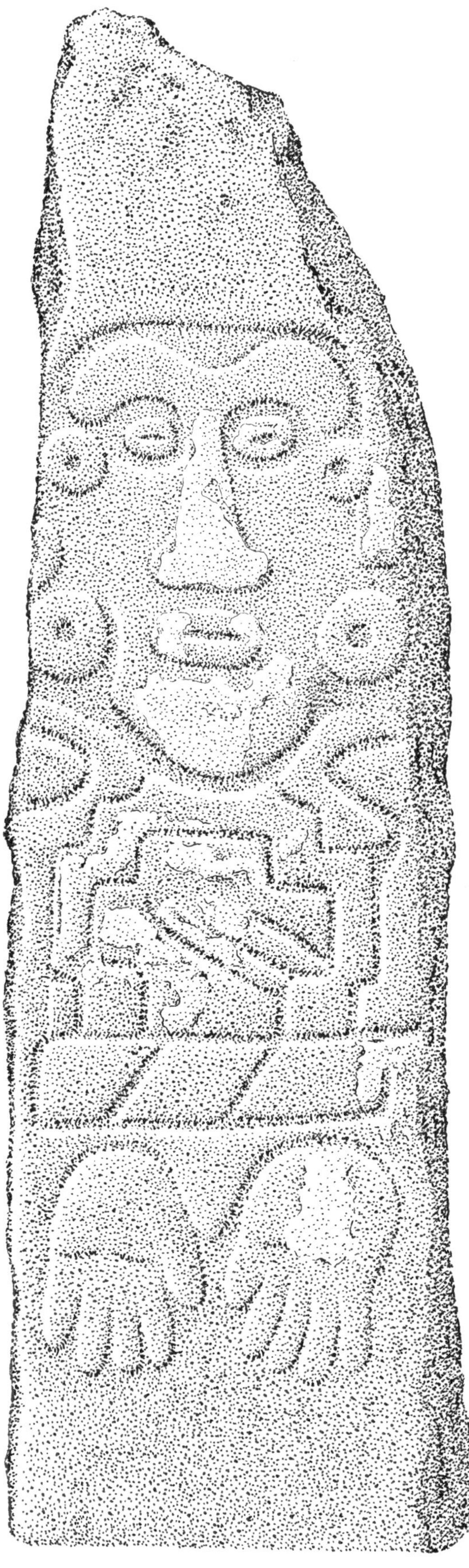

Figure 14.38. This statue from Zaachila measures 110 x 55 cm. While its date is uncertain, the individual's hands are treated in a crude fashion, similar to the way hands and feet were treated on Period V carvings from Teotitlán del Valle (Chapter 17). The man wears earplugs, a pectoral similar to that shown on many urns, and a nose ornament similar to those known from Period V. Drawing by Mark Orsen.

Figure 14.39. This circular stone slab was found at La Ciénega, a site just south of Zaachila; it measures 43 cm in diameter and 6 cm in thickness. The monument features cartouches of the kind that typically encircle important Zapotec nobles and ancestors. There are side scrolls, halfway down the left and right sides of the slab, which Caso (1928:113) and others have interpreted as plants. At the top of the carving we see a bird descending from an abbreviated version of the Jaws of the Sky. Nearby we see the hieroglyph 4E or 6E, which may be the name of an ancestor. Lower down we see a marital pair sitting on a single hill sign, suggesting that they co-ruled that town. The man, at left, seems to be named 5 Owl (5F). The woman, at right, seems to be named 2E; she holds an unidentified object and may be conjuring up a metamorphosed ancestor. Lord 5 Owl seems to be associated with two ancestors; one is named 4 Skull (4H), shown above and behind 5 Owl, while the other seems to be named 6E. Lady 2E is also associated with two ancestors, who seem to be named 10 O (10 Monkey) and 3H (3 Skull); the latter is shown above and behind Lady 2E. Centrally placed above the marital couple's heads is a hieroglyph that Caso interpreted as 12E. This name might be either (1) that of an apical ancestor invoked by the couple, or (2) that of an ancestor—depicted as a bird—descending from the Jaws of the Sky. Drawing by Mark Orsen.

Figure 14.40. This monument is set in a wall at Santa Inés Yatzeche. At the top we see Glyph E and Glyph O; below we see two serpents with upturned snouts (Marcus 1976a:135). At the lower left is a figure wearing a costume suggesting that he is a *Cociyo* impersonator; he holds a crosshatched object, similar to that shown on a monument from Zaachila (see Figure 14.30). Photo by the author.

Centrally placed above the marital couple's heads is a hieroglyph that Caso (1928:32; Figure 8, XIV) interpreted as 12E. This might be either (1) the name of an apical ancestor invoked by the couple, or (2) the name of the ancestor depicted as a dove descending from the Jaws of the Sky.

The Santa Inés Yatzeche Monuments

In 1973 the town of Santa Inés Yatzeche was almost entirely inhabited by monolingual Zapotec speakers who did not welcome outsiders. On my first visit I was surprised, but pleased, to see a man using the traditional *cerbatana* (blowgun) to hunt birds, followed by a woman collecting grasshoppers in a traditional net bag. They were just as surprised (but less pleased) to see a vehicle bearing North American archaeologists.

A young boy who spoke some Spanish came forward to greet us and to show us the archaeological site. On our way to what turned out to be a large ceremonial center on a natural promontory, we passed a series of well-made circular basins that had been carved into the living rock. Kowalewski et al. (1989:229) estimate that during its Classic heyday, Yatzeche had at least 26 mounds.

Ignacio Bernal and Lorenzo Gamio had visited the site in the 1950s, and told me about a few carved stones that they had seen but were not permitted to photograph. They encouraged me to go to Yatzeche to see if I could photograph them. One of those carved stones (Figure 14.40) displays a Glyph E and a Glyph O at the top; below we see two serpents with upturned

Figure 14.41. This carved stone from Santa Inés Yatzeche features a skull associated with the hieroglyph 10E (Marcus 1976a: Fig. 22, p. 135). Photo by the author.

snouts (Marcus 1976a:135). At the lower left is a figure wearing a costume that suggests he is a *Cociyo* impersonator. He holds a circular crosshatched object, similar to the unidentified object shown on a monument from Zaachila (see Figure 14.30).

Another carved stone from Santa Inés Yatzeche (Figure 14.41) shows only a skull associated with a hieroglyph that may be 10E (Marcus 1976a: Figure 22, page 135).

Monuments from Rancho Tejas de Morelos

The Valley of Oaxaca Settlement Pattern Project found 28 artificial mounds at Rancho Tejas de Morelos. That team assigned a population estimate of 1937 to the site during its Classic heyday (Feinman and Nicholas 2017:70; Kowalewski et al. 1989:227–229).

In the early 1970s, looters at Rancho Tejas discovered three unusual stone monuments, some of which may have been from a tomb. These carved stones can be seen in Figures 14.42–14.44. Figure 14.42, a possible lintel, displays a sacrificial knife and a stylized bleeding human heart with signs for blood. Figure 14.43 shows an animal carved in the round. Figure 14.44 depicts a person conducting a ritual.

What Can We Say About the Carved Stones of the Valle Grande?

The biggest problem with the monuments of the Valle Grande is that so many of them were found by looters or collectors, leaving their original context unknown. That having been said, they show some clear differences from the stones of the Etla and Tlacolula subvalleys. None of the Valle Grande stone monuments so far discovered share the funerary crate theme seen on several monuments in the Etla subvalley. If our current sample of Valle Grande monuments can be said to display one dominant theme, it would be scenes of noble descendants (often marital pairs) performing various rituals to honor or conjure up their metamorphosed or apical ancestors.

Figure 14.42 (above). This possible tomb lintel is from Rancho Tejas. Among other things, it displays a large sacrificial knife above a trilobed heart and the symbols for flowing blood (see Neys and von Winning 1946). *a* is a photo taken by the author; *b* is a drawing by Mark Orsen.

Figure 14.43. This unique monument from Rancho Tejas consists of an animal carved in the round. Maximum height: 2.58 m. *a* is a photo taken by the author; *b*, created by John Klausmeyer, is based on a drawing by Mark Orsen.

Figure 14.44. This monument from Rancho Tejas shows a figure seated in a circular cartouche. Photo taken by the author.

15

Monuments of the Tlacolula Region

In the eastern, or Tlacolula, arm of the Valley of Oaxaca an estimated 35 sites with artificial mounds date to Period IIIb–IV. Among the best-known sites with carved stones are Macuilxóchitl, Tlacochahuaya, Lambityeco, and Yagul (Figure 15.1).

This arm of the valley presents us with three major challenges. One is dating unprovenienced carved stones. A second is determining the Period IIIb–IV political hierarchy. There is no guarantee of a correlation between political importance, on the one hand, and the number of mounds, height of mounds, and population estimate on the other. Nevertheless, the Valley of Oaxaca Settlement Pattern Project has generated some population estimates that serve as a starting point for thinking about political hierarchies—Macuilxóchitl (6200 people), Tlacochahuaya (5300), Lambityeco (2700), and Yagul (1200) (Kowalewski et al. 1989:260–261, 287).

A third challenge has been distinguishing Period IIIb pottery from Period IV pottery. Tlacolula is the one arm of the valley where some success has been achieved, simply because more imitation Fine Orange (Balancan Z) pottery has been found in that region. That type of Fine Orange is one of the key diagnostics used to define Period IV (Kowalewski et al. 1978:191–192; Kowalewski et al. 1989).

The Valley of Oaxaca Settlement Pattern Project has provided data showing that population trajectories differed from subvalley to subvalley. Feinman and Nicholas (2017:83–84) have characterized Etla's and Tlacolula's population trajectories in the following way: the Etla subvalley and the area around Monte Albán had a large population in Period IIIb; it declined in Period IV and rebounded in Period V. In contrast, the Tlacolula subvalley had a large population in Period IIIa, declined in IIIb, recovered during Period IV, and expanded even more dramatically in Period V.

Feinman and Nicholas emphasize that even within the Tlacolula subvalley, there were major differences between the western sector and the eastern sector. For example, when populations declined during Period IIIb in the western sector of the Tlacolula subvalley, populations were increasing in the eastern sector. To the east of Lambityeco, in particular, settlements grew significantly during Periods IV and V (see Chapter 17).

The eastern half of the Tlacolula arm ultimately became the demographic center of the region, accounting for 62% of that subvalley's population. It is believed to have become a commercial center by producing salt, cotton, and maguey for other parts of the valley (Canseco [1580]1905; Faulseit 2012, 2013; Faulseit et al. 2018; Feinman and Nicholas 2017).

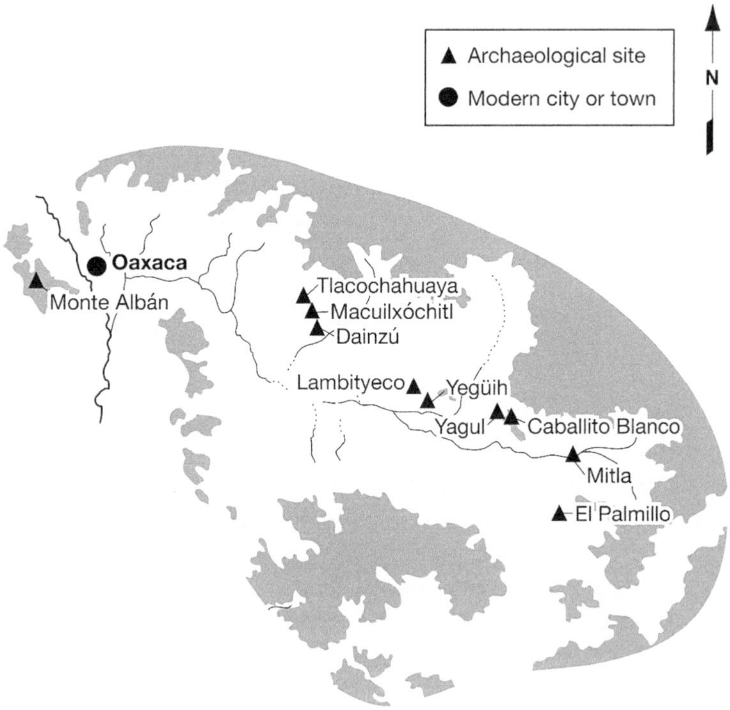

Figure 15.1. Map of the Tlacolula arm of the valley, showing key sites (see also Feinman and Nicholas 2017: Chapter 6). Drawing by John Klausmeyer.

The Monuments of Lambityeco

Approximately two kilometers west of the modern town of Tlacolula lies Yegüih, an archaeological zone covering more than 75 ha (Paddock et al. 1968; Peterson 1976). Some of the (approximately) 250 mounds in that zone reveal occupation going back to 800 BC or earlier.

The northwestern sector of Yegüih has 70 mounds that Paddock (1983d:197) regarded as having been occupied during Period IV. This northwestern sector is locally called "Lambityeco," a hybrid term (part Spanish, part Zapotec) that refers to salt production. Such a name is apt because one of the ancient activities documented there was the production of salt from local saline springs, beginning by ca. 300 BC and becoming increasingly important over time.

Lambityeco's site core was carefully planned, with all buildings having the same orientation. Its palaces were positioned on the north side of the ceremonial center, as was the case at Monte Albán (Feinman and Nicholas 2017:88). A ballcourt similar in size and orientation to the one in Monte Albán's Main Plaza was also built there.

Late in Period IIIb–IV, Monte Albán began a slow decline. At that point local elites at secondary centers, including Lambityeco, had a chance to create their own trade networks and commission their own monuments, including genealogical registers honoring their own noble lineages.

Both at Lambityeco and at El Palmillo near Matatlán, the palaces of nobles were growing in size. They came to be organized around two interior patios, a significant departure from the earlier one-patio Zapotec palaces. The civic-ceremonial core of Lambityeco was remodeled, along with the ballcourt. This remodeling of the ballcourt made it less similar to those at Monte Albán (Feinman and Nicholas 2011; Feinman and Nicholas 2016b). In addition, Lambityeco's ballcourt was now located between two palaces, making it readily accessible to members of two noble households. Such a location differed from that of Monte Albán's Main Plaza ballcourt.

Lambityeco's Mound 195

John Paddock selected Lambityeco's Mound 195 for excavation based largely on its accessibility—a mere 35 meters south of the Panamerican Highway. Excavation of Mound 195, which was six meters high, revealed six superimposed elite residences. Successive generations of nobles had occupied these residences and were later buried below them (Lind and Urcid 1983, 2010; Miller 1995; Rabin 1970; see also Batres 1901; Bernal 1965b; Bernal and Gamio 1974; Holmes 1895; Pohl 1999, 2005).

The earliest residence, Structure 195-6, consisted of four rooms around a central patio. Beneath the room on the east side was Tomb 5, an original component of the overall residential plan. The final and uppermost building in the sequence was Structure 195-3, which covered 434 m^2 and featured two impressive interior patios surrounded by several rooms.

Figure 15.2. Tomb 6 at Lambityeco was opened at least six times during a period of ca. 100 years (see Fig. 11.5, Chapter 11). Multiple generations of noble couples were venerated on stucco friezes in front of the tomb, including Lord 4Ñ and Lady 10 Monkey (depicted on the north frieze). That couple was succeeded by others, including Lord 8 Owl and Lady 3E (depicted on the south frieze). Note that each male ruler brandishes his predecessor's femur, symbolic of his right to rule. Drawing by John Klausmeyer.

Tomb 5 at Lambityeco was largely destroyed when the main chamber of a later tomb (Tomb 6) intruded into it (see Figure 11.5, Chapter 11). Over the entrance to Tomb 6 appeared large stucco depictions of a marital pair that Emily Rabin has designated Lady 10J (10 Maize) and Lord 1L or 1P (Rabin 1970:12 and Figure 18). More recently, Lind and Urcid (2010) have interpreted the husband's name as Lord 1Ñ or 1 Lachi (1 Ballcourt).

Lord 1 Lachi and Lady 10 Maize probably lived in Structure 195-3 sometime between AD 775 and 800. Sometime after their stucco portraits had been attached to the tomb's façade, the modeled heads were covered over and protected from damage with a layer of mud and a mat. The impression of the mat was still visible in the mud covering the portraits, which suggested to the excavators that these portraits were uncovered every time the tomb was reopened, then covered and protected every time it was closed.

In front of the portraits, there is evidence that visitors had come to pay their respects. They left behind several miniature vessels, a number of which depict *Cociyo*. While some of these vessels actually represent Lightning, others likely represent humans impersonating a range of supernatural beings (Marcus 1983b).

Like the tomb entrances at Xoxocotlán (Chapter 14), the area immediately in front of Tomb 6 at Lambityeco witnessed a series of rituals involving eating, drinking, offering libations, and burning incense. These rites were probably conducted on the anniversaries of the interment of the tomb occupants. The final offerings placed in front of Lady 10 Maize and Lord 1 Lachi were arranged in two groups. Two small human male effigies and a jaguar effigy were placed near Lord 1 Lachi. Associated with Lady 10 Maize was a vessel depicting a bearded male, who may represent her husband (Lind and Urcid 2010).

Six skeletons were found in Tomb 6; they were missing nine of the expected twelve femora. An explanation for the missing femora can be found in the stucco friezes placed on the outside of the tomb (Figure 15.2). Those friezes show four men brandishing human femora (*chita baala*), leading us to conclude that each successive ruler retrieved his father's femur as proof of his genealogical right to rule. Each of the men shown brandishing a femur is depicted with his wife.

Arthur Miller (1995:147–149) has reconstructed three of the generations of married couples in the Tomb 6 friezes as follows:

Generation 1: Lord 1 Lachi and Lady 10 Maize ("Ancestral Couple" on the Tomb Façade)
Generation 2: Lord 4 Lachi and Lady 10 Monkey (North Frieze)
Generation 3: Lord 8 Owl and Lady 3 Earthquake (South Frieze)

To account for the six skeletons in the tomb, Miller reconstructed three successive marital pairs, leaving out a fourth couple in the friezes, Lord 8 Death and Lady 5 Reed. For their part, Lind and Urcid (1983:88) offered a reconstruction of four generations:

Generation 1: Lord 4 Lachi and Lady 10 Monkey
Generation 2: Lord 8 Owl and Lady 3 Earthquake
Generation 3: Lord 1 Lachi and Lady 10 Maize
Generation 4: Lord 8 Death and Lady 5 Reed

Finally, in a more recent reconstruction, Lind and Urcid (2010) have identified five generations leading back to an apical ancestor named 2 Chilla. Their expanded reconstruction is as follows:

Generation 1: 2 Chilla or 2 Lagarto (an apical ancestor) (AD 650 to 675)
Generation 2: Lord 4 Lachi and Lady 10 Monkey (AD 675 to 700) (North Frieze)
Generation 3: Lord 5 Jaguar and Lady 4 ? (AD 700 to 725) (buried in Tomb 5?)
Generation 4: Lord 8 Laala and Lady 3 Earthquake (AD 725 and 750) (buried in Tomb 6?) (South Frieze)
Generation 5: Lord ? and Lady 5 Maize (AD 750 and 775) (buried in Tomb 6?)
Generation 6: Lord 1 Lachi and Lady 10 Maize (AD 775 to 800) (buried in Tomb 6?)

In contrast to Miller (1995), Lind and Urcid (2010) surmise that Lady 10 Maize was the last person to be buried in Tomb 6. They suggest that the descendants of Lord 1 Lachi took his remains with them when they moved away from the residential compound (Lind and Urcid 2010:189).

Note that the removal of an important ancestor has numerous precedents in Oaxaca—going all the way back to the Rosario phase (700–500 BC), when the skeletal remains from Tomb 10 at San José Mogote were removed (Marcus and Flannery 1996:132–133). Left behind in Tomb 10 were a patella, a few ribs, and 11 small projectile points, all of which may have been overlooked because they were hidden by a thick deposit of red pigment.

Tomb 6 at Lambityeco was evidently opened multiple times over approximately 100 years, and several marital pairs were venerated at this locality (Joseph Mogor, field notes). The exact number of marital pairs is still not certain, because sections of the external friezes were in fragments (Rabin 1970). Nevertheless, two things are clear: (1) the exterior stucco friezes were designed to express dynastic continuity by depicting married couples through whom descendants could claim privileges and rights; and (2) genealogical continuity and noble descent were illustrated by showing each son holding the femur of his father. Exterior tomb friezes clearly constitute horizontal propaganda, serving the needs of noble descendants even more than they served the needs of the deceased.

The Lambityeco data reinforce two longstanding Zapotec practices. To begin with, honoring a sequence of married couples had a long history in Oaxaca, one that continued into the Colonial era. For example, in a sixteenth-century document called the *Etla Genealogy*, we see a founding couple depicted in front of a building that represents a lineage house; then we see all the married couples that succeeded the founders (Whitecotton 1990: Figures 3.2–3.5). During the earliest generations recorded in the *Etla Genealogy*, marriages took place between first-born sons and first-born daughters; whether this pattern also characterized Period IIIb–IV is not known.

A second point is that the retrieval of femora was not restricted to Lambityeco. Recent excavations by Lacey Carpenter (2019) at Tilcajete have documented the removal of femora from burials, one as early as Period Ia. Excavations by Feinman et al. (2010) at the Mitla Fortress (two kilometers west of the town of Mitla) have revealed that the right femur was the only large bone removed from the grave of a Late Classic male 44–50 years of age. Feinman et al. (2010:1099) conclude that "the descendants of an important person carefully reopened his burial cist well after death to extract the individual's right femur." Where such femora were stored after they had been removed is not known.

Monuments of Macuilxóchitl

Macuilxóchitl, which lies to the west of Lambityeco, was one of a cluster of sites with Period IIIb–IV stone monuments (see also Faulseit 2012, 2013; Paddock 1983d; Whitecotton 1977, 1982, 1983). This cluster included Macuilxóchitl, Teotitlán del Valle, and Tlacochahuaya (as well as Dainzú; see Chapter 8). According to the Valley of Oaxaca Settlement Pattern Project, the site with the largest IIIb–IV population in the Tlacolula arm of the valley was Macuilxóchitl. Macuilxóchitl also ranked highest in mound height and volume.

More than two dozen carved stones believed to be from the site of Macuilxóchitl have been found in the nearby town's churches, streets, walls, and houses; evidently they were considered readily available construction material in Colonial and recent times. Most, but not all, have been published by Bernal and Seuffert (1973); one that was not is Monument 26 (see below).

The Macuilxóchitl sculptors used stone that was easy to carve, and unfortunately when exposed to the elements it was also highly vulnerable to spalling and rapid deterioration. Bernal and Seuffert (1973:9) noted that "all the pieces are carved from a local stone which unfortunately is of a bad quality and erodes easily; flakes of it chip off, damaging the surface."

Since Bernal and Seuffert have already published many of the Macuilxóchitl monuments, I will present only a sample of them here.

Monument 1

Monument 1 of Macuilxóchitl, found in the façade of the church, has a height of 1.51m. Bernal and Seuffert assigned this stone to Period IIIb.

The stone shows an older man holding a bag in his left hand. His right hand appears to be in the act of scattering (Figure 15.3). By analogy with individuals on other monuments of this era, this man may have been divining by scattering corn kernels or incense beads that he had been carrying in his bag.

The man wears an elaborate headdress decorated with feathers and has a short cape tied around his throat. He wears possible knee guards and a cloth band around the knees. His headdress and sandals signal that he is a high-status individual.

The name of the man on Monument 1 is apparently given above his headdress. The number 13 is legible, but the element inside the cartouche is not; it might be Caso's Glyph E. In addition to his calendric name, the man has a sign in front of his face that may be a nickname. This sign seemingly includes a reed-like element and either flowing water or blood. Bernal and Seuffert (1973:11) suggested that his name + nickname might be "13 Turquoise-Water-Flower." This kind of composite name is similar to several of those included in the murals of Tombs 104 and 105 at Monte Albán (Chapter 9). Alternatively, I would read it as "13 Earthquake + Water/Blood + Reed."

Monument 2

Monument 2 of Macuilxóchitl, which was also found in the church, has a width of 70 cm. The uppermost part of Monument 2 is somewhat eroded, but seems to show a person sitting cross-legged on a box or possible toponym or place name (Figure 15.4). Bernal and Seuffert (1973:10–11) suggest that the motif inside the box might be a depiction of Lightning.

Monument 3

Monument 3 measures 90 cm in width and displays a noble couple conducting a ritual inside a cartouche (Figure 15.5). The Zapotec cartouche usually consists of a frame with scrolls at the midpoint of its left and right sides, and this example is no exception.

At the top of Monument 3 is an abbreviated version of the Jaws of the Sky. Descending from that motif is an element that could be interpreted either as the head of a bird or a human hand. Bernal and Seuffert (1973:11) characterized this element as "a hand with two outstretched fingers reaching down from the sky. This divine intervention appears in almost all the similar scenes we know." I would add that sometimes the descending figure is more avian than human, and sometimes more human than avian. Often the figure holds strands of beads, leaves, or yet-to-be-identified items.

Inside Monument 3's ancestor cartouche we see a man and a woman, each associated with a speech scroll. The man's hieroglyphic name (at far left) includes the number "12," but no day sign is given. He is seated cross-legged with his arms folded across his chest, wearing earspools and a necklace of large beads. He also seems to be wearing a cloth headdress.

The woman (at right) is shown kneeling. The number "3" appears in the upper right corner, but just as we saw with the man's name, the day sign is not given. This woman has a hieroglyph

Figure 15.3. Macuilxóchitl was a major settlement with many Period IIIb–IV carved stones. Monument 1 shows 13E, a man whose name appears above his headdress. A compound sign, consisting of reed + water, appears in front of his face (see Bernal and Seuffert 1973:11). In his left hand he holds a bag, possibly containing items to be cast in divination. Drawing by Lois Martin.

Figure 15.4. Monument 2 of Macuilxóchitl shows a person seated cross-legged on a box that may also serve as a toponym (see Bernal and Seuffert 1973:11). Drawing by John Klausmeyer.

Figure 15.5. Monument 3 of Macuilxóchitl features a noble couple inside a frame with side scrolls. At the top of the monument is a variant of the Jaws of the Sky motif, with what may be a bird head or a human hand descending from it. The most unusual feature of this monument is its lack of day signs (see Bernal and Seuffert 1973:11). Associated with the man (at left) is the number 12; associated with the kneeling woman (at right) is the number 3. The only day sign in the scene is that held by the woman; it is Glyph J (maize). Drawing by John Klausmeyer.

in her outstretched hand—Glyph J, which is the depiction of a corncob. Possibly her name was 3 Maize (see also Bernal and Seuffert 1973:11).

Monument 4

Monument 4 measures 84 cm in height (Figure 15.6). This is the depiction of a ballplayer or gladiator with his helmet and faceguard; it is so similar to the gladiators from Dainzú that Bernal and Seuffert (1973, 1979) suggested that this stone was actually brought from Dainzú to Macuilxóchitl (see also Taube and Zender 2009). As in the case of the Dainzú gladiators, there are ruffs of scrolls or volutes below the helmet.

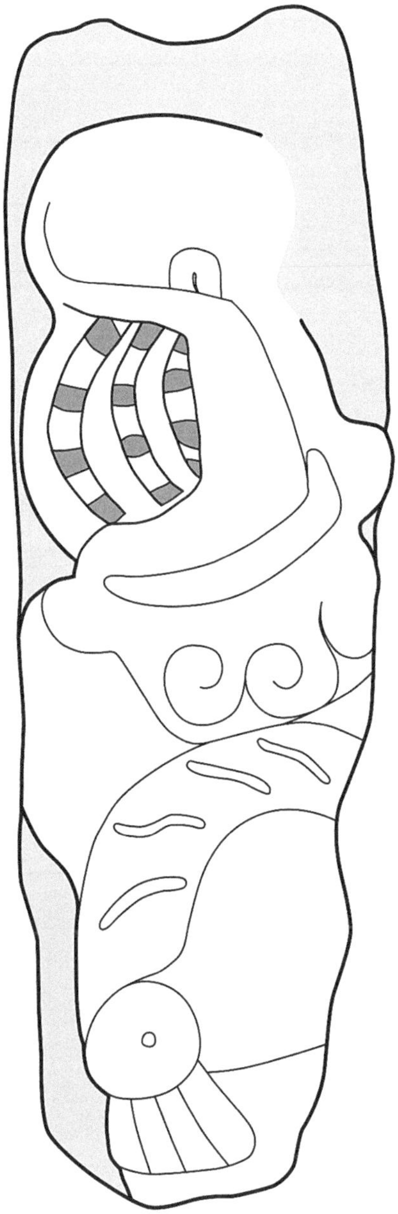

Figure 15.6. Monument 4 of Macuilxóchitl is so similar to the helmeted gladiators on carved stones at Dainzú (see Chapter 8) that Bernal and Seuffert (1973:13) suggested that this stone might have been brought from the latter site. Drawing by John Klausmeyer.

Monument 5

The left portion of Monument 5 is missing (Figure 15.7). The height of the surviving fragment is 1.5 m. At the upper right we see a reptilian creature with an upturned snout, similar to those shown on ballcourt markers and in many tombs. Below we see an animal head, followed by a jaguar with a bar and two dots, suggesting the name 7 Jaguar. The huge glyph at the center of this monument, although damaged, appears to be the Year 10E. See Color Plate VI, this volume.

Monument 11

Although Bernal and Seuffert (1973:15) thought the hieroglyph on this stone might be a flower, it could also be reconstructed as 3 Knot (3A) (Figure 15.8).

Monument 12

This stone measures 78 cm in height. I suspect that this isolated hieroglyph may represent 3 or 8 Rain (i.e., 3C or 8C). Bernal and Seuffert (1973:17), however, reconstruct it as 3 Maize (3J) (Figure 15.9).

Monument 13

The seated figure on this stone has a cape decorated with crosshatching. This monument's height is 33 cm (Figure 15.10).

Monument 17

This monument, which has a width of 23 cm, shows one isolated glyph that I believe corresponds to 4E (Figure 15.11).

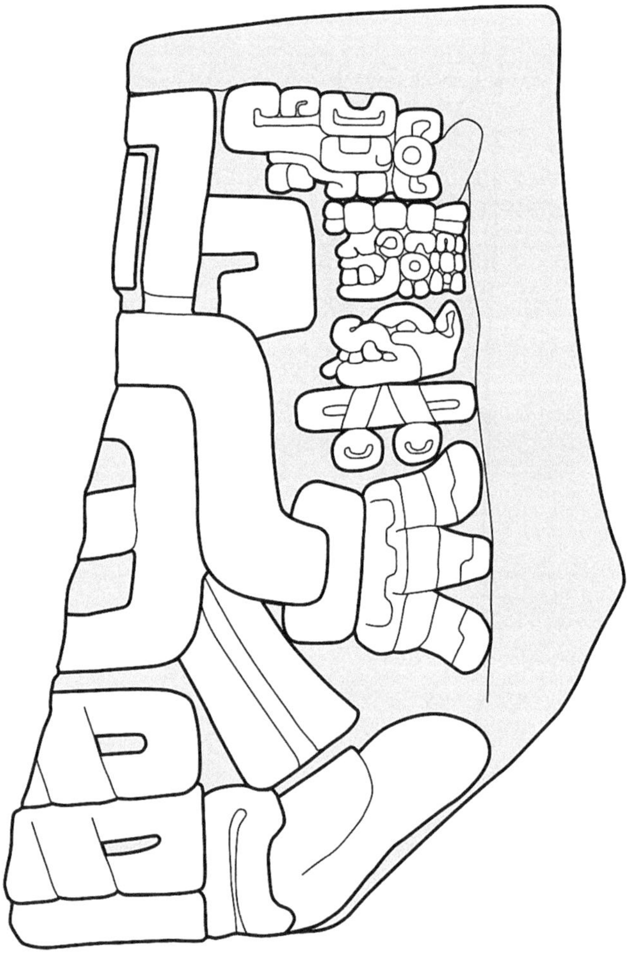

Figure 15.7. Monument 5 of Macuilxóchitl displays a short hieroglyphic text (at right) that begins with a reptilian creature with an upturned snout and ends with the name 7 Jaguar (see Bernal and Seuffert 1973:13). The huge hieroglyph at the center of the monument (of which less than half remains) appears to be the Year 10E. Drawing by John Klausmeyer. See Color Plate VI, this volume.

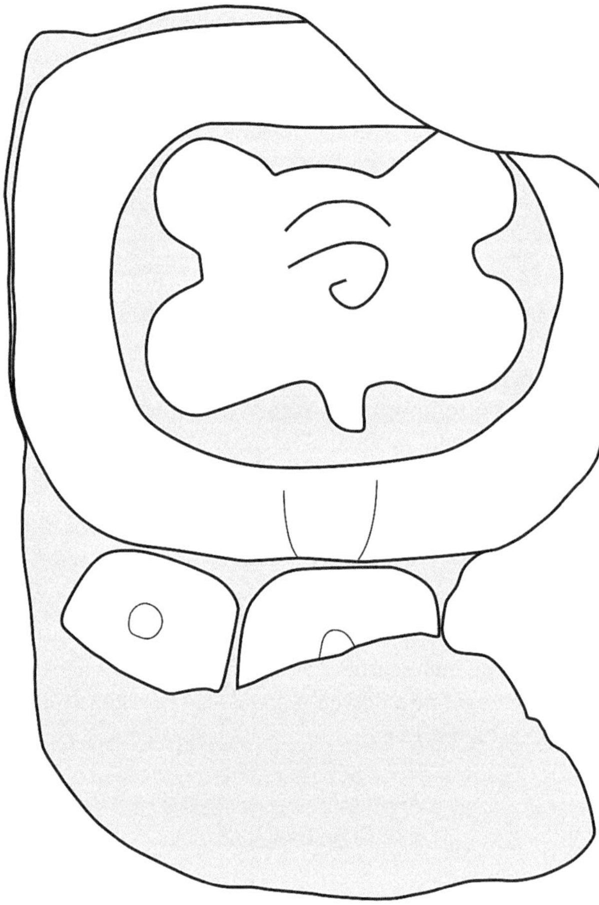

Figure 15.8. Monument 11 of Macuilxóchitl may be interpreted as 3 Knot, although other possibilities exist (see Bernal and Seuffert 1973:15). Drawing by John Klausmeyer.

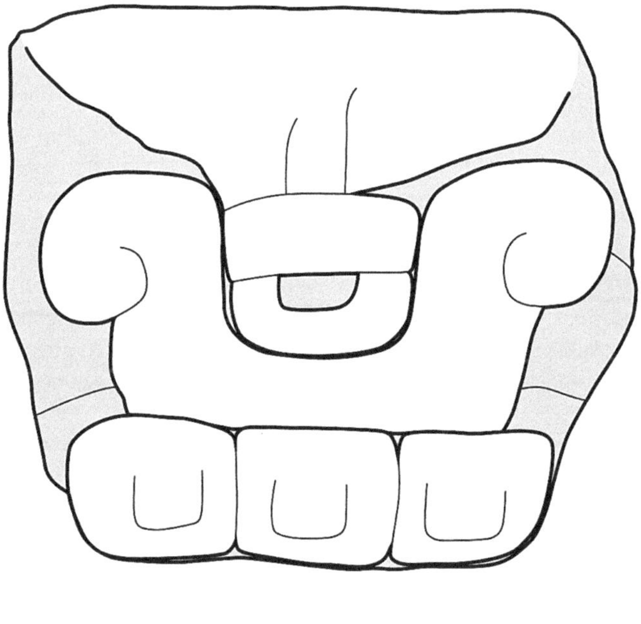

Figure 15.9. Monument 12 of Macuilxóchitl displays what may be Glyph 3C or 8C (see Bernal and Seuffert 1973:17). Drawing by John Klausmeyer.

Figure 15.10. Monument 13 of Macuilxóchitl shows a seated figure wearing a cape (see Bernal and Seuffert 1973:17). Drawing by John Klausmeyer.

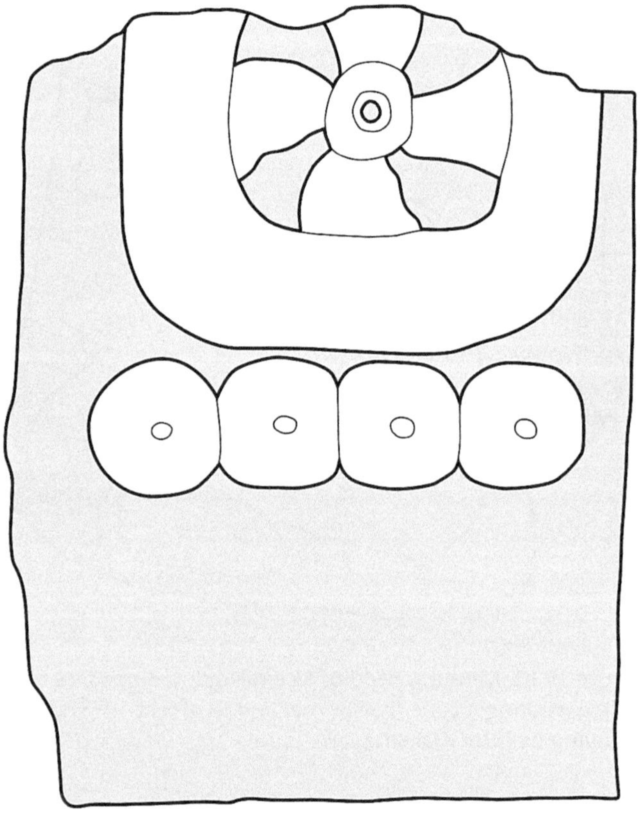

Figure 15.11. Monument 17 of Macuilxóchitl shows one isolated glyph, which appears to be 4E (see Bernal and Seuffert 1973:17). Drawing by John Klausmeyer.

Monument 22

This fragment has a height of 80 cm. It was once part of a beautifully carved stone that seems to show the Jaws of the Sky, below which we see an elaborate headdress that includes the downturned snout of a supernatural bird; the rest of the individual who wears this headdress must be on another fragment (Figure 15.12a).

Monument 23

This monument has a width of 95 cm and is carved on two sides. On one side we see 6 Jaguar inside a hill sign; on the other side we see a year sign (see Figure 7.12, Chapter 7).

Monument 26

Monument 26 shows the Year 8E and the Day 5E. We also see (at right) a cluster of signs that refers to anniversaries and mortuary offerings; that cluster includes a skull, a hand, and the Maltese cross (Figure 15.12b).

Monuments of Tlacochahuaya

The archaeological site of Tlacochahuaya lies directly across the Panamerican Highway from Macuilxóchitl and probably had strong ties to the latter site (see also Faulseit 2013). Since Bernal and Seuffert (1973) have already published the monuments of Tlacochahuaya, I have only chosen a sample in order to illustrate the similarities they share with carved stones from sites nearby.

Monument 1

Monument 1, which measures 110 cm in height, shows a man wearing an elaborate costume with a jaguar headdress and a mask or trophy head suspended from a cord around his neck (see Figure 15.13).

Monument 8

Monument 8 is now only a fragment some 80 cm high (Figure 15.14). The face of the person depicted is largely eroded, but we can see feathers and a necklace.

Monument 9

This monument, which features a serpent with an upturned snout, was probably once part of a much larger group of stones set in a

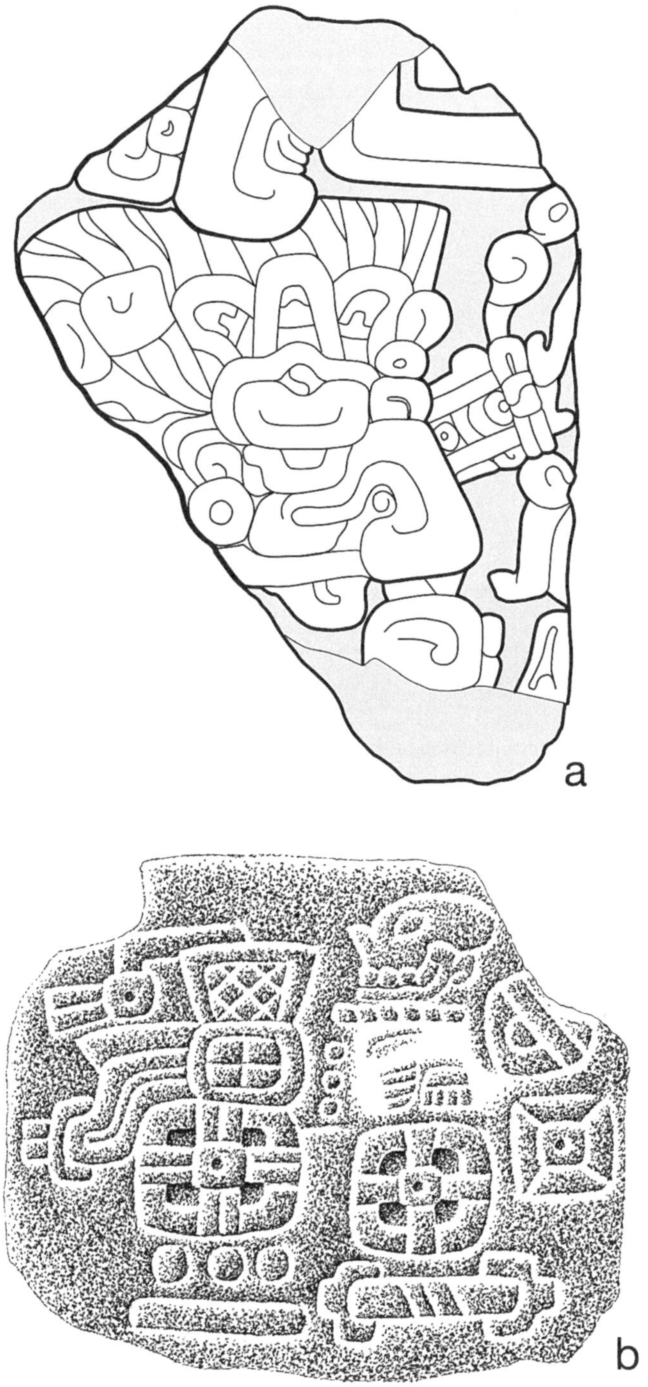

Figure 15.12. Carved stones from Macuilxóchitl. *a*, Monument 22 seems to show an elaborate headdress that includes the same downturned snout of a bird also seen in the Jaws of the Sky above. *b*, Monument 26 displays the Year 8E and a date of 5E. We also see a cluster of signs (at right) that includes the Maltese cross, a glyph associated with anniversaries and mortuary offerings. Drawing in *a* is by John Klausmeyer; *b* was drawn by Lois Martin.

Figure 15.13. Monument 1 of Tlacochahuaya shows a man wearing an elaborate costume, with a mask or trophy head suspended from a cord around his neck (see Bernal and Seuffert 1973:23). This is an in-the-field sketch by Mark Orsen.

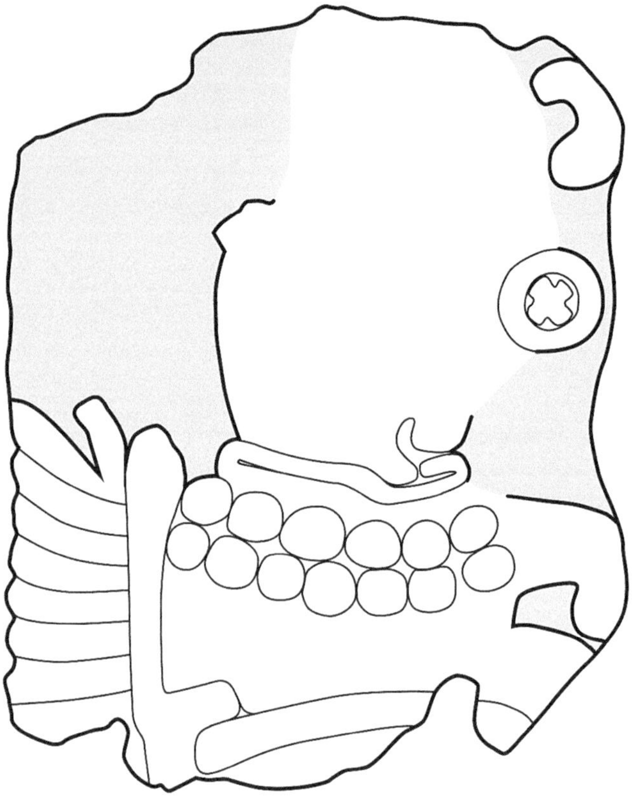

Figure 15.14. Monument 8 of Tlacochahuaya may show the eroded face of a person who wears a necklace with two rows of beads (see Bernal and Seuffert 1973:25). Drawing by John Klausmeyer.

building (Figure 15.15). The stone's width is 80 cm (Bernal and Seuffert 1973).

Monument 11

This stone, with a diameter of 45 cm, is now located in the belfry of the Tlacochahuaya church (Figure 15.16). The hieroglyphic name is 9 Jaguar (Bernal and Seuffert 1973:27).

The Monuments of Yagul

Yagul, a mesa-top site near Tlacolula, was an important community during Period IIIb–IV. The site was divided into three sectors (Bernal and Gamio 1974). At the center was an enormous artificial platform that supported temples and palaces; on the surrounding slopes was a large residential zone. During Period V a palace with multiple patios was built at Yagul.

Excavations on a terrace in the residential zone yielded a tomb with three important carved stones; two of these were lintels, and the third was the door to the tomb. This tomb (Tomb 28) had an outer vestibule, an antechamber (with Lintel 1), and a burial chamber (with Lintel 2). The door stone was no longer in its original position; it had been left face down—presumably after the tomb's final reopening, at which time it appears that all skeletons were removed. During the 1958 field season, directed by John Paddock, project members William O. Payne and Kent V. Flannery excavated Tomb 28.

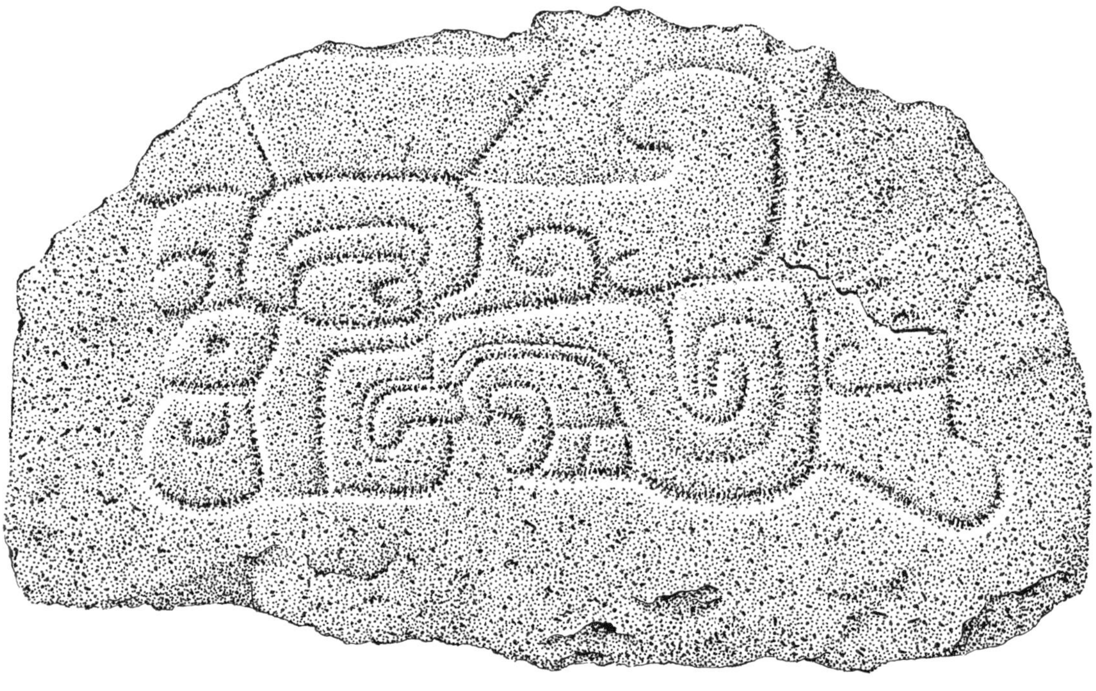

Figure 15.15. Monument 9 of Tlacochahuaya features a serpent with an upturned snout similar to that on the *yahui* or *xicàni* (see Bernal and Seuffert 1973:25). Drawing by John Klausmeyer.

The Carved Door of Tomb 28

When the door of Tomb 28 was discovered, its carved surface was face down and in good condition, given that it had been protected from the elements. At its top center we see the Maltese cross (Glyph I), which often appeared in mortuary settings and was likely associated with offerings and anniversaries (Figure 15.17). Glyph I, in this case, is associated with the number "1" and a descending footprint.

As Caso (1928:35) noted, Glyph I could occur with or without a numeral and was often associated with tomb doors and jambs, with a human head that had its mouth open and eyes closed, or with a human figure or statuette. The use of Glyph I and the number "1" on this door may indicate that offerings were made on the first anniversary of the occupant's interment. Flanking Glyph I are two pairs of glyphs that may refer to marital pairs.

The two rows of text are as follows:

Upper: 13 Lightning	1+I	8 Monkey
Lower: 10? Chilla	7+Z	4 Chilla

Lintel 1 of Tomb 28

Lintel 1 overlooks the entrance to the antechamber (Figure 15.18); three large hieroglyphs dominate the text. At the left is 8 Monkey (8O). The middle hieroglyph is the Year 6 Lightning (6M). On the right is 7 Jaguar (7B).

Noteworthy in this tomb is the repetition of the name 8 Monkey, who may be mentioned as many as three times. Unfortunately, it is not clear whether 8 Monkey was (1) the principal occupant of the tomb, (2) an apical ancestor from whom everyone else claimed descent, or (3) the descendant who would benefit the most by commissioning these carved stones.

Lintel 2 of Tomb 28

Lintel 2, set over the entrance to the burial chamber, mentions the Year 2M (Figure 15.19). The central position of this year sign suggests that 2M may be either the year in which the principal occupant died or the name of an apical ancestor. We are uncertain how many years separated the Year 6M on Lintel 1 and the Year 2M on Lintel 2. If 6M was the starting date and 2M the final date, some 48 years would have elapsed. If, on the other hand, 2M was the start and 6M the finish, only 4 years would have elapsed. The latter scenario may be more likely, since Saville (1904) cited four years as the period after which Zapotec visitors would return to honor the dead.

Finally, the name 3 or 8 Owl or Night occurs to the left of the Year 2M, while the name 8 Monkey occurs to the right. This leads us to wonder whether 3 Owl (or 8 Owl) was 8 Monkey's spouse.

Clearly, the story of 8 Monkey and his relatives is being told by the door and lintels of Yagul's Tomb 28. We just need

Figure 15.16. Monument 11 of Tlacochahuaya, which bears the name 9 Jaguar, is now set high in the wall of the local church (see Bernal and Seuffert 1973:27). Photo by the author.

Figure 15.17. Yagul, a mesa-top site, was another important community during Period IIIb–IV. Excavations on a terrace in the residential zone of Yagul yielded Tomb 28, which featured three carved stones. Shown here is the tomb door that seems to mention two marital couples. Facing each other at the top are 13M and 8 Monkey, separated by a 1 + Glyph I. Facing each other at the bottom are 10 Chilla and 4 Chilla, separated by Glyph 7Z. Drawing by Mark Orsen.

Figure 15.18. In addition to its carved door, Tomb 28 of Yagul had two carved lintels. At the entrance to the antechamber was Lintel 1, which shows three large hieroglyphs: 8 Monkey + Year 6 Lightning + 7 Jaguar. Note that this is the second mention of 8 Monkey (see Figure 15.17). Drawing by Mark Orsen.

Figure 15.19. Lintel 2 of Tomb 28 was set over the entrance to the burial chamber. The name 8 Owl occurs at left; then we see the Year 2 Lightning; and, at right, the name 8 Monkey. The fact that 8 Monkey's name appears three times (on the tomb door and on Lintels 1 and 2) leads us to suspect that he was either the principal occupant of the tomb or an apical ancestor. Drawing by Mark Orsen.

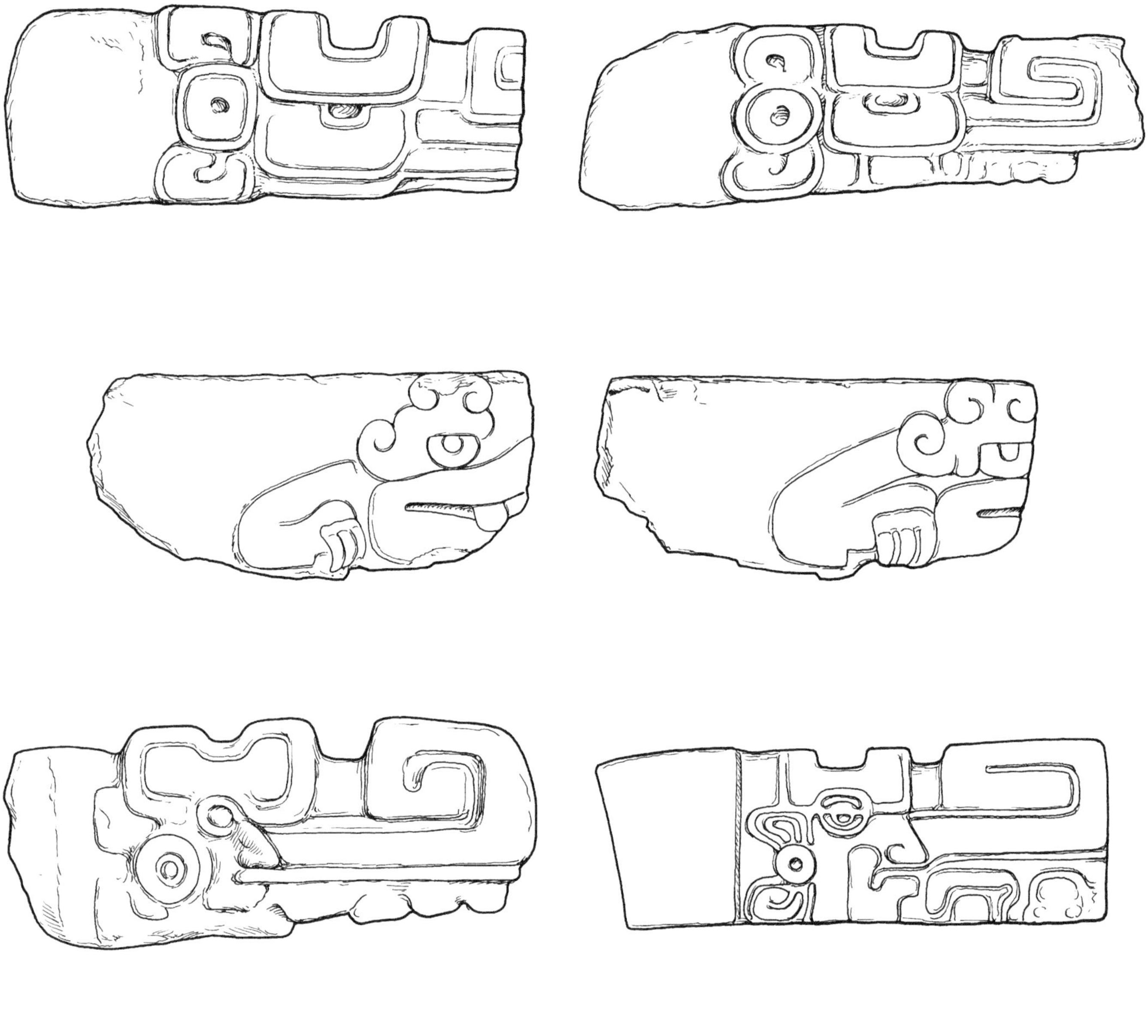

Figure 15.20. These carved stones were found in the Sola Valley, to the south of the Valley of Oaxaca. They appear to have functioned as tenons that had been inserted into walls. Andrew Balkansky, who systematically surveyed the Sola Valley, suggested that some of these stones came from his Site 111. All depict a long-nosed supernatural being who shares crocodilian attributes with carved stones in the Valley of Oaxaca. Redrawn by John Klausmeyer from Balkansky 2002, Berlin 1951, and Marcus 2002.

to decipher all the hieroglyphs to understand 8 Monkey's life more fully.

Ballcourt Monuments

Tenoned stones have been found at a number of sites in the Tlacolula subvalley (for example, at Yagul, Lambityeco, and Mitla), as well as at Zapotec sites outside the Valley of Oaxaca (e.g., Sola de Vega). We are confident that many of these stones functioned as tenons, based on their shape and the sizable portion of the stone's shaft that was left uncarved. The shaft would have been inserted into a building wall, façade, or stairway.

Heinrich Berlin (1946, 1951) was the first to see an association between tenons and ballcourts. His fieldwork focused on the Sola Valley, to the south of the Valley of Oaxaca and west of Ejutla. Among the 40 carved stones that Berlin found at Sola were several tenons, many of which depict reptilian or crocodilian creatures with upturned snouts (Figure 15.20). During his systematic survey of the Sola Valley, Andrew Balkansky located another example of this kind of carved stone in the center of a ballcourt at his Site 39 (Balkansky 2002; Marcus 2002: Figures 7.15–7.18).

During the 1954 excavations at Yagul, Oriol Pi-Sunyer and Charles Wicke found a carved stone in the ballcourt (Wicke 1957: Figure 30). This ballcourt stone is described as follows:

> This was a large block of stone carved in the shape of a serpent head which had been re-used to make up part of the wall. The head is very stylized and exhibits arms and hands. The hands show five fingers with nails. The arm develops an earplug from which a feather extends upward. The rectangular eye is pitted by a deep pupil and a superior and inferior plate surrounds it. The nose, which turns upon itself, is continuous with and balanced by the mouth, which also turns in a similar manner. The prominent front teeth are set in equally prominent gums that jut out slightly (Wicke 1957:68).

Although found in the Yagul ballcourt (to be specific, in the southwest corner of the eastern end zone), this tenoned "serpent stone" was no longer *in situ* (Figure 15.21). The Yagul ballcourt is oriented east-west, in contrast to the ballcourts at Reyes Etla, San José Mogote, and Monte Albán's Main Plaza.

Tomb 7 at Mitla has produced a carved stone which, although removed from its original context, shares some features with the aforementioned tenons (Figure 15.22). It has been described as follows:

> At the back of the tomb was found a carved stone, which was utilized as part of the construction material and covered with stucco. It undoubtedly represents the god Cocijo's eye and ear adorned with an earplug. (Oliver 1955:64–66, citing Caso and Rubín de la Borbolla 1936).

Monuments of Santiago Matatlán

The modern town of Santiago Matatlán lies below the steep ridge where the archaeological site of El Palmillo can be found. It seems likely that many of the stone monuments now incorporated into buildings at Matatlán originated at El Palmillo.

El Palmillo extends from the summit of the ridge (at about 2010 m) to multiple stepped terraces that extend down to 1760 m. This site is in one of the most arid parts of the Valley of Oaxaca and is associated with many drought-resistant plants, including eight species of maguey (Carpenter et al. 2012; Feinman and Nicholas 2001, 2002, 2004, 2011). Maguey is grown today in the region to produce ropes, cords, nets, and cloth. It is likely that such items were also produced and traded by El Palmillo during its heyday (AD 600–900).

Monument 1 of Matatlán

One of the carved stones likely brought to Matatlán from El Palmillo is now in the American Museum of Natural History (catalogue #30.3/1211–12). It is a genealogical register with an older couple in the lower register and a younger couple in the upper register (Figure 15.23; see also Figure 7.6, Chapter 7).

In both of these registers the woman is seated at the left. The woman in the upper register is named 3L and the name of her probable husband is 1 Monkey. The woman in the lower register is named 10 Deer and her husband is 1N or 6N. Both couples appear to be conducting rituals that involve the burning of copal or rubber (Masson and Orr 1998a: Figure 1). A metamorphosed ancestor, descending from the Jaws of the Sky, appears to be decorated with leaves or similar items.

Monument 2 of Matatlán

Among the plaster casts of carved stones stored in Mexico City's Museo Nacional is one that Alfonso Caso called "Lápida 14" (Caso 1928: Figure 94). Although Caso was able to study the cast, he apparently did not know where the actual stone was located. In the 1970s I photographed several carved stones in the Tlacolula arm of the valley, including a stone fragment set in the wall of the Méndez family's house on Calle Independencia in Santiago Matatlán (see Figures A.1–A.3). The stone, which measures 62 x 53 cm, appears to be the Lápida 14 from which the cast was made. It shows two marital pairs, with the men at the left and the women on the right.

At the top of Monument 2 is the Jaws of the Sky. Descending from it are two prominent leaves, which resemble tobacco leaves and a possible bird. The descending item—whether a bird or something else—almost touches the handheld staff, which has two leaves that also resemble tobacco leaves and a possible owl head. This bird at the top of the staff replicates the bird in the

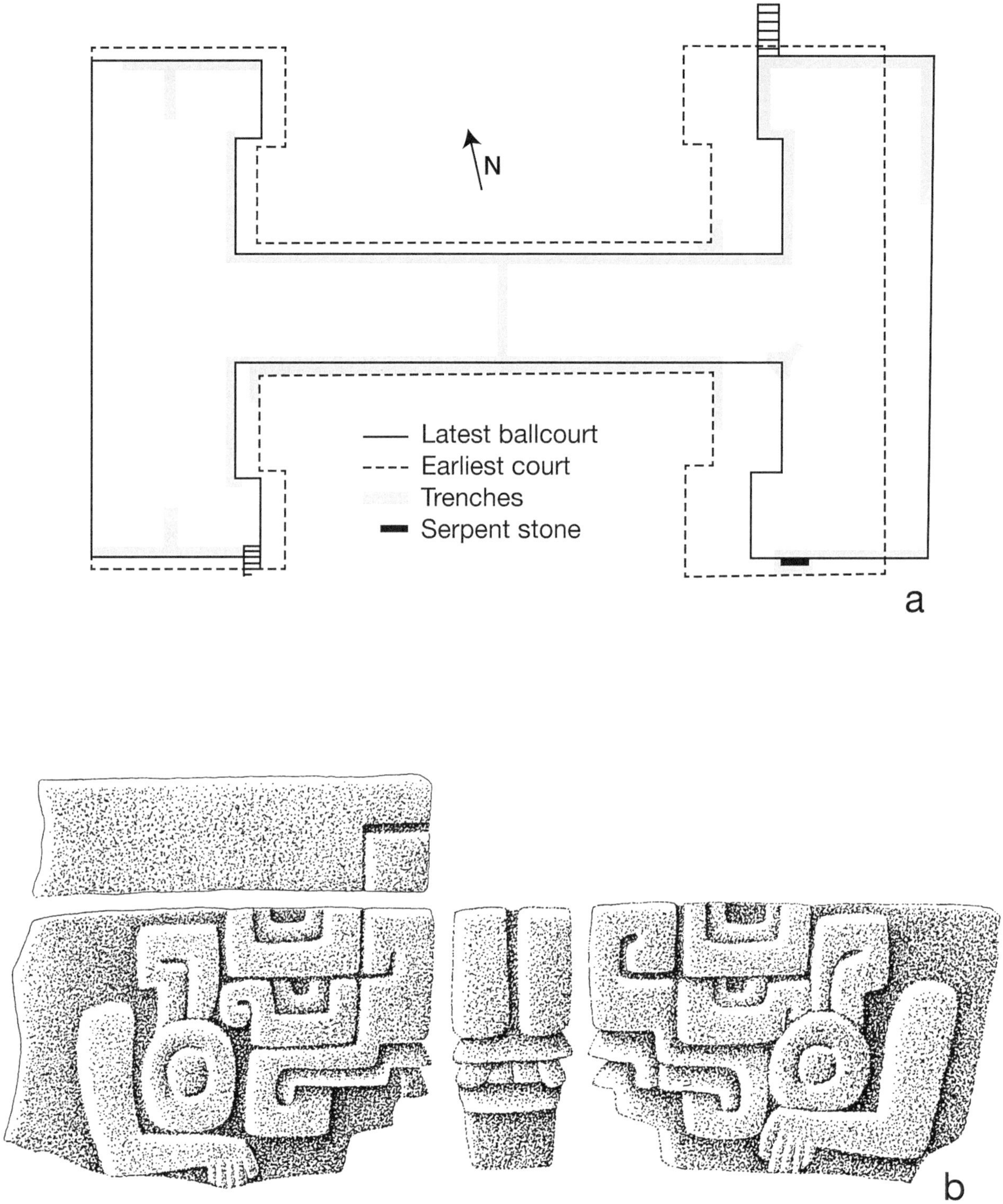

Figure 15.21. Ballcourt and "serpent stone" at Yagul. *a* is a plan of the Yagul ballcourt, showing where the stone (illustrated at *b*) was found. This stone (*b*) features a version of the supernatural being the Zapotec called *xicàni* and the Mixtec called *yahui* (Pohl 1994:67). It combines the upturned snout of a reptilian creature with human arms. Redrawn by John Klausmeyer from Wicke 1957: Fig. 30.

Figure 15.22. This carved stone was found in Tomb 7 at Mitla. Redrawn by John Klausmeyer from Oliver 1955: Fig. 39.

upper left corner, which is associated with the man seated at the upper left (see Figure A.3). This man—probably 13 Owl—has a beard, wrinkles, an ear ornament, and a prominent speech scroll. Caso (1928:121) gave this man's name as 1F or 6F (1 Owl or 6 Owl); however, if I add up all the numerical elements floating on the upper left, I can suggest that this bearded man may have been named 10 Owl or 13 Owl. Feathers are attached to his turban-like headgear, similar to the feathers associated with his female companion, who grasps in both hands the bird staff.

The man at the lower left is known only from his head, because the monument is broken below his chin. This man is presumably from a younger generation, since he lacks wrinkles and a beard. His name is not clear, but I have interpreted it as 10 Maize (10J).

The right half of the stone depicts two women from different generations. The seated woman, whose name I reconstruct as 11C, seems to be the most prominent performer in the bird staff ritual because she grasps a staff with leaves and a bird's head. (Note that these are the same elements seen descending from the Jaws of the Sky.) The woman at lower right (shown only as a bust) is associated with a speech scroll. (Thus the only person not associated with a speech scroll is the woman grasping the bird staff.)

The artifact that I have designated a "bird staff" is not restricted to the Zapotec. A similar staff (called a "tree staff" by V. Garth Norman) is seen on Izapa's Stela 25, as well as on Lintels 2 and 5 at Yaxchilan (Norman 1976: Figure 3.28).

In the lintel above the central doorway of Temple 33 at Yaxchilan we see a boy named Chel Te' Chan K'inich. On Lintel 2, that boy and his father (Bird Jaguar IV) perform a dance that evidently required both of them to hold a bird staff (Schele and Freidel 1990:289). The occasion that called for this dance was the fifth anniversary (AD 757) of his father's accession to office, which took place in AD 752. On Lintel 5 at Yaxchilan, the same

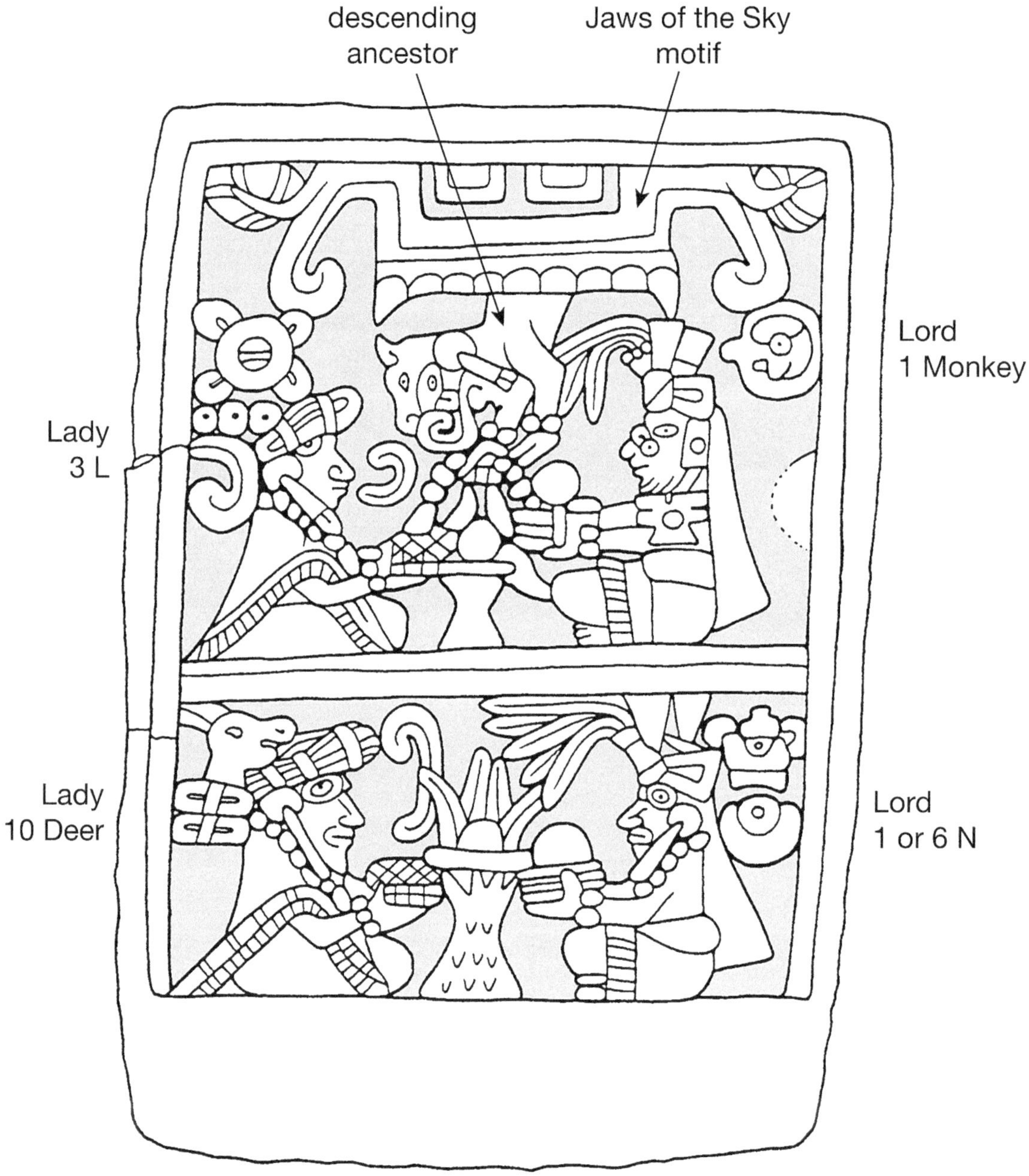

Figure 15.23. The original provenience of this genealogical register may be the archaeological site of El Palmillo, near Matatlán. In the lower register we see a likely marital pair, Lady 10 Deer and Lord 1N (or possibly 6N). In the upper register we see Lady 3L and Lord 1 Monkey. Height: 51 cm. American Museum of Natural History, catalogue #30.3/1211–12. Drawing by John Klausmeyer.

Figure 15.24. Monument 3, probably from Matatlán, is a stone column showing a person wearing an animal headdress while conducting a rite of divination. *Left*, the column. *Right*, a rollout of the column. Drawing by Mark Orsen.

ruler (Bird Jaguar IV) again holds two bird staffs, one in each hand; this occasion seems to have been the completion of Bird Jaguar IV's first 40 days in office. While we cannot be sure exactly what these bird staffs meant to the Zapotec, we can say that for the Maya they were used to mark the end of notable periods of time or anniversaries during a ruler's term of office.

Returning to Monument 2 at Matatlán, we note that the outer frame of the carving is associated with spirals or side scrolls; their presence usually establishes that a scene includes nobles. Thus this monument features two generations of nobles, conducting a rite that involved the holding of a staff.

Monument 3 of Matatlán

Monument 3 is a carved column showing a person with an elaborate headdress in the act of conducting a ritual, possibly divining (Figure 15.24).

Monument 4 of Matatlán

Monument 4 displays a footprint + leaf (Figure 15.25). The footprint + leaf motif also appears on monuments at Monte Albán

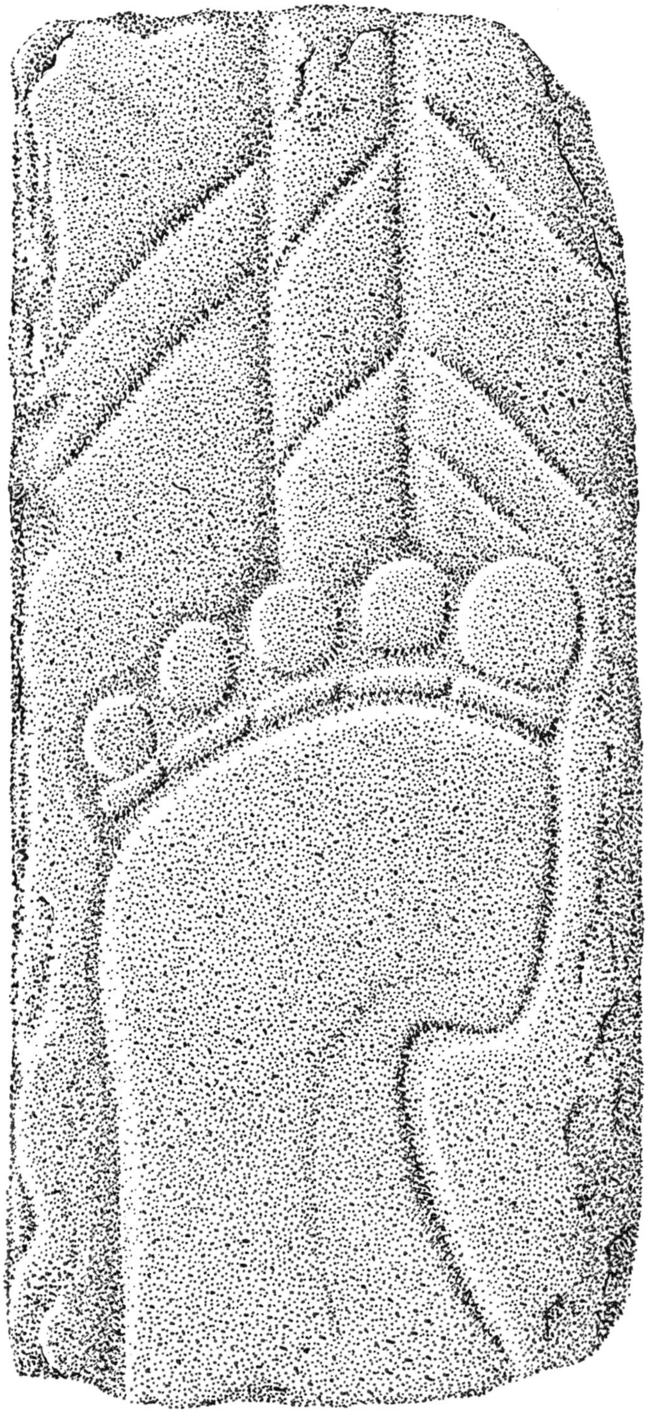

Figure 15.25. Monument 4, probably from Matatlán, shows a footprint and a leaf. This same combination appears on an unprovenienced ceramic sculpture and on stone sculptures at Monte Albán and Zaachila. Drawing by Mark Orsen.

(e.g., one associated with the North Platform) and on the back of an unprovenienced hollow ceramic sculpture (see Chapter 16).

Summary: Monuments of the Tlacolula Subvalley

The Period IIIb–IV monuments of the Tlacolula subvalley contrast with those of Etla. Nowhere in the eastern valley do we see stone monuments of deceased rulers transported in funerary crates. Instead, we see multiple generations of noble marital pairs, sometimes conducting rituals or commemorating ancestors. Time will tell whether these differences represent a true contrast in political strategy or merely sampling error.

16

Monuments without Provenience

When carved stones have been commissioned as a group and are found *in situ* (for example, still arranged in order in the façade of a building), we can often discern their overall message. In contrast, when they are no longer arranged in order (or even worse, no longer associated with an archaeological site), we are forced to spend a considerable amount of time speculating about the stones' original context, provenience, message, and targeted audience.

When the Spaniards arrived in Oaxaca in AD 1521, they began to build churches, municipal buildings, and residences, and to expedite their construction they borrowed any stones conveniently exposed on archaeological sites. Additional monuments were removed by farmers, explorers, looters, and art collectors, some of whom put the carved stones into private collections, churches, restaurant patios, houses, or museums.

Although there are scores of Zapotec monuments that lack provenience, I have selected only a sample to illustrate a few points. The most obvious point is that a great deal of information has been lost. Another point is that monuments have often been attributed to a known site without real evidence. Finally, some of the buildings from which unprovenienced monuments were extracted may still contain related sculptures or carved fragments that were not removed. It might therefore be productive to compile a comprehensive inventory of all broken fragments—published to the same scale—with the goal of tracing monument fragments to their original source (e.g., Boos and Shaplin 1969; Caso 1928; Dieseldorff 1933; Masson and Orr 1998a, 1998b; Paddock 1966a). In the Andes, for example, careful photos and drawings made it possible to show that a broken monument from Tiwanaku (Bolivia) was the missing half of the Thunderbolt Stela from Arapa (Peru) (Chávez 1975; Chávez and Jorgenson 1980).

A Monument from the Etla Arm?

Figure 16.1 shows a beautifully carved, unprovenienced Oaxaca monument of modest size (42 x 34 cm). With advancements in decipherment and the recovery of more genealogical registers, we may one day be able to tie the names of the nobles illustrated on this stone to a specific site. Urcid and Winter (1989) have suggested that this stone was carved near Atzompa, in the Etla arm of the valley. While currently unprovable, such an attribution is plausible, since this monument was carved from raw material

Figure 16.1. This unusual version of a genealogical register (42 x 34 cm) has two vertical bands made up of the blood motif (circle + triangle). These bands divide the stone into three panels, with the central panel mentioning a person named 5 Deer and the Year 11E. At the bottom of the stone we see the eyes of the crocodile, which the Zapotec called *chilla*. Drawing by John Klausmeyer.

still quarried in that area. Moreover, some of its iconographic and stylistic elements are similar to those on monuments from other Etla sites. For example, the depiction of the eyes of the crocodile and the "rolling waves" of primordial waters is known from a San Lorenzo Cacaotepec monument (see Figure 7.8, Chapter 7) and from tomb murals at Monte Albán and Cerro de la Campana (Fahmel Beyer 2005b). To be sure, similar rolling waves and volutes are also known from Izapa (Chiapas), where that motif was used to indicate ground level and primordial waters (e.g., Stela 67, Izapa; see Norman 1976: Figure 3.43).

Layout of the Monument

Vertical bands divide this unprovenienced stone into three parts that are side-by-side. Compartments are also used in genealogical registers (see Chapters 12–15; Martínez Gracida 1910: Vol. II, Plate 45), but it is more typical for such registers to be arranged vertically, showing one generation above another. Genealogical registers also typically include depictions of individuals with their associated name glyphs (e.g., Figures 7.6, 7.7).

This all-glyph monument does not depict individual nobles, but refers to them using only hieroglyphs. The vertical bands dividing the slab into three divisions are ribbon-like strips of blood, advising us that the subject matter is "bloodlines."

Each vertical band is composed of the circle + triangle motif (blood droplet + flowing blood) (see Figures 16.1, 16.2). We first saw the circle + triangle motif on a Middle Formative shell pendant from Fábrica San José (ca. 850–700 BC). Our next example was on Monument 3 at San José Mogote (ca. 600 BC) (see Figures 6.5 and 6.9 in Chapter 6). I originally proposed that the circle + triangle alluded to blood after seeing the motif used at those two Formative sites in the Etla arm of the valley (Drennan 1976; Marcus 1976a). It now appears that this motif endured in the Etla

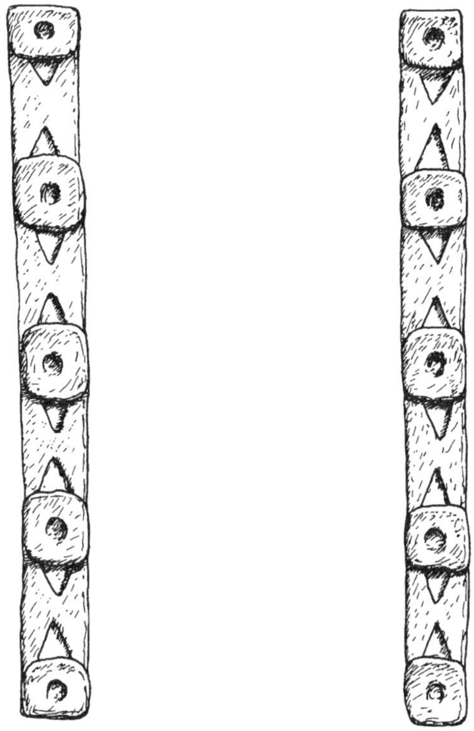

Figure 16.2. The vertical bands on the monument shown in Figure 16.1 display the blood motif, whose origins can be found in the Middle Formative (see Chapter 6). In this context they convey the concept of blood descent. Drawing by John Klausmeyer.

region in modified form. The vertical bands of blood on the Figure 16.1 stone define the content of this monument as genealogical.

It seems likely to me that this stone was originally set inside a palace, interior patio, or tomb, where it constituted horizontal propaganda. Its content is, in fact, reminiscent of a monument found in Tomb 1 at Cuilapan (Bernal 1958) and Lápida 1 del Museo Nacional (see below).

Interpretation of the Hieroglyphs on the Figure 16.1 Monument

At the bottom of the Figure 16.1 monument are a year sign and year bearer. This fact suggests that the reading order was from bottom to top, the same order displayed by many genealogical registers. The names of probable ancestors or marital pairs flank the central date (Figure 16.3).

The text can be interpreted as follows:

9Ñ	5 Deer	6(?)
6M	Year 11E	6J

Significantly, the central panel commemorates a person named 5 Deer, whose name is shown directly above the Year 11 Earthquake. 5 Deer may have been either an apical ancestor or a principal tomb occupant, which raises two possibilities:

if 5 Deer was an apical ancestor, the left and right panels might refer to descendants or to marital pairs;

if, on the other hand, 5 Deer was the most recent tomb occupant and the vertical bands divided three generations, the sequence (from left to right) might refer to grandparents, son, and grandchildren.

Because no depictions of actual people accompany these glyphs, we know neither the gender nor the generations of the individuals named (Urcid and Winter 1989). Usually the Zapotec

Figure 16.3. The central hieroglyph of the monument shown in Figure 16.1 is 5 Deer, which may be the name of an apical ancestor. Below 5 Deer we see the Year 11E. The flanking pairs of hieroglyphs might refer to two marital couples. Drawing by John Klausmeyer.

solved these problems by depicting one couple with wrinkles (to indicate an older generation) and the other without wrinkles (to indicate youth). They could also distinguish women and men by their dress and posture (i.e., kneeling vs. sitting cross-legged). Furthermore, the oldest generation was often placed in the lowest register.

In sum: the subject matter of the unprovenienced monument in Figure 16.1 is typical of Period IIIb–IV, but its layout is unusual. Although most of the hieroglyphs seem to refer to individuals, it is impossible to determine the gender or generation of the named individuals without having their depictions.

Lápida 1 del Museo Nacional de Antropología

Another unprovenienced genealogical register—Lápida 1 del Museo Nacional—is notable for its list of 13 names. This is the second longest list that I have seen, almost as long as the 15 names on Lintel 3 of Xoxocotlán (see Figures 14.12, 14.13, 14.21 in Chapter 14). Lápida 1 del Museo Nacional (Figure 16.4), as its name suggests, is on exhibit in the Museo Nacional (Caso 1928: Figure 81; see also Spinden 1924: Vol. VI, No. 4, Plate 2; Marcus 1983c: Figure 7.4). A photograph of this monument (60 x 38 x 8 cm) was first published in 1924 by Herbert Spinden (1924: Vol. VI, No. 4, Plate 2). A few years later, Alfonso Caso (1928: Figure 81, page 109) published it and gave it its current name.

The layout of Lápida 1 is typical of genealogies in being divided into upper and lower registers (Caso 1928: Figure 81). The layout of the text, however, is unusual—the hieroglyphs begin at the bottom and then ascend the right edge of the stone (see also Figure 5.9, Chapter 5). Thus the text, which begins with the year 8N, was read first from left to right and then from bottom to top. (Caso [1928:110–111], in contrast, read this text from top to bottom.)

Based on other genealogical registers, I consider the list to include an apical ancestor, followed by six marital pairs. Reading from bottom to top, the 13 names are 13A, 10L, 5B, 4E, 4C,

Figure 16.4. Lápida 1 del Museo Nacional is a genealogical register whose text begins at the bottom with the Year 8N and three glyphs—an open hand, a Maltese cross, and a bird. What follows is the name of a likely apical ancestor (13 Knot), then a vertical column of six possible marital pairs. One of those pairs—Lady 3M and Lord 6L—is shown in the upper register (see also Figure 5.9). Drawing by Mark Orsen.

Figure 16.5. Miniature Zapotec temple models. The provenience of the model at *a* is unknown; *b* is said to be from Tlacolula (Caso 1969: Fig. 26c); *c* may have been commissioned by the descendants of a Lord 3E, who wanted to honor their ancestor; *d* honors Lord 12L (whose name is given on the roof of the model). Drawing by John Klausmeyer.

4G, 1F, 2Z, 1N, 6L, 3M, 13J, and 10Y. The last four names are of particular interest. The names 6L and 3M appear not only in the vertical column of hieroglyphs but also in the upper register, where they identify the man and woman depicted. The nine names preceding 6L and 3M probably refer to an apical ancestor and four marital pairs. As for the names following 6L and 3M, it is logical to assume that they refer to younger people, possibly the offspring of 6L and 3M.

Now let us turn to the relationship between the 13 people in the list and the phrase that precedes them: an open hand, the Maltese cross, and a bird. As we have seen, the Maltese cross (Glyph I) was a sign associated with mortuary contexts and offerings marking the anniversaries of a deceased's death. This is not the only case in which Glyph I is seen to be associated with a cluster of signs that can include an open hand, a bird, a stone figurine, or a human head with mouth open or eye closed.

Turning now to the lower register of the monument, we see a woman on the left—perhaps an older woman, judging by her wrinkles. Her name is apparently 11 Monkey; on the right is a bearded man named 8N. This elderly pair is seated on hill signs. The man is associated with a decorated speech scroll, indicating that he is speaking or singing.

This lower register clearly depicts an older generation, while the upper register presents a younger generation. This format tends to reinforce the reading order of the column of hieroglyphs, i.e. from ancestors at the bottom to descendants at the top.

Finally, let us return to the upper register. At the top we see the Jaws of the Sky, ornamented with scrolls. A man, possibly holding a string of jade beads, is descending from the jaws. Kneeling on the left is Lady 3M (3 Lightning) and seated on the right is Lord 6L (6 Eye); a plant separates them. This noble couple is conducting a ritual in which each holds a vessel, possibly containing a liquid such as chocolate or pulque.

This monument, believed by Spinden to be from Zaachila, might once have been placed in the antechamber of a tomb or the wall of a palace.

Other Stones without Provenience

In Figure 16.5 we see examples of stone models that were relatively easy to carry from place to place. Their very portability ensured that such models rarely stayed in meaningful contexts. Many of these models appear to be miniature temples, and some are carved with the names of individuals, possibly revered nobles (Figure 16.5c). We would certainly know more if these models could be tied to particular buildings.

At the top of the unprovenienced monument shown in Figure 16.6 is a three-dimensional human head that protrudes from the stone (see also Figure 16.5d). I suspect that the emergent figure in Figure 16.6 represents the apical ancestor who is thought to supervise a ritual. The ancestor wears a necklace of large beads, ear ornaments, an elaborate headdress, and perhaps a mask. The position of this three-dimensional ancestor is similar to that

Figure 16.6. On this unprovenienced monument, an apical ancestor (top) oversees a possible conjuring rite conducted by Lord 7 Skull (at left) and Lady 10 Owl (at right). Drawing by Mark Orsen.

occupied by the *Cociyo* displayed on Mound 190 at Lambityeco (Lind and Urcid 2010:113).

The ritual itself is being conducted by two nobles, a man named 7H (7 Black/Skull) and a woman named 10F (10 Owl or 10 Night). The woman is either drinking or offering a liquid contained in a vessel (see Marcus 1992a: Figure 8.12; Masson and Orr 1998a: Figure 1b). The man seems to be offering an item as well.

The theme of this monument is one we have seen before—a noble marital pair engaged in ritual with an ancestor whose spirit oversees their activity.

Hollow Ceramic Figurine with Incised Hieroglyphic Text

Equally frustrating are unprovenienced ceramic sculptures with hieroglyphs carved on their neck, back, or arms. One such sculpture was once part of Howard Leigh's collection. The text carved on the figure's back (Figure 16.7d) includes a year sign, possibly the Year 8M. Below that is the name 7 Serpent (7Y), which is associated with a footprint and a leaf. Below 7 Serpent is the name 8E, associated with the bag glyph. On the figure's left arm is a 5P (Figure 16.7a), and on his right arm is 7 Jaguar (7B) and the Maltese cross (Figure 16.7c).

Placing an inscription on a human body is known from earlier times. Like some sacrificial victims in the Building L Prisoner Gallery at Monte Albán, where hieroglyphs were seemingly "branded" into a prisoner's body (for example, on Monument D-55; see Figure 6.38, Chapter 6), this ceramic sculpture shows that a man's skin could display his name and the bag glyph.

In the case of the Leigh Collection sculpture, the hieroglyphs on the figure's back seem to include the year of his death (Year 8M), his own name (7Y), and perhaps his wife's name (8E). The bag glyph may indicate that one or both are deceased. The

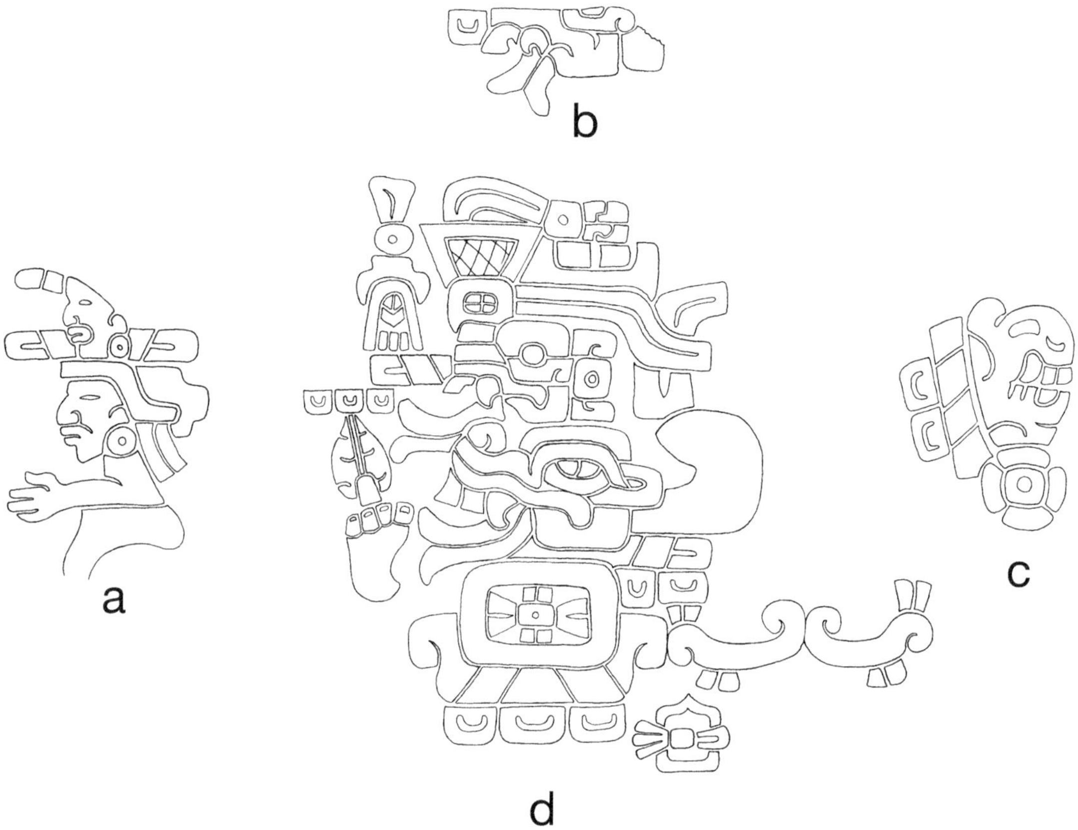

Figure 16.7. The text shown here was incised on the hollow ceramic figure of a man. The hieroglyphs occur in four locations—on his left arm (*a*), his neck (*b*), his right arm (*c*), and his back (*d*). The provenience of this sculpture is unknown and we can only speculate as to why the carvers wanted to put these glyphs on a portable object, rather than a stationary monument. Drawing by Mark Orsen.

additional names carved on the figure's neck and arms may be those of ancestors. The glyph carved on his neck (Figure 16.7b) is possibly 1M. Sadly, we will never know whether this sculpture was found in a cache, in a tomb, in a temple, or in an elite residence. It is simply one more example of a piece that would be even more valuable if we knew its original context.

Another Stone from the Leigh Collection

Another piece from Leigh's collection is shown in Figure 16.8. On one of my visits to Mitla, Howard Leigh graciously allowed Mark Orsen to draw this carved stone for me. The monument seems to depict a ritual being conducted inside a building, perhaps a palace or tomb where privacy was ensured; it likely constitutes horizontal propaganda.

The focus of the ritual scene is an incense burner with a round ball of burning copal or rubber, giving off huge volutes of smoke. On a low platform, we see a woman seated behind a man who was seemingly named 12E. The man wears a cape or cloak with three round circles or disks, reminiscent of the cloaks worn by the men on the San Lázaro Etla tomb jambs (Chapter 12). It looks as if the woman's name may have been given above her head, and that is unfortunately where the stone is damaged. (See also Color Plate III in this volume.)

A Fragment without Provenience

The stone shown in Figure 16.9 is only a fragment. Its left margin reveals that the hieroglyphs were contained within a scene delimited by scrolls; we have seen that such cartouches often contain the names of marital pairs or ancestors. We see the name

Figure 16.8. This monument commemorates a ritual that may have been conducted by a marital pair. The rite featured a ball of burning copal or rubber, which gave off huge volutes of smoke. The name of the man wearing the cape may be 12E. The name of the woman seated behind him is unknown, because that part of the stone is largely missing. Drawing by Mark Orsen.

Figure 16.9. This fragment of a monument may have been an ancestor or noble cartouche, based on the side scroll at left. Drawing by Rubén Méndez.

7 Reed below a footprint, and at the center we see the left half of a sign that may have been 7N or 8N. At the bottom of the fragment is the possible sign for 1 Water (1Z) or 1 Chilla. As always, we would know so much more if this stone were *in situ* and complete.

A Monument from the Museo Regional

In Figure 16.10 we see the inscription on a stone that was on display in the Museo Regional de Oaxaca at the time that Lois Martin sketched it for me. One's attention is immediately drawn to the four large hieroglyphs that wrapped around this rectangular stone block (1.23 x 1.14 m). The position of the glyphs on the block, however, required one to crane his neck to see them. Starting at the top and moving clockwise, we see the Year 4 Deer; then 8 Reed; then a possible jaguar + accession glyph; and finally the name 5 Jaguar, who was likely an individual acceding to office.

A Stone from "La Mansión"

Figure 16.11 shows a small stone monument that was once displayed in the patio of the restaurant La Mansión in the city of Oaxaca. The stone shows a pair of men, both with beards, conducting a ritual that seems to involve the burning of copal or rubber in a vessel. The man on the right seems to be manipulating a strand of beads, an action we have seen undertaken on several occasions by ancestors descending from the Jaws of the Sky; behind him we see an animal and a possible tree. The man on the left has a possible figurine tucked under his arm.

Four Miscellaneous Stones without Provenience

Figure 16.12 shows a stone with a ritual scene involving a woman (at left) and a bearded man (at right). The couple appears to hold a box containing the hieroglyph L ("Eye").

Figure 16.10. Here we see four hieroglyphs, each of which wraps around two surfaces. This monument may have commemorated an accession that took place in the Year 4 Deer. Drawing by Lois Martin.

Figure 16.11. This carved stone, which was set in the wall of the restaurant La Mansión, shows two men conducting a ritual. Drawing by Mark Orsen.

Figure 16.13 shows a stone on which two women are conducting a ritual. The most unusual feature is the abbreviated nature of the women's names—only bars and dots are given; the day signs are omitted.

In Figure 16.14 we see a stone with glyphs but no actual depictions of people. Among the glyphs are the names of a possible apical ancestor named 10 Reed (uppermost) plus individuals named 13 Water (at lower left) and 7N or 8N (at right).

Figure 16.15 illustrates a carved stone (said to be from Santito las Margaritas) on which a barefoot woman named 7 Maize (7J) is shown carrying a vessel.

A Carved Stone Bowl with Hieroglyphs

Figure 16.16 shows the hieroglyphs carved on a stone bowl that has a diameter of 39 cm. Although the bowl is sometimes attributed to Zimatlán, no one is certain about this item's provenience.

Figure 16.12. Between the woman (left) and the bearded man (right) we see a box containing the hieroglyph "L," which was possibly the name of an apical ancestor. Drawing by Mark Orsen.

Figure 16.13. This unprovenienced monument is unusual in that it depicts two women whose names are incompletely rendered. Numerals are given (possibly 11 and 6), but the expected calendar day signs are not. This is also the case with Monument 3 at Macuilxóchitl (Figure 15.5). 31 x 22 x 10 cm. Drawing by Mark Orsen.

Figure 16.14. This monument begins (at the top) with the name 10 Reed; below it we see the names 13 Water (lower left) and 8 Chilla (lower right). Drawing by Rubén Méndez.

Figure 16.15. This carved stone (currently in the Museo Nacional de Antropología) has been attributed to Las Margaritas, located to the east of the Valley of Oaxaca. We see a barefoot woman standing on the hill sign, and in her skirt we see the name 7 Maize. She points with her left index finger, while she holds a bowl in her right hand. Given the shape of the stone, it might have been a tomb jamb or a stela. Height: 1.06 m. Drawing by Mark Orsen.

Figure 16.16. A rollout of the carving on a stone bowl with a diameter of 39 cm and a height of 28 cm. This piece has been attributed to Zimatlán; today it is in the Museo de las Culturas de Oaxaca. Drawing by Mark Orsen.

Plate I. Photo of Monument 3, San José Mogote, shortly after discovery (see Chapter 6).

Plate II. Photo of Structure J, Monte Albán; the loose stones in the foreground were never incorporated into the reconstructed building (see Chapter 8).

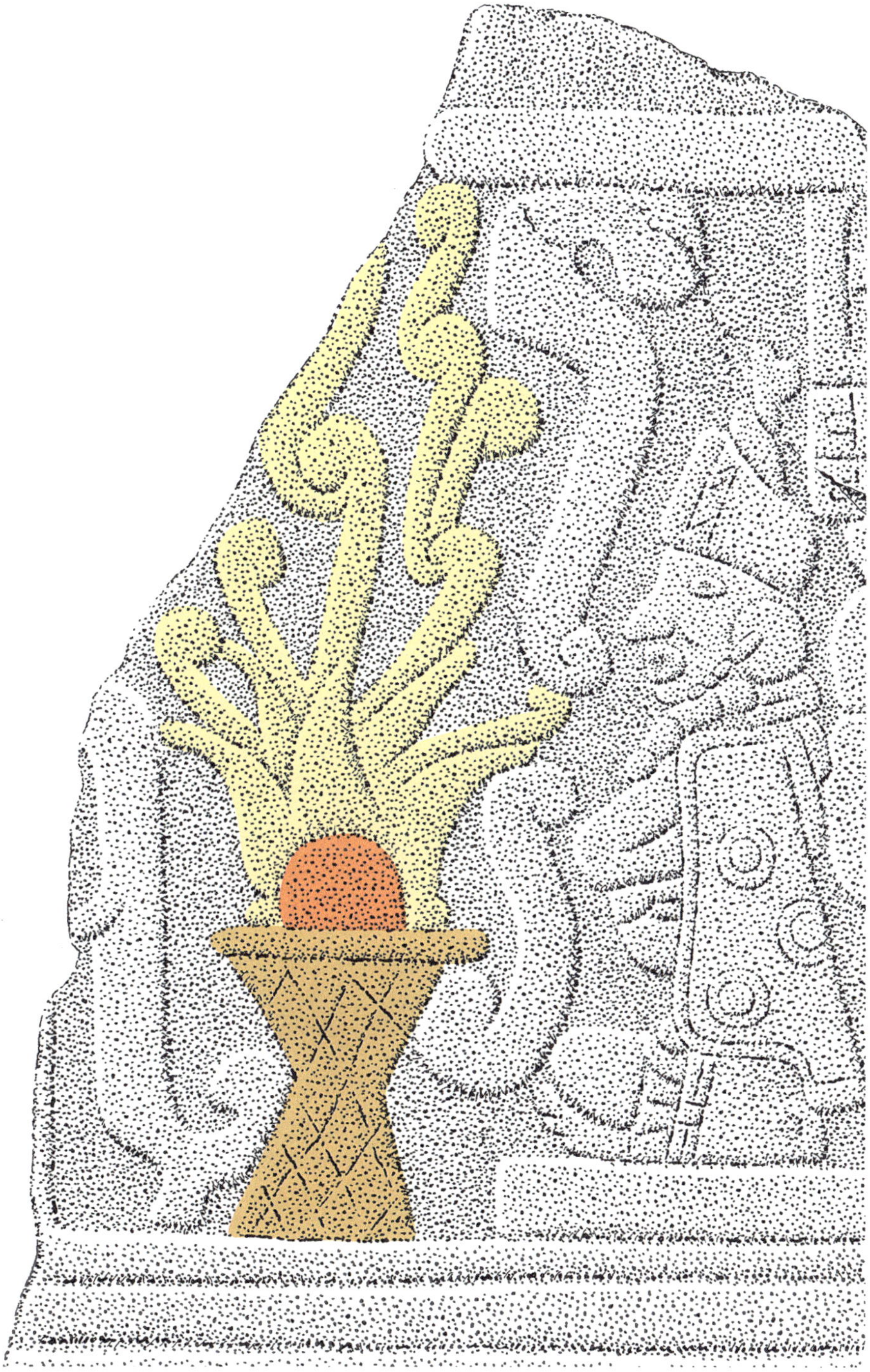

Plate III. Unprovenienced stone shows the burning of an offering, possibly a ball of copal or rubber (see Chapter 16). Color has been added to enhance key features.

Plate IV. A monolith on display at Zaachila, probably Postclassic in date (see Chapter 14).

Plate V. Ceramic box that depicts maize and water (see Chapter 8). This is one of five painted ceramic boxes found in the Adoratorio of Mound H, Monte Albán.

Plate VI. Monument 5 from Macuilxóchitl has been reused—incorporated into a wall as construction material. Perhaps the missing left half will be found in a meaningful context some day (see Chapter 15).

Plate VII. A monument from Rancho Tejas, showing a possible toponym that includes a sacrificial knife, a heart, and the blood motif (see Chapter 14).

Plate VIII. The actual stone from Tomb 5 at Cerro de la Campana is covered with red pigment. Here, in this line drawing, we show key features by adding color to them. In red is the deceased Lord 13 Monkey; in yellow, his son 12 Monkey; in brown, the quail his son offers and 13 Monkey's funerary crate (see Chapter 12).

Plate IX. The central portion of a turquoise-inlaid carved bone from Tomb 7 at Monte Albán. This is Bone 203b (see Chapter 17).

Plate X. Examples of surviving murals from the lintels at Mitla surrounding the interior patios in the North (Church) Group and the Arroyo Group (see Chapter 17).

Part V

Declining Use of Hieroglyphic Writing

17

Monte Albán Ceases to be the Capital

By AD 900, the Valley of Oaxaca was no longer dominated by Monte Albán. Many of its former secondary centers were now powerful and independent. The sociopolitical landscape was a network of interconnected noble families, palaces, and courts, headed by powerful couples who administered the petty kingdoms later called *señoríos* or *cacicazgos* by the Spaniards.

The era was one of political decentralization, with changes in trade partners, an increase in certain craft specialization, and the establishment of advantageous marital alliances (see Berdan et al. 1996, 2003; Boone 1982; Byland and Pohl 1994; Feinman and Nicholas 2017:97; Flannery 1983b:290–295; Flannery 1983d:318–322; Flannery and Marcus 1983d:295–300; Marcus 1983g:314–318; Marcus 1989b; Marcus and Flannery 1983:217–226, 1990; McCafferty 1994b; Nicholson and Quiñones Keber 1994; Oudijk 2002, 2008; Smith and Berdan 2003).

The Early Postclassic in the Valley of Oaxaca (AD 900–1200) continues to be poorly known. Many of our so-called "Postclassic" accounts are really descriptions of the **Late** Postclassic (AD 1200–1500), a period when multiregional interaction among royal courts and great houses is evident in the codices and other sixteenth-century documents. Many Postclassic nobles adopted an art style that crosscut ethnic and linguistic boundaries and has come to be known as the "Mixteca-Puebla" or "Postclassic International Style" (e.g., Balkansky 1999; Berdan et al. 1996, 2003; Boone 1982; Boone and Smith 2003; Brown and Andrews 1982; Díaz et al. 2005; Masson 2000; McCafferty 1994a; Miller 1995; Nicholson 1960, 1971, 1982; Paddock 1966a, 1966b, 1983a, 1983b; Pohl and Byland 1994; Robertson 1970; Smith and Berdan 2003; Vaillant 1938).

In the Valley of Oaxaca, the overly long phase known as Period V (AD 900–1500) was a time of political realignment and economic opportunity, especially for former Tier 2 and Tier 3 sites (Caso 1969; Feinman and Nicholas 2017). We do not know the exact number of *señoríos* in the Valley of Oaxaca, but the number probably fluctuated between 10 and 20. In the Mixteca Alta, by comparison, the number was about 30. Thus there was ample opportunity for noble families to form trade alliances with several polities and to pursue one or more suitable foreign spouses for their offspring.

Monte Albán's political collapse—once regarded as an abrupt event—is now considered a long and gradual process that significantly affected nobles but did not profoundly affect the daily lives of most commoners (e.g., Feinman and Nicholas 2011, 2016a, 2017). Two of the major changes that affected nobles were the increased autonomy of noble families and the new decision-making powers of the *coquì* and *xonàxi* (lords and ladies) who were able to fill the political vacuum. The lords residing at Tier 2 and Tier 3 sites probably viewed Monte Albán's political decline as a golden opportunity for them to form new alliances. In other respects there was continuity—e.g., in ancestor veneration, in building elite residences with interior patios and family crypts, and in noble-to-noble gift giving and event hosting (see Berlin 1957; Bernal and Gamio 1974; Flannery and Marcus 1983b, 1983c; Markens 2004; Middleton et al. 1998; Miller 1995; Séjourné 1960).

Nobles often formed peaceful alliances that crosscut ethnic and linguistic boundaries, but they also had conflicts with other noble houses. When participating in battles they used slings, bows and arrows, spears, and wooden broadswords with obsidian blades set in the edges—a weapon called *macana* by the Taínos, *macuahuitl* by the Aztecs, and likely *yagaqueça pitanco* by the Zapotec.

The hallmarks of earlier Zapotec civilization—the elaborate funerary urns, the polychrome murals, the hieroglyphs carved on wall slabs, lintels, jambs, and tomb doors—were all disappearing. Noble families in each *cacicazgo* continued to enjoy a busy ritual life in their respective palaces, where they could honor their ancestors in private or with a few guests. Nevertheless, fewer and fewer families commissioned hieroglyphic texts. When Period V nobles did turn to hieroglyphs, they usually created them in stucco on tomb walls (e.g., Tomb 1 at Zaachila), painted them on palace interiors (e.g., Mitla), or incised them on animal bones that could be incorporated into mummy bundles (e.g., Tomb 2 at Zaachila and Tomb 7 at Monte Albán).

Another change for the Valley of Oaxaca was the appearance of new palaces and royal courts. Some of the larger palaces were located at sites near Monte Albán (e.g., Zaachila, Cuilapan, and Xoxocotlán) or in the Tlacolula region (e.g., Macuilxóchitl, Teotitlán del Valle, Yagul, Lambityeco, and Mitla) (Figure 17.1).

During Period V, the Tlacolula arm appears to have been the most densely settled part of the valley. Since Period V lasted 600 to 700 years, however, we do not know how many of these Tlacolula palaces were occupied at the same time.

Several ways to subdivide Period V have been proposed (Flannery and Marcus 1983c; Marcus and Flannery 1983:217–226; Markens 2008; Markens et al. 2008; Oudijk 2000, 2002, 2008). For example, Ignacio Bernal (1966) suggested three subdivisions—Early V, Middle V, and Late V (Marcus and Flannery 1990:199–200). Early V, which featured local G3M grayware and imported Yanhuitlán Red-on-cream, lacked polychrome pottery. Middle V added polychrome ceramics of Mixteca-Puebla style to G3M grayware and Yanhuitlán Red-on-cream pottery, but still had no metal. Late V had all the pottery that Middle V had, plus metal (Bernal 1966:361). An alternative to Bernal's scheme is Michel Oudijk's (2008) division of Period V into four phases—AD 963–1100, 1100–1280, 1280–1440, and 1440–1521. Since Oudijk's divisions are based on his study of genealogical and ethnohistorical data, however, they do not provide us with the archaeological diagnostics of each phase.

Rather than revealing ethnic boundaries, the distribution of so-called "Mixtec" polychromes simply shows us where noble families lived and entertained other nobles. Indeed, "we can view the Postclassic as having a series of specialized pottery-making centers whose products were distributed by a network of regional market systems, actually crosscutting ethnic boundaries. In this view, a Zapotec farmer might use locally made G3M pottery whereas the Zapotec nobility used a mixture of G3M, imported Yanhuitlán Red-on-cream, and Mixteca or Cholula polychrome" (Marcus and Flannery 1983:224–225).

Period V is regarded as a fascinating era because of its multiethnic and multiregional character and its unique mix of evidence from sixteenth-century documents, codices, dictionaries, settlement patterns, and tombs. Many items seem to have been used by all noble families, whether they were Zapotec, Mixtec, Nahua, Cuicatec, Chinantec, or even the offspring of Zapotec-Mixtec or Zapotec-Nahua marriages (e.g., Carrasco Pizana 1974).

Over the years the multiethnicity of Period V has remained controversial (e.g., Bernal 1966; Blomster 2008). Some scholars have argued that the impact of the Mixtec was quite localized (e.g., Feinman and Nicholas 2016a; Flannery and Marcus 1983b:277–279; Marcus and Flannery 1983:221), while others have suggested that the Mixtec actually invaded the Valley of Oaxaca and had a major impact (e.g., Bernal 1966; Caso 1966; Paddock 1966b, 1983b).

Few scholars today believe in a wholesale Mixtec invasion, but they do see evidence for Mixtec-Zapotec noble marriages and for significant interaction between elite families and multiple ethnic groups across the State of Oaxaca (Pohl 2003a, 2003b). The enduring and widespread distribution of Zapotec speakers, as well as continuity in mortuary customs and architectural styles, make it clear that the Valley of Oaxaca remained Zapotec. There were, however, pockets of Mixtec speakers in Cuilapan and Xoxocotlán in the 1890s, as noted by Marshall Saville (1899).

What seems to have happened is that during Period V, former Tier 2 and Tier 3 centers began to arrange marriages that tied them to noble families both inside and outside the Valley of Oaxaca (Byland and Pohl 1994; Caso 1966; Jansen et al. 1998; Miller 1995; Oudijk 2000; Paddock 1966b; Pohl 1994, 1999). For example, the 1580 *Relación de Teozapotlan* (Zaachila) reports a marriage between a member of the Zaachila dynasty and a Mixtec princess that took place ca. AD 1280 (Mata 1580:190–191). The Codex Nuttall records the marriage of a man named 9 Serpent and a woman named 11 Rabbit; their offspring, Lord 5 Flower, married a woman named 4 Rabbit Quetzal, a Mixtec princess from Teozacoalco. Much later, one of 5 Flower's descendants moved from Zaachila to Tehuantepec to establish a new dynastic seat (see Figure 5.5, Chapter 5). In the 1960s, Caso made a good case that the Lord 5 Flower mentioned in the Codex Nuttall was the same Lord 5 Flower depicted on the wall of Tomb 1 at Zaachila (Caso 1966: Plate 14; de la Cruz 2014).

Such Mixtec-Zapotec noble marriages would have been politically and economically advantageous, particularly when the prospective spouse was more highly ranked and had control of lands, laborers, and followers. In some cases a noble Mixtec bride arrived with a large retinue, establishing an enclave of Mixtec

Figure 17.1. The Postclassic (AD 900–1500) was an era of increasing ties between the noble houses of the Mixtec and the Zapotec; some marriage alliances led to actual movements of courts and commoner followers. This map gives the location of Mixtec-speaking towns (from Tequixtepec to Tilantongo) and Zapotec communities (from Huitzo to Juchitán).

speakers in the Valley of Oaxaca. Such marriage alliances were often so beneficial that Zapotec lords sought to have multiple wives, each marriage adding more resources and followers. In the 1579 *Relación de Cuilapan* we read of a Mixtec lord who married the daughter of the Zapotec lord of Zaachila (Barlow 1945; Salazar 1581). That Mixtec son-in-law was fortunate enough to be awarded land in Cuilapan from his Zapotec father-in-law, which helps to explain why a group of Mixtec speakers once resided in Cuilapan (Caso 1966:329).

Period V Texts and Iconography

We will now look at a few of the murals, carved bones, carved stones, and stucco figures of Period V. They come from Huitzo (Flannery 1983d: Figure 8.37; Moser 1969a, 1969b), Monte Albán (Caso 1932a, 1932b, 1969), Zaachila (Acosta 1972; Gallegos Ruiz 1962, 1978; Sánchez Santiago 2014), Mitla (Bandelier 1884; Flannery and Marcus 1983d; Miller 1995; Pohl 1999), and Teotitlán del Valle (López Zárate 2014; Seler 1904b:298–299).

Tomb 1 of Barrio del Rosario Huitzo

The University of Michigan's 1967 excavations at Barrio del Rosario Huitzo exposed Tomb 1 (AD 1200–1500), a Late Postclassic sepulcher (Figure 17.2). Near the tomb lay ten other burials of Period V date; most of these were young males associated with military weapons.

Tomb 1 was a two-room stone masonry structure with a corbel-vault roof (Flannery 1983d:319). The floor was painted red, as were the lower sections of the interior walls. The lintel of Tomb 1 has received considerable attention because of the four crania depicted on it, and because of the painting technique used. Moser (1969a, 1969b) noted that the painted red background was used to highlight the unpainted white crania. Miller (1995:160–162) also commented on this painting technique—a kind of resist or negative painting—in which the background was painted red and the unpainted area left white to show four skulls, a series of circles, and the framing lines on the top and sides of the lintel (Flannery 1983d: Figure 8.37).

It is noteworthy that a similar resist technique was used in the painting of the Postclassic murals in major buildings at Mitla. Huitzo and Mitla are, at present, the only known Period V sites that utilized this negative or resist technique in painting lintels. The use of dark red paint, however, has deep roots in the Valley of Oaxaca; indeed, the earliest known tomb murals at Monte Albán featured red on red (Caso 1965b; Miller 1995).

Huitzo's Tomb 1 façade displayed relatively large carved stones to either side of the tomb entrance; both stones, however, were reused rather than in primary context (see Chapter 7). We know that these stones were reused, not only because they are damaged fragments and in an earlier sculptural style, but also because one of them was set upside down (Figure 17.2).

The stone set to the right of the tomb door shows a lord with a shield and atlatl; Moser (1969a, 1969b) compares this stone to a carved monument found at the site of Tilantongo in the Mixteca (Paddock 1966a: Figure 248). Three other carved stone fragments had been set in the tomb façade (Flannery 1983d:319), and a small offering box had been placed in front of the tomb door.

The principal skeleton in Huitzo's Tomb 1 was a man in his twenties, lying supine and fully extended. Around his neck was a necklace that included 34 beads of amethyst, 35 beads of lost-wax cast gold over a carbon nucleus, and 29 beads of jade; he was accompanied by three matched pairs of polychrome vessels and three local G3M grayware vessels. Near his head were some backed and truncated obsidian blades that are likely the remains of a *macana*, an obsidian-edged wooden broadsword. This man had turquoise in his mosaic earspools. At his feet were the remains of other adults—possibly marital pairs, since both males and females were present. More skeletal remains were discovered in the fill outside the tomb, just as we have seen at Xoxocotlán, Lambityeco, and other sites.

The other male burials found nearby ranged in age from 17 to 35, typical ages for warriors. One of these was Burial 4, which included four quartz arrow points of the Harrell type. Burial 6 had an obsidian arrow point and a copper axe; Burial 7 had four *macana* blades. Such an array of young Monte Albán V men, buried with broadswords or arrow points, suggests that we may be dealing with a group of warriors who died defending Huitzo in some battle. That the main individual in the tomb was a noble officer, while the nearby burials were of common foot soldiers, is further suggested by his sumptuary goods and the fact that his bone strontium levels indicate that his diet included more meat than that of the soldiers nearby.

Tomb 7 of Monte Albán

By Period V the once-great urban center of Monte Albán had declined in population to perhaps 4000 to 6000 inhabitants, a sharp retreat from its Period III peak of 30,000 (Blanton 1978). Monte Albán's Main Plaza had fallen into disrepair, although commoners still occupied the lower terraces around the base of the mountain. The summit of Monte Albán, however, was still considered a sacred place, so much so that it became a kind of necropolis. Its Period V inhabitants discovered some of its earlier tombs and reused them for special burials.

Tomb 7, the most famous funerary venue at Monte Albán, was found by Alfonso Caso in January of 1932. This tomb lies northeast of the North Platform in an area called the Cementerio Norte (Caso 1932a, 1932b, 1969). Tomb 7 had originally been constructed during Period III, at which time it was decked out with Classic funerary urns and a carved stone door with hieroglyphs (Figure 17.3). Above it lay a two-room temple, with columns to either side of the doorway (Figure 17.4).

The Period V inhabitants who found the tomb inserted its former door stone into the roof of the antechamber and removed

Figure 17.2. Tomb 1 at Huitzo featured a painted lintel, as well as jambs consisting of reused carved stones. The lintel showing four crania provides an example of resist or negative painting, similar to that used in the Postclassic dichromatic murals at Mitla. (See Flannery 1983d:320; Miller 1995; Moser 1969a, 1969b.)

Figure 17.3. Before being reused in the roof of Tomb 7 at Monte Albán, this square stone may have served as a tomb door. The style of the hieroglyphs—which record the Year 8M and the day or name 1 Reed—suggests that this text was carved hundreds of years prior to the tomb's Postclassic reuse (Caso 1969: Fig. 246).

some of the original tomb contents to make way for a series of Postclassic bundle burials. (While these bundle burials are traditionally called "secondary," Middleton et al. [1998] prefer the term "ongoing use" to indicate the diverse kinds of activity seen during multiple reentries.) At any rate, Tomb 7 became the final resting place for at least nine incomplete skeletons. These incomplete skeletons are thought to include both the Period V bundle burials and the remains of the original Period III individuals, who were shoved aside to make room for the new interments.

Tomb 7 is long and narrow, with two chambers (Figure 17.4). According to Rubín de la Borbolla (1969), the principal skeleton was that of a 55-year-old man with deliberate cranial deformation and filed teeth. Most of the other skeletons in Tomb 7 were males and fell into two age groups—either 16–20 years old or 45–55 years old. There were also bones from two women and an infant, whom Rubín de la Borbolla considered not to have been part of the bundle burials. Here is a case where DNA analysis could greatly clarify our understanding of the relationships among individuals.

After Tomb 7 had been resealed, the Period V people left an offering above the tomb; it consisted of three jade earspools, 36 jade beads, and a series of marine shells, including a conch shell trumpet (Caso 1969: Lámina III). Among the 500 items left inside the tomb were objects of gold and rock crystal, as well as a trophy skull covered with turquoise mosaic (Caso 1969: Lámina IV). Some of the gold beads were lost-wax cast with carbon nuclei, similar to the beads found in Tomb 1 at Huitzo.

Of direct relevance to the theme of this book is the set of carved bones found in Tomb 7. Thirty-four of these bones were carved with hieroglyphs or pictorial scenes (Figure 17.5). The subject matter varies; some bones provide the names of people and places, while others show sequences of days and years, or display repetitive or alternating motifs (Caso 1969:179).

Caso suggested that some of the carved bones found in Tomb 1 at Zaachila (discussed later in this chapter) had been produced by the same craftsman responsible for the carved bones in Tomb 7 of Monte Albán. Although the carvings are similar—which suggests that Zaachila's Tomb 1 and Monte Albán's Tomb 7 were broadly contemporaneous—I am less convinced that the bones were carved by the same craftsman.

Caso (1969) referred to the writing on the Tomb 7 bones as "Mixtec." Scholars today, however, would likely argue that

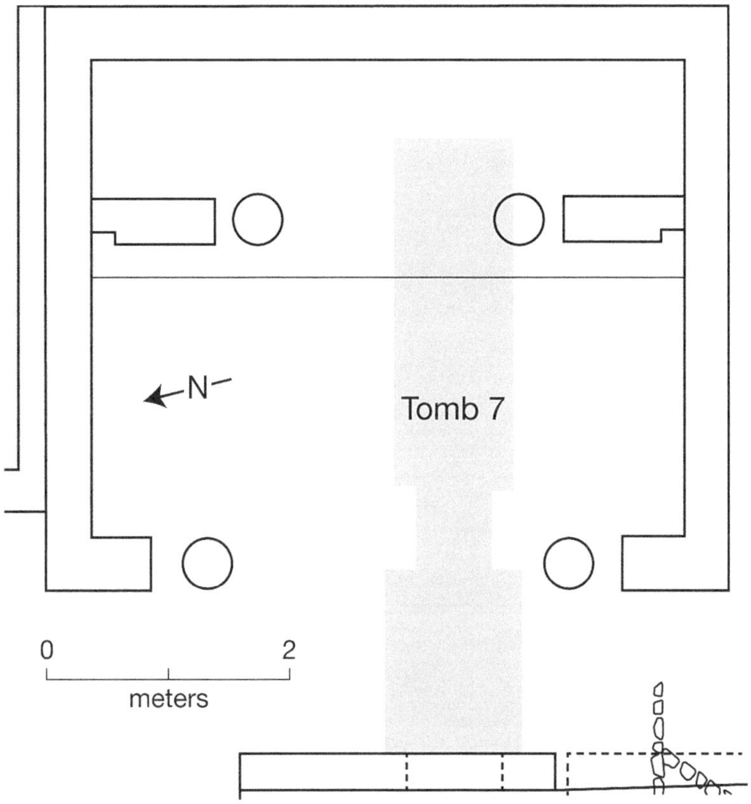

Figure 17.4. Tomb 7 at Monte Albán was found beneath a two-room temple. Although most of the tomb's contents were of Postclassic date, the tomb itself had been constructed much earlier. The shaded area shows the location of the tomb (Caso 1969: Plano II; Marcus 2008b: Fig. XV.1, 182).

after AD 1300 both the Zapotec and the Mixtec were employing a Nahuatl-influenced symbol system. "The effectiveness of pictographic communication was apparently such that it seemed not to bother either group [Zapotec and Mixtec] to do so; they simply continued to apply their own terminology for the signs" (Pohl and Urcid Serrano 2006:230). Indeed, the widespread symbol system and pictographs of this era can be regarded as a Postclassic "international style," used by multiple ethnic and linguistic groups from the Basin of Mexico to the east coast of Yucatán (see Boone and Smith 2003; Lothrop 1924; Miller 1982; Quirarte 1982; Tozzer 1957).

Although some have considered the Tomb 7 bones to be weaving battens (e.g., Brumfiel 1994; McCafferty and McCafferty 1994), I am not convinced. The historical and calendrical content of the carved bones, the use of tiny pieces of turquoise to highlight the white areas, and the very delicate nature of the carvings make it unlikely these bones had a utilitarian function. It seems more likely that they played a role in divination, calendric rituals, and storytelling. Postclassic priests or *colanij* (diviners) used such items as mnemonic devices—for example, for naming children and recalling the protagonists in mythical and historical events.

With such ritual purposes in mind, let us look at a few of the carved bones from Tomb 7. Bone 42 (Figure 17.5a) shows animal heads suspended from two bands. The upper band has circles that may be interpreted as jade beads, alternating with interlocking scrolls and stylized feathers. The lower band has a row of feathers interrupted by animal heads. Starting on the far right, we see the possible shaft of a spearthrower with four feather balls attached. Next we see what Caso called a cloud-serpent, with four strips (regarded by Caso as rain) descending from its mouth. Then comes an arrow, decorated on either side with a small feather ball and jade bead; the end has a jade bead, followed by the head of an eagle with several strips descending from its mouth. Next we see the head of another cloud-serpent, and a deer head with a human hand + flower. Finally we see a stylized flower, a serpent head, the head of another eagle, and more stylized flowers. The symbolism of Bone 42 may relate to the sky and its associated celestial beings; if so, it seems to be a sun-filled sky, as opposed to the star-filled night sky depicted on Bones 203l and 203j (Caso 1969).

Bone 37a (Figure 17.5b) features a decorative eagle at both ends, serving as its first and last elements. The text between the eagles lists 13 consecutive years, reading from right to left—1

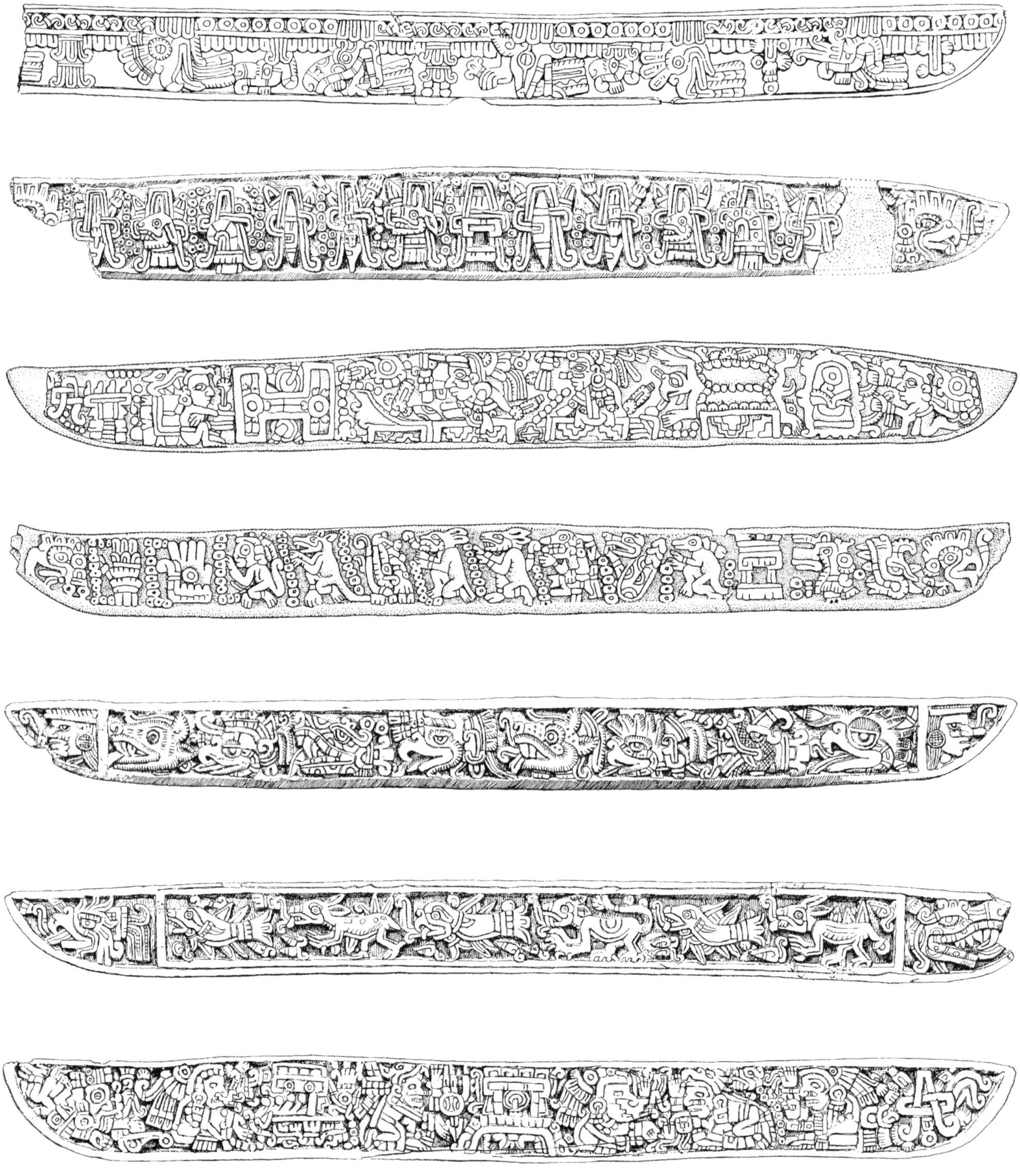

a

b

c

d

e

f

g

Figure 17.5. A sample of carved bones from Tomb 7, Monte Albán. Their historical and calendric content, as well as their delicate turquoise inlay, suggests that two of their functions were as mnemonic devices and for divination (Caso 1965c:957; Caso 1969; see also Color Plate IX, this volume).

Reed, 2 Flint, 3 House, 4 Rabbit, 5 Reed, 6 Flint, 7 House, 8 Rabbit, 9 Reed, 10 Flint, 11 House, 12 Rabbit, and 13 Reed. This 13-year sequence is the first quarter of the 52-year Calendar Round used by the Zapotec, Mixtec, and Aztec. We also see the A-O year sign. (The Mixtec year is regarded as beginning with 1 Reed, while the Aztec year began with 1 Rabbit.)

Bone 203b (Figure 17.5c; also see Color Plate IX) seems to report conquests, seemingly recording a slice of history that can be compared to events painted in both the Codex Selden and the Codex Bodley. Caso (1969:183) argued that this bone was designed to be read from right to left, even though we see a year sign and day sign at the far left.

On the far right of Bone 203b we see 7 Rain, a date or name associated with a man holding ropes attached to a place sign; he seems to be pulling a hill that contains a jade disk and a corn plant. The next sign is another toponym, a turtle on a wall decorated with grecas. Then comes the day 8 House, apparently associated with the name of a conquered place (shown by an arrow shaft piercing a greca-decorated platform). Above the place glyph we see a wall and a warrior or deity who sports a feather headdress, a horizontal noseplug, an earspool, and a pectoral with bells. Next we see the date 7 Motion, which is probably the day this place was conquered.

Next in sequence comes another wall with grecas; above it is the bust of a man richly decked out in a feather headdress, nose ornament, jade earspool, and pectoral with gold bells. Apparently this place was also conquered, since one can see the arrow thrust into it. Between this item and the next one in sequence we see a flint knife; we cannot say whether this represents a date, since no number is included. We next see a third conquered place whose name is represented by a wall with grecas, associated with the hieroglyph used in Codex Nuttall 73 to signify a steep bank.

Next in sequence comes another place, conquered on the day 3 or 5 Rain, and another wall with grecas, once again associated with the hieroglyph for a steep bank (Codex Nuttall 73). Then comes the day 4 Flower, followed by a ballcourt marked with two disks (possibly of gold or jade); in the interior of the court are disks with gold bells. We can only assume that the ballcourt stands for another conquered place. Our last toponym is a river with the date 5 Lagarto. Finally, on the far left of the bone is a year, possibly 8 House.

Bone 172i (Figure 17.5d) is another with eagles carved at both ends (see Caso 1969: Figure 213). Between those decorative eagles is a complete 13-day period (or *trecena*) that would have been read from right to left. Beginning on the far right, we see the days 1 Crocodile, 2 Wind, 3 House, 4 Lizard, 5 Serpent, 6 Death, 7 Deer, 8 Rabbit, 9 Water, 10 Dog, 11 Monkey, 12 Grass, and 13 Reed. The Maya were also known to carve bones giving the day signs in order. For example, a bone reportedly found on the island of Jaina shows an individual casting maize kernels, as well as a list of the Maya day signs in order (Barthel 1967).

The carving on Tomb 7's Bone 114 (Figure 17.5e) begins and ends with a human head, in contrast to those bones that feature an animal on either end. In between—from right to left—we see an eagle, a crocodile, an eagle, perhaps a jaguar, then an eagle, a crocodile, an eagle and perhaps a dog.

Animals appear at the ends of Bone 50 (Figure 17.5f). There is an eagle head at the left end and a serpent head at the right end, each set in its own compartment. Six more animals are depicted in a kind of procession in the central compartment, all facing to the left. From right to left we see a rabbit, a fish, a jaguar, a fish with the head of an eagle, then a deer and a fish. This sequence of six animals may relate to an origin myth; presenting them in this particular order may have helped a diviner tell a story.

Bone 124 (Figure 17.5g) was evidently meant to be read from right to left, beginning with the year 1 Reed. There are six figures on this bone; the two individuals on the right end face left, while the remaining four face right. There are also two prominent temples. One is the Temple of Water, and then—close to the center of the bone—comes the Temple of Jade, with a cavern below it. The two seated individuals facing left may well be impersonators of deities; between them we see the day 8 Serpent. Next comes a goddess, or a woman impersonating a goddess, with an elaborate nose ornament; in front of the ornament is a possible year sign.

Next in order we see a place sign with a below-ground cavern, followed by a kneeling man with the helmet of a coyote; he has a shield, arrows, and a curved *macana*. 4 Flower appears behind the kneeling man's back. Then comes the Temple of Water with an earth monster below it; facing the temple is a goddess or deity impersonator named 6 Water, whose costume is decorated with beads. Finally, on the far left we see a Lightning or Rain deity descending from the sky. This bone appears to convey ritual information, and may have served as a mnemonic device to make sure that the performers of the ritual (including deity impersonators) followed the correct sequence of actions.

The discussion above barely scratches the surface of the Tomb 7 bones. The overwhelming impression they leave is that they were a collection of memory aids used by priests or state personnel when called upon to convey important historical accounts, origin myths, or elaborate ritual sequences. I suspect that the bones belonged more to an office (a sacred religious post) than to an individual.

Tombs 1 and 2 at Zaachila

Zaachila, thought to be the Zapotec capital throughout the latter half of Period V, once had at least ten archaeological mounds (Figure 17.6). In 1962 Roberto Gallegos Ruiz focused his excavations on the summit of Mound A, where he exposed a palace and the two tombs that lay below its interior patio.

Tomb 1's main chamber contained two individuals, while an additional nine were discovered in its antechamber. Among the many items in Tomb 1 were sets of carved bones and fine polychrome vessels, including a unique cup with a hummingbird sipping from it (Caso 1966: Plates 18–20).

Like many of the elite tombs at Monte Albán, Cerro de la Campana, and Mitla, the tombs on Mound A at Zaachila

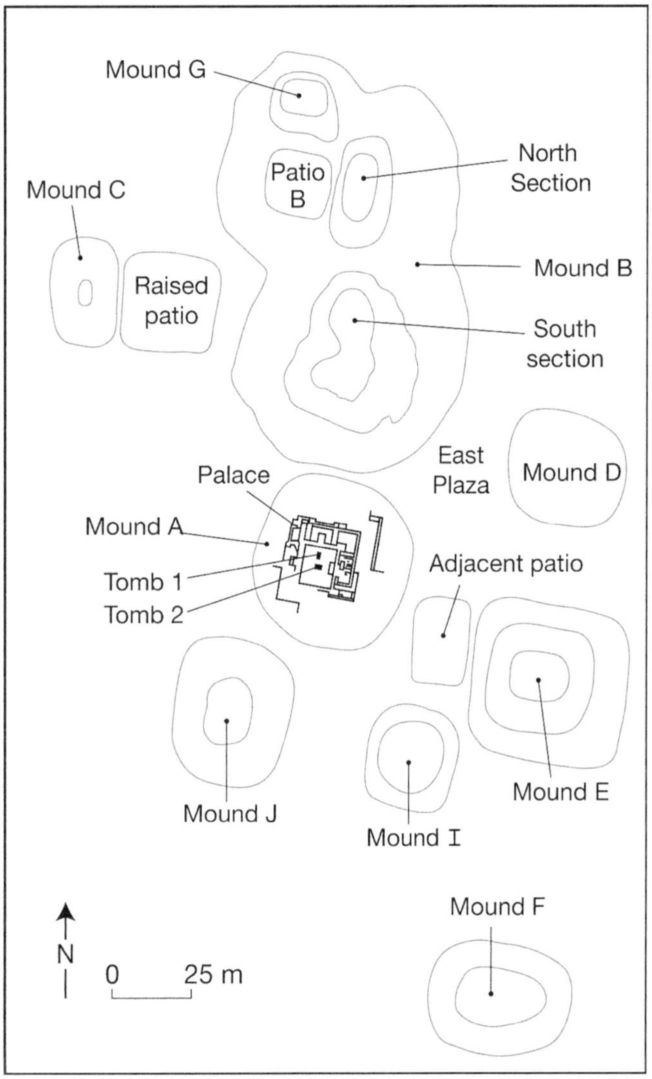

Figure 17.6. On the summit of Mound A at Zaachila (at the center of this map) stood a palace whose interior patio had steps leading down to Tombs 1 and 2. There its rulers were buried with polychrome ceramics and gold. Drawing by John Klausmeyer.

were reached from an interior patio of the palace. These multichambered tombs were so long that they reached beyond the patio and extended below the rooms of the palatial residence. Such a location ensured that the deceased lay immediately below the rooms where his descendants continued to go about their daily lives (Caso 1966:321; Miller 1995).

The stairway leading to Tomb 1, oriented north-south, descended from the center of the patio. The stairway had three high steps that led down to a small antechamber. While excavating the antechamber, Gallegos Ruiz encountered two feline heads that may have been placed to either side of the tomb entrance—a detail reminiscent of Tomb 7 at Dainzú (see Chapter 9).

The most unusual features in Tomb 1 were the stucco figures on the walls (Figure 17.7). During earlier periods we would have expected polychrome murals and carved stones. Instead, two owls had been modeled in stucco on the walls of the antechamber, one on the west and one on the east. The owls appear above niches that probably once contained offerings (Caso 1966:323). The precise meaning of these stucco owls is not known, but based on what we know of Oaxacan ethnoscience it is likely that these birds were considered nocturnal messengers, able to fly between the land of the living and the land of the dead.

In the main chamber of Tomb 1 were additional stucco figures. On the west wall we see a hummingbird, flying above a skeletal figure that likely represents a God of Death. A nearly identical figure on the east wall is another God of Death. This presumed God of Death (showing Postclassic Mixtec or Nahua influence) has a human body and a fleshless skull, a sacrificial knife protruding from his nose, and a human heart suspended from a rope around his neck (Caso 1966: Plates 16, 17). These two gods of the underworld faced the entrance and would have greeted any visitor making offerings.

On the west wall of the tomb we also see the stucco figure of a man named 5 Flower (Caso 1966: Plates 14, 22). The stucco figure of a man named 9 Flower appears on the east wall. Caso (1966) attempted to link these Tomb 1 stucco figures to the founders of a Mixtec dynasty recorded on page 33 of the Codex Nuttall, noting that the two people in Tomb 1 wear the same headdress as the rulers shown on that page.

Caso (1966:319) went on to say: "Although we cannot be sure that Nine Flower of Zaachila is the same person as Nine Serpent of Nuttall, we can be confident that Five Flower is the same mentioned in Nuttall 33 and that he is the great-grandfather of 6 Water 'Colored Strips'." Other scholars have disagreed with Caso's interpretation, as a result of which there has been considerable discussion about 9 Flower (e.g., de la Cruz 2014; Fahmel Beyer 1994; Gallegos Ruiz 1978).

Although Caso thought the discrepancy in names between 9 Flower and 9 Serpent might be explained as a simple scribal error, Víctor de la Cruz (2014:72–74) offers a different solution. In his view,

> (1) Lord 5 Flower was the founder of a dynasty at Zaachila, with Yagul as one of its subjects.

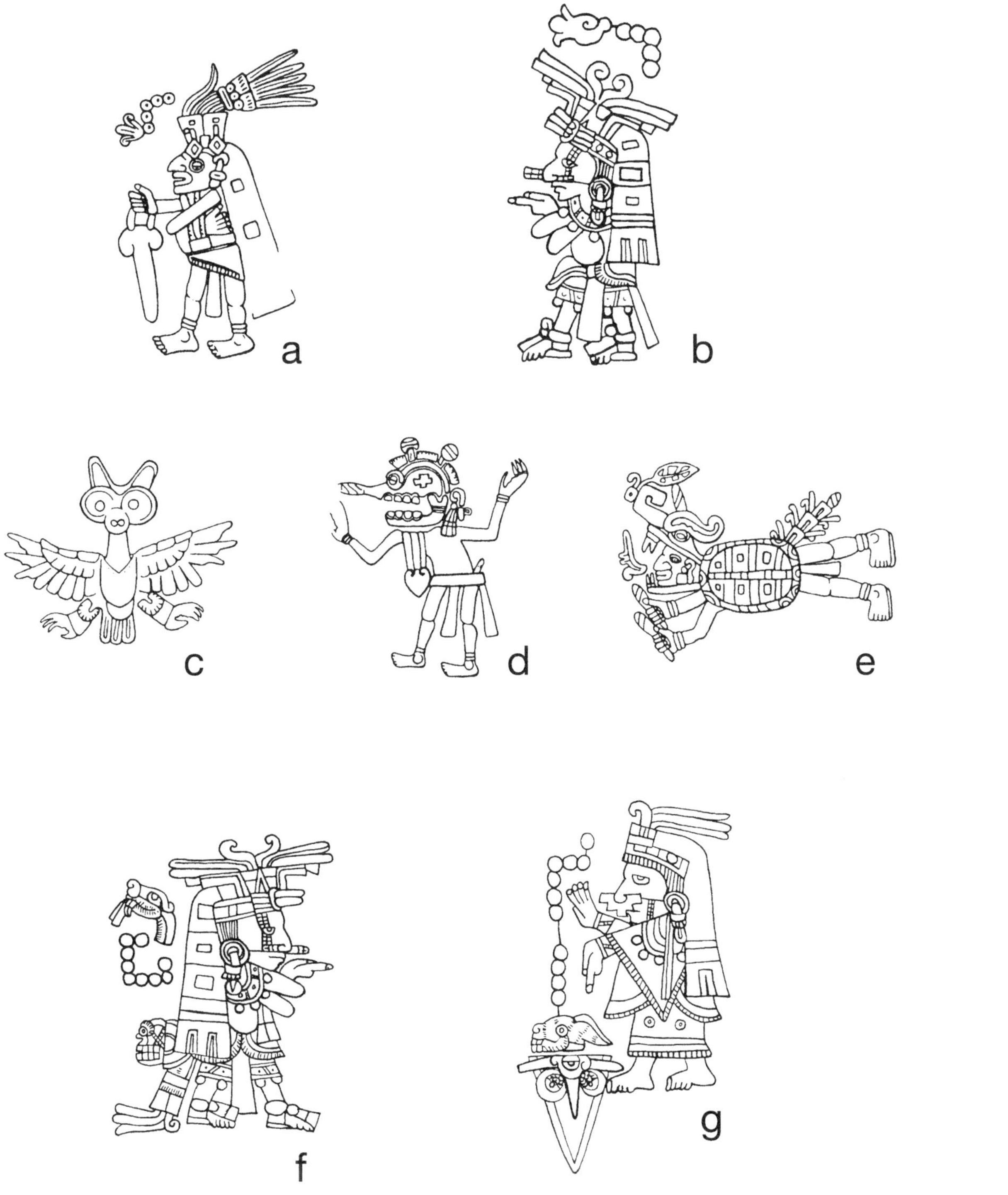

Figure 17.7. Postclassic protagonists. *a*, a stucco figure of Lord 5 Flower on the west wall of Tomb 1 at Zaachila. *b*, Lord 5 Flower as painted in the Codex Nuttall. *c*, the stucco figure of an owl attached to the wall of Tomb 1, Zaachila. *d*, the God of Death from Tomb 1, with claw-like hands, a sacrificial knife protruding from his nose, and a human heart suspended from a rope around his neck. *e*, the stucco figure of a sorcerer whose torso is the carapace of a turtle and whose limbs are those of a human; this flying figure is called a *yahui* by the Mixtec and a *xicàni* by the Zapotec (Pohl 1994:67). This stucco figure is displayed above the niche on the back wall of Tomb 1, Zaachila. *f*, Lord 9 Serpent as painted in the Codex Nuttall. *g*, Lady 11 Rabbit as painted in the Codex Nuttall (see Byland and Pohl 1994; Gallegos Ruiz 1978; Hermann Lejarazu 2009; Jansen and Pérez Jiménez 2011; Lind 2015; Markens 2014; Paddock 1966a: Pl. 13–17; Vicente Cruz and Sánchez Santiago 2014: Lám. XIV–XV).

(2) Lord 5 Flower had at least two sons, 9 Serpent and 9 Flower.
(3) One son, 9 Serpent, governed Zaachila and later Yagul, ultimately leaving the Valley of Oaxaca to take up residence in the Isthmus of Tehuantepec, where he died and was buried.
(4) The other son, 9 Flower, governed Zaachila and died there.
(5) 9 Flower and 5 Flower were both buried in Tomb 1 at Zaachila, and stucco depictions of them were placed on opposite walls of the main chamber.

Finally, on the back wall of the main chamber of Tomb 1 is the stucco figure of a man who holds a sacrificial knife in each hand. His most unusual attributes are (1) his ability to fly and (2) the large turtle carapace he wears. Similar beings are depicted in both the Codex Nuttall and the Selden Roll (e.g., Hermann Lejarazu 2009; Jansen and Pérez Jiménez 2011; Lind 2015; Pohl 1994; M. E. Smith 1973b; Terraciano 1994).

Mary Elizabeth Smith (1973b:60–64) has offered an explanation for such "flying turtle men." After studying annotations in the Códices Muro and Sánchez Solís, she determined that *yahui* was the word that the Mixtec used to refer to this "flying turtle-Xiuhcoatl sacrificer." A *yahui* had special abilities—he could transform himself into butterflies, eagles, and other animals that could fly through mountains and caves; he was a sorcerer, a wizard, an impersonator, a sacrificer, a supernatural being, and apparently the *nagual* or spirit of the deceased (Augsburger 2003; Caso 1964b:27, 75; Caso 1969: Figure 121; Hermann Lejarazu 2009; Parsons 1931; Pohl 1994:67).

Given turtle-man's prominent location on the rear wall of Zaachila's Tomb 1, we wonder if he was the *tona*, *nagual*, or alter ego of one of the tomb's occupants (see Alcina Franch 1971; Brinton 1894; Kaplan 1956; Saler 1977). His ability to transform himself into a creature that could fly would allow him to exit the tomb and presumably communicate with the descendants of 5 Flower and 9 Flower. Unfortunately, the widespread nature of such concepts in Postclassic culture makes it impossible to resolve the question of whether Tomb 1's occupants were Zapotec, Mixtec, or the offspring of a multiethnic marriage.

In Zaachila's Tomb 1 the turtle-man holds a sacrificial knife in each hand, perhaps ready to make human and/or animal sacrifices (Marcus 1983c); he also serves as a mediator between the living and the dead. The part man/part turtle may represent a dead noble who has metamorphosed into a supernatural being with all of these special powers—the ability to fly, to sacrifice, to perform divination, and to speak with remote ancestors. I have suggested that this figure was sometimes regarded as an apical ancestor who acquired these abilities after death (Caso 1965a:942; Marcus 1983c, 1983e).

The Mitla Murals

Mitla is estimated to have been a town of more than 10,000 people in Period V (Kowalewski et al. 1989:321). It featured five major clusters of public buildings: (1) the Church (or North) Group, (2) the Adobe Group, (3) the Arroyo Group, (4) the Group of the Columns, and (5) the South Group. Excavations by Caso and Rubín de la Borbolla (2003) showed that the Church Group, the Arroyo Group, and the Group of the Columns were all Period V in date.

Early European visitors described Mitla's amazingly well-preserved buildings, and especially their decorated walls with their intricate mosaic step-frets and grecas. Motolinía (1951:254) described Mitla's Period V buildings as being more beautiful than those in any other part of New Spain. William Henry Holmes (1895:264–265) noted that the grecas on the walls stood out because they were painted white, while the wall panels surrounding them were painted dark red. The step-fret variants—so reminiscent of textile and basketry designs—form a highly attractive geometric decoration that breaks up the monotony of large expanses of wall.

When Holmes visited Mitla in the 1890s he noted murals on door jambs, pillars and lintels, often in restricted-access interior spaces. Although early sources agree that several Period V buildings once had murals, only a few survived to be published by Caso (2002:2), Díaz et al. (2005), León (1901), Miller (1995), Pohl (1999), and Seler (1904b).

What was the content of the Mitla murals? Unfortunately, today we can see only the uppermost remnants (see Color Plate X, this volume), which present the sky with stars and planets, the sun, the moon, Venus, and some possible constellations. Pohl (1999, 2005) has suggested that the murals related origin myths. Of some interest is the fact that the technique used to paint the Mitla murals is reminiscent of the resist technique used to paint the lintel of Tomb 1 at Huitzo, which also dates to Period V.

The Monuments of Teotitlán del Valle

Eduard Seler (1904b) was one of the first scholars to document a group of stylistically related carved stones at Teotitlán del Valle in the Tlacolula region (Figures 17.8–17.14). He noted that by the time he arrived, the stones had been removed from their original context and reset in the walls of the town's houses and churches. Although we know little about their original setting, their style suggests a Period V date.

> Nothing remains to-day of the magnificent buildings of the Zapotec Teotitlan del valle [sic], but portions of the ancient buildings, stone mosaics with geometric designs of the fashion of those of Mitla and fragments of reliefs are here and there found embedded in the walls of houses and churches in Teotitlan, as well as in those of the neighboring Macuilxochic [sic]. (Seler 1904b:298)

Most of the Teotitlán stones are so similar as to suggest that they were commissioned as a group. Many of the carvings show men holding a weapon or a shield, wearing the animal

Figure 17.8. This monument from Teotitlán del Valle shows a man with a large circle behind him and another on his chest. The spirals (one at his left elbow and one at his ear) and the style of his feet (in which the front half hangs down) are features shared with other Postclassic monuments. Drawing by Rubén Méndez.

Figure 17.9. Monument from Teotitlán del Valle that shows a man with a weapon in his right hand (see also Seler 1904b: Fig. 69a). The way his right hand projects directly from his garment, without showing his arm, is another Postclassic feature. Drawing by Rubén Méndez.

costumes of a celebrated warrior, or encased in padded, quilted garments that would have protected them during battle. What makes the ten known Teotitlán del Valle stones so distinctive are the oversized garments and the unusual treatment of the men's hands and feet. Sometimes the front half of the foot is shown curved over or bending down; sometimes the arms are signaled just by showing the hands. One monument even shows hands and feet attached directly to the oversized garment, without any legs or arms depicted. Stylistically, the droopy feet of the Teotitlán monuments remind us of other Period V works, such as the stucco figures on the walls of Tomb 1 at Zaachila and the simplified hands depicted on a statue-in-the-round at Zaachila (see Chapter 14, Figure 14.38).

Summary

The corpus of Period V stone sculptures is small and limited to a handful of sites. The nobles of this era were more likely to invest in stucco modeling and the painting of murals or lintels, rather than carving scenes on stone. Rare indeed were the very large stone monuments of earlier times, with their vertical propaganda. The role of hieroglyphic writing was declining, and when writing did occur it was often found on objects as small as carved bones or gold jewelry (Caso 1969).

The Period V palace and its associated tombs remained one locus for artistic and iconographic display, almost certainly because that is where noble families would host others and conduct the affairs of state. The investment in expanding palaces so that they had two or more interior patios—for example, in the Tlacolula arm of the valley—may have had something to do with situating the seat of government in the great houses of prominent noble families. In a sense, the enlarged palaces of Period V had made obsolete many of the places of assembly featured in the Classic era. One theme that did continue from earlier times was warfare, with its representation of armed warriors wearing animal costumes on carved stones and the depiction of conquered towns on carved bones. This theme was often displayed, however, in venues where horizontal propaganda is the most plausible explanation.

Figure 17.10. Monument from Teotitlán del Valle that shows a figure wearing an animal costume (see also Seler 1904b: Fig. 70b). Drawing by Rubén Méndez.

Figure 17.11. Monument from Teotitlán del Valle showing a man holding a shield (see also Seler 1904b: Fig. 69b). Drawing by Rubén Méndez.

Figure 17.12. Monument from Teotitlán del Valle, depicting a person in what may be an animal costume. Drawing by Rubén Méndez.

Figure 17.13. Monument from Teotitlán del Valle, depicting a man in animal costume (see also Seler 1904b: Fig. 70a). Drawing by Rubén Méndez.

Figure 17.14. Monument from Teotitlán del Valle, showing a man wearing a garment similar to the one in Figure 17.9. The hand, rather than the arm, projecting from the garment and the spiral at his ear are typical of Teotitlán's Postclassic monuments. Drawing by Mark Orsen.

Part VI

Shifting Strategies in the Use of Zapotec Writing

18

The Evolution of Zapotec Writing and Political History

It is generally accepted that the Zapotec created one of Mesoamerica's oldest writing systems (Caso 1928, 1965a). The early appearance of writing in Oaxaca fits well with the fact that that region can also be credited with early agriculture (8000 BC), early rank societies (1150 BC), and a 300-year period (300 BC to AD 1) of political and military competition that led to one of Mesoamerica's first states (Feinman and Marcus 1998; Flannery 1976, 1986; Flannery and Marcus 2012; Marcus and Feinman 1998; Marcus and Flannery 1996; Sherman et al. 2010; Spencer 2003, 2007, 2009, 2010; Spencer and Redmond 2004a, 2005, 2006; Spencer et al. 2008).

Zapotec writing appeared between 600 and 500 BC in the context of chiefly competition. The carvers of Monument 3 at San José Mogote needed to specify the name of a sacrificed rival; the victim was carved on a stone threshold so that anyone entering or exiting a corridor would step on his body (see Flannery and Marcus 2015:180–193). By specifying the victim's name, the Zapotec, like the Maori of New Zealand, suggested that no battle was memorable unless it involved the capture or death of a chiefly individual whose name was known (Buck 1949).

While this first appearance of Zapotec writing was limited to the naming of an individual, the use of writing expanded greatly between 500 BC and 200 BC. During Period Ia, Monte Albán carved 300 images of sacrificed captives and virtually monopolized writing within the Valley of Oaxaca. Zapotec texts came to reflect the use of two calendars, one secular (365 days) and one ritual (260 days). By combining their 365-day and 260-day calendars, the Zapotec created a 52-year Calendar Round. They did not, however, add a base date to create a Long Count. That accomplishment was first recorded at Chiapa de Corzo (Mexico) around 36 BC, followed by southern Guatemala in AD 37 and northern Guatemala in AD 292. The fact that the Zapotec lacked the Long Count means that we cannot assign precise dates to Zapotec monuments the way we can for Isthmian, Chiapan, and Maya monuments.

Period I writing was concerned with names, dates, the taking of captives, and accession to office. We are confident that Period I writing was related to the spoken Zapotec language because (1) it employs the rebus principle, using tone pairs and homonyms that work only in Zapotec; and (2) the order of the glyphs reflects Zapotec syntax. Period I also produced our first "pure text": columns of hieroglyphs unaccompanied by images and scenes (Stelae 12, 13, 14, 15, 17 at Monte Albán).

The earliest Zapotec monuments focused on "vertical propaganda"—that is, messages conveyed from the nobles to the commoners. These monuments were set up in public venues where literate personnel could communicate their content to those who could not read. Most hieroglyphic texts were accompanied by scenes that helped explain the message. One interesting strategy was to place carvings of slain enemies in places that allowed them to be trod upon—an idea later borrowed by the Maya and by the architects of Cacaxtla in Tlaxcala (e.g., Brittenham 2015:73–74; Dillon 1982; Foncerrada de Molina 1980, 1993; Lombardo de Ruiz 1986; López de Molina 1979; Marcus 1974).

At AD 100 the Zapotec were still preoccupied with sacrifice, subjugated rivals, conquest, and territorial expansion, but to write about such expansion they had to create a standardized "hill" or "place" glyph. This hill sign allowed the architects of Monte Albán's Building J to list more than 60 places that the Zapotec likely considered to be part of their expanding empire—a theme later borrowed by the site of Xochicalco in Morelos (Berlo 1989; Hirth 1989). The Zapotec used the presence of upside-down heads with closed eyes to indicate that a place had been conquered, and a hill sign without an upside-down head to show that a place had capitulated peacefully.

Soon Valley of Oaxaca pottery (especially the graywares) started to appear at sites outside the valley, identifying them as communities that were now part of Monte Albán's political sphere. Some of these sites commissioned sculptures with hieroglyphs, showing a desire to emulate the Valley Zapotec (e.g., Gaxiola 1976; Marcus 1983h). At first it was easier for the Zapotec to dominate less politically developed areas outside the Valley of Oaxaca; their most powerful rivals within the valley resisted, and as a result it took longer to subdue them (Marcus 1992c; Spencer 1982, 2007; Spencer and Redmond 2001a, 2003).

By AD 300 the themes the Zapotec selected to memorialize had become more varied. To be sure, there were still depictions of war captives; now, however, it was more common to see a living captive portrayed with his arms tied than to see a slain and mutilated victim. Moreover, some of the bound captives were associated with scenes of royal inauguration; we suspect that it was now more important to display elaborately costumed captives at one's accession to the throne than to show their nude and mutilated corpses.

A significant theme during the period from AD 200 to 600 was that of diplomatic relations between Monte Albán and Teotihuacán. Visitors wearing Teotihuacán-style tassel headdresses and sandals were shown meeting a Zapotec ruler and attending building dedications (Acosta 1958–1959; Caso 1965a, 1965b; C. Millon 1973, 1988). The Teotihuacanos carried harmless pouches rather than weapons, and one carved stone suggests that they burned incense and conducted rites with the Zapotec.

The Period III data show that (1) Monte Albán and Teotihuacán left a buffer zone between their spheres of influence, situated to the north of Quiotepec (Redmond 1983; Spencer 1982); (2) there was active trade between these two superpowers, with Teotihuacán-controlled obsidian reaching Oaxaca, and Monte Albán-controlled mica reaching Teotihuacán (Armillas 1944; Manzanilla et al. 2017); and (3) Teotihuacán accepted an enclave of Oaxacan peoples within its urban boundaries (R. Millon 1981, 1992; Spence 1992; White et al. 2004). Although Teotihuacán and Monte Albán readily expanded against their weaker neighbors, their relationship with each other was clearly one of détente and active trade. Among the items Monte Albán received were Thin Orange pottery and obsidian, and among the items Monte Albán likely sent to Teotihuacán were mica and cochineal.

After AD 700, both Teotihuacán and Monte Albán began to decline in political power. By AD 900 the buildings in Monte Albán's Main Plaza were no longer being repaired, and various of its former secondary centers were becoming the capitals of politically independent petty states. The surge of prestigious noble lineages at many secondary sites fundamentally changed the political system, as well as the distribution and nature of Zapotec hieroglyphic monuments. The most notable theme of the new monuments was the establishment of the genealogical right to rule. This message seems to have been aimed mainly at other nobles, and as a result, horizontal (noble-to-noble) propaganda became more common than vertical (noble-to-commoner) propaganda.

The genealogical registers and ancestor veneration monuments of this era were more likely to be placed in areas of restricted access, such as palaces and tombs, than on the exterior walls of public buildings. Even the few freestanding stone stelae of AD 600–900 were not necessarily examples of vertical propaganda, because the majority were set up in places to which commoners had limited access. One stela, for example, was placed in the *patio hundido* of the North Platform at Monte Albán, and another was placed just south of Building e on the North Platform (Marcus 2009b: Figure 8). The patio associated with Buildings d, g, and e was the most private venue in all of Monte Albán, a space that virtually no commoners would have been able to enter (Blanton 1978:61–63).

At the same time that Monte Albán stopped maintaining the buildings around the Main Plaza, some noble families at secondary centers were seeking to attract more followers and arrange favorable alliances with their peers. These secondary centers were fomenting the manufacture of new craft goods and increased participation in trade networks. As Monte Albán became weaker, its former Tier 2 sites began forging new marriage alliances to elevate their status. Many former Tier 2 and Tier 3 towns were growing in population and prestige, investing in impressive palaces, genealogical registers, and elaborate tombs (Feinman and Nicholas 2017; Marcus 1989b). Monte Albán, in contrast, was investing less manpower in major construction projects and was occasionally reusing old tombs, as we will see later.

Among the former Tier 2 communities now creating elaborate tombs and carved stones were (1) sites in the northern valley (Reyes Etla, San Lázaro Etla, Huitzo, and Cerro de la Campana); (2) sites in the Valle Grande (Cuilapan, Xoxocotlán, and Zaachila); and (3) sites in the eastern valley (Lambityeco, Macuilxóchitl, Teotitlán del Valle, El Palmillo, and Yagul). The largest settlement in the valley at that time was actually Jalieza, which grew to cover more than 5 km^2 by AD 900; despite its size, Jalieza has yet to yield hieroglyphic texts.

Areas south and east of Monte Albán seem to have been the first to break away from its control. Lords at secondary sites during

Period IIIb–IV often pursued a three-step plan: secede from Monte Albán, avoid reincorporation, and work to forge a new polity by subordinating others (Marcus 1976a, 1992c, 2003b).

Each noble family had to establish new ties to other nobles to maintain its status, privileges, and trade relations. To find a suitable person of noble birth one often had to look to other towns, and over time such inter-site marriages led to an extensive web of horizontal links. Although symmetrical relations linked sites for a time, those links would later evolve into asymmetrical and hierarchical relations. Carved stones featured genealogies, apical ancestors, bundled corpses in funerary crates, and semi-divine marital pairs performing a diverse set of rites including conjuring, sacrificing quails, offering beverages, and burning incense.

During Period IIIb–IV communities such as Cuilapan, Lambityeco, El Palmillo, Mitla, Suchilquitongo, Xoxocotlán, Yagul, and Zaachila gained greater prominence. If a noble family chose the right strategy, its community had a chance to move up in the political hierarchy. Noble families commissioned tomb jambs, doors, lintels, and genealogical registers, as well as tomb murals and elaborate façades on family mausolea (Marcus 1989b).

Establishing legitimacy and asserting dynastic continuity were two of the motivations for making claims about genealogy, military prowess, and one's lineage and dynastic founders. Nobles commissioned texts not only to preserve history but also to effect specific results, such as establishing ritual contact with ancestors, legitimizing the claims of their descendants, and memorializing the names of those in ascendant generations (Marcus 1992a; Masson and Orr 1998a; Whitecotton 1977, 1982, 1983).

Nobles also forged ties to other nobles through reciprocal obligations—attending their funerals and marking the anniversaries of their interments, especially those of dynastic founders and important marital pairs. Visitors and participants sometimes spent time at tomb doors, where they arranged a group of urns, usually five in number, bearing the image of *Cociyo* or Lightning. In front of many tombs archaeologists have also found evidence of incense burning (braziers); food consumption (bowls, jars); the offering of precious items (jade, shells); and the drinking of pulque (*nupi*) or chocolate (*niça pizoya*) from beakers.

The most elaborate Zapotec family tombs were carved into bedrock, often before the residential structures above them were built (Flannery 1983c:134–135). Some tombs came to include people from multiple generations, establishing legitimacy for them and their descendants. In Zapotec cosmology, the living and the dead coexisted in a seamless continuum.

Multigenerational use, which required reopening the tomb, made the private interior patio of the palace a key locus for rituals. A tomb might be opened several times to add family members from other generations; Tomb 6 at Lambityeco is a good example, because it was evidently opened six times (Lind 2003, 2015; Lind and Urcid 1983, 2010).

The Zapotec elite had special abilities, such as (1) communicating with deified ancestors, (2) impersonating supernatural forces, (3) metamorphosing into beings that were half-human and half-animal, (4) mediating between celestial and terrestrial beings, and (5) flying to heaven and returning with messages or gifts (Flannery and Marcus 1976b; Marcus 1992a, 2006b). As early as AD 100, an important ancestor might be depicted as a flying figure who had attributes of *Cociyo*, turtles, or crocodiles. For example, an offering box below Structure 35 at San José Mogote contained seven ceramic pieces arranged in a scene. The principal actor in the scene was a metamorphosed flying figure who rested atop the roof of a miniature tomb (Flannery and Marcus 2015:268–269; Marcus and Flannery 1994, 1996:186–188).

What seems to have been happening during Period IIIb–IV is that a stratified society, once dominated by royal dynasties at Monte Albán, was evolving into one in which a whole series of "noble houses" were establishing themselves at multiple centers around the valley. Long ago, Bernal (1965b:847) pointed out that prior to Period III, more effort went into the construction of temple pyramids than palaces; from Period IIIb onward, however, more effort went into the construction of the palace. Royal residences in the Tlacolula subvalley came to have multiple patios instead of one central open space (e.g., Bernal and Gamio 1974), while temples were less likely to be set on steep pyramidal structures. The "noble house" of the Postclassic period often possessed a large tomb where deceased family members continued to be added for generations to come.

This emphasis on funerary settings for horizontal propaganda continued into the period AD 1200–1500. By then, however, the use of Zapotec hieroglyphic writing was on the wane. Warfare continued (López Zárate 2014), but none of the petty states of the Late Postclassic was worthy of the term "expansionist." Rival nobles warred over the right to rule relatively small territories, and Zapotec nobles sometimes reached beyond the valley to marry Mixtec nobles, in order to consolidate power. In the end, a Zapotec-Mixtec military alliance prevented the Aztec from taking over the Valley of Oaxaca (Flannery 1983b, 1983d; Marcus 1983g).

Themes in Zapotec Writing

Let us now recapitulate, roughly in chronological order, some of the dominant themes in Zapotec monuments and hieroglyphic writing; we will begin with those themes that seem to have been there from the beginning.

Naming People

The earliest theme so far known in Zapotec writing was the naming of individuals. To do this, the Zapotec used that person's calendric name as a caption to accompany his image.

The oldest known example of Zapotec writing (Monument 3, San José Mogote) provided the name of a sacrificial victim (see Chapter 6). On later Zapotec monuments we see names like 7 Monkey, 8 Deer, 9 Jaguar, and 10 Maize, names that included bars for "5" and dots for "1." We are fortunate that the Zapotec named their children after the day of their birth in the 260-day calendar, because the bars and dots in their names are so easy to recognize (Chapter 3).

More than 90 years ago, Alfonso Caso (1928) published the first catalog of Zapotec hieroglyphs, and many of them proved to be the names of people. Such calendric names were carved in stone as early as the Middle Formative and continued well into the Colonial era, where they were recorded in wills, *lienzos*, *genealogías*, and codices (e.g., Caso 1964a, 1966; Oudijk 1998, 2000; Romero Frizzi 2003; Whitecotton 1977, 1983, 1990, 2003).

Anchoring Events in Time

In addition to using hieroglyphs to identify the people depicted in their monuments, the Zapotec wanted to date political and ritual events; to do so, they used the 52-year Calendar Round (Caso 1928). In their creation of a year sign, the Zapotec drew inspiration from the diadem or headband that was traditionally tied around a ruler's head (see Chapters 3 and 14, e.g., Figures 3.8 and 14.28). Once developed, the Zapotec year sign would be combined with one of the four days that could begin a year (i.e., the year bearer). The resulting 52-year period allowed monument carvers to place events into that unit of time (Chapter 3).

The 52-year Calendar Round was used throughout Mesoamerica. The lowlands added a new wrinkle, however, by selecting a base date in the fourth millennium BC. Lowland groups then calculated the number of days that had elapsed since that datum point. This Long Count system was superior because its dates were firmly anchored, whereas those in the Calendar Round can only be tied to a floating 52-year period (Boone 2000; Edmonson 1988; Morley 1915; Satterthwaite 1965; Thompson 1950).

Our earliest example of a Zapotec year sign and year bearer appears on Stela 12 at Monte Albán. Dating to 500–300 BC, Stela 12 was an orthostat set up at the south end of the Building L Prisoner Gallery on the west side of the Main Plaza (see Chapter 6). Stela 12 appears to commemorate the year a Zapotec leader took office, an event evidently accompanied by the sacrifice of hundreds of captives displayed in the Building L gallery (Alcina Franch 1969; Caso 1928:95; Dupaix [1834]1969; Marcus 1980). That display suggests that the show of military prowess was not only a prerequisite for assuming office, but also worthy of being memorialized in stone. The Prisoner Gallery of Building L had no rival in the annals of Oaxaca prehistory. Never again were so many monuments carved for a single outpouring of vertical propaganda.

Although the Zapotec appear to have been the first to use the Calendar Round, this 52-year period continued to provide the principal calendric framework throughout highland Mexico. Two millennia later, the Mixtec and Aztec were still recording events in the 52-year Calendar Round (see Figure 3.1). Figure 18.1 shows an Aztec dedication stone that features the year bearer "8 Reed" (the day that began the year AD 1487). That date marked the year the emperor Ahuitzotl took office, and the Aztecs rededicated the Temple of Huitzilopochtli. The carvers of this monument even engaged in a bit of fake news: they depicted Ahuitzotl participating in a bloodletting rite with his predecessor Tizoc, who had actually died prior to this alleged event. Such a scene, though historically inaccurate, was needed to establish legitimacy for Ahuitzotl, who was a mere child at the time and had therefore not taken the captives required for his inauguration.

Creating Place Names

In addition to specifying the dates of events, the Zapotec needed a way to record the names of places. For this purpose they created the "hill" or "place" sign. This glyph appeared by 50 BC during the course of Zapotec state formation.

Hill signs + qualifiers were used to specify the name of a place (Chapter 8). The Zapotec were then able to specify places that they claimed to have subjugated, places from which sacrificed enemies had originated, places from which royal spouses came, and places where a royal ally resided. Some of the earliest place names positioned the place-specifier (e.g., a rabbit) just above the hill sign; later, some place-specifiers (e.g., a heart) were literally placed inside the hill sign (Caso 1928; Marcus 2009b; Neys and von Winning 1946).

While the Zapotec appear to have been the first to use a place sign, other highland and lowland peoples picked up the idea; eventually the Maya, Mixtec, and Aztec also created hill signs (Marcus 1992a). By AD 900, Xochicalco in Morelos had listed more than a dozen subjugated places on its Building of the Plumed Serpent. Xochicalco even added a glyph for "tribute," to leave no doubt about what it was claiming (Berlo 1989; Hirth 1989).

Taking Office

The first possible accession glyph appeared on Monte Albán's Stela 12, a Middle Formative monument. During Period III, Stela 1 in Monte Albán's South Platform depicted a newly accessioned ruler seated on a huge throne; the stelae nearby showed a procession of jaguar-costumed prisoners with their arms tied behind their backs (Chapter 9).

In addition to showing the new ruler seated on his throne, a procession of prisoners to be sacrificed, and the rededication of a temple, Zapotec accession ceremonies added a variety of rituals over time. One of the most unusual was the brandishing of the old ruler's femur by his successor (Chapter 15).

Offerings and Sacrifices

At least three kinds of sacrifice were practiced in ancient Mesoamerica—autosacrifice, animal sacrifice, and human sacrifice. Infant sacrifice was one of the oldest versions, since it is known from the Archaic era in the Tehuacán Valley (Fowler and MacNeish 1975; MacNeish 1962). Autosacrifice (or ritual

Figure 18.1. This Aztec dedication monument shows the emperor Ahuitzotl (at upper right) and his predecessor Tizoc (upper left) performing a ritual. Together they let blood from their earlobes, allowing it to flow down to an opening in the earth. Below Ahuitzotl and Tizoc is a huge date marking the Year 8 Reed (which corresponds to AD 1487); this was the year when the Temple of Huitzilopochtli was rededicated and Ahuitzotl took office. This ritual could not have included Tizoc, since he died before Ahuitzotl was named ruler; the monument was carved to reinforce Ahuitzotl's credentials. Redrawn from Klein 1987: Fig. 15 by John Klausmeyer.

bloodletting), although probably practiced just as early, is more difficult to document, until actual stingray spines begin to appear in Oaxaca's Early Formative villages (Flannery and Marcus 2005; Marcus 1999a, 1999b). Although the Maya often depicted women and men in the act of bloodletting, the Zapotec rarely elected to show autosacrifice on stone monuments.

By 600 BC we see evidence of adult sacrifice (heart removal) on Monument 3 at San José Mogote; that stone placed the sacrificed enemy in a position to be stepped upon by anyone entering the corridor between two Middle Formative temples (see Figure 6.15, Chapter 6). By 300 BC Monte Albán had constructed an impressive Prisoner Gallery—a powerful example of vertical propaganda—in which hundreds of naked, mutilated, and humiliated captives were displayed on a building that faced the Main Plaza.

Animal sacrifice in Oaxaca included deer, turtles, dogs, turkeys, and more than one species of wild bird. The sacrifice of birds seems to have been a particularly important part of funerary rites. For example, during Period II at San José Mogote, a sacrificed quail was part of a miniature ritual scene of metamorphosis (Flannery and Marcus 2015:268–269; Marcus and Flannery 1996:187). Bird sacrifice also accompanied several funerals at Lambityeco (Lind and Urcid 2010). On one Zapotec stone model we see a bird descending from an apical ancestor, carrying messages or auguries from the dead to the living (see Figure 16.5d, Chapter 16). Quail were sometimes shown being decapitated and offered to a mummy bundle in later codices from the Mixteca Alta (for example, see Figure 12.3 in Chapter 12; M. E. Smith 1973a; pages 4, 6, 20, 81 in the Codex Nuttall).

Conjuring and Communing

Over time the role of apical ancestors increased significantly for noble families, judging from the frequency with which they featured them in monuments and murals. On many Period IIIb–IV monuments we see a man and a woman performing rites in the presence of a downward-gazing apical ancestor.

These apical ancestors took different forms. Some had a human head, some wore a mask, and others had metamorphosed into a downward-diving bird or a flying creature with an upturned snout. Still others had human legs and arms attached to a torso resembling a turtle carapace (Caso 1966: Figure 20). Among the items held in their hands were sacrificial knives, birds, leaves, strands of beads, and a range of other objects that have yet to be identified (Caso 1965b: Figure 22; Hermann Lejarazu 2009; M. E. Smith 1973a, 1973b; see Figure 9.16).

Apical ancestors could communicate with the humans depicted below them on the monument; they could also mediate between humans and supernatural beings, some of whom combined the attributes of bats, birds, snakes, jaguars, crocodiles, and/or Lightning (e.g., Caso and Bernal 1952; Masson 2001). Carving apical ancestors on stones kept their names alive.

Some monuments depicted the Zapotec burning materials whose smoke reached the noses and eyes of their ancestors (see Figure 16.8 in Chapter 16). On some occasions they burned rubber or copal in braziers; on others they offered vessels containing beverages (see Figures 7.7, 14.36, 16.15). Some of the rites depicted seem to have involved divination, conjuring, or inducing an apical ancestor to descend from the sky. Often the ancestor dominated the scene, either by protruding three-dimensionally from the stone or by being centrally positioned on the monument.

The depiction of such rites was usually horizontal propaganda. Noble families displayed such monuments in their palaces, tombs, and private patios. As Monte Albán's power declined, noble families in each town became even more concerned with recording the names of their ancestors and keeping track of the marital pairs from whom they had descended. At the apogee of Monte Albán's power, the founder couple Lord 1 Jaguar and Lady 2 Maize had been featured (Marcus 2008b). By Period IIIb–IV there was a multiplicity of founder couples, and this pattern continued into the era of the Postclassic codices.

Establishing Noble Genealogies

The appearance of genealogical registers during Period IIIb–IV allowed Zapotec nobles to establish their right to rule by featuring founder couples, apical ancestors, and noble relatives. Generational differences were often shown by giving individuals of older generations wrinkles or beards.

Many genealogical registers were meant to be read from bottom to top, with the older generation in the compartment at the bottom of the monument. Such carved stones were typically displayed in private settings such as palaces, interior patios, and tombs—places where no commoner was likely to see them. Tomb-based monuments could be consulted on the anniversary of an ancestor's interment, at which time relatives might (1) re-enter a tomb and paint a lintel (e.g., Stela 5 at Cerro de la Campana) or (2) leave red or vermilion stripes on each niche or offering box (e.g., Monte Albán's Tomb 104). It was on such anniversaries that the Maltese cross (Glyph I) was often carved.

The Bundling and Crating of Deceased Nobles

One Period IIIb–IV theme often depicted in the Etla arm of the valley is worth mentioning. In that region, monuments suggest that deceased rulers were bundled, placed in a wooden box or crate, and carried from place to place on a litter. It may be that this bundling and crating was done by the deceased's descendants and served to legitimize the dead ruler's heir. It may have been the equivalent of the Tlacolula region's custom of having the heir brandish his predecessor's femur. The underlying principle may have been that the legitimate heir, and only he, had access to all or part of his predecessor's corpse.

Similarities and Differences between Zapotec and Maya Writing

Two of the ancient states that made the greatest use of hieroglyphs on stone were the Zapotec and the Maya. Let us now look at some of the similarities and differences between them.

One of the most obvious similarities was in the way military victory was shown. The Zapotec showed prisoners with their arms bound; so did the Maya at sites such as Toniná, Caracol, and Yaxchilan. The Zapotec also displayed prisoners on thresholds (Monument 3, San José Mogote) or stairways (Building L, Monte Albán), so that they could tread on the depictions of their defeated rivals. The Maya similarly showed their enemies being trod underfoot or in stairways (e.g., at Naranjo, Dos Pilas, Tamarindito, Tikal, Yaxchilan, and Dzibanché; see Chapter 6, Figures 6.10–6.11).

The Zapotec and Maya selected many of the same themes for their respective monuments—accession to office, depicting enemies, naming prisoners, conjuring ancestors, burning incense, divination, metamorphosis, and showing the deceased as a mummy bundle propped up in a box or on a bench (Figure 18.2).

The Zapotec and Maya also carved bones to use as mnemonic devices. Both groups carved the days of the calendar so that they could be consulted for divining and prognostication. For example, a bone reportedly found on the island of Jaina shows an individual casting maize kernels, as well as a complete list of the Maya day signs in order (Barthel 1967). Similar content is displayed on several carved bones from Tomb 7 at Monte Albán (Caso 1969; see also Chapter 17).

One of the obvious differences between the Zapotec and Maya lay in kinship. Both the Zapotec and Mixtec, who spoke Otomanguean languages (see Chapter 5), used what are called Hawai'ian kinship terms. They reckoned descent through both parents, taking differences in rank into account. The Maya, on the other hand, were more likely to reckon descent through the male line. These differences between Otomanguean and Maya descent help to explain one of the most noticeable differences in their monuments—the greater frequency with which the Zapotec depicted marital pairs in noble genealogies. Maya rulership was typically envisioned as involving one man on a throne, whereas the Zapotec and Mixtec often viewed a married couple as co-ruling a polity.

Let us look at Copán's Altar Q, a monument commissioned by that site's sixteenth ruler. On the four sides of the altar we see carved a succession of sixteen male rulers, beginning with the alleged dynasty founder (Yax K'uk' Mo'o) and ending with the ruler commissioning the monument. Nowhere on Altar Q is a royal woman mentioned. The contrast with most Zapotec genealogical registers, which feature several generations of marital pairs, could not be greater (see Chapters 12, 13). Even the primordial founders of Monte Albán's Period IIIa royal dynasty—Lord 1 Jaguar and Lady 2 Maize—were a husband and wife. In contrast, no known Maya king list begins with a marital pair.

That is not to say that royal women were never depicted on Maya monuments; some were. Most, however, were featured only because they were the bride, widow, mother, or daughter of a male ruler. This is not unexpected in a system which even today uses patronymics (e.g., Restall 1997; Roys 1940, 1943).

Another significant difference was that the Maya possessed the Long Count, while the Zapotec had only the 52-year Calendar Round. This allowed the Maya to produce monuments with dates that can be placed in absolute time and correlated with today's Western calendar. The dates of many Maya rulers' births, accession to the throne, marriage, and death can be reconstructed in ways that are simply not possible for the Zapotec (see Chapter 11). Many Period IIIb–IV genealogical registers give us the names of Zapotec marital pairs from several generations. The dates of their respective reigns, however, are floating in time; they cannot be securely correlated with our Western calendar. The Zapotec and Mixtec named their children after the day on which they were born, but the Maya did not. The Maya were more likely to use serpent, peccary, jaguar, or turtle names.

Another major difference was the kinds of monuments the Maya and Zapotec created. The pairing of the stela and the altar was typical of the lowlands (e.g., Tikal, Caracol). Not only were true stelae rare in the Valley of Oaxaca, they were also never paired with altars. The stela-altar pairing extended from lowland sites as far apart as Tres Zapotes in the west to Caracol in the east.

Possible Zapotec influence on the Maya may be seen in the appearance of tomb niches and continuous wraparound murals, such as those that appeared suddenly at Río Azul around AD 400. Although the Zapotec and Maya both constructed elaborate tombs for their nobles, the Zapotec were the first to create tombs with polychrome murals, usually placing a huge hieroglyph on the back wall that gave the name of an apical ancestor. The Zapotec painted hieroglyphs naming the marital pairs, often walking in processions, who were coming to pay tribute to the apical ancestor named on the back wall of the tomb. The tomb niches often contained offerings, sacred boxes, bundles, and ceramics, as well as the bones of ancestors. The Maya rarely painted polychrome murals, and most of their royal tombs featured a single ruler. Sometimes servants or sacrificial victims were placed immediately in front of the tomb door, as in the case of K'inich Janaab' Pakal at Palenque (see Figure 11.2).

Future Goals

Despite the fact that Zapotec monuments have appeared in print off and on since the 1800s, I am left with the impression that the systematic study of Zapotec writing is still in its initial stages. The most identifiable glyphs are still those related to the 260-day calendar, year signs, year bearers, and the 52-year Calendar Round. (Think how lucky we are that the Zapotec named their children after days in the sacred calendar; were that not the case, we might not know the name of a single Zapotec noble.)

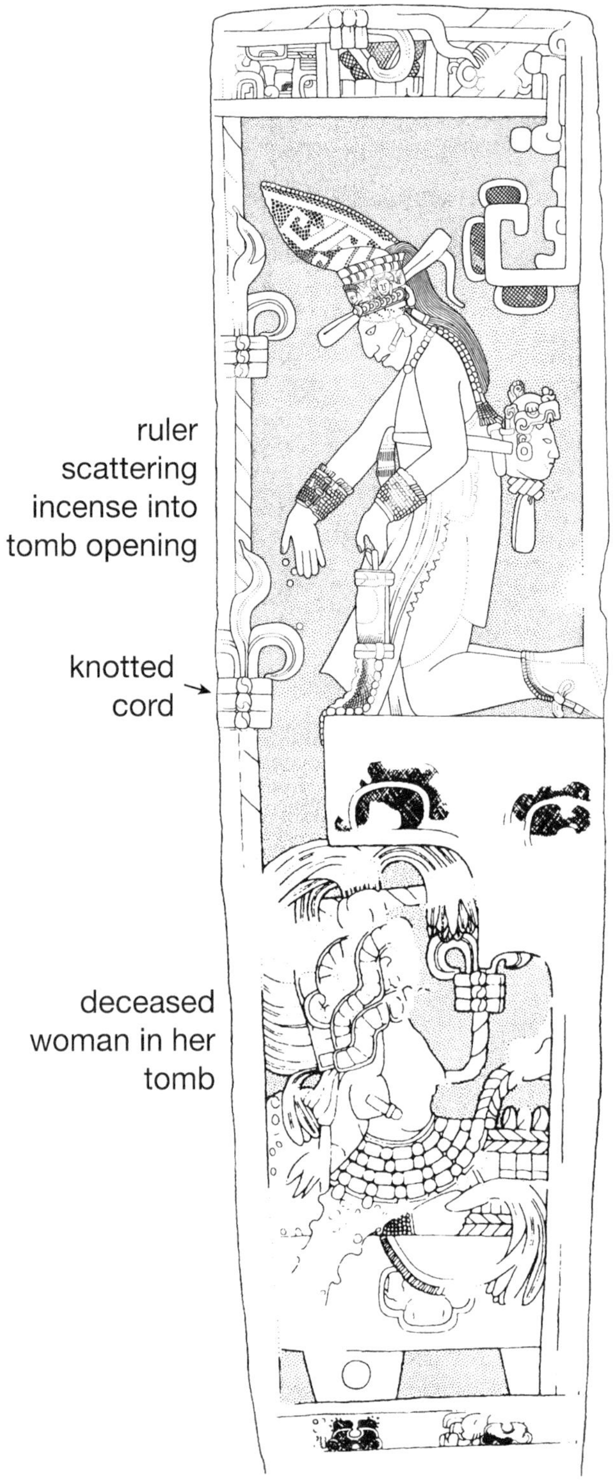

Figure 18.2. Like Zapotec elites, Maya elites wanted to have access to their relatives' tombs. On this stela, we see a Maya ruler kneeling above the tomb of his deceased mother. Like the corpses propped up in wooden crates on the San Lázaro Etla monuments, his mother is propped up on a bier or stone bench. The knotted cord running down the left side of the carving leads to her nose, allowing her to smell the copal incense being offered by her son; this provides her with a lifeline to the world of the living. This is Stela 40 of Piedras Negras, Guatemala. Redrawn from Martin and Grube (2000:149) by John Klausmeyer.

Perhaps the second most recognizable group of Zapotec hieroglyphs are those relating to places, using the well-known "hill sign." One of our future challenges will be to link more of these hill signs to actual places on the landscapes—not an easy task, since many of Oaxaca's places now have Spanish or Nahuatl names.

One of our most significant future needs is to identify more of the glyphs that represent verbs and nouns. Working in our favor is the fact that we now know that Oaxaca's hieroglyphic texts used Zapotec word order and syntax. Working against us is the fact that so many verbs and nouns appear only once or twice on monuments. Maya epigraphers have taken advantage of a monument corpus that is many times larger, and in which many Maya verbs and nouns occur dozens of times (e.g., Schele 1982; Thompson 1962).

Many Maya monuments have very long texts and repetitive clauses. Some of our longest Zapotec texts are on Lápida 1 del Museo Nacional (see Figure 16.4), Lintel 3 at Xoxocotlán (see Figure 14.12), and Stela 5 at Cerro de la Campana (see Figure 12.11); each of these texts has fewer than 25 hieroglyphs arranged in columns! All of these Zapotec examples pale by comparison with Copán's Hieroglyphic Stairway, with its 2000 hieroglyphs; Palenque's wall panels in the Temples of the Inscriptions, Cross, Foliated Cross, and Sun, with their hundreds of hieroglyphs; and Tikal's Stela 31, with its more than 250 glyphs.

To be sure, the recovery of more Zapotec monuments would help, but we need for them to be found *in situ*. Once a monument has been looted and reset in the wall of a church, half its information has been lost. For the earlier periods of the Oaxaca sequence, we are likely to benefit from exposing buildings, since that is where so many examples of vertical propaganda were displayed. For the later periods we are likely to benefit from exposing noble palaces and tombs, where so many examples of horizontal propaganda were displayed.

In addition to the more general goals of identifying verbs and nouns and establishing grammatical structures, there are a number of specific topics we need to explore. One of these topics is subvalley-to-subvalley differences. Early studies of Oaxaca monuments relied on a small sample and emphasized their similarities—now, with monuments from many more sites in each arm of the valley, we can see some of the intriguing regional differences, e.g., among Monte Albán, Etla, Valle Grande, and Tlacolula.

At a time when Monte Albán had more than its share of monuments and a virtual monopoly on the use of hieroglyphs, Dainzú in the Tlacolula region stands out by having literally scores of carved stones. Dainzú featured helmeted gladiators who used stone balls as weapons (Baudez 2011; Berger 2011; Hammond 2017; T. A. Joyce 1933; Orr 2003; Taube and Zender 2009). Dainzú's hillside boulders featured more than 50 decapitated heads (Bernal and Seuffert 1973, 1979). During Period IIIb–IV, when the Etla region was emphasizing deceased nobles propped up in funerary boxes (Caso 1965b: Figure 23), Tlacolula featured marital pairs conjuring images of their ancestors and conducting an array of rituals. By Period V, the Tlacolula arm was producing more monuments than any other part of the valley (Seler 1904b).

Each subvalley—Etla, Tlacolula, Valle Grande—used themes seen outside its own region, but also displayed unique features. These local and regional differences will only come into sharper focus as the number of monuments known for each region increases.

Finally, we need to understand the transition from a highly stratified society—dominated by Monte Albán's royal families—to a society in which palatial "great houses"—with multiple patios and multigenerational tombs—competed with each other for advantageous marriage alliances and trading partners. Excavation and settlement pattern survey will surely contribute to our understanding of this transition. To create a more complete picture, however, we need to know how the competing nobles themselves saw the situation. Monuments that reveal the nobles' political strategies and horizontal propaganda—especially if we can find them *in situ*—will go a long way toward fleshing out the picture.

Resumen en español

Soren Frykholm

La escritura jeroglífica zapoteca es ampliamente reconocida como una de las más antiguas de Mesoamérica. Apareció por primera vez entre el 600 y el 500 a.C., en el contexto de una intensa competencia militar y política entre sociedades de jefatura en el Valle de Oaxaca. El Monumento 3 de San José Mogote es un monolito grabado que fue utilizado como umbral de un pasillo entre dos templos del Formativo Medio. Representa a un prisionero sacrificado, presumiblemente un rival noble, cuyo nombre incluye el número 1 y el Glifo L definido por Alfonso Caso. Este primer monumento zapoteco, en otras palabras, sirvió como propaganda para un jefe victorioso en su lucha por subyugar a su rival y mencionar su nombre. A este respecto, la escritura zapoteca se asemeja a la del Egipto temprano, la cual se empleó para registrar los acontecimientos históricos y los nombres de los líderes políticos. No se parece por ello a la escritura mesopotámica temprana, que se usaba principalmente para consignar transacciones económicas.

Para el 500 a.C., 2000 personas de San José Mogote y sus aldeas satélites ya se habían trasladado a la cima de esa montaña defendible que llamamos Monte Albán. Mientras libraba la guerra contra sus rivales, Monte Albán incrementó enormemente la costumbre de erigir monumentos de piedra, con o sin escritura jeroglífica. Durante el Período I, en Monte Albán se tallaron 300 imágenes de cautivos sacrificados y se monopolizó la escritura dentro del Valle de Oaxaca.

Los textos zapotecos atestiguan el uso de dos calendarios, uno secular (365 días) y otro ritual (260 días). Al combinar ambos calendarios, los zapotecos crearon un ciclo calendárico mayor o rueda de 52 años. No establecieron, empero, una fecha base para anclar la llamada Cuenta Larga. Ese logro se registró por primera vez en Chiapa de Corzo (México) alrededor del 36 a.C., seguido por los mayas del sur de Guatemala en el 37 d.C. y los del norte en el 292 d.C. El hecho de que los zapotecos carecieran de una Cuenta Larga propia significa que no podemos asignar en la actualidad fechas precisas a los monumentos de esa civilización de la misma manera en que lo hacemos para los monumentos istmeños, mayas y chiapanecos.

La escritura de la Época I se refería a los nombres, las fechas, la captura de cautivos y el acceso al poder. Estamos seguros de que la escritura del Período I estaba relacionada con el idioma zapoteco hablado porque empleaba ejemplos del principio *rebus* (basado en homónimos o palabras similares al sonido) que sólo funcionaban en zapoteco. Cuando dos palabras en zapoteco se pronunciaban de la misma manera, pero una era fácil de dibujar y la otra difícil, los zapotecos elegían el signo más fácil para transmitir el término. Por ejemplo, dado que la palabra zapoteca *yobi* significaba tanto "pulgar" como "primogénito" los talladores preferían representar un pulgar para mostrar que algún gobernante era el "primogénito" de su antecesor. Los jeroglíficos zapotecos también parecen seguir la secuencia típica de las frases zapotecas, es decir, tiempo + verbo + sujeto + objeto.

Para el año 20 a.C. Monte Albán había derrotado a todos sus rivales y creado un estado zapoteco expansionista. Los monumentos de esta época se enfocaron en la "propaganda vertical", es decir, en mensajes transmitidos por los nobles a los plebeyos. Estos monumentos se instalaron en lugares públicos donde la gente alfabetizada podía comunicar su contenido a aquellos que no sabían leer. La mayoría de los textos jeroglíficos estaban acompañados por escenas que ayudaron a explicar el mensaje. Una estrategia interesante fue colocar relieves con imágenes de enemigos asesinados en lugares donde era posible pisarlos, una práctica luego implementada tanto por los mayas como por los arquitectos de Cacaxtla en Tlaxcala.

En el 100 d.C., los zapotecos seguían estando interesados en el sacrificio, los jefes subyugados, la conquista y la expansión territorial, pero para representar estos temas en la escritura tenían que crear el glifo estandarizado de "cerro" o "lugar". Este glifo toponímico les permitió enumerar en el Edificio J de Monte Albán más de 60 lugares que los zapotecos probablemente consideraban parte de su imperio en expansión, un tema que luego se repetiría en el Templo de las Serpientes Emplumadas en Xochicalco, Morelos. Los zapotecos usaron imágenes de cabezas invertidas con los ojos cerrados para indicar que un lugar había sido conquistado, y un cerro sin cabeza invertida para mostrar que un lugar había capitulado pacíficamente.

Hacia el 300 d.C. los temas que los zapotecos seleccionaron para conmemorar eventos se hicieron más variados. Todavía se representaban cautivos de guerra; pero ahora era más común ver la escena de un cautivo vivo con los brazos atados que a una víctima desnuda y mutilada. Además, algunos de los cautivos atados aparecían en escenas de entronización; quizás ahora era más importante figurar cautivos ricamente ataviados en una ceremonia de acceso al trono que plasmar sus cadáveres desnudos y mutilados.

Un tema importante durante el período comprendido entre el 200 y el 600 d.C. fue el de las relaciones diplomáticas entre Monte Albán y Teotihuacan. A visitantes que llevaban sandalias y tocados de borlas al estilo teotihuacano se les figuró presentándose ante un gobernante zapoteca y asistiendo a la dedicación de edificios. Los teotihuacanos portaban bolsas (posiblemente de copal) en lugar de armas, y una talla sugiere que quemaron incienso y realizaron ritos junto con los zapotecos.

Los datos del Período III muestran que (1) Monte Albán y Teotihuacan dejaron una zona de amortiguación (tierra de nadie), situada al norte de Quiotepec, entre sus respectivas esferas de influencia; (2) hubo comercio activo entre estas dos superpotencias, que involucraba obsidiana controlada por Teotihuacan y exportada a Oaxaca, y mica monopolizada por Monte Albán y enviada a Teotihuacan, y (3) Teotihuacan aceptó el asentamiento de un enclave de oaxaqueños dentro de sus límites urbanos. Aunque Teotihuacan y Monte Albán se expandieron fácilmente sobre los territorios de sus vecinos más débiles, la relación entre ellos fue claramente de distensión y de un activo comercio e intercambio.

Después del 700 d.C., el poder político de Teotihuacan y Monte Albán comenzó a disminuir. Hacia el 900 d.C., los edificios en la Plaza Principal de Monte Albán ya no estaban siendo reparados, y varios de sus antiguos centros secundarios se estaban convirtiendo en capitales de pequeños estados independientes. El surgimiento de linajes nobles prestigiosos en muchos sitios secundarios transformó substancialmente el sistema político, así como la distribución y el carácter de los monumentos jeroglíficos zapotecas. El tema más notable de los nuevos monumentos fue el del derecho genealógico a gobernar. Este mensaje parece haber estado dirigido principalmente a otros nobles, y, como resultado, la propaganda horizontal (de noble a noble) se hizo más común que la propaganda vertical (de noble a plebeyo).

Los registros genealógicos y los monumentos para la veneración de los antepasados erigidos en esta época tenían más probabilidad de ubicarse en áreas de acceso restringido, como palacios y tumbas, que en los muros exteriores de los edificios públicos. Inclusive, las escasas estelas de piedra exentas del 600–900 d.C. no fueron necesariamente ejemplos de propaganda vertical, porque fueron colocadas en lugares donde los plebeyos tenían un acceso limitado.

Entre las comunidades originalmente del Nivel 2 que ahora crearon tumbas elaboradas y monumentos escultóricos había (1) sitios en el valle norte (Reyes Etla, San Lázaro Etla, Huitzo y Cerro de la Campana); (2) sitios en el Valle Grande (Cuilapan, Xoxocotlán y Zaachila), y (3) sitios en el valle oriental (Lambityeco, Macuilxóchitl, Teotitlán del Valle, El Palmillo y Yagul).

El establecimiento de la legitimidad y la afirmación de la continuidad dinástica fueron dos de las motivaciones para hacer declaraciones sobre la genealogía, la destreza militar, los antepasados nobles y los fundadores dinásticos. Los nobles comisionaron textos no sólo para preservar la memoria histórica, sino también para alcanzar resultados específicos, como entablar contacto ritual con los antepasados, legitimar los postulados de sus descendientes y recordar los nombres de los individuos de generaciones pasadas.

Los nobles también forjaron vínculos con sus homólogos a través del cumplimiento de obligaciones recíprocas: asistir a sus funerales y marcar los aniversarios de sus exequias, especialmente los de los fundadores dinásticos y las parejas matrimoniales importantes. Los visitantes y los participantes a veces se aproximaban a los accesos de las tumbas, donde disponían un grupo de urnas, generalmente cuatro o cinco en número, con la imagen de *Cociyo,* dios del Rayo. Frente a las tumbas, los arqueólogos han encontrado evidencias de combustión de incienso (braseros), consumo de alimentos (cajetes, vasos), oblación de artículos preciosos (jade, conchas) y consumo de bebidas en jarras que podrían haber contenido pulque (*nupi*) o chocolate (*niça pizoya*).

Las tumbas familiares más elaboradas fueron esculpidas en la roca madre, muchas veces construidas con anterioridad a las estructuras residenciales que se encuentran sobre ellas. Algunas tumbas alojaron los cadáveres de individuos pertenecientes a múltiples generaciones, legitimándolos a ellos y a sus descendientes. En la cosmología zapoteca, los vivos y los muertos coexistían en un continuo ininterrumpido.

El uso multigeneracional de una tumba, que implicaba su reapertura, convirtió el patio interior privado del palacio en un lugar clave para los rituales. Una tumba podría abrirse varias veces para agregar los cuerpos de familiares pertenecientes a otras generaciones. La Tumba 6 en Lambityeco es un buen ejemplo, pues fue reabierta en seis ocasiones.

El subvalle de Etla ha contribuido con una serie de monumentos que muestran los envoltorios de momias de los antepasados reales siendo transportados en cajas de madera llamadas “angarillas” o “andas de muertos”. La exploración de este subvalle también ha producido una estela (en la Tumba 5 del Cerro de la Campana) que ejemplifica la sintaxis prototípica zapoteca en un texto jeroglífico.

El subvalle de Tlacolula, por otro lado, es el origen de monumentos en los que la veneración de los antepasados parece ser el tema central. Igualmente importantes durante el período 600–900 d.C. son las pinturas murales de tumbas que muestran escenas de nobles visitándolas.

Lo que parece haber estado sucediendo en este momento es que una sociedad estratificada, alguna vez dominada por dinastías reales en Monte Albán, se estaba convirtiendo en una sociedad distinta, en la que una serie completa de “casas nobles” se establecían en numerosos centros alrededor del valle. Hace mucho tiempo, Ignacio Bernal señaló que, antes de la Época III, se dedicaron más esfuerzos a la construcción de las pirámides templarias que a los palacios. De la Época IIIb en adelante, se invirtió un mayor esfuerzo a la construcción de los palacios. Las residencias reales en el subvalle de Tlacolula llegaron a tener varios patios en lugar de un único espacio central abierto; era menos probable que los templos se levantaran sobre estructuras piramidales. La “casa noble” del período Posclásico muchas veces poseía una gran tumba, donde los miembros fallecidos de la familia continuaron siendo inhumados para las generaciones venideras.

Similitudes y diferencias entre la escritura zapoteca y la maya

Dos de los estados antiguos que hicieron el mayor uso de los jeroglíficos tallados en piedra fueron el zapoteca y el maya. Veamos ahora algunas de las similitudes y diferencias existentes entre ambos.

Una de las similitudes más obvias fue la forma en que se representó la victoria militar. Los zapotecas figuraban a los prisioneros con los brazos atados; también lo hicieron los mayas en sitios como Toniná, Caracol y Yaxchilán. Los zapotecas también plasmaban a los prisioneros en umbrales (Monumento 3 de San José Mogote) o escaleras (Edificio L de Monte Albán) para que se pudieran pisar las imágenes de sus rivales derrotados. De manera similar, los mayas mostraron que sus enemigos eran pisoteados con los pies o en las escaleras (por ejemplo, en Naranjo, Dos Pilas, Tamarindito, Tikal, Yaxchilán y Dzibanché).

Los zapotecas y los mayas recurrieron a temas semejantes para sus respectivos monumentos: la representación de enemigos, el nombramiento de prisioneros, la conjura de antepasados, la quema de incienso, la adivinación, la metamorfosis y la figuración de la imagen del difunto como un bulto apoyado sobre una caja.

Los zapotecas y los mayas también tallaron huesos para usarlos como dispositivos mnemotécnicos. Ambos grupos esculpieron en la piedra los días del calendario para que pudieran ser consultados para adivinar y pronosticar el futuro. Por ejemplo, un hueso que supuestamente fue encontrado en la isla de Jaina muestra a un individuo arrojando granos de maíz, así como una lista completa y en orden de los signos mayas de los días. Hay casos análogos en los huesos posclásicos de la Tumba 7 de Monte Albán.

El parentesco era una de las diferencias obvias entre los zapotecas y los mayas. Se utilizaron los términos del llamado parentesco hawaiano tanto en el zapoteco como en el mixteco que eran lenguas otomangues. Consideraron la descendencia por líneas paterna y materna, teniendo en cuenta las diferencias de rango. Los mayas, por otro lado, eran más propensos a establecer la descendencia a través de la línea masculina. Estas diferencias entre la ascendencia otomangue y la maya ayudan a explicar una de las diferencias más notables en sus monumentos: la mayor frecuencia con que los zapotecas representaban parejas maritales en las genealogías nobiliarias. El gobierno maya normalmente involucraba a un hombre solo en el trono, mientras que los zapotecas y mixtecos concebían a una pareja casada como co-gobernantes de un sistema de gobierno.

Analicemos el Altar Q de Copán, un monumento encargado por el decimosexto gobernante de ese sitio. En los cuatro lados del altar observamos una sucesión de 16 gobernantes varones, comenzando con el supuesto fundador de la dinastía (Yax K'uk' Mo'o) y terminando con quien comisionó el monumento. En ninguna parte del Altar Q se alude a una mujer de la realeza. No podría ser mayor el contraste con la mayoría de los registros genealógicos zapotecas, que presentan varias generaciones sucesivas de parejas matrimoniales. Incluso los fundadores primigenios de la dinastía real de Monte Albán —Señor 1 Jaguar y Señora 2 Maíz— eran marido y mujer. Por el contrario, las listas de reyes mayas nunca comienzan con parejas matrimoniales.

Eso no significa, empero, que las mujeres de la realeza nunca fueron representadas en los monumentos mayas: existen excepciones. La mayoría, sin embargo, se figuraron solo porque eran la esposa, la viuda, la madre o la hija de un gobernante varón. Esto no es inesperado en un sistema que todavía hoy usa patronímicos.

Otra diferencia significativa es que los mayas poseían la Cuenta Larga, mientras que los zapotecas tenían únicamente el ciclo calendárico o rueda de 52 años. Esto les permitió a los mayas producir monumentos con fechas que se pueden colocar en tiempo absoluto y correlacionarse con nuestro calendario occidental. Las fechas de los nacimientos, las entronizaciones, los matrimonios y las defunciones de muchos gobernantes mayas se pueden reconstruir de una manera que es imposible para el caso de los zapotecas. Muchos registros genealógicos del período IIIb–IV nos informan de los nombres de las parejas matrimoniales zapotecas pertenecientes a varias generaciones. Las fechas de sus respectivos reinados, sin embargo, están flotando en el tiempo; no pueden correlacionarse de manera segura con nuestro calendario occidental. Los zapotecos y los mixtecos llamaban a sus hijos dependiendo del día en que habían nacido, pero los mayas no lo acostumbraban de la misma forma, sino que preferían usar nombres como *Serpiente*, *Pecarí*, *Jaguar* o *Tortuga*.

Otra diferencia importante fue el tipo de monumentos que erigieron los mayas y los zapotecos. El par escultórico estela-altar era típico de las tierras bajas (por ejemplo, Tikal y Caracol). Las verdaderas estelas no sólo eran raras en el Valle de Oaxaca, sino que nunca se asociaron con altares.

La posible influencia zapoteca entre los mayas puede verse en la aparición de nichos de tumbas y murales continuos envolventes, como los que aparecieron repentinamente en Río Azul alrededor del 400 d.C. Aunque los zapotecas y los mayas construyeron tumbas elaboradas para sus nobles, los zapotecas fueron los primeros en crear tumbas con pinturas murales policromas, en las que representaban un enorme jeroglífico en la pared posterior que daba el nombre de un antepasado apical. Los zapotecas pintaron jeroglíficos que evocaban a las parejas matrimoniales que, en procesión, acudían a rendir homenaje a ese ancestro apical en la pared posterior de la tumba. Los nichos de las tumbas muchas veces contenían ofrendas y cajas, bultos y cerámica sagrada, así como los huesos de los antepasados. Los mayas rara vez pintaban murales policromos en las tumbas, y la mayoría de sus tumbas reales contenían los restos de un solo gobernante. En ocasiones, sin embargo, los servidores o las víctimas del sacrificio fueron colocados inmediatamente enfrente de la puerta de la tumba, como en el caso de K'inich Janaab' Pakal en Palenque.

Bibliography

A

Acosta, Jorge R.

n.d. Exploraciones en Monte Negro, Tilantongo, Oaxaca. Unpublished manuscript. Archivo del Instituto Nacional de Antropología e Historia, Centro de Oaxaca, México.

1958–1959 Exploraciones arqueológicas en Monte Albán, XVIII temporada. *Revista Mexicana de Estudios Antropológicos* 15:7–50.

1965 Preclassic and Classic architecture of Oaxaca. In *Archaeology of Southern Mesoamerica*, Part 2, edited by Gordon R. Willey, pp. 814–836. Handbook of Middle American Indians, Vol. 3, Robert Wauchope, general editor. University of Texas Press, Austin.

1972 Nuevos descubrimientos en Zaachila (1971). *Boletín del Instituto Nacional de Antropología e Historia*, Época II (3):27–34.

1974 Informe: XIV temporada de exploraciones en la zona arqueológica de Monte Albán, 1945-46. *Cultura y Sociedad* 1(2):69–82.

Acosta, Jorge R. and Javier Romero

1992 *Exploraciones en Monte Negro, Oaxaca: 1937-38, 1938-39 y 1939-1940*. Antologías, Serie Arqueología, Instituto Nacional de Antropología e Historia, Mexico.

Adams, Richard E. W.

1999 *Río Azul: An Ancient Maya City*. University of Oklahoma Press, Norman.

Adams, Robert McCormick

1966 *The Evolution of Urban Society: Early Mesopotamia and Prehispanic Mexico*. Aldine Publishing Co., Chicago.

Adams, Robert McCormick and Hans J. Nissen

1972 *The Uruk Countryside: The Natural Setting of Urban Societies*. University of Chicago Press, Chicago.

Agüero, Cristóbal de

1666 *Confessionario en la mesma lengua zapoteca. Misceláneo espiritual, en el idioma zapoteco*. John Carter Brown Library, Brown University, Providence, Rhode Island.

Alcina Franch, José

1966 Calendarios zapotecos prehispánicos según documentos de los siglos XVI y XVII. *Estudios de Cultura Náhuatl* 6:119–133.

1969 *Expediciones acerca de los antiguos monumentos de la Nueva España (1805/1808) por Guillermo Dupaix*. Colección Chimalistac de libros y documentos acerca de la Nueva España, No. 27. Ediciones José Porrúa Turanzas, Madrid.

1971 Nahuales y nahualismo en Oaxaca: siglo XVII. *Anuario del Instituto de Antropología e Historia* VII–VIII:23–30. Caracas, Venezuela.

1972 Los dioses del panteón zapoteco. *Anales de Antropología* 9:9–38.

1979 Calendario y religión entre los zapotecos serranos durante el siglo XVII. In *Mesoamérica: homenaje al doctor Paul Kirchhoff*, pp. 212–224. Instituto Nacional de Antropología e Historia, Mexico.

1993 *Calendario y religión entre los zapotecos*. Instituto de Investigaciones Históricas, Serie de Culturas Mesoamericanas 3. Universidad Nacional Autónoma de México, Mexico.

Algaze, Guillermo
1993a Expansionary dynamics of some early pristine states. *American Anthropologist* 95(2):304–333.
1993b *The Uruk World System: The Dynamics of Expansion of Early Mesopotamian Civilization*. University of Chicago Press, Chicago.

Alleman, Vera Mae
1952 *Vocabulario zapoteco del Rincón*. Instituto Lingüístico de Verano, México, D.F.

Alvarado Tezozómoc, Fernando
1944 *Crónica mexicana*, edited by Manuel Orozco y Berra. Editorial Leyenda, Mexico.

Amiet, Pierre
1966 Il y a 5000 ans les Elamites inventaient l'écriture. *Archéologia* 12:20–22.
1972 *Glyptique susienne des origines à l'époque des Perses achéménides cachets, sceaux-cylindres et empreintes antiques découverts à Suse de 1913 à 1968*. P. Guethner, Paris.

Anders, Ferdinand, Maarten Jansen, and Gabina Aurora Pérez Jiménez
1992a *Crónica Mixteca: el rey 8 Venado "Garra de Jaguar" y la dinastía de Teozacualco-Zaachila: libro explicativo del llamado Códice Zouche-Nuttall*. Fondo de Cultura Económica, Mexico City.
1992b *Origen e historia de los reyes mixtecos: libro explicativo del llamado Códice Vindobonensis Mexicanus I*. Fondo de Cultura Económica, Mexico City.

Anderson, Carolyn and Brook Danielle Lillehaugen
2016 Negation in Colonial Valley Zapotec. *Transactions of the Philological Society* 114(3):391–413.

Angulo, Jaime de
1925 The linguistic tangle of Oaxaca. *Language* 1(3):96–102.
1926a The development of affixes in a group of monosyllabic languages of Oaxaca. *Language* 2(1):46–61; 2(2):119–133.
1926b Tone patterns and verb forms in a dialect of Zapotek. *Language* 2(4):238–250.

Angulo, Jaime de and L. S. Freeland
1935 The Zapotekan linguistic group: a comparative study of Chinanteco, Chocho, Mazateco, Cuicateco, Mixteco, Chatino, and especially of Zapoteco proper and its dialects. *International Journal of American Linguistics* 8(1):1–38; 8(2):111–130. Baltimore.

Angulo Villaseñor, Jorge
2008 Intercambio étnico y cultural en algunos asentamientos de Oaxaca. In *La pintura mural prehispánica en México, Vol. III: Oaxaca*, tomo III (Estudios), edited by Beatriz de la Fuente, pp. 17–57. Universidad Nacional Autónoma de México, Instituto de Investigaciones Estéticas, Mexico City.

Arkush, Elizabeth and Charles Stanish
2005 Interpreting conflict in the ancient Andes. *Current Anthropology* 46(1):3–28.

Armillas, Pedro
1944 Exploraciones recientes en Teotihuacan. *Cuadernos Americanos* 4:121–136.

Augsburger, Deborah
2003 Traduciendo a la brujería. "Bruxos, hechizeros y hechizeria" en el vocabulario de Córdova. In *Escritura zapoteca: 2500 años de historia*, edited by María de los Ángeles Romero Frizzi, pp. 241–263. CIESAS, CONACULTA-INAH.

Aung-Thwin, Michael
1983 Divinity, spirit, and human: conceptions of classical Burmese kingship. In *Centers, Symbols, and Hierarchies: Essays on the Classical States of Southeast Asia*, edited by Lorraine Gesick, pp. 45–86. Monograph Series number 26. Yale University Southeast Asia Studies Program, New Haven, Connecticut.

Aveni, Anthony F. and Robert M. Linsley
1972 Mound J, Monte Alban: possible astronomical orientation. *American Antiquity* 37(4):528–531.

Ayala, Maricela
2002 *El bulto ritual de Mundo Perdido, Tikal y los bultos mayas*. Instituto de Investigaciones Filológicas, Cuadernos del Centro de Estudios Mayas 27. Universidad Nacional Autónoma de México, México.

B

Baines, John
1983 Literacy and ancient Egyptian society. *Man* n.s. 18:572–599.
1989 Communication and display: the integration of early Egyptian art and writing. *Antiquity* 63(240):471–482.
1994 On the status and purposes of ancient Egyptian art. *Cambridge Archaeological Journal* 4(1):67–94.
1999 Writing, invention and early development. In *Encyclopedia of the Archaeology of Ancient Egypt*, edited by Kathryn Bard, pp. 882–885. Routledge, London.

Balkansky, Andrew K.
1997 Archaeological settlement patterns of the Sola Valley, Oaxaca, Mexico. *Mexicon* 19(1):12–18.
1998a Origin and collapse of complex societies in Oaxaca (Mexico): Evaluating the era from 1965 to the present. *Journal of World Prehistory* 12(4):451–493.
1998b Urbanism and early state formation in the Huamelulpan Valley of southern Mexico. *Latin American Antiquity* 9:37–67.
1999 Settlement pattern studies in the Mixteca Alta, Oaxaca, 1966–1996. In *Settlement Pattern Studies in the Americas: Fifty Years since Virú*, edited by Brian Billman and Gary M. Feinman, pp. 191–202. Smithsonian Institution Press, Washington, D.C.
2002 *The Sola Valley and the Monte Albán State: A Study of Zapotec Imperial Expansion*. Memoirs of the University of Michigan Museum of Anthropology, No. 36. Ann Arbor.

Balkansky, Andrew K., Verónica Pérez Rodríguez, and Stephen A. Kowalewski
2004 Monte Negro and the urban revolution in Oaxaca, Mexico. *Latin American Antiquity* 15(1):33–60.

Balsalobre, Gonzalo de
1892 [1656] Relación auténtica de las idolatrías, supersticiones, vanas observaciones de los indios del Obispado de Oaxaca. *Anales del Museo Nacional de México*, primera época, Vol. 6, pp. 225–260. Mexico.

Bandelier, Adolf F.
1884 *Report of an Archaeological Tour in Mexico in 1881*. Papers of the Archaeological Institute of America, American Series 2. Cupples, Upham, Boston.

Bard, Kathryn A.
2015 *An Introduction to the Archaeology of Ancient Egypt*. Second edition. Wiley Blackwell, Chichester, England.

Barlow, Robert H. (see also Agustín de Salazar)
1945 Dos relaciones antiguas del pueblo de Cuilapan, Estado de Oaxaca. *Tlalocan* II(1):18–28.

Barthel, Thomas S.
1967 Notes on the inscription on a carved bone from Yucatan. *Estudios de Cultura Maya* 6:223–241.

Bartholomew, Doris A.
1983 *Gramática zapoteca. Diccionario zapoteco de Juárez*. Compiled by Neil Nellis and Jane Goodner de Nellis, pp. 336–444. Instituto Lingüístico de Verano, México, D.F.

Batres, Leopoldo
1888 *Arqueología mexicana. Civilización de las diferentes tribus que habitaron el territorio hoy mexicano en la antigüedad*. Imprenta del Gobierno Federal en el ex-arzobispado, Mexico.
1901 *Lyobaa o Mictlan*. Tipografía y Lit. La Europea.
1902 *Explorations of Monte Albán*. Casa Editorial Gante, Mexico.

Baudez, Claude-François
2011 Las batallas rituales en Mesoamérica: Parte 1. *Arqueología Mexicana* 112:20–29. Editorial Raíces, México.

Bauer, Brian S.
2004 *Ancient Cuzco: Heartland of the Inca*. University of Texas Press, Austin.

Beals, Ralph
1969 Southern Mexican highlands and adjacent coastal regions: introduction. In *Ethnology*, edited by Evon Z. Vogt, pp. 315–328. Handbook of Middle American Indians, Vol. 7, Robert Wauchope, general editor. University of Texas Press, Austin.

Beam de Azcona, Rosemary G.
2004 A Coatlán-Loxicha Zapotec grammar. Ph.D dissertation, University of California at Berkeley, Berkeley, California.

Belmar, Francisco
1901 *Idiomas indígenas del estado de Oaxaca: breve noticia del idioma papabuco del pueblo de Elotepec*. Imprenta del Comercio, Oaxaca.
1902 *Idiomas del estado de Oaxaca: investigaciones sobre la lengua chatina*. Imprenta del Comercio, Oaxaca.
1905 *Lenguas indígenas de México: familia mixteco-zapoteco y sus relaciones con el Otomí. Familia zoque-mixe. –Chontal.— Huave y mexicano*. Imprenta Particular, Mexico.
1921 *Glotología indígena mexicana. Estudio comparativo y clasificación de las lenguas indígenas de México*. Mexico.

Berdan, Frances F.
1987 Cotton in Aztec Mexico: production, distribution and uses. *Mexican Studies/Estudios Mexicanos* 3(2):235–262. University of California Press and the Universidad Nacional Autónoma de México.

Berdan, Frances F. and Patricia Rieff Anawalt
1997 *The Essential Codex Mendoza*. University of California Press, Berkeley, Los Angeles, and London.

Berdan, Frances F., Richard E. Blanton, Elizabeth Hill Boone, Mary G. Hodge, Michael E. Smith, and Emily Umberger
1996 *Aztec Imperial Strategies*. Dumbarton Oaks Research Library and Collection, Washington, D.C.

Berdan, Frances F., Susan Kepecs, and Michael E. Smith
2003 A perspective on Late Postclassic Mesoamerica. In *The Postclassic Mesoamerican World*, edited by Michael E. Smith and Frances F. Berdan, pp. 313–317. University of Utah Press, Salt Lake City.

Berger, Martin
2011 The ballplayers of Dainzú? An alternative interpretation of the Dainzú iconography. *Mexicon* 33(2):46–51.

Berlin, Heinrich
1946 Three Zapotec stones. *Notes on Middle American Archaeology and Ethnology*, No. 66, pp. 34–36. Carnegie Institution of Washington, Division of Historical Research, Washington, D.C.
1951 A survey of the Sola region in Oaxaca (Mexico). *Ethnos* 16(1–2):1–17.
1957 *Las antiguas creencias en San Miguel Sola, Oaxaca, México*. Beiträge zur mittelamerikanischen Völkerkunde, Herausgegeben von Hamburgishen Museum für Völkerkunde und Vorgeschichte, No. 4.
1958 El glifo 'emblema' en las inscripciones mayas. *Journal de la Société des Américanistes* n.s. 47:111–119.
1959 Glifos nominales en el sarcófago de Palenque. *Humanidades* 2(10):1–8. Universidad de San Carlos, Guatemala.
1977 *Signos y significados en las inscripciones mayas*. Instituto Nacional de Patrimonio Cultural de Guatemala, Guatemala.

Berlo, Janet Catherine
1989 Early writing in central Mexico: in Tlilli in Tlapalli before A.D. 1000. In *Mesoamerica after the Decline of Teotihuacan A.D. 700-900*, edited by Richard A. Diehl and Janet Catherine Berlo, pp. 19–47. Dumbarton Oaks Research Library and Collection, Washington, D.C.

Bernal, Ignacio
1958 *Exploraciones en Cuilapan de Guerrero, 1902-1954*. Dirección de Monumentos Prehispánicos, Informe No. 7. Instituto Nacional de Antropología e Historia, México, D.F.
1960 Exploraciones arqueológicas en Noriega, Oaxaca. In *Homenaje a Rafael García Granados*, pp. 83–88. Instituto Nacional de Antropología e Historia, México, D.F.
1965a Archaeological synthesis of Oaxaca. In *Archaeology of Southern Mesoamerica*, Part 2, edited by Gordon R. Willey, pp. 788–813. Handbook of Middle American Indians, Vol. 3, Robert Wauchope, general editor. University of Texas Press, Austin.

1965b Architecture in Oaxaca after the end of Monte Alban. In *Archaeology of Southern Mesoamerica,* Part 2, edited by Gordon R. Willey, pp. 837–848. Handbook of Middle American Indians, Vol. 3, Robert Wauchope, general editor. University of Texas Press, Austin.
1966 The Mixtecs in the archeology of the Valley of Oaxaca. In *Ancient Oaxaca: Discoveries in Mexican Archeology and History,* edited by John Paddock, pp. 345–366. Stanford University Press, Stanford, California.
1967 Excavaciones en Dainzu. *Boletín del Instituto Nacional de Antropología e Historia* 27:7–13.
1968 The ball players of Dainzu. *Archaeology* 21(4):246–251.
1973 Stone reliefs in the Dainzú area. In *The Iconography of Middle American Sculpture*, pp. 13–23. The Metropolitan Museum of Art, New York.
1976 The jaguar façade tomb at Dainzú. In *To Illustrate the Monuments: Essays on Archaeology Presented to Stuart Piggott on the Occasion of his Sixty-fifth Birthday*, edited by J. V. S. Megaw, pp. 295–300. Thames and Hudson, London.
1985 *Guía oficial. Valle de Oaxaca*. Instituto Nacional de Antropología e Historia, Salvat, Mexico.

Bernal, Ignacio and Lorenzo Gamio
1974 *Yagul: el palacio de los seis patios*. Instituto de Investigaciones Antropológicas, Universidad Nacional Autónoma de México, México, D.F.

Bernal, Ignacio and Rubén Méndez
1974 *Bajorrelieves en el Museo de Arte Zapoteco de Mitla, Oaxaca*. Corpus Antiquitatum Americanensium, No. VII. Instituto Nacional de Antropología e Historia, Mexico.

Bernal, Ignacio and Arturo Oliveros
1988 *Exploraciones arqueológicas en Dainzú, Oaxaca*. Colección Científica No. 167. Serie Arqueología, Instituto Nacional de Antropología e Historia, México, D.F.

Bernal, Ignacio and Andy Seuffert
1973 *Esculturas asociadas del valle de Oaxaca*. Corpus Antiquitatum Americanensium, No. VI. Instituto Nacional de Antropología e Historia, Mexico.
1979 *The Ballplayers of Dainzu*. Akademische Druck-u. Verlagsanstalt, Graz, Austria.

Berrin, Kathleen, editor
1988 *Feathered Serpents and Flowered Trees: Reconstructing the Murals of Teotihuacan.* Fine Arts Museum, San Francisco.

Billman, Brian R.
1999 Reconstructing prehistoric political economies and cycles of political power in the Moche Valley, Peru. In *Settlement Pattern Studies in the Americas: Fifty Years since Virú*, edited by Brian R. Billman and Gary M. Feinman, pp. 131–159. Smithsonian Institution Press, Washington, D.C.

Black, Cheryl A.
2000 *Quiegolani Zapotec Syntax: A Principles and Parameters Account*. Publications in Linguistics 136. Summer Institute of Linguistics, Dallas, and the University of Texas, Arlington.

Blanton, Richard E.
1978 *Monte Albán: Settlement Patterns at the Ancient Zapotec Capital*. Academic Press, New York.
1983 The founding of Monte Albán. In *The Cloud People*, edited by Kent V. Flannery and Joyce Marcus, pp. 87–90. Academic Press, New York.

Blanton, Richard, Stephen A. Kowalewski, Gary Feinman, and Jill Appel
1982 *Monte Albán's Hinterland, Part I: Prehispanic Settlement Patterns of the Central and Southern Parts of the Valley of Oaxaca, Mexico.* Memoirs of the University of Michigan Museum of Anthropology, No. 15. Ann Arbor.

Blanton, Richard, Stephen A. Kowalewski, Gary M. Feinman, and Laura Finsten
1993 *Ancient Mesoamerica: A Comparison of Change in Three Regions*. Second edition. Cambridge University Press, Cambridge.

Bloch, Maurice
1971 *Placing the Dead: Tombs, Ancestral Villages and Kinship Organizaton in Madagascar*. Seminar Press, New York.

Blomster, Jeffrey P., editor
2008 *After Monte Albán: Transformation and Negotiation in Oaxaca, Mexico*. University Press of Colorado, Boulder.

Boas, Franz
1913 Notes on the Chatino language of Mexico. *American Anthropologist* 15:78–86.

Boltz, William G.
1986 Early Chinese writing. *World Archaeology* 17:420–436.
1996 Early Chinese writing. In *The World's Writing Systems*, edited by Peter T. Daniels and William Bright, pp. 191–199. Oxford University Press, Oxford and New York.

Boone, Elizabeth Hill
1982 *The Art and Iconography of Late Post-Classic Central Mexico*. Dumbarton Oaks Research Library and Collection, Washington, D.C.
2000 *Stories in Red and Black: Pictorial Histories of the Aztec and Mixtec*. University of Texas Press, Austin.

Boone, Elizabeth Hill and Michael E. Smith
2003 Postclassic international styles and symbol sets. In *The Postclassic Mesoamerican World*, edited by Michael E. Smith and Frances F. Berdan, pp. 186–193. University of Utah Press, Salt Lake City.

Boos, Frank
1966a *Colecciones Leigh and Museo Frissell de Arte Zapoteca*. Instituto Nacional de Antropología e Historia, Mexico.
1966b *The Ceramic Sculptures of Ancient Oaxaca*. A. S. Barnes, South Brunswick, New Jersey.

Boos, Frank H. and Philippa D. Shaplin
1969 A Classic Zapotec tile frieze in St. Louis. *Archaeology* 22(1):36–43.

Borhegyi, Stephan F. de
1961 Ball-game handstones and ball-game gloves. In *Essays in Pre-Columbian Art and Archaeology*, edited by Samuel K. Lothrop et al., pp. 126–151. Harvard University Press, Cambridge, Massachusetts.
1967 Piedras semiesféricas con asas para el juego de pelota y "manoplas" en Mesoamérica: una posible alternativa para su función. *Estudios de Cultura Maya* 6:215–219.

Bradomín, José María
1980 [1955] *Toponímia de Oaxaca*. Second edition. Imprenta Arana, Mexico.

Braswell, Geoffrey, editor
2003 *The Maya and Teotihuacan: Reinterpreting Early Classic Interaction*. University of Texas Press, Austin.

Briggs, Elinor
1961 *Mitla Zapotec Grammar*. Summer Institute of Linguistics and Centro de Investigaciones Antropológicas de México, Mexico City.

Brinton, Daniel Garrison
1870 The ancient phonetic alphabet of Yucatan. *American Bibliopolist* 2:143–148.
1886 The phonetic elements in the graphic systems of the Mayas and Mexicans. In *Essays of an Americanist*, pp. 195–212. F. H. Revell, Chicago.
1893 The native calendars of Central America and Mexico: a study in linguistics and symbolism. *Proceedings of the American Philosophical Society* 31(142):258–314.
1894 *Nagualism: A Study in Native American Folk-lore and History*. MacCalla & Company, Philadelphia.

Brittenham, Claudia
2015 *The Murals of Cacaxtla: The Power of Painting in Ancient Central Mexico*. University of Texas Press, Austin.

Broadwell, George Aaron
2003 Review of "Quiegolani Zapotec Syntax: A principles and parameters approach" [sic] by Cheryl Black. *The Linguistic Review* 20:95–107.
2015 The historical development of the progressive aspect in central Zapotec. *International Journal of American Linguistics* 81(2):151–185.

Brockington, Donald L.
1973 *Archaeological Investigations at Miahuatlán, Oaxaca*. Vanderbilt University Publications in Anthropology No. 7. Nashville, Tennessee.

Brockington, Donald, María Jorrín, and Robert Long
1974 *The Oaxaca Coast Project Reports*, Part 1. Vanderbilt University Publications in Anthropology No. 8. Nashville, Tennessee.

Broda (de Casas), Johanna
1969 The Mexican calendar as compared to other Mesoamerican systems. *Acta Ethnologica et linguistics* 15. Engelbert Stiglmayr, Vienna, Austria.
1971 Las fiestas aztecas de los dioses de la lluvia: Una reconstrucción según las fuentes del siglo XVI. *Revista Española de Antropología Americana* 6:245–327.

Brown, Jennifer S. H. and E. Wyllys Andrews V, editors
1982 *Aspects of the Mixteca-Puebla Style and Mixtec and Central Mexican Culture in Southern Mesoamerica*. Middle American Research Institute, Tulane University, Occasional Paper No. 4. New Orleans.

Brumfiel, Elizabeth M.
1994 Comments on "Engendering Tomb 7 at Monte Albán: respinning an old yarn" by Sharisse D. McCafferty and Geoffrey G. McCafferty. *Current Anthropology* 35(2):153.

Buck, Peter H. (Te Rangi Hiroa)
1949 *The Coming of the Maori*. Whitcombe and Tombs, Wellington, New Zealand.

Buigues, Santiago Vicente
1993 The Archaeology and Iconography of Monte Albán's Mound J. Master's thesis, University of Calgary, Calgary, Canada.

Burdick, Catherine E.
2016 Held captive by script: interpreting "tagged" prisoners in Late Classic Maya sculpture. *Ancient Mesoamerica* 27:31–48.

Burgoa, Francisco de
1934 [1674] *Geográfica descripción…* Publicaciones del Archivo General de la Nación, Vols. 25-26. Talleres Gráficos de la Nación, Mexico.

Butler Haworth, Inez M.
1980 *Gramática zapoteca: zapoteco de Yatzachi El Bajo*. Serie Gramática de Lenguas Indígenas de México, No. 4. Instituto Lingüístico de Verano, Mexico City.

Byland, Bruce E. and John M. D. Pohl
1994 *In the Realm of 8 Deer: The Archaeology of the Mixtec Codices*. University of Oklahoma Press, Norman.

C

Cahn, Robert and Marcus Winter
1993 The San José Mogote dancer. *Indiana* 13:39–64.

Campbell, Eric
2011 Zenzontepec Chatino aspect morphology and Zapotecan verb classes. *International Journal of American Linguistics* 77(2):219–246.

Canseco, Alonso de
1905 [1580] Relación de Tlacolula y Mitla hecha en los días 12 y 23 de agosto respectivamente. *Papeles de Nueva España, Segunda Serie, Geografía y Estadística,* Vol. 4, edited by Francisco del Paso y Troncoso, pp. 144–154. Est. Tipográfico "Sucesores de Rivadeneyra," Madrid.

Carman, John
1999 Beyond the Western way of war: ancient battlefields in comparative perspective. In *Ancient Warfare: Archaeological Perspectives*, edited by John Carman and Anthony F. Harding, pp. 39–55. Sutton, Stroud, Gloucestershire.

Carneiro, Robert L.
1970 A theory of the origin of the state. *Science* 169:733–738.

Carnie, Andrew and Eithne Guilfoyle
2000 *The Syntax of Verb Initial Languages*. Oxford University Press, Oxford.

Carpenter, Lacey B.
2019 Households and Political Transformation: Daily Life during State Formation at Tilcajete, Oaxaca, Mexico. PhD dissertation, Department of Anthropology, University of Michigan, Ann Arbor.

Carpenter, Lacey B., Gary M. Feinman, and Linda M. Nicholas
2012 Spindle whorls from El Palmillo: economic implications. *Latin American Antiquity* 23(4):381–400.

Carrasco Pizana, Pedro
1951 Una cuenta ritual entre los zapotecos del sur. In *Homenaje al Doctor Alfonso Caso*, edited by Ignacio Bernal, pp. 91–100. Editorial Nuevo Mundo, Mexico City.
1974 Sucesión y alianzas matrimoniales en la dinastía teotihuacana. *Estudios de Cultura Náhuatl* 11:235–242.
1984 Royal marriages in ancient Mexico. In *Explorations in Ethnohistory: Indians of Central Mexico in the Sixteenth Century*, edited by Herbert R. Harvey and Hanns J. Prem, pp. 41–81. University of New Mexico Press, Albuquerque.

Carter, Howard and A. C. Mace
1923 *The Tomb of Tutankhamen*. Cassell and Company, London.

Carter, Nicholas P.
2017 Epigraphy and empire: reassessing textual evidence for Formative Zapotec imperialism. *Cambridge Archaeological Journal* 27(3):433–450.

Caso, Alfonso
1928 *Las estelas zapotecas.* Monografías del Museo Nacional de Arqueología, Historia y Etnografía. Publicaciones de la Secretaría de Educación Pública. Talleres Gráficos de la Nación, Mexico.
1932a La tumba 7 de Monte Albán es mixteca. *Universidad de México* 4 (2):117–150.
1932b Monte Albán, richest archaeological find in America. *National Geographic Magazine* LXII:487–512.
1932c *Las exploraciones de Monte Albán: temporada 1931-1932.* Instituto Panamericano de Geografía e Historia, Publicación 7. México.
1935 *Las exploraciones en Monte Albán: temporada 1934-1935.* Instituto Panamericano de Geografía e Historia, Publicación 15. México.
1936 Culturas mixteca y zapoteca. *El Libro de la Cultura* 6:227–262. Editorial González Porto. Salvat Editores S.A. Barcelona, Spain.
1938 *Exploraciones en Oaxaca, quinta y sexta temporadas 1936-1937.* Instituto Panamericano de Geografía e Historia, Publicación número 34. Tacubaya, D.F., Mexico.
1947 Calendario y escritura de las antiguas culturas de Monte Albán. Reprint of the original that appeared in *Obras completas de Miguel Othón de Mendizábal, un homenaje*, Vol. 1, pp. 5–102. Talleres de la Nación, Mexico.
1949 El mapa de Teozacoalco. *Cuadernos Americanos* Año VIII, Vol. 47, No. 5, pp. 145–181. Mexico.
1956 El calendario mixteco. *Historia Mexicana* 5-20:481–497.
1964a Los señores de Yanhuitlán. *Acta of the 35th International Congress of Americanists*, Vol. 1, pp. 437–448. Mexico.
1964b *Interpretación del Códice Selden 3135 (A. 2)/ Interpretation of the Codex Selden 3135 (A. 2).* Translated by Jacinto Quirarte and revised by John A. Paddock. Sociedad Mexicana de Antropología, Mexico.
1965a Zapotec writing and calendar. In *Archaeology of Southern Mesoamerica,* Part 2, edited by Gordon R. Willey, pp. 931–947. Handbook of Middle American Indians, Vol. 3, Robert Wauchope, general editor. University of Texas Press, Austin.
1965b Sculpture and mural painting of Oaxaca. In *Archaeology of Southern Mesoamerica,* edited by Gordon R. Willey, pp. 849–870. Handbook of Middle American Indians, Vol. 3, Robert Wauchope, general editor. University of Texas Press, Austin.
1965c Mixtec writing and calendar. In *Archaeology of Southern Mesoamerica,* edited by Gordon R. Willey, pp. 948–961. Handbook of Middle American Indians, Vol. 3, Robert Wauchope, general editor. University of Texas Press, Austin.
1965d Lapidary work, goldwork, and copperwork from Oaxaca. In *Archaeology of Southern Mesoamerica,* edited by Gordon R. Willey, pp. 896–930. Handbook of Middle American Indians, Vol. 3, Robert Wauchope, general editor. University of Texas Press, Austin.
1966 The lords of Yanhuitlán. In *Ancient Oaxaca: Discoveries in Mexican Archeology and History,* edited by John Paddock, pp. 313–335. Stanford University Press, Stanford, California.
1967 *Los calendarios prehispánicos.* Instituto de Investigaciones Históricas, Universidad Nacional Autónoma de México, Mexico.
1969 *El tesoro de Monte Albán.* Memorias del Instituto Nacional de Antropología e Historia, No. 3. Instituto Nacional de Antropología e Historia, México.
1977 *Reyes y reinos de la mixteca.* Fondo de Cultura Económica, México.
1979 *Reyes y reinos de la mixteca.* Fondo de Cultura Económica, México.
2002 Una pintura desconocida de Mitla. In *Obras 1: El México Antiguo (mixtecas y zapotecas)*, pp. 1–5. El Colegio Nacional, Mexico City.

Caso, Alfonso and Ignacio Bernal
1952 *Urnas de Oaxaca.* Memorias del Instituto Nacional de Antropología e Historia, No. 2. Instituto Nacional de Antropología e Historia, Mexico.
1965 Ceramics of Oaxaca. In *Archaeology of Southern Mesoamerica,* edited by Gordon R. Willey, pp. 871–895. Handbook of Middle American Indians, Vol. 3, Robert Wauchope, general editor. University of Texas Press, Austin.

Caso, Alfonso, Ignacio Bernal, and Jorge R. Acosta
1967 *La cerámica de Monte Albán.* Memorias del Instituto Nacional de Antropología e Historia, No. 13. México, D.F.

Caso, Alfonso and Lorenzo Gamio
1961 *Informe de exploraciones en Huamelulpan.* Manuscript in Archivo del Instituto Nacional de Antropología, Mexico City.

Caso, Alfonso and Daniel F. Rubín de la Borbolla
1936 *Exploraciones en Mitla, 1934-1935.* Instituto Panamericano de Geografía e Historia, Publicación 21. Mexico.
2003 Las exploraciones en Mitla: temporadas 1934-1935. In *Obras 2: El México Antiguo* (*mixtecas y zapotecas*), pp. 349–437. El Colegio Nacional, Mexico City.

Černý, Jaroslav
1965 *Hieratic Inscriptions from Tut'ankhamun's Tomb.* Griffith Institute at the University Press, Oxford.

Chávez, Sergio Jorge
1975 The Arapa and Thunderbolt stelae: a case of stylistic identity with implications for Pucara influences in the area of Tiahuanaco. *Ñawpa Pacha: Journal of Andean Archaeology* 13:3–25.

Chávez, Sergio Jorge and David Bruce Jorgenson
1980 Further inquiries into the case of the Arapa-Thunderbolt stela. *Ñawpa Pacha: Journal of Andean Archaeology* 18:73–80.

Childe, Vere Gordon
1950 The urban revolution. *Town Planning Review* 21:3–17.

Clark, James Cooper, editor and translator
1938 *Codex Mendoza: The Mexican manuscript known as the collection of Mendoza and preserved in the Bodleian Library, Oxford*. 3 volumes. Waterlow and Sons, London.

Cline, Howard F.
1975 Ancient and Colonial Zapotec and Mixtec calendars: a revisionist view. *The Americas* 31(3):272–288.

Clune, Francis J., Jr.
1963 Borhegyi's interpretation of certain Mesoamerican objects as ball-game handstones. *American Antiquity* 29(2):241–242.

Cobean, Robert H. and Alba Guadalupe Mastache
1995 Tula. In *Xochicalco y Tula*, edited by Leonardo López Luján, Robert H. Cobean, and Alba Guadalupe Mastache F., pp. 143–229. Editoriale Jaca Book, Mexico.

Codex Bodley (see Jansen and Pérez Jiménez 2005)

Codex Mendoza (see Berdan and Anawalt 1997)

Codex Nuttall (see Anders et al. 1992a; Nuttall 1902, 1975)

Coe, Michael D.
1962 *Mexico*. Frederick A. Praeger, New York.
1976 Early steps in the evolution of Maya writing. In *Origins of Religious Art and Iconography in Preclassic Mesoamerica*, edited by Henry B. Nicholson, pp. 107–122. UCLA Latin American Studies Series, Vol. 31. Latin American Center Publications, University of California at Los Angeles.

Coe, William R.
1967 *Tikal: A Handbook of the Ancient Maya Ruins*. University of Pennsylvania Museum of Archaeology and Anthropology, Philadelphia.
1990 *Excavations in the Great Plaza, North Terrace and North Acropolis of Tikal*. Tikal Report No. 14, Vol. III. University Museum Monograph 61. University of Pennsylvania Museum of Archaeology and Anthropology, Philadelphia.

Coggins, Clemency Chase
1988 Maya metaphors of death and life. *RES: Anthropology and Aesthetics* 16:64–84.

Córdova, fray Juan de
1942 [1578a] *Vocabulario en lengua zapoteca*. Pedro Charte y Antonio Ricardo, Mexico.
1886 [1578b] *Arte del idioma zapoteco*. Casa de Pedro Balli, Imprenta del Gobierno, Morelia, Mexico.
1942 *Vocabulario en lengua zapoteca*, edited by Wigberto Jiménez Moreno. Instituto Nacional de Antropología e Historia, Mexico.

Corona Núñez, José
1964 Explicaciones. In *Antigüedades de México: basadas en la recopilación de Lord Kingsborough*. 2 volumes. Secretaría de Hacienda y Crédito Público, Mexico.

Covarrubias, Miguel
1946 *Mexico South: The Isthmus of Tehuantepec*. Alfred A. Knopf, New York.

Crespo, Ana María and Alba Guadalupe Mastache
1981 La presencia en el área de Tula, Hidalgo, de grupos relacionados con el barrio de Oaxaca en Teotihuacan. In *Interacción cultural en el México central*, edited by Evelyn C. Rattray, Jaime Litvak King, and Clara Luz Díaz Oyarzábal, pp. 99–106. Instituto de Investigaciones Antropológicas, Universidad Nacional Autónoma de México, México, D.F.

Croissier, Michelle
2007 The Zapotec presence at Teotihuacan, Mexico: political ethnicity and domestic identity. PhD dissertation, Department of Anthropology, University of Illinois at Urbana-Champaign.

Cruz, Wilfrido C.
1935 *El tonalamatl zapoteco*. Imprenta del Gobierno del Estado de Oaxaca de Juárez, Oaxaca, México.
1936 Los binigulaza. *Neza* 2 (11). Órgano Mensual de la Sociedad Nueva de Estudiantes Juchitecos, México, D.F.
1946 *Oaxaca recóndita: razas, idiomas, costumbres, leyendas y tradiciones del Estado de Oaxaca, México*. Oaxaca, Mexico.

D

Dahlgren de Jordan, Barbro
1954 *La Mixteca: su cultura e historia prehispánicas*. Colección Cultura México 11. Imprenta Universitaria, Mexico.

Damerow, Peter
2006 The origins of writing as a problem of historical epistemology. *Cuneiform Digital Library Journal* 1:1–10.

Daniels, Peter T.
2018 *An Exploration of Writing*. Equinox, Bristol, Connecticut.

Daniels, Peter T. and William Bright, editors
1996 *The World's Writing Systems*. Oxford University Press, Oxford and New York.

Davletshin, Albert and Alfonso Lacadena
2019 Signos numéricos y registros de cuenta en la escritura jeroglífica náhuatl. *Revista Española de Antropología Americana* 49:301–328.

De Cicco, Gabriel and Donald L. Brockington
1956 *Reconocimiento arqueológico en el suroeste de Oaxaca*. Dirección de Monumentos Prehispánicos, Informe 6. Instituto Nacional de Antropología e Historia, México, D.F.

DeFrancis, John
1989 *Visible Speech: The Diverse Oneness of Writing Systems*. University of Hawaii Press, Honolulu.

de la Cruz, Víctor
1995 Los nombres de los días en el calendario zapoteco *piye* en comparación con el calendario nahua. *Estudios de Cultura Náhuatl* 25:149–176.

2014 Los señores 5 y 9 Flor de Zaachila. In *Zaachila y su historia prehispánica: Memoria del quincuagésimo aniversario del descubrimiento de las tumbas 1 y 2*, edited by Ismael G. Vicente Cruz and Gonzalo Sánchez Santiago, pp. 63–74. CONACULTA, Oaxaca, Mexico.

del Castillo, Cristóbal
2001 *Historia de la venida de los mexicanos y de otros pueblos e historia de la conquista*. Traducción y estudio introductorio de Federico Navarrete, Consejo Nacional de la Cultura y las Artes, México.

del Paso y Troncoso, Francisco
1905 *Relaciones geográficas de Oaxaca. Papeles de Nueva España. Segunda Serie, Geografía y Estadística*, Vol. IV. Tipográfico "Sucesores de Rivadeneyra," Madrid.

Desroches-Noblecourt, Christine
1978 *Tutankhamen: Life and Death of a Pharaoh*. New York Graphic Society, New York.

Díaz Castro, Susana
2008 Representaciones de glifos de espacio en la pintura mural de Oaxaca. In *La pintura mural prehispánica en México III, Oaxaca, Tomo II, Catálogo*, edited by Beatriz de la Fuente, pp. 469–511. Universidad Nacional Autónoma de México, Instituto de Investigacionces Estéticas, Mexico City.

Díaz Oyarzábal, Clara Luz
1980 *Chingú: un sitio clásico del área de Tula, Hidalgo*. Colección Científica No. 90. Instituto Nacional de Antropología e Historia, México, D.F.
1981 Chingú y la expansión teotihuacana. In *Interacción Cultural en México Central*, edited by Evelyn C. Rattray, Jaime Litvak King, and Clara Díaz Oyarzábal, pp. 107–112. Universidad Nacional Autónoma de México, México, D.F.

Díaz Castro, Susana, Laura Piñeirúa Menéndez, and Dionisio Rodríguez Cabrera
2005 Mitla. In *La pintura mural prehispánica en México III: Oaxaca*—Tomo II: Catálogo, edited by Beatriz de la Fuente, pp. 268–337. Universidad Nacional Autónoma de México, Instituto de Investigaciones Estéticas, Mexico City.

Dibble, Charles E.
1940 El antiguo sistema de escritura en México. *Revista Mexicana de Estudios Antropológicos* Vol. IV, Nos. 1–2, pp. 105–128. Sociedad Mexicana de Antropología, Mexico.
1955 The Aztec writing system. In *Readings in Anthropology*, edited by E. Adamson Hoebel, Jesse D. Jennings, and Elmer R. Smith, pp. 296–302. McGraw-Hill Book Co., New York.
1971 Writing in central Mexico. In *Archaeology of Northern Mesoamerica*, Part 1, edited by Gordon F. Ekholm, and Ignacio Bernal, pp. 322–332. Handbook of Middle American Indians, Vol. 10, Robert Wauchope, general editor. University of Texas Press, Austin.

Diehl, Richard A. and Janet Catherine Berlo, editors
1989 *Mesoamerica after The Decline of Teotihuacan AD 700-900*. Dumbarton Oaks Research Library and Collection, Washington, D.C.

Dieseldorff, Erwin Paul
1933 *Kunst und Religion der Mayavölker* III. L. Friederichsen & Co., Hamburg, Germany.

Dillon, Brian D.
1982 Bound prisoners in Maya art. *Journal of New World Archaeology* 5(1):24–50.

Diringer, David
1962 *Writing*. Frederick A. Praeger, New York.

Donnan, Christopher
1988 Unraveling the mystery of the Warrior Priest. *National Geographic* 174:551–555.

Dow, J. W.
1967 Astronomical orientations at Teotihuacán, a case study in astro-archaeology. *American Antiquity* 32:326–334.

Drennan, Robert D.
1976 *Fábrica San José and Middle Formative Society in the Valley of Oaxaca*. In The Prehistory and Human Ecology of the Valley of Oaxaca series, Vol. 4, edited by Kent V. Flannery. Memoirs of the University of Michigan Museum of Anthropology, No. 8. Ann Arbor.
1983 Monte Albán I and II settlement in the Mountain Survey Zone between the Valleys of Oaxaca and Nochixtlán. In *The Cloud People: Divergent Evolution of the Zapotec and Mixtec Civilizations*, edited by Kent V. Flannery and Joyce Marcus, pp. 110–111. Academic Press, New York.

Dreyer, Günter
1992 Recent discoveries at Abydos Cemetery U. In *The Nile Delta in Transition, 4th-3rd Millennium BC*, edited by Edwin C. M. van den Brink, pp. 293–299. Israel Exploration Society, Tel Aviv.

Dreyer, Günter, Ulrich Hartung, and Frauke Pumpenmeier
1993 Umm el-Qaab: Nachuntersuchungen im Frühzeitlichen Königsfriedhof 5./6. Bericht, *Mitteilungen des Deutschen Archäeologischen Instituts Abteilung Kairo* 49:23–62.
1998 *Umm el-Qaab I*. Philipp von Zabern, Mainz, Germany.

Drucker, Philip
1952 *La Venta, Tabasco: A Study of Olmec Ceramics and Art*. Smithsonian Institution, Bureau of American Ethnology, Bulletin 153. U.S. Government Printing Office, Washington, D.C.

Drucker, Philip, Robert F. Heizer, and Robert J. Squier
1959 *Excavations at La Venta, Tabasco, 1955*. Smithsonian Institution, Bureau of American Ethnology, Bulletin 170. U.S. Government Printing Office, Washington, D.C.

Duncan, William N., Andrew K. Balkansky, Kimberly Crawford, Heather A. Lapham, and Nathan J. Meissner
2008 Human cremation in Mexico 3,000 years ago. *Proceedings of the National Academy of Sciences* 105(14):5315–5320.

Dupaix, Guillermo
1969 [1834] *Antiquités mexicaines: relation des trois expéditions du Capitaine Dupaix. 1805, 1806, 1807*. 2 volumes. Paris. (See also Expediciones acerca de los antiguos monumentos de Nueva España, 1805-1808. Edición, introducción, y notas por José Alcina Franch. 2 volumes. Ediciones José Porrúa Turanzas, Madrid.)

Durán, fray Diego
1964 [1581] *The Aztecs: The History of the Indies of New Spain.* Translated with notes by Fernando Horcasitas and Doris Heyden. Orion Press, New York.

E

Earl, Robert
1968 Rincón Zapotec clauses. *International Journal of American Linguistics* 34(4):269–274.

Easby, Elizabeth Kennedy and John F. Scott
1970 *Before Cortés: Sculpture of Middle America.* The Metropolitan Museum of Art, New York.

Edmonson, Munro S.
1988 *The Book of the Year: Middle American Calendrical Systems.* University of Utah Press, Salt Lake City.

Edwards, I. E. S.
1976 *Treasures of Tutankhamun.* Ballantine Books, New York.

Ellul, Jacques
1973 *Propaganda: The Formation of Men's Attitudes.* Vintage Books, New York.

Elson, Christina
2007 *Excavations at Cerro Tilcajete: A Monte Albán II Administrative Center in the Valley of Oaxaca.* Memoirs of the University of Michigan Museum of Anthropology, No. 42. Ann Arbor.

Emery, Walter B.
1961 *Archaic Egypt.* Viking Penguin Books, Harmondsworth, New York.

Englund, Robert K.
1988 Administrative timekeeping in ancient Mesopotamia. *Journal of the Economic and Social History of the Orient* 31:121–185.
1994a Proto-cuneiform account-books and journals. In *Creating Economic Order: Record-keeping, Standardization, and the Development of Accounting in the Ancient Near East*, Vol. IV, edited by Michael Hudson and Cornelia Wunsch, pp. 23–46. CDL Press, Bethesda, Maryland.
1994b *Archaic Administrative Texts from Uruk: The Early Campaigns.* Gebr. Mann, Berlin.

Esparza Olguín, Octavio and Vania E. Pérez Gutiérrez
2009 Archaeological and epigraphic studies in Pol Box, Quintana Roo. *The PARI Journal* 9(3):1–16.

Espíndola, Nicolás de
1905a [1580] Relación de Chichicapa y su partido. In *Papeles de Nueva España. Segunda Serie, Geografía y Estadística,* Vol. 4, edited by Francisco del Paso y Troncoso, pp. 115–119. Tipográfico "Sucesores de Rivadeneyra," Madrid.
1905b [1580] Relación de Ocelotepeque. In *Papeles de Nueva España. Segunda Serie, Geografía y Estadística*, Vol. 4, edited by Francisco del Paso y Troncoso, pp. 137–143. Tipográfico "Sucesores de Rivadeneyra," Madrid.

Eubanks, Mary W.
1999 *Corn in Clay: Maize Paleoethnobotany in Precolumbian Art.* University Press of Florida, Gainesville.

F

Fahmel Beyer, Bernd W. F.
1991 *La arquitectura de Monte Albán.* Instituto de Investigaciones Antropológicas, Universidad Nacional Autónoma de México, Mexico.
2000 Las lápidas del Montículo J de Monte Albán y el surgimiento del estado en los valles centrales de Oaxaca. *Anales de Antropología* 34:81–104.
2005a Xoxocotlan, tumbas de los montículos 5, 8 y 9. In *La pintura mural prehispánica en Oaxaca, México*, edited by Beatriz de la Fuente, pp. 338–339. Instituto de Investigaciones Estéticas, Universidad Nacional Autónoma de México, Mexico City.
2005b Suchilquitongo. In *La pintura mural prehispánica en Oaxaca, México III*, Oaxaca—Tomo I, edited by Beatriz de la Fuente, pp. 146–215. Instituto de Investigaciones Estéticas, Universidad Nacional Autónoma de México, Mexico City.

Fash, Barbara W., William L. Fash, Rudy Larios, Sheree Lane, Linda Schele, Jeffrey Stomper, and David Stuart
1992 Investigations of a Maya council house from Copán, Honduras. *Journal of Field Archaeology* 19:419–442.

Fash, William L.
1991 *Scribes, Warriors and Kings: The City of Copán and the Ancient Maya.* Thames and Hudson, London.

Fash, William L. and Barbara W. Fash
1996 Building a worldview: visual communication in Classic Maya architecture. *RES: Anthropology and Aesthetics* 29-30:127–147.

Faulseit, Ronald K.
2012 State collapse and household resilience in the Oaxaca Valley of Mexico. *Latin American Antiquity* 23(4):401–425.
2013 *Cerro Danush: Excavations at a Hilltop Community in the Eastern Valley of Oaxaca, Mexico.* Memoirs of the University of Michigan Museum of Anthropology, No. 54. Ann Arbor.

Faulseit, Ronald K., Gary M. Feinman, and Linda Nicholas
2018 Household economic strategies and social resilience in the Valley of Oaxaca, Mexico. In *City, Craft, and Residence: Research Papers in Honor of Dan M. Healan*, edited by Ronald K. Faulseit, Nezahualcoyotl Xiuhtecutli, and Haley Holt Mehta, pp. 11–31. Middle American Research Institute, Tulane University, Publication 72. New Orleans.

Feinman, Gary M. and Joyce Marcus, editors
1998 *Archaic States.* School of American Research Press, Santa Fe, New Mexico.

Feinman, Gary M. and Linda M. Nicholas
1990 At the margins of the Monte Albán state: Settlement patterns in the Ejutla Valley, Oaxaca, Mexico. *Latin American Antiquity* 1:216–246.

1993 Shell-ornament production in Ejutla: Implications for highland-coastal interaction in ancient Oaxaca. *Ancient Mesoamerica* 4:103–119.

1995 Household Craft Specialization and Shell Ornament Manufacture in Ejutla, Mexico. *Expedition* 37(2):14–25.

2001 Excavations at El Palmillo: A hilltop terrace site in Oaxaca, Mexico. *In the Field Magazine* 2-5. Field Museum of Natural History, Chicago.

2002 Residential terrace excavations at El Palmillo, Oaxaca, Mexico. *Antiquity* 76:27–28.

2004 Unraveling the prehispanic highland Mesoamerican economy. In *Archaeological Perspectives on Political Economies*, edited by Gary M. Feinman and Linda M. Nicholas, pp. 167–188. University of Utah Press, Salt Lake City.

2005 More than alluvial land and water: the late pre-Hispanic emergence of eastern Tlacolula, Oaxaca, Mexico. In *Settlement, Subsistence and Social Complexity*, edited by Richard E. Blanton, pp. 229–259. Cotsen Institute of Archaeology, University of California at Los Angeles.

2011 The ballcourt at El Palmillo: implications for Late Classic Oaxaca, Mexico. *Mexicon* 33:98–104.

2016a Reconsiderando la "invasión mixteca" del valle de Oaxaca en el Posclásico. *Anales de Antropología* 50:247–265.

2016b Crocodilian sculpture discovered at Lambityeco, Oaxaca. *Mexicon* 38:114–115.

2017 *Settlement Patterns in the Albarradas Area of Highland Oaxaca, Mexico: Frontiers, Boundaries, and Interaction.* Fieldiana n.s. No. 46. Field Museum of Natural History, Chicago.

2019 Civic-ceremonial transition at Lambityeco, Oaxaca, Mexico. In *Historical Ecologies, Heterarchies and Transtemporal Landscapes*, edited by Celeste Ray and Manuel Fernández-Götz, pp. 248–264. Routledge, Abingdon-on-Thames.

Feinman, Gary M., Linda M. Nicholas, and Lindsey C. Baker

2010 The missing femur at the Mitla Fortress and its implications. *Antiquity* 84:1089–1101.

Feria, fray Pedro de

1567 Doctrina cristiana en lengua castellana y çapoteca. Casa de Pedro Ocharte, Mexico City.

Fernández Dávila, Enrique

1997 San José Mogote, Etla: origen y desarrollo de la civilización zapoteca. *Arqueología Mexicana* V(26):18–23. Editorial Raíces, Mexico.

Fernández de Miranda, María Teresa

1995 *El Protozapoteco.* Edition prepared by Michael J. Piper and Doris A. Bartholomew. El Colegio de México, Instituto Nacional de Antropología e Historia, México, D.F.

Fernández de Miranda, María Teresa, Mauricio Swadesh, and Roberto J. Weitlaner

1960 El panorama etno-lingüístico de Oaxaca y el Istmo. *Revista Mexicana de Estudios Antropológicos* 16:137–157.

Field, Frederick V.

1967 *Thoughts on the meaning and use of pre-Hispanic Mexican sellos.* Studies in Pre-Columbian Art and Archaeology No. 3, pp. 1–48. Dumbarton Oaks Library and Research Collection, Washington, D.C.

Finsten, Laura

1983 The Classic-Postclassic Transition in the Valley of Oaxaca, Mexico: A Regional Analysis of the Process of Political Decentralization in a Prehistoric Complex Society. PhD dissertation, Department of Anthropology, Purdue University, West Lafayette, Indiana. University Microfilms, Ann Arbor.

Flannery, Kent V.

1976 *The Early Mesoamerican Village*. Academic Press, New York.

1983a Monte Negro: a reinterpretation. In *The Cloud People: Divergent Evolution of the Zapotec and Mixtec Civilizations*, edited by Kent V. Flannery and Joyce Marcus, pp. 99–102. Academic Press, New York.

1983b Major Monte Alban V sites: Zaachila, Xoxocotlán, Cuilapan, Yagul, and Abasolo. In *The Cloud People: Divergent Evolution of the Zapotec and Mixtec Civilizations*, edited by Kent V. Flannery and Joyce Marcus, pp. 290–295. Academic Press, New York.

1983c The legacy of the early urban period: an ethnohistoric approach to Monte Albán's temples, residences, and royal tombs. In *The Cloud People: Divergent Evolution of the Zapotec and Mixtec Civilizations*, edited by Kent V. Flannery and Joyce Marcus, pp. 132–136. Academic Press, New York.

1983d Zapotec warfare: archaeological evidence for the battles of Huitzo and Guiengola. In *The Cloud People: Divergent Evolution of the Zapotec and Mixtec Civilizations*, edited by Kent V. Flannery and Joyce Marcus, pp. 318–322. Academic Press, New York.

1986 *Guilá Naquitz: Archaic Foraging and Early Agriculture in Oaxaca, Mexico*. Academic Press, Orlando.

1998 The ground plans of archaic states. In *Archaic States*, edited by Gary M. Feinman and Joyce Marcus, pp. 15–57. School of American Research Press, Santa Fe, New Mexico.

Flannery, Kent V. and Joyce Marcus

1976a Evolution of the public building in Formative Oaxaca. In *Cultural Change and Continuity*, edited by Charles E. Cleland, pp. 205–221. Academic Press, New York.

1976b Formative Oaxaca and the Zapotec cosmos. *American Scientist* 64:374–383.

1983a The earliest public buildings, tombs, and monuments at Monte Albán, with notes on the internal chronology of Period I. In *The Cloud People: Divergent Evolution of the Zapotec and Mixtec Civilizations*, edited by Kent V. Flannery and Joyce Marcus, pp. 87–91. Academic Press, New York.

1983b An editorial position on the Mixtec impact. In *The Cloud People: Divergent Evolution of the Zapotec and Mixtec Civilizations*, edited by Kent V. Flannery and Joyce Marcus, pp. 277–279. Academic Press, New York.

1983c An introduction to the Late Postclassic. In *The Cloud People: Divergent Evolution of the Zapotec and Mixtec Civilizations*, edited by Kent V. Flannery and Joyce Marcus, pp. 217–226. Academic Press, New York.

1983d Urban Mitla and its rural hinterland. In *The Cloud People: Divergent Evolution of the Zapotec and Mixtec Civilizations*, edited by Kent V. Flannery and Joyce Marcus, pp. 295–300. Academic Press, New York.

1994 *Early Formative Pottery of the Valley of Oaxaca*. Memoirs of the University of Michigan Museum of Anthropology, No. 27. Ann Arbor.

2003 The origin of war: New ^{14}C dates from ancient Mexico. *Proceedings of the National Academy of Sciences* 100(20):11801–11805.

2005 *Excavations at San José Mogote 1: The Household Archaeology*. Memoirs of the University of Michigan Museum of Anthropology, No. 40. Ann Arbor.

2012 *The Creation of Inequality*. Harvard University Press, Cambridge, Massachusetts.
2015 *Excavations at San José Mogote 2: The Cognitive Archaeology*. Memoirs of the University of Michigan Museum of Anthropology, No. 58. Ann Arbor.

Folan, William J., Joyce Marcus, Sophia Pincemin, María del Rosario Domínguez, Laraine Fletcher, and Abel Morales
1995 Calakmul: New Data from an Ancient Maya Capital in Campeche, Mexico. *Latin American Antiquity* 6:310–334.

Foncerrada de Molina, Marta
1980 Mural painting in Cacaxtla and Teotihuacán Cosmopolitanism. In *Third Palenque Round Table, 1978*, edited by Merle Greene Robertson, Vol. V, Part 2, pp. 183–198. University of Texas Press, Austin.
1993 *Cacaxtla: La iconografía de los olmeca-xicalanca*. Universidad Nacional Autónoma de México and Instituto de Investigaciones Estéticas, Mexico City.

Foreman, John and Brook Danielle Lillehaugen
2017 Positional verbs in Colonial Valley Zapotec. *International Journal of American Linguistics* 83(2):263–305.

Fowler, Melvin L. and Richard S. MacNeish
1975 Excavations in the Coxcatlan locality in the alluvial slopes. In *The Prehistory of the Tehuacan, Vol. 5: Excavations and Reconnaissance*, edited by Richard S. MacNeish, Melvin Fowler, Angel García Cook, Frederick Peterson, Antoinette Nelken-Terner, and James Neely, pp. 219–340. University of Texas Press, Austin.

Franco Brizuela, María Luisa
1993 *La tumba zapoteca de Huijazoo en Oaxaca*. EPSON, Cavallari Impresores y Editores, S.A. de C.V., Mexico City.

Franco C., José Luis
1959 La escritura y los códices. In *Esplendor del México Antiguo*, edited by R. Noriega, Carmen Cook de Leonard, and J. R. Moctezuma, pp. 361–378. Centro de Investigaciones Antropológicas, México.

Freidel, David A. and Stanley Paul Guenter
2006 Soul bundle caches, tombs, and cenotaphs: creating the places of resurrection and accession in Maya kingship. In *Sacred Bundles, Ritual Acts of Wrapping and Binding in Mesoamerica*, edited by Julia Guernsey and F. Kent Reilly III, pp. 59–79. Boundary End Archaeology Research Center, Barnardsville, North Carolina.

Freidel, David A., Marilyn A. Masson, and Michelle Rich
2017 Imagining a complex Maya political economy: counting tokens and currencies in image, text and the archaeological record. *Cambridge Archaeological Journal* 27(1):29–54.

Freidel, David A., Linda Schele, and Joy Parker
1993 *Maya Cosmos: Three Thousand Years on the Shaman's Path*. William Morrow and Company, New York.

Friberg, Jöran
1999 Counting and accounting in the proto-literate Middle East: examples from two new volumes of proto-cuneiform texts. *Journal of Cuneiform Studies* 51:107–137.

Fuente, Beatriz de la, editora
2008 *La pintura mural prehispánica en México, Vol. III, Oaxaca*—Tomos III, IV. Instituto de Investigaciones Estéticas, Universidad Nacional Autónoma de México, Ciudad Universitaria, Coyoacán, México, D.F.

Fuson, Robert H.
1969 The orientation of Mayan ceremonial centers. *Annals of the Association of American Geographers* 59:494–511.

G

Gadow, Hans
1908 *Through Southern Mexico, being an account of the travels of a naturalist*. C. Scribner's Sons, New York.

Gaida, María
2011 Un cofre mexica de piedra de la Colección de Bauer, 1904. *Arqueología Mexicana* 110:78–83. Editorial Raíces, México.

Galant, Michael
2011 Kinship terms in Colonial Valley Zapotec. In *Tradition and Innovation in Mesoamerican Cultural History: A Homage to Tatiana A. Proskouriakoff*, edited by Roberto Cantú and Aaron Sonnenschein, pp. 65–73. Lincom Studies in Anthropology, No. 16. Lincom Europa, Muenchen.

Galindo y Villa, Jesús
1905 Algo sobre los zapotecas y los edificios de Mitla. *Anales del Museo Nacional de México*, segunda época, tomo 2, Nos. 4–6, pp. 193–258. Imprenta del Museo Nacional, Mexico.

Gallegos Ruiz, Roberto
1962 Exploraciones en Zaachila, Oaxaca. *Boletín del Instituto Nacional de Antropología e Historia* 8:6–8. Mexico City.
1963 Zaachila: the first season's work. *Archaeology* 16(4):226–233. Translated by Dudley T. Easby, Jr.
1964 Exploraciones arqueológicas en Zaachila, Oaxaca, 1962. MA tesis, Escuela Nacional de Antropología e Historia, Mexico.
1978 *El Señor 9 Flor en Zaachila*. Universidad Nacional Autónoma de México, Mexico.

Gamio, Lorenzo
1944 *Informe de la exploración llevada a cabo en la tumba de Zaachila, Oaxaca*. Archivo de la Dirección de Monumentos Prehispánicos, Tomo 87, Vol. 4: Nos. 702–723. Instituto Nacional de Antropología e Historia, México, D.F.

García Moll, Roberto, Donald W. Patterson Brown, and Marcus C. Winter
1986 *Monumentos escultóricos de Monte Albán*. Verlag C. H. Beck, München, Germany.

Gaxiola, Margarita
1976 *Excavaciones en San Martín Huamelulpan, Oaxaca, 1974*. Tesis profesional, Escuela Nacional de Antropología, México, D.F.

Gelb, Ignace Jay
1952 *A Study of Writing*. Routledge and K. Paul, London.

Gendrop, Paul
1998 *Río Bec, Chenes, and Puuc Styles in Maya Architecture*. Labyrinthos, Culver City, California.

González Licón, Ernesto
2003 Social Inequality at Monte Albán, Oaxaca: Household Analysis from the Terminal Formative to Early Classic. PhD dissertation, Department of Anthropology, University of Pittsburgh.

Graham, Ian and Eric von Euw
1975 *Naranjo*. Corpus of Maya Hieroglyphic Inscriptions 2(1). Peabody Museum, Harvard University, Cambridge, Massachusetts.

Graham, John Allen
1971 Commentary on: calendrics and writing. In *Observations on the Emergence of Civilization in Mesoamerica*, edited by Robert F. Heizer and John A. Graham, pp. 133–140. University of California Archaeological Research Facility, Contribution 11. Berkeley, California.

Green, Margaret W. and Hans J. Nissen, editors
1987 *Zeichenliste der archaischen Texte aus Uruk. Ausgrabungen der Deutschen Forschungsgemeinschaft in Uruk-Warka 11*. Archaische Texte aus Uruk 2. Gebrüder Mann Verlag, Berlin.

Greene, Merle, Robert L. Rands, and John A. Graham
1972 *Maya Sculpture from the Southern Lowlands, Highlands, and Pacific Piedmont*. Lederer, Street and Zeus, Berkeley, California.

Grube, Nikolai
2012 Maya writing. In *The Oxford Handbook of Mesoamerican Archaeology*, edited by Deborah L. Nichols, pp. 1–10. Oxford University Press, Oxford.

Guernsey, Julia
2006 *Ritual and power in stone: the performance of rulership in Mesoamerican Izapan style art*. University of Texas Press, Austin.
2010 A consideration of the quatrefoil motif in Preclassic Mesoamerica. *RES: Anthropology and Aesthetics* 57/58:75–96.

Guernsey, Julia and F. Kent Reilly, editors
2006 *Sacred Bundles: Ritual Acts of Wrapping and Binding in Mesoamerica*. Boundary End Archaeology Research Center, Barnardsville, North Carolina.

H

Hall, Grant D.
1984 Tombs at Río Azul: 1983. In *Río Azul Report*, No. 1, edited by Richard E. W. Adams, pp. 53–62. Center for Archaeological Research, San Antonio, Texas.
1986 Results of tomb investigations at Río Azul: 1984. In *Río Azul Report*, No. 2, edited by Richard E. W. Adams. Center for Archaeological Research, San Antonio, Texas.
1989 Realm of Death: Royal Mortuary Customs and Polity Interaction in the Classic Maya Lowlands. PhD dissertation, Department of Anthropology, Harvard University, Cambridge, Massachusetts.

Hammond, Norman
2017 Boxing day: a Maya polychrome pot from southern Belize. *Antiquity* 91:1–7.

Hassig, Ross
1988 *Aztec Warfare: Imperial Expansion and Political Control*. University of Oklahoma Press, Norman.

Hendrickx, Stan
2006 Predynastic-Early Dynastic chronology. In *Ancient Egyptian Chronology*, edited by Erik Hornung, Rolf Krauss, and David A. Warburton, pp. 55–93. Brill, Leiden, The Netherlands.

Henestrosa, Andrés
1936 Vini-Gundah-Zaa. *Neza*, año II, No. 10. Órgano Mensual de la Sociedad Nueva de Estudiantes Juchitecos, México, D.F.

Hermann Lejarazu, Manuel A.
2008 Religiosidad y bultos sagrados en la Mixteca prehispánica. *Desacatos* 27:75–94.
2009 La serpiente de fuego o *yahui* en la Mixteca prehispánica: iconografía y significado. *Anales del Museo de América* 17:64–77.

Hernández Reyes, Carlos
1990 Un enclave zapoteco en el valle de Mezquital. *Atalaya* 1(1):3–10.
1994 Rescate de una tumba zapoteca en Tepeji del Río. In *Simposio sobre arqueología en el Estado de Hidalgo: Trabajos recientes, 1989*, edited by Enrique Fernández Dávila, pp. 125–149. Colección Científica, Vol. 282. Instituto Nacional de Antropología e Historia, México, D.F.

Herrera y Tordesillas, Antonio de
1947 [1601] *Historia general de los hechos de los castellanos en las islas y tierra firme del Mar Océano*, Vol. VI. Academia de la Historia, Madrid.

Hirth, Kenneth
1989 Militarism and social organization at Xochicalco, Morelos. In *Mesoamerica after the Decline of Teotihuacan A.D. 700-900*, edited by Richard A. Diehl and Janet C. Berlo, pp. 68–81. Dumbarton Oaks Research Library and Collection, Washington, D.C.

Hirth, Kenneth G. and Jorge Angulo Villaseñor
1981 Early state expansion in central Mexico: Teotihuacan in Morelos. *Journal of Field Archaeology* 8(2):135–150.

Hocart, Arthur Maurice
1927 *Kingship*. Oxford University Press, London.

Holmes, William Henry
1895 *Archaeological Studies among the Ancient Cities of Mexico*. Field Columbian Museum, Chicago.
1907 On a nephrite statuette from San Andrés Tuxtla, Vera Cruz, Mexico. *American Anthropologist* 9(4):691–701.

Holt Mehta, Haley
2018 More than an enclave? Ethnic identity and cultural affiliations at El Tesoro, a Classic period Zapotec site in the Tula area. In *City, Craft, and Residence: Research Papers in Honor of Dan M. Healan*, edited by Ronald K. Faulseit, Nezahualcoyotl Xiuhtecutli, and Haley Holt Mehta, pp. 125–134. Middle American Research Institute, Tulane University, Publication 72. New Orleans.

Houston, Stephen D.
1984 An example of homophony in Maya script. *American Antiquity* 49:790–805.

Houston, Stephen D., editor
2004 *The First Writing: Script Invention as History and Process*. Cambridge University Press, Cambridge.

Houston, Stephen D. and Michael D. Coe
2003 Has Isthmian writing been deciphered? *Mexicon* XXXV:151–161.

Hunn, Eugene S.
1998 Mixtepec Zapotec ethnobiological classification: a preliminary sketch and theoretical commentary. *Anthropologica* XL:35–48.

Hunn, Eugene S. and Donato Acuca Vásquez
2001 La etnobiología en el *Vocabulario en lengua Çapoteca* de fray Juan de Córdova, comparación con la actual de San Juan Mixtepec. *Cuadernos del Sur* año 7(16):21–32.

Hvidtfeldt, Arild
1958 *Teotl and *ixiptlati: Some Central Conceptions in Ancient Mexican Religion, with a General Introduction on Cult and Myth*. Munksgaard, Copenhagen, Denmark.

I

Isaac, Barry L.
1983 Aztec warfare: goals and battlefield comportment. *Ethnology* 22(2):121–131.

J

Jaeger, Jeri J. and Robert D. Van Valin, Jr.
1982 Initial consonant clusters in Yateé Zapotec. *International Journal of American Linguistics* 48(2):125–138.

Janák, Jiri
2011 A question of size: a remark on early attestations of the ba hieroglyph. *Studien zur Altägyptischen Kultur* Bd. 40:143–153.

Jansen, Maarten E. R. G. N. and Gabina Aurora Pérez Jiménez
2005 *Codex Bodley: A Painted Chronicle from the Mixtec Highlands, Mexico*. Bodleian Library, Oxford.
2011 *The Mixtec Pictorial Manuscripts: Time, Agency, and Memory in Ancient Mexico*. Brill, Leiden.

Jansen, Maarten, Peter Kröfges, and Michel R. Oudijk, editors
1998 *The Shadow of Monte Albán: Politics and Historiography in Postclassic Oaxaca*. Research School of Asian, African, and Amerindian Studies, Leiden University, Leiden.

Jiménez Moreno, Wigberto
1961 Diferente principio del año entre diversos pueblos y sus consecuencias para la cronología prehispánica. *El México Antiguo: Homenaje al Dr. Hermann Beyer*, Vol. 4, pp. 137–152. Mexico.

Johnson, Gregory Alan
1972 Local Exchange and Early State Development in Southwestern Iran. PhD dissertation, Department of Anthropology, University of Michigan, Ann Arbor.
1973 *Local Exchange and Early State Development in Southwestern Iran*. Anthropological Papers of the University of Michigan Museum of Anthropology, No. 51. Ann Arbor.

Johnson, Irmgard W.
1936 A Chinantec calendar. *American Anthropologist* 38:197–201.

Jones, Christopher and Linton Satterthwaite
1982 *The Monuments and Inscriptions of Tikal: The Carved Monuments*. Tikal Report No. 33, Part A. University Museum Monograph No. 44. University of Pennsylvania Museum of Archaeology and Anthropology, Philadelphia.

Jones, Ted E. and Lyle M. Knudson
1977 Guelavía Zapotec phonemes. In *Studies in Otomanguean Phonology*, edited by William R. Merrifield, pp. 163–180. Summer Institute of Linguistics and University of Texas at Arlington.

Joyce, Arthur A.
1991 Formative Period occupation in the Lower Río Verde Valley, Oaxaca, Mexico: interregional interaction and social change. PhD dissertation, Department of Anthropology, Rutgers University, New Jersey.
2003 Imperialism in pre-Aztec Mesoamerica: Monte Alban, Teotihuacan, and the lower Río Verde Valley. In *Ancient Mesoamerican Warfare*, edited by M. Kathryn Brown and Travis M. Stanton, pp. 49–72. AltaMira Press, Walnut Creek, California.
2013 (ed.) *Polity and Ecology in Formative Period Coastal Oaxaca*. University Press of Colorado, Boulder.
2014 Warfare in Late/Terminal Formative-period Oaxaca. In *Embattled Bodies, Embattled Places: War in Pre-Columbian Mesoamerica and the Andes*, edited by Andrew K. Scherer and John W. Verano, pp. 117–141. Dumbarton Oaks Research Library and Collection, Washington, D.C.

Joyce, Arthur A., Hector Neff, Mary S. Thieme, Marcus Winter, J. Michael Elam, and Andrew Workinger
2006 Ceramic production and exchange in Late/Terminal Formative period Oaxaca. *Latin American Antiquity* 17(4):579–594.

Joyce, Thomas A.
1933 The pottery whistle-figurines of Lubaantun. *Journal of the Royal Anthropological Institute* LXIII:xv–xxv. London.

Just, Bryan R.
2005 Modifications of ancient Maya sculpture. *RES: Anthropology and Aesthetics* 48:69–82.

Justeson, John S.
1975 The identification of the emblem glyph of Yaxha, El Peten. In *Studies in Ancient Mesoamerica* II, edited by John A. Graham, pp. 123–129. University of California Archaeological Research Facility, Contribution 27. Berkeley, California.
1986 The origin of writing systems: Preclassic Mesoamerica. *World Archaeology* 17(3):437–458.

2012 Early Mesoamerican writing systems. In *The Oxford Handbook of Mesoamerican Archaeology*, edited by Deborah L. Nichols and Christopher Pool, pp. 830–844. Oxford University Press, Oxford.

Justeson, John S. and Lyle Campbell, editors
1984 *Phoneticism in Mayan Hieroglyphic Writing*. Institute for Mesoamerican Studies, Publication No. 9. State University of New York, Albany.

Justeson, John S. and Terrence Kaufman
1993 A decipherment of epi-Olmec hieroglyphic writing. *Science* 259:1703–1711.
1997 A newly discovered column in the hieroglyphic text on La Mojarra Stela 1: a test of the Epi-Olmec decipherment. *Science* 277:207–210.
2010 Zapotec grammatical constructions in the Preclassic inscriptions of Monte Albán. Paper presented in Coloquio sobre Lenguas Otomangues y Vecinas, April 16–18.

Justeson, John S. and Peter Mathews
1990 Evolutionary trends in Mesoamerican hieroglyphic writing. *Visible Language* 24(1):88–132.

K

Kahl, Jochem
2001 Hieroglyphic writing during the fourth millennium BC: an analysis of systems. *Archéo-Nil* 11:103–134.

Kaplan, Lucille N.
1956 Tonal and nagual in coastal Oaxaca. *Journal of American Folklore* 69:363–368.

Kaufman, Terrence and John Justeson
2004a Zapotec. Appendix 3. In *The Cambridge Encyclopedia of the World's Ancient Languages*, edited by Roger D. Woodard, pp. 1109–1111. Cambridge University Press, Cambridge.
2004b Epi-Olmec. In *The Cambridge Encyclopedia of the World's Ancient Languages*, edited by Roger D. Woodard, pp. 1071–1108. Cambridge University Press, Cambridge.

Keightley, David N.
1989 The origins of writing in China: scripts and cultural contexts. In *The Origins of Writing*, edited by Wayne M. Senner, pp. 171–202. University of Nebraska Press, Lincoln.

Kelley, David H.
1966 A cylinder seal from Tlatilco. *American Antiquity* 31(5):744–746.
1968 Kakupacal and the Itzas. *Estudios de Cultura Maya* 7:255–268.
1976 *Deciphering the Maya Script*. University of Texas Press, Austin.

Kerr, Justin
1989 *The Maya Vase Book: a corpus of rollout photographs of Maya vases*. Vol. 1. Kerr and Associates, New York.

Kidder, Alfred V., Jesse D. Jennings, and Edwin M. Shook
1946 *Excavations at Kaminaljuyu, Guatemala*. Carnegie Institution of Washington, Publication 561. Washington, D.C.

Kirchhoff, Paul
1950 The Mexican calendar and the founding of Tenochtitlan-Tlatelolco. *Transactions of the New York Academy of Sciences*, Series II, 12(4):126–132. New York.
1954–1955 Calendarios Tenochca, Tlatelolca y otros. *Revista Mexicana de Estudios Antropológicos* 14(1-2):257–267.

Kirchhoff, Paul, Linda Odena Güemes, and Luis Reyes García
1976 *Historia Tolteca-Chichimeca*. CISINAH, Instituto Nacional de Antropología e Historia, Mexico.

Klein, Cecelia F.
1987 The ideology of autosacrifice at the Templo Mayor. In *The Aztec Templo Mayor: A Symposium at Dumbarton Oaks, 8th and 9th October, 1983*, edited by Elizabeth Hill Boone, pp. 293–370. Dumbarton Oaks Research Library and Collection, Washington, D.C.

Kowalewski, Stephen A., Charles S. Spencer, and Elsa M. Redmond
1978 Ceramic appendix. In *Monte Albán: Settlement Patterns at the Ancient Zapotec Capital*, by Richard E. Blanton, pp. 167–193. Academic Press, New York.

Kowalewski, Stephen A., Gary M. Feinman, Laura Finsten, Richard E. Blanton, and Linda M. Nicholas
1989 *Monte Albán's Hinterland, Part II: Prehispanic Settlement Patterns in Tlacolula, Etla, and Ocotlán, the Valley of Oaxaca, Mexico*. Memoirs of the University of Michigan Museum of Anthropology, No. 23. 2 volumes. Ann Arbor.

Kowalski, Jeff Karl
1999 *Mesoamerican Architecture as a Cultural Symbol*. Oxford University Press, Oxford.

Krebernik, Manfred
1994 Review of Green and Nissen 1987. *Orientalistische Literaturzeitung* 89:380–386.

L

Lacadena García-Gallo, Alfonso
2008 Regional scribal traditions: methodological implications for the decipherment of Nahuatl writing. *The PARI Journal* 8(4):1–22.

Langley, James C.
1986 *Symbolic Notation of Teotihuacan: Elements of Writing in a Mesoamerican Culture of the Classic Period*. BAR International Series, No. 313. Oxford, UK.

Leal, Mary
1950 Patterns of tone substitution in Zapotec morphology. *International Journal of American Linguistics* 16(3):132–136.

Leal, Mary and Otis Leal
1954 Noun possession in Villa Alta Zapotec. *International Journal of American Linguistics* 20(3):215–216.

Lee, Felicia
2000 VP remnant movement and VSO in Quiaviní Zapotec. In *The Syntax of Verb Initial Languages*, edited by Andrew Carnie and Eithne Guilfoyle, pp. 143–162. Oxford University Press, Oxford and New York.

Leigh, Howard
1966 The evolution of the Zapotec Glyph C. In *Ancient Oaxaca: Discoveries in Mexican Archeology and History*, edited by John Paddock, pp. 256–269. Stanford University Press, Stanford, California.

León, Nicolás
1901 *Lyobaa o Mictlan: Guía Histórico-Descriptive Guide*. La Europea, Mexico City.
1933 *Códice Sierra*. Imprenta del Museo Nacional de Arqueología, Historia y Etnografía. Mexico.

Lerner, Daniel, editor
1951 *Propaganda in War and Crisis*. George W. Stewart, New York.

Levanto, fray Leonardo
1776 [1732] *Cathecismo de la doctrina christiana en lengua zaapoteca*. Imprenta del Colegio Real de San Ignacio de la Puebla de los Angeles.

Lieberman, Stephen J.
1980 Of clay pebbles, hollow clay balls, and writing: a Sumerian view. *American Journal of Archaeology* 84:339–358.

Lillehaugen, Brook Danielle
2006 Expressing Location in Tlacolula Valley Zapotec. Ph.D. dissertation, University of California at Los Angeles.

Lillehaugen, Brook Danielle and Aaron Huey Sonnenschein, editors
2012 *Expressing Location in Zapotec*. Lincom Europa, Munich, Germany.

Lind, Michael
2003 Lambityeco—Tomb 6. In *Homenaje a John Paddock*, edited by Patricia Plunket, pp. 45–66. Universidad de las Américas, Cholula, Puebla, Mexico.
2015 *Ancient Zapotec Religion: An Ethnohistorical and Archaeological Perspective*. University Press of Colorado, Boulder.

Lind, Michael and Javier Urcid
1983 Lords of Lambityeco and their nearest neighbors. *Notas Mesoamericanas* 9:76–111. Universidad de las Américas, Fundación Puebla, Cholula, Mexico.
2010 *The Lords of Lambityeco: Political Evolution in the Valley of Oaxaca during the Xoo Phase*. University Press of Colorado, Boulder.

Linné, Sigvald
1942 *Mexican Highland Cultures: archaeological researches at Teotihuacan, Calpulalpan, and Chalchicomula in 1934-1935*. Ethnographical Museum of Sweden, Stockholm.

Lombardo de Ruiz, Sonia
1986 La pintura. In *Cacaxtla: El lugar donde muere la lluvia en la tierra*, pp. 209–499. Gobierno del Estado de Tlaxcala and Instituto Nacional de Antropología e Historia, Mexico City.
2008 Los estilos en la pintura mural de Oaxaca. In *La pintura mural prehispánica en México III: Oaxaca*, tomo III (Estudios), edited by Beatriz de la Fuente, pp. 89–175. Universidad Nacional Autónoma de México, Instituto de Investigaciones Estéticas, Mexico City.

López Chiñas, Jeremías
1937 Algunos animales y plantas que conocieron los antiguos zapotecas. *Neza* 3(1):12–24.

López de Molina, Diana
1979 Excavaciones en Cacaxtla, Tercera Temporada. *Comunicaciones* 16:141–148.

López Luján, Leonardo
2012 El *tepetlacalli* de la colección Leof: imagen cuatripartita del tiempo y el espacio. *Estudios de Cultura Náhuatl* 43:7–46.

López Zárate, José Leonardo
2014 Instrumentos bélicos en la imaginería zapoteca prehispánica. In *Zaachila y su historia prehispánica: Memoria del quincuagésimo aniversario del descubrimiento de las tumbas 1 y 2*, edited by Ismael G. Vicente Cruz and Gonzalo Sánchez Santiago, pp. 219–242. CONACULTA, Oaxaca, Mexico.

Lothrop, Samuel Kirkland
1924 *Tulum: An Archaeological Study of the East Coast of Yucatan*. Carnegie Institution of Washington, Publication 335. Washington, D.C.

Lounsbury, Floyd G.
1974 The inscription of the sarcophagus lid at Palenque. In *Primera Mesa Redonda de Palenque*, Part 2, edited by Merle Greene Robertson, pp. 5–19. Robert Louis Stevenson School, Pebble Beach, California.
1978 Maya numeration, computation, and calendrical astronomy. In *Dictionary of Scientific Biography*, edited by Charles C. Gillispie, Vol. 15, pp. 759–818. Charles Scribner's Sons, New York.
1988 A Palenque king and the planet Jupiter. In *World Archaeoastronomy*, edited by Anthony F. Aveni, pp. 246–249. Cambridge University Press, Cambridge.

Lupo, Alessandro
1999 Nahualismo y tonalismo. *Arqueología Mexicana* VI (35): 16–23.

Lyman, Larry
1964 The verb syntagmemes of Choapan Zapotec. *Linguistics* 7:16–41.

Lyman, Larry and Rosemary Lyman
1977 Choapan Zapotec phonology. In *Studies in Otomanguean Phonology*, edited by William R. Merrifield, pp. 137–161. Summer Institute of Linguistics, Publications in Linguistics No. 54. University of Texas at Arlington.

M

Macgowan, Kenneth
1945 The orientation of Middle American sites. *American Antiquity* 11(2):118.

MacLaury, Robert E.
1989 Zapotec body-part locatives: prototypes and metaphoric extensions. *International Journal of American Linguistics* 55(2):119–154.

MacNeish, Richard S.
1962 *Second Annual Report of the Tehuacán Archaeological-Botanical Project*. R. S. Peabody Foundation for Archaeology, Phillips Academy, Andover, Massachusetts.

Macri, Martha J. and Laura M. Stark
1993 *A sign catalog of the La Mojarra script*. Monograph 5 of the Pre-Columbian Art Research Institute. San Francisco.

Malmström, Vincent H.
1992 Geographical diffusion and calendrics in pre-Columbian Mesoamerica. *The Geographical Review* 82(2):113–127.

Manzanilla, Linda R.
2009 Corporate life in apartment and barrio compounds at Teotihuacan, central Mexico: craft specialization, hierarchy, and ethnicity. In *Domestic Life in Prehispanic Capitals: A Study of Specialization, Hierarchy, and Ethnicity,* edited by Linda R. Manzanilla and Claude Chapdelaine, pp. 21–42. Memoirs of the University of Michigan Museum of Anthropology, No. 46. Ann Arbor.

Manzanilla, Linda R., Xim Bokhimi, Dolores Tenorio, Melania Jiménez-Reyes, Edgar Rosales, Cira Martínez, and Marcus C. Winter
2017 Procedencia de la mica de Teotihuacan: control de los recursos suntuarios foráneos por los élites gobernantes. *Anales de Antropología* 51:23–38.

Marcus, Joyce
1972 Field report on Zapotec monuments, Parts 1 and 2. Manuscript prepared for Ford Foundation.
1973 Territorial organization of the lowland Classic Maya. *Science* 180:911–916.
1974 The iconography of power among the Classic Maya. *World Archaeology* 6(1):83–94.
1975 The Zapotec calendar. Submitted to the National Endowment for the Humanities, Washington, D.C.
1976a The iconography of militarism at Monte Albán and neighboring sites in the Valley of Oaxaca. In *The Origins of Religious Art and Iconography in Preclassic Mesoamerica*, edited by Henry B. Nicholson, pp. 123–139. Latin American Center at the University of California at Los Angeles.
1976b An analysis of the ancient Zapotec writing system. Report to National Endowment for the Humanities, Washington, D.C.
1976c The origins of Mesoamerican writing. *Annual Review of Anthropology* 5:35–67.
1976d *Emblem and State in the Classic Maya Lowlands*. Dumbarton Oaks Research Library and Collection, Washington, D.C.
1978 Archaeology and religion: A comparison of the Zapotec and Maya. *World Archaeology* 10:172–191.
1980 Zapotec writing. *Scientific American* 242:50–64.
1983a The genetic model and the linguistic divergence of the Otomangueans. In *The Cloud People: Divergent Evolution of the Zapotec and Mixtec Civilizations*, edited by Kent V. Flannery and Joyce Marcus, pp. 4–9. Academic Press, New York.
1983b Rethinking the Zapotec urn. In *The Cloud People: Divergent Evolution of the Zapotec and Mixtec Civilizations*, edited by Kent V. Flannery and Joyce Marcus, pp. 144–148. Academic Press, New York.
1983c Changing patterns of stone monuments after the fall of Monte Albán, A.D. 600-900. In *The Cloud People: Divergent Evolution of the Zapotec and Mixtec Civilizations*, edited by Kent V. Flannery and Joyce Marcus, pp. 191–197. Academic Press, New York.
1983d Stone monuments and tomb murals of Monte Albán IIIa. In *The Cloud People: Divergent Evolution of the Zapotec and Mixtec Civilizations*, edited by Kent V. Flannery and Joyce Marcus, pp. 137–143. Academic Press, New York.
1983e Zapotec religion. In *The Cloud People: Divergent Evolution of the Zapotec and Mixtec Civilizations*, edited by Kent V. Flannery and Joyce Marcus, pp. 345–351. Academic Press, New York.
1983f The first appearance of Zapotec writing and calendrics. In *The Cloud People: Divergent Evolution of the Zapotec and Mixtec Civilizations*, edited by Kent V. Flannery and Joyce Marcus, pp. 91–96. Academic Press, New York.
1983g Aztec military campaigns against the Zapotecs: The documentary evidence. In *The Cloud People: Divergent Evolution of the Zapotec and Mixtec Civilizations*, edited by Kent V. Flannery and Joyce Marcus, pp. 314–318. Academic Press, New York.
1983h The style of the Huamelulpan stone monuments. In *The Cloud People: Divergent Evolution of the Zapotec and Mixtec Civilizations*, edited by Kent V. Flannery and Joyce Marcus, pp. 125–126. Academic Press, New York.
1983i Lintel 2 at Xoxocotlán. In *The Cloud People: Divergent Evolution of the Zapotec and Mixtec Civilizations*, edited by Kent V. Flannery and Joyce Marcus, pp. 150–152. Academic Press, New York.
1984 Monumentos mayas en el Museo "Rufino Tamayo," Oaxaca. *Estudios de Cultura Maya*, Vol. XV, pp. 97–115. Universidad Nacional Autónoma de México, Mexico City.
1987 *The Inscriptions of Calakmul: Royal Marriage at a Maya City in Campeche, Mexico*. Technical Report 21, University of Michigan Museum of Anthropology, Ann Arbor.
1989a Zapotec chiefdoms and the nature of Formative religions. In *Regional Perspectives on the Olmec*, edited by Robert J. Sharer and David C. Grove, pp. 148–197. School of American Research and Cambridge University Press, Santa Fe, New Mexico.
1989b From centralized systems to city-states: possible models for the Epiclassic. In *Mesoamerica after the Decline of Teotihuacan A.D. 700-900*, edited by Richard A. Diehl and Janet Catherine Berlo, pp. 201–208. Dumbarton Oaks Research Library and Collection, Washington, D.C.
1992a *Mesoamerican Writing Systems: Propaganda, Myth, and History in Four Ancient Civilizations*. Princeton University Press, New Jersey.
1992b Royal families, royal texts: examples from the Zapotec and Maya. In *Mesoamerican Elites: An Archaeological Assessment*, edited by Diane Z. Chase and Arlen F. Chase, pp. 221–241. University of Oklahoma Press, Norman.
1992c Dynamic cycles of Mesoamerican states. *National Geographic Research & Exploration* 8(4):392–411. Washington, D.C.
1994 A Zapotec inauguration in comparative perspective. In *Caciques and Their People: a volume in honor of Ronald Spores*, edited by Joyce Marcus and Judith Francis Zeitlin, pp. 245–274. Anthropological Papers of the University of Michigan Museum of Anthropology, No. 89. Ann Arbor.
1995 Writing, literacy, and performance in the New and Old Worlds. *Cambridge Archaeological Journal* 5(2):325–331.
1996 Writing systems. In *Encyclopedia of Cultural Anthropology*, edited by David Levinson and Melvin Ember, Vol. 4, pp. 1387–1391. Human Relations Area Files at Yale University. A Henry Holt Reference Book. Henry Holt and Company, New York.

1998a *Women's Ritual in Formative Oaxaca: Figurine-making, Divination, Death and the Ancestors*. Memoirs of the University of Michigan Museum of Anthropology, No. 33. Ann Arbor.

1998b The peaks and valleys of ancient states: an extension of the Dynamic Model. In *Archaic States*, edited by Gary M. Feinman and Joyce Marcus, pp. 59–94. School of American Research Press, Santa Fe, New Mexico.

1999a Early architecture in the Valley of Oaxaca: 1350 B.C.-A.D. 500. In *Mesoamerican Architecture as a Cultural Symbol*, edited by Jeff Karl Kowalski, pp. 58–75. Oxford University Press, Oxford.

1999b Men's and women's ritual in Formative Oaxaca. In *Social Patterns in Pre-Classic Mesoamerica,* edited by David C. Grove and Rosemary A. Joyce, pp. 67–96. Dumbarton Oaks Research Library and Collection, Washington, D.C.

2000 Cinco mitos sobre la guerra maya. In *La Guerra entre los Antiguos Mayas: Memoria de la Primera Mesa Redonda de Palenque, Mexico*, edited by Silvia Trejo, pp. 225–243. Instituto Nacional de Antropología e Historia, Mexico.

2001a Epigraphy: Zapotec writing. In *The Oxford Encyclopedia of Mesoamerican Cultures: The Civilization of Mexico and Central America,* edited by Davíd Carrasco, Vol. 1, pp. 387–388. Oxford University Press, Oxford.

2001b Breaking the glass ceiling: the strategies of royal women in ancient states. In *Gender in Pre-Hispanic America*, edited by Cecelia F. Klein, pp. 305–340. Dumbarton Oaks Research Library and Collection, Washington, D.C.

2002 Carved stones from the Sola Valley. In *The Sola Valley and the Monte Albán State: A Study of Zapotec Imperial Expansion,* by Andrew K. Balkansky, pp. 103–121. Memoirs of the University of Michigan Museum of Anthropology, No. 36. Ann Arbor.

2003a The Maya and Teotihuacan. In *The Maya and Teotihuacan: Reinterpreting Early Classic Interaction*, edited by Geoffrey E. Braswell, pp. 337–356. University of Texas Press, Austin.

2003b Monumentality in archaic states: lessons learned from large-scale excavations of the past. In *Theory and Practice in Mediterranean Archaeology,* edited by John K. Papadopoulos and Richard M. Leventhal, pp. 115–134. Cotsen Institute of Archaeology, University of California at Los Angeles.

2003c Escritura y representación en el Viejo y el Nuevo Mundo. In *Escritura Zapoteca: 2500 años de historia*, edited by María de los Ángeles Romero Frizzi, pp. 73–93. CIESAS, CONACULTA-INAH.

2005 Place glyphs and polity boundaries: two Zapotec cases. In *Painted Books and Indigenous Knowledge in Mesoamerica*, edited by Elizabeth Hill Boone, pp. 91–108. Middle American Research Institute, Tulane University, New Orleans.

2006a Mesoamerica: scripts. In *Encyclopedia of Language and Linguistics*, Vol. VIII, edited by Peter T. Daniels, pp. 16–25. Second edition. Elsevier Press, Oxford & San Diego.

2006b Identifying elites and their strategies. In *Intermediate Elites in Pre-Columbian States and Empires*, edited by Christina M. Elson and R. Alan Covey, pp. 212–246. University of Arizona Press, Tucson.

2006c The roles of ritual and technology in Mesoamerican water management. In *Agricultural Strategies*, edited by Joyce Marcus and Charles Stanish, pp. 221–254. Monograph 50, Cotsen Institute of Archaeology series, University of California at Los Angeles.

2007 Rethinking ritual. In *The Archaeology of Ritual*, edited by Evangelos Kyriakidis, pp. 43–76. Cotsen Institute of Archaeology, University of California at Los Angeles.

2008a The archaeological evidence for social evolution. *Annual Review of Anthropology* 37:251–266.

2008b *Monte Albán*. Fideicomiso Historia de las Américas, Serie Ciudades. El Colegio de México, Fondo de Cultura Económica, Mexico.

2009a Understanding houses, compounds, and neighborhoods. In *Domestic Life in Prehispanic Capitals*, edited by Linda Manzanilla and Claude Chapdelaine, pp. 256–266. Memoirs of the University of Michigan Museum of Anthropology, No. 46. Ann Arbor.

2009b How Monte Albán represented itself. In *The Art of Urbanism*, edited by William L. Fash and Leonardo López Luján, pp. 77–110. Dumbarton Oaks Research Library and Collection, Washington, D.C.

2012 Maya political cycling and the story of the *Kaan* polity. In *The Ancient Maya of Mexico: Reinterpreting the Past of the Northern Maya Lowlands*, edited by Geoffrey E. Braswell, pp. 88–116. Equinox Press, London.

2019 Studying figurines. *Journal of Archaeological Research* 27(1):1–47.

Marcus, Joyce and Gary M. Feinman

1998 Introduction. In *Archaic States*, edited by Gary M. Feinman and Joyce Marcus, pp. 3–13. School of American Research Press, Santa Fe, New Mexico.

Marcus, Joyce and Kent V. Flannery

1978 Ethnoscience of the sixteenth-century Valley Zapotec. In *The Nature and Status of Ethnobotany*, edited by Richard I. Ford, pp. 51–79. Anthropological Papers of the University of Michigan Museum of Anthropology, No. 67. Ann Arbor.

1983 The Postclassic balkanization of Oaxaca: an introduction to the Late Postclassic. In *The Cloud People: Divergent Evolution of the Zapotec and Mixtec Civilizations*, edited by Kent V. Flannery and Joyce Marcus, pp. 217–226. Academic Press, New York.

1990 Science and science fiction in Postclassic Oaxaca: or, yes Virginia, there is a Monte Albán IV. In *Debating Oaxaca Archaeology*, edited by Joyce Marcus, Anthropological Papers of the University of Michigan Museum of Anthropology, No. 84, pp. 191–205. Ann Arbor.

1994 Ancient Zapotec ritual and religion: an application of the direct historical approach. In *The Ancient Mind*, edited by Colin Renfrew and Ezra B.W. Zubrow, pp. 55–74. Cambridge University Press, Cambridge.

1996 *Zapotec Civilization: How Urban Society Evolved in Mexico's Oaxaca Valley*. Thames and Hudson, New York.

Markens, Robert J.

2004 Ceramic chronology in the Valley of Oaxaca, Mexico, during the Late Classic and Postclassic Periods and the Organization of Ceramic Production. PhD dissertation, Department of Anthropology, Brandeis University, Waltham, Massachusetts.

2008 Advances in defining the Classic-Postclassic portion of the Valley of Oaxaca ceramic chronology: occurrence and phyletic seriation. In *After Monte Albán: Transformation and Negotiation in Oaxaca, Mexico*, edited by Jeffrey P. Blomster, pp. 49–94. University Press of Colorado, Boulder.

2014 Análisis del conjunto arquitectónico de las tumbas 1 y 2 de Zaachila. In *Zaachila y su historia prehispánica: Memoria del quincuagésimo aniversario del descubrimiento de las tumbas 1 y 2*, edited by Ismael G. Vicente Cruz and Gonzalo Sánchez Santiago, pp. 75–98. CONACULTA, Secretaría de las Culturas y Artes de Oaxaca, Mexico.

Markens, Robert, Marcus Winter, and Cira Martínez López
2008 Ethnohistory, oral history, and archaeology at Macuilxochitl: perspectives on the Postclassic period (800–1521 CE) in the Valley of Oaxaca. In *After Monte Albán: Transformation and Negotiation in Oaxaca, Mexico*, edited by Jeffrey P. Blomster, pp. 193–218. University Press of Colorado, Boulder.

Markman, Charles W.
1981 *Prehispanic Settlement Dynamics in Central Oaxaca, Mexico: A View from the Miahuatlán Valley*. Vanderbilt University Publications in Anthropology, No. 26. Nashville, Tennessee.

Marlett, Stephen A. and Velma B. Pickett
1987 The syllable structure and aspect morphology of Isthmus Zapotec. *International Journal of American Linguistics* 53(4):398–422.

Marquina, Ignacio
1951 *Arquitectura prehispánica*. Instituto Nacional de Antropología e Historia, Mexico.
1964 *Arquitectura prehispánica*. Second edition. Instituto Nacional de Antropología e Historia, Mexico.

Martin, Simon
2000 At the periphery: the movement, modification and re-use of early monuments in the environs of Tikal. In *The Sacred and the Profane: Architecture and Identity in the Southern Maya Lowlands*, edited by Pierre R. Colas, Kai Delvendahl, Marcus Kuhnert, and Annette Schubart, pp. 51–61. Acta Mesoamericana 10. Verlag Anton Saurwein, Hamburg, Germany.
2003 In line of the founder: a view of dynastic politics at Tikal. In *Tikal: Dynasties, Foreigners & Affairs of State,* edited by Jeremy A. Sabloff, pp. 3–45. School of American Research Press, Santa Fe, New Mexico.

Martin, Simon and Nikolai Grube
2000 *Chronicle of the Maya Kings and Queens*. First edition. Thames and Hudson, London.
2008 *Chronicle of the Maya Kings and Queens*. Second edition. Thames and Hudson, London.

Martínez Gracida, Manuel
1883 *Colección de cuadros sinópticos de los pueblos, haciendas y ranchos del Estado libre y soberano de Oaxaca*. Gobierno del Estado de Oaxaca, Oaxaca, Mexico.
1910 *Los indios oaxaqueños y sus monumentos arqueológicos*. 5 volumes. Biblioteca Pública Central del Estado de Oaxaca, Mexico.

Martínez López, Cira
1994 La cerámica de estilo teotihuacano en Monte Albán. In *Monte Albán: Estudios Recientes*, coordinated by Marcus C. Winter, pp. 25–54. Contribución del Proyecto Monte Albán 1992-1994. Oaxaca de Juárez, Oaxaca, Mexico.

Martínez López, Cira, Marcus Winter, and Pedro Antonio Juárez
1995 Entierros humanos del Proyecto Especial Monte Albán 1992-1994. In *Entierros Humanos de Monte Albán: Dos Estudios*, coordinated by Marcus Winter, pp. 79–247. Centro Regional del Instituto Nacional de Antropología e Historia, Oaxaca, Mexico.

Masson, Marilyn A.
2000 *In the Realm of Nachan Kan: Postclassic Maya Archaeology at Laguna de On, Belize*. University Press of Colorado, Niwot.
2001 El sobrenatural Cocijo y poder de linaje en la antigua sociedad zapoteca. *Mesoamérica* año 22, número 41:1–30.

Masson, Marilyn A. and Heather Orr
1998a The role of Zapotec genealogical records in late Precolumbian Valley of Oaxaca political history. *Mexicon* XX(1):10–16.
1998b The writing on the wall: political representation and sacred geography at Monte Alban. In *The Sowing and the Dawning: Termination, Dedication, and Transformation in the Archaeological and Ethnographic Record of Mesoamerica*, edited by Shirley Boteler Mock, pp. 165–175. University of New Mexico Press, Albuquerque.

Mata, Juan de
1580 Relación de Teozapotlan. In *Papeles de Nueva España: segunda serie, geografía y estadística*, Vol. 4, edited by Francisco del Paso y Troncoso, pp. 190–195. Est. Tipográfico "Sucesores de Rivadeneyra," Madrid.

Matrícula de Tributos
1980 *Matrícula de Tributos* (Códice de Moctezuma), edited by Frances F. Berdan and Jacqueline de Durand-Forest. Akademische druck- und Verlagsanstalt, Graz, Austria.

Mattessich, Richard
2002 The oldest writings, and inventory tags of Egypt. *The Accounting Historians Journal* 29(1):195–208.

McCafferty, Geoffrey G.
1994a The Mixteca-Puebla stylistic tradition at Early Postclassic Cholula. In *Mixteca-Puebla: Discoveries and Research in Mesoamerican Art and Archaeology*, edited by Henry B. Nicholson and Eloise Quiñones Keber, pp. 53–77. Labyrinthos, Culver City, California.
1994b The conquered women of Cacaxtla: gender identity or gender's ideology? *Ancient Mesoamerica* 5(2):159–172.

McCafferty, Sharisse D. and Geoffrey G. McCafferty
1994 Engendering Tomb 7 at Monte Albán: respinning an old yarn. *Current Anthropology* 35(2):143–166.

Mead, Sidney M.
1985 Nga Timunga Me Nga Paringa o Te Mana Maori: The Ebb and Flow of Mana Maori and the Changing Context of Maori Art. In *Te Maori: Art from New Zealand Collections*, edited by Sidney M. Mead, pp. 20–36. Harry N. Abrams, New York.

Meissner, Nathan J., Katherine E. South, and Andrew K. Balkansky
2013 Figurine embodiment and household ritual in an early Mixtec village. *Journal de la Société des Américanistes* 99-1:7–43.

Méluzin, Sylvia
1992 The Tuxtla Statuette: steps toward decipherment based on La Mojarra Stela 1. *Latin American Antiquity* 3(4):283–297.
1995 *Further investigations of the Tuxtla script: an inscribed mask and the La Mojarra Stela 1*. Papers of the New World Archaeological Foundation 65. Brigham Young University, Provo, Utah.

Méndez Martínez, Enrique
1988 La Tumba 5 de Huijazoo. *Arqueología* 2:7–16. Dirección de Monumentos Prehispánicos, Instituto Nacional de Antropología e Historia, México.

Merrill, Elizabeth D.
2008 Tilquiapan Zapotec. *Journal of the International Phonetic Association* 38(1):107–114.

Michalowski, Piotr
1990 Early Mesopotamian communicative systems: art, literature, and writing. In *Investigating Artistic Environments in the Ancient Near East*, edited by Anne C. Gunter, pp. 53–69. Smithsonian Institution, Washington, D.C.
1993 Tokenism. *American Anthropologist* n.s. 95(4):996–999.
1994 Writing and literacy in early states: a Mesopotamianist perspective. In *Literacy: Interdisciplinary Conversations*, edited by Deborah Keller-Cohen, pp. 49–70. Hampton Press, Cresskill, New Jersey.
1996 Cuneiform: origins. In *The World's Writing Systems*, edited by Peter T. Daniels and William Bright, pp. 33–36. Oxford University Press, Oxford and New York.

Middleton, William D., Gary M. Feinman, and Guillermo Molina Villegas
1998 Tomb use and reuse in Oaxaca, Mexico. *Ancient Mesoamerica* 9(2):297–307.

Miles, Suzanne Whitelaw
1952 An analysis of modern Middle American calendars. In *Acculturation in the Americas. International Congress of Americanists Proceedings and Selected Papers*, edited by Sol Tax, pp. 273–284. University of Chicago Press, Chicago.

Miller, Arthur G.
1973 *The Mural Painting of Teotihuacan*. Dumbarton Oaks Research Library and Collection, Washington, D.C.
1982 On the Edge of the Sea: Mural Painting at Tancah-Tulum, Quintana Roo, Mexico. Dumbarton Oaks Research Library and Collection, Washington, D.C.
1991 The carved stela in Tomb 5, Suchilquitongo, Oaxaca, Mexico. *Ancient Mesoamerica* 2:215–224.
1995 *The Painted Tombs of Oaxaca, Mexico: Living with the Dead*. Cambridge University Press, New York.

Millon, Clara
1973 Painting, writing, and polity in Teotihuacan, Mexico. *American Antiquity* 38(3):294–314.
1988 A reexamination of the Teotihuacan Tassel Headdress insignia. In *Feathered Serpents and Flowering Trees: Reconstructing the Murals of Teotihuacan*, edited by Kathleen Berrin, pp. 114–134. The Fine Arts Museum, San Francisco.

Millon, René
1973a Urna de Monte Albán IIIA encontrada en Teotihuacan. *Boletín del Instituto Nacional de Antropología e Historia* 29:42–44.
1973b *The Teotihuacan Map*, Part 1. University of Texas Press, Austin.
1981 Teotihuacan: city, state, and civilization. In *Archaeology*, edited by Jeremy A. Sabloff, pp. 198–243. Supplement to the Handbook of Middle American Indians, Vol. 1, Victoria R. Bricker, general editor. University of Texas Press, Austin.
1992 Teotihuacan studies: from 1950 to 1990 and beyond. In *Art, Ideology, and the City of Teotihuacan*, edited by Janet Catherine Berlo, pp. 339–429. Dumbarton Oaks Research Library and Collection, Washington, D.C.

Mora-Marín, David F.
1997 The origins of Maya writing: the case for portable objects. In *U Mut Maya VII*, edited by Tom and Carolyn Jones, pp. 133–164. Humboldt State University, Arcata, California.
2005 Kaminaljuyu Stela 10: script classification and linguistic affiliation. *Ancient Mesoamerica* 16:63–87.
2009 Early Olmec writing: reading format and reading order. *Latin American Antiquity* 20(3):395–412.
2018 Izapan writing: classification and preliminary observations. *Ancient Mesoamerica* 29:93–112.

Morley, Sylvanus G.
1915 *An Introduction to the Study of Maya Hieroglyphs*. Smithsonian Institution, Bureau of American Ethnology Bulletin 57. Government Printing Office, Washington, D.C.

Morris, Craig and Adriana von Hagen
2011 *The Incas: Lords of the Four Quarters*. Thames and Hudson, London, England.

Moser, Christopher L.
1969a Tomb 1 at Barrio del Rosario, Huitzo, Oaxaca. *Katunob* 7(1):17–21.
1969b La Tumba 1 del Barrio del Rosario, Huitzo, Oaxaca. *Boletín del Instituto Nacional de Antropología* 36:41–47. México, D. F.
1973 *Human Decapitation in Ancient Mesoamerica*. Studies in Precolumbian Art and Archaeology, No. 11. Dumbarton Oaks Research Library and Collection, Washington, D.C.

Motolinía, Toribio
1951 *Motolinía's History of the Indians of New Spain*. Academy of Franciscan History, William Byrd Press, Richmond, Virginia.

Müller, Florencia
1948 Chimalacatlan. *Acta Antropológica* Vol. 3, Número 1. Escuela Nacional de Antropología e Historia, Mexico City.

Munro, Pamela
2002 Hierarchical pronouns in discourse: third-person pronouns in San Lucas Quiaviní Zapotec narratives. *Southwest Journal of Linguistics* 21:37–65.
2011 Evidence about proto-Zapotec from a Colonial document. In *Tradition and Innovation in Mesoamerican Cultural History: A Homage to Tatiana A. Proskouriakoff*, edited by Roberto Cantú and Aaron Sonnenschein, pp. 39–53. Lincom Studies in Anthropology, No. 16. Lincom Europa, Muenchen.

Munro, Pamela and Felipe López
1999 *San Lucas Quiaviní Zapotec Dictionary*. UCLA Chicano Studies Research Center Press, University of California at Los Angeles.

N

Nalda, Enrique, editor
2004 *Los cautivos de Dzibanché*. Instituto Nacional de Antropología e Historia, Mexico.

Navarijo Ornelas, María de Lourdes
2008 Las aves en los contextos funerarios. In *La pintura mural prehispánica en Oaxaca, México III*, Tomo III: Estudios, edited by Beatriz de la Fuente, pp. 245–283. Instituto de Investigaciones Estéticas, Universidad Nacional Autónoma de México, México.

Navarrete, Carlos
1974 *The Olmec Rock Carvings at Pijijiapan, Chiapas, Mexico and Other Olmec Pieces from Chiapas and Guatemala.* Papers of the New World Archaeological Foundation No. 35. Brigham Young University, Provo, Utah.

Nellis, Donald G. and Barbara E. Hollenbach
1980 Fortis versus lenis in Cajones Zapotec phonology. *International Journal of American Linguistics* 46:92–105.

Nellis, Neil and Jane Goodner de Nellis
1983 *Diccionario de Juárez: zapoteco-español, español-zapoteco: Ca titsa' qui'ri'u.* Instituto Lingüístico de Verano, Serie de Vocabularios y Diccionarios Indígenas "Mariano Silva y Aceves," número 27. Mexico.

Neys, Horace and Hasso von Winning
1946 The treble scroll symbol in the Teotihuacan and Zapotec cultures. In *Notes on Middle American Archaeology and Ethnology* 74:82–89. Carnegie Institution of Washington, Washington, D.C.

Nicholson, Henry B.
1960 The Mixteca-Puebla concept in Mesoamerican archaeology: A reexamination. In *Men and Cultures: Selected Papers from the Fifth International Congress of Anthropological and Ethnological Sciences, September 1-9, 1956*, edited by Anthony Wallace, pp. 612–617. University of Pennsylvania, Philadelphia.
1971 Religion in Pre-Hispanic Central Mexico. In *Archaeology of Northern Mesoamerica*, Part 1, edited by Gordon F. Ekholm and Ignacio Bernal, pp. 395–446. Handbook of Middle American Indians, Vol. 10, Robert Wauchope, general editor. University of Texas Press, Austin.
1973 Phoneticism in the late pre-Hispanic Central Mexican writing systems. In *Mesoamerican Writing Systems*, edited by Elizabeth P. Benson, pp. 1–46. Dumbarton Oaks Research Library and Collection, Washington, D.C.
1982 The Mixteca-Puebla concept revisited. In *The Art and Iconography of Late Post-Classic Central Mexico*, edited by Elizabeth Hill Boone, pp. 227–254. Dumbarton Oaks Research Library and Collection, Washington, D.C.

Nicholson, Henry B. and Eloise Quiñones Keber
1994 Introduction. In *Mixteca-Puebla: Discoveries and Research in Mesoamerican Art and Archaeology*, edited by Henry B. Nicholson and Eloise Quiñones Keber, pp. vii–xv. Labyrinthos, Culver City, California.

Nissen, Hans J.
1986 The Archaic texts from Uruk. *World Archaeology* 17:317–334.

Nissen, Hans J., Peter Damerow, and Robert K. Englund
1993 *Archaic Bookkeeping: Early Writing and Techniques of Economic Administration in the Ancient Near East.* University of Chicago Press, Chicago.

Noguera, Eduardo
1940 Excavations at Tehuacan. In *The Maya and Their Neighbors*, edited by Clarence L. Hay, Ralph Linton, Samuel K. Lothrop, Harry Shapiro, and George C. Vaillant, pp. 306–319. Appleton-Century, New York.

Norman, V. Garth
1973 *Izapa Sculpture*. Part 1: Album. Papers of the New World Archaeological Foundation, No. 30. Brigham Young University, Provo, Utah.
1976 *Izapa Sculpture*. Part 2: Text. Papers of the New World Archaeological Foundation, No. 30. Brigham Young University, Provo, Utah.

Nuttall, Zelia
1902 *Codex Nuttall, facsimile of an ancient Mexican Codex Belonging to Lord Zouche of Harynworth, England.* Cambridge, Massachusetts.
1975 *The Codex Nuttall: A Picture Manuscript from Ancient Mexico.* Introduction by Arthur G. Miller. Dover Publications, New York.

O

Oliver, James P.
1955 Architectural similarities of Mitla and Yagul. *Mesoamerican Notes* 4:49–68. Department of Anthropology, Mexico City College, Mexico.

Oliveros, Arturo
1997 Dainzú-Macuilxóchitl. *Arqueología Mexicana* 5(26):4–29. Editorial Raíces, México.

Operstein, Natalie
2003 Personal pronouns in Zapotec and Zapotecan. *International Journal of American Linguistics* 69(2):154–185.
2012 Proto-Zapotec *tty/*ty and *ttz/*tz. *International Journal of American Linguistics* 78:1–40.
2017 Suppletion in Zapotec. *Linguistics* 55(4):739–782.

Oppenheim, A. Leo
1959 An operation device in Mesopotamian bureaucracy. *Journal of Near Eastern Studies* 18:121–128.

Orozco y Berra, Manuel
1864 *Geografía de las lenguas y carta etnográfica de México, precedidas de un ensayo de clasificación de las mismas lenguas y de apuntes para las inmigraciones de las tribus.* Imprenta de J. M. Andrade and F. Escalante, Mexico.

Orr, Heather S.
1997 Power Games in the Late Formative Valley of Oaxaca: The Ballplayer Carvings at Dainzú. PhD dissertation, Department of Art and Art History, University of Texas, Austin.
2001 Processional rituals and shrine sites: the politics of sacred space in the Late Formative Valley of Oaxaca. In *Landscape and Power in Ancient Mesoamerica*, edited by Rex Koontz, Kathryn Reese-Taylor, and Annabeth Headrick, pp. 55–79. Westview Press, Boulder, Colorado.
2003 Stone balls and masked men: ballgame as combat ritual, Dainzú, Oaxaca. *Ancient America* 5:73–104. Center for Ancient American Studies, Barnardsville, North Carolina.

Oudijk, Michel Robert
1998 La genealogía de San Lucas Quiaviní. *Acervos* 10:21–25. Oaxaca, Mexico.

2000 *Historiography of the Bènizàa: The Postclassic and Early Colonial Periods (1000–1600 A.D.)*. Research School CNWS Vol. 84. Leiden University, Leiden, The Netherlands.
2002 The Zapotec city-state. In *A Comparative Study of Thirty City-State Cultures, Supplement*, edited by Mogens Hansen, pp. 73–90. The Royal Danish Academy of Sciences and Letters, Copenhagen, Denmark.
2008 The Postclassic period in the Valley of Oaxaca: the archaeological and ethnohistorical records. In *After Monte Albán: Transformation and Negotiation in Oaxaca, Mexico*, edited by Jeffrey P. Blomster, pp. 95–118. University Press of Colorado, Boulder.

Oudijk, Michel and Maarten Jansen
1998 Tributo y territorio en el Lienzo de Guevea. *Cuadernos del Sur* 12:53–102. CIESAS, Oaxaca, Mexico.
2000 Changing history in the Lienzos de Guevea and Santo Domingo Petapa. *Ethnohistory* 47(2):281–331.

P

Paddock, John
1966a Oaxaca in ancient Mesoamerica. In *Ancient Oaxaca: Discoveries in Mexican Archeology and History*, pp. 83–242. Stanford University Press, Stanford, California.
1966b (ed.) *Ancient Oaxaca: Discoveries in Mexican Archeology and History*. Stanford University Press, Stanford, California.
1983a *Lord 5 Flower's Family: Rulers of Zaachila and Cuilapan*. Vanderbilt University Publications in Anthropology No. 29. Nashville, Tennessee.
1983b Mixtec impact on the Postclassic Valley of Oaxaca. In *The Cloud People: Divergent Evolution of the Zapotec and Mixtec Civilizations*, edited by Kent V. Flannery and Joyce Marcus, pp. 272–277. Academic Press, New York.
1983c The Oaxaca Barrio at Teotihuacan. In *The Cloud People: Divergent Evolution of the Zapotec and Mixtec Civilizations*, edited by Kent V. Flannery and Joyce Marcus, pp. 170–175. Academic Press, New York.
1983d Lambityeco. In *The Cloud People: Divergent Evolution of the Zapotec and Mixtec Civilizations*, edited by Kent V. Flannery and Joyce Marcus, pp. 197–204. Academic Press, New York.
1983e Monte Albán II in the Yagul-Caballito Blanco area. In *The Cloud People: Divergent Evolution of the Zapotec and Mixtec Civilizations*, edited by Kent V. Flannery and Joyce Marcus, pp. 115–117. Academic Press, New York.
1983f Comments on the Lienzos of Huilotepec and Guevea. In *The Cloud People: Divergent Evolution of the Zapotec and Mixtec Civilizations*, edited by Kent V. Flannery and Joyce Marcus, pp. 308–313. Academic Press, New York.

Paddock, John, Joseph Mogor, and Michael Lind
1968 Lambityeco Tomb 2: a preliminary report. *Boletín de Estudios Oaxaqueños* No. 25. Mitla, Oaxaca.

Palomares Rodríguez, María Teresa
2013 The Oaxaca Barrio in Teotihuacan: mortuary customs and ethnicity in Mesoamerica's greatest metropolis. Master's thesis, Southern Illinois University, Carbondale.

Pareyón Moreno, Eduardo
1960 Exploraciones arqueológicas en la Ciudad Vieja de Quiotepec, Oaxaca. *Revista Mexicana de Estudios Antropológicos* 16:97–104.

Parsons, Elsie Clews
1931 Curanderos in Oaxaca. *Scientific Monthly* 32:60–68.
1936 *Mitla: Town of the Souls and other Zapoteco-Speaking Pueblos of Oaxaca, Mexico*. University of Chicago Press, Chicago.

Peeler, Damon E. and Marcus Winter
1992 Mesoamerican site orientations and their relationship to the 260-day ritual period. *Notas Mesoamericanas* 14:37–62.
1995 Building J at Monte Albán: a correction and reassessment of the astronomical hypothesis. *Latin American Antiquity* 6(4):362–369.

Peñafiel, Antonio
1885 *Nombres geográficos de México*. Catálogo alfabético de los nombres de lugar pertenecientes al idioma "Nahuatl." Estudio jeroglífico de la Matrícula de los Tributos del Códice Mendocino. 2 volumes. Secretaría de Fomento, México.
1890 *Monumentos del arte mexicano antiguo*. 3 volumes in 5 bindings. Berlin.
1893 *Arqueología zapoteca*. Trabajos para la exposición colombina de Chicago. Secretaría de Fomento, México.

Pérez Báez, Gabriela
2011 Spatial frames of reference preferences in Juchitán Zapotec. *Language Sciences* 33:943–960.

Pérez Báez, Gabriela and Terrence Kaufman
2016 Verb classes in Juchitán Zapotec. *Anthropological Linguistics* 58(3):217–257.

Peterson, David
1976 *Ancient Commerce*. PhD dissertation, Department of Anthropology, State University of New York at Binghamton.

Pickett, Velma B.
1953 Isthmus Zapotec verb analysis I. *International Journal of American Linguistics* 19:292–296.
1955 Isthmus Zapotec verb analysis II. *International Journal of American Linguistics* 21:217–232.
1959 *Castellano-Zapoteco, Zapoteco-Castellano*. Instituto Lingüístico de Verano, México, D.F.
1960 The grammatical hierarchy of Isthmus Zapotec. *Language* 36 3-101. Linguistic Society of America, Baltimore, Maryland.
1967 Isthmus Zapotec. In *Linguistics*, edited by Norman A. McQuown, pp. 291–310. Handbook of Middle American Indians, Vol. 5, Robert Wauchope, general editor. University of Texas Press, Austin.
1990 Comparación de dos 'dialectos' zapotecos. In *Homenaje a Jorge A. Suárez*, edited by Beatriz Garza Cuarón and Paulette Levy, pp. 407–436. El Colegio de México, México, D.F.

Pickett, Velma Bernice and collaborators
1988 *Vocabulario zapoteco del Istmo*. Serie de Vocabularios Indígenas Mariano Silva y Aceves, No. 3. Instituto Lingüístico de Verano, Mexico.

Pike, Eunice V.
1948 Problems in Zapotec tone analysis. *International Journal of American Linguistics* 14:161–170.

Pike, Kenneth L.
1945 Tone puns in Mixteco. *International Journal of American Linguistics* 11:129–139.

1948 *Tone Languages: A Technique for Determining the Number and Type of Pitch Contrasts in a Language, with Studies in Tonemic Substitution and Fusion*. University of Michigan Publications: Linguistics IV. University of Michigan Press, Ann Arbor.

Plumb, May Helena
2019 Conjunction in Colonial Valley Zapotec. *International Journal of American Linguistics* 85(2):213–245.

Pohl, John Martin Deland
1994 *The Politics of Symbolism in the Mixtec Codices*. Vanderbilt University Publications in Anthropology, Vol. 46. Nashville, Tennessee.
1999 The lintel paintings of Mitla and the function of the Mitla palaces. In *Mesoamerican Architecture as a Cultural Symbol*, edited by Jeff Karl Kowalski, pp. 176–197. Oxford University Press, New York.
2003a Ritual ideology and commerce in the southern Mexican highlands. In *The Postclassic Mesoamerican World*, edited by Michael E. Smith and Frances F. Berdan, pp. 172–177. The University of Utah Press, Salt Lake City.
2003b Royal marriage and confederacy building among the eastern Nahuas, Mixtecs, and Zapotecs. In *The Postclassic Mesoamerican World*, edited by Michael E. Smith and Frances F. Berdan, pp. 243–248. The University of Utah Press, Salt Lake City.
2005 The Arroyo Group lintel painting at Mitla, Oaxaca. In *Painted Books and Indigenous Knowledge in Mesoamerica: Manuscript Studies in Honor of Mary Elizabeth Smith*, edited by Elizabeth Hill Boone, pp. 109–127. Middle American Research Institute, Publication 69, Tulane University, New Orleans.

Pohl, John M. D. and Bruce E. Byland
1994 The Mixteca-Puebla style and Early Postclassic sociopolitical interaction. In *Mixteca-Puebla: Discoveries and Research in Mesoamerican Art and Archaeology*, edited by Henry B. Nicholson and Eloise Quiñones Keber, pp. 189–199. Labyrinthos, Culver City, California.

Pohl, John M. D. and Javier Urcid Serrano
2006 A Zapotec carved bone. In *The Princeton University Library Chronicle* 67(2):225–236.

Pohl, Mary E. D., Kevin O. Pope, and Christopher von Nagy
2002 Olmec origins of Mesoamerican writing. *Science* 298:1984–1987.

Pope, Maurice
1999 *The Story of Decipherment: From Egyptian Hieroglyphs to Maya Script*. Thames and Hudson, London and New York.

Postgate, Nicholas, Tao Wang, and Toby Wilkinson
1995 The evidence for early writing: utilitarian or ceremonial? *Antiquity* 69:459–480.

Powell, Barry B.
2009 *Writing: Theory and History of the Technology of Civilization*. Wiley-Blackwell, Oxford, UK.

Prem, Hanns J.
1971 Calendrics and writing in Mesoamerica. In *Observations on the Emergence of Civilization in Mesoamerica*, edited by Robert F. Heizer and John A. Graham, pp. 112–132. University of California Archaeological Research Facility, Contribution 11. Berkeley, California.
1973 A tentative classification of non-Maya inscriptions in Mesoamerica. *Indiana* 1:29–59.

Proskouriakoff, Tatiana
1946 *An Album of Maya Architecture*. Carnegie Institution of Washington, Publication 558. Washington, D.C.
1950 *A Study of Classic Maya Sculpture*. Carnegie Institution of Washington, Publication 593. Washington, D.C.
1960 Historical implications of a pattern of dates at Piedras Negras, Guatemala. *American Antiquity* 25(4):454–475.
1963 Historical data in the inscriptions of Yaxchilan, part 1. *Estudios de Cultura Maya* 3:149–167.
1964 Historical data in the inscriptions of Yaxchilan, part 2. *Estudios de Cultura Maya* 4:177–201.
1968 The jog and the jaguar signs in Maya writing. *American Antiquity* 33(2):247–251.
1973 The hand-grasping-fish and associated glyphs on Classic Maya monuments. In *Mesoamerican Writing Systems: A Conference at Dumbarton Oaks, October 30th and 31st*, edited by Elizabeth P. Benson, pp. 165–178. Dumbarton Oaks Library and Collection, Washington D.C.
1993 *Maya History*. University of Texas Press, Austin.

Q

Quibell, James E.
1898–1900 *Hierakonpolis*. Bernard Quaritch, London.

Quilter, Jeffrey
2002 Moche politics, religion, and warfare. *Journal of World Prehistory* 16(2):145–195.

Quiñones Keber, Eloise
1995 *Codex Telleriano-Remensis: Ritual, Divination, and History in a Pictorial Aztec Manuscript*. University of Texas Press, Austin.

Quirarte, Jacinto
1973 *Izapan-style Art: A Study of its Form and Meaning*. Studies in Pre-Columbian Art and Archaeology, No. 10. Dumbarton Oaks Research Library and Collection, Washington, D.C.
1977 Early art styles of Mesoamerica and Early Classic Maya art. In *The Origins of Maya Civilization*, edited by Richard E. W. Adams, pp. 249–283. University of New Mexico, Albuquerque.
1981 Tricephalic units in Olmec, Izapan-style and Maya art. In *The Olmec and Their Neighbors: Essays in Memory of Matthew W. Stirling*, edited by Elizabeth P. Benson, pp. 289–308. Dumbarton Oaks Research Library and Collection, Washington, D.C.
1982 The Santa Rita murals: a review. In *Aspects of the Mixteca-Puebla Style and Mixtec and Central American Culture in Southern Mesoamerica*, edited by Jennifer Brown and E. Wyllys Andrews V, pp. 43–59. Papers from a symposium organized by Doris Stone, Middle American Research Institute. Occasional Paper 4. Tulane University, New Orleans.

R

Rabin, Emily
1970 The Lambityeco friezes: notes on their content, with an appendix on C14 dates. *Boletín de Estudios Oaxaqueños*, No. 33. Mitla, Mexico.

Radin, Paul
1925 The distribution and phonetics of the Zapotec dialects: a preliminary sketch. *Journal de la Société des Americánistes de Paris* 17:27–76.
1930 Preliminary sketch of the Zapotec language. *Language* 6:64–85.

Rattray, Evelyn Childs
1990a New findings on the origins of Thin Orange ceramics. *Ancient Mesoamerica* 1:181–195.
1990b Nuevos hallazgos sobre los orígenes de la cerámica Anaranjada Delgado. *La época clásica: nuevos hallazgos, nuevas ideas*, edited by A. Cardoso, pp. 89–106. Instituto Nacional de Antropología e Historia, Mexico City.
1993 *The Oaxaca Barrio at Teotihuacan*. Instituto de Estudios Avanzados, Universidad de las Américas, Puebla, Mexico.
2001 *Teotihuacan: Ceramics, Chronology, and Cultural Trends*. University of Pittsburgh, Pittsburgh; Instituto Nacional de Antropología e Historia, Mexico City.

Rattray, Evelyn C. and Garman Harbottle
1992 Neutron activation analysis and numerical taxonomy of Thin Orange ceramics from the manufacturing sites of Río Carnero, Puebla, Mexico. In *Chemical Characterizations of Ceramic Pastes in Archaeology*, edited by Hector Neff, pp. 221–231. Prehistory Press, Madison, Wisconsin.

Ray, J. D.
1986 The emergence of writing in Egypt. *World Archaeology* 17(3):307–316.

Redmond, Elsa M.
1983 *A Fuego y Sangre: Early Zapotec Imperialism in the Cuicatlán Cañada, Oaxaca*. Memoirs of the University of Michigan Museum of Anthropology, No. 16. Ann Arbor.
1994 *Tribal and Chiefly Warfare in South America*. Memoirs of the University of Michigan Museum of Anthropology, No. 28. Ann Arbor.

Redmond, Elsa M. and Charles S. Spencer
1983 The Cuicatlán Cañada and the Period II frontier of the Zapotec state. In *The Cloud People: Divergent Evolution of the Zapotec and Mixtec Civilizations*, edited by Kent V. Flannery and Joyce Marcus, pp. 117–120. Academic Press, New York.
1994 The *cacicazgo*: an indigenous design. In *Caciques and Their People: A Volume in Honor of Ronald Spores*, edited by Joyce Marcus and Judith F. Zeitlin, pp. 189–225. Anthropological Papers of the University of Michigan Museum of Anthropology, No. 89. Ann Arbor.
2006 From raiding to conquest: warfare strategies and early state development in Oaxaca, Mexico. In *The Archaeology of Warfare: Prehistories of Raiding and Conquest*, edited by Elizabeth N. Arkush and Mark W. Allen, pp. 336–393. University Press of Florida, Gainesville.
2013 Early (300–100 B.C.) temple precinct in the Valley of Oaxaca, Mexico. *Proceedings of the National Academy of Sciences* 110(19):E1707–E1715.
2017 Ancient palace complex (300–100 B.C.) discovered in the Valley of Oaxaca, Mexico. *Proceedings of the National Academy of Sciences* 114(15):3805–3814.

Reeck, Roger
1982 Sixteenth-century central valley Zapotec: a challenge for linguistics and ethnohistory. In *Native American Ethnohistory, Papers in Anthropology*, Vol. 23, No. 2, edited by Joseph W. Whitecotton and Judith Bradley Whitecotton, pp. 369–375. University of Oklahoma Press, Norman.

Reents-Budet, Dorie
2006 Power material in ancient Mesoamerica: the roles of cloth among the Classic Maya. In *Sacred Acts of Wrapping and Binding in Mesoamerica*, edited by Julia Guernsey and F. Kent Reilly III, pp. 105–126. Boundary End Archaeology Research Center, Barnardsville, North Carolina.

Reents-Budet, Dorie, Joseph Ball, Ronald Bishop, Virginia Fields, and Barbara MacLeod
1994 *Painting the Maya Universe: Royal Ceramics of the Classic Period*. Duke University Press, Durham, North Carolina and London.

Reeves, Nicholas
1990 *The Complete Tutankhamun: The King, The Tomb, The Royal Treasure*. Thames and Hudson, London.

Regulski, Ilona
2008 The origin of writing in relation to the emergence of the Egyptian state. In *Egypt at its Origins 2. Proceedings of the International Conference "Origin of the State: Predynastic and Early Dynastic Egypt," Toulouse, September 5-8, 2005*, edited by B. Midant-Reynes, Y. Tristant, J. Rowland, and S. Hendrickx, pp. 983–1008. Peeters, Leuven, Belgium.
2016 *The origins and early development of writing in Egypt*. Oxford Handbooks Online.

Reh, Emma S.
1928 Ancient Mexican carvings in church floor. *El Palacio* 24(11):203–206.

Relaciones geográficas (see del Paso y Troncoso)
1905 [1579–1581] In *Papeles de Nueva España. Segunda Serie, Geografía y Estadística*, Vol. IV, edited by Francisco del Paso y Troncoso. "Sucesores de Rivadeneyra," Madrid, Spain.

Rendón, Juan José
1967 Relaciones internas de las lenguas de la familia zapoteco-chatino. *Anales de Antropología* 4:187–190. Universidad Nacional Autónoma de México, Mexico.
1969 Nuevos datos sobre el origen del vocabulario en lengua zapoteca del padre Córdova. *Anales de Antropología* 6:115–129. Instituto de Investigaciones Antropológicas, Universidad Nacional Autónoma de México, México, D.F.
1995 Diversificación de las lenguas zapotecas. Instituto Oaxaqueño de las Culturas, Centro de Investigaciones y Estudios Superiores de Antropología Social, Oaxaca, Mexico.

Restall, Matthew
1997 *The Maya World: Yucatec Culture and Society, 1550-1850*. Stanford University Press, Stanford, California.

Restall, Matthew, Lisa Sousa, and Kevin Terraciano
2005 *Mesoamerican Voices: Native-Language Writings from Colonial Mexico, Oaxaca, Yucatan, and Guatemala.* Cambridge University Press, Cambridge.

Reyes, fray Antonio de los
1976 [1593] *Arte en lengua mixteca.* Vanderbilt University Publications in Anthropology, No. 14. Nashville, Tennessee.

Rickards, Constantine George
1910 *The Ruins of Mexico.* Vol. 1. H. E. Shrimpton, London, England.
1918 Aspectos generales sobre lápidas y petroglifos del estado de Oaxaca. *Boletín de la Sociedad Mexicana de Geografía y Estadística (quinta época)* 8:17–24.
1938 Monograph on ornaments on Zapotec funerary urns. In *Journal de la Société des Américanistes* 30(1):147–166.

Robertson, Donald
1970 The Tulum murals: The International Style of the Late Post-Classic. In *Verhandlungen del XXXVIII Internationalen Amerikanisten-Kongres*, Stuttgart-München, 1968, Vol. 2, pp. 77–88. Klaus Renner, Munich, Germany.

Robertson, Merle Greene
1983 *The Sculpture of Palenque. Volume I: The Temple of the Inscriptions.* Princeton University Press, New Jersey.

Robicsek, Francis
1975 *A Study in Maya Art and History: The Mat Symbol.* Washburn Press, Charlotte, North Carolina, and the Heye Foundation Museum of the American Indian, New York.

Robinson, Dow F.
1963 *Field notes on Coatlán Zapotec.* Hartford Studies in Linguistics, No. 7. Hartford Seminary Foundation, Hartford, Connecticut.

Rodríguez Martínez, María del Carmen, Ponciano Ortíz Ceballos, Michael D. Coe, Richard A. Diehl, Stephen D. Houston, Karl A. Taube, and Alfredo Delgado Calderón
2006 Oldest writing in the New World. *Science* 313:1610.

Rojas Torres, Rosa María
2009 La categoría 'adjetivo' en el *Arte del idioma zapoteco* (1578) y el *Vocabulario en lengua çapoteca* (1578) de Juan de Córdova. Historiographia Linguistica XXXVI (2/3):259–279.

Romero Frizzi, María de los Ángeles, editora
2003 *Escritura zapoteca: 2500 años de historia.* CIESAS, CONACULTA-INAH.

Rosenbaum, Harvey
1974 *Language Universals and Zapotec Syntax.* PhD dissertation, University of Texas, Austin.

Rostworowski, María and Craig Morris
1999 The Fourfold Domain: Inca Power and its Social Foundations. In *The Cambridge History of the Native Peoples of the Americas, Vol. III, Part I: South America*, edited by Frank Salomon and Stuart B. Schwartz, pp. 769–863. Cambridge University Press, Cambridge.

Royce, Anya Peterson
2011 *Becoming an Ancestor: The Isthmus Zapotec Way of Death.* State University of New York Press, Albany.

Roys, Ralph L.
1940 *Personal Names of the Maya of Yucatan.* Carnegie Institution of Washington, Publication 523, Contribution 31. Washington, D.C.
1943 *The Indian Background of Colonial Yucatan.* Carnegie Institution of Washington, Publication 548. Washington, D.C.

Ruppert, Karl and John H. Denison, Jr.
1943 *Archaeological Reconnaissance in Campeche, Quintana Roo, and Peten.* Carnegie Institution of Washington, Publication 543. Washington, D.C.

Ruz Lhuillier, Alberto
1973 *El Templo de las Inscripciones, Palenque.* Colección Científica No. 7. Arqueología. Instituto Nacional de Antropología e Historia, Universidad Autónoma de México, México.

S

Sáenz, César A.
1961 Tres estelas en Xochicalco. *Revista Mexicana de Estudios Antropológicos* XVII: 39–65.
1964 Las estelas de Xochicalco. *Actas y Memorias del XXXV Congreso Internacional de Americanistas*, celebrado en la ciudad de México en 1962, Tomo 2:69–86. Mexico.
1968 Cuatro piedras con inscripciones en Xochicalco, México. *Anales de Antropología* V(1):181–198. Universidad Nacional de Autónoma de México, Mexico.

Sahagún, Bernardino de
1981 *Florentine Codex, Book 2—The Ceremonies.* Translated by Charles E. Dibble and Arthur J. O. Anderson. School of American Research and the University of Utah, Provo, Utah, and Santa Fe, New Mexico.

Salazar, Agustín de
1581 Relación de Cuylapa. English translation by Douglas S. Butterworth. *Boletín de Estudios Oaxaqueños* 23:36–41. Museo Frissell, Mitla, Oaxaca.

Saler, Benson
1977 Supernatural as a Western category. *Ethnos* 5(1):31–53.

Samaniego, Lorenzo, Enrique Vergara, and Henning Bischof
1985 New Evidence on Cerro Sechín, Casma Valley, Peru. In *Early Ceremonial Architecture of the Andes*, edited by Christopher B. Donnan, pp. 165–190. Dumbarton Oaks Research Library and Collection, Washington, D.C.

Sampson, Geoffrey
1985 *Writing Systems: A Linguistic Introduction.* Hutchinson, London.

Sánchez Santiago, Gonzalo
2014 El complejo serpiente-buho en los silbatos zapotecos del clásico. In *Zaachila y su historia prehispánica: Memoria del quincuagésimo aniversario del descubrimiento de las tumbas 1 y 2*, edited by Ismael G. Vicente Cruz and Gonzalo Sánchez Santiago, pp. 243–260. CONACULTA, Oaxaca, Mexico.

Sandstrom, Alan
1991 *Corn is our Blood: Culture and Ethnic Identity in a Contemporary Aztec Indian Village*. University of Oklahoma Press, Norman.

Satterthwaite, Linton
1958 *The problem of abnormal stela placements at Tikal and elsewhere*. Tikal Report 3, pp. 61–83. University Museum Monograph No. 15. University of Pennsylvania Museum of Archaeology and Anthropology, Philadelphia.
1965 Calendrics of the Maya lowlands. In *Archaeology of Southern Mesoamerica*, edited by Gordon R. Willey, pp. 603–631. Handbook of Middle American Indians, Vol. 3, Robert Wauchope, general editor. University of Texas Press, Austin.

Saturno, William A., David Stuart, and Boris Beltrán
2006 Early Maya writing at San Bartolo, Guatemala. *Science* 311:1281–1283.

Saville, Marshall H.
1899 Exploration of Zapotecan tombs in southern Mexico. *American Anthropologist* 1(2):350–362.
1904 Funeral urns from Oaxaca. *The American Museum Journal* 4(3):49–60.
1909 *The Cruciform Structures of Mitla and Vicinity*. In Anthropological Essays presented to Frederick Ward Putnam, pp. 151–190. New York.
1922 *Turquois* [sic] *Mosaic Art in Ancient Mexico*. Museum of the American Indian, Heye Foundation, Vol. VI. Heye Foundation, New York.

Schele, Linda
1982 *Maya Glyphs: The Verbs*. University of Texas Press, Austin.

Schele, Linda and David A. Freidel
1990 *A Forest of Kings: The Untold Story of the Ancient Maya*. William Morrow and Company, New York.

Schele, Linda and Peter Mathews
1999 *The Code of Kings: The Language of Seven Sacred Maya Temples and Tombs*. A Touchstone Book, Simon & Schuster, New York.

Schmandt-Besserat, Denise
1977 An archaic recording system and the origin of writing. *Syro-Mesopotamian Studies* 1(2):1–32.
1978 The earliest precursor of writing. *Scientific American* 238(6):50–58.
1979 An archaic recording system in the Uruk-Jemdet Nasr period. *American Journal of Archaeology* 83:19–48.
1992 *Before Writing: From Counting to Cuneiform*, Vols. I and II. University of Texas Press, Austin.

Schmieder, Oscar
1930 *The Settlements of the Tzapotec and Mije Indians, State of Oaxaca, Mexico*. University of California Publications in Geography, Vol. 4:1–184. Berkeley.

Schortman, Edward M. and Patricia Urban, editors
1992 Sociopolitical Hierarchy and Craft Production: The Economic Bases of Elite Power in a Late Classic Southeastern Polity, Part II. Instituto Hondureño de Antropología e Historia and Kenyon College, Gambier, Ohio.

Scott, John F.
1965 Figural posture in early Mesoamerican relief. Master's thesis, Columbia University, New York.
1978 *The Danzantes of Monte Albán, Part I (Text) and Part II (Catalogue)*. Studies in Pre-Columbian Art & Archaeology No. 19. Dumbarton Oaks, Trustees for Harvard University, Washington, D.C.

Scott, Sue
1993 *Teotihuacán Mazapan figurines and the Xipe Totec statue: a link between the Basin of Mexico and the Valley of Oaxaca*. Vanderbilt University Publications in Anthropology, No. 44. Nashville, Tennessee.

Séjourné, Laurette
1960 El simbolismo de los rituales funerarios en Monte Albán. *Revista Mexicana de Estudios Antropológicos* 16:77–90.

Seler, Caecilie
1900 *Auf alten wege in Mexiko und Guatemala*. Dietrich Reimer, Berlin.

Seler, Eduard
1904a The Mexican chronology, with special reference to the Zapotec calendar. In *Mexican and Central American Antiquities, Calendar Systems, and History*, pp. 11–56. Bureau of American Ethnology Bulletin 28. Government Printing Office, Smithsonian Institution, Washington, D.C.
1904b Wall paintings of Mitla: a Mexican picture writing in fresco. In *Mexican and Central American Antiquities, Calendar System, and History*, pp. 243–324. Bureau of American Ethnology Bulletin 28. Government Printing Office, Smithsonian Institution, Washington, D.C.
1906 Das Dorfbuch von Santiago Guevea. *Zeitschrift für Ethnologie* 38:121–155.
1960 [1904] Die archäologischen Ergebnisse meiner ersten mexikanischen Reise. In *Gesammelte Abhandlungen zur Amerikanischen Sprach- und Alterthumskunde* Band II:289–367. A. Ascher & Co., Berlin.
1986 *Plano jeroglífico de Santiago Guevea*. Translated by Carlos Enrique Delgado. Ediciones Guchachi' Reza, Mexico.
1991 Archaeological results of my first trip to Mexico. In *Collected Works in Mesoamerican Linguistics and Archaeology*, edited by Frank Comparato, Vol. II, pp. 155–202. Labyrinthos, Culver City, California.

Sellen, Adam T.
2002 Storm-god impersonators from ancient Oaxaca. *Ancient Mesoamerica* 13(1):3–19.
2011 Sowing the blood with the maize: Zapotec effigy vessels and agricultural ritual. *Ancient Mesoamerica* 22:71–89.

Senner, Wayne M., editor
1989 *The Origins of Writing*. University of Nebraska Press, Lincoln, Nebraska.

Sharer, Robert J.
1994 *The Ancient Maya*. Fifth edition. Stanford University Press, Stanford, California.

Sharer, Robert J., Loa P. Traxler, David W. Sedat, Ellen E. Bell, Marcello A. Canuto, and Christopher Powell
1999 Early Classic Architecture Beneath the Copan Acropolis: A Research Update. *Ancient Mesoamerica* 10:3–23.

Sherman, Robert J., Andrew K. Balkansky, Charles S. Spencer, and B. D. Nicholls
2010 Expansionary dynamics of the nascent Monte Albán state. *Journal of Anthropological Archaeology* 29:278–301.

Sicoli, Mark A.
2007 Tono: a linguistic ethnography of tone and voice in a Zapotec region. PhD dissertation, Department of Anthropology, University of Michigan, Ann Arbor.

Smith, Mary Elizabeth
1973a *Picture Writing from Ancient Southern Mexico: Mixtec Place Signs and Maps.* University of Oklahoma Press, Norman.
1973b The relationship between Mixtec manuscript painting and the Mixtec language: a study of some personal names in Códices Muro and Sánchez Solís. In *Mesoamerican Writing Systems: A Conference at Dumbarton Oaks,* edited by Elizabeth P. Benson, pp. 47–98. Dumbarton Oaks Research Library and Collection, Washington, D.C.
1983 Codex Selden: a manuscript from the Valley of Nochixtlan? In *The Cloud People: Divergent Evolution of the Mixtec and Zapotec Civilizations*, edited by Kent V. Flannery and Joyce Marcus, pp. 248–255. Academic Press, New York.

Smith, Michael E. and Frances Berdan, editors
2003 *The Postclassic Mesoamerican World.* University of Utah Press, Salt Lake City.

Smith, Michael E. and Michael D. Lind
2005 Xoo-phase ceramics from Oaxaca found at Calixtlahuaca in central Mexico. *Ancient Mesoamerica* 16:169–177.

Smith, Virginia G.
1984 *Izapa Relief Carving: Form, Content, Rules for Design, and Role in Mesoamerican Art, History, and Archaeology*. Studies in Pre-Columbian Art and Archaeology, No. 27. Dumbarton Oaks Research Library and Collection, Washington, D.C.

Smith Stark, Thomas C.
2001 Las clases verbales del zapoteco cordovés. Paper presented at the VI Congreso Nacional de Lingüística. Mérida, Mexico.
2002 Dioses, sacerdotes y sacrificio: una mirada a la religión zapoteca a través del *Vocabulario en Lengua Çapoteca* (1578) de Juan de Córdova. In *La religión de los Binnigul'sa'*, edited by Víctor de la Cruz and Marcus C. Winter, pp. 89–195. Instituto Estatal de Educación Pública de Oaxaca y el Instituto Oaxaqueño de las Culturas, Colección Voces del Fondo, Oaxaca, Mexico.
2003 La ortografía del zapoteco en el Vocabulario de fray Juan de Córdova. In *Escritura zapoteca: 2500 años de historia*, edited by María de los Ángeles Romero Frizzi, pp. 173–239. CIESAS, CONACULTA-INAH.
2007 Algunas isoglosas zapotecas. In *Clasificación de las lenguas indígenas de México, Memorias del III Coloquio Internacional de Lingüística Mauricio Swadesh*, edited by Cristina Buenrostro, Samuel Herrera Castro, Yolanda Lastra, Juan José Rendón, Otto Schumann, Leopoldo Valiñas and María Aydée Vargas Monroy, pp. 69–133. Universidad Nacional Autónoma de México and Instituto Nacional de Lenguas Indígenas.

Sonnenschein, Aaron H.
2005 *A Descriptive Grammar of San Bartolomé Zoogocho Zapotec.* Lincom Europa, Munich, Germany.

Spence, Michael W.
1989 Excavaciones recientes en Tlailotlacan, el barrio oaxaqueño de Teotihuacán. *Arqueología* 5:81–104.
1992 Tlailotlacan, a Zapotec enclave in Teotihuacan. In *Art, Ideology, and the City of Teotihuacan*, edited by Janet C. Berlo, pp. 59–88. Dumbarton Oaks Research Library and Collection, Washington, D.C.
1996 A comparative analysis of ethnic enclaves. In *Arqueología mesoamericana: homenaje a William T. Sanders*, Vol. 1, edited by Alba Guadalupe Mastache, Jeffrey R. Parsons, Robert S. Santley, and Mari Carmen Serra Puche, pp. 333–353. Instituto Nacional de Antropología e Historia, Mexico City.
2004 A Zapotec diaspora network in Classic-period Central Mexico. In *The Archaeology of Colonial Encounters*, edited by Gil J. Stein, pp. 173–205. School for Advanced Research Press, Santa Fe, New Mexico.

Spencer, Charles S.
1982 *The Cuicatlán Cañada and Monte Albán: A Study of Primary State Formation.* Academic Press, New York.
1990 On the tempo and mode of state formation: neoevolutionism reconsidered. *Journal of Anthropological Archaeology* 9:1–30.
1998 A mathematical model of primary state formation. *Cultural Dynamics* 10:5–20.
2003 War and early state formation in Oaxaca, Mexico. *Proceedings of the National Academy of Sciences* 100:11185–11187.
2007 Territorial expansion and primary state formation in Oaxaca, Mexico. In *Latin American Indigenous Warfare and Ritual Violence*, edited by Richard J. Chacon and Ruben G. Mendoza, pp. 55–72. University of Arizona Press, Tucson.
2009 Testing the morphogenesist model of primary state formation: the Zapotec case. In *Macroevolution in Human Prehistory: Evolutionary Theory and Processual Archaeology*, edited by Anna Marie Prentiss and James C. Chatters, pp. 133–155. Springer, New York.
2010 Territorial expansion and primary state formation: the Zapotec case. *Proceedings of the National Academy of Sciences* 107(16):7119–7126.
2019 Cultural macroevolution and social change. In *Handbook of Evolutionary Research in Archaeology*, edited by Anna M. Prentiss, pp. 183–213. Springer, New York.

Spencer, Charles S. and Elsa M. Redmond
1997 *Archaeology of the Cañada de Cuicatlán, Oaxaca.* American Museum of Natural History Anthropological Paper No. 80. American Museum of Natural History, New York.
2001a The chronology of conquest: implications of new radiocarbon analyses from the Cañada de Cuicatlán, Oaxaca. *Latin American Antiquity* 12:182–201.

2001b Multilevel selection and political evolution in the Valley of Oaxaca, 500-100 B.C. *Journal of Anthropological Archaeology* 20:195–229.

2003 Militarism, resistance, and early state development in Oaxaca, Mexico. *Social Evolution and History* 2(1):25–70.

2004a Primary state formation in Mesoamerica. *Annual Review of Anthropology* 33:173–199.

2004b A Late Monte Albán I phase (300-100 B.C.) palace in the Valley of Oaxaca. *Latin American Antiquity* 15(4):441–455.

2005 Institutional development in Late Formative Oaxaca: the view from San Martín Tilcajete. In *New Perspectives on Formative Mesoamerican Culture*, edited by Terry G. Powis, pp. 171–182. BAR International Series 1377. BAR, Oxford, UK.

2006 Resistance strategies and early state formation in Oaxaca, Mexico. In *Intermediate Elites in Pre-Columbian States and Empires*, edited by Christina M. Elson and R. Alan Covey, pp. 21–43. University of Arizona Press, Tucson.

Spencer, Charles S., Elsa M. Redmond, and Christina M. Elson

2008 Ceramic microtypology and the territorial expansion of the early Monte Albán state in Oaxaca, Mexico. *Journal of Field Archaeology* 33:321–341.

Spinden, Herbert J.

1913 The picture writing of the Aztecs: words are rebuses made up of conventionalized pictures as syllables. *The American Museum Journal* 13:31–38.

1924 *The Reduction of Maya Dates*. Papers of the Peabody Museum of Archaeology and Ethnology, Vol. VI, No. 4. Harvard University, Cambridge, Massachusetts.

Spores, Ronald

1974 Marital alliance in the political integration of Mixtec kingdoms. *American Anthropologist* 76:297–311.

Spores, Ronald and Kent V. Flannery

1983 Sixteenth-century kinship and social organization. In *The Cloud People: Divergent Evolution of the Zapotec and Mixtec Civilizations*, edited by Kent V. Flannery and Joyce Marcus, pp. 339–342. Academic Press, New York.

Stenzel, Werner

1968–1970 The sacred bundles in Mesoamerican religion. In *Actas del 38th International Congress of Americanists*, Vol. II, pp. 347–352. Stuttgart and Munich, Germany.

Stirling, Matthew W.

1943 *Stone Monuments of Southern Mexico*. Smithsonian Institution Bureau of American Ethnology, Bulletin 138. U.S. Government Printing Office, Washington, D.C.

Stocker, Terrance L. and Michael W. Spence

1973 Trilobal eccentrics at Teotihuacan and Tula. *American Antiquity* 38(2):195–199.

Strauss, Stephanie M.

2018 Negotiating narrative domains: Izapa's place in the discourse on early hieroglyphic writing. *Ancient Mesoamerica* 29:347–359.

Stuart, David

1985 *The Yaxha emblem glyph as* Yax-ha. Research Reports on Ancient Maya Writing, No. 1, pp. 1–6. Center for Maya Research, Washington, D.C.

Stubblefield, Morris and Carol Miller de Stubblefield

1991 *Diccionario zapoteco de Mitla, Oaxaca*. Serie de Vocabularios y Diccionarios Indígenas Mariano Silva y Aceves 31. Instituto Lingüístico de Verano, México, D.F.

Suárez, Jorge A.

1990 La clasificación de las lenguas zapotecas. In *Homenaje a Jorge A. Suárez*, edited by Beatriz Garza Cuarón and Paulette Levy, pp. 41–68. El Colegio de México, Mexico.

Swadesh, Morris

1947 The phonemic structure of proto-Zapotec. *International Journal of American Linguistics* 13:220–230.

1949 El idioma de los zapotecos. In *Los zapotecos: monografía histórica, etnográfica y económica*, edited by Lucio Mendieta y Núñez, pp. 415–448. Imprenta Universitaria, Universidad Nacional Autónoma de México, Mexico.

1967 Lexicostatistic classification. In *Linguistics*, Part 1, edited by Norman A. McQuown, pp. 79–115. Handbook of Middle American Indians, Vol. 5, Robert Wauchope, general editor. University of Texas Press, Austin.

T

Taladoire, Eric

2003 Could we speak of the Super Bowl at Flushing Meadows? *La pelota mixteca*, a third pre-Hispanic ballgame, and its possible architectural context. *Ancient Mesoamerica* 14:319–342. Cambridge University Press, Cambridge.

Taube, Karl

1996 The Olmec maize god: The face of corn in Formative Mesoamerica. *RES: Anthropology and Aesthetics* 29/30:39–81.

Taube, Karl and Marc Zender

2009 American gladiators: ritual boxing in ancient Mesoamerica. In *Blood and Beauty: Organized Violence in the Art and Archaeology of Mesoamerica and Central America*, edited by Heather Orr and Rex Koontz, pp. 161–220. Cotsen Institute of Archaeology Press, University of California at Los Angeles.

Tello, Julio C.

1956 *Arqueología del Valle de Casma, Culturas Chavín, Santa o Huaylas*. Editorial San Marcos, Lima.

Terraciano, Kevin

1994 Ñudazhui History: Mixtec Writing and Culture in Colonial Oaxaca. PhD dissertation, University of California at Los Angeles.

2001 *The Mixtecs of Colonial Oaxaca*. Stanford University Press, Stanford, California.

Thomas, Cyrus

1893 Are the Maya hieroglyphs phonetic? *American Anthropologist* 6:241–270.

Thompson, J. Eric S.

1939 *Excavations at San Jose, British Honduras*. Carnegie Institution of Washington, Publication 506. Washington, D.C.

1950 *Maya Hieroglyphic Writing: Introduction*. Carnegie Institution of Washington, Publication 589. Washington, D.C.

1962 *A Catalog of Maya Hieroglyphs*. University of Oklahoma Press, Norman.
1970 *Maya History and Religion*. University of Oklahoma Press, Norman.

Torres Rodríguez, Alfonso, Juan Cervantes, and Patricia Fournier García
1999 Las relaciones entre el centro y la periferia: El caso de las comunidades del clásico en la región de Tula, México. *Boletín de Antropología Americana* 35:73–93.

Townsend, Richard F.
1987 Coronation at Tenochtitlan. In *The Aztec Templo Mayor: A Symposium at Dumbarton Oaks, 8th and 9th October, 1983*, edited by Elizabeth Hill Boone, pp. 371–409. Dumbarton Oaks Research Library and Collection, Washington, D.C.
1992 *The Aztecs*. Thames and Hudson, London.

Tozzer, Alfred M.
1941 *Landa's Relación de las cosas de Yucatán*, edited by Alfred M. Tozzer. Papers of the Peabody Museum of Archaeology and Ethnology, Vol. 18. Harvard University, Cambridge, Massachusetts.
1957 *Chichen Itza and its Cenote of Sacrifice: A Comparative Study of Contemporaneous Maya and Toltec*. Memoirs of the Peabody Museum of Archaeology and Ethnology, Vols. 11 and 12. Harvard University, Cambridge, Massachusetts.

Trigger, Bruce G.
1998 Writing systems: a case study in cultural evolution. *Norwegian Archaeological Review* 31(1):38–62.

Trujillo de los Santos, Axel
1986 Huijazoo: esplendor pictórico de la cultura zapoteca. *México Desconocido* 112:14–19.

U

Umberger, Emily
1987 Events commemorated by date plaques at the Templo Mayor: further thoughts on the solar metaphor. In *The Aztec Templo Mayor: A Symposium at Dumbarton Oaks, 8th and 9th October, 1983*, edited by Elizabeth Hill Boone, pp. 411–449. Dumbarton Oaks Research Library and Collection, Washington, D.C.

Urcid Serrano, Javier
1995 Comentarios a una lápida zapoteca en el Museo Nacional de Historia Natural, Smithsonian Institution en Washington, D.C. *Cuadernos del Sur* 3(8-9):8–27. CIESAS, Oaxaca, Mexico.
1999 La lápida grabada de Noriega: tres rituales en la vida de un noble zapoteca. *Indiana* 16 (12):211–264. Berlin.
2001 *Zapotec Hieroglyphic Writing*. Studies in Pre-Columbian Art and Archaeology, No. 34. Dumbarton Oaks Research Library and Collection, Washington, D.C.
2003a La conquista por el señor 1 Muerte: inscripción zapoteca en un cilíndro cerámico. In *Escritura zapoteca: 2500 años de historia*, edited by María de los Ángeles Romero Frizzi, pp. 95–142. Instituto Nacional de Antropología e Historia, CONACULTA and Editorial Porrúa.
2003b Las urnas del barrio zapoteco de Teotihuacan. *Arqueología Mexicana* 11(64):54–57. Editorial Raíces, México.
2003c A Zapotec slab in Santiago Matatlán, Oaxaca. *Mesoamerican Voices* 1:65–90.
2005 Zapotec Writing: Knowledge, Power and Memory in Ancient Oaxaca. Foundation for the Advancement of Mesoamerican Studies website (www.famsi.org/zapotecwriting).
2008 El arte de pintar las tumbas: sociedad e ideología zapotecas (400-800 d.C.). In *La pintura mural prehispánica en México III: Oaxaca*, tomo IV (Estudios), edited by Beatriz de la Fuente, pp. 513–628. Universidad Nacional Autónoma de México, Instituto de Investigaciones Estéticas, México.
2011 The written surface as a cultural code: a comparative perspective of scribal traditions from southwestern Mesoamerica. In *Their Way of Writing: Scripts, Signs, and Pictographies in Pre-Columbian America*, edited by Elizabeth Hill Boone and Gary Urton, pp. 111–148. Dumbarton Oaks Research Library and Collection, Washington, D.C.

Urcid, Javier and Arthur A. Joyce
2014 Early transformations of Monte Albán's Main Plaza and their political implications, 500 BC-AD 200. In *Mesoamerican Plazas*, edited by K. Tsukamoto and Takeshi Inomata, pp. 149–167. University of Arizona Press, Tucson.

Urcid, Javier and Adam Sellen
2009 A forgotten house of ancestors from ancient Xoxocotlán. *Baessler-Archiv* 56:177–224.

Urcid, Javier and Marcus Winter
1989 ¿Una genealogía prehispánica zapoteca? *Arqueología* 2:61–67. Instituto Nacional de Antropología e Historia, México.

Urcid, Javier, Marcus Winter, and Raúl Matadamas
1994 Nuevos monumentos grabados en Monte Albán, Oaxca. In *Proyecto Especial Monte Albán 1992-1994*, Contribución No. 4, coordinated by Marcus C. Winter, pp. 2–52. Oaxaca, Mexico.

V

Vaillant, George C.
1938 A correlation of archaeological and historical sequences in the Valley of Mexico. *American Anthropologist* 40(4):535–573.
1941 *Aztecs of Mexico*. Doubleday, New York.

Valdespino, Andrés
1887 *Gramática de la lengua zapoteca / por autor anónimo que agregó á su obra otro "Arte" por Andrés Valdespino, las reglas de las partículas por Juan de Córdova*. Edición dirigida por Antonio Peñafiel. Oficina Tipográfica de la Secretaría de Fomento, México.

van Meer, Ron
2000 Análisis e interpretación de un libro calendárico zapoteco: el manuscrito de San Antonio Huitepec. *Cuadernos del Sur* año 6, número 15:37–74.

Velásquez García, Erik
2004 Los escalones jeroglíficos de Dzibanché. In *Los cautivos de Dzibanché*, edited by Enrique Nalda, pp. 79–103. Instituto Nacional de Antropología e Historia, Mexico.

Vicente Cruz, Ismael G. and Gonzalo Sánchez Santiago, coodinators and editors
2014 Zaachila y su historia prehispánica. In *Zaachila y su historia prehispánica: Memoria del quincuagésimo aniversario del descubrimiento de las tumbas 1 y 2*. CONACULTA, Oaxaca, Mexico.

Villagra Caleti, Agustín
n.d. Unpublished drawings and photos. Courtesy of Ignacio Bernal.
1939 "Los danzantes." Piedras grabadas del Montículo 'L,' Monte Albán, Oaxaca. *Vigesimoseptimo Congreso Internacional de Americanistas* 27(2):143–158. Mexico.

Villagutierre Soto-Mayor, Juan de
1983 [1701] *History of the Conquest of the Province of the Itza*. Translated by Robert D. Wood, edited by Frank E. Comparato. Labyrinthos, Culver City, California.

Vogt, Evon Z.
1969 *Zinacantan: A Maya Community in the Highlands of Chiapas*. Belknap Press of Harvard University Press, Cambridge, Massachusetts.
1976 *Tortillas for the Gods: A Symbolic Analysis of Zinacanteco Rituals*. Harvard University Press, Cambridge, Massachusetts.

von Müller, Johann Wilhelm
1864–1865 *Reisen in den Vereinigten Staaten Canada und Mexico*. 3 volumes. Borckhaus, Leipzig.

von Winning, Hasso
1947 Representations of temple buildings as decorative patterns on Teotihuacan pottery and figurines. Carnegie Institution of Washington, Division of Historical Research, No. 83. Washington, D.C.

W

Wang, Haicheng
2014 *Writing and the Ancient State: Early China in Comparative Perspective*. Cambridge University Press, Cambridge.

Weitlaner, Robert J. and Gabriel De Cicco
1962 La jerarquía de los dioses zapotecos del sur. *Actas del XXXIV Congreso Internacional de Americanistas*, pp. 695–710. Vienna, Austria.

Weitlaner, Robert J., Gabriel De Cicco, and Donald Brockington
1958 Calendario de los zapotecos del sur. *Actas del XXXII Congreso Internacional de Americanistas*, pp. 296–299. Munksgaard, Copenhagen, Denmark.

Whallon, Robert
1992 A statistical analysis of Mixtec nobles' names. In *Mesoamerican Writing Systems*, by Joyce Marcus, pp. 447–463. Princeton University Press, New Jersey.

White, Christine D., Michael W. Spence, Fred J. Longstaffe, and Kimberley R. Law
2000 Testing the nature of Teotihuacan imperialism at Kaminaljuyu using phosphate oxygen-isotope ratios. *Journal of Anthropological Research* 56(4):535–558.
2004 Demography and ethnic continuity in the Tlailotlacan enclave of Teotihuacan: the evidence from stable oxygen isotopes. *Journal of Anthropological Archaeology* 23:385–403.

Whitecotton, Joseph W.
1977 *The Zapotecs: Princes, Priests, and Peasants*. University of Oklahoma Press, Norman.
1982 Zapotec pictorials and Zapotec naming: towards an ethnohistory of ancient Oaxaca. In *Native American Ethnohistory, Papers in Anthropology*, Vol. 23(2), edited by Joseph W. Whitecotton and Judith B. Whitecotton, pp. 285–343. University of Oklahoma Press, Norman.
1983 The genealogy of Macuilxóchitl: a 16th-century Zapotec pictorial from the Valley of Oaxaca. *Notas Mesoamericanas* 9:59–75.
1990 *Zapotec Elite Ethnohistory: Pictorial Genealogies from Eastern Oaxaca in Late Prehispanic and Early Colonial Times*. Vanderbilt University Publications in Anthropology, No. 39. Nashville, Tennessee.
2003 Las genealogías del valle de Oaxaca: Época Colonial. In *Escritura zapoteca: 2500 años de historia*, edited by María de los Ángeles Romero Frizzi, pp. 305–339. Instituto Nacional de Antropología e Historia and CIESAS, Mexico.

Whitecotton, Joseph W. and Judith Bradley Whitecotton
1993 *Vocabulario zapoteco-castellano*. Vanderbilt University Publications in Anthropology, No. 45. Nashville, Tennessee.

Whittaker, Gordon
1980 The Hieroglyphics of Monte Albán. PhD dissertation, Department of Anthropology, Yale University, New Haven, Connecticut.
1982 The tablets of Mound J at Monte Alban. In *The Indians of Mexico in Pre-Columbian and Modern Times*, edited by Maarten E. R. G. N. Jansen and Ted J. J. Leyenaar, pp. 50–86. Leiden, Netherlands.
1983 The structure of the Zapotec calendar. In *Calendars in Mexico and Peru: Proceedings of the 44th International Congress of Americanists, Manchester 1982*, edited by Anthony Aveni and Gordon Brotherston, pp. 101–133. BAR International 174, Oxford and London.
1992 The Zapotec writing system. In *Epigraphy*, edited by Victoria R. Bricker, pp. 5–19. Supplement to the Handbook of Middle American Indians, Vol. 5, Victoria R. Bricker, general editor. University of Texas Press, Austin.
2009 The principles of Nahuatl writing. *Göttinger Beiträge zur Sprachwissenschaft* 16:47–81.
2018 Aztec hieroglyphics: a name-based writing system. *Language and History* 61:60–76.

Whorf, Benjamin L.
1933 *The phonetic value of certain characters in Maya writing*. Papers of the Peabody Museum of Archaeology and Ethnology, Vol. 13. Harvard University, Cambridge, Massachusetts.

Wichmann, Soren, editor
2004 *The Linguistics of Maya Writing*. University of Utah Press, Salt Lake City.

Wicke, Charles
1957 The ball court at Yagul, Oaxaca: a comparative study. *Mesoamerican Notes* 5:37–76. Department of Anthropology, Mexico City College, Mexico.

Wilson, David J.
1988 *Prehispanic Settlement Patterns in the Lower Santa Valley, Peru: A Regional Perspective on the Origins and Development of Complex North Coast Society*. Smithsonian Institution Press, Washington, D.C.

Winter, Marcus, Javier Urcid, Raúl Matadamas, Damon E. Peeler, and Benjamín Maldonado
1994 *Escritura zapoteca prehispánica: nuevas aportaciones*. Contribución No. 4 del Proyecto Especial Monte Albán 1992–1994. Oaxaca, Mexico.

Workinger, Andrew and Arthur A. Joyce
2009 Reconsidering warfare in Formative period Oaxaca. In *Blood and Beauty: Organized Violence in the Art and Archaeology of Mesoamerica and Central America*, edited by Heather Orr and Rex Koontz, pp. 3–38. Cotsen Institute of Archaeology Press, University of California at Los Angeles.

Wright, Henry T. and Gregory A. Johnson
1975 Population, exchange, and early state formation in southwestern Iran. *American Anthropologist* 77:267–289.

Y

Yasugi, Yoshiho
1995 *Native Middle American Languages: An Areal-Typological Perspective*. Senri Ethnological Studies No. 39. National Museum of Ethnology, Senri Expo Park, Suita, Osaka, Japan.

Z

Zehnder, Luise Wiltraud
1977 Los Danzantes de Monte Albán. PhD dissertation, Instituto de Investigaciones Estéticas de la Universidad Nacional Autónoma de México.

Zeitlin, Robert N. and Arthur A. Joyce
1999 The Zapotec-imperialism argument: insights from the Oaxaca coast. *Current Anthropology* 40(3):383–392.

Zimansky, Paul E.
1993 Review of Denise Schmandt-Besserat's *Before Writing*. *Journal of Field Archaeology* 20:513–517.

Zúñiga, Rosa María
1982 *Toponímias zapotecas: desarrollo de una metodología*. Serie Lingüística, Instituto Nacional de Antropología e Historia, México, D.F.

Index

A

B

C

D

E

F

G

H

I

J

K

L

M

N

O

P

U

V

W

X

Y

Z